PATRIOTISM, PERSEVERANCE, POSTERITY

**The Story of the
National Japanese
American Memorial**

PATRIOTISM

PERSEVERANCE

POSTERITY

The Story of the National Japanese American Memorial

National Japanese American Memorial Foundation

Washington, DC

Editorial Board:　Bill Hosokawa, Maj. Gen. James H. Mukoyama, Jr.,
　　　　　　　　　Kaz Oshiki, Dr. Mae Takahashi, Cherry Y. Tsutsumida
Layout, Design Supervisor: Cheron D. Carlson
Cover Illustration: Hisako Terasaki

Library of Congress Catalog Card Number: 00-134132
Publisher's Cataloging-in-Publication:
Patriotism, Perseverance, Posterity : the Story of the Japanese American National
Memorial. -- 1st ed.
　p. cm.
　ISBN: 0-9678422-0-4

1. World War 1939-1945--Japanese Americans.　2. Japanese Americans--Civil rights--
History--1933-1945.　3. Japanese Americans--Evacuation and relocation, 1942-1945.
4. Patriotism--United States　I. Japanese American Memorial Foundation.

D753.8.P38 2000　　　　　　　940.54'0895673　　　　　　QBI00-500144

Special Acknowledgements

The National Japanese American Memorial Foundation extends its eternal gratitude to the 20,000 donors whose generosity and unwavering loyalty brought this national project to fruition. This Memorial and this book are for you, for our Issei parents and grandparents, for the thousands of Nisei veterans who served our country, and for generations to come.

The Foundation would like to thank the individuals whose dedicated efforts in creating this book were indispensable. In particular, this book could not have been completed without the expert guidance of Bill Hosokawa, who chaired the editorial committee composed of Dr. Mae Takahashi, Kaz Oshiki, and James Mukoyama. A veteran newspaper editor and reporter for metropolitan newspapers, including the Denver Post, Hosokawa is the author of ten books. Among his honors is recognition by the Freedom Forum's "Newseum" of newspaper history in Arlington, Virginia. As a noted contemporary historian of Japanese Americans, Hosokawa's contribution to this work was invaluable. The Foundation also thanks Cheron Carlson for her creative talent and sensitivity to Japanese American history which resulted in the attractive, thought provoking layout of this book.

It is hoped that this product of innumerable drafts, discussions, rewrites and editorial sessions will be a memorable keepsake that will remain in families from generation to generation.

Contents

The Capitol stands majestically near the Memorial site on Federal land reserved for memorials commemorating the most significant events in our history. An audience of an estimated 2,000 attended the Dedication Ceremony on November 9, 2000.

Foreword

*T*his book tells the story of a time between February 19, 1942 when President of the United States Franklin D. Roosevelt signed the infamous Executive Order 9066, and November 9, 2000 when the Japanese American National Memorial to Patriotism was dedicated in the Nation's Capital. It is a story about men, women and children, who by that order were removed from their homes and sent to concentration camps in the harsh and desolate interior, or placed under martial law in Hawaii solely because of their ancestry. Almost fifty years after the War was over, the Nation recognized the injustice that had been done and issued a Presidential apology as well as token compensation.

Importantly, Congress has given this story one of the very limited significant sites saved only for the most important historic events in our Nation. And the National Park Service will assure its upkeep in perpetuity. It is an affirmation of this Nation's ability and greatness to redress grievances when committed even under the stress of war.

In Nina Akamu's studio, Cherry Tsutsumida offers perspective on the height of a working model of the crane statue which stands at the center of the Memorial.

The right to build a memorial in the nation's capital is a profound privilege and responsibility. By this right we become the reservoir and resonator of an important chapter of American history.

These are the public facts about the Memorial. But behind the scene are also many facts which have made the building of this Memorial a triumph by which we end the Twentieth century. This Memorial was built because the Japanese American community represented by more than 20,000 donors became a mobilized force to assure that the dark chapter during World War II shall never be repeated in these United States. They also enlisted friends and organizations of good will representing various sectors of America.

It is a Memorial which expresses the diversity of our community. It is honed by generational differences: one generation to whom WWII is the pivotal point of their courage and loyalty; another generation who served in integrated units during the Korean War, and the youngest generation to whom the Vietnam War protests remain the awakening of their American conscience. This book is an attempt to show that the choices and actions taken reflect the complexity and variety of views within our communities, from the brave men and women who volunteered to fight as their own families were unjustly behind barbed wire fences, to the women, many separated from their husbands, who held the families together giving security to their families at a time of excruciating uncertainty, to the incarcerated men who on Constitutional principle resisted the draft, to the woman and men who challenged evacuation through the courts. In a real sense, the Japanese Americans fought in two conflicts during that period: one a cataclysmic war overseas to secure a free world; one at home to assure these same freedoms to all Americans.

The two cranes entwined by barbed wire symbolize this saga. The cruelty and the injustice of the barbed wire do not conquer the spirit of a valiant people to aspire, to struggle and to break out and rise to the limitless horizons of freedom.

This book is an American parable which leaves a powerful legacy for which we can all be proud. We leave it to this Nation in memory of our Issei parents who were the first believers in the American dream and to their brave sons who gave their lives to continue that dream.

Cherry Yuriko Tsutsumida
Executive Director

The Dedication Ceremony of the Memorial on November 9, 2000 celebrated a Nation and a democracy, as well as what it means to be American.

Chapter One

The principle on which this country
was founded and by which it has always
been governed is that Americanism
is a matter of the mind and heart;
Americanism is not, and never was,
a matter of race or ancestry.

Franklin D. Roosevelt

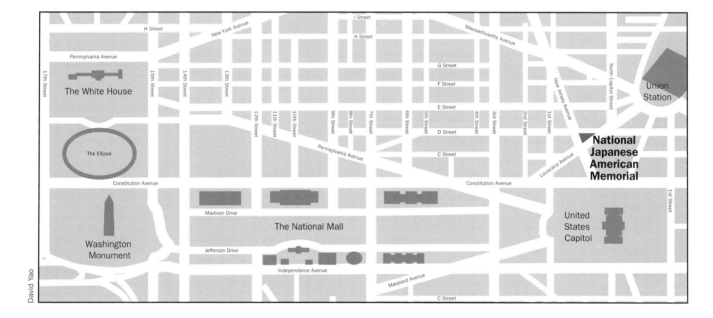

Computerized map of the Washington D.C. Capitol Hill area depicting location of Memorial relative to familiar landmarks. The site is the triangular piece of land at the intersection of New Jersey and Louisiana Avenues and D Street, N.W.

The Memorial

Midway between the Capitol and Union Station along the heavily traveled thoroughfare called Louisiana Avenue Northwest in Washington, D.C., a gently curving wall of tall gray granite slabs stands half-concealed by young flowering cherry trees. Completed in the spring of 2001, the site's beauty has yet to achieve maturity.

Yet, even from street level there is something haunting, something deeply moving about the stone and greenery that stand on the triangular site, and the symbolism of the burnished wingtips of some giant bird reaching for the skies above the wall.

What is this monument in a city of proud memorials? What distinguishes it among the scores in the nation's capital that commemorate highlights of a long and distinguished history?

John Harrington

Congressional Medal of Honor recipients George Sakato and Hiroshi "Hershey" Miyamura among a patriotic audience salute the Color Guard at the Memorial's Dedication, November 9, 2000.

This Memorial, authorized by Act of Congress in 1992, honors the steadfast allegiance to the United States demonstrated by Americans whose roots reach back to Japan. By its approval, Congress acknowledged the nation's error in imprisoning 120,000 of these Americans for no reason other than their ethnic roots. Further, it recommitted itself to the historic ideals of justice and equality for all. Consequently the volunteer National Japanese American Memorial Foundation (NJAMF) undertook to memorialize this tragic and triumphant chapter of the nation's history. More than 20,000 donors contributed in excess of $13 million to create the physical manifestation of this commitment. For the record, let it be noted that ground was broken on a bright, sunny October 22, 1999. The Memorial was dedicated on November 9 the following year and its completion celebrated on the 29th of June, 2001.

A report to the House of Representatives, dated July 27, 1992, contains these words attributed to Judge William Marutani, chairman emeritus of NJAMF: "The Memorial is a tribute to the indomitable spirit of a segment of our citizenry — defined not by themselves but by the government — who remained steadfast in their faith in this democratic system of government and fought for its preservation. It is a celebration of our system of government which demonstrated its strength and integrity by admitting a wrong and correcting it."

His reference to the admission and correction of a wrong was the Civil Liberties Act of 1988, passed by Congress and signed by President Ronald Reagan on August 10 of that year. In it the nation admitted a wrong had been committed against Japanese Americans in the heat of World War II and offered an apology. The Act also provided a token payment of $20,000 to each surviving internee.

That remarkable history is remembered for posterity in stone and bronze and flowing water on a triangle of land provided by the federal government, quietly reflecting on a powerful statement by another President for all Americans to ponder: "The principle on which this country was founded and by which it has always been governed is that Americanism is a matter of the mind and heart; Americanism is not, and never was, a matter of race or ancestry."

The fact that the nation, including the then President Franklin Delano Roosevelt, abandoned the truth of his words in 1942, resulted in the sad episode of the nation's history now remembered on this wooded one-third acre plot.

The Memorial was designed as a place for inspiration, for meditation, for learning about the price and power of freedom and a reminder that the Constitution's promise requires vigilant defense.

Into the enduring granite panels is etched the outline of the Japanese American experience in World War II and the nation's apology for that violation of their rights. Detailed on these pages is the rest of their story and how the Memorial became reality.

The historic narrative begins with the arrival in the United States more than a century ago of immigrants from an Asian land seeking, like other immigrants, freedom and opportunity in the New World. It recounts the Americanization of their offspring and their poignant saga in the crucible of war. Although the early history of immigrants from Japan is an important prelude, the Memorial of necessity focuses on the experiences of their descendants in World War II.

Preserved for posterity on the panels are the names of more than 800 of their men who, in that war, gave their lives in the service of their country. And so that no one shall ever forget, cut into the stone are the names of the camps which during those war years imprisoned approximately 120,000 men, women and children — two-thirds of whom were native-born Americans — and their foreign-born parents whose only crime was their ethnicity.

Congressional Medal of Honor recipients Hershey Miyamura and George Sakato place a ceremonial wreath before the Died In Service wall during the Veterans Memorial Service, November 11, 2000.

Softly cascading water and a reflecting pool speak of continuity. In the pool are boulders to break the tranquility of the surface, for history has not been tranquil. Some see the craggy rocks as representing the generations commemorated here — the Issei immigrants who left their parents to transplant their roots into

HERE WE HONOR THOSE WHO DIED IN SERVICE DURING WORLD WAR II

John Harrington

New World soil, their American-born Nisei children who fought injustice to claim their rights as citizens, and the subsequent generations which are enriching the American heritage of fidelity, achievement and courage.

John Harrington

Above: bell sculpted by Paul Matisse. Below: bronze statue by Nina Akamu, surrounded by granite walls bearing the War Relocation Authority camp names.

There is also an innovative bronze-aluminum tube whose deep resonance when struck, reminiscent of an ancient temple bell, is a contemporary invitation to gather, to learn, to meditate.

The centerpiece is a powerful metaphor in bronze. It is a statue that depicts two cranes struggling from barbed wire shackles toward the freedom of the skies.

Together, these elements create a Memorial which celebrates an American epic, a lesson for the ages.

Internees at the Manzanar War Relocation Authority camp demonstrate that loyalty is not a matter of ancestry.

Chapter Two

"...a monument in our nation's
Capital would be a constant
reminder to all Americans
that the slant of one's eyes does not
reflect the slant of one's heart..."

Mike M. Masaoka

John Harrington

The vision would effectively unite the Japanese American community, as well as many individuals and organizations not of Japanese descent, as evidenced by the audience at the Dedication ceremony witnessing the project's fruition.

The Vision

The Japanese American Memorial did not just happen. It began as a vision of one of the men in U.S. Army uniform who had known the violence of the war against tyranny in Europe and seen his comrades die in battle. His name is Mike M. Masaoka. Prior to enlisting he was spokesman for the Japanese American Citizens League (JACL) through its most trying times. Postwar, he had spearheaded JACL's civil rights campaigns against injustices through corrective legislation and through public education. It was largely through his efforts that Congress enacted the laws that gave Asians the right to become naturalized citizens, and repealed the so-called Oriental Exclusion Act which banned immigration from Asia. Meanwhile the courts, in a number of suits instigated by Masaoka, overturned other discriminatory laws, not the least of which was a racist measure that state governments had used to

Masaoka in southern France in 1945 working with the 442nd Regimental Combat Team's public information office.

deprive resident aliens of the fundamental American right to property.

The records show that Masaoka was thinking of some way to honor Japanese American servicemen even as he was training at Camp Shelby, Mississippi prior to joining Nisei troops already bloodied in Europe. In a 165-page "Final Report" to JACL, dated April 22, 1944, he had included a suggestion for a memorial in Arlington National Cemetery "as a lasting and irrefutable monument to the loyalty, fidelity and Americanism of the Japanese American society which gave so generously of its young manhood that their country would not perish."

A decade later, in 1954 Masaoka raised the idea again, in *Pacific Citizen*, JACL's weekly publication. He proposed that the Japanese American community consider:

"...the placing of an appropriate monument to our heroic dead in the nation's Capital where, among the nation's heroes, it would be in proper company as a constant reminder to all Americans that the slant of one's eyes do not reflect the slant of one's heart, that the cost of racial intolerance runs high, that all Americans are of a common patriotism..."

The idea remained in Masaoka's mind for more than another 30 years while other urgent matters such as remedial legislation took precedence.

In 1987, the Smithsonian Institution in Washington opened an exhibit titled "A More Perfect Union: Japanese Americans and the Constitution," reflecting a growing national interest in the experience of ethnic Japanese in the United States during World War II. The exhibit told a vivid and moving story, little known to the general public, of the discrimination faced by this American minority and its remarkable response to this injustice. At a dinner of Nisei veterans celebrating the opening of the exhibit, Masaoka shared anew his vision of a military memorial to that experience that would stand together with those commemorating the deeds of other valiant Americans.

The Smithsonian Museum of American History, which houses this permanent installation, is the third most visited museum in the world, hosting millions of visitors annually.

Smithsonian Institution and National Archives

John Harrington

Members of the Go For Broke National Veterans Association share a moment of silent prayer at the Veterans Memorial Service, November 11, 2001.

The following year he presented the idea to a group of Japanese American veterans at a reunion in Reno, Nevada. The reaction was enthusiastic.

Encouraged, Masaoka rallied some of his fellow veterans into an organization named Go for Broke National Veterans Association (GFBNVA). "Go for Broke," a Hawaiian expression for "shoot the works," had been the battle cry of Nisei combat troops in World War II. It was incorporated as a non-profit entity in California in 1989 with extensive pro bono legal help from Mark Kiguchi of Los Angeles. Judge William Marutani of Philadelphia, who had served as a commissioned officer with U.S. troops in occupied Japan, was named president. The Association's purpose was to erect a memorial to the sacrifice made by Nisei who had died in military service.

However, this was just the beginning. Not the least of problems was the matter of public support. While the veterans were ready to spearhead the effort as their final service to the nation, they realized the project should have the backing of the entire Japanese American community. The veterans were aware that there might be other national and local Japanese American organizations with ideas of their own about a memorial, some led by individuals who had opposed Nisei volunteering for military service. The organizers were sensitive to the concern that internal disunity might stir up groups outside the community which still harbored prewar prejudices.

Masaoka foresaw problems involving his own role in Japanese American history. The minutes of an organizing meeting held by Go for Broke National Veterans Association in late 1988, compiled by Toro Hirose of Hyattsville, Maryland, includes this paragraph:

"Though no specific actions were decided upon as to what might be done to minimize or avert any calamitous consequences, Masaoka readily acknowledged that much of the criticisms were directed at him. As the sole remaining surviving leader of the Japanese American Citizens League (JACL) who participated in most of the events and activities

After the war Mike Masaoka became the representative of the JACL in Washington, D.C. as a full-time lobbyist until 1953 and part-time for another twenty years.

complained about by so-called activists and dissenters, he understands why he is the scapegoat for much of the frustrations and criticisms, most by those who were not directly involved in the decision-making in that period and who are not intimately acquainted with the facts and temper of the times. He explained that he felt he could explain each and every criticism in terms of the general good, the national welfare, and the major achievements won by the evacuees in general and by the Japanese American veterans specifically, but he volunteered his willingness to resign from any and all GFBNVA activities immediately because he believed that so much is at stake that only a united association of individuals with a common goal and objectives could succeed. No one asked for Masaoka's resignation or replacement...."

Unknown to GFBNVA, the path to building a memorial in the nation's capital was blocked by a maze of federal red tape. To guide the proposal through the legislative labyrinth, Kaz Oshiki, a former serviceman with 32 years experience as administrative assistant to Congressman Robert Kastenmeier of Wisconsin, was enlisted. It took four months of intense spadework before Representative Norman Y. Mineta and Senator Daniel K. Inouye introduced, in June of 1991, identical bills to authorize a memorial on federal land "honoring Japanese American veterans."

All bills to authorize a memorial in the Capital area must by law be referred to the National Capital Memorial Commission for a recommendation. Within a month the Commission disapproved the memorial, stating it did not conform to the provisions of the Commemorative Works Act which decreed there would be no further memorials for any particular military unit for any ethnic group.

Mineta promptly asked for a re-hearing. "This memorial," Mineta wrote, "serves an important purpose, as a reminder that the lessons learned during this extraordinary and dark chapter in our nation's history will not be forgotten and will not be allowed to happen again to any segment of our citizenry, regardless of race, religion or national origin."

In its response, the Commission told Mineta the denial was final.

All Nikkei members of Congress — Mineta, Bob Matsui and Patricia Saiki joined by important colleagues in the House, and Senator Inouye — then sent a letter to Interior Secretary Manuel Lujan, Jr., requesting reconsideration on the grounds that the proposal was for more than an ethnic or military monument, but to an event of great historical significance.

A second hearing was held April 28, 1992. Judge Marutani, speaking as president of GFBNVA, said: "If all we were doing here is asking you to endorse a memorial to Japanese American veterans, I'd say forget it. It is far, far beyond that. It is an important segment but it is not solely a military memorial. It is, indeed, a significant chapter in American history. What other government apologizes to its citizens for having committed a wrong? That's beautiful. It makes me proud to be an American."

Marutani was referring to then President Ronald Reagan's remarks at the signing of the so-called Redress Bill on

August 10, 1988. Congressional approval of the Redress Bill was a key to the approval of the Memorial and is detailed later in this chapter.

Mineta, referring to Marutani's statement, then added: "To me the most telling part of that legislation was the part that says, 'And on behalf of the Congress and on behalf of the Nation, the Congress apologizes.' At that moment I think the people felt that their dignity was being restored."

A commission member, James Whitaker, was moved to comment: "...I think there is a much broader story (in the memorial) in terms of recognition of wrong, of repentance, of forgiveness. If it can be cast in historical significance and that kind of thing, and isn't this a wonderful country that we can turn ourselves around...."

Flags of the Color Guard with the Capitol dome as backdrop symbolically celebrate Japanese American patriotism at the Dedication Ceremony, November 9, 2001.

John Harrington

After further consultation with the Commission the purpose of the Memorial was broadened to read:

"The Go for Broke National Veterans Association (GFBNVA) is authorized to establish a memorial on Federal land in the District of Columbia or its environs *to honor Japanese American patriotism in World War II.*"

What is patriotism? The simple dictionary definition is "love for or devotion to one's country." There was no doubt that the word was being employed properly.

Thus the concept was expanded from a war memorial to one to preserve the memory of the unprecedented trials to which the Japanese American minority had been subjected, and the courageous way in which the people had endured and overcome the injustice.

The House passed the measure on July 28, 1992 with the Senate giving its approval the following October 7. President George Bush signed the bill, designated as Public

Law 102-502, on October 24, 1992. Masaoka had died a year and a half earlier.

Specifically, the bill authorized a memorial to "Commemorate the experience of American citizens of Japanese ancestry and their parents who patriotically supported this country despite their unjust treatment during World War II." Further, the bill said the memorial will "serve as a reminder of the lessons learned and as a constant reminder that those errors will not be repeated to the detriment of any segment of the population."

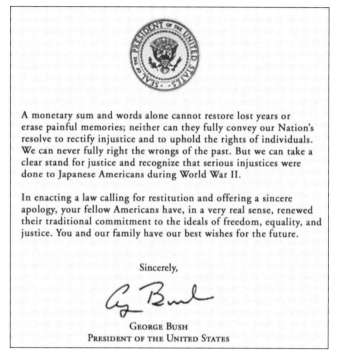

A monetary sum and words alone cannot restore lost years or erase painful memories; neither can they fully convey our Nation's resolve to rectify injustice and to uphold the rights of individuals. We can never fully right the wrongs of the past. But we can take a clear stand for justice and recognize that serious injustices were done to Japanese Americans during World War II.

In enacting a law calling for restitution and offering a sincere apology, your fellow Americans have, in a very real sense, renewed their traditional commitment to the ideals of freedom, equality, and justice. You and our family have our best wishes for the future.

Sincerely,

GEORGE BUSH
PRESIDENT OF THE UNITED STATES

Copy of President Bush's letter of apology and redress to Japanese Americans, October 1990. Bush also signed the legislation authorizing the establishment of the memorial.

Early on, it had become evident that GFBNVA, deeply dedicated as it was to honoring the sacrifice of their comrades, must broaden its base of support if the mission were to succeed. GFBNVA had been founded with an initial nation-wide membership of fewer than 35. For seed money to launch its memorial program, the original members donated approximately $15,000. The records show that the first contributors were Peter Okada, Chet Tanaka, Mike Masaoka, Herbert Sasaki, Mel Tominaga, Jun Yamamoto, Wilson Makabe, Frank Morimoto, Tosh Okamoto, George Kihara, Jiro Futamachi, Tom Kawaguchi, Koichi Furutani, Orville Shirey, Dr. Toshi Kuge, Monte Fujita, Budd Fukei, Ed Okazaki, Art Morimitsu, Dr. Harold Harada and William Marutani. Thanks largely to the efforts of Dr. Harada, $100,000 had been accumulated. But now it was time to share the responsibility with the Japanese American public.

Go for Broke National Veterans Association at its annual meeting in 1993 named James Suzuki to head a search for public-spirited men and women to serve as trustees of a reorganized committee with a greatly expanded mission.

After a nation-wide search, Suzuki's committee recruited 11 individuals here named alphabetically: George Aratani, Bill Hosokawa, Helen Kawagoe, Hideto Kono, William (Mo) Marumoto, Jun Mori, Tomio Moriguchi, Cressey Nakagawa, Dr. Franklin Odo, Francis Sogi and Dr. Rita Takahashi. They were joined by three founding members of Go for Broke: Marutani, Peter Okada and Hitoshi (Mike) Shimizu. Today the Board numbers 47, including a dozen from the predecessor Go for Broke membership. Most of them had spent time in the camps.

Suzuki's logo of a waving flag conveys both patriotism and ethnic heritage.

Members of the Board, listed later in this publication, accepted appointment knowing full well the idea for the Memorial was far larger than the visible resources. Their personal contribution to the cause, in addition to cash donations, has been estimated at more than a million dollars in time, travel expenses, and subsidies to local fund-raising efforts.

At an organizational meeting at El Segundo, CA in December of 1994, called by Marutani as the convening chair, the Board changed the name to National Japanese American Memorial Foundation. The most difficult problem was finding a chairman with the skills and leadership to head a huge and daunting project and, equally important, the means to donate the time and dedication that the responsibility required. That man turned out to be Mo Marumoto who headed a consulting firm in Washington, D.C. and had been a member of President

Richard Nixon's White House staff in charge of recruiting minorities for federal positions. At a meeting in Honolulu, the Board elected Marumoto as chairman, and established an office in Washington, with George Wakiji as executive director.

A retired veteran of federal Civil Service , Wakiji had the job of organizing the Foundation's secretariat, setting up an office and arranging for everything from ordering stationery to scheduling meetings to making lists of people important to the Foundation. Wakiji enlisted a friend, Tom Suzuki, one of the nation's most distinguished graphic artists, to design the organization's distinctive logo.

The Foundation set four objectives:

1. To raise funds and build a Memorial which would:

2. Tell the story of what happened to Japanese Americans and their Issei parents in World War II.

3. Help ensure that such a gross violation of the rights of citizens is never again forced on any other American minority.

4. Reflect on the greatness of a nation which, through Congressional action, would admit it had wronged Japanese Americans in World War II.

That admission of wrong-doing was the result of a tremendous and dedicated national grassroots effort by a number of Japanese American organizations, including JACL which had adopted Redress as a League objective in 1978.

Led by JACL Redress Executive Director Grayce Uyehara, the strategy then was to educate Congressional leaders about the history of Japanese Americans — their internment in violation of their civil rights, the patriotism of their civilians and the sacrifice of their soldiers — about which many were unaware. JACL raised funds to establish an office in Washington to lobby for Redress. With the guidance of Nisei members of Congress, calls were made on key leaders to ask for support in righting a historic wrong.

Congressman Barney Frank, a Massachusetts Democrat, as chair of the subcommittee of the House Judiciary Committee with jurisdiction over the redress issue, took great personal interest in helping the bill over the numerous hurdles. Thanks in large part to his efforts, the Redress Bill, titled HR 442 in honor of the 442nd Regimental Combat Team, was approved

THE WHITE HOUSE
WASHINGTON
November 9, 2000

Over fifty years ago, the United States
Government unjustly interned, evacuated, or
relocated you and many other Japanese Americans.
Today, on behalf of your fellow Americans, I
offer a sincere apology to you for the actions
that unfairly denied Japanese Americans and
their families fundamental liberties during
World War II.

In passing the Civil Liberties Act of
1988, we acknowledged the wrongs of the past
and offered redress to those who endured
such grave injustice. In retrospect, we understand
that the nation's actions were rooted deeply in
racial prejudice, wartime hysteria, and a lack
of political leadership. We must learn from
the past and dedicate ourselves as a nation to
renewing the spirit of equality and our love of
freedom. Together, we can guarantee a future
with liberty and justice for all. You and your
family have my best wishes for the future.

Bill Clinton

After the signing of the Civil Liberties Act of 1988, the disbursement of the compensatory funds to former internees was spread over several years covering the Reagan, Bush, and Clinton Administrations.

by the House by a vote of 243 to 141 on Sept. 17, 1987. The Senate version passed 69 to 27 on April 20, 1988. The two versions were reconciled in July, and President Ronald Reagan signed the bill on Aug. 10, 1988. The legislation provided for a symbolic payment and apology for "a historic injustice" to survivors of the World War II imprisonment.

"What is most important in this bill," the President said at the signing ceremony, "has less to do with property than with honor. For here we admit a wrong. Here we affirm our commitment as a nation to equal justice under the law."

Chapter Three

Japanese by blood

Hearts and minds American

With honor unbowed

Bore the sting of injustice

For future generations

Akemi Dawn Matsumoto Ehrlich

The Isseis' knowledge of intensive farming enabled them to make a living and cultivate rich, highly productive farmland.

The Beginnings

To understand and honor the patriotism of Japanese Americans in World War II, it is necessary to know their history. It begins with the arrival on these shores of immigrants from Japan in the waning decades of the 19th Century and the early years of the 20th. Their motives for leaving the homeland were not unlike those of earlier waves of immigrants from Europe — to seek freedom and find opportunity for improving their lives.

There were jobs aplenty in the burgeoning West for men with willing hands and strong backs. But the Japanese also found something else: Prejudice, codified by laws that denied them citizenship because of race and, after 1925, a total ban against further immigration from Asia.

Like the Blacks of an earlier time in the Deep South, the Japanese in America were accepted so long as they remained in their place. That "place" was unskilled labor and permanent alien status. They could work as farmhands, but as aliens barred from citizenship they were not permitted to own the land they tilled. They could struggle to get an education, but few professions were open to them.

Yet they persisted. They helped lay and maintain the rails that stitched the West together. Their labor built irrigation systems, mined coal, harvested fish and timber. On rented land they cleared the brush and coaxed rich crops out of once desolate soil. They married, nurtured families and urged their children — citizens by birth — to study hard, work hard, and

love America. And many of them — truly an amazing number considering the circumstances — by perseverance became successful professionals and businessmen, merchants and pioneers in the West's expanding agricultural industries. Despite the extreme handicap of permanent alien status, theirs was a true American success story.

It was not until Congress, under intense lobbying by JACL, passed the Walter-McCarran Immigration and Naturalization Act of 1952, that all Asians could apply for citizenship. Thousands of elderly Issei survivors of the immigrant generation, tutored in the intricacies of U.S. civics by their American-born sons and daughters, eagerly lined up to be sworn in as citizens. How much more might they have contributed to America had they received the rights of citizenship earlier in life?

Pacific Citizen

When war came in 1941 with the attack on Pearl Harbor, the Issei generation after decades of struggle was in its most productive years but politically powerless. Their offspring, the Nisei generation, were still young and inexperienced and just beginning to find a niche in their country. Neither group was prepared for the shock that would devastate the Japanese American community in the weeks to follow. In the light of the historical antipathy toward and lingering prejudice against Japanese Americans, perhaps it was inevitable if grossly unjust that the nation's frustration and anger should be directed against anyone who looked like the enemy.

88,000 resident aliens, 85,000 of whom were of Japanese ancestry, became eligible for citizenship through the Walter-McCarran Act.

National Archives

120,000 men, women and children were placed into internment camps surrounded by barbed wire and armed guards. Dispossessed of their homes and belongings, most were unprepared for the harsh winters which would face them.

Seventy-three days after the outbreak of war, on February 19, 1942, President Roosevelt signed Executive Order 9066. It authorized, as a "military necessity," the apprehension and removal of "any or all persons" from any war-sensitive area, which was defined as all of California, Alaska and Hawaii, the southern portion of Arizona, and the western halves of Oregon and Washington.

And except in Hawaii, where the reality was that Japanese Americans were the indispensable backbone of the economy, "any or all persons" turned out to be everyone of Japanese ancestry, "aliens and non-aliens" alike in the official jargon.

The term "non-alien" was particularly disingenuous. By any interpretation, classifying an American citizen as a "non-alien" was a cruel and offensive euphemism to evade the fact that the rights of citizens were being violated. It was a denial of the promise that all citizens are entitled equally to the protections enunciated in the Constitution. Imprisonment was on the basis of race; under E.O. 9066, citizenship counted for no more than a scrap of paper.

The Constitution's Fifth Amendment states that no person shall be "deprived of life, liberty, or property without due process of law." Soldiers with bayonets, not due process, dispossessed Japanese Americans and drove them into detention.

The Fourteenth Amendment further provides that no person shall be denied "the equal protection of the laws".

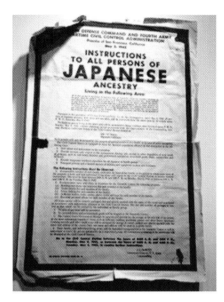

Stark instructions posted after the signing of Executive Order 9066. Non-citizen Issei and citizen Nisei alike were forcibly evacuated to assembly centers while permanent WRA camps were being constructed.

In 1942 the laws were not applied equally to a minority of citizens who had a physical resemblance to the enemy.

Such was the temper of the times that the Executive Order created hardly a ripple of protest in the general public. Any concern for Constitutional rights was overwhelmed by fear of people who looked like the enemy. Federal officials, aware of the enormity of a program to move 120,000 men, women and children away from the West Coast, considered the possibility of a voluntary exodus. In early spring of 1942 they summoned governors of Western states to Salt Lake City to ask their cooperation in accepting the evacuees.

All except one tossed up their hands in horror. If these people were too dangerous to the national security to be allowed to stay on the West Cost, certainly they were unwanted in their states. The one exception was Gov. Ralph Carr of Colorado who pointed out that unwanted "persons of Japanese ancestry" had been accused of nothing, had every legal right to live where they pleased, and would be welcome to his state.

This demonstration of moral courage ended Carr's political career. Carr lost his subsequent campaign for the United States Senate and returned to private life.

Under the authority of the Executive Order, more than 120,000 persons of Japanese ancestry — men, women and children, two-thirds of them citizens by birth — were ordered out of their homes in the spring of 1942 and herded into Army-controlled holding pens set up in fairgrounds and race tracks. The Japanese Americans were imprisoned in these temporary concentration camps while more permanent impoundments were being constructed in desolate and isolated sites in the nation's interior.

Those subject to the Executive Order did not know where they would be taken or when they would be able to return. Under military armed guard, such pertinent questions would remain unanswered.

Weeks and months later the people were moved inland to the ten camps administered by the hastily established civilian War Relocation Authority (WRA) but still guarded by the Army. The government told its prisoners that it was their patriotic duty to accept imprisonment.

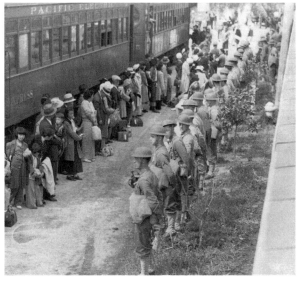

National Archives

National Archives

Disheartened and confused but obedient under the threat of armed force, all complied except for three young citizens — Minoru Yasui, Gordon Hirabayashi and Fred Korematsu. In individually filed test cases, they went to court to assert, without success, their Constitutional right to freedom in the absence of due process. A fourth litigant, Mitsue Endo, succeeded in challenging in court the government's authority to keep her imprisoned after her loyalty had been ascertained.

Armed soldiers boarding a mother and two young children as hundreds more stand awaiting further instructions.

Years later, in what were called the *coram nobis* cases, the three men sought reversal of the convictions on the basis that newly uncovered material showed the government had distorted and falsified evidence against them, suppressing documents that contradicted Lt. Gen. John L. DeWitt's contention that Japanese Americans were dangerous and disloyal. The evidence of misconduct by government attorneys was overwhelming. As a result, a new generation of government attorneys admitted wrongdoing by their predecessors and asked that the convictions be reversed, a request the courts granted without delay.

Chapter Four

Haiku

O, America

Imperfect, stumbling, striving;

Lessons from the past

Bill Hosokawa

The ten War Relocation Camps established to intern the 120,000 Japanese Americans and Issei parents evacuated from areas in California, Oregon, Washington, Arizona, and Alaska. Other camps existed for men taken into custody in Hawaii, as well as those considered potential security risks by the Justice Department.

The Camps

In that fearful summer of 1942, ten huge concentration camps sprang up in the American interior to relocate the men, women and children languishing in intolerable temporary holding pens on the West Coast. Eight of the camps were in the desolate high deserts of the interior West, two in the boggy river bottoms of Arkansas. For Japanese Americans their names are unforgettable: In eastern California, Manzanar near Death Valley and Tule Lake where there is no lake; in sun-scorched Arizona, Poston and Gila River; in Utah, Topaz in the Sevier Desert; in Idaho, Minidoka not far from the Snake River; in windblown Wyoming, Heart Mountain; in southeastern Colorado once buffeted by Dust Bowl storms, Amache; in Arkansas, Rohwer and Jerome. Their names, seared into the memories of the imprisoned, are cut into the stone of the Memorial together with the number each held as an eternal reminder of what was.

National Archives

Successful, well-respected members of society were considered highly suspect and separated from their families.

When evacuation orders were issued, fear and uncertainty shook both the young and the old.

National Archives

The WRA camps, administered by civilians but ringed by barbed wire and guarded by armed troops in watch towers, housed prisoners who were accused of nothing more than being ethnic Japanese. For more than two thousand non-citizen males listed by the Justice Department as potential security risks, but never charged with or convicted of anything other than being of Japanese blood, there were separate isolation camps away from their families. There were also "family" camps which housed Peruvians of Japanese ancestry who were taken from their homes and held hostage for the duration of the war.

Whether operated by WRA or the Justice Department, the camps were barracks cities with a minimum of amenities. In the WRA camps entire families were housed in uninsulated single rooms where privacy was impossible. There was no water in the barracks. Feeding was in mess halls. Until the inmates took it upon themselves to build partitions, intimate human functions were performed in stark rows of communal toilets in central latrines. For the elderly, young children and nursing mothers, it was a nightmare. The medical care available in inadequately equipped hospitals was minimal. Japanese American physicians and nurses, being paid $19 and $16 a month, worked alongside Caucasian care-givers employed at Civil Service salaries. Schools had no desks and, at first, not even books. Here again, qualified Japanese American educators being paid the standard minimal compensation did the same work as their federally employed Caucasian counterparts.

National Archives

Yukiko Okinaga's expression, tagged and awaiting further instruction, exemplifies the feelings at the time of loss and uncertainty.

The intangible losses to families, such as the cohesiveness commonly attributed to Japanese American communities, were immeasurable.

Parents watched in dismay as their authority eroded and family cohesiveness disintegrated. Yet, somehow, the inmates endured the heat, cold and dust and struggled to make sense of this regimented reality so cruelly different from the homes and communities from which they had been driven.

National Archives

National Archives

Intensive nurturing was required to coax crops out of desolate soil.

They staffed the mess halls, hauled the coal to heat their cubicles, scrubbed the clothes, schooled the children, tended the ailing and supported each other. They prayed and wept together. They broke ground, as the Issei had done in their youth, and dug ditches to channel water to the desert to grow food and, remarkably, flowers.

It is impossible to underestimate the impact that the imprisonment experience had on impressionable young Japanese Americans, particularly those of school age. All that they had learned about democracy, freedom and the opportunity of America had been wiped out by harsh racist military orders. Yet, somehow, they persevered and retained their faith. The mood of those times is reflected in two moving poems, composed that first paralyzing winter at the Heart Mountain camp by two young California teen-agers and published in the camp newspaper. The first is by Miyuki Aoyama:

Snow upon the rooftop
Snow upon the coal,
Winter in Wyoming —
Winter in my soul.

The other is by Kay Masuda:

Father you have wronged me grievously,
I know not why you punish me
For sins not done nor reasons known
You have caused me misery.

But through this all I look on you
As a child would look on parents true
With tenderness co-mingling in
Anguishment and bitter tears.
My heart still beats with loyalty
For you are my father,
I know no other.

Early in 1943 the Army announced plans for an all-Nisei unit to be called the 442nd Regimental Combat Team. Its ranks would be filled, in the government's view, by volunteers from the camps rushing to demonstrate their loyalty by enlisting to fight

Issei parents with young sons volunteering for service were filled with both pride and fear. More than 800 of the young Nisei would die serving their country.

for their country. And anticipating early restoration of Selective Service responsibility for all Japanese Americans, the Army prepared a loyalty questionnaire to be answered by all men of draft age.

WRA, seeing this as an opportunity to determine the loyalty to the United States of all its prisoners-without-hearing, mandated that everyone over 17 years of age respond to the same questionnaire. That was a mistake that provoked fear, confusion and anger. The scars of that mandate still fester in Japanese American communities.

Question 27 asked: "Are you willing to serve in the armed forces of the United States on combat duty, wherever ordered?"

The detainees, who had experienced little reasonableness from the government, were understandably cautious about what appeared to be an invitation to suicide. Men beyond draft age, and women, were reluctant to say they were ready to march off into battle. When some cautiously checked the "No" box, they automatically were classified as of suspected loyalty.

Question 28 asked: "Will you swear unqualified allegiance to the United States of America and faithfully defend the United States from any or all attack by foreign or domestic forces, and foreswear any form of allegiance or obedience to the Japanese emperor…?"

The question sounded suspiciously like a trap. Nisei as citizens suspected that to foreswear allegiance to the Japanese emperor might be interpreted as admission that such allegiance had existed even though none had. And the Issei, barred from American citizenship, feared they would be people without a country if they renounced the only citizenship they possessed.

Cautiously, some answered "No" and under the questionnaire's inflexible rules, they also became suspect of disloyalty.

The federal government then offered to send to Japan at the first opportunity anyone who wanted to go, segregating them at the Tule Lake camp until transportation could be arranged. Most of the minority who accepted were aliens who had given up on America, and their minor children. At war's end, a total of 4,732 Japanese Americans left the United States as repatriates or expatriates, but many were U.S.-born minors who later applied for restoration of citizenship and were allowed to return.

Somehow, despite government blunders and insensitivity, the Japanese Americans displayed remarkable fortitude as unindicted exiles in their own land.

There is a bitter lesson in this experience. Now in this less stressful time, every government agency should review the Army's conduct during World War II as a case study of injustices and violations of the basic law of the land, injustices based upon ignorance, expedience and thoughtlessness.

Chapter Five

They risked their lives

above and beyond the call of duty

and in doing so, they did more

than defend America.

In the face of painful prejudice,

they helped to define America at its best.

President William J. Clinton
White House Ceremony
for Congressional Medal of
Honor Recipients

The irony of this billboard is easily captured with President Franklin D. Roosevelt's quote in the upper right hand corner: "Americanism is a matter of the heart; Americanism is not, and never was, a matter of race or ancestry...." Though the majority of Japanese Americans in current military service were discharged after war broke out in 1941, many would ultimately volunteer for service while their families were behind barbed wire, as is indicated by this photo taken at Minidoka Relocation Center.

The Call

Only days after war broke out in 1941, hundreds of Japanese American draftees already in U.S. Army uniform were discharged without explanation other than that it was "for the convenience of the government." Of those retained in service, many were disarmed and transferred from combat units to menial and degrading assignments amounting in many cases to no more than latrine cleaners and officers' houseboys. At the same time the draft status of every Nisei civilian was changed automatically to 4-C — aliens ineligible for military service — despite their U.S. citizenship.

But in one sector, pragmatism prevailed. A handful of Nisei with a working knowledge of the Japanese language had been in training in a hush-hush school, organized by two Army language officers named John Weckerling and Kai Rasmussen at the Presidio in San Francisco, to become combat intelligence specialists. In June of 1942, even as their families were being imprisoned, some of these Nisei specialists were rushed to the Aleutians to help repel a Japanese invasion. They proved to be so valuable that the Army brass took notice and the prison camps were scoured for additional linguists. But so Americanized were the Nisei that only a limited number could meet the Army's requirement of fluency. Ironically, the best linguists were largely Kibei — Nisei who had received some of their education in Japan and therefore had been considered to be most likely to be disloyal to the U.S. Again, the Army could not have been more wrong.

Nisei linguists proved to be priceless assets to the military in translation, interpretation and interrogation of prisoners.

The most able linguists were inducted, given hurried training and flown to far Pacific fronts. Their assignment was to translate captured documents, interrogate prisoners and decipher enemy battle orders and other critically important data. Often they were so close to the front lines that they tapped enemy telephone lines and intercepted orders. Ultimately thousands of Nisei whose skills were sharpened in the language school were sent off to participate in every major Pacific campaign, in the front lines of island-hopping jungle fighting and in response to calls for help from the Navy, Marines, Air Corps and Australian, British and Canadian allies.

At war's end some Nisei linguists were aboard the battleship Missouri for the surrender ceremony in Tokyo Bay. On the Asian mainland, Nisei were with Chinese troops accepting Japanese surrender and among the Yanks parachuting into PW camps to free American prisoners. During America's seven-year occupation and rehabilitation of the defeated Japan, Nisei soldiers played a key part in easing the inevitable stress and securing the peace.

But this utilization of Nisei skills was not generally the case in the beginning. On December 7 the Hawaii Territorial Government mobilized the Territorial Guard made up largely of University of Hawaii students in the reserve officer training program. Two months later Nisei members of the Territorial

Guard were discharged without explanation. Dismayed, they formed the Varsity Victory Volunteers who took on any construction and other non-combat jobs the Army asked of them to demonstrate their loyalty.

The Nisei in the Hawaiian National Guard whose officers were primarily Caucasians, not to be confused with the Territorial Guard, remained in service. On May 30, 1942, 1,315 National Guardsmen were assembled at Schofield Barracks and told the unit was to become the Hawaii Provisional Infantry Battalion and was being sent to the mainland for training. Within days they were on their way. On June 12, 1942, when their transport docked in Oakland, the men learned they would be designated as the 100th Battalion (Separate), which would train at Camp McCoy, Wisconsin. The members of the VVV group, averaging perhaps 10 years younger than the National Guardsmen, later became the core of the 442nd Regimental Combat Team.

So well did the 100th Battalion perform in training that the Army accelerated its plans for another unit of Japanese

Americans to be designated as the 442nd. It was to be a combat team composed of the 442nd Infantry Regiment, the 522nd Field Artillery Battalion, the 232nd Combat Engineer Company, and Cannon, Headquarters and Service Companies and a medical detachment. In January, 1943, many mainland Nisei still serving in various units around the mainland were sent to Camp Shelby in Mississippi as cadre to train those who would come later to be integrated into the 442nd.

442nd RCT training at Camp Shelby, Mississippi. The unit comprised roughly 5,000 Americans of Japanese descent who would soon be sent to service at the front.

An Army representative, at Manzanar, was received with mixed feelings and foreboding.

Meanwhile, recruiting teams were sent to the WRA camps to sign up volunteers to fill the ranks. But again the government miscalculated. Unquestionably, there was something incongruous about the Army inviting Nisei to put their lives on the line while their families were held in U.S. camps. Instead of thousands of volunteers as the Army had anticipated, there were hundreds.

"We are ready to go to war if drafted," the majority seemed to be saying, "but before volunteering to possibly give up our lives, we want freedom for our families." It was an understandable position.

Seattle veterans Bob Sato (left), Joe Kamikawa (center) and Tosh Okamoto were leaders in immortalizing the record set by the Nisei during WWII.

Later, after Selective Service responsibilities were re-instituted for all Japanese Americans, a handful of Nisei as a matter of conscience refused military service so long as their families were imprisoned, and they paid the consequences of violating the Selective Service Act.

Because of the limited initial response on the mainland the Army looked to Hawaii, where there had been no mass imprisonment, to fill out the ranks of the 442nd. The Army sought 1,500 men in Hawaii and 10,000 volunteered. Ultimately 3,000 Japanese Americans from Hawaii were selected to join 1,500 from the mainland to form the 442nd Regimental Combat Team.

While the 442nd proceeded with its training, the 100th left the U.S. for North Africa on August 11, 1943, and landed in Oran on September 2. The 100th was attached to the battle-tested 133rd Infantry of the 34th Division and set foot on the Italian peninsula for the first time at the Salerno beachhead on Sept. 22, D-day plus 13. In the following months the 100th at heavy cost (It was to become known as the Purple Heart Battalion) joined the drive up the Italian peninsula. The 34th Division, including the Nisei, took heartbreaking losses in repeated assaults on German positions on the mountain known as Cassino in January of 1944. The official U.S. Army booklet, "Go for Broke," reports:

Ultimately, over 30,000 young Japanese American men served in uniform; more than 800 names of those who died in service are remembered on the walls of the Memorial.

"History will record that when the line was finally broken and the enemy reeled back, five fresh divisions took on the job that one division (the 34th) so gallantly attempted and so nearly completed.

John Harrington

National Archives

*Group in training at
Camp Shelby.*

History will also record that among the foremost in the ranks of that division were the men of the 100th Infantry Battalion." In just one bloody day the 100th had lost four officers and 38 men killed; 15 officers and 130 men wounded or injured; six men died of wounds; two men missing; and one officer and one man, prisoners.

That was only the beginning. Casualties mounted at an alarming rate in subsequent battles. To replace them the Army drew on troops from the 442nd Combat Team training at Camp Shelby. Thus, when it was time for the 442nd to go overseas and some of the men had been left behind to train new recruits, the Combat Team had been reduced to two battalions. They caught up with the 100th in the middle of June, 1944, at Civitaveccia north of Rome.

There the battle-tested 100th joined the 442nd Regiment as its 1st Battalion, a decision the booklet "Go for Broke" describes as "only fitting since the original 1st Battalion of the 442nd had been bled dry to furnish replacements for the 100th during the long winter campaign." The gutsy performance of the combined 100th/442nd in the months that followed is now legend. After its critical role in fierce fighting that sealed the fate of the Axis nations in central Italy, the regiment was dispatched to France where an offensive was being launched against the southern German flank in the Vosges mountains. The objective was to retake the railroad center of Bruyeres.

One of the streets in Bruyeres with the name "442nd Regiment American Infantry Liberator of Bruyeres October 1944"

The 100th/442nd was involved in 25 days of nearly continuous action in rain and raw cold. It was in this battle that the Nisei rescued the Texas "Lost Battalion" trapped by the Germans, losing more men in the effort than were saved. In all, the 100th/442nd paid a terrible price in the Vosges, suffered 814 casualties — one out of every five men, including 140 dead — while taking every objective. During this bloody three and a half weeks of action the 100th/442nd won five of its seven Presidential Unit Citations.

Appreciation plaque presented to the 442nd Infantry Regiment for its aid and rescue of the 1st Bn., 141st Infantry Regiment near Biffontaine, France.

After the battle, the "Go for Broke" booklet says: "Average company strength in the regiment was 35 men. Company I had a total of five riflemen, plus a few men from the weapons platoon. Company K was commanded by S/Sgt. Tsutomu Yoshida, a squad leader (later lieutenant)... The month the Combat Team spent with the 36th Division had been a month of great heroism and great tragedy. At the time they went into the lines these had been the only fresh troops the Seventh Army possessed. They were committed against an enemy whose orders were to hold to the last man. In destroying this enemy, the Combat Team was so badly battered that it was impossible to go on without reinforcements and these were not forthcoming.

"Perhaps if it had not been for the urgency of the mission to reach the 'Lost Battalion', casualties would have been lower, but even this is doubtful. Suffice it to say that the 442nd Combat Team contributed mightily to the drive of the Seventh Army when its contribution was needed most.

That, after all, is the highest accolade of any regiment of infantry."

After a winter of relative quiet patrolling the forests of the rugged French-Italian Alps while replacements from Camp Shelby were being

National Archives

Military funerals such as this were an unfortunate common occurrence for Issei parents.

hardened, the 100th/442nd was called back to Northern Italy to help dislodge German forces dug into the mountain stronghold of the Gothic line. Instead of attempting another frontal assault, the strategists picked the Nisei for a critical "end-around" attack. In the dark of night Nisei troops silently climbed the precipitous face of a 3,000-foot mountainside, lay hidden the next day, then launched a pre-dawn flank attack that led to breaking the back of the Gothic line.

The Presidential Unit Citation read by Gen. Dwight D. Eisenhower said: "The 442nd Regimental Combat Team... is cited for outstanding accomplishment in combat...

National Archives

by executing a diversionary attack on the Ligurian coast (Carrara, Italy, April 1945)… a daring and skillful flanking attack on the positions which formed the western anchor of the formidable Gothic line. In 4 days, the attack destroyed positions which

Sixteen of the twenty-one Congressional Medals of Honor awarded to the 100th Bn/442nd RCT were earned on the battlefronts in Italy.

1st Lt. Shigeru Tsubota, pictured, was serving with the 100th Battalion before his hospitalization for a shrapnel wound.

had withstood efforts…for five months. The 442nd drove forward despite heavy casualties…allowing the enemy no time for rest or reorganization…liberated the city of Carrara, seized the heights beyond…and opened the way for advances on the key road center and ports of La Spezia and Genoa…The successful accomplishment of this mission turned a diversionary action into a full-scale and victorious offensive…an important part in the final destruction of the German armies in Italy."

But the war was not over. After the campaign in the Vosges Mountains the 522nd Field Artillery Battalion had been detached for special duty supporting U.S. divisions assaulting the Siegfried

Line between central France and Germany. In true irony the Nisei of the 522nd, some of whom had relatives under detention back home, were among the troops that liberated prisoners in one of the impoundments at the Nazi death camp known as Dachau.

In all, the 100th and 442nd fought in seven campaigns in two countries. Their members were awarded 18,143 individual decorations, including more than 9,500 Purple Heart Medals for battle wounds, 5,200 Bronze Stars, 588 Silver Stars, 52 Distinguished Service Crosses and one Medal of Honor to Pvt. Sadao Munemori. After wiping out two enemy machine gun nests, Munemori sacrificed his own life by throwing himself on a German grenade to save two of his comrades.

National Archives

Young Nisei and Issei parents alike suffered tragic losses in battle.

In this photo Lt. General John W. O'Daniel awards the Bronze Star Medal posthumously to Gazo Shiroma, father of Private First Class Yoshinobu Gusukuma of Kaneohe, Oahu, killed in action in Korea, 1952.

Congressional Medal of Honor, highest military decoration awarded by the President of the United States, authorized by Congress.

The Medal of Honor, which must be authorized by Congress, is the nation's highest award for extraordinary heroism. Why the 100th/442nd received only one Medal of Honor and 52 of the next highest decoration, the Distinguished Service Cross, plus seven Presidential Unit Citations, puzzled many. In 1996 Senator Daniel Akaka of Hawaii sponsored legislation to look into this seeming discrepancy. After a thorough review of the records, the names of 104 Asian American veterans were submitted to the Army Decorations Board which recommended that 22 of the awards be upgraded to Medal of Honor. Twenty were members of the 100th/442nd.

Their names: Pvt. Barney F. Hajiro, Pvt. Mikio Hasemoto, Pvt. Joe Hayashi, Pvt. Shizuya Hayashi, 2nd/Lt. Daniel K. Inouye, T/Sgt. Yeiki Kobashigawa, S/Sgt. Robert T. Kuroda, Pfc. Kaoru Moto, Pfc. Kiyoshi K. Muranaga, Pvt. Masato Nakae, Pvt. Shinyei Nakamine, Pfc. William K. Nakamura, Pfc. Joe M. Nishimoto, S/Sgt. Allan M. Ohata, T/Sgt. James Okubo, T/Sgt. Yukio Okutsu, Pfc. Frank H. Ono, S/Sgt. Kazuo Otani, Pvt. George T. Sakato, T/Sgt. Ted T. Tanouye.

The other two were 2nd Lt. Rudolph B. Davila who served with the 7th Infantry Division, and Capt. Francis B. Wai, 24th Infantry Division.

White House ceremony for Congressional Medal of Honor recipients, June 21, 2000.

Eight of the 22 were killed in action and seven had died since World War II. One of the seven, James Okubo, was an unarmed combat medic who had twice exposed himself to murderous fire to rescue wounded buddies.

The survivors, including Senator Inouye, were presented their Medals of Honor at the White House on June 21, 2000. President Clinton observed: "They risked their lives above and beyond the call of duty and in doing so, they did more than defend America. In the face of painful prejudice, they helped to define America at its best."

The Nisei performance in battle added great luster to the history of American military valor. More significantly,

National Archives

A Hawaiian family welcoming home their Nisei son and soldier.

the men of the 100th/ 442nd focused worldwide attention on the fact that Americans were of many ethnic groups committed to the cause of freedom. While the 100th/442nd is usually described as an all-Nisei outfit, most of its officers were Caucasians.

Battlefield commissions for Nisei — ultimately as many as 88 — with outstanding leadership qualities helped increase the number of Nisei officers in combat. And as the Army gained confidence in the Nisei, more and more of them were selected for Officer Candidate School. (The current U.S. Army Chief of Staff, Gen. Eric Shinseki, is a Japanese American.)

In battle, strong ties of affection and trust grew between the Nisei troops and their Caucasian officers. Lieut. Col. James M. Hanley, commander of the 442nd's 2nd Battalion, was outraged when he received a clipping from his hometown newspaper in Mandan, S.D., which made a crack about there being "some good Jap-Americans in this country but it didn't say where they were buried." Colonel Hanley wrote to the editor:

"Yes, Charlie, I know where there are some GOOD Japanese Americans — there are some 5,000 of them in this unit. They are American soldiers — and I know where some of them are buried. I wish I could show you some of them."

Hanley cited the stories of several Japanese Americans who had lost their lives in battle and continued:

Nisei of the 442nd assemble for inspection.

"I wish I could tell you the number of Japanese Americans who have died in this unit alone. I wish the boys in the 'Lost Battalion' could tell you what they think of Japanese Americans. I wish that all the troops we have fought beside could tell you what they know. The marvel is,

National Archives

Charlie, that these boys fight at all — they are good soldiers in spite of the type of racial prejudice shown by your paragraph.

"I know it makes a good joke — but it is the kind of joke that prejudice thrives upon. It shows a lack of faith in the American ideal. Our system is supposed to make good Americans out of anyone — it certainly has done it in the case of these boys. You, the Hood River Legion Post, Hearst and a few others make one wonder just what we are fighting for. I hope it isn't racial prejudice. Come over here, Charlie, I'll show you where 'some good Japanese Americans' are buried."

Members of this regiment were not the only Nisei to fight and, too often, die for their country. Japanese Americans served with other combat units in Europe and the Southwest Pacific, with the Army Air Corps, the Office of Strategic Services, as front-line intelligence specialists in such bloody battlefronts as New Guinea, China, Burma, Guadalcanal and Okinawa, Iwo Jima and the Philippines, Tarawa and the Aleutians. Some of the best of the linguists were too valuable to be sent overseas. They worked secretly in a Maryland headquarters checking and analyzing and reviewing information hurriedly decoded in the field while others manned a highly classified radio listening post in Portland, Oregon monitoring Japanese domestic broadcasts.

In the Pacific Theater, no major unit was without a team of Nisei language specialists. Said Maj. Gen. Charles Willoughby, Gen. Douglas MacArthur's chief of intelligence: "Never before in history did an Army know so much concerning its enemy, prior to actual engagement, as did the Army during most of the Pacific campaigns…The Nisei saved a million lives and shortened the war by two years."

At a California burial service for S/Sgt. Kazuo Masuda who was killed in Italy, Gen. Joseph Stilwell who had served with Nisei in Burma remarked: "The Nisei bought an awful big hunk of America with their blood. You're damned right those Nisei boys have a place in the American heart, now and forever."

Belatedly, as the War Department in 2000 reviewed and upgraded the decorations of Nisei deserving of the Medal of Honor, a Presidential Unit Citation was awarded those who

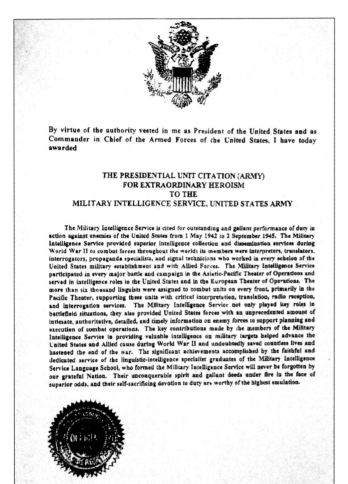

By virtue of the authority vested in me as President of the United States and as Commander in Chief of the Armed Forces of the United States, I have today awarded

THE PRESIDENTIAL UNIT CITATION (ARMY)
FOR EXTRAORDINARY HEROISM
TO THE
MILITARY INTELLIGENCE SERVICE, UNITED STATES ARMY

The Military Intelligence Service is cited for outstanding and gallant performance of duty in action against enemies of the United States from 1 May 1942 to 2 September 1945. The Military Intelligence Service provided superior intelligence collection and dissemination services during World War II to combat forces throughout the world; its members were interpreters, translators, interrogators, propaganda specialists, and signal technicians who worked in every echelon of the United States military establishment and with Allied Forces. The Military Intelligence Service participated in every major battle and campaign in the Asiatic-Pacific Theater of Operations and served in intelligence roles in the United States and in the European Theater of Operations. The more than six thousand linguists were assigned to combat units on every front, primarily in the Pacific Theater, supporting these units with critical interpretation, translation, radio reception, and interrogation services. The Military Intelligence Service not only played key roles in battlefield situations, they also provided United States forces with an unprecedented amount of intimate, authoritative, detailed, and timely information on enemy forces to support planning and execution of combat operations. The key contributions made by the members of the Military Intelligence Service in providing valuable intelligence on military targets helped advance the United States and Allied cause during World War II and undoubtedly saved countless lives and hastened the end of the war. The significant achievements accomplished by the faithful and dedicated service of the linguistic-intelligence specialist graduates of the Military Intelligence Service Language School, who formed the Military Intelligence Service will never be forgotten by our grateful Nation. Their unconquerable spirit and gallant deeds under fire in the face of superior odds, and their self-sacrificing devotion to duty are worthy of the highest emulation.

Presidential Unit Citation awarded to the Military Intelligence Service

had served with the Military Intelligence Service in World War II. The award, presented by General Shinseki at a dinner honoring Nisei veterans, was unprecedented in U.S. military history since it is given only to combat units and not to a "service" such as the MIS. A special act of Congress was necessary to give the intelligence service this recognition.

From the outset, GFBNVA and its successor, NJAMF, wanted more than just a monument honoring Japanese Americans who fought in World War II. One idea discussed was a memorial building in addition to a monument, the building to serve as the official repository, in the words of GFBNVA minutes, "for the records, documents, memorabilia, artifacts, pictures, and other mementos of those of Japanese ancestry who served in all of America's wars, from the Spanish-American War, down through World War I and II, Korea, Vietnam and Grenada, as well as the Nisei Colonel (Ellison Onizuka) in the Space Shuttle Challenger."

Indeed, seven Japanese serving in the U.S. Navy had been killed in the sinking of the battleship Maine in 1898 in Havana Harbor that led to the Spanish-American War. Let their names be recorded here: Suke Chingi, Otogiro Ishida, Yukichi Kitagata, Tomekichi Nagamine, Mas Ohye, Isa Sugisaki, Kashitaro Suzuki. An eighth Japanese, Katsusaburo Kushida, survived. Two decades later nearly 700 Issei and a handful of Nisei had served in various U.S. Army units in World War I.

In World War II, while most Nisei had been segregated in the 100th/442nd or Military Intelligence, there were many others who served in a variety of units on the same basis as other Americans, a notable example being Sgt. Ben Kuroki, Army Air Corps gunner who flew hair-raising bombing missions over Europe and

President Eisenhower pins the Congressional Medal of Honor on Hershey Miyamura for his service in the Korean War. Hershey was drafted into the Army in 1944 and served with the 442nd in Italy. He received his Medal of Honor in 1953.

National Archives

National Archives

Pvt. Shizuko Shinagawa, a native of Arizona, was visiting in California at the time of the evacuation and was confined in Poston for 10 months before being inducted into the Women's Army Corps in August 1943.

Japan. There were Nisei combat surgeons, such as Maj. Robert Kinoshita of the 7th Armored Division. In the space of a month in the summer of 1944 he won a Silver Star Medal and an Oak Leaf Cluster representing a second Silver Star. These were for extraordinary valor in four separate actions in which he rescued and cared for wounded GIs while under enemy fire in France. Kinoshita, who had to fight his way into the Army, won seven combat medals and was wounded three times. 2nd Lt. Harry Yanagimachi, who was graduated from Officer Candidate School after the war had ended in Europe, found himself leading his infantry platoon on missions against Japanese in the jungles of the Philippines.

Nor must we overlook the Nisei women who served as Army nurses and in the Women's Army Corps, and the psychological warfare specialists undermining Japanese morale with propaganda broadcasts and leaflets. In September, 1943, 47 Nisei were inducted into the Women's Army Corps, the first of more than 300 to serve in uniform. After basic training some of them volunteered for the Military Intelligence

Service Language School at Fort Snelling, Minnesota, and after Japan's surrender many served with Occupation forces.

By the outbreak of the Korean War in 1950, racial segregation in the Armed Forces had ended. Nisei and Sansei, some of whom were veterans of World War II who had been recalled into service, fought with great distinction in racially integrated units. At least 247 Japanese Americans, including 15 who had served in World War II, gave their lives in the Korean conflict. One of the World War II veterans, Sgt. Hershey Miyamura, won the Medal of Honor in Korea but the award was kept secret until he was released from a Communist prisoner of war camp.

Army Chief of Staff Gen. Eric Shinseki with Vietnam veteran and Board Member Maj. Gen. James H. Mukoyama Jr. (Ret) at Groundbreaking Ceremony, October 22, 1999.

In Vietnam, members of a new generation of Japanese Americans had served not only as infantrymen but as Air Force and Naval officers, helicopter and fighter pilots and technical specialists in a racially integrated defense establishment. Two Japanese Americans, Rodney

John Harrington

Yano and Terry Kawamura were awarded the Medal of Honor. At least 121 Japanese Americans were among the dead. In the brief invasion of Grenada in 1983, one of the few American fatalities was a Sansei.

Each of these men who gave his life deserves recognition on a memorial to Japanese American patriotism, but NJAMF was bound by the restrictions, limiting honors to World War II, written into the Congressional authorization.

A Chicago Sansei member of the NJAMF Board, James H. Mukoyama Jr., a retired major general, veteran of service in Korea and Vietnam and the first Nikkei to command a U.S. Army division, volunteered to take on the responsibility of identifying the names to appear on the Memorial. The work, with assistance of another member of the Board, Kelly Kuwayama, and James Yamashita from the AJA World War II Memorial Alliance, was a two-year effort. It involved coordination with the 100th/442nd Veterans Club in Honolulu, the World War II AJA Alliance in Los Angeles, and research in the National Archives. In addition the list was posted on a website and the public helped to add and delete names. "I volunteered for the project as a labor of love and accept full responsibility for its accuracy," Mukoyama declared.

Since military records did not identify soldiers as Japanese Americans, numerous pieces of information were considered in evaluating a serviceman for listing: family name, first name, middle initial, rank, serial number, unit, date of death, place of death, and place of burial. One of the key sources of information was the official 1946 War Department Honor Roll List. In some cases confirmation had to be requested of families. Not all qualifying elements were obtained for every individual. If not enough elements were available to justify listing, the name was placed on an unconfirmed list until additional information became available. As a final precaution, Shiuko Sakai, a regular Foundation volunteer, double and triple checked each name before it was chiseled into stone.

The Memorial Foundation has been able to identify over 800 Japanese Americans — and Caucasians who served with the Nisei in the 100th/442nd — who gave their lives in

John Harrington

The names engraved on the Memorial wall convey the harsh reality of the sacrifices of the young Nisei. Board Member and GFBNVA President, Tom Masamori, and hundreds of others were deeply moved at the Dedication Ceremony, November 9, 2000.

World War II. Their names, in honored glory, are engraved in the stone of five of the Memorial's panels and reproduced on these pages. In every sense the Memorial is a tribute to their courage, patriotism and sacrifice. The poem that appears adjacent to the names, written in the classic Japanese tanka form, is the work of Akemi Dawn Matsumoto Ehrlich of San Mateo, California, selected after a nation-wide competition.

It reads:

LEGACY

Japanese by blood

Hearts and minds American,

With honor unbowed

Bore the sting of injustice

For future generations

On the Memorial are etched the following names:

*A*BE, CHESTER K.
AJITOMI, MATSUEI
AJITOMI, TOKIO
AKIMOTO, JOHN
AKIMOTO, VICTOR
AKIYAMA, HIDEO
AKIYAMA, ZENTARO G.
AMABE, EUGENE T.
AMAKAWA, NOBUO
ANDERSON, DANIEL J.
ANZAI,JAMES H.
AOYAMA,YOSHIHARU N.
ARAKAKI, HIDEO W.
ARAKAWA, HAROLD J.
ARAKAWA, JAMES Y.
ARAKI, MASASHI
ARIKAWA, FRANK N.
ARITA, HIROAKI
ASADA, TATSUMI
ASAHINA, SHIRO
ASAI, RALPH Y.
ASAKAWA, JACK
ASATO, SHOTARO H.
ASAUMI, KENNETH I.
ASHIKAWA, SHIGEO

*B*ETSUI, DANIEL D.
BOODRY, JAMES
BURT, HOWARD V.
BYRNE, JOSEPH L.

*C*HIBANA, HENRY M.

CHINEN, GICHI
CHINEN, JENHATSU
CHINEN, ONSO
CHORIKI, DANNY K.
CONNER, CLOUDY G.
CRONE, WALTER M.

*D*OI, HARUO

*E*ATON, KENNETH E.
EBATA,TETSUO T.
EJI, WILLIAM K.
EKI, GEORGE
ENDO, HIROO H.
ENDO, MASAHARU
ENDO, ROBERT T.
ENOMOTO, KANAME
ENOMOTO, KIYOZO
ENSMINGER, RALPH B.
ETHRIDGE, HAROLD C.

*F*ARNUM, CHARLES O. JR.
FRITZMEIER, FRED H.
FUJI, ABE M.
FUJII, MASAO
FUJII, RICHARD T.
FUJII, YUTAKA
FUJIKAWA, JITSURO
FUJIKAWA, MASAKI
FUJIKI, HIDEO
FUJIMOTO, TOSHIAKI

FUJINAKA, NOBORU
FUJINO, RUSSELL T.
FUJINO, YASUO
FUJINO, YOSHIMI
FUJIOKA, TERUO
FUJIOKA, TERUO T.
FUJIOKA, WENDELL S.
FUJITA, SADAMI
FUJITANI, ROSS K.
FUJIWARA, PETER K.
FUJIYAMA, TAKEO
FUKAGAWA, MASAMI
FUKEDA, AKIRA W.
FUKUBA, SHIGEO G.
FUKUHARA, HERBERT M.
FUKUI, EDWIN Y.
FUKUMOTO, ROY S.
FUKUMURA, ICHIJI
FUKUNAGA, CHESTER T.
FUKUOKA, ARTHUR M.
FUKUSHIMA, KATSUMI
FUKUYAMA, KAORU
FUNAI, STANLEY K.
FURUKAWA, SATOSHI
FURUKAWA, TATSUMI
FURUKAWA, TSUYOSHI
FURUKIDO, KENNETH K.
FURUSHIRO, HENRY T.
FURUUCHI, MITSUO
FUTAMATA, GEORGE M.
FUYUMURO, SHIGETO E.

*G*AGNON, ROLAND J.
GANEKO, SEKICHI
GODA, HIROSHI
GOSHIKOMA, RALPH M.
GOTO, YOSHITO
GOYA, KAZUO
GOYA, YEIKO
GUSHIKEN, GEORGE

*H*ACHIYA, FRANK T.
HADA, VICTOR K.
HADANO, HATSUJI
HAITA, EIICHI F.
HAJI, TOM S.
HAMADA, TETSUO
HAMAMOTO, KATSUYOSHI
HAMAMOTO, SEIICHI
HAMANAKA, FRED Y.
HANA, CLIFFORD H.
HANAUMI, RICHARD S.
HANIDA, TAMOTSU
HARA, BEN K.
HARADA, CHARLES K.
HARANO, JOHN Y.
HASEGAWA, KIYOSHI
HASEMOTO, MIKIO

HASHIMOTO, DENNIS M.
HASHIMOTO, JOHN T.
HASHIZUME, HISAO
HATANAKA, MASAO
HATTORI, KUNIO
HAYAKAWA, HARRY M.
HAYAMA, MAKOTO
HAYAMI, STANLEY K.
HAYASHI, DONALD S.
HAYASHI, JOE J.
HAYASHI, ROBERT N.
HAYASHI, TADAO
HAYASHI, TORAO
HAYASHIDA, HENRY Y.
HAYASHIDA, HIDEYUKI
HEMPSTEAD, ROBERT L.
HIDAKA, EIJI
HIGA, CHARLES S.
HIGA, EDDIE K.
HIGA, KATSUMORI P.
HIGA, MASAO
HIGA, TAKEMITSU
HIGA, TOSHIO
HIGA, WILSON E.
HIGA, YEIKO
HIGASHI, BERT K.
HIGASHI, HAROLD T.
HIGASHI, JAMES T.
HIGUCHI, MASAMI H.
HIKICHI, HARRY N.
HIRAHARA, TOMOSU
HIRAKI, MITSUO
HIRAMATSU, KAZUO L.
HIRAMOTO, HIROYUKI
HIRANO, FREDRICK M.
HIRANO, ROBERT R.
HIRAOKA, GENICHI W.
HIRAOKA, SATORU
HIRATA, GEROME M.
HIRATANI, HIMEO
HIRAYAMA, YASUO
HIRAYAMA, YUTAKA
HISANO, MASAO
HISAOKA, GARY T.
HIYAMA, YEIICHI
HONDA, RICHARD M.
HORINOUCHI, JAMES J.
HORIUCHI, PAUL F.
HOSHINO, ROBERT S.
HOSODA, EARL
HOSODA, MAX M. JR.
HOTTA, KIHACHIRO J.
HOZAKI, TOSHIO
HUNT, LEON I.

*I*CHIKI, STANLEY T.
ICHIMURA, KENICHI
IDE, EDWARD Y.
IGARASHI, SHIGEO

IGUCHI, KIYOSHI
IHA, MASAO
IHARA, KAZUO
IIDA, GEORGE U.
IIDA, MARTIN M.
IKEDA, GEORGE
IKEDA, GEORGE T.
IKEDA, ISAMU
IKEDA, KATSUMI
IKEDA, MASAO
IKEDA, ROY Y.
IKEDA, WILLIAM Y.
IKEFUGI, LLOYD
IKEHARA, HENRY S.
IKEHARA, KIKUCHIRO D.
IKEMOTO, HARUYUKI
IKEMOTO, KANAMAE
IKENO, JAMES S.
IMAI, SABURO
IMAI, TOMIO
IMAMOTO, WILLIAM I.
IMAMURA, LARRY M.
IMANO, SUSUMU
IMOTO, WILLIAM S.
INADA, THOMAS T.
INAKAZU, BEN M.
INAMINE, SEIJI
INATSU, MASAMI
INKYO, SUEICHI
INOUE, MINORU
INOUYE, ITSUTOMU
INOUYE, KAZUYOSHI
INOUYE, MASATO
IRIE, MASAJI
IRIGUCHI, TADAYOSHI
ISERI, MITSUO M.
ISHIDA, HARUO
ISHIDA, MINORU
ISHII, GEORGE F.
ISHII, MASAYUKI
ISHII, RICHARD H.
ISHIKI, WALTER S.
ISOBE, KOSAKU
ITO, HACHIRO
ITO, TAKASHI
ITO, TETSUO
IWAHIRO, ROBERT K.
IWAI, HISASHI
IWAMASA, YOSHIO
IWAMOTO, LAWRENCE T.
IZUMIZAKI, HENRY S.

*J*ICHAKU, THOMAS M.
JINNOHARA, KATSUI
JOHNSON, JOHN A. JR.

*K*ADOOKA, CHITOSHI W.
KADOYAMA, JOE Y.

KAGAWA, YASUO
KAGIHARA, JAMES J.
KAIURA, RICHARD K.
KAJIKAWA, TSUGITO
KAJIWARA, NOBUO
KAMAI, WILLIAM K. JR.
KAMEDA, FRED Y.
KAMEOKA, BOB T.
KAMETANI, SHINOBU
KAMI, MITSUO
KAMIKAWA, SHIZUTO
KANADA, JAMES J.
KANAYA, WALTER E.
KANAZAWA, JOHN S.
KANDA, FRANK T.
KANDA, TAKEZO
KANEICHI, TAKEO
KANEMITSU, KATSUHIRO
KANESHIRO, SEICHI
KANESHIRO, YASUO
KANETANI, ISAMU
KANETOMI, JIRO
KANZAKI, AKIRA
KARATSU, JAMES S.
KARIMOTO, HARUO
KASHIWAEDA, KENNETH G.
KASHIWAGI, KAZUO
KATAOKA, YOSHITAKA
KATAYAMA, NORITADA
KATO, JOHN J.
KATO, JOSEPH H.
KATO, KENJI
KATO, YOSHIO
KATSUDA, MASAICHI C.
KAWAGUCHI, JOHN R.
KAWAHARA, RICHARD HIROO
KAWAKAMI, TETSURO
KAWAMOTO, HARUO
KAWAMOTO, HARUO
KAWAMOTO, SADAO
KAWAMOTO, TOSHIO
KAWAMOTO, YUTAKA
KAWANISHI, KIKUMATSU F.
KAWANO, CIKE C.
KAWANO, GEORGE U.
KAWANO, TETSUO
KAWANO, YASUO
KAWATA, ALBERT G.
KAYA, SATOSHI
KAYA, STEPHEN M.
KENMOTSU, YASUO
KEY, LEWIS A.
KIJIMA, TADASHI
KIKUCHI, LEO T.
KIMURA, MATSUICHI
KIMURA, PAUL JR.
KIMURA, PAUL T.
KIMURA, TSUGUO
KINA, SHOMATSU E.
KINOSHITA, FRANCIS T.

KINOSHITA, MAMORU
KINOSHITA, RICHARD K.
KINYONE, JOSEPH F.
KIRITO, TOSHIO
KISHI, ROBERT T.
KITAGAWA, ROY J.
KITSUSE, PAUL T.
KIYABU, RONALD S.
KIYOTA, EDWARD Y.
KODA, KIICHI
KOHARA, SADAICHI
KOITO, SADAMU
KOIZUMI, HAYATO
KOIZUMI, YUTAKA
KOJAKU, SHAW
KOJIMA, TADASHI
KOKAME, NOBUO
KOKUBU, JIMMIE T.
KOMATSU, JAMES K.
KOMATSU, KATSUTO
KOMEDA, FRED H.
KOMOTO, NOBUO
KONDO, HARUSHI B.
KONDO, HENRY
KONDO, HERBERT Y.
KONDO, HOWARD N.
KOTSUBO, SEICHI
KUBA, SHIGEO
KUBO, TADASHI
KUBO, YOSHIO
KUBOKAWA, JAMES K.
KUBOYAMA, MITSUHARU
KUGE, THOMAS T.
KUNIMATSU, ISAMU
KURAOKA, JERRY S.
KURATA, MINORU
KURODA, ICHIJI H.
KURODA, ROBERT T.
KUROKAWA, BEN S.
KUTAKA, SHOSEI
KUTARA, MASAJI H.
KUWADA, JOSEPH T.
KUWAHARA, SUNAO T.
KYONO, JOHN H.

*L*AFFIN, WILLIAM
LANG, CLARENCE E.
LUNA, LEONARD H.

*M*ADOKORO, HARRY F.
MAEHARA, SABURO
MAGARIFUJI, RICHARD K.
MAKI, ALBERT E.
MAKISHI, MATSUTADA
MANA, SEISO J.
MASAOKA, BEN F.
MASAOKA, KAY K.
MASAOKA, PETER S.

MASHITA, MASATOMO
MASUDA, DICK Z.
MASUDA, ESO
MASUDA, KAZUO
MASUDA, YOSHITO
MASUMOTO, GEORGE H.
MASUMOTO, NORIYUKI
MASUMURA, LAWRENCE K.
MASUNAGA, KIYOSHI
MASUOKA, PETER S.
MATSUDA, CARL G.
MATSUI, MASAO
MATSUKAWA, HIROSHI
MATSUKAWA, ISAMIE
MATSUMOTO, DICK Y.
MATSUMOTO, GORO
MATSUMOTO, KIYUICHI
MATSUMOTO, SADAO
MATSUMOTO, TOMMY T.
MATSUMURA, RENKICHI
MATSUNAGA, KANAME
MATSUOKA, SATOSHI
MATSUSHIMA, KAZUO
MATSUSHITA, SHIZUO J.
MAYEDA, GEORGE M.
MEKATA, THOMAS T.
MIGITA, TORAO
MIHO, KATSUAKI
MINAMI, YOSHIO T.
MINATODANI, ISAMU
MINE, KIYOSHI
MISUMI, TOM T.
MITANI, KAZUO
MITO, KAZUO
MIURA, JACK E.
MIURA, LARRY N.
MIURA, TOSHIO
MIYABE, CHARLES M.
MIYAGI, MASAYOSHI
MIYAGUCHI, MASAYUKI J.
MIYAKE, TETSUO
MIYAMOTO, JAMES H.
MIYAMOTO, THOMAS T.
MIYAMOTO, YASUO R.
MIYAOKA, GEORGE S.
MIYASATO, ISAMI
MIYATA, TAMOTSU
MIYAZONO, TOKIO
MIYOGA, TSUYOSHI
MIYOKO, MITSURU E.
MIYOKO, NOBORU
MIZOKAMI, TIMOTHY I.
MIZUKAMI, WILLIAM S.
MIZUMOTO, LARRY T.
MIZUMOTO, MORIO
MIZUTARI, YUKITAKA T.
MOCHIZUKI, HENRY T.
MORAN, EDWARD V.
MORI, KIYOTO
MORI, SHIGERU

MORIGUCHI, HALUTO
MORIGUCHI, ROKURO
MORIHARA, ARTHUR A.
MORIHIRO, ROY T.
MORIKAWA, HARUTO
MORIKAWA, HIROMU
MORIMOTO, TOSHIAKI
MORISAKI, HAROLD H.
MORISHIGE, JOSEPH
MORISHITA, TAKEO
MORITA, IWAO
MORIWAKI, GEORGE K.
MOSELEY, DAVID L.
MOTOISHI, HIROSHI
MOTOKANE, WILFRED M.
MOTONAGA, SUSUMU
MOTOYAMA, SUSUMU
MUKAI, HACHIRO
MUNEMORI, SADAO S.
MURAKAMI, ISAMU
MURAKAMI, KIYOSHI
MURAKAMI, LESTER T.
MURAKAMI, SAKAE
MURAKAMI, TADATAKA L.
MURAKAMI, TOKIWO
MURAKAMI, TOSHIO T.
MURAMOTO, MASARU
MURANAGA, KIYOSHI K.
MURASHIGE, RICHARD K.
MURATA, ROBERT S.
MURONAKA, LARRY H.
MURONAKA, MITSUGI

NAEMURA, ROY I.
NAGAJI, GROVER K.
NAGAMI, HIROSHI
NAGANO, HIROSHI F.
NAGANO, SETSUO
NAGANUMA, MARTIN M.
NAGAO, GOICHI
NAGAOKA, HITOSHI
NAGATA, HIDEO
NAGATA, JIM
NAGATA, TAICHI
NAGATO, FUMITAKE
NAITO, KAORU
NAJITA, HITOSHI
NAKAGAKI, MASARU
NAKAGAWA, HIRAO E.
NAKAHARA, SHOICHI
NAKAI, HITOSHI
NAKAMA, MASAO R.
NAKAMA, SHIGENORI
NAKAMINE, SHINYEI
NAKAMOTO, JOE K.
NAKAMOTO, SEICHI
NAKAMURA, EDWARD E.
NAKAMURA, GEORGE I.
NAKAMURA, GEORGE S.

NAKAMURA, HENRY Y.
NAKAMURA, IWAO
NAKAMURA, JOHN M.
NAKAMURA, KOSEI
NAKAMURA, MASAKI H.
NAKAMURA, NED T.
NAKAMURA, TADAO
NAKAMURA, WILLIAM K.
NAKAMURA, YOSHIMITSU
NAKANISHI, MASAO
NAKANO, TSUTOMU
NAKASAKI, ROBERT K.
NAKASHIMA, RAITO R.
NAKASHIMA, WATARU
NAKATA, ALFRED Y.
NAKAUYE, DONALD T.
NAKAYA, KIYOSHI C.
NAKAYAMA, MINORU
NAKAZATO, SABURO B.
NARIMATSU, JOHN T.
NEZU, YUTAKA
NII, YOSHITO
NIIDE, SHIGETO
NILGES, EDWARD J.
NINOMIYA, BAN
NINOMIYA, TAKAO T.
NISHI, CHIKAO
NISHI, TAKANORI A.
NISHIHARA, KAZUO
NISHIKAWA, AKIO
NISHIMOTO, JOE M.
NISHIMOTO, TOM T.
NISHIMURA, SHIGEKI
NISHIMURA, WILFRED K.
NISHISHITA, CHARLES J.
NISHITANI, CHIETO
NISHITANI, TARO
NITTA, KONGO
NODA, SUEO
NORITAKE, YOSHITO
NOZAKI, ALBERT Y.
NOZAKI, TADASHI
NOZAWA, ALFRED S.
NUMA, TOSHIO

OBA, MASAYOSHI
OBA, SANICHI G.
OBA, STANLEY T.
OCHIAE, LARRY M.
OGATA, BENJAMIN F.
OGATA, FRED S.
OGATA, MASARU
OGATA, MASAYOSHI
OGATA, TSUGIO
OGAWA, EDWARD
OGAWA, JOHN N.
OGAWA, SADAO
OGOMORI, YOSHIO W.
OHAMA, ABRAHAM G.

OHKI, ARNOLD
OISHI, TEIJI T.
OJIRI, AKIRA
OKADA, JOHN T.
OKAMOTO, DONALD M.
OKAMOTO, JAMES S.
OKAMOTO, JAMES T.
OKAMOTO, RALPH S.
OKAMOTO, TOMISO
OKAZAKI, ISAO
OKAZAKI, TAKAAKI
OKIDA, KATSUNOSHIN
OKIDO, SHOJI
OKIMOTO, RICHARD M.
OKU, MUNEO L.
OKUMA, SEIEI
OKUMURA, TOYOKAZU
OKURA, SUSUMU
OLIVER, HARRY E.
OMOKAWA, GEORGE
OMURA, KENNETH
ONAGA, TAKEYASU T.
ONODERA, SATORU
ONOYE, LLOYD M.
OSATO, REGINALD M.
OSHIRO, CHOYEI
OSHIRO, KENNETH C.
OSHIRO, SAM Y.
OSHIRO, SEIKICHI
OSHIRO, WALLACE H.
OSHIRO, YEISHIN
OTA, DANIEL C.
OTA, GEORGE
OTA, RANDALL M.
OTA, ROY
OTAGURO, TADASHI
OTAKE, MASANAO R.
OTANI, DOUGLAS K.
OTANI, KAZUO
OTSUBO, AKIRA R.
OTSUKA, JIRO
OYABU, HARUMATSU
OYAKAWA, FRANCIS K.
OZAKI, ROBERT Y.
OZAWA, GEORGE Y.

PERRAS, FRANCIS J.
PETERSON, ROY T.
POTTER, RALPH J. JR

RAY, NEIL M.
RIYU, MASATSUGU
ROGERS, BEN W. JR.

SADAYASU, HERBERT K.
SAGAMI, YOHEI
SAGIMORI, THOMAS T.

SAHARA, ATSUO
SAIKI, MASAMI
SAITO, CALVIN T.
SAITO, CHUJI
SAITO, GEORGE S.
SAITO, KINJI
SAITO, TSUKASA
SAKADO, MASUTO
SAKAI, RICHARD M.
SAKAI, YOSHINORI
SAKAMOTO, ATSUSHI
SAKAMOTO, LOUIS K.
SAKAMOTO, MASAMI
SAKAMOTO, NOBORU
SAKAMOTO, ROBERT I.
SAKAMOTO, UICHI W.
SAKOHIRA, TODD T.
SAMESHIMA, GEORGE S.
SANMONGI, UETARO W.
SASAKI, YOSHIO F.
SASANO, TOSHIO
SASAOKA, ITSUMI
SASE, ANDREW Y.
SATO, SABURO
SATO, SHIN
SATO, SHUKICHI
SATO, TADAO
SATO, TAKEO
SATO, YUKIO
SAWADA, GEORGE K.
SCHEMEL, KURT E.
SEIKI, TOLL
SEKIMURA, KOICHI K.
SESHIKI, HIHUMI
SHIBATA, GEORGE MITSUO
SHIBATA, KENNETH K.
SHIGAYA, TETSUO
SHIGEMURA, MASAO F.
SHIGETA, HIDEO
SHIGEZANE, MASAO
SHIGIHARA, TAKESHI
SHIIGI, SHINICHI
SHIKATA, GEORGE M.
SHIKIYA, TED T.
SHIMABUKU, ROY K.
SHIMABUKURO, HIDEO
SHIMABUKURO, TOMOAKI
SHIMADA, GEORGE M.
SHIMATSU, AKIRA R.
SHIMIZU, GORDON S.
SHIMIZU, JIMMY T.
SHIMIZU, TAKEO
SHINTANI, TAKEO
SHIOMICHI, JOE A.
SHIOZAWA, ROY R.
SHIRAKAWA, RAYMOND H.
SHIRAMIZU, KIYOSHI J.
SHIROISHI, SHIGEOMI
SHIROKANE, KIZO
SHIYAMA, HENRY M.

SHOJI, TOSHIAKI
SOGI, MASARU
SOKEN, YEISHUN
SUDA, DAVID I.
SUEOKA, SADAMU R.
SUEOKA, THEODORE T.
SUGAHARA, SHINICHI
SUGAWARA, KENJI
SUGIYAMA, HIROSHI
SUGIYAMA, ITSUO
SUGIYAMA, TOGO S.
SUMIDA, MICHIRU
SUNADA, ALBERT M.
SUWA, NOBUYUKI
SUYAMA, GEORGE W.
SUZAWA, JIRO
SUZUKI, TAKASHI
SWEITZER, EDWARD H.

*T*ABATA, TERUO
TABUCHI, SHIGEO
TAGAMI, YOSHIO
TAGUCHI, HITOSHI B.
TAHARA, COOPER T.
TAHIRA, GEORGE Y.
TAIRA, MASARU
TAIRA, SEITOKU
TAKAGI, BOON E.
TAKAHASHI, ITSUO
TAKAHASHI, IWAO A.
TAKAHASHI, MON
TAKAO, THOMAS T.
TAKARA, RONALD K.
TAKASAKI, GORDON K.
TAKASUGI, KATSUMI L.
TAKATA, SHIGEO J.
TAKAYAMA, JOHN N.
TAKAYAMA, YOSHITO J.
TAKEBA, MASAHARU
TAKEHARA, SHOICHI J.
TAKEI, YOSHINOBU
TAKEMOTO, HARUO
TAKEMOTO, IWAO B.
TAKEMOTO, TAMI T.
TAKEMURA, ISAO S.
TAKENAKA, TOORU
TAKEO, ROBERT M.
TAKETA, JIMMY Y.
TAKETA, SHIGETO
TAKETA, WILLIAM H.
TAKEUCHI, ICHIRO S.
TAKEUCHI, TADASHI T.
TAKUBO, KENJI
TAMANAHA, KUNIO D.
TAMANAHA, MASAO H.
TAMASHIRO, THOMAS T.
TAMURA, MASARU R.
TAMURA, TOYOSHI
TANAHASHI, KEI

TANAKA, HARLEY
TANAKA, JACK M.
TANAKA, JIRO
TANAKA, JOHN Y.
TANAKA, KEICHI
TANAKA, KO
TANAKA, MATSUSABURO
TANAKA, SEIJI
TANAMACHI, SABURO
TANI, BUSHICHI
TANIMOTO, LARRY T.
TANIMOTO, TERUTO
TANIMOTO, YUKIO E.
TANJI, MITSUO
TANOUYE, KATSUSHI
TANOUYE, TED T.
TASHIMA, MASARU
TATEYAMA, HARUYOSHI H.
TATSUMI, GEORGE U.
TENGAN, MASARU
TENGWAN, YOSHIO
TERADA, HENRY M.
TERAMAE, TED A.
TERAMOTO, LLOYD M.
TERAMOTO, SHIZUO
TERAMOTO, TOSHI
TERUYA, HERMAN T.
TERUYA, KENKICHI K.
TESHIMA, MICHIO
TESHIMA, ROBERT T.
TEZUKA, THEODORE T.
TODA, ROBERT L.
TOGO, SHIRO
TOKUNAGA, CLIFFORD T.
TOKUSATO, HIDETOSHI
TOKUSHIMA, HARRY H.
TOKUSHIMA, PATRICK M.
TOKUYAMA, MINORU
TOMA, TSUGIYASU
TOMA, YASUKICHI J.
TOMIKAWA, CALVIN T.
TOMITA, HIROICHI
TOMITA, ISAMI
TOMITA, NOBUAKI
TONAI, TARO
TORI, JOHN A.
TOSAKA, MINORU
TOYAMA, RICHARD K.
TOYAMA, SHINSUKE
TOYOTA, SHICHIZO
TSUKAMOTO, DANIEL Y.
TSUKANO, ICHIRO
TSUMAKI, KENICHI
TSUNEMATSU, BERTRAM A.
TSUNO, ISAO J.
TSUTSUI, KAZUMI

*U*CHIMA, YASUJI M.
UEJO, JAMES K.

UEMOTO, KAZUMI
URABE, HOWARD M.
UYEDA, MORIICHI
UYENO, THEODORE T.

𝒲ADA, DANIEL M.
WAKITA, MASUO
WASADA, KENNETH Y.
WASANO, SHIGEO
WATANABE, HIROSHI
WATANABE, KIYOTOSHI
WATANABE, THEODORE H.
WHEATLEY, JAMES D. JR.
WHITE, FLOYD E. JR.

𝒴AGI, STEVE S.
YAMADA, HIDEO
YAMADA, RAYMOND T.
YAMAGUCHI, GEORGE
YAMAGUCHI, ROBERT M.

YAMAJI, IWAO B.
YAMAMIZU, TORAO
YAMAMOTO, FRED M.
YAMAMOTO, GEORGE I.
YAMAMOTO, JOHN H.
YAMAMOTO, JOHN T.
YAMAMOTO, MASARU
YAMAMOTO, TAKEO
YAMANAGA, THOMAS I.
YAMAOKA, TSUTOMU
YAMASAKI, HARRY S.
YAMASHIRO, GORDON K.
YAMASHIRO, LEI S.
YAMASHITA, KAZUO R.
YAMASHITA, SETSURO
YAMAUCHI, CHIYOAKI J.
YAMAURA, GORDON G.
YANO, ALBERT H.
YASUDA, FRED S.
YASUDA, JOE R.
YASUHIRA, ARATA
YASUI, HIDEO

YASUI, YOJI O.
YETO, MITSURU T.
YOGI, MATSUICHI
YONAMINE, HIDEO F.
YONEKURA, SATOSHI
YONEMURA, HITOSHI
YONEMURA, YONEZO
YOSHIDA, KENJIRO
YOSHIDA, MINORU
YOSHIDA, YOSHIHARU E.
YOSHIGAI, MITSUICHI
YOSHIHARA, MAKOTO
YOSHIHARA, TORAICHI
YOSHIMURA, JACOB Y.
YOSHIMURA, MINORU
YOSHIMURA, SABURO
YOSHINAGA, AKIRA
YOSHIOKA, ISAMI
YOSHIOKA, SHIGEO
YOSHIZAKI, TATSUO
YUNOKI, SHIYOJI

Computers on the site contain a directory for locating the specific panel and line where a name can be found.

Chapter Six

Here we admit a wrong.

Here we affirm our commitment

- as a nation -

to equal justice under the law.

President Ronald W. Reagan
Upon Signing the Civil Liberties Act
August 1988

John Harrington

John Harrington

The veterans and Honorary Color Guard at the October 22, 1999 Groundbreaking Ceremony commanded utmost respect from a large, reverent audience.

The Change

As World War II ground to a close, the military record of Nisei servicemen and the fortitude of those still imprisoned slowly softened hostile public attitudes toward the Japanese Americans. In an unprecedented and well-publicized gesture, President Harry S Truman honored the 100th/442nd with a review on the White House grounds and presented it with its seventh Presidential Unit Citation in July of 1946 when the regiment came home from Europe.

"I can't tell you how much I appreciate the privilege of being able to show you just how the United States of America thinks of what you have done," the President said. "You fought not only the enemy, but you fought prejudice — and you won. Keep up that fight, and we will continue to win — to make this great republic stand for what the

Constitution says it stands for: The welfare of all the people all the time."

His message was a far cry from the racist rantings that had driven Japanese Americans into detention camps only a few years previously. Times were changing. Some years later, Senator Inouye posed an interesting question:

"Does anyone truly believe Hawaii would have become a state in 1959 if the 100th/442nd had not been formed, if Japanese Americans remained satisfied with their 4-C Selective Service status? Do you think the Oriental Exclusion Act that had established race as a barrier to naturalization and immigration would have been repealed if so many of our friends and loved ones had not served and died so bravely?…I would like to believe that our wartime sacrifice had something to do with the extension of civil rights and dignity, not only to Japanese Americans, but all citizens of this nation."

The impact of the sacrifice was more than just the "something" that the Senator mentioned. Although Japanese

Americans do not claim credit for the new national concern with civil rights, certainly their example of patriotism and loyalty helped prick the collective conscience and stimulate an awareness.

United Press International

On February 19, 1976 prominent members of Congress and the JACL were present when President Gerald R. Ford officially rescinded Executive Order 9066. Among those pictured are Helen Kawagoe, Daniel K. Inouye, Patsy Mink, Norman Y. Mineta, Mike M. Masaoka, Spark Matsunaga, Hiram Fong, and Shig Sugiyama.

As young Japanese Americans struggled to re-establish themselves, little by little opportunities opened for this minority. For the first time impressive numbers of well-qualified Japanese American men and women worked their way into important roles in business, government and politics, the military, the law and the judiciary, the media and the arts, medicine, education, social work, large-scale food production, the sciences and the space program, and other positions — even the cabinets of two Presidents where Norman Mineta sat, first as Bill Clinton's Secretary of Commerce and later as Secretary of Transportation in the George W. Bush administration — from which they could contribute to the nation's well-being.

John Harrington

"I would like to believe that our wartime sacrifice had something to do with the extension of civil rights and dignity, not only to Japanese Americans, but all citizens of this nation."

Sen. Inouye's words were a profound echo among the guests and dignitaries at the Groundbreaking Ceremony. Pictured left to right: Senator Daniel Inouye, Chief of Staff General Eric Shinseki, Major General James H. Mukoyama, Jr., and acting assistant Attorney General Bill Lann Lee.

Indeed, the wartime sacrifice and fidelity of Japanese Americans had important national repercussions and is an essential part of the story the Memorial seeks to tell. Their ultimate vindication is contained in a blunt report from the Commission on Wartime Relocation and Internment of Civilians to Congress in 1982 — 40 years after the event it was investigating. Its conclusion read:

"The promulgation of Executive Order 9066 was not justified by military necessity, and the decisions which followed from it — detention, ending detention and ending exclusion — were not driven by analysis of military conditions. The broad historical causes which shaped these decisions were race prejudice, war hysteria and a failure of political leadership...A grave injustice was done to American citizens and resident aliens of Japanese ancestry who, without individual review or any probative evidence against them, were excluded, removed and detained by the United States during World War II."

On the basis of this report, and under intense prodding from Japanese Americans and others concerned with justice,

Congress as recounted earlier passed and President Ronald Reagan signed on August 10 the Civil Liberties Act of 1988. In it the nation admitted a wrong had been committed against Japanese Americans in 1942 and offered an apology and token payment.

Senator Daniel Inouye and Secretary of Commerce Norman Mineta were two of the dignitaries participating in the Groundbreaking Ceremony, October 22, 1999.

In memorializing the history that led to this apology, NJAMF vows to prevent anything like it from happening ever again to any American.

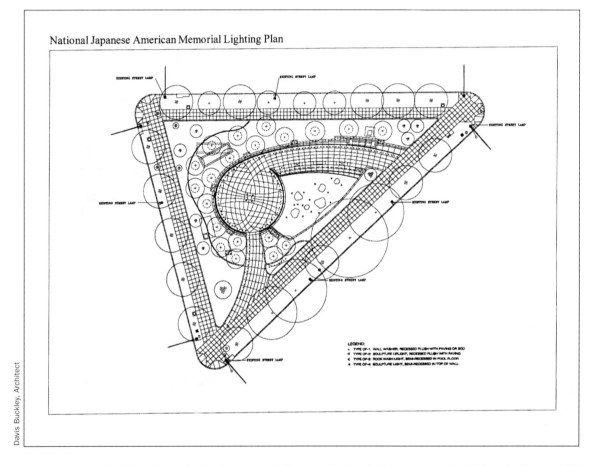

National Japanese American Memorial Lighting Plan

Preliminary sketch of the lighting plan for the Memorial illustrates the detailed planning involved before the first spadeful of earth was turned.

Chapter Seven

What combination of stone, bronze,

water and trees would tell the

Japanese American story honestly,

with beauty and impact?

What would be the role of words

- and what words would be chosen -

to articulate the message?

James Ritchie/Associates

Small-scale architectural rendering of the Memorial created by Davis Buckley, Architect. On the triangular piece of land a curved granite wall carries the narrative, camp names, and list of those who died in service. A bronze sculpture of two cranes stands at the center, while a solemnly resounding bell and reflecting pool offer closure at the Memorial's exit.

The Concept

After Marumoto was elected chairman in 1995 NJAMF gradually enlarged the Board, enlisting the help of men and women with diverse talents who were happy to volunteer their time and energy to the Memorial project. Some were skilled at fund-raising, or had the means to contribute liberally. Others had organizational abilities, or were experienced in the arts, the law, business, education, the military, accounting or construction. Widespread geographical distribution was sought. What the members of the Board had in common was a determination to create a Memorial worthy of the Japanese American experience.

Early on, it was established that members of the Board would receive no compensation and would pay their own expenses to meet quarterly at various locations so that, while conducting NJAMF business, they could tell their story to a broad audience, encourage contributions and gather local input, pro and con. It turned out that these strong-minded individuals were rarely unanimous on anything other than their dedication to the project. They knew that they wanted a Memorial, but from the beginning had only vague ideas about what it should look like, what it would say and how it would say it.

What shape should the Memorial take? Should it be a towering obelisk like the Washington Monument? Should it have the classic lines of a Greek temple like the Lincoln Memorial? A stark, dark wall below ground level, like the Vietnam Memorial, that epitomized the mood of that time? A heroic tableau like the flag-raising on Iwo Jima depicted in the Marine Corps Memorial outside Arlington National Cemetery? What combination of stone and bronze and water and trees would tell the Japanese American story honestly, with beauty and impact, and stand the test of time? How would what was proposed fit on the site and how much would it cost? The idea of a combat-weary infantryman with Asian features was considered, but for a long time the Board could agree only that the Memorial would not be a stereotypical mounted military figure on a pedestal.

More and more the Board wisely depended on the experience and know-how of Davis Buckley, a monument designer and planning consultant familiar with Washington and the exacting government regulations concerning memorials. Buckley's association with the project precedes NJAMF. In the spring of 1992 Buckley had written to Congressman Mineta, with whom he had had earlier contacts, saying he had heard about the Nisei veterans memorial project and offering to help. Davis's letter was referred to Kaz Oshiki who was representing GFBNVA in seeking passage of the original bill to authorize a memorial.

"Davis was very helpful to me as the bill made its way through Congress," Oshiki says, "and once the bill became law, he was generous with his time and advice." When it became evident GFBNVA would have difficulty in pursuing the site selection process, Buckley was retained as a paid consultant. He was assisted by a conscientious and extremely competent second in command, Tom Striegel, who was an excellent supervisor of day to day operations. That was in April, 1993, more than a year and a half before NJAMF was organized as successor to GFBNVA.

In the spring of 1994 federal authorities sent Buckley a list of sites, all owned by the National Park Service, available for the Memorial. None was attractive and the wait continued. Then, one day, John G. Parsons of the National Park Service suggested a small site, controlled by the Capital Memorial Commission, between the classic marble Supreme Court Building and the Hart Senate Office Building. It seemed to be the perfect location and Davis was instructed to ask for it. The request was on the agenda of the next Capital Memorial Commission meeting, but a week before it could convene Davis was told that the Capitol Architect, a member of the Commission, would object to offering the site. The Capitol Architect's reasoning was that the site logically was part of the Capitol grounds, an area including the Senate Office Buildings, the Supreme Court, the Library of Congress, the House Office Buildings and the Capitol itself.

"We didn't want to give up the site," Oshiki says, "but Davis and I concluded that if the Capitol Architect, who is a member of the National Capital Memorial Commission would object to a site, the other members would go along with his wishes. Later, the Capitol Architect suggested the location that eventually became the site for our Memorial."

Some members of the NJAMF Board were not unaware of the irony that might be posed by placing the Memorial in close proximity to the Supreme Court. In 1944 a majority of the Supreme Court upheld the legality of uprooting and imprisoning Japanese Americans in the cases brought by Gordon Hirabayashi, Minoru Yasui and Fred Korematsu, with a minority protesting "this legalization of racism." Justice Robert H. Jackson, speaking for the minority, had written that the Court majority had validated the principle of racial discrimination in an emergency, and that this principle is a "loaded weapon" available even today to anyone who can convince others by whipping up hysteria or by any other device that there is a need to use it again.

Triangular plot of land granted by the Federal Government, at the intersection of Louisiana and New Jersey Avenues and D Street, N.W.

Despite Congressional admission of wrong-doing and Presidential apologies, the Supreme Court's validation of the Evacuation had never been overturned. Wouldn't a memorial to the patriotism of Japanese Americans in the face of injustice, standing in the shadow of the Court's hallowed home, underscore the irony?

Congressman Mineta asked Buckley, among others, what might be done to make the Supreme Court site available. Buckley remembers that he was in the office of House Speaker Tom Foley, a powerful Washington figure, when Foley picked up his telephone and spoke directly — and forcefully — to some bureaucrat in the Capitol Architect's office to express his displeasure at the withdrawal. But to no avail. In the end, GFBNVA decided not to press its request for the Supreme Court site.

Some months later the Capitol Architect told Buckley that there was a small, triangular National Park Service site on Louisiana Avenue N.W., near the Capitol Hill Hyatt Regency Hotel, which might be made available for the projected Memorial. In May of 1995, with NJAMF now taking over, members of the Board toured several possible sites, then voted to request the parcel near the Hyatt Regency. It had much going for it, including a reasonable amount of space in a well-traveled area.

The site is only a few blocks from Union Station, which has some eight million visitors annually, and the Capitol is roughly equidistant on the other side. But only after many months of cutting through red tape was the exchange formalized and the site made available for the Memorial.

The transfer of the land from the jurisdiction of the Capitol Architect to the National Park Service, and then to the NJAMF, was not completed until 1996. But there were strings attached. The Foundation faced a deadline of October, 1999 to show it had a design, and enough money in the bank to construct the Memorial. If the deadline was not met, the land would revert to the government. Enlisting public support and raising sufficient funds before that deadline seemed to be an insurmountable challenge in the absence of a design which potential donors could see and evaluate.

Davis Buckley was assigned to create with all possible dispatch a concept for the Memorial that, within the restrictions of the site, would be beautiful, compelling, and tell a dramatic story. To begin with, he set his thoughts down in two succinct paragraphs:

John Harrington

*Architect Davis Buckley
presents design at
press conference
for the Memorial's
Groundbreaking
Ceremony.*

"Every memorial is, in essence, a symbol. Whether a particular memorial is abstract or literal, object or landscape, text or graphic, or any combination of these, the memorial is a representation of something beyond itself which holds great significance for an individual or a society.

"By nature of being a symbol, it is an abstraction of the story it memorializes. To gain access to what it communicates, therefore, one must go beyond the physical reality and engage its meaning through its symbolism. A successful memorial provides an appealing means to negotiate this change of levels and experience the story personally."

Now he set out to seek some indication of general community feelings in focus groups. Sessions were held in Washington, D.C., San Francisco and Honolulu. The San Francisco gathering was attended by about 25 individuals representing a cross-section of the Nikkei community. Davis found most of them had not given much thought to the specifics of the project and thus responded only positively or negatively to his ideas. He had focus group participants fill out questionnaires and then sent questionnaires to a number of Japanese Americans in the Seattle area and Japan. In addition, meetings were held at Asian American studies departments at the University of Pennsylvania and Columbia University.

The findings signaled a warning of many difficult decisions ahead about the design, and more important, the precise message the Memorial was to convey and how that would be accomplished. However, several basic themes were identified. A question as to the most important elements to be incorporated in the Memorial drew the following responses:

Establishing a legacy for future generations was of utmost priority from the beginning stages of the project. Mrs. Eric Shinseki and Congressional Medal of Honor Recipient George Sakato are pictured here at the Dedication Ceremony with grandchildren of Foundation supporters, Mr. and Mrs. Tom Shiba.

The majority thought that the military accomplishments of the Japanese Americans, particularly the 100th/ 442nd should be incorporated into the Memorial. Nearly as many said loyalty and

Mr. and Mrs. Tom Shiba and family

patriotism should be featured and the internment camps represented. Lesser numbers wanted the perseverance of previous generations featured while others stressed the U.S. government's error as an essential element of the Memorial. A small minority was concerned with civil rights violations and about the same number suggested emphasis on garden elements such as rocks, trees and water to represent aspects of Japanese American culture.

One basic question asked at the various meetings was: "If you brought a child to the Memorial, what would you want him or her to remember?"

The replies were varied. The largest number emphasized the sacrifice of previous generations of Japanese Americans. Others voted for focusing on the loyalty and patriotism of Japanese Americans despite violations of their civil rights, including their military sacrifice, and the lessons learned from the government's mistakes. There was general agreement that in commemorating the Japanese American experience, it was desirable to weave the lessons learned into the nation's struggle to create "a more perfect union". It was argued that in a nation where diversity has not been easily understood, the Japanese American experience could contribute to awareness of the essence of America.

All were worthy suggestions. But there were knotty questions to be answered. What was the order of importance of these points and how many could be incorporated? How could these abstract concepts be dramatized in inanimate stone and metal? What would be the role of words — and what words would be chosen — to articulate the message?

At a free-wheeling session in San Francisco, Board members reviewed an abundance of ideas about what the Memorial should say to the viewer, even without words. Buckley had sketched three different concepts for study.

Concept A proposed a park-like setting with a path leading past a rock garden and a cascading water course, and 10 cast glass "tablets" representing the ten internment camps. There would be individual monuments within the overall composition to honor Nisei military units.

Construction crew pauses for a photo during a visit to the site by architect Davis Buckley and Executive Director Cherry Tsutsumida. Below: Bell sculptor Paul Matisse at the site with Tsutsumida.

Concept B featured an oval lawn containing stones representing the generations of Japanese Americans interned in the camps. A circular pavilion with ten columns representing the ten camps would sit at the edge of the path surrounding the lawn. Within the pavilion would be a ring of ten glass slabs with inscriptions telling the story of the camps. In the center would be a fountain symbolizing the spirit of cooperation under duress.

Concept C treated the memorial as an architectural assemblage featuring a 10-column pavilion structure hovering in a pool linked to an arbor. Within the pavilion would be glass slabs referring to the internment camps and a channel cascading water into a pool.

Somehow, none seemed to convey the proper "feel" and that was not unexpected. Famed landscape architect Hideo Sasaki, with a deep interest in the project despite failing health, volunteered to assemble a committee of specialists as consultants. Architect Noboru Nakamura offered to do whatever he could to help. Sasaki; Richard Bender, professor of architecture at the University of California, Berkeley; Donald H. Hisaka, FAIA, of Berkeley; Barney F. Matsumoto of MLA Design Studio, San Diego; and Gyo Obata, FAIA, of Hellmuth, Obata and Kassabaum of St. Louis, met with Buckley over a weekend at Noboru Nakamura's architectural office in Oakland. Also present were Peter Okada, chairman of the NJAMF facilities committee, and several members of the Board. And out of their wide-ranging discussions, other concepts began to take shape.

John Harrington

Board Member and founding member of GFBNVA, Peter Okada (left), pictured here as the Amache representative at the Groundbreaking Ceremony. Okada is also a veteran of the Military Intelligence Service.

Masaji Inoshita (right) represented Gila River and has chaired efforts for its historic preservation.

Chapter Eight

This Memorial, like all others
in this Nation's commemorative
landscape here in Washington, will
exist for centuries and will tell this
story to unborn generations to come.

The National Park Service as stewards
of this memorial is charged with
interpreting its message in perpetuity.

John Parsons
National Park Service

Etsu Masaoka (wife of the late Mike Masaoka) and her granddaughter, Michelle Amano, stand before the first three panels of the Memorial which contain the quotes of Norman Y. Mineta, Mike M. Masaoka, and Robert T. Matsui.

The Inscription

While the design of the Memorial was under study, another committee began work on an equally difficult task — to craft the words that would help the granite tell the story. There were two basic questions:

What should be said? How should it be said?

There was much to be written on the Memorial but there would be space to include no more than a terse outline of the Japanese American story. Some questioned whether such an outline would get the job done. Repeatedly the committee was reminded by the review commissions that no sweaty tourist on a hot summer day could be expected to decipher, much less understand, the message contained in long rows of words carved into a stone wall. And without understanding, the Memorial would fail in its purpose of making an impression.

Yet, in the absence of adequate background, an abbreviated message might be without meaning. The narrative would have to be complete, accurate, compelling, understandable. And brief. The complex history of a people and their response to that history had to be told dramatically and in no more than the arbitrary limit of 1,000 words set by the National Park Service.

Over a period of two years seventeen different inscriptions were drafted, each differing in both wording and approach. The trustees agreed that the first draft was much too long. It read like a textbook, which would be appropriate in a classroom but not on a memorial. Each succeeding version was considered an improvement in content or tone over the previous draft, but unanimous approval seemed impossible.

In the later versions a new approach was tried. Rather than employing a running narrative, the technique highlighted historic milestones or turning points with a memorable quotation followed by a brief explanation. For example, Lieut. Gen. John L. DeWitt's infamous statement urging mass imprisonment: "A Jap's a Jap... it makes no difference whether he is an American citizen..."

The quotation is vivid testimony of the racism and disregard of legal rights involved in the imprisonment of Japanese Americans and its use on the Memorial was intended to underscore the bitterness and irrationality of the times. But there were some Board members who insisted strongly that neither DeWitt's name nor the hated word "Jap" had a place on the Memorial in any context. DeWitt was dropped.

Ironically, the most controversial figure turned out to be Mike Masaoka who originally had proposed the Memorial. In spite of his record as a human rights advocate, his name was anathema to some.

Masaoka's name had appeared in early drafts but had been eliminated in later versions. Then at a meeting in

Washington, D.C., Board member Grant Ujifusa asked for reconsideration. He proposed that in addition to Senator Inouye, quotations from Congressman Matsui, the late Senator Spark Matsunaga, civil rights activist Minoru Yasui, and Masaoka be included on the Memorial.

None of the quotations other than Masaoka's was questioned. But in the merciless process of elimination, the eminently quotable Yasui, who had been the first to challenge the discriminatory wartime restrictions in court, lost out in the interests of brevity.

The Masaoka quotation had been written in 1940 when the possibility of war with Japan was a distant but ominous cloud, and Nisei felt the need to assert their Americanism. The portion proposed for use was:

"I am proud that I am an American of Japanese ancestry. I believe in this nation's institutions, ideals and traditions; I glory in her heritage; I boast of her history; I trust in her future."

Masaoka's affirmation of faith had been adopted by the Japanese American Citizens League and became known as the Japanese American Creed. Some members of the Board argued that there was no such thing as a Japanese American Creed and the quotation's origin should not be identified as such. But before long it became apparent the opposition was to Masaoka's name appearing on the Memorial in any context, and was based less on what he had said than what he was alleged to have done as a JACL leader in the desperate days leading up to the evacuation.

Chairman Rear Admiral Melvin H. Chiogioji (Ret.) stands before one of the inscriptions, a tanka written by Akemi Dawn Matsumoto Ehrlich.

Opponents argued that Masaoka was unworthy because he had not been "authorized" to speak for Japanese Americans, and had urged cooperation with government orders to move into the camps when, in their opinion, he should have counseled mass resistance to a discriminatory and unjust order. Before long the NJAMF Board found Masaoka being made a public issue with arguments being aired in lengthy letters in the Japanese American press.

Primarily the active objectors were young Japanese Americans whose first-hand awareness of war was the controversial Vietnam War. They were critical generally of their elders' obedience to the military's imprisonment order in 1942, and specifically of Masaoka for urging compliance. From their viewpoint, a half century after the event, Japanese Americans should have defied government orders in 1942 instead of accepting an illegal mandate.

Contrary to one of the charges opponents made, there is no evidence that the JACL under Masaoka's leadership was in "collusion" — one critic's choice of words — with the government in the imprisonment program. NJAMF's legal counsel, Gerald H. Yamada, writing as a private citizen, responded that JACL had vigorously fought incarceration, and only after it became inevitable did the organization adopt a policy of cooperation with the government even though there were strong protests that Constitutional rights were being infringed upon.

Even before the outbreak of the Pacific war, Japanese Americans faced widespread racial discrimination. In some areas of California they were required to attend segregated schools. Public facilities such as swimming pools were closed to them. Mostly, they lived in "Japan town" settlements and the discrimination was intensified as Japanese military aggression in Asia stirred up anti-Japanese feeling. The Pearl Harbor attack only intensified hostility against Japanese Americans. The Commission on Wartime Relocation and Internment of Civilians, appointed by Congress to review history and quoted earlier, said in its report published in 1982:

"The violence against ethnic Japanese on the West Coast cannot be dismissed lightly. Between Pearl Harbor and Feb. 15, five murders and 25 other serious crimes — rapes, assaults, shootings, property damage, robbery or extortion — were reported against ethnic Japanese."

The report quotes sociologist Jacobus tenBroek: "During March an attempt was made to burn down a Japanese-owned hotel at Sultana. On April 13 at Del Ray five evacuees were involved in a brawl with the local constable

— following which a crowd of white residents, some armed with shotguns, threatened violence to a nearby camp of Japanese Americans. On succeeding nights the windows of four Japanese stores were smashed, and similar incidents occurred in Fresno. In northern Tulare County, a group known as the 'Bald Eagles' — described by one observer as a 'guerrilla army of nearly 1,000 farmers' — armed themselves for the announced purpose of 'guarding' the Japanese in case of emergency. A similar organization was formed in the southeast part of the county, where a large number of evacuees were concentrated."

Secretary of War Henry Stimson, who had authorized the evacuation, wrote in his autobiography: "Japanese raids on the West Coast seemed not only possible but probable in the first months of the war, and it was quite impossible to be sure that the raiders would not receive important help from individuals of Japanese origin. More than that, anti-Japanese feeling on the West Coast had reached a level which endangered the lives of all such individuals, incidents of extra-legal violence were increasingly frequent."

In Seattle, Mayor Earl Millikin announced a horse-mounted patrol was ready to escort local "Japs" over the mountains into Eastern Washington in case of emergency. In Wyoming, Gov. Nels Smith warned there would be "Japs" hanging from every tree if they moved into his state. And later, Col. Karl R. Bendetsen revealed troops had been prepared in case of resistance to complete in 24 hours the job of uprooting more than 100,000 men, women and children.

The camp names etched in the Memorial's granite walls are an emotional reminder of what is permanently burned into the memories of former internees.

Japanese Americans were well aware of their rights as citizens and desperate to assert them. But they also knew of the indigenous racism that permeated so many parts of local, state and federal governments. (The archives reveal that the State Department was seriously considering "deportation" of all Japanese Americans after the war. Assistant Secretary of State Breckinridge Long noted: "We have quite a number of these Japanese of American nationality serving in our Army whom we could not in justice kick out of the United States after they had fought with us…")

John Harrington

Masaoka wrote in his autobiography:

"My most difficult decision was to urge cooperation with the federal government in the suspension of our rights as Americans as our patriotic contribution to the war effort. We were told this was a matter of military necessity and we had no way of disputing that contention, nor could we risk the possibility of bloodshed if we stood on our rights and resisted military orders."

Masaoka's testimony before the Tolan Committee included the following paragraphs:

"With any policy of evacuation definitely arising from reasons of military necessity and national safety, we are in complete agreement. As American citizens, we cannot and should not take any other stand. But, also, as American citizens believing in the integrity of our citizenship, we feel that any evacuation enforced on grounds violating that integrity should be opposed.

"If, in the judgment of military and federal authorities, evacuation of Japanese residents from the West Coast is a primary step toward assuring the safety of this nation, we will have no hesitation in complying with the necessities implicit in that judgment. But if, on the other hand, such evacuation is primarily a measure whose surface urgency cloaks the desires of political or other pressure groups who want us to leave merely for motives of self-interest, we feel we have every right to protest and to demand equitable judgment on our merits as American citizens."

MILITARY AREA LEGEND

Prohibited Zone

Restricted Zone

Masaoka relates in his autobiography that confinement following removal never came up in conversations with key federal civilian officials. "Our government," he wrote, "was asking us to cooperate in the violation of what we considered to be our fundamental rights. The first impulse was to refuse, to stand up for what we knew to be right.

Executive Order 9066 dispossessed thousands of families from all war-sensitive areas, defined as all of California, Alaska and Hawaii, the southern portion of Arizona and the western halves of Oregon and Washington.

"But on the other hand there were persuasive reasons for working with the government. First of all was the matter of loyalty. In a time of great national crisis the government, rightly or wrongly, fairly or unfairly, had demanded a sacrifice.

"Moreover, we feared the consequences if Japanese Americans resisted evacuation orders and the Army moved in with bayonets to eject the people forcibly. JACL could not be party to any decision that led to violence and bloodshed. At a time when Japan was still on the offensive, the American people could well consider us saboteurs if we forced the Army to take drastic action against us. This might place our future — and the future of our children and our children's children — as United States citizens in jeopardy…I was determined that JACL must not give a doubting nation further cause to confuse the identity of Americans of Japanese origin with the Japanese enemy. The officers had made it clear to us that we could cooperate or they would do it the Army way."

In retrospect, there seems to be little doubt that a powerful affirmation such as Masaoka had expressed fortified the Nisei determination to maintain their faith in America in the face of hysterical persecution, a faith that led eventually to Congressional and Presidential apology.

However, even as work on the Memorial proceeded, a campaign protesting inclusion of Masaoka's name began.

J. Carter Brown, chairman of the Commission on Fine Arts which had final responsibility for the design of the Memorial, received many communications pro and con about the Masaoka quotation*. One of the letters of support was from Congressman Robert Matsui who, putting the issue in perspective, said in part:

"…The controversy over this proposed inscription is not just a manifestation of objections to the actual words of the creed, it is, moreover, an attack on the man who wrote the words to the creed, Mr. Mike Masaoka. I know a small number of Mike's detractors have been in contact with you through the commission's open meetings and in writing. From what I have heard, much of what has been said by this group about Mike has been either grossly overstated or just plain wrong. As such, I wanted to add my voice to the debate as someone who feels that Mike is not only worthy of inclusion on the Memorial, he is, in fact, one of the real giants in Japanese American history — a true hero…. As with any great leader there will be detractors, but I

---

*One member of the NJAMF editorial board, Kaz Oshiki, has requested this footnote placing him on record as opposing the inclusion in this publication of the following: All material on this page and ending with the paragraph on Page 127 closing with the words: "…only three of the over 20,000 donors to the Memorial asked for return of their contributions." Oshiki explained that he strongly believes that such a lengthy discussion of one controversial issue is neither appropriate nor deserving, particularly since the final inscription does include the Masaoka quotation.

can assure you that Mike's place in our history is secure, and I would hope that his place on the Memorial is equally safe."

Brown replied: "...I believe everyone here on the Commission found Mr. Masaoka's words eloquent. Our public recommendation asked the Foundation address the divisiveness of this one issue in a democratic forum. I understand that our recommendation has been honored, although the outcome, as is often the case with memorials, did not please everyone.

"A concern raised by several members of the Commission apparently has been settled. This focused on removing the title from Mr. Masaoka's inscription. It was felt that the title could be misleading to the majority of the public visiting the memorial, in that the Creed would be assumed to represent all Japanese Americans, which, judging from the volume of letters received by this office, seems not to be the case. The Commission is eager to see the Japanese American National Memorial completed. I believe that it will have an important and necessary impact."

Removing the title was no problem. But the Foundation, seeking public unity, went further. It examined a dozen or so other quotations from Masaoka's speaking and writing but decided ultimately the original one was appropriate.

But this did not settle the issue. Even though the Board had voted at the previous meeting, 22 to 7 with 5 abstentions, to accept the inscription approved by the federal agencies, it was brought up for further consideration at the Board's quarterly meeting in San Diego in the spring of 2000 after the stonework had begun. Following a two-hour discussion another vote was taken — the fifth over a period of years. Again the Board approved the inscription, including the Masaoka quotation, this time by a vote of 27 to 6 with one abstention.

Still, the matter was not concluded. One of the Board's members declared the inscription unacceptable despite the majority decision, and said he was considering legal steps to overturn the Board's action on the grounds that the process had not been "open". The Board then authorized the chairman to "take all actions necessary" to fight any possible lawsuit. No suit was filed.

Regardless of any sponsor's wishes the Fine Arts Commission, although open to negotiation, exercises absolute control over the design of a memorial while the National Park Service has jurisdiction over the inscriptions that appear on it. In affirming final approval, the National Park Service in a letter by Parsons stated:

"...This Memorial, like all others in this Nation's commemorative landscape here in Washington, will exist for centuries and will tell this story to unborn generations to come. The National Park Service as stewards of this memorial is charged with interpreting its message in perpetuity...This brings us to the issue of including Mike Masaoka among the people whose quotations are on the Memorial.... Whether he is being mischaracterized for his action or not, it is clear to us that the current |controversy surrounding him is not going to be resolved if his name is removed from the Memorial. The Memorial has simply heightened a debate which has been ongoing for many years and will continue into the future. Further, it is evident to us that no one would contest that Mr. Masaoka was an important national figure in this story.

"Thus we believe that including his name and the words from the Japanese American Creed, but deleting the reference to it, is the best compromise. We agree with the action of the Board in this regard and trust that those who may be disappointed in our decision will understand our rationale in coming to this conclusion."

The finalized inscriptions and names engraved on the Memorial wall serve an educational function as well as a moving tribute to those who gave their lives during World War II.

This did not satisfy an element in the Japanese American community which had taken little interest in the Memorial project until Masaoka's name came up. While the inscription finally approved for the National Japanese American Memorial has little resemblance to those first proposed, the majority of NJAMF's board accepts it as an accurate and appropriate telling of the story of a people in keeping with the objectives of the Memorial.**

**In November, 2000, as the Memorial was being dedicated, two members of the Board, Francis Y. Sogi and Yeiichi (Kelly) Kuwayama, published and distributed a 24-page booklet titled "Japanese Americans Disunited" stating their opposition to use of the Masaoka quotation.

But even as the stone masons were cutting the inscription into the granite, opponents continued their campaign. A group calling itself the JA Voice established a computer website and invited dissidents to sign a petition demanding revisions. Eventually the group announced it had submitted a petition with some 1,000 signatures to the National Park Service.

That led Scott Yamasaki, a Sansei from Canton, Michigan to launch what he called the "Grassroots Signature Support Campaign for Mike Masaoka" in support of the NJAMF Board. "It is important to show the American public the real depth of the admiration that is still accorded to Mike by Japanese Americans and others who knew of him and his accomplishments," he wrote.

Perhaps it is most telling that despite the heat of the controversy, only three of the over 20,000 donors to the Memorial asked for return of their contributions.

Following is the text of the inscription on the National Japanese American National Memorial:

THE NATIONAL JAPANESE AMERICAN MEMORIAL TO PATRIOTISM DURING WORLD WAR II

PANEL 1

MAY THIS MEMORIAL BE A TRIBUTE
TO THE INDOMITABLE SPIRIT OF OUR CITIZENRY
IN WORLD WAR II WHO REMAINED STEADFAST
IN THEIR FAITH IN OUR DEMOCRATIC SYSTEM.

NORMAN Y. MINETA
U.S. Congressman
Internee, Heart Mountain

PANEL 2

I AM PROUD THAT I AM AN AMERICAN
OF JAPANESE ANCESTRY.
I BELIEVE IN THIS NATION'S INSTITUTIONS,
IDEALS AND TRADITIONS;
I GLORY IN HER HERITAGE;
I BOAST OF HER HISTORY;
I TRUST IN HER FUTURE.

MIKE M. MASAOKA
Staff Sergeant, 442nd Regimental Combat Team
Civil Rights Advocate

PANEL 3

OUR ACTIONS HERE ARE ESSENTIAL
FOR GIVING CREDIBILITY
TO OUR CONSTITUTIONAL SYSTEM
AND REINFORCING OUR TRADITION OF JUSTICE.

ROBERT T. MATSUI
U.S. Congressman
Internee, Tule Lake

PANELS 10, 11, 12

ON FEBRUARY 19, 1942, 73 DAYS AFTER THE UNITED STATES ENTERED WORLD WAR II, PRESIDENT FRANKLIN D. ROOSEVELT ISSUED EXECUTIVE ORDER 9066 WHICH RESULTED IN THE MASS REMOVAL OF 120,000 JAPANESE AMERICAN MEN, WOMEN AND CHILDREN FROM THEIR HOMES IN THE WESTERN STATES AND HAWAII.

ALLOWED ONLY WHAT THEY COULD CARRY, FAMILIES WERE FORCED TO ABANDON HOMES, FRIENDS, FARMS AND BUSINESSES TO LIVE IN TEN REMOTE RELOCATION CENTERS GUARDED BY ARMED TROOPS AND SURROUNDED BY BARBED WIRE FENCES FOR THREE YEARS OR MORE. IN ADDITION, 4,500 WERE ARRESTED BY THE JUSTICE DEPARTMENT AND HELD IN INTERNMENT CAMPS, SUCH AS SANTA FE, NEW MEXICO AND THE FAMILY CAMP IN CRYSTAL CITY, TEXAS, WHERE 2,500 WERE HELD.

ANSWERING THE CALL TO DUTY, YOUNG JAPANESE AMERICANS ENTERED INTO MILITARY SERVICE, JOINING MANY PRE-WAR DRAFTEES. THE 100TH INFANTRY BATTALION AND THE 442ND REGIMENTAL COMBAT TEAM, FIGHTING IN EUROPE, TOGETHER WERE THE MOST HIGHLY DECORATED ARMY UNIT FOR ITS SIZE AND LENGTH OF SERVICE IN THE HISTORY OF THE U.S. ARMY. THE JAPANESE AMERICANS IN THE MILITARY INTELLIGENCE SERVICE, WITH BILINGUAL SKILLS SHORTENED THE WAR IN THE PACIFIC AND THUS SAVED COUNTLESS AMERICAN LIVES. THE 1399TH ENGINEER CONSTRUCTION BATTALION HELPED FORTIFY THE INFRASTRUCTURE ESSENTIAL FOR VICTORY.

IN 1983, ALMOST FORTY YEARS AFTER THE WAR ENDED, THE FEDERAL COMMISSION ON WARTIME RELOCATION AND INTERNMENT OF CIVILIANS FOUND THAT THERE HAD BEEN NO MILITARY NECESSITY FOR THE MASS IMPRISONMENT OF JAPANESE AMERICANS AND THAT A GRAVE INJUSTICE HAD BEEN DONE.

IN 1988, PRESIDENT RONALD W. REAGAN SIGNED THE CIVIL LIBERTIES ACT WHICH APOLOGIZED FOR THE INJUSTICE, PROVIDED MINIMAL COMPENSATION AND REAFFIRMED THE NATION'S COMMITMENT TO EQUAL JUSTICE UNDER THE LAW FOR ALL AMERICANS.

PANELS 20 AND 21

HERE WE ADMIT A WRONG.
HERE WE AFFIRM OUR COMMITMENT AS A NATION
TO EQUAL JUSTICE UNDER THE LAW.

PRESIDENT RONALD W. REAGAN
Upon Signing The Civil Liberties Act
August 1988

In addition to the narrative and the quotations, the walls also bear the names of the ten internment camps.

PANEL 34

LEGACY
JAPANESE BY BLOOD
HEARTS AND MINDS AMERICAN
WITH HONOR UNBOWED
BORE THE STING OF INJUSTICE
FOR FUTURE GENERATIONS

AKEMI DAWN MATSUMOTO EHRLICH

PANEL 37

WE BELIEVED A THREAT TO THIS NATION'S DEMOCRACY
WAS A THREAT TO THE AMERICAN DREAM
AND TO ALL FREE PEOPLES OF THE WORLD.

SPARK M. MATSUNAGA
U.S. Congressman
U.S. Senator
Captain, 100th Battalion

PANEL 44

YOU FOUGHT NOT ONLY THE ENEMY,
BUT YOU FOUGHT PREJUDICE — AND YOU WON.
KEEP UP THAT FIGHT, AND WE WILL CONTINUE TO WIN —
TO MAKE THIS GREAT REPUBLIC STAND FOR
JUST WHAT THE CONSTITUTION SAYS IT STANDS FOR:
THE WELFARE OF ALL OF THE PEOPLE ALL OF THE TIME.

PRESIDENT HARRY S TRUMAN
1946 White House Ceremony for
the 100th Battalion and
442nd Regimental Combat Team

PANEL 52

THE LESSONS LEARNED MUST REMAIN
AS A GRAVE REMINDER
OF WHAT WE MUST NOT ALLOW
TO HAPPEN AGAIN TO ANY GROUP.

DANIEL K. INOUYE
U.S. Congressman
U.S. Senator
Captain, 442nd Regimental Combat Team

AMACHE, COLORADO
7,318

ROHWER, ARKANSAS
8,475

GILA RIVER, ARIZONA
13,348

MANZANAR, CALIFORNIA
10,046

POSTON, ARIZONA
17,814

TOPAZ, UTAH
8,130

MINIDOKA, IDAHO
9,397

TULE LAKE, CALIFORNIA
18,789

JEROME, ARKANSAS
8,497

HEART MOUNTAIN, WYOMING
10,767

The name and population of each camp is engraved linearly across the tops of the walls.

Central crane statue designed by Nina Akamu symbolizes the Japanese American struggle for freedom and the injustice of oppression; and depicts the sacrifices of all Americans in the fight for justice and liberty.

A curved wall leads visitors along a path depicting a narrative of the Japanese American experience punctuated by historically significant quotes to create an understanding of the events of World War II.

Cherry blossom trees line the perimeter of the site, creating an attractive setting for quiet reflection.

Also engraved along this wall are the names of those who died in service for their country, many serving for the legendary combined 100th Battalion and 442nd Regimental Combat Team, and the Military Intelligence Service.

Reflecting pool containing five large rocks, representing the generations of Japanese Americans. A serene setting, the pool will provide a quiet place to reflect on the wrongs committed during WWII and how each and every citizen can be affected.

Resounding bell designed by Paul Matisse provides an opportunity for visitors to interact by making a sound in response to the Memorial's message. Its deep and quieting tone will be heard at the end of the visit to express closure on the conflicting difficulties and tragedies of the events described.

There is a discrepancy between the total number of evacuees in the 10 camps listed on the inscription (117,556, WRA's figures), and the figure of 120,000 engraved on the Monument wall. The population of the individual camps changed almost daily as individuals died and babies were born, as college students were released to continue studies, as individuals with skills critical to the war effort were summoned to super-secret jobs in Washington, as men left to help local farmers with their harvest, as members of families separated among several camps were reunited, and as husbands and fathers were released by the Justice Department to join their families in the WRA camps.

Board Member Dennis Otsuji inspects a template for the inscriptions in Minnesota. Otsuji was instrumental in overseeing the design and construction phases, and served as a liaison between the architect and the NJAMF.

Aside from those sent to the camps, nearly 5,000 Japanese Americans fled inland from the forbidden zones to avoid imprisonment during a brief period early in 1942 when the Army was permitting what it called "voluntary migration". After often hazardous trips, most of them found shelter with friends or relatives in Utah, Idaho and Colorado.

The Board also discussed at length the feasibility of listing the Justice Department camps which held approximately 2,000 non-citizens, mostly foreign-born men suspected as Japanese sympathizers, but never charged with endangering the national security. Among the camps were those in Missoula, Montana; Bismarck, North Dakota; Santa Fe and Lordsburg, New Mexico; Kooskia, Idaho; Seagoville and Crystal City, Texas; Fort Sill and Stringtown, Oklahoma; Tulahoma, Tennessee; Fort Livingston, Louisiana; Fort Mead, Maryland; Fort Richardson, Alaska, and Sand Island and Honouliuli, Hawaii. In addition WRA operated two small, temporary camps to house dissidents. However, the decision was to list only the principal WRA camps.

Chapter Nine

A pair of cranes -
symbols for happiness,
longevity and auspiciousness -
emerge from a pedestal,
wings reaching high into the sky
for freedom as they seek release
from entangling barbed wire.

The Cranes

The concept of a memorial-in-process is as likely to draw as much adverse comment as the inscription. Yet, rarely does an idea or concept for a project strike like a bolt out of the blue. Most often it is the product of endless thinking and doodling and experimenting by the architect until a vision begins to take shape.

Following the meeting with architects in Oakland, Davis Buckley had a fairly good idea what the Memorial should look like. But an architect commissioned to build a monument in Washington, D.C. does more than draw pictures. In addition to producing a design satisfactory to his employer, he must have every detail of his work approved by a variety of federal boards charged with keeping Washington beautiful.

Their names suggest the complexity of the approval process: the U.S. Commission of Fine Arts, National Park Service, National Capital Memorial Commission, District of Columbia Historic Preservation Review Board, National Capital Planning Commission and the Washington Metropolitan Area Transit Authority which is concerned with traffic patterns. They review not only the overall design, but also such details as the precise placement of each of its components, the grading and planting plan as well as the text of the inscription. Buckley was responsible for dealing with all of them on behalf of NJAMF. In addition his firm would supervise selection of materials, prepare detailed construction plans and select and oversee the work of contractors including soil-testers, earthmovers, plumbers, electricians, stone masons, landscapers, tree-planters and others. A member of the NJAMF Board with expertise in design and construction, Dennis Otsuji, exercised time-consuming oversight, traveling as needed from his home in San Diego to Washington and the quarry in Cold Spring, Minnesota.

Buckley's final design called for a curving wall of granite panels with a statue, standing in the plaza formed by the panels, as a centerpiece. The various inscriptions would be carved into the panels. Opposite the wall of panels, on the other side of the plaza, would be a reflecting pond with five huge boulders representing the generations of Japanese Americans swept into confinement. Flowering trees would be planted outside the wall of panels.

The statue would be the key to the Memorial's effectiveness. Ideally, it would project a sense of struggle against oppression, courage, and ultimate triumph. But how would that be done? The Board's memorial facilities committee headed by Peter Okada studied proposals from some 20 sculptors. One of the two finalists was Ruth Asawa, the eminent California Nisei artist whose bas-relief panels recounting the Japanese American experience add drama to a public square in San Jose, California, among other places. The other was a Sansei named Nina Akamu, also with an impressive list of credits. Nina was born in Oklahoma where her father, a career Air Force serviceman from Hawaii of Chinese and Japanese extraction, had been stationed.

Nina Akamu

*Akamu in her studio
working on an early
model of the crane
sculpture.*

Akamu emerged the winner. At the time she was commissioned, Akamu was completing an assignment to sculpt a 24-foot-tall bronze statue of a mighty warhorse envisioned, but never created, by the great Leonardo Da Vinci about the time Columbus was embarking on his epic voyages. The sculpture was unveiled in late 1999 with much acclaim before it was cut into segments and flown to Milan, Italy, where it was re-assembled and put on permanent display.

As a child Nina and her father would go fishing in Pearl Harbor where the rusting remains of ships destroyed in the Japanese attack could still be seen. She was aware of Pearl Harbor for another reason. Her grandfather, Hisahiko Kokubo, an immigrant from Japan who had lived on the island of Kauai for more than 40 years, was among the first in Hawaii to be jailed by federal officials after the outbreak of war because of unsubstantiated suspicion of disloyalty. Kokubo was interned on Sand Island near Honolulu Harbor. Three months later he died of a heart attack, the first Japanese American in Hawaii to die in internment.

"The death of my grandfather," Akamu says, "stripped of his civil liberties, is a powerful metaphor for the fragility of human freedoms." Her feelings are projected in the Memorial's center. A pair of cranes — symbols for happiness, longevity and auspiciousness — emerge from a pedestal, wings reaching high into the sky for freedom as they seek release from entangling barbed wire. The action symbolizes the Japanese American experience of freeing themselves from a deeply painful time. The sculpture, in bronze, is 14 feet tall. Half of it is visible from outside the Memorial wall, symbolic of efforts to rise beyond restrictions to freedom. Akamu's proposal for bas-relief panels depicting the Japanese

The crane sculpture towers above viewers at the Dedication Ceremony. Also visible to the left are three of the panels carrying inscriptions.

John Harrington

American experience was, unfortunately, among the ideas turned down by the Commission in the interests of simplicity.

Another feature of the Memorial is the bell designed by Paul Matisse who had lived 12 years in Japan. The bell is a horizontal tube, 16 feet long, and represents a new technology. When struck by an electronic clapper activated by a button, a deep, solemn and resonant sound emanates from the tube. Several tubes were cast before Matisse was satisfied with the tone. Matisse experimented many hours on a grand piano in his study to achieve the precise key of G-sharp sound that he sought.

The five stones in the pool were picked by Dennis Otsuji and Davis Buckley from granite found in Minnesota. They provide the stability within a flowing pool of water recalling the past, as one meditates the future.

Chapter Ten

The scene was more than a

half century and a million miles

removed from the dusty tarpaper barracks,

the malevolent barbed wire,

the tears of anger and bitter frustration...

this time the tears were of

joy and redemption.

Camp banners gently fluttered as a backdrop for the representatives participating in the Groundbreaking Ceremony, October 22, 1999. From left to right: Peter K. Okada, Masaji Inoshita, Ellen Nakamura, Bacon Sakatani, Paul Bannai, Ron Shiozaki, Department of the Interior Secretary Bruce Babbitt, Joanne Iritani, Barry Saiki, Daisy Satoda, Tomio Moriguchi, Hershey Miyamura

The Groundbreaking

At long last the groundbreaking was held at the Memorial site on a bright, sunny Friday afternoon, the 22nd day of October, 1999. A military band played as some 300 hundred Japanese Americans and their friends from all parts of the country gathered for the ceremony. Banners representing the 10 WRA camps fluttered in the breeze. Among the celebrities on the bunting-draped stage under the trees were a cabinet secretary, Bruce Babbitt of the Department of Interior whose agency so long ago had run the WRA camps; Army Chief of Staff Gen. Eric Shinseki; a United States senator, Daniel Inouye; a retired rear admiral and chairman of NJAMF, Melvin Chiogioji; an acting assistant attorney general, Bill Lann Lee. Norman Mineta, former congressman, deputy chairman of the NJAMF Board and future member of the cabinets of Presidents Clinton and Bush, was master of ceremonies.

Seated in the front rows were a Medal of Honor winner who had seen combat in two of America's wars, Hershey Miyamura; a retired two-star general and member of the NJAMF Board, James H. Mukoyama; beribboned and graying veterans of World War II in overseas caps who formed an honorary color guard. With them were a man or woman internee from each of the ten WRA detention camps to turn the traditional first spade of earth. There were moving speeches, prayers of gratitude and thanksgiving, and stirring songs of patriotism and glory by a serviceman from Hawaii with a gifted voice.

It was, as all agreed, a moving ceremony, long overdue. The scene was more than a half century and a million miles removed from the dusty tarpaper barracks, the malevolent barbed wire fences, the tears of anger and bitter frustration, the despair of being unjustly suspected of disloyalty, that Japanese Americans had known. The scene was justification and recognition of their steely determination to prove their right to share the American promise. This time the tears were of joy and redemption.

And when the crowd was gone and the chairs hauled away, the site was ready for the men in thick-soled shoes and rough clothing entrusted with the privilege of constructing a Memorial to remember a tragedy and celebrate a triumph. Now, nothing could block its construction. Not even the discovery six feet underground of the remnants of a patterned Colonial brick walkway, an ancient bottle, one shoe, and a possibly archaeologically significant bone that turned out to be merely bovine.

But nothing would come easily. Land under the District of Columbia is a tangle of unanticipated obstacles — unmarked sewer lines, inaccurately charted electrical conduits, subway vents that seemed to appear out of nowhere. Excavation for the Memorial had to be delayed for weeks as the bureaucracies sought to overcome the obstacles in the way of construction. The weather refused to cooperate. Costs and schedules had to be re-assessed and contracts re-negotiated repeatedly. Delays are not unusual in the creation of memorials. From the very beginning, as the NJAMF directors learned, there are many concepts about how the Memorial should appear and what it should say. Then there is the problem of paying for the project.

Paul Bannai

Photo of construction site taken shortly after Groundbreaking. It would be several months before the site would take on distinctive shape.

By contrast to the NJAMF effort, the Memorial to the WWII veterans went through nearly a half century of controversy before its construction on Washington's mall was finally approved by Congress just before Memorial Day 2001. Now its sponsors must agree on the design and raise the monies necessary to begin work.

The NJAMF was determined that whatever the barriers, the Memorial would be dedicated on time, and in record time for this Nation's capital. The wait had been too long for further delay.

That promise was kept, but not quite as planned.

Chapter Eleven

The enthusiasm caught on.

In two years, more than

20,000 donors from every part

of the nation made gifts

ranging from $1 to $500,000.

The Support

The National Japanese American Memorial could not have been built without money. Early estimates put the cost of the project at $8.6 million including $1 million for educational purposes. Inflation, construction delays and other unanticipated costs such as the addition of a computerized information kiosk at the site raised the total cost by another $3 million. It was the Board's responsibility to find that money. Three members — Cressey Nakagawa of San Francisco, Tomio Moriguchi of Seattle, Robert Sakata of Brighton, Colorado — headed the Standing Capital Campaign committee to lead the way.

The general wisdom in fund-raising is that one-third of the goal should be pledged by major donors before approaching the general population. But NJAMF faced

Board Member Cressey Nakagawa from San Francisco co-chaired the Capital Campaign committee.

a unique situation. Many potential major donors had committed generous gifts only recently to a number of worthy projects in the community, not least of them the Japanese American National Museum. It would be necessary to depend heavily on popular support.

"We knew it could be done," says Nakagawa in speaking for the committee. "In talks around the country we could identify an uniqueness of this project, based on an appreciation of civil liberties, that had an appeal that would encourage people to give whatever their economic status."

The committee divided the country into fifteen geographic regions, and based on the estimated Japanese American population, each region was assigned an arbitrary goal. The Greater Los Angeles area, with the largest number of Japanese American residents, was given the largest goal — $2.6 million. Other major areas centered around Chicago, San Francisco, Seattle and Honolulu.

The directors from each region set up a soliciting strategy best suited for their own areas. And the directors themselves set the pace, giving of time and energy to spread the word as well as donating from their own pockets.

Their enthusiasm caught on. In two years, more than 20,000 donors from every part of the nation made gifts ranging from $1 to $500,000. Young and old Japanese Americans and their families, church groups, war veterans individually and through their clubs, youth organizations, unaffiliated individuals, chapters of the Japanese American Citizens League, participated. The Japanese American Memorial is indeed a community-wide project — and triumph — reflecting the pride of a people. When a limited direct mail campaign was undertaken with the cooperation of the Japanese American Museum in Los Angeles, NJAMF's response was close to 20 percent instead of the 2 percent return considered usual for mailings.

Members of West Valley JACL Next Generation present a $25,000 donation to the Foundation.

John Harrington

*George Aratani pictured
with Bishop Watanabe
and Ambassador Yanai
at the Gala Dinner.*

*Dr. Paul Terasaki
speaking at a
fund-raising event.*

As expected, the Greater Los Angeles area led the way with more than 6,700 donors giving approximately $3 million. John Saito took on the responsibility of fund-raising coordinator without pay and pledged to spread the word at every community bazaar, every festival celebration, every organizational dinner where he would be welcome. Bilingual Hitoshi (Mike) Shimizu spoke frequently to groups of new immigrants from Japan and Issei in retirement homes. The two leading donors were George T. Aratani and his wife Sakaye with $500,000, and Dr. Paul Terasaki and his wife Hisako, who designed the cover of this publication, with $250,000.

Aratani, a one-time California farm boy and a NJAMF director, had prospered after World War II in electronics and fine Mikasa dinnerware, and is widely known as a generous supporter of good causes in the Japanese American community. Dr. Terasaki, another member of the Board, had pioneered a test for tissue compatibility that was a major milestone in advancing transplant surgery.

The second most productive area, with more than 2,300 donors giving in excess of $2.8 million, was Chicago's Greater Midwest region which included Illinois,

The "Chicago trio" from left to right: Maj. Gen. James H. Mukoyama, Jr., Masaru Funai, and Shiro Shiraga. The record-setting Greater Midwest Region raised more than 200% of their goal.

Ohio, Wisconsin, Michigan, Minnesota and Indiana. With a limited population of Japanese Americans, the fund-raisers demonstrated what enthusiasm, hard work, and knowledge of the community could do. A quartet of directors — Shiro Shiraga, James Mukoyama, the late Art Morimitsu and Masaru Funai who succeeded Morimitsu — spent countless hours soliciting in Chicago and carrying their message to outlying areas.

For starters, the Thomas Masuda Foundation and the law firm of Masuda, Funai, Eifert and Mitchell came up with a $200,000 challenge grant. When the public matched that grant, the Foundation contributed another $250,000, thanks to the commitment of Masuda's widow, Kay. Another major gift,

$300,000, was received from the estate of Thomas Arai, a Chicago war veteran.

The contributions were not always monetary. Morimitsu persuaded his friend, Kenshin Nawa, a prize-winning Japanese video producer studying in the United States, to donate his talents in creating a 10-minute promotional video which was used extensively in fund-raising events. Another Midwesterner, Brian Nagata, enrolled the pro bono services of video producer Bill Klavon, which resulted in a lengthier educational tape, titled "Suspicious People", targeted toward younger and non-Nikkei viewers. Mukoyama also recruited Robert Wilson to establish and maintain the Foundation's website (www.njamf.org) dealing with Japanese American history. Mukoyama's securities firm, Regal Discount Securities, provided commission-free handling of stocks and bonds given to the Foundation.

Also in the Midwest region two Buddhist temples made sizable contributions and the Wisconsin chapter launched JACL support nationally with a gift of $20,000, a substantial portion of their treasury. Shiro Shiraga, a Chicago businessman, and his wife Catherine gave $100,000, then persuaded a business associate, Herbert L. Stern Jr., to match the gift. Stern died before the Memorial's completion. Shiraga then increased his gift to $200,000.

Early on, when contributions were lagging in 1998, Funai contacted Shigeo Takayama of Tokyo, a Nisei who had done well in the electronics business in Japan. He sent in $100,000 and challenged Californians to match it. Gifts from Takayama and his wife Megumi total more than $300,000.

Shiro Shiraga was responsible for seeing that the organization ran a tight financial ship.

In the Pacific Northwest, Bob Sato and Tosh Okamoto, with the help of a part-time employee, June Hirose, directed a productive campaign out of office space contributed by the Seattle JACL chapter. The campaign, pushed by a committee of 73 members, was begun in September of 1997. Twenty months later Northwesterners had raised a million dollars more than the original $500,000 goal and it was reason for a victory celebration. One of the more unusual Seattle donations with the help of

Bob Sato (right) pictured with Board Member Tomio Moriguchi (left) and Washington Governor Gary Locke. The Pacific Northwest Region exceeded its goal by more than 200%.

Frank Sato was Wilce Shiomi who with his wife Mitsuko donated farmland valued at $250,000. The Foundation liquidated it in a favorable real estate market. Shiomi died several months before he could make his lovingly anticipated trip to the dedication. Another major donor was Dr. Toshio Inahara of Portland, Oregon, who with his wife gave $250,000.

Frank Sato, along with several family members, was not only instrumental in bringing in significant donors, but also made generous personal donations to the Foundation.

Spokane JACL President Dean Nakagawa, Denny Yasuhara and National JACL President Floyd Mori present check meeting the Spokane JACL's pledge.

Seattle's donor list contains more than 2,600 names. They include friends from places like Hawaii, Florida, Michigan, Tennessee and Australia, and communities in the Northwest like Moses Lake, Olympia, Tacoma and the Puyallup Valley, Wapato and Spokane, Boise and Ontario in Oregon, and Alaska. In Spokane, with only a handful of Japanese American residents, the former National JACL president Denny Yasuhara organized a fund-raising dinner at which NJAMF Chairman Chiogioji spoke. That community also met its goal.

A major dispersal problem was faced in the Northeast where a limited number of Japanese Americans are

scattered over a large area without a community newspaper. Nonetheless, the team of Dr. Harry F. Abe, Frank Sogi and Henry Daty surpassed their $250,000 goal by more than $100,000. Giving them important support were Ted Oye and his wife of the Seabrook, N.J. JACL chapter. John Fuyuume was a major donor as well as a fund-raiser. In Philadelphia, Grayce Uyehara took charge when it seemed the fund-raising effort was bogged down and before long the goal was met.

Grayce Uyehara, pictured with her husband Hiroshi, is often described as a "firecracker". Her energy and enthusiasm are incomparable.

Mae Takahashi epitomized the grassroots efforts which brought this project to fruition.

In Central California Mae Takahashi, another member of the Board, rounded up a small army of volunteers to make sure her region would carry its share of the Memorial's cost. A campaign committee of 30, in addition to inviting friends to their homes to learn about the Memorial, sent out solicitation letters to 3,500 households and more than 1,200 responded with donations. The NJAMF staff opening mail in Washington was surprised to find along with checks many personal notes crediting Mae's efforts for the donation. Among the volunteers was Janet Tanaka, a nurse who spent two tours of military duty in Vietnam and took the Memorial's message to numerous mainstream service organizations.

The San Francisco bay area was one of four (the others were Greater Los Angeles, Greater Midwest, and Pacific Northwest) to raise more than one million dollars. Board member Cressey Nakagawa mobilized volunteers in surrounding areas, like Toko Fujii in Sacramento, Fred Oshima and Mas Hashimoto in Salinas, and Edwin T. Endow and his wife Debra in Stockton. The total number of donors — close to 5,000 — was second only to the Greater Los Angeles area.

Four primary supporters in the Capital area, Mr. and Mrs. Toshio and Doris Hoshide, and Mr. and Mrs. Shig and Jean Kariya (Board Member).

In the Washington D.C. area 1,800 donors contributed more than $800,000. In addition, many members of the community volunteered their services in the NJAMF office and undertook much of the preparatory work for the groundbreaking and dedication programs.

When Tom Shiba, a mango importer and packer in Mission, Texas, heard of the Foundation's campaign, he sent in a check for $100,000. Then he and his wife hosted a country club reception at which gifts from friends — including a donation of $100,000 in stock from Shigemori Narahara and his wife — put Texas well over its goal.

The Shiba family was an inspiring representation of the legacy at the Dedication Ceremony with their children and grandchildren in attendance.

Colorado's campaign was kicked off with a dinner sponsored by Leo Goto at his posh Wellshire Inn restaurant. Ben and Florence Miyahara, a husband and wife team and both retired physicians, organized the fund-raising with monthly meetings in their home. Florence had served as an Army nurse before earning her medical degree, and when she was elected commander of Go for Broke, she joined the NJAMF Board. With such leadership, backed by Bob Sakata's appeals to larger donors, Colorado topped its quota quickly.

Dr. Florence Miyahara (center) at one of the numerous fund-raising meetings held in the Colorado region.

Bob Sakata (right) and Cressey Nakagawa co-chairs of the Capital Campaign. Sakata Farms was recently recognized by the U.S. Department of Agriculture for outstanding contributions to our Nation.

In Hawaii, Warren Haruki, Rodney Shinkawa, Margaret Oda, Robert Katayama and Hideto Kono worked to get big and small donations from all the islands, being especially successful in winning the support of the various veterans groups and the financial community. Their total donor list is approaching 4,500 — third only to the Los Angeles and San Francisco areas — with gifts approaching $1 million.

The largest single gift was the half million dollars from George Aratani and his wife Sakaye. The most modest contribution was $1, received gratefully for the sentiment it represented. The youngest individual contributor was seven-year-old David Dolifka of Niwot, Colorado, who took $15 from his own savings to send to the Foundation. The acknowledgment letter told David "Your money will help build a historic monument which will tell the story of how your grandfather and grandmother and 120,000 other Japanese Americans maintained their courage and loyalty to the United States..."

In San Jose, California, Board Members Yosh Uchida and Harry Fukuhara wanted to avoid a drawn-out fund-raising campaign. With help from Roger Minami they arranged a community dinner where their $200,000 goal was reached in a single night. Minami also accompanied Bob Sakata on a tour of California coastal areas to carry the message to large-scale Japanese American vegetable producers, not least among them George Higashi and the Tanimura brothers. West Valley Next Generation, a JACL chapter of young adults in the San Jose area, also raised $25,000. That made it the nation's most successful JACL fund-raiser followed by the Wisconsin chapter's $20,000. Many Japanese Americans employed by firms with matching gift programs were able to double their donations with company contributions.

Board Member Harry Fukuhara is a retired colonel of the Military Intelligence Service.

Board Member Yosh Uchida, former chairman of the National Museum, has been a grassroots supporter of the Foundation.

Organizations from all parts of the country other than JACL were generous contributors. So were literally hundreds of individual war veterans and their clubs. The original Go For Broke National Veterans Association got the campaign rolling with their $100,000 gift. The Club

100, made up of veterans of the 100th Infantry Battalion, gave $50,000. Giving $10,000 or more were organizations like the 442nd RCT Foundation, the 442nd Veterans Club, and JAVA (Japanese American Veterans Associ-

Among a crowd of locals as well as tourists for the National Cherry Blossom Festival, a member of the Go For Broke National Veterans Association participated in the Cherry Blossom Freedom Walk, an annual fund-raiser in Washington DC for the Foundation.

ation of Washington, D.C.). One dedicated Board member, who supported the Foundation even though she could not attend meetings, was Sharon Saito of Spokane who faithfully mailed in her $150 contribution like clockwork each month.

But the greatest number were gifts of $100 or less, given by thousands of Japanese Americans and their friends. Notable among these contributors was Jean Lee, a non-Japanese Florida retiree who mailed in $25 every month.

There were many donors with interesting stories to tell, and perhaps the most unusual of them was Cal Taggart of Sun

City, Arizona and Lovell, Wyoming. As a teenager he had worked as a carpenter erecting barracks at the Heart Mountain camp in the summer of 1942. Taggart wrote a check for $100.

The Washington Post ad generated an unprecedented amount of publicity. The staff was inundated with inquiries and requests for additional information.

Professional fundraisers marvel at the quick response the Memorial received from such a broad segment of the community. Obviously the project was something wanted, and needed, to bring to full circle the Japanese American story. On November 8, 2000, the Washington Post published a full-page advertisement, sponsored by the Foundation's donors, announcing the gift of the Memorial to

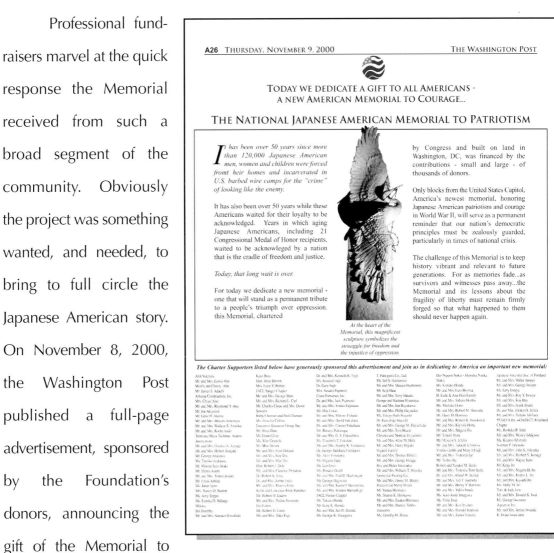

Regional Support for NJAMF, 2001

Area	# of Gifts	Total Contributions
Greater Los Angeles Area	6718	$ 2,945,272.72
Greater Bay Area	4759	$ 1,161,948.60
Central California	1643	$ 482,906.43
Greater San Diego	1021	$ 200,650.50
San Jose	1563	$ 424,533.11
Hawaii	4484	$ 977,253.00
Greater Capital Area *(DC, MD, VA)*	1861	$ 810,242.92
Colorado	956	$ 379,435.10
Southwest *(AZ, NM, NV, UT)*	505	$ 111,747.00
Greater Northeast *(NY, MA, CT, NJ)*	1141	$ 385,079.78
Pacific Northwest *(AK, OR, WA)*	2615	$ 1,690,275.33
Pennsylvania	265	$ 202,696.03
Greater Midwest *(IL, OH, WI, MI, MN, IN)*	2335	$ 2,766,713.82
Texas	201	$ 295,473.00
Mountain Area *(MT, WY, ID)*	59	$ 8,135.00
Miscellaneous *(Unassigned States)*	601	$ 113,466.01
Japan-Canada	90	$ 142,568.42

The planners of the Memorial wanted to assure that no one was deprived of an opportunity to help build the Memorial. This meant an aggressive grassroots plan where Regional teams explained the vision of the Memorial and solicited their support. A multitude of community organizations including veterans groups and the Japanese American Citizens League chapters mobilized teams to raise funds from friends, neighbors and local businesses. At a key point, the Foundation launched a direct mail campaign which proved to be a strong indicator that the support to build the Memorial was indeed there. The Foundation has always been proud that fund- raising costs have been a small percentage of its operating and construction costs.

the nation as a symbol of the aspirations of a free people in these United States.

As is appropriate in the nation's capital, the purpose of this notice was to make the dedication of the Monument a part of the public record. In less than a month more than 400 donors contributed to this project.

Stewardship of all funds collected was monitored by Rick Lefever, CPA, who supervised the annual financial audit required by the Department of Interior. All funds were balanced quarterly and reports submitted to NJAMF's treasurer, Mike Shimizu, and the financial chairman, Shiro Shiraga.

Supervising this vast effort, building on the start made by Wakiji and his immediate successor, Mary Ann Yoden, was a tireless and innovative woman, Cherry Tsutsumida, a one-time California farm girl who had been sent to the Gila River camp in Arizona. After the war she was involved in persuading the Arizona legislature to repeal both the Alien Land Law and the Anti-Miscegenation Act. As a veteran of the federal civil service, she was well acquainted with the ins and outs of Washington. As executive director of NJAMF with a minimal staff assisted by volunteers from the Washington area, she managed to keep the Foundation's efforts on track, acknowledge every donation, answer every inquiry, settle misunderstandings, pay the bills, joust with the bureaucrats, and shepherd the project to a successful conclusion. Hers was an indispensable role in a nationally significant achievement.

Attorney General Janet Reno's eloquent words at the Dedication Ceremony re-affirmed the Nation's commitment to preserve this chapter of history as a lesson for future government officials and civilians alike.

For Japanese Americans the Twentieth has been, to say the least, a momentous Century. The Japanese American National Memorial in the nation's capital is testimony for eternity of the patriotism of this segment of America in its time of travails during that Century, the courageous way it overcame them, the faith it demonstrated in the greatness of their country, and the justification of that faith, as Janet Reno would note, by the apology voiced by Congress on

John Harrington

behalf of the American people. "This site will be as much a civil rights memorial as a war memorial. It will be a reminder to us all about racism, suffering, injustice and courage...."

The Memorial campaign provided an important lesson about making democracy work with patience and commitment. The Memorial's dedication, with deserved pomp and ceremony and not a few tears, and the celebration that followed, were from the Ninth to Eleventh days of the month of November in the year 2000.

Chapter Twelve

May this Memorial be a tribute

to the indomitable spirit

of a citizenry in World War II

who remained steadfast

in their faith

in our Democratic system.

Norman Y. Mineta

The Dedication Ceremony dais was constructed to resemble the granite walls of the Memorial. The inscription on the wall behind the participants is Reagan's quote "Here we admit a wrong. Here we affirm our commitment as a nation to equal justice under the law."

John Harrington

The Dedication

As D-day approached the pace of activity quickened and the lights burned longer at NJAMF headquarters in downtown Washington. A three-day dedication program had been scheduled and there were what seemed like a million details to be addressed by the staff, the co-chairs of the local dedication committee, Barbara Nekoba and Nancy Yamada, and a host of volunteers.

But nothing goes smoothly in a project as large as the Memorial. The timetable was disrupted by a combination of misfortunes — weather that delayed construction, a tangle of federal red tape that messed up the schedule, and unforeseen problems that seemed to pop up with each yard of earth moved and every load of concrete poured. Cherry Tsutsumida learned to her dismay that the Memorial

Staff (left to right) Neal Motonaga,Cheron Carlson, Erica Kent, Shiho Ochiai Thompson, and Heather Kanemoto with artist Nina Akamu (center).

Below: Dedication committee co-chairs Barbara Nekoba and Nancy Yamada.

could not possibly be completed by November 9. Would a week's delay help?

Not a chance. The contractors were talking in terms of weeks or maybe even months of delay. But postponement posed other problems. Some 2,000 celebrants were expected, mostly from distant places. Hundreds of hotel and travel reservations would have to be canceled and re-booked. Speakers and entertainment would have to be re-scheduled. And after November, the weather was unpredictable.

There was only one solution. Hold the dedication as scheduled. And then have a grand opening celebration in the spring when everything, including the landscaping, would be completed.

And so the dedication was celebrated over three days, November 9, 10 and 11 as originally scheduled. By then, much of the Memorial was in place. The granite slabs, properly engraved, created a protective semi-circle to form the plaza. Nina Akamu's statue, more striking than anyone had imagined, stood tall on its pedestal in the center of the plaza area and the bell resounded properly when its button was pressed. The principle missing element was the reflecting pool fed by a waterfall, and the symbolic boulders that were to be in it. There was nothing to do but leave the area covered and invite the public to return for the grand opening celebration in the spring.

Sculptress Nina Akamu and Chairman Melvin H. Chiogioji stand proudly before the crane statue as it reflected brilliant sunlight from the center of the plaza.

As November approached, the already frenetic pace at NJAMF offices was stepped up further. Have you ever planned a dinner for 1,400 guests? Space at the Marriott Wardman Park Hotel had to be confirmed and re-confirmed. Programs had to be coordinated with the Smithsonian. A fleet of busses had to be reserved to transport celebrants from the Wardman Park, where most of them stayed, to the Memorial site.

John Harrington

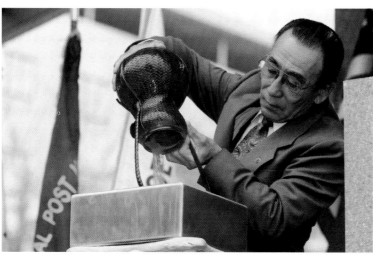

John Harrington

Since the Memorial, even if completed, could not have accommodated the expected 2,000 attendees, a platform for the dignitaries had to be built just outside the entrance and hundreds

Bacon Sakatani adds soil collected from the camps to the Memorial's foundation as distinguished ceremony participants and media crews capture the moment's symbolism.

of folding chairs placed on blocked-off New Jersey Avenue. And not to be forgotten was a battery of Porta-johns.

John Harrington

There were other details to be pinned down. Would President Bill Clinton speak? The White House had indicated he just might be able to schedule it. And who else should be on the platform? Who should sing and who should give the invocation and dedication? The hotel was clamoring for a decision on the menu for the banquet for 1,400 guests. You can't have a banquet without a speaker and a program.

What arrangements should be made for events outside of the formal ceremonies? What about a ceremony at the Tomb of the Unknowns? How do you move a thousand people to the memorial site. And the souvenir booklet — it had to be a professional product and it had to carry enough advertising to be self-supporting.

Two-time Emmy-award winning news anchor Ann Curry provided an energetic opening as the Mistress of Ceremonies.

"Today, two generations of Americans join together to witness these ceremonies. For one, the memory of the events of WWII are living and personal. For the other, they are stories passed down through family ties - stories that seem like a distant past that cannot touch us today."

"But touch us they do."

November 9th dawned misty. The crowd, later estimated at more than 2,000, began to assemble nearly two hours before the scheduled 1 p.m. starting time. There were not seats for all, but the overflow stood patiently until Ann Curry, the television network anchorperson who had come from New York for the event, opened the ceremonies.

The list of attendees underscored, as nothing else could do, how widely dispersed Japanese Americans had become. They were no longer concentrated in and around metropolitan areas on the West Coast like Los Angeles, San Francisco and

Seattle. They and their friends came from homes in places like Cabin John, MD (Mildred Ikeda) and Dobbs Ferry, NY (Sam and Sumi Koide). They came from Oak Lawn, IL (Chikaji and Yoneko Tsurusaki) and Sherman Oaks, CA (Theresa Yee and Paul Barker). Jimmie Kanaya came from Gig Harbor, WA and Joseph and Tamie Kimura from Cardiff by the Sea, CA Cheryl Miyazaki Lund and Kevin Miyazaki came from Wauwatosa, WI and Vernon and Joy Nishimura Frerking came from Cle Elum, WA. In addition to the large delegations from

Ceremony participants after the dedication of the wreath at the Died in Service wall. Left to right: Norman Mineta, Ann Curry, Melvin Chiogioji, Robert Matsui, Robert Katayama, Rudy Tokiwa, Richard Morishige,Rudy deLeon, Rev. Garrett Yamada, Bishop Watanabe, Bacon Sakatani.

John Harrington

metropolitan areas, they came from places like Wappinger Falls, NY; Basking Ridge, NJ; Wyomissing, PA; Leominster, MA; Tehachapi, CA, Chappaqua, NY, Pewaukee, WI, and Indian Head Park, IL. Miye and Ronald Yoshida came from Northridge, CA and Mary Ann and Masami Yoshinari from Norridge, IL. Records for distance traveled were set by Sylvia Kobayashi who flew in from Anchorage, AL and Melissa Kwee from Singapore. What brought them all together was the shared memory of long-ago pain.

John Harrington

From near and far the crowd of an estimated 2,000 began to assemble on an overcast morning to witness a moment of vindication and celebration.

One by one the honorables spoke, their words echoing off the buildings nearby. Two of the more eloquent were Rudy Tokiwa, a war veteran who struggled to the podium on crutches, and Cherry Tsutsumida who reminded the audience of the tears and sacrifice and fortitude of women in the history being commemorated.

John Harrington

Ceremony participant Rudy Tokiwa pictured with Congressional Medal of Honor recipients Hershey Miyamura and George Sakato, and Secretary of the Army Louis Caldera.

The President did not appear, but he sent a moving letter. It said in part: "Nearly six decades ago, as this nation fought for freedom throughout the world, more than 120,000 Americans of Japanese ancestry were denied their freedom and forcibly relocated to internment camps simply because of their ethnic heritage...

"The National Park Service has just released a study of Japanese American internment sites. Today I am directing the Secretary of the Interior to examine ways to preserve these important sites so that Americans never forget this sad chapter in our history.

"We are diminished when any American is targeted unfairly because of his or her heritage. This memorial and the internment sites are powerful reminders that stereotyping, discrimination, hatred, and racism have no place in this country.

And if we can overcome them, there is no limit to what we can accomplish together as Americans."

The principal speaker was Attorney General Janet Reno whose Justice Department had failed in 1942 to see that justice was done. A few of her most pertinent paragraphs follow:

Executive Director Cherry Tsutsumida spoke of the strength of the women:

"We take time out at this Dedication to also honor the women, who despite turmoil and uncertainty including being separated from their fathers, husbands and even their sons, maintained their strength to make the unbearable bearable."

"The lessons of World War II are not simple ones. That is why it is so important that future generations learn about how Japanese American families suffered grave injustices and hardships, and still triumphed over racial hatred....

"...It is no easy task to balance civil rights and liberties with national security, because during difficult times, complex considerations shape our decisions. That was the case in our country during World War II. And that will be the case at other unforeseen times when consciences will be tried, and civil liberties challenged. The story of the Japanese American community has also involved national redemption. High government officials played an ignoble role in the internment of Japanese Americans, elevating racism to policy.

"To the credit of the Japanese American community leaders along with Congressman Bob Matsui and now Secretary Norman Mineta, these misdeeds have not gone unchallenged in the historical record...All Americans can take pride in the fact that our government issued a public apology acknowledging that the internment was wrong when Congress in 1988 enacted the Civil Liberties Act...

Congressman and Mrs. Robert Matsui speak with Former Senator Bob Dole at the Gala Dinner. Dole, a fellow WWII veteran who met Daniel Inouye in a medical ward, has been a strong supporter of the Memorial project.

John Harrington

"Nothing will redress the pain and humiliation of internment for those who lived through it. But redress has vindicated the faith in this country of those who shed their blood on foreign battlefields while their families at home were held under armed sentries. They did not fight in vain...

"The lesson of the Japanese American experience is that a community's abiding faith in our national promise was vindicated through peaceful petition and lawful redress. That lesson gives hope to every American in our nation's on-going struggle to achieve equality and justice. That lesson must not be forgotten. It is, after all, those ideals that bind us together as a people.

"This site will be as much a civil rights memorial as a war memorial. It will be a reminder to us all about racism, suffering, injustice and courage..."

There was a long silence as the first woman to serve as Attorney General of the United States completed her address, and then the thunder of applause.

That night, a banquet celebrated victory. Former Senator Bob Dole, who had shared a hospital ward with Senator-to-be Dan Inouye after one bloody battle in

Senator Daniel Inouye, unable to attend the Ceremonies in person, created a videotaped message to be played at the Gala Dinner congratulating the Japanese American community on the success of the project.

John Harrington

John Harrington

Jon Nakamatsu played a collection of classical pieces as well as a Japanese song, Koko Ni Sachi Ari, a sentimental Hawaiian favorite for the audience.

Italy, spoke. The hit of the evening was California-born Jon Nakamatsu, in 1997 the first American since 1981 to win the gold medal of the 10th Van Cliburn International Piano Competition. His piano seemed to express in music all the emotion of an audience that was celebrating an exhilarating triumph after surviving an unforgettable ordeal.

Many days later, Grant Ujifusa in a letter to George Aratani, expressed his emotions in these words: "I still feel so good about the dedication. It was about as perfect a thing in life as I have experienced. When there were no words for how I felt, Jon Nakamatsu expressed it in music, which is for me more perfect even than mathematics because a quadratic equation has never brought tears to my eyes. I only wish that Mike and Min and Grandma and Grandpa could have been there."

Postscript

As this was written, the Grand Opening of the Memorial was set for June 29 and 30, 2001, when at long last the final stones would be in place, the trees planted and the reflecting pool with its five rocks would bring together the harmony of past generations and the present. This time it would be a "family" affair in cost and in ceremony. Of course, a military color guard would be there, and the dignitaries including Senator Daniel Inouye, Secretary Norman Mineta and Congressman Robert Matsui would give the appropriate messages.

The banquet would have its distinguished tables sponsored by generous supporters of the Memorial; but there would also be discounted family tables where children could attend at a nominal cost. By popular demand, Senator Inouye who had to miss the last Dedication, would be the keynote speaker. World renown baritone Christopheren Nomura would entertain.

The whole event would symbolize a transition — from the Memorial's inception, nurtured and built by private community resources to a public National Memorial to be preserved for posterity by the National Park Service. The evening's program will also symbolize a transition as some of our great leaders recapture the past in recognition of a proud heritage. It would close with songs by the future generation conveying in bilingual chorus the joy of the legacy they inherit.

But the mission would not be ended. Some members feel that this Memorial will serve to awaken a new consciousness about the history it commemorates. There is, they believe, an even greater need for supplementary literature to provide a fuller account of the history remembered here, and for working out cooperative educational arrangements with more permanent institutions such as the Japanese

American National Museum, the Northern California Historical Society and the Smithsonian Institute in the nation's capital.

According to the survey conducted by Peter D. Hart Research Associates, Inc., when asked about their knowledge of the internment of 120,000 Japanese Americans during World War II, 32% answered either unsure or denied that the internment took place. Knowledge levels about the internment varied among age groups and gender groups as well: 38% of adults between 18-34 and 31% of adults 65 and older are not aware of the internment camps. Almost half of the women polled did not know about the camps.

Despite the number of Japanese Americans who served, many Americans were unaware of the role they played in the Allied effort. Of those polled 51% of Americans reported awareness of Japanese Americans' military service in World War II, but only 41% of high school graduates/students recalled the formation of all-Japanese American troops.

Meanwhile this volume brings to a close the construction phase of the Memorial. It would not be possible without the encouragement and support of the 20,000 who believed in it.

This book is dedicated to all of them, but in particular, to those supporters who did not live to see the completion of the project, not the least of whom is Hideo Sasaki who played such a large part in the Memorial's ultimate design. And most specially to two faithful members of the Board:

Hideo Sasaki 1919 - 2000

Art Morimitsu 1912 - 1998

Dr. Mae Takahashi 1935 - 2001

Honor Roll of Donors

The Japanese American Memorial

is indeed a community-wide project

-- and triumph --

reflecting the pride of a people.

The Gala Dinner was the highlight of the celebration during the Dedication Ceremonies. Fitting for the occasion, the elegant ballroom was decorated with patriotic flags for 1,500 guests. Congressman Robert Matsui was the Master of Ceremonies with Former Senator Bob Dole delivering the keynote. Seated at the head table from left to right: Rev. and Mrs. Canon Kitagawa, Mrs. Norman Y. Mineta, Chairman Melvin Chiogioji, Congressman Robert Matsui, Mrs. Robert Matsui, Ambassador Shunji Yanai, Mr. George T. Aratani, and Bishop Hakubun Watanabe.

Our Supporters

$500,000 and Over

Mr. and Mrs. George T. Aratani
Thomas Masuda Memorial Foundation Group
  Masuda, Funai, Eifert & Mitchell, Ltd.
  Mr. and Mrs. Bryan Y. Funai
  Mr. and Mrs. Masaru Funai
  Mr. and Mrs. Colin Hara
  Mr. and Mrs. Dayne Kono
  Ms. Nancy Sasamoto
  Douglas Weingarten

$250,000 - $499,999

The Estate of Thomas Arai
Dr. and Mrs. Toshio Inahara
Mr. (deceased) and Mrs. Wilce Shiomi
Mr. and Mrs. Shiro F. Shiraga
Shigeo and Megumi Takayama Family
Dr. and Mrs. Paul Terasaki

$100,000 - $249,999

Mr. and Mrs. Jack Hirose
Ms. Nobuko Mitokawa
Mitsui High-tec Inc. - Yoshiaki Mitsui
Mr. Cressey H. Nakagawa
Mr. and Mrs. Shigemori Narahara
Hiroaki, Elaine, Lawrence Kono Foundation
  Dr. Margaret Oda
Peter and Muts Okada and Family
Mr. and Mrs. Tom Shiba Family
Mr. and Mrs. Herbert L. Stern, Jr.
Mr. Matsuo Takabuki
Dr. Warren H. Watanabe

$50,000 - $99,999

Bigston Foundation
Mr. Melvin H. Chiogioji
Club 100 - Veterans 100th Battalion
Mr. Robert Haraga and Family
George and Janice Higashi Family
Mrs. Chiyoko D. Hoshide
Ikeda Brothers and Families:
  Kazuo, Saburo (deceased), Seirin
Mr. and Mrs. Robert N. Katayama
Mr. and Mrs. Gary Kawaguchi
In Memory of Otoichi Kawana
  and Kensaku Ochi Families
Kenwood Corporation
Clarence and John Nishizu Families
Dr. and Mrs. Sanbo S. Sakaguchi
Robert Sakata Family
Mr. and Mrs. Masamori Sato Family:
  Mr. and Mrs. Michael Sato
  Mr. and Mrs. Richard Sato
  Yoshi and Betty Maekawa
  Brian and Leslie Okura
  Mr. and Mrs. Frank Sato
  Mr. and Mrs. John Sato
  Mr. and Mrs. Martin Brinitzer
  Mr. and Mrs. Marvin Hernandez
  Mr. and Mrs. Robert Sato
  Mr. and Mrs. Stanley Sato
  Ms. Amy M. Sato
  Ms. Rose M. (Sato) Stults
  Ms. Jennifer Stults
  Mr. Andy Stults
  Mr. and Mrs. Kent Sato
Tanimura Land Co., LLC
Mr. and Mrs. Masayoshi 'Massey' Tomooka
Mr. Akira Uehara
Mr. and Mrs. Tadao Yamada

$25,000 - $49,999

442nd RCT Foundation
Dr. Harry F. Abe
Mr. and Mrs. Tick Akiyoshi
Anonymous
Dr. and Mrs. Ben Chikaraishi
Mr. Henry I. Daty
Col. and Mrs. Sunao Ishio
Col. and Mrs. Jimmie Kanaya
Mrs. Shig Kariya
Maruchan, Inc.
Mr. and Mrs. William H. Marumoto
Mr. and Mrs. William M. Marutani
Mrs. Etsu M. Masaoka
Mr. and Mrs. Reiso Miyamoto
Mr. and Mrs. Jun Mori
Mr. Tomio Moriguchi
Ms. Ayako Murakami
Dr. and Mrs. Raymond S. Murakami
Mr. and Mrs. James Y. Nishimura
Mr. and Mrs. Dennis Otsuji
Dr. Sakaye Shigekawa
Taisho Pharmaceutical Co., Ltd.
Dr. Mae Takahashi (deceased)
Mr. and Mrs. Takeshi Tanimoto
Mr. and Mrs. Don S. Tokunaga
Ms. Cherry Y. Tsutsumida
Umeya Rice Cake Co.
  Tak Hamano
Guy Watanabe Partnership
Mr. and Mrs. Tadashi Yamagata

$10,000 - $24,999

442nd Veterans Club
Mr. and Mrs. Arthur Abe
Mr. and Mrs. Mitsuji M. Abe
Mr. and Mrs. Hatsuro Aizawa
Dr. Ronald H. Akashi
Mr. Hajime Amemiya
American Honda Motor Co., Inc.
Mr. and Mrs. George Asakawa
Mr. and Mrs. George Azumano
Bank of America
Central Pacific Bank
Citigroup Foundation
Ms. Toshiko Dairiki
Mrs. Violet K. De Cristoforo
Mr. Ernest Doizaki
Mr. and Mrs. Takeshi Endo
Fifty-Eight Investors
First Hawaiian Foundation
Jerry Fukui, Christine Kohler and
Catherine Tanaka
Mr. Roy Fukunaga
Mr. Yuji Fukunaga

Mr. Takeshi Funahashi
Mr. and Mrs. John N. Fuyuume
GM Super Sales Co., Inc.
Good Samaritan Hospital
Dr. and Mrs. Masaro Harada
Hiraki Enterprise, Inc
Mr. and Mrs. Manabi Hirasaki
Mr. and Mrs. William Y. Hirose
Hiroshima Kenjin Kai
Mr. and Mrs. Noboru Honda
Hosiden America Corporation
Mr. and Mrs. William D. Hughes
Ms. Kimi Inadomi
Mr. and Mrs. Minoru Inoshita
Mr. and Mrs. Ray Inouye
Mr. and Mrs. Tomio Ito
Ito-Kogyo, Ltd
JACL Arizona Chapter
JACL Diablo Valley Chapter
JACL Pacific Southwest Council
JACL San Francisco Chapter
JACL Spokane Chapter
JACL Wisconsin Chapter
JAVA Washington, DC
Japanese Association of Colorado
Japanese Chamber of Commerce (LA)
Japanese Chamber of Commerce of NY
Japanese Women Volunteers of Chicago
Mr. and Mrs. Bruce T. Kaji
Messers. Jim and George Kanemoto
Kapolei Holding Corp.
Kawabe Memorial Fund
Ms. Helen S. Kawagoe
Mr. and Mrs. Herbert G. Kawahara
Mr. and Mrs. James Kawamoto
Heiji and Kita
Mrs. Keiko Kitayama
Mr. and Mrs. Samuel Kumagai
Dr. and Mrs. Glen Kumasaka
Ms. Sumi Kuriyama
Ms. Julia N. Kuroda
Aya and Yeiichi Kuwayama
Ms. Donna Aratani Kwee
MBL (USA) Corporation
Mikasa, Inc.
Hon. Norman Y. Mineta
Drs. Ben and Florence Miyahara
Mr. and Mrs. Harrison Y. Miyahira
Mr. and Mrs. Takashi Momoda
Mr. and Mrs. Eddie I. Moriguchi
Messrs. Kenichi and Art Morimitsu
Mr. and Mrs. Kazuo G. Murakami
Ms. Masako Murakami
Mr. and Mrs. Yoshio Murakami
Mr. and Mrs. Jack Nagano
Mr. Jim Naganuma
Mr. and Mrs. Robert S. Nagata
Mr. Shigeru Nakahira

Mr. Robert Nakamoto
Mr. and Mrs. Ted Nakanishi
Nisei Farmers League
Mr. and Mrs. Frank K. Nishimura
Mr. S. John Nitta
Mrs. Yvonne H. Noguchi-Oji
Mr. and Mrs. Wallace K. Nunotani
Mr. and Mrs. Toshikazu Okamoto
Mr. and Mrs. Muneo M. Okusa
Mr. and Mrs. Kaz Oshiki
Dr. and Mrs. Frank Sakamoto
Sanken Electric Co., Ltd.
Mr. and Mrs. James Satake
Mr. and Mrs. Joseph Scott
Mr. Kimitaka Sekiguchi
Mr. and Mrs. T. Thomas Sera
Mr. and Mrs. Yoshimi Shibata
Ms. Yuko Shibata
Mr. and Mrs. Zenji Shibayama
Mr. and Mrs. Mike Shimizu
G. Shimoura Family
Rodney R. and Sandy J. Shinkawa
Mr. and Mrs. Francis Y. Sogi
Sonnenberg and Anderson
Mr. and Mrs. Ted K. Soyeshima
Mr. and Mrs. Jack K. Sugihara
Ms. Masako Suyehiro
Mr. and Mrs. James T. Suzuki
Ms. Masako M. Suzuki
Dr. and Mrs. James Taguchi
Mr. and Mrs. Henri Takahashi
Mr. and Mrs. Kats Tanino
Dr. and Mrs. Roy T. Tanoue
Mr. Shigeru Tasaka
Toko America, Inc.
Ms. Chiye Tomihiro
Mr. and Mrs. Minoru Tonai
Ms. Michi Tsukada
Union Bank of CA, N.A.
Mr. and Mrs. Otto A. Uyehara
Mr. and Mrs. Henry Wakabayashi
Elizabeth and Joseph Yamada
Mr. and Mrs. Gerald H. Yamada
Mr. and Mrs. Gordon T. Yamada
Mr. and Mrs. Dick Yamagami
Ms. Kristi Yamaguchi
Mr. and Mrs. George M. Yamamoto
Mrs. William Yamamoto and
Mr. and Mrs. Daniel Yoshida
Yaskawa Electric America
Mr. and Mrs. Ted T. Yasuda
Mr. and Mrs. George Yasui
YKK Corporation of America
Mr. and Mrs. Ronald Yoshino
Yoshinoya D&C
T. Yuki Family

$5,000 - $9,999

AT&T, Inc.
Mr. and Mrs. T. Aigaki
Ms. Mary Akashi
Anti-Defamation League
Mr. and Mrs. Moto Asakawa
Ms. Judith Y. Asano
Bridge Media, Inc.
Brighton JA Assoc.
Buddhist Church of Stockton
Buddhist Temple of Chicago
California-Nevada United Methodist
  Foundation
Crane & Norcross
Mr. David Dolifka
Edwin Endow and Debra Hatanaka
Benito Fresquez and Iris Kobayashi
Mr. and Mrs. Kiyoshi Fujihara
Ms. Yukiko Fujii
Mr. Ralph Fujimoto
Dr. and Mrs. Charles K. Fujisaki
Mr. and Mrs. Mitsuo J. Fujishima
Garden Grove Japanese Language School
Mr. Frank K. Hamada
Mae Mayko Hara
Mr. and Mrs. Yoshiro Harada
Mr. and Mrs. Warren H. Haruki
Mr. and Mrs. Makiji Hase
Helen, Craig, Bruce and Ted Hasegawa
Heart Mountain Comm. of Southern CA
Mr. and Mrs. Ken Higashi
Dr. Michael R. Higashi
Mr. and Mrs. Francis I. Hirakawa
Mr. and Mrs. Richard M. Hirata Family
Mr. and Mrs. Shurei Hirozawa
Mr. Garret S. Hokada
Mr. and Mrs. Paul Y. Hosoda
Mr. and Mrs. Peter Hosokawa
Mr. Bill Hosokawa
Mr. and Mrs. Joseph Ichiuji
Ms. May M. Ideta
Mr. and Mrs. Sho Iino
Mr. and Mrs Ken M. Iseri
Mrs. Kuniko Ishii
Mr. and Mrs. Joseph R. Ishizaki
Dr. and Mrs. Harvey Itano
Mrs. Koharu Ito
Mr. Koji Iwata
Dr. Victor S. Izui
JACL Detroit Chapter
JACL Florin Chapter
JACL Lodi Chapter
JACL Marysville Chapter
JACL New Mexico Chapter
JACL Placer County Chapter
JACL Sacramento Chapter
JACL San Jose Chapter
JACL Stockton Chapter
JACL Washington, DC Chapter
Japan Commerce Association of Washington, DC
Mr. Eddie Jonokuchi

Ms. Emi Kamachi
Mr. Noritashi Kanai
Dr. and Mrs. John Kanda
Mr. and Mrs. Hiroji Kariya
Mr. and Mrs. Kazuo Kato
Mr. Keizo Katori
Mr. and Mrs. Lester G. Katsura
Mr. Ben Kawahata
Mr. Hayato Kihara
Mr. Roy Kirita
Mr. and Mrs. Albert Koga
Mr. Michael Komai
Mr. and Mrs. Hideto Kono
Mrs. Ruth Kosaka
S. Kosasa Foundation
Mr. and Mrs. Satoru Kuroda
Mr. and Mrs. Paul H. Kusuda
MIS Assoc. of Northern CA
Mr. and Mrs. George Y. Masunaga
Ms. Michi Masunaga
Mr. and Mrs. Hisao Matsumoto
Dr. Ayako Wada Mayeda
Midwest Buddhist Temple
Dr. and Mrs. Warren Minami
Mr. and Mrs. George Miyada
Mr. Jim J. Miyazaki
Mr. Tom Moon
Mrs. Kay T. Morishita
Mr. and Mrs. Takashi Moriuchi
The Mukai Family
Mr. and Mrs. James H. Mukoyama, Jr.
Mr. and Mrs. Fred K. Murakami
Mr. and Mrs. Patrick N. Nagano
Mr. Albert Nakai
Mrs. Lillian Y. Nakamoto
Mr. and Mrs. Hiro Ray Nakanishi
Mr. and Mrs. Nobuyuki Nakashima
Mr. and Mrs. Robert Nakasone
Ms. Yuri Nakata
Mr. and Mrs. Tadashi Nakauchi
Nanka Kenjinkai Kyogikai
Mr. and Mrs. Mike Y. Niimoto
Mr. David T. Nikaido
Nisei Veterans Committee, Inc.
Dr. and Mrs. A. Hirotoshi Nishikawa
Dr. and Mrs. Roy M. Nishikawa
Mr. and Mrs. Shigeshi Nishikawa
Mr. and Mrs. Francis A. Nishimura
Dr. and Mrs. Akira Nishizawa
Mr. and Mrs. Henry Nishizu
Mr. and Mrs. Akira P. Nose'
Oda Family Charitable Foundation
Mr. and Mrs. Claude Ohanesian
Mr. and Mrs. Paul T. Ohtaki
Mr. Sammy Oi
Mr. and Mrs. K. Patrick Okura
Mrs. Mary J. Okura
Mr. and Mrs. Akira Omachi
S. Omura & Sons, Inc.
Mr. and Mrs. Jim S. Onchi
Mr. and Mrs. Hideo S. Onoda

Heizo and Hide Oshima
Dr. and Mrs. Richard K. Otagaki
PhilipMorris, Inc.
SBD Group, Inc.
Mr. and Mrs. Barry Saiki
Mrs. Bess M. Saito and Stephanie Allyn
Ms. Sharon Ann Saito
Mr. and Mrs. Henry K. Sakai
Ms. Shiuko Sakai
Mr. Yozo Sakai
Ms. Cherry I. Sakakida
Mr. Harumi (Bacon) Sakatani
Johnny K. and Grace M. Sakioka and Family
Dr. and Mrs. Edwin Sasaki
Mr. Naoharu Satake
Mr. and Mrs. John Y. Sato
Mr. and Mrs. Tokuye Sato
Dr. and Mrs. Haruto Sekijima
Servco Foundation
Mr. and Mrs. Mark M. Sese
Mr. and Mrs. S. Don Shimazu
Ms. Nami V. Shio
Mr. and Mrs. Sho Shiraga
Mr. and Mrs. Toshiyuki Shiraga
Mr. and Mrs. Ernie Shirakawa
Mr. Shinsaku Sogo
Solectron California Corporation
Stockton Aichi Shinboku Kai
Mr. and Mrs. Sterling S. Suga
Mr. Go Sugiura
Jennett and Tatsumi Tada
Ms. Violet Tagawa
Mr. and Mrs. Harry I. Takagi
Mr. and Mrs. Nobukazu Takahashi
Mrs. Masako Tanaka
Mr. Toshiaki Tanaka
Ms. Virginia Tanaka
Thomas and Kazuko Tanigawa
Mr. Barry K. Taniguchi
Mr. and Mrs. Gary Tanimura
Mr. and Mrs. Hiroshi Tateyama
Toyota Motor Company
Ms. Marielle Tsukamoto
Mr. and Mrs. Hiroshi Uyehara
Venice Japanese Community Center
Ms. Takeko Wakiji
Mrs. Hatayo H. Wallen
Mr. Dale L. Watanabe
Mr. and Mrs. George Watanabe
Mr. and Mrs. Samuel Watanabe
Mr. Carl T. Yamada
Mr. and Mrs. Kelly K. Yamada
Mr. Shoji S. Yamada
Mr. and Mrs. Yoshio Yamada
Carole S. and Jerry M. Yamaki
Mr. and Mrs. Shiroku Yamamoto
Mr. and Mrs. Tom Y. Yanagihara
Mr. and Mrs. Kentaro Yasuda
Mr. and Mrs. Mas Yonemura
Mr. and Mrs. Masami Samuel Yoshinari
Yoshinoya West, Inc.

$1,000 - $4,999

100th/442nd Veterans Association
232nd Engineers-Band Chapter 206
442nd Veterans Club 171st Chapter, HI
442nd Veterans Club Anti-Tank Chapter
442nd Veterans Club Co. I RCT - Honolulu
442nd Veterans Club Fox Chapter, HI
442nd Veterans Club HQ 2nd Battalion, HI
442nd Veterans Club HQ 3rd Chapter, HI
442nd Veterans Club Mike Chapter, HI
442nd Veterans Club Okinawa Chapter
442nd Veterans Club Service Chapter
552nd FAB, 442nd RCT, Mainland Chapter
552nd FAB Historical Book Committee, HI
AARP
A V Travel, Inc.
Mrs. Kimiko Abe
Mr. and Mrs. Lewis Abe
Masaru and Sadano Abe
Morris and Cherry Abe
Mr. and Mrs. Victor Abe
Mr. James S. Adachi
Mr. and Mrs. Kazuo Adachi
Aihama Construction, Inc.
Daiei Hawaii Investments
Mrs. Chiyo Aiso
Ms. Tsuyako Ajari
Mr. and Mrs. Raymond Y. Aka
Mr. James Akagi
Mr. Joe Akiyama
Mr. Joseph S. Akiyama
Mr. Gene H. Akutsu
Alpha Data Services, Inc.
Mr. Richard K. Amano
Mr. and Mrs. Minoru Amemiya
American Commercial, Inc., Mikasa
American Legion Post #185
Ameritech Foundation
Mr. and Mrs. Minoru Amimoto
Mr. and Mrs. Wallace S. Amioka
Mr. and Mrs. Joe K. Ando
Mr. and Mrs. Koshi Ando
Mr. and Mrs. Roy Andow
Tomi and Masy Tashima Andow
Anonymous
Mr. and Mrs. Yorio Aoki
Mr. and Mrs. Gordon A. Aoyagi
Mr. Katsumi Aoyama
Aquamar, Inc.
Mr. and Mrs. Hebert Aragaki
Ms. Adele Arakawa
Mr. George Arakawa
Mr. and Mrs. Paul Arakawa
Ms. Toyoko Arakawa
Janet Y. and James T. Araki Family
Mr. Minoru Sam Araki
Mr. and Mrs. Raymond M. Arao
Mr. Shinta Asami
Mr. and Mrs. Yoneo Asano
Mr. and Mrs. Ted T. Asato
Mr. Frank Ashida
Mr. and Mrs. Dange Atagi
Ms. Janet Ayers
Mr. Gregory Barlow
Mrs. Nancy O. Barrett
David and Miyoko I. Bassett
Mrs. Isabel M. Benson
Ms. Amy Beppu
Mr. and Mrs. Richard Berman
Ms. Loretta D. Billings
Mr. and Mrs. Edmund J. Birch
Warren, Susan, Steven and Stephanie Boatright
Mrs. Mabel Shoji Boggs
Iku Boothby
Mr. Paul J. Bowlby
Mr. and Mrs. Sumiko Brinsfield
Broadway HS Alumni Assoc.
Mr. Tom Brokaw
Brokers West
Mr. James Broussard
Hon. Jesse Brown
Mr. and Mrs. Robert Brown
Buddhist Temple of Chicago
Buddhist Temple of Chicago Asoka Society
Mrs. Lucy Y. Buhler
Mr. Stimson Bullitt
Mrs. Frances Bushell
Mr. and Mrs. George Buto
Mr. and Mrs. Jaroslav Byma
California Flower Market
Calvary Presbyterian Church, California

Canal High School Reunion
Cannon Land Co.
Mr. and Mrs. Richard L. Carl
Castle & Cooke Homes Hawaii, Inc.
Central Valley Jewish & Japanese American Forum
Ms. Lucia Cha and Mr. Jerry Hiura
Mr. Charles Chase and Mrs. Dawn Sawada Chase
Chicago Japanese American Council
Chicago-Nisei Post
Mr. Ray Chikahisa
Ruby Chuman and Paul Chuman
Chuo Bussan Corporation
City Bank, HI
Mr. and Mrs. Stephen Clapp
Coast Nurseries, Inc.
The Coca-Cola Company
Coldwell Banker - Gay Dales
Mr. Patrick Collins
Ms. Priscilla Collins
Mr. Robert Cullum
Mr. Daniel Date
Mr. and Mrs. Kazuo Henry Date
Mr. Shoji Date
Mr. and Mrs. Davidson
Ms. Mae Deguchi
Denver Buddhist Temple
Denver Buddhist Women's Assoc.
Denver Central Optimist Club
Devon Church of Jesus Christ
Denver Nikkei Singles Club
Raymond B. Dingman and Susan Vogel
Mr. Moe Dinner
Disabled Amerian Veteran Nisei Chapter #100
Mr. and Mrs. Fred Dohzen
Mr. and Mrs. Mas Doi
Mr. and Mrs. Paul Doi
Mr. and Mrs. Roy Doi
Dr. Susan C. Doi
Dr. and Mrs. Tom T. Doi
Hon. Robert J. Dole
Mr. George Domon
Mr. and Mrs. Clarence Donahoe
Mr. Willis Edel
Dr. Robert K. Emy
Dr. and Mrs. Arthur Endo
Mr. and Mrs. Harry Endo
Mr. and Mrs. Kenneth Endo
Keith and Lawrence Endo Families
Mr. and Mrs. Minoru Endo
Mr. and Mrs. Robert M. Endo
Mr. and Mrs. Edward Endow
Mr. Robert O. Endow
Mr. and Mrs. Jerry J. Enomoto
Mr. and Mrs. Toshio Enomoto
Mrs. Rinko Shimasaki Enosaki
Equus Las Vegas Assoc.
Eto Farms
Executive Resource Group, Inc.
Mr. and Mrs. Darrel K. Fiske
Mr. Robert H. Foote
Fuji Flour Milling Co., Ltd
Mr. and Mrs. Atsushi Fujii
Dr. Gary Fujii
Mr. Joe Yuzuru Fujii and Family
Dr. John K. Fujii
Ms. Kazumi Fujii
Mr. and Mrs. Kazuo Fujii
Dr. and Mrs. Kenneth K. Fujii
Mr. Satoru Dick Fujii
Mr. and Mrs. Toko Fujii
Mrs. Yasuko Fujimori
Dr. and Mrs. Jack Fujimoto
Mr. and Mrs. James Fujimoto
Mr. William T. Fujimoto
Ms. Fusayo Fujimura
Mr. and Mrs. Yoshio Fujimura
Mr. and Mrs. Henry H. Fujiura
Mr. Mas Fukai
Mr. Budd Fukei
Mr. and Mrs. Makoto Fukuda
Ms. Satoko Fukuda
Mr. and Mrs. Chester Fukuhara
Mr. and Mrs. David Fukuhara
Mr. and Mrs. Harry K. Fukuhara
Mr. and Mrs. Michael Fukuma
Mr. and Mrs. Harold K. Fukunaga
Ms. Ritsuye Fukunaga
Mr. and Mrs. G. S. Fukushima
Mr. and Mrs. Edgar Fukutaki
Ms. Elizabeth T. Fukutaki
Funaei Co., Ltd.
Funakoshi-Ito Insurance Services, Inc.
Mr. and Mrs. Hideo Furiya
Mr. Akira Furukawa
Dr. George Tadaharu Furukawa

Mr. and Mrs. George H. Furukawa
Dr. and Mrs. James M. Furukawa
Mr. and Mrs. Stanley K. Furukawa
Mr. Chester Furuto
Galleria Enterprise, Inc.
GeeTee Company
Gila River Reunion '97
Goda & Associates, Inc.
Mr. Paul Gordon
Mr. and Mrs. Kazuo Goto
Mr. Leo Goto
Gotoh Distribution Services, Inc.
Ms. Rosalie Gould
Mr. and Mrs. Paul B. Hackmeyer
Mr. Kerry S. Hada
Mr. George Hagiwara
Hakuto Co., Ltd.
Mr. and Mrs. Shig Hamachi
Raymond Noboru Hamamoto and Jean Hirasuna
Mr. and Mrs. Kenneth Hamamura
Mr. and Mrs. Joseph Hamanaka
Mr. and Mrs. Kintaro Hamashige
Mr. and Mrs. Edgar Hamasu
Mr. Mitsuhiro Hanawa
Mr. Takuzo Handa
Mr. and Mrs. Don Hara
Mr. Gary K. Harada and Mr. Masayoshi Harada
Dr. and Mrs. Harold S. Harada
Mr. and Mrs. Kei D. Harada
Harken Foundation
Mr. and Mrs. Andrew Hasegawa
Mr. George K. Hasegawa
T. Hasegawa Co., Ltd.
Ms. Yoshino Hasegawa
Mr. and Mrs. Richard T. Hashi
Mr. Hiroshi James Hashimoto
Mr. and Mrs. Masaru Hashimoto
Ms. Ruth Y. Hashimoto
Mr. Ted S. Hashimoto
Mr. Seiji Hata
Mrs. Yoshie Hata
Mr. Yoshio Hata
Mr. and Mrs. Terry Hatada
George and Kashina Hatamiya
Mr. and Mrs. Roy Hatamiya
Dr. and Dr. Rick N. Hattori
Hawaii Nikkei History Editorial Board
Mr. and Mrs. Jun Hayakawa
Mr. and Mrs. Robert Hayamizu
Mr. and Mrs. Philip Hayasaka
Mr. and Mrs. Joshua Hayase
Mr. and Mrs. Haruo Hayashi
Dr. Kazushige Hayashi
Dr. Tom Y. Hayashi
Ms. Yukiyo Ruth Hayashi
Mr. and Mrs. George M. Hayashida
Mr. John M. Hayashida
Mr. and Mrs. Tom Heard
Heart Mountain Class of 1947
Mr. William G. Hessler
Chiyoko and Norman Heyamoto
Mr. Henry K. Hibino
Mr. and Mrs. Allan M. Hida
Mr. Wallace S. Higa
Mr. and Mrs. Harry Higaki
Mr. Gary Higashi
Kenneth and Lyn Higashi Family
Shari Higashi Family
Mr. and Mrs. Fred Hikida
Mr. and Mrs. Thomas Hikida
Mr. Grant H. Hirabayashi
Mr. and Mrs. George Hiraga
Dr. Bernice K. Hirai
Roy and Helen Hiramatsu
Mr. and Mrs. Dick Hirano
Mr. and Mrs. William T. Hiraoka
Mas and Mary Hirashima
Mr. and Mrs. Henry M. Hirata
Richard and Merry Hirata
Mr. Yoshiomi H. Hirata
Mrs. Yukiko Hirata
Mr. Shigeki Hiratsuka
Mr. Yutaka Hiratsuka
Ms. Sharon K. Hirokawa
Mr. David Hiromura
Mr. and Mrs. Eisaku Hiromura
Mr. and Mrs. Paul Hiromura
Hiroshima Doshikai Stockton
Mr. and Mrs. Stanley Tariho Hirozawa
Ms. Dorothy M. Hiura
Mr. and Mrs. Pearce Hiura
Mr. and Mrs. Wilfred Hiura
Dai-Nippon Nokai - Hokubei Nanka Shikai
Mr. and Mrs. Garry L. Holloway
Hollywood Japanese Cultural Institute

Mr. and Mrs. Harry K. Honda
Ms. Kazuko Honda
Mr. and Mrs. Masami Honda
Mr. and Mrs. Lizo Honma
H. Earle and Ann Hori Family
Saburo Hori Family
Mr. and Mrs. Takashi Hori
Mr. and Mrs. Saburo Horiba
Mr. and Mrs. Tak Horiba
Ms. Michiko Horio
Mr. and Mrs. Kaz Horita
Mr. and Mrs. Robert M. Horiuchi
Mr. and Mrs. Lloyd Hoshide
Mr. Harry H. Hoshiko
Mr. and Mrs. Fred Y. Hoshiyama
Dr. Michael C. Hosokawa
Mr. and Mrs. Robert R. Hosokawa
Mr. and Mrs. Kiyoshi Hotta
Mr. and Mrs. Steven Hotta
Ms. Ayako Okubo Hurd
Mr. and Mrs. Shigeru Iba
Dr. and Mrs. Shozo Iba
Mr. Terashi Ibara
Mr. Masami S. Ichiba
Mr. Mikio Ichiba
Ms. Nancy Ichikawa
Mr. and Mrs. Takaaki Ichikawa
Mr. and Mrs. Paul T. Ichiuji
Yoshiko Edith and Mary Ichiuji
Mr. and Mrs. Edward H. Ichiyama
Ida-Ore Nikkeijinkai, Inc.
Mr. and Mrs. Tsutomu Ige
Mr. and Mrs. Ted Iida
Mr. and Mrs. Joe G. Ike
Mr. Toshio Ike
Mr. and Mrs. Dale Ikeda
Robert and Yasuko M. Ikeda
Mr. and Mrs. Tsuguo Ikeda
Mr. and Mrs. Tsutomu Tom Ikeda
Dr. and Mrs. Alfred W. Ikefuji
Ms. Midori Ikegami
Mr. and Mrs. Henry Y. Ikemoto
Ms. Noriko Ikemoto
Mr. and Mrs. Ted T. Ikemoto
Mr. and Mrs. Nobo Ikuta
Mr. and Mrs. Eiichi Imada
Mr. and Mrs. Yukio Imada
Ms. Aiko Asaki Imagawa
Eskridge and Theresa Imai
Ms. Viola Imai
Mr. and Mrs. Ken Imatani
Dr. Raymond J. Imatani
Mr. Wayne Inaba
Mr. and Mrs. Donald Inadomi
Mr. George Inai
Mr. and Mrs. James Inatomi
Mr. and Mrs. Yutaka Inokuchi
Mr. and Mrs. Chikateru Inouye
Mr. and Mrs. George Inouye
Dr. and Mrs. Henry S. Inouye
Mr. Jerry Inouye
Mr. and Mrs. Roger Inouye
Mr. and Mrs. Roy Y. Inouye
Dr. Ruby A. Inouye
Mr. and Mrs. Walter Inouye
Mr. and Mrs. Roy Inui
Mr. and Mrs. Jerry Irei
Mr. and Mrs. Frank Iritani
Mr. George Ishibashi
Mr. and Mrs. Henry J. Ishida
Dr. and Mrs. Hiraku H. Ishida
Mr. and Mrs. Lonny M. Ishihara
Mr. and Mrs. Tadashi Ishihara
Ms. Hoshiko B. Ishii
Ms. Marion K. Ishii
Mr. and Mrs. Paul R. Ishikawa
Mr. and Mrs. Wesley Ishikawa
Ms. Kazuyo Ishimaru
Mrs. May Asaki Ishimoto
Norman P. Ishimoto
Mr. and Mrs. John K. Ishizuka
Mr. Sam S. Isokane
Mr. and Mrs. Herbert S. Isonaga
Akio and Gladys Itamura
Dr. and Mrs. Masashi Itano
Mr. and Mrs. Wayne Itano
Mr. and Mrs. Arthur Ito
Ms. Dolly M. Ito
Mr. Kenji Ito
Mr. and Mrs. Kensaku Ito
Mr. and Mrs. Kiyoshi Ito
Mr. and Mrs. Martin L. Ito
Mr. and Mrs. Shigeru H. Ito
Dr. and Mrs. Susumu Ito
Mr. and Mrs. Yonejiro Ito

Toru and Judy Iura
Mr. and Mrs. Donald K. Iwai
Mr. Warren T. Iwai
Brooks Iwakiri
Mr. George Iwamoto
Mrs. Mary Iwaoka
Mr. and Mrs. Akira Iwasaki
Mr. and Mrs. Arthur Iwasaki
Mr. and Mrs. George Iwasaki
K. Iwata Associates
Mr. and Mrs. Norio Iwata
Mr. Richard S. Iwata
Mr. and Mrs. Roy Tadashi Iwata
Mr. and Mrs. Susumu Iwatake
In memory/honor of Peter O. and
  David K. Iwatsu
Mr. and Mrs. Takumi Izuno
JA Resource Center/Museum
JACL Alaska Chapter
JACL Berkeley Chapter
JACL Cincinnati Chapter
JACL Cleveland Chapter
JACL Clovis Chapter
JACL Cortez Chapter
JACL Eastern District Council
JACL Eden Township Chapter
JACL Fort Lupton Chapter
JACL Fresno Chapter
JACL Gardena Valley Chapter
JACL Imperial Valley Chapter
JACL Japan Chapter
JACL Mile-Hi Chapter
JACL Mountain Plains District
JACL New York Chapter
JACL No. CA-West Nevada
JACL Orange County Chapter
JACL Philadelphia 98 Chapter
JACL Philadelphia Chapter
JACL Pocatello-Blackfoot Chapter
JACL Puyallup Valley Chapter
JACL Reedley Chapter
JACL Reno Chapter
JACL Riverside Chapter
JACL Salinas Valley Chapter
JACL San Diego Chapter
JACL Sanger Chapter
JACL Santa Maria Valley Chapter
JACL Seattle Chapter
JACL Sequoia Chapter
JACL St. Louis Chapter
JACL Tri Valley Chapter
JACL Venice Culver Chapter
JACL Ventura County Chapter
JACL West Los Angeles Auxiliary
JACL West Los Angeles Chapter
JACL-Central California District Council
Ms. Merle Jack
Japanese Ancestral Soc. of Portland
Japanese Chamber of Commerce of Northern
  California, SF
Japanese Community Health, Inc.
Japanese Community of Delano
Japanese Community Pioneer Ct
Japanese Presbyterian Church, Seattle, WA
Mr. Carl W. Jarvie
Jerome Camp Reunion
Mr. and Mrs. Jacob S. Jichaku
Jiji Press America, Ltd.
Ms. Junko J. Jofuku
Ms. Tomoko Joichi
Mr. and Mrs. Wallace K. Kagawa
Mr. Arthur Y. Kageyama
Mr. and Mrs. Reynold S. Kagiwada
Kahma Corporation
Mr. and Mrs. Willy S. Kai
Mr. and Mrs. Thomas K. Kaihara
Mr. and Mrs. Arthur S. Kaihatsu
Mr. Kazumi Kaita
K Company Veterans Club
Mr. Arthur N. Kaku
Mr. Hiroshi Kaku
Ms. James Kambara
Mr. and Mrs. Fred Kamemoto
Mr. Alden T. Kamikawa
Mr. Milton Kanatani
Mr. and Mrs. Enoch H. Kanaya
Mr. Brett S. Kanazawa
Mr. and Mrs. Edward Kanazawa
Ms. Saji Kanazawa
Ms. Catherine N. Kanda
Mr. and Mrs. Mamoru E. Kanda
Mr. and Mrs. Ben Kaneda
Dr. Robert R. Kaneda
Mr. and Mrs. Jerry Kaneko
Mr. and Mrs. Wayne M. Kanemoto
Mr. and Mrs. Stanley Kaneshiki

Mr. and Mrs. Sadao Kaneshiro
Ms. Rose S. Kanno
Mr. and Mrs. Satoru Kanzaki
Mr. Henry Karatsu
Mr. Scott T. Kariya
Dr. Steven T. Kariya
Ms. Grace Kasahara
Mr. Mitsugi M. Kasai
Mr. and Mrs. Kenneth Kasamatsu
Ms. Louise Kashino and Family
Mr. and Mrs. Bill Kasuga
Messrs. Jiro and Hirotaka Kasuga
George Katagiri and Michiko Kornhauser
Harry and Rose Kataoka
Kato Brothers
Dr. Eugene Kato
Ms. Eva M. Kato
Mr. and Mrs. Tadashi Kato
Ms. Toshiko Kato
Mr. and Mrs. Fred Katsuyama
Mr. and Mrs. John Kawachi
Mrs. Sadako Kawaguchi
Dr. and Mrs. George Kawahara
Mrs. Elsie Kawahata
Mr. and Mrs. George Kawakami
Mr. and Mrs. Mike Kawamoto
Dr. and Mrs. Shigeo Kawamoto and Family
Ms. Hamako Kawamura
Mr. and Mrs. Shigeru Kawanami
Mr. and Mrs. Tami Kawano
Mr. and Mrs. Thomas Kawano
Mr. and Mrs. Masuo Kawasaki
Mr. Eric H. Kawashima
Mr. Nobuyuki Kawata
Mr. and Mrs. Ray S. Kayano
Dr. Ernest Kazato
Ms. Edna S. Kazue
Gail, Bruce, Judy, M. Keikoan
Ms. Carolyn Kelly
Susan Kelty and Tracy and Jody Oshita
Mr. and Mrs. Lawrence Kern
Mr. and Mrs. Mark Kiguchi
Mr. and Mrs. Shigeya Kihara
Ms. Kimiko Kikuchi
Dr. and Mrs. Thomas Kikuchi
Mr. and Mrs. Eugene T. Kimura
Mr. and Mrs. Joe Kimura
Ms. Lillian C. Kimura
Mr. and Mrs. Tom K. King
Dr. and Mrs. Dennis K. Kinoshita
Dr. and Mrs. Eugene H. Kinoshita
Dr. and Mrs. Jin H. Kinoshita
Mr. and Mrs. Mas Kinoshita
Mr. and Mrs. Masao Kinoshita
Ms. Ruth Kinoshita
Ms. Kimiko Kishi
Mr. and Mrs. Sherman Kishi
Ms. Helen Kishimoto
Mr. Shunichiro Kishioka
Mr. and Mrs. Moss Kishiyama
Ms. Fumiko Kita
Ms. Kyoko Kita
Mrs. Yoshiko M. Kita
Dr. and Mrs. Holly Kitagawa
Mr. and Mrs. Fred S. Kitajima
Mr. and Mrs. Kenji Kitamura
Mr. Ken Kitasaki
Ms. Mabel E. Kitsuse
Dr. and Mrs. William Kiyasu
Mr. and Mrs. George Kiyomoto
Mr. and Mrs. Hideo Kiyomura
Kiyota Greenhouse, Inc.
Mr. Toshiro Kizaki
Mr. and Mrs. Shig T. Kizuka
Dr. and Mrs. Joe Kobara
Mr. and Mrs. Ken Kobara
Kobara Farm
Mr. and Mrs. Toru Kobara
Mr. and Mrs. Elmer W. Kobashi
Kay Kobata
Dr. and Mrs. Albert Kobayashi
Mr. Harry Kobayashi
Mr. and Mrs. Kazuo Kobayashi
Ms. Kyoko Kobayashi
Ms. M. Jane Kobayashi
Ms. Marian S. Kobayashi
Mr. and Mrs. Nelson Kobayashi
Dr. and Mrs. Ronald M. Kobayashi
Ms. Sumiko Kobayashi
Mr. and Mrs. Kaoru Kodama
Dr. Richard Y. Kodama
Mr. and Mrs. Roy K. Kodama
Max and Yuri Koga
Ms. Mitsuko Kohatsu
Mr. and Mrs. Ruvern H. Kohaya
Dr. and Dr. Sam Koide

Dr. and Mrs. Masaru Koike
Mr. and Mrs. Mits Kojimoto
Mr. and Mrs. Ryo Komae
Mr. and Mrs. Thomas Kometani
Ms. Fumiko Komori
Drs. Sam and Nori Komorita
Mr. and Mrs. Bill Komoto
Mr. and Mrs. James A. Komura
Dr. and Mrs. Ben Konishi
Mr. and Mrs. Hitoshi Kono
Ms. Marilyn Korenaga
Mr. and Mrs. Takeshi Kosakura
Mrs. Neil Kosasa and Family
Mr. and Mrs. William Koseki
Ms. Mieko Kosobayashi
Mr. Hiroshi Kotoh
Mr. and Mrs. Kenso Koura
Mr. Joe Koyama
Mr. James I. Kozen
Mr. and Mrs. Ard K. Kozono
Mr. and Mrs. George Kozu
Mr. and Mrs. Shinji Kozu
Mr. and Mrs. Eiji (Ed) Kubokawa
Mr. and Mrs. Riley Kumagai
Mrs. Chiyeko Kumano
Dr. and Mrs. Yukio Kumasaka
Ms. Yuriko K. Kumasaka
Mr. Raymond Kunita
Mr. and Mrs. Milnes Kurashige
Mr. Edward M. Kurata
Mr. and Mrs. Joseph Kurata
Mr. Paul Kurata
Mr. and Mrs. Lloyd Kurihara
Walter and Marie Kurihara and Family
Mr. Arden S. Kuroda
Mr. and Mrs. Tokuo Kurosaka
Ms. May Kushida
Mr. Masami Kusumoto
Mr. Roy T. Kusumoto
Dr. and Mrs. Roger K. Kuwabara
Mr. Clyde Y. Kuwahara
Mr. and Mrs. Frank Kuwahara
Mr. and Mrs. Satoshi Kuwamoto
Lake Park United Methodist Church
Mr. Frank F. Lau
Ms. Jean Lee
Mrs. Leanne M. Lee
Gordon and Janet Livengood
Mr. Terry J. Lundgren
MIS Northwest Association
MIS Vets Club Hawaii
MIS Vets Club Rocky Mountain
Louise S. Maehara and Miki Rotman
Ms. Tomi M. Maeno
Mr. and Mrs. Tai Makino
Mr. and Mrs. Jun Makishima
Mr. Herbert Mameda
Mr. and Mrs. Royal L. Manaka
Mr. and Mrs. Tim Manaka
Mr. and Mrs. Tosh Mano
Mr. and Mrs. Deairwood Manzo
Marina Gardeners Association, Inc.
Marshall & Sullivan, Inc.
Dr. and Mrs. George Marumoto
Mr. Greg Marutani
Nancy Marutani-Hackmeyer and Paul Hackmeyer
Dr. and Mrs. Herbert A. Maruyama
Ms. Amy Masaki
Mr. and Mrs. Tom Masamori
Mr. and Mrs. Harry Masatani
Master Sheet Metal, Inc.
Mr. and Mrs. George M. Masuda
Mr. and Mrs. James Masuda
Mr. and Mrs. Kaoru Masuda
Ms. Nori Masuda
Mr. Hiromu Masumoto
Mr. and Mrs. Shig Masunaga
Dr. and Mrs. David Masuoka
Nobuko, Connie, Neva and Loren Masuoka
Mr. and Mrs. Hiroshi Matoba
Mr. Hiroshi Matsubara
Mr. and Mrs. Frank T. Matsuda
Mr. and Mrs. Tadao Matsuda
Mr. and Mrs. Tatsuo Matsuda
Mr. and Mrs. John T. Matsudaira
Mr. and Mrs. Taro Matsui
Dr. and Mrs. Richard K. Matsuishi
Mr. and Mrs. Paul S. Matsuki
Drs. Alan and Julie Matsumoto
Ms. Alyce K. Matsumoto
Mr. and Mrs. Frank Y. Matsumoto
Mr. and Mrs. George Y. Matsumoto
Col. and Mrs. Glenn K. Matsumoto
Mr. and Mrs. Jerry K. Matsumoto
Mrs. Kaoru Matsumoto
Mr. and Mrs. Katsuo Matsumoto

Ms. Kazuko Matsumoto
Mrs. Masako Matsumoto
Mr. Robert J. Matsumoto
RGR. and Mrs. Roy H. Matsumoto
Mrs. Ruth Y. Matsumoto
Ms. Tayeko M. Matsumoto
Mr. and Mrs. Walter Matsumoto
Mr. and Mrs. George M. Matsumura
Ms. Helene H. Matsunaga
Mr. and Mrs. James K. Matsunaga
Mr. Keith Matsuo
Mr. and Mrs. Theodore Matsuo
Mr. and Mrs. George I. Matsuoka
Mr. and Mrs. Jack Matsuoka
James and Amy Matsuoka
Mrs. Kazuye K. Matsuoka
Mr. and Mrs. John Matsushima
Matsuyama-Sacramento Sister City Corporation
Mr. and Mrs. Hiro Mayeda
Mr. and Mrs. James H. Mayeda
Mr. and Mrs. Sam Mayeda
Mr. and Mrs. Tadashi Mayeda
Toshiko and Sibyl Yau Mayeda
Mr. and Mrs. Jim McClure
Mr. and Mrs. Calvin McGinnis
Mr. Colin McLennan
Mr. Neal McLens
Mrs. Debbra K. McQuilken
Mr. Allen H. Meyer
Mr. Noboru Mikasa
Mr. Claude Mimaki
Mr. and Mrs. Ronald S. Minami
Mr. and Mrs. Wayne Minami
Dr. and Mrs. Wayne H. Minami
Mr. and Mrs. Ben N. Minamide
Mr. and Mrs. Thomas T. Minamide
Mr. and Mrs. Howard Minato
Christopher Mincks and Lisa Shakerin
Mr. Tom I. Mine
Dr. and Mrs. Albert Mineta
MIS Northwest Association
MIS Veterans Club Rocky Mountain
Mr. and Mrs. James Mita
Mr. and Mrs. Harold Mitobe
Mr. and Mrs. Sam M. Mitsui
Messrs. Wataru Miura
Kenji Miyahara
Mrs. Kiyo Miyahara
Akemi Miyake
Mr. and Mrs. Bob Miyamoto
Mr. James Y. Miyamoto
Mr. Hiroshi Miyamura
Mr. and Mrs. Walter H. Miyao
Shuichi and Pearl Miyasaki
Miyasaki, Tateishi Family
Mr. and Mrs. Victor M. Miyata
Mr. Perry Mizota
Mr. Setsuo Tom Mizote
Mr. Frank Y. Mizukami
Mr. and Mrs. Yoshito Mizuta
Mr. Jun L. Mizutani
Mr. and Mrs. Mitsuo Mizutani
Mr. and Mrs. Minoru Mochizuki
Dr. and Mrs. Milton Momita
Mr. and Mrs. Gerald Momoda
Mr. John Momoyo
Mr. Patrick T. Moran and Mrs. Malli Ueno Moran
Bruce, Irene and Meriko Mori
Mr. and Mrs. Jerold H. Mori
Mr. and Mrs. Perry T. Mori
Mr. and Mrs. Robert Moriguchi
Mr. and Mrs. George Morimitsu
Kathryn, Carol, and Phil Morimitsu
Ms. Joni Morishita
Mrs. Mitsuko Murao Morishita
Mr. and Mrs. Deen Morita
Mr. and Mrs. Takashi Morita
Mr. and Mrs. William Morita
Mr. and Mrs. Frank Moriya
Dr. and Mrs. Iwao M. Moriyama
Dr. Elizabeth D. Morningstar
Mr. John S. Mortimer
Motoda Foundation
Mr. and Mrs. Ben Motoike
Mr. and Mrs. Junichi Mugihira
Cromwell and Kyoko Mukai
Mr. George M. Mukasa
Mr. and Mrs. Harold T. Murai
Mr. Craig Murakami
Ms. Momoko Murakami
Mr. and Mrs. Richard Murakami
Dr. and Mrs. Wesley K. Murakami
Christine, Ted and Kokoro Murakishi
Ms. Ruth Muramatsu
Mr. and Mrs. Takeo Muramoto
Mr. Shigesato Murao

Mr. Victor T. Muraoka
Ms. Alice U. Murashige
James and Sumi I. Murashima
Dr. Alice Kishiye Murata
Mr. and Mrs. Kiguma Murata
Dr. Makio Murayama
Ms. Mary Muto
NB Corporation of America
Mr. and Mrs. Michio Nagai
Mr. and Mrs. Willie T. Nagai
Mr. and Mrs. William N. Naganuma
Mrs. Mas Nagasawa
Mr. Craig Nagasugi
Dr. and Mrs. James K. Nagatani
Mr. and Mrs. Mitsu J. Naito
Mr. and Mrs. Richard H. Naito
Mr. and Mrs. Shig Naito
Mr. Nicholas T. Nakabayashi
Mr. and Mrs. Edward T. Nakagawa
Mr. Fred Nakagawa
Mr. and Mrs. Giro Nakagawa
Mr. and Mrs. Henry Nakagawa
Ms. Mary H. Nakagawa
Ms. Ruby Nakagawa
Sam and Martha Nakagawa
Mr. and Mrs. Sam Nakagawa
Mr. and Mrs. Shunichi Nakagawa
Mr. and Mrs. Togo Nakagawa
Ms. Tsune S. Nakagawa
Mr and Mrs. Juan Nakagi
Mrs. Midori Nakaguchi
Ms. Lucille S. Nakahara
Mr. and Mrs. Steve Nakaji
Dr. and Mrs. William Nakamoto
Mrs. Ellen Ayako Noguchi Nakamura
Mr. and Mrs. Frank Y. Nakamura
Mr. Harry Nakamura
Mr. James M. Nakamura
Ms. Janice Nakamura
Mr. and Mrs. Kennon Nakamura
Mr. and Mrs. Norman Nakamura
Mr. and Mrs. Robert M. Nakamura
Ms. Shigeyo Jane Nakamura
Mr. T. T. Nakamura
Nakamura & Tyau, Inc.
Mrs. Yoshimi K. Nakamura
Mr. and Mrs. Toshio Nakanishi
Mr. and Mrs. Calvin Y. Nakano
Gerry Nakano
Ms. Grace K. Nakano
Mr. Tsutomu Nakano
Mr. William H. Nakano
Mrs. Yayoi Margaret Nakano
Mr. and Mrs. Arthur Nakashima
Mr. and Mrs. Tom Nakashima
Mr. and Mrs. Don Nakata
Mr. and Mrs. Roy Nakata
Mrs. Kayo A. Nakatani
Mr. and Mrs. James Nakawatase
Dr. and Mrs. Don K. Nakayama
Ms. Mineko Nakayama
Ms. Rose N. Nakayama
Mr. and Mrs. Tommy Nakayama
Ms. Riya Nakazono
Nalco Chemical Comp.
Mr. Mark Namba
Mr. and Mrs. Joe A. Naritoku
National Council of AJA Veterans
National Japanese American Historical Society
Natori Company, Inc.
Mr. and Mrs. Donald K. Negi
Motomu and Moe Neishi
Col. and Mrs. Francis Nekoba
Ms. Mable M. Nemoto
New Horizons
Ms. Miyako Yahata Newell
Mr. Donald Nii
Judy Niizawa and Rudy Tokiwa
Mr. Hisashi Nikaidoh
Nikkei International Association
Nikkei Matsuri
Messrs. Pro Takanori and Smokey Saburo Nimura
Mr. and Mrs. H. Harold Nishi
Mr. Ken Nishi
Sumio and Grace Nishi
Ms. Jane T. Nishida
Ms. Kyoko Nishida
Ms. Asako Nishimura
Mr. George I. Nishimura
Mr. and Mrs. Paul Nishimura
Mr. and Mrs. Paul T. Nishimura
Mr. Scott Nishioki
Mr. and Mrs. Hideo Nishita
Sen Nishiyama
Mr. David K. Nitta

Mr. Hank Nogawa
Mr. and Mrs. Raymond Nogawa
Dr. and Mrs. Henry Noguchi and Family
Hideyuki Noguchi
Mr. and Mrs. Toshio Noma
Mr. and Mrs. Kazuo Nomi
Mr. George M. Nomura
Mr. Tadashi Nomura
Mr. and Mrs. Walter Nomura
Ms. Shinako Noritake
North San Diego Church
North San Diego County Fujinkai
Mr. James C. Nose'
Ms. Miyoko M. O'Neill
Oahu AJA Veterans Council
Ms. Joanne C. Obata
Mr. and Mrs. Roger S. Obata
Dr. and Mrs. Robert T. Obi
Mr. James and Dr. Mary Oda
Ms. June Oda
Ms. Craney Ogata
Mr. and Mrs. Dye Ogata
Mr. and Mrs. Gen Ogata
Ms. Tamaki Ogata
Mrs. Chiyeko Hayashi Ogawa
Mr. Abraham Ohama, II
George and Haru Ohama
Mr. Leo H. Ohashi
Mr. and Mrs. Robert Ohashi
Mr. Katashi Oita
Dr. Chester S. Oji
Mr. and Mrs. Sukeo Oji
Ms. Sandra Ojiri
Mr. and Mrs. Kenichi Okabe
Mr. and Mrs. Tetsuo Okabe
Mrs. Sue Okada
Mr. and Mrs. Tomiaki Okada
Mr. and Mrs. Yoshitaka Okada
Mr. and Mrs. Herbert M. Okamoto
Mr. and Mrs. John Okamoto
Mr. and Mrs. Paul Y. Okamoto
Mr. Richard Katsumi Okamoto
Mr. and Mrs. Robert Okamoto
Mr. and Mrs. Ted T. Okamoto
Mr. and Mrs. William I. Okamoto
Mr. Randy Okamura
Okaya (USA), Inc.
Mr. and Mrs. Seiichi J. Okazaki
Mr. and Mrs. Kazuichi Okigawa
Mr. and Mrs. Ebo Okiyama
Mr. and Mrs. Robert Oku
Mr. and Mrs. H. Okumura
Mr. and Mrs. Arthur Okuno
Mr. Dale Okuno
Okura Mental Health Leadership Foundation
Ms. Patsy Omata
Dr. and Mrs. Robert R. Omata
Mr. and Mrs. Frank K. Omatsu
Mr. and Mrs. Ernest S. Omiya
Dr. and Mrs. Thomas Omori
Mr. and Mrs. Craig Omoto
Mr. and Mrs. Taketo Omoto
Mrs. Claire Fujita Omura
Onishi Florist, Inc.
Mr. and Mrs. Allen K. Ono
Mr. and Mrs. Paul Ono
Dr. Bright Onoda
Ms. Susan Onuma
Mr. Kazuo Ooka
Orange Coast Optimist Club of Garden Grove
Orange County Nikkei Coordinating Council
Orange County Sansei Singles
Ms. Mary Reiko Osaka
Mr. and Mrs. Walter K. Osaka
Mr. and Mrs. James Oshika
Mr. and Mrs. Mas Oshiki
Mr. Fred K. Oshima
Sanshiro and Ise Oshima
Ms. Janet S. Oshiro
Mr. and Mrs. Joe S. Oshiro
Mr. and Mrs. Frank K. Oshita
Mr. and Mrs. Hosen Oshita
Mr. and Mrs. James Osuga
Mr. and Mrs. Mas Ota
Mr. and Mrs. Robert Y. Ota
Mr. Kihei Otani
Mr. Michael Otani
Mr. Ted M. Oto
Mr. and Mrs. George Otsuki
Mr. and Mrs. Lloyd N. Ouye
Mr. and Mrs. Saburo Sam Owada
Patrick and Sally Oyabe
Mrs. Albert Oyama
Ms. Joyce Y. Oyama
Mr. Leo Oyama

Ms. Margaret Oyama
Ms. Mitsuye Oyama
Mr. Wright Oyama
Mr. and Mrs. Ron Oye
Mr. and Mrs. Ted T. Oye
Mr. and Mrs. Harry Ozawa
Ms. Marie Ozawa
Dr. and Mrs. Roy Ozawa
Pacific Advisory Services, Inc.
Pacific Heritage Bank
Stephen and Sandy Paolini
Ms. Kazuyo T. Parsch
Dr. Haakon Radge
Mr. and Mrs. Eugene F. Redden
Mr. Melvin Renge
Mr. Joseph A. Reyes
Mr. and Mrs. Paul Rohrer
Rohwer Reunion II Committee
Rich and Eileen Roulier
SO-PHIS of Orange County
Safeco Insurance, Co.
Mr. Masao Sagara
Ms. Shuny Sagara
Ms. Jane S. Sahara
Mr. and Mrs. Tamotsu Sahara
Mr. and Mrs. Albert K. Saiki
Mrs. Irene Y. Saiki
Mr. Tee T. Saisho
Mr. Henry H. Saito
Mr. and Mrs. John J. Saito
Mrs. Mary M. Saito
Mr. and Mrs. Minoru Saito
Natsu Taylor Saito
Ms. Jean Sakahara
Mr. Akira J. Sakai
Mrs. Carolyn Sakai
Mr. and Mrs. Katsu Sakai
Mr. and Mrs. Lawson Sakai
Ms. Lilly Sakai
Mr. and Mrs. Yukio Sakai
Ms. Tadashi Sakaida
Mr. and Mrs. Thomas S. Sakamoto
Mr. and Mrs. Roy Sakasegawa
Sakata Seed America, Inc.
Mr. George Sakato
Ms. Suzy S. Sakato
Dr. Carolyn Sakauye
Mr. and Mrs. Eiichi E. Sakauye
Mr. Isaac Sakuma
Mr. and Mrs. Isao Sakurai
Mr. and Mrs. Hitoshi G. Sameshima
Mr. Jack Sameshima
Sankosha Corporation
R.A. Sano Farms, Inc.
Mr. Kenneth K. Saruwatari
Mr. and Mrs. Calvin Sasai
Mr. and Mrs. Samuel Y. Sasai
Mr. Edward S. Sasaki
Dr. and Mrs. Gordon Sasaki
Mr. Paul Sasaki
Dr. and Mrs. Raymond Sasaki
Mr. Sam I. Sasaki
Ms. Shirley K. Sasaki
Mr. and Mrs. Steve Sashihara
Hayami and Teruma Sato
Mr. John S. Sato
Mr. and Mrs. Kenichi Sato
Mr. and Mrs. Mitsuho Sato
Mr. Stephens N. Sato
Ms. Susie Sato
Mr. and Mrs. Thomas Sato
Mr. and Mrs. Yone Satoda
Dr. and Mrs. Gregg K. Satow
Dr. Kathleen Y. Sawada
Mr. and Mrs. Yukio Ken Sawada
Dr. and Dr. Mark Schaefer
Mr. and Mrs. Lawrence D. Schectman
Ms. Irene Schoon
Seattle Sansei
Ben S. and Grace M. Segawa Family
Mr. and Mrs. S. Benjamin Seike
Mr. and Mrs. Sam Seiki
Seinan Senior Citizens Club, Inc.
Mr. and Mrs. Duzo Seko
Ms. Sachi Wada Seko
Dr. Laura L. Semba
Senba Foods Co., Ltd.
Mr. and Mrs. Kane Senda
Ms. Ruth Akiko Senda
Mr. and Mrs. Joseph T. Seto
Mrs. Virginia Shapiro
Ms. May Sagawa Shelton
Mr. Jerry Y. Shibata
Ms. Naomi Shibata
Shibayama & Karasawa, Inc.

Ms. Laura Y. Shibuya
Mr. Tad Shibuya
Ms. Satsuki Shigekawa
Mr. and Mrs. Charles Shikuma
Mr. and Mrs. Terry Shima
Mr. and Mrs. Robert T. Shimada
Mr. and Mrs. Bill Shimamoto
Mr. and Mrs. George Shimamoto
Mr. Ira Shimasaki
Mr. Joe S. Shimashita
Mrs. Akiko Shimatsu and Masao Mikami
Mr. George Shimizu
Ms. Kazuko Shimizu
Mr. and Mrs. Paul Shimizu
Mr. and Mrs. Kenneth Shimokochi
Ms. Janice T. Shimokubo
Ms. Tsugiye Fujii Shimokubo
Dr. and Dr. Wesley T. Shimomaye
Mr. and Mrs. George Shimotsu
Mr. and Mrs. Harry H. Shimotsu
Mr. John Shinkai
Mr. Francis S. Shinohara
Ms. Susan Shio
Ms. Kathryn S. Shioi
Mr. and Mrs. Tom Shiokari
Ms. Leila W. Shiozawa
Mr. and Mrs. Harry M. Shirachi
Ms. Carole A. Shiraga
Ms. Elizabeth M. Shiraga
Ms. Susan L. Shiraga
Ms. Vivian Shiraga
Mr. and Mrs. Toru Shiraki
Ms. Shizuko Shiramizu
Mr. and Mrs. Takeo H. Shirasawa
Mr. Katashi K. Shiroishi
Mr. and Mrs. Tak Shishino
Mr. and Mrs. Kazuo Shitama
Mr. John F. Shoji
Mr. and Mrs. Mack Shoji
Ms. Dorothy Ito Shundo
Mr. Robert H. Smith
Dr. and Mrs. Marvin Snell
Mr. and Mrs. Milton A. Snyder
Mr. and Mrs. Mitsuyoshi B. Sogioka
Mr. and Mrs. Yoshimaro Sogioka
Ms. Elsie Sogo
Ms. Mitsu Sonoda
Sons and Daughters of the 442nd Veterans
South Bay F.O.R.
Southern California Japanese Women's Society
Mr. and Mrs. B. P. Spoon
Dr. and Mrs. George Suda
Dr. and Mrs. Otto H. Suda
Ms. Itsuko Sueoka
Ms. Frances Sugai
Mr. and Mrs. Henry Sugai
Ms. Renee Sugasawara
Mr. and Mrs. Michael Sugawara
Ms. Madeleine S. Sugimoto
Choye Sugita
Mr. Garrret Sugiyama
Mr. and Mrs. Yone J. Sugiyama
Mr. Eddie Suguro
Ms. Gladyce T. Sumida
Sunnyside Packing Co.
Ms. Toshiko Sunohara
Mr. and Mrs. Tom Suyama
Tatsuye and Mitsuko Suyeishi
Mr. and Mrs. Hideo Suyetsugu
Ms. Marumi M. Suyeyasu
Mr. and Mrs. Hiroshi Suzuki
Mrs. Janet Y. Tabata
Ms. Ayako Tagashira
Jean and Patricia Tahara
Mr. and Mrs. Willie H. Tahara
Mr. and Mrs. Robert R. Taira
Mr. and Mrs. George Takabayashi
Mr. Yoshiki Takada
Mr. and Mrs. Calvin Takagi
Ms. Rosie Kazuko Takagi
Mr. and Mrs. Gene Takahashi
Mr. and Mrs. Hideo Takahashi
Ms. Rita Takahashi
Mr. and Mrs. Robert C. Takahashi
Mr. and Mrs. Sakae Takahashi
Mr. and Mrs. Ted Takahashi
Mr. and Mrs. Tom H. Takahashi
Takahashi Foundation and Trust
Mr. and Mrs. Roy Takai
The Sachiko, Mel, Alan Takaki Families
Dr. and Mrs. James Takano
Mr. and Mrs. Katsumi J. Takashima
Mr. Joseph Takata
Mr. and Mrs. Tetsuo Takayanagi
Mr. Juichiro Takeda

Kenneth and Mary Takeda
Mrs. May Ichinaga Takeda
Mr. and Mrs. Robert Takefuji
Mr. George H. Takei
Henry and June Takei
Mr. and Mrs. Katsuto Takei
Mr. and Mrs. Kazuo Takei
Mr. and Mrs. Taketsugu Takei
Mr. and Mrs. Yutaka D. Takekawa
Mr. and Mrs. Sadaichi Takemoto
Mr. and Mrs. Victor M. Takemoto
Mr. and Mrs. George M. Takeno
Mr. Grayson Taketa
Mr. and Mrs. Kazuto Taketa
Mr. and Mrs. S. Tom Taketa
Mr. Tom Taketa
Dr. Lisa Takeuchi
Mr. and Mrs. William K. Takimoto
Ms. May Takizawa
Mr. and Mrs. Hiroshi Takusagawa
Mr. and Mrs. Tadashi Tamagawa
Dr. and Mrs. Tom Tamaki
Mr. and Mrs. Frank Tamura
Mr. and Mrs. Masato Tanabe
Mr. and Mrs. Takao Tanabe
Mr. Yoshinori Tanada
Mr. and Mrs. Floyd Tanaka
Mr. and Mrs. Henry T. Tanaka
Mr. Hiroshi Tanaka
Ms. Jeanne Tanaka
Dr. and Mrs. Kouichi R. Tanaka
Mr. Mickey M. Tanaka
Mr. and Mrs. Richard Y. Tanaka
Mr. and Mrs. Robert M. Tanaka
Mr. Shigenobu Tanaka
Dr. and Mrs. Shiro Tanaka
Mr. and Mrs. Taro Tanaka
Mr. and Mrs. Walter Tanaka
Mr. Yukio Tanaka
Mr. and Mrs. Kaz T. Tanemura
Ms. Karen E. Tani
Mr. and Mrs. Akira Taniguchi
Mr. Fred Taniguchi
Mr. and Mrs. Richard Taniguchi
Mr. and Mrs. Toshio Taniguchi
Mr. Yayono Taniguchi
Mr. and Mrs. Tetsu T. Tanimoto
Ms. Susan S. Tanimura
Mrs. Dorothy Tanita
Mr. and Mrs. Haruo Tashiro
Mr. Minoru Tateishi
Mr. Dave Tatsuno
Mr. Ted Tawa
Ms. Deneen Taylor-Colston
Mr. and Mrs. Elmer S. Tazuma
Mr. Kiyoshi Temma
Dr. and Mrs. James H. Terada
Mr. Joe Terada
Mr. Stanley H. Terada
Mr. and Mrs. Thomas S. Teraji
Dr. and Mrs. Tsutomu T. Teraji
Ms. Mary M. Teramoto
Mr. and Mrs. John Teranishi
Mr. and Mrs. Denis Teraoka
Mr. and Mrs. Sam Terasaki
Terminal Islanders
Mr. and Mrs. Ben Terusaki
Mr. and Mrs. Roy Teshima
Mr. and Mrs. Yoshio Teshima
Ms. Mary Toda
Mr. and Mrs. Terrance Toda
Mr. and Mrs. Hachiro J. Togashi
Mr. Frank Tokubo
Mr. and Mrs. Sei Tokuda
Mrs. Mary Akiyama Tokuhisa
Mr. and Mrs. Byon J. Tokunaga
Mr. and Mrs. Joe Tokunaga
Yoshio Tokunaga
Mr. and Mrs. Shiro Tokuno
Mr. Kazuo Tomasa
Ms. Mary S. Tominaga
Mr. and Mrs. Isao Tomita
Ms. Virginia Tomita
Mr. and Mrs. Yoshio Tomita
Mr. and Mrs. Tak Tomiyama
Ms. Kayuko Tomokiyo
Topaz Reunion Fund
Dr. and Mrs. Kenji Torigoe
Toyota Motor Sales
Toyota Tsusho America, Inc.
Mr. and Mrs. Frank A. Tsuboi
Mr. and Mrs. Roy S. Tsuboi
Mr. and Mrs. Minoru Tsubota
Mr. and Mrs. James M. Tsuda
Mr. and Mrs. Masuo Tsuda

Mr. James Tsuji
Mr. Joe Tsujimoto
Dr. and Mrs. Himeo Tsumori
Dr. and Mrs. Warren M. Tsuneishi
Mr. and Mrs. Robert Tsuru
Mr. and Mrs. Eddie Hisao Tsuruta
Dr. Mike and Lillian Uba and Family
Mr. and Mrs. George S. Uchida
Ms. Susan S. Uchida
Mr. George Y. Uchima
Mr. and Mrs. Masayoshi Uchimura
Mr. and Mrs. Minoru Uchimura
Mr. Sam Uchiumi and Ruth Matsumoto
Mr. M. Uchiyama
Mr. and Mrs. Taro Uchizono
Ms. Chiyoko and Ms. Sugako Ueda
Mr. and Mrs. Itsuo Uenaka
Mr. Grant M. Ujifusa
Mr. and Mrs. Ben T. Umeda
Mr. and Mrs. Tom S. Umeda
Mr. Henry Umeki
Mr. and Mrs. Tosh Umemoto
Mr. and Mrs. George M. Umemura
United Way of The National Capital Area
Mr. and Mrs. Ernest Uno
Mrs. Haruyo Uota
UPS Foundation, Inc.
Mr. and Mrs. Kay Urakawa
Mr. and Mrs. Marvin T. Uratsu
Mr. and Mrs. Masaji G. Uratsu
Mr. and Mrs. Uratsu
Mr. and Mrs. Tsutomu T. Uratsu
Dr. and Mrs. Masashi Uriu
Mr. Mitsuo 'Mits' Usui
Lt. Col. and Mrs. Robert S. Utsumi
Mr. and Mrs. Takeo Utsumi
Mr. Tom Utsunomiya
Ms. Fumiye Uyeda
Ms. Sharon Uyeda
Mr. and Mrs. Isamu Uyehara
Mr. and Mrs. Roy T. Uyehata
Mr. Toshio Uyeji
Mr. and Mrs. Satoru Sats Uyekubo
Uyematsu, Inc.
VFW Post #9902
VFW Post #9938
Visa, USA
Mrs. Ruth U. Voorhies
Ms. Florence F. Wada
Ms. Lynne Wada
Ms. V. Hideko Wada
Mr. and Mrs. Yooichi Wakamiya
Ms. Irene N. Wakatsuki
Mr. and Mrs. George M. Wakiji
Bruce Waldman and Sharon Shiraga
Mr. and Mrs. Ben G. Watada
Ms. Chiyeko Watanabe
Mr. and Mrs. Guy Watanabe
Mr. and Mrs. Hideo Watanabe
Dr. James Watanabe
Mr. and Mrs. Jimmy Watanabe
Ms. Mari R. Watanabe
Marion Watanabe
Mr. and Mrs. Masao Watanabe
Ms. Ruth K. Watanabe
Ms. Sachiko Watanabe
We Are One
Ms. Michi Weglyn (deceased)
Ms. Linda Murakishi Whitted
Y-E Data Company
Mr. and Mrs. George Yagi
Ms. Suma Yagi
Mr. and Mrs. Kenji Yaguchi
Ms. Ayako Yamachika
Mrs. Ayako Yamada
Ms. Hattie H. Yamada
Dr. and Mrs. Henry Yamada
Mr. Kiyo Yamada
Sachiko Yamada
Yamada & Assoc., P.C.
Mr. and Mrs. George S. Yamadera
Ms. Futami Terri Yamaguchi
Mr. and Mrs. John K. Yamaguchi
Mr. and Mrs. Kazuo Yamaguchi
Mr. and Mrs. Kent T. Yamaguchi
Masu and Michio Yamaguchi
Mr. Tak Yamaguchi
Mrs. Ayako Yamakoshi
Ms. Carole Yamakoshi
B.K. Yamamoto Family
Mr. and Mrs. Floyd Yamamoto
Dr. and Mrs. Joe Yamamoto
Dr. Joseph M. Yamamoto
Mr. and Mrs. Masatsuki Yamamoto
Mr. and Mrs. Michitaro Yamamoto
Minoru and Miyoko Yamamoto

Mr. and Mrs. Richard Sus Yamamoto
Mr. Steve S. Yamamoto
Mr. and Mrs. Ben S. Yamanaka
Mr. and Mrs. George J. Yamanaka
Mr. and Mrs. Craig Yamane
Mr. and Mrs. Dick Yamane
Mr. and Mrs. Frank Yamane
Mr. and Mrs. George Yamane
Mr. and Mrs. George K. Yamaoka
Mr. and Mrs. George Yamasaki
Mrs. June Yamasaki
Ms. Mary Yamasaki
Mr. and Mrs. Masao Yamashiro
Mr. Alan Yamashita
Mr. K. Yamashita
Lt. Col. and Mrs. Kanshi Yamashita
Mr. and Mrs. Kiyoshi Yamashita
Mr. and Mrs. Shigeru Yamashita
Ms. Emi Yamauchi
Dr. and Mrs. Paul Yamauchi
Ms. Ruth Yamauchi
Dr. and Mrs. James N. Yamazaki
Ms. Margaret Yanagimachi
Mr. Dale Yanari
Yanmar Diesel America Corp.
Mr. Jim T. Yasuda
Mr. Masami Yasuda
Mr. and Mrs. Roderick K. Yasuda
Morio Roy and Setsu Yasuhira
Mr. and Mrs. Homer Yasui
Dr. and Mrs. Wm. Toshio Yasutake
Mrs. Miyo Yatabe
Mr. and Mrs. Mot Yatabe
Dr. and Mrs. Frank Yatsu
Mr. and Mrs. Lawrence Yatsu
Ms. Takako Yoda
Tomoegawa (USA), Inc.
Mr. and Mrs. Feb S. Yokoi
Mr. and Mrs. Frank Yokoi
Dr. Eric T. Yokota
Mr. Harry Masaru Yokoyama
Ms. Jean T. Yonemoto
Ronald and Emiko Yonemoto
Yonsei Basketball Association
Mr. and Mrs. Arthur Yorimoto
Ms. Toshie P. Yorioka
Mr. and Mrs. Arthur Yorozu
Mr. Akira Yoshida
Mr. and Mrs. Ronald Y. Yoshida
Ms. Toshiko Yoshida
Ms. Isami Yoshihara
Capt. and Mrs. Tak Yoshihara
Mr. and Mrs. Taro Yoshihara
Mrs. Chiyo Yoshihashi
Mr. Dan O. Yoshii
Mr. and Mrs. Dick N. Yoshimura
Mr. and Mrs. Hideo David Yoshimura
Ms. Kiyo Yoshimura
Mrs. Teruyo T. Yoshimura
Mr. and Mrs. Ben Yoshinaga
Mr. and Mrs. Jimmy Yoshinaka
Mary Ann and Holly Yoshinari
Mrs. Ben Yoshioka
Ms. June Yoshioka
Ms. Marian Yoshioka
Ms. Mieko Yoshiura
Mr. and Mrs. Arthur Yoshizawa
Ms. Jean T. Yoshizuka
Mr. and Mrs. Junji Yukawa
Mr. Thomas M. Yuki
Mr. and Mrs. Wallace Yuki and Family
Zaibei Mie Kenjinkai
Mr. Richard H. Zukemura

Up to $999

41st District Democrats
442 Vet Club Fox Chapter
442nd Club I Company Southern CA
442nd Medics
442nd Veterans Club H Chapter
522nd B Chapter
522nd C Chapter
732nd Railroad Operation WWII Battalion
85th Division
8th National JACL Singles Convention
AARP Downtown Chapter 3686
ABC Imaging
ABC Nursery
ACLU South Bay Chapter
ADC Telecommunications
AJA Veterans Council
A.Y. Dental Lab
Abacus Products, Inc.

Ms. Donna Kishi Abbot
Ms. Jane Abbott
Akira Abe
Akira and Kiyoko Abe
Mr. Al K. Abe
Mr. and Mrs. Albert Abe
Ms. Amy Abe
Ms. Betty Y. Abe
Mr. Calvin Abe
Mr. Calvin J. Abe
Ms. Cara M. Abe
Mr. and Mrs. Casey Abe
Mr. Charles M. Abe
Mr. and Mrs. Davis S. Abe
Mr. and Mrs. Douglas Abe
Mr. Duwayne Abe
Ms. Etsuko Abe
Ms. Florence Abe
Mr. Frank Abe
Mr. Fred I. Abe
George and Keiko Abe
George and Jean Abe
Mr. George Abe and Mrs. Helen Oda Abe
Mr. George J. Abe
Ms. Hanayo Abe
Mr. and Mrs. Hideo Abe
Mr. Hiroshi Abe
Mr. and Mrs. James Abe
Mr. James Y. Abe
Mrs. Janet K. Abe
Ms. Janice Abe
Mr. and Mrs. Joe Abe
Mr. and Mrs. Joe K. Abe
Mr. John Abe
Mr. John Y. Abe
Mr. Joseph M. Abe
Mr. Kenneth Abe
Mr. Kenneth H. Abe
Mr. and Mrs. Kokichi Abe
Mr. Kunitsugu K. Abe
Mr. Makato Abe
Mr. and Mrs. Martin Abe
Mary and Shirley Abe
Mr. and Mrs. Masaji Abe
Mr. Masaru Abe
Ms. Maxine Abe
Ms. Mieko Abe
Mr. and Mrs. Mikio Abe
Ms. Nora Abe
Mr. Norman I. Abe
Mrs. Pam R. Abe
Mr. Patrick Abe
Mr. and Mrs. Paul Abe
Mr. Richard Abe
Mr. Roy Abe
Sokichi Abe
Mr. and Mrs. Stanley Abe
Toshi Abe and Nancy Hall
Mr. Toshito L. Abe
Mr. Walter Abe
Mr. Roy F. Abo
Dr. and Mrs. Fredrick Abrams
Mr. and Mrs. Keith R. Abrams
Mrs. Emiko Aburamen
Mr. Anthony T. Accetta
Mr. and Mrs. Charles Acebo
Ms. Susan Achikbashian
Mr. Albert Ackerman
Mr. and Mrs. Bill Adachi
Ms. Chieko Adachi
Miss Chiyo Adachi
Mr. and Mrs. Eiichi Adachi
Mr. Harry Adachi
Mr. John Adachi
Mr. Kelly Adachi
Mr. Koichi Adachi
Ms. Leatrice Adachi
Ms. Lucy Adachi
Ms. Mitsuko Adachi
Mr. Nathan S. Adachi
Mr. and Mrs. Richard Adachi
Mr. and Mrs. Sam Adachi
Seiichi Adachi
Mr. Yasumasa Adachi
Ms. Yuriko Adachi
Mr. and Mrs. Jack L. Adair
Mr. and Mrs. Joseph W. Adams
Ms. Lily Adams
Mr. and Mrs. Michael Adams
Ms. Miya L. Adams
Mr. Robert Adams
Mr and Mrs. Thomas Adams
Mr. Henry Adaniya
Mr. and Mrs. Bill Adler
Advocates for the Rights of Korean Americans
Mr. Frederick S. Afuso

Ms. Jane N. Agawa
Mr. and Mrs. Robert Agawa
Mr. Timothy Agawa
Mr. Richard Agemura
Mr. and Mrs. Kazuo Agena
Mr. Sudhir Aggarwal
Mr. and Mrs. Robert Agner
Mr. Joe Aguilar
Mr. and Mrs. Gordon Ah Tye
Mr. Thomas G. Ahajanian
Mr. and Mrs. Ken K. Aiba
Mr. and Mrs. Joe Aiboshi
Mr. Mike M. Aida
Mr. Neno J. Aiello
Mr. Jimmy S. Aigaki
Mr. Edward K. Aihara
Mr. and Mrs. George T. Aihara
Mr. and Mrs. Luis Aihara
Mr. Sam K. Aihara
Dr. and Mrs. Jerry K. Aikawa
Mr. Mark G. Aikawa
Mr. Satoshi Aimoto
Mr. and Mrs. Francis Aisaka
Mrs. Mary Aisawa
Mr. Robert Aisawa
Mr. Shiro Aisawa
Mr. Daniel I. Aiso
Ms. Katharine Aiso
Mr. Nobuo Aito
Mr. and Mrs. Kinziro Aizawa
Mr. and Mrs. Seiji Aizawa
Mr. and Mrs. Tad Aizumi
Col. and Mrs. Henry Ajima
Ms. Junko Ajima
Mr. and Mrs. Richard Ajimine
Mr. and Mrs. Thomas Ajimura
Mr. and Mrs. George S. Ajioka
Mr. and Mrs. Thomas T. Ajisaka
Mr. and Mrs. Yoshimori Aka
Mr. and Mrs. Jun Akaba
Mr. Kenji Akaba
Mrs. Mieko Akada
Ms. Elaine Akagi
Mr. and Mrs. Harry Akagi
Mr. James H. Akagi
Mr. and Mrs. Mark Akagi
Mr. and Mrs. Nelson Akagi
Dr. and Mrs. Noboru Akagi
Mr. Richard Akagi
Mr. Sachio Akagi
Mr. and Mrs. Terry Akagi
Mr. and Mrs. Ted Akahori
Mrs. Doris Akahoshi
Mr. and Mrs. Frank Akahoshi
Mr. and Mrs. Kenji Akahoshi
Mr. Masato Akahoshi
Mr. and Mrs. Tadashi Akaishi
Hon. Daniel K. Akaka
Mr. and Mrs. Paul T. Akama
Mr. and Mrs. Ed Akamatsu
Mr. Masaru Akamatsu
Mr. Robert Akamatsu
Mr. Robert T. Akamatsu
Mr. and Mrs. T. John Akamatsu
Mr. Yasuka Akamatsu
Mr. and Mrs. Akira Akamine
Mr. and Mrs. David Akamine
Mr. and Mrs. Eishin Akamine
Mr. and Mrs. Eric Akamine
Mr. and Mrs. George K. Akamine
Mr. and Mrs. Herbert Akamine
Ms. Karen Akamine
Mr. and Mrs. Seitoku Akamine
Mr. and Mrs. Shigeru Akamine
Mr. Takemitsu Akamine
Mr. Paul Akana
Ms. Kathleen K. Akao
Ms. Shizuko Akasaki
Dr. and Mrs. Takeo Akasaki
Ms. Kathy R. Akashi
Mrs. Kiyomi Akazawa
Ms. Sally Akazawa
Rev. and Mrs. George Aki
Mr. and Mrs. Iwanaga Aki
Mrs. Mariko Aki
Mr. and Mrs. Hiroshi Akiagi
Mr. and Mrs. Akira Akimoto
Mr. Bob Akimoto
Mr. Harding K. Akimoto
Mr. and Mrs. Martin Akimoto
Mr. Ned E. Akimoto
Mr. Tsunetoshi Akimoto
Mr. and Mrs. Jim Akioka
Mr. and Mrs. Sam Akioka
Jitsumyo Akira

Ms. Beatrice Akita
Mr. Byron Akita
Mr. Guy Akita
Mr. and Mrs. Hiram G. Akita
Mr. Tsutomu Akita
Ms. Mary S. Akitomo
Mr. and Mrs. Edward Akiya
Albert and Nina Akiyama
Ms. Betty Akiyama
Mr. David K. Akiyama
Ms. Emiko Akiyama
Ms. Emmy Akiyama
Mr. and Mrs. Frank M. Akiyama
Mr. and Mrs. George Akiyama
Mr. Glenn Y. Akiyama
Mr. and Mrs. Hisano Akiyama
Mr. John Taro Akiyama
Mr. Lawrence L. Akiyama
Mr. and Mrs. Mark Akiyama
Mr. and Mrs. Mas Akiyama
Mr. and Mrs. Masaji Akiyama
Mr. Michihiko Akiyama
Mr. and Mrs. Soichi Akiyama
Ms. Sue Akiyama
Ms. Sunae Akiyama
Mr. and Mrs. Tak Akiyama
Mr. and Mrs. Takehiko Akiyama
Mr. and Mrs. Toshio Akiyama
Mr. Utaka Akiyama
Mr. and Mrs. Yoshio Akiyama
Ms. Alice Akiyoshi
Mr. and Mrs. George Akiyoshi
Mr. Minoru Akiyoshi
Mr. Rod T. Akiyoshi
Satsuki Akiyoshi and Yumiko Miyakawa
Mr. and Mrs. William J. Akiyoshi
Mr. and Mrs. David Akizuki
Mr. Gary Akizuki and Carrie Parks
Ms. Sumie Akizuki
Mr. and Mrs. Kenichi Akutagawa
Mrs. Aimee T. Akutsu
Mr. Arthur P. Alberts
Bob and Kay Albright and
Ricky and Kerry Williams Families
Mr. R.G. Alden
Ms. May S. Alexander
Natsuyo Alexander
Ms. Jasmine Alinder
Mr. Wayne A. Alkire
Mr. and Mrs. Frank Allard
Mr. Bruce Allen
Mr. and Mrs. James Allen
Kerry Kenn Allen
Ms. Sandra Allen
Mr. and Mrs. Joseph Roy Allman
Mr. Denis R. Alonso
Jay, Colleen, Brenna and Alaina Alvarez
Mr. and Mrs. Ralph Alvarez
Amache Relocation Center
Ms. Joanne Amaki
Mr. Naoto Amaki
Mr. and Mrs. Arthur Amano
Mr. Earl A. Amano
Mr. Herbert Amano
Mr. and Mrs. Herbert T. Amano
Mr. James K. Amano
Mr. and Mrs. Joe Amano
Mr. and Mrs. Kazumi Amano
Mr. and Mrs. Kenneth Amano
Ms. Merian K. Amano
Mr. and Mrs. Mitsuru Harry Amano
Mr. Robert Amano
Mr. Tom Amano
Ms. Ellen Amasaki
Mr. and Mrs. K. Mike Amate
Mr. and Mrs. Stanley Ambo
Dr. Stanley S. Amdurer
Mr. and Mrs. George H. Amemiya
Ms. Kay Amemiya
Mrs. Mary Amemiya
Mr. and Mrs. Minoru M. Amemiya
Prof. and Mrs. Takeshi Amemiya
Mr. and Mrs. Kenneth S. Amer
American Citizens of Taiwan Orgin
American Legion Cathay Post #186
American Legion Fresno Post #4
American Legion Fresno Post #509
American Legion Post #166
American Petroleum Institute
American Pool Service, Inc.
American Security Equipment Company
American Venture Enterprises
Ameritech
Mr. Eugene Amimoto
Ms. Myrna Amimoto

Mr. and Mrs. Yosh Amino
Mr. Ronald Amioka
Mr. and Mrs. Chuck Amos
Mr. E. Harrison Amos
Warren and Cindy Amuro
Mr. and Mrs. George Anbe
Anderson-Taylor Assoc.
Ms. Lorraine Andersen
Ms. Courtney Anderson
Ms. Dee Anderson
Mr. Everend Anderson
Mr. and Mrs. Jack E. Anderson
Mrs. Julie K. Anderson
Ms. Karen Lee Anderson
Ms. Meri Lou Anderson
Ms. Nancy Anderson
Mr. and Mrs. Albert Ando
Mr. and Mrs. Allen Ando
Mr. and Mrs. Arthur Ando
Mr. and Mrs. Bob Ando
Ms. Doris Ando
Mr. and Mrs. Eddie Ando
Ms. Elizabeth S. Ando
Mr. and Mrs. Ernest Ando
Mr. James S. Ando
Mr. Kenji Ando
Dr. Kerry J. Ando
Mr. and Mrs. Lloyd Ando
Mr. Manabu Ando
Ms. Masako Ando
Mr. Norman H. Ando
Ms. Pauline K. Ando
Mr. Tobin Ando
Mr. and Mrs. Toshio Ando
Mr. David Andow
Mr. and Mrs. Eric Andow
Ms. Grace Andow
Mr. Jose Andow
Mr. and Mrs. Jose Andow
Mr. Kengi Andow
Dr. Kenneth L. Andow
Ms. Patricia Andow
Ms. Hilary Andrews
Ms. Katherine D. Andrus
Mr. James L. Angel
Mr. and Mrs. Fred Animoto
Mr. John Annala
Mr. and Mrs. Yoshito Anno
Anonymous
Ms. Michi Anraku
Mr. and Mrs. Tatsuo Anraku
Mr. and Mrs. Russell Ansai
Mr. Daniel S. Antinozzi
Ms. Amy K. Antoku
Marion C. Antoku
Dr. and Mrs. Alan K. Anzai
Mr. Hideo Anzai
Mr. and Mrs. Hideo Anzai
Mr. Mark M. Anzai
Mr. Masao Anzai
Mr. Sakuo Anzai
Mr. and Mrs. Shiro Aochi
Mrs. Anna Aoki
Mr. and Mrs. Buntaro Aoki
Ms. Cheryl J. Aoki
Mrs. Cheryl M. Aoki
Mr. Donald Aoki
Ms. Doris Aoki
Ms. Elizabeth Aoki
Ms. Eva Aoki
Mrs. Grace Y. Aoki
Mr. and Mrs. Hidecomi Aoki
Mr. and Mrs. Hitoshi Aoki
Mr. James Aoki
Dr. Jeffrey E. Aoki
Mr. and Mrs. Jimmy Aoki
Joan and Kathy Aoki Aoki
Mr. Kazuo Aoki
Mr. and Mrs. Lawrence S. Aoki
Ms. Lenna M. Aoki
Mr. Lloyd J. Aoki
Mr. Marvin Aoki
Mr. and Mrs. Mas Aoki
Mr. and Mrs. Masahiro Aoki
Mr. Mits Aoki
Mr. Mitsuho B. Aoki
Mr. Mitsuo Aoki
Mr. and Mrs. Norio Aoki
Mr. and Mrs. Otomatsu Aoki
Mr. Peter Aoki
Mr. Richard Aoki
Mr. and Mrs. Roy Aoki
Mrs. Rubi Aoki
Shea Aoki
Mr. and Mrs. Shiro Aoki

Mr. and Mrs. Takao Aoki
Drs. Thomas and Susan Aoki
Mr. and Mrs. Thomas Aoki
Mr. Toru Aoki
Mr. Toshitsugu Aoki
Mr. Ulysses Aoki
Dr. and Mrs. Vincent Aoki
Mr. and Mrs. Wayne Aoki
Mr. Yoshiyuki Aoki
Ms. Lynell N. Aono
Mr. and Mrs. Tom Aono
Mr. Akio Aotaki
Mr. Harold Aoyagi
Mr. Hitoshi Aoyagi
Ms. Joyce Aoyagi
Ms. Miyoko Aoyagi
Mr. Toshio Aoyagi
Mr. and Mrs. Akira Aoyama
Mr. Alan Y. Aoyama
Mr. David T. Aoyama
Mr. Fred Aoyama
Mr. George Aoyama
Mr. and Mrs. Harold Aoyama
Mr. and Mrs. Isami Aoyama
Ms. Lillian Aoyama
Mr . and Mrs. Marc Aoyama
Mr. and Mrs. Masayoshi Aoyama
Mr. and Mrs. Tsugio Aoyama
Appell Dental Group
Mr. and Mrs. Fred Aragaki
Ms. Mieno Aragaki
Mr. Noriaki Aragaki
Mrs. Kathy Aragaki-Van Horn
Mr. Ben Arai
Mr. Garric Arai
Mr. and Mrs. Geoffry Arai
Ms. Haruno Arai
Ms. Hatsue Arai
Mr. Kaz Arai
Ms. May M. Arai
Ms. Sumie Arai
Mr. and Mrs. Theodore Arai
Mr. and Mrs. Yoshiaki Arai
Mr. and Mrs. Alfred Arakaki
Mr. Carl Arakaki
Mrs. Cheryl Arakaki
Mr. Eugene Arakaki
Mr. and Mrs. James Arakaki
Mr. and Mrs. Jiro Arakaki
Mrs. May M. Arakaki
Mr. Minoru Arakaki
Mr. Robert S. Arakaki
Shane and Cantigny Arakaki
Mr. Stanley K. Arakaki
Mr. Yasuki Arakaki
Mr. and Mrs. Yusuke Arakaki
Mr. Yutaka Arakaki
Ms. Aileen Arakawa
Mr. Atlas H. Arakawa
Mr. and Mrs. Elbert G. Arakawa
Ms. Eva E. Arakawa
Mr. Gary H. Arakawa
Mr. and Mrs. Harry Arakawa
Mr. and Mrs. J. Masakiyo Arakawa
Mr. James Arakawa
Mr. Jerry Arakawa
Mr. Kenneth H. Arakawa
Ms. Mary Arakawa
Mr. and Mrs. Michael S. Arakawa
Mr. and Mrs. Paul Arakawa
Mr. Raymond Arakawa
Mr. Richard Arakawa
Mr. and Mrs. Robert Arakawa
Mr. Robert N. Arakawa
Mr. and Mrs. Roy and Terri Arakawa
Mr. and Mrs. S. E. Arakawa
Mr. S. K. Arakawa
Mr. Shigeru Arakawa
Mrs. Sue S. Arakawa
Ms. Sueko Arakawa
Mr. and Mrs. Wallace Arakawa
Mr. and Mrs. Brian Araki
Ms. Elizabeth Araki
George and June Araki
Mr. George S. Araki
Mr. Hajime Araki
Mr. and Mrs. Ken Araki
Mr. Mamoru Araki
Mr. and Mrs. Norman G. Araki
Mrs. Peggy Araki
Mr. and Mrs. Scotty Araki
Mr. and Mrs. Tad Araki
Mr. and Mrs. William Araki
Yoshiaki Araki
Ms. Joanne M. Araki-Faulkner

Mr. Hideo Aramaki
Mr. Saige Aramaki
Ms. Fumi Arao
Mr. and Mrs. Henry Arao
Mr. and Mrs. Lawrence Gerald Arao
Mr. Michael Arao
Mr. Michael S. Arao
Mr. Motomi Arao
Mr. and Mrs. Chosei Arasaki
Mr. Martin Arase
Mr. Paul Arase
Mr. Sid S. Arase
Mr. Ted Arase
Mr. Verne Arase
Ms. Carolyn Arashiro
Mr. Daniel Arashiro
Mr. Steven Y. Arashiro
Mr. Thomas M. Arashiro
Mr. Don T. Arata
Mr. and Mrs. Henry Arata
Ms. Kathleen J. Arata
Mr. Brian H. Aratani
Ms. Diane E. Aratani
Mr. and Mrs. James Aratani
Mr. and Mrs. Jiro Aratani
Ms. Lori Aratani
Mr. and Mrs. Terry Aratani
Mr. and Mrs. Mark Archterman
Mrs. Jerianne K. Arellanes
Ms. Barbara Ann Arentz
Mr. and Mrs. Kenneth Arie
Ms. Michiko Ariga
Mr. John Y. Arii
Mr. and Mrs. Lawrence Arii
Mrs. Martha Arii
Mr. and Mrs. Mum Arii
Mr. August Y. Arikawa
Mr. Ben T. Arikawa
Mr. Fred Arikawa
Mr. and Mrs. Seigo Arikawa
Mr. Sam Ariki
Dr. and Mrs. Donald Arima
Dr. and Mrs. Hisao Arima
Mr. and Mrs. Jim T. Arima
Ms. Memie Arima
Mr. Yoshio Arima
Dr. and Mrs. Howard K. Arimoto
Mr. Ichiro Arimoto
Mr. and Mrs. Bob Arimura
Mr. and Mrs. Hiroshi Arisumi
Mr. Lloyd K. Arisumi
Mr. Mark T. Arisumi
Mr. and Mrs. Mitsuo Arisumi
Mr. and Mrs Art Arita
Ms. Carol K. Arita
Mr. and Mrs. David Arita
Mr. Don Arita
Mr. Frank Y. Arita
Mr. and Mrs. Henry Arita
Mr. Katsuki Arita
Mary M., Allan and John Arita
Mr. Michael J. Arita
Mr. Ted T. Arita
Mr. Thomas Arita
Mrs. Janice M. Aritomi
Sandy, Andy, Kevin and Kiana Ariyama
Mr. Larry Ariyasu
Ms. Linda Ariyasu
Mr. and Mrs. Reginald G. Ariyasu
Mr. and Mrs. Douglas Ariyoshi
Hon. George R. Ariyoshi
Arlington Songfellows
Mrs. Mary Jane Arnam
Mr. and Mrs. Steven Arnam
Mr. and Mrs. Marvin Arnold
Mr. Murray Aronson
Mr. and Mrs. Robert Arpke
Mr. and Mrs. Yukie S. Arthur
Hiroshi and Midori Aruga
Ms. Pauline Asaba
Mr. and Mrs. Takahiko Asaba
Ms. Carol Asada
Mr. and Mrs. Mark Asada
Mr. Michael Asada
Mr. Kiyoshi Asaeda
Mr. John Asahara
Mr. John M. Asahara
Mr. Seicho Asahi
Ms. Margot Asahina
Mr. Richard Asahina
Mr. and Mrs. Thomas Asahino
Asai Family
Mr. and Mrs. Akira Asai
Mr. Eugene Asai
Mr. and Mrs. George Asai
Mr. Haruo J. Asai

Mr. and Mrs. Ken Asai
Rev. and Mrs. Sadaichi Asai
Mr. and Mrs. Vincent Asai
Mr. and Mrs. Woodrow W. Asai
Ms. Cori Asaka
Mr. Dennis Asaka
Mr. and Mrs. Gary Asaka
Mr. and Mrs. Bruce Asakawa
Mr. Gilbert K. Asakawa
Ms. Junko M. Asakawa
Mr. and Mrs. Masato Asakawa
Mr. Shoichi Mike Asakawa
Mr. and Mrs. Goro G. Asaki
Mr. Hidemo Asaki
Mr. and Mrs. Howard Asaki
Mr. and Mrs. Jack Asaki
Mr. and Mrs. Sam Asaki
Mr. Hidetoshi Asakura
June, Memi and Dane Asakura
Mr. and Mrs. Lowell Asakura
Mr. and Mrs. Takaya Asakura
Mrs. Yoshiko Asakura
Mr. Yukio Asakura
Dr. and Mrs. Richard Asami
Ms. Hazel K. Asamoto
Mr. and Mrs. Mickey Asamoto
Mr. and Mrs. Noboru B. Asamoto
Mr. and Mrs. Richard A. Asamoto
Mr. Rick Asamoto
Mr. and Mrs. Akira Asano
Mr. Fred Asano
Ms. Fumiko Asano
Ms. Hisako Asano
Ms. Mary S. Asano
Mr. Paul Asano
Ms. Roberta Asano
Mrs. Sayoko Asano
Mrs. Setsuko E. Asano
Mr. and Mrs. Fujio Asao
Ms. Yoshinori Asao
Mr. and Mrs. Henry T. Asaoka
Mr. and Mrs. Kanao Asaoka
Tomiji Asari
Mr. Dennis Asato
Mr. and Mrs. Donald Asato
Mr. and Mrs. Evan Asato
Ms. Flora T. Asato
Mr. George Asato
Mr. and Mrs. George Asato
Mr. Goro Asato
Mr. and Mrs. Harry Asato
Mr. and Mrs. Herbert Asato
Mr. Hiroshi Asato
Mr. Maxie Asato
Mr. and Mrs. Minoru Asato
Mrs. Misao Asato
Mr. Richard Asato
Mr. and Mrs. Satoshi Asato
Mrs. Setsuko H. Asato
Mr. and Mrs. Shigeo Asato
Mr. Thomas S. Asato
Mr. and Mrs. Tom Asato
Mr. Yoshiaki Asato
Mr. Yoshito Asato
Charles and Michi Asawa and Family
Mr. and Mrs. Jimmie Asayama
Mr. Esam Asazawa
Mr. and Mrs. Eugene Asazawa
Mr. Shoichi Mike Asazawa
Mr. and Mrs. Randy Asher
Dr. Ellyn R. Ashida and Mr. Paul W. Poareo
Mr. and Mrs. Hisao Buddy Ashida
James. H. Ashida
Ms. Michelle Ashitomi
Mr. Carl Ashizawa
Mr. Phillip Ashizawa
Mr. Roy Yoshio Ashizawa
Asian American Bar Association of the
    Delaware Valley
Asian Pacific American Heritage Council, Inc.
Ms. Joy Aso
Associated West Imports
Mr. and Mrs. Archie Atagi
Mr. and Mrs. Richard Atagi
Mr. Lawrence Atsumi
Mr. and Mrs. Roy Atsumi
Mr. and Mrs. Mark Au
Mr. and Mrs. Wayne W. Aubert
Ms. Hideko Aubry
Ms. Selma Auernheimer
Mr. Pierre P. Augustin
Mr. and Mrs. Leonard Auslender
Mr. and Mrs. Robert F. Austin
Mr. and Mrs. Robert W. Avery
Mr. Yoshio Awakuni
Mr. George Awaya

Mr. Marvin B. Awaya
Mr. Robert Awaya
Mr. Susumu Awaya
Ms. Gail Awaya-Fujii
Ms. Carol H. Azama
Mr. and Mrs. Gilbert Azama
Mr. Takeo Azama
Mr. and Mrs. Nobuyoshi Azebu
Mr. Calvin Azeka
Mr. and Mrs. Itsuo Azeka
Mr. and Mrs. Alyse Azuma
Mr. Eric Azuma
Mr. and Mrs. George Azuma
Ms. Katherine Azuma
Mr. and Mrs. Kenneth I. Azuma
Mr. Mike M. Azuma
Ms. Mitsy Azuma
Mr. and Mrs. Paul Azuma
Mr. and Mrs. Robert T. Azuma
Mr. Ronald Azuma
Mr. Shoji Azuma
Mr. Steven Azuma
Ms. JoAnn Azzaro
Mr. and Mrs. Frank S. Baba
Mr. George K. Baba
Mr. and Mrs. George S. Baba
Mr. Kazuhiro T. Baba
Ms. Mary Baba
Ms. Nancy E. Baba
Dr. Robert Baba
Mrs. Toshiyuki Baba
Fred and Ruth Shayman Babbin
Dr. Joan Roberts Baber
Mrs. Deborah Black Babson
Ms. Barbara Back
Ms. Mirla R. Baclig
Mr. and Mrs. Andrew Bacnik
Mr. and Mrs. Bryan Bacon
Ikuko Bacon
Mr. Thomas C. Baek
Mr. and Mrs. June Baensch
Mr. Hans H. Baerwald
Mr. and Mrs. Thad Baggaley
Bainbridge Island Japanese American Community
Mrs. Katherine Baishiki
Mr. and Mrs. Rod Baishiki
Mr. and Mrs. Sadao Baishiki
Ms. Clara Bajio
Ms. Beverly H. Baker
Mr. and Mrs. Donald R. Baker
Mr. Jonathan Scot Baker
Dr. Samuel J. Bakersville
Mr. and Mrs. Earl E. Bakken
Mr. George Ball
Ms. Kathy S. Fujii Ball
Mr. and Mrs. L. Duane Ball
Ms. Marjory Ball
Ms. Gladys H. Ballard
Ms. Theresa Balogh
Mr. Eugene Balter
Mrs. Shimako Ban
Bank of America
Ms. Harumi Banno
Mr. Kent Banno
Dr. and Dr. Steven E. Bansbach
Ms. Hester F. Barfoot
Mr. and Mrs. Jack Barker
Mr. Gus Barlas
Ms. Elizabeth I. Barnes
Ms. Joan A. Barnes
Mr. and Mrs. William Barnes
Mr. Robert O. Barnhart
Mr. and Mrs. Bob Barr
Mr. and Mrs. John Barreto
Lt. Col. James Barrett
Mr. and Mrs. Steve Barrow
Ms. June Barrows
Ms. Kathleen E. Barry
Ms. Norma Barsness
Ms. Cathy Nakano Basak
Mr. William A. Basinger
Mr. and Mrs. Norman Batchelder
Mr. and Mrs. Robert W. Batchelder
Ms. Amy Batcheldor
Mr. and Mrs. Bruce Batcheller
Mr. Sam Batt
Dr. and Mrs. Donald Battaglia
Mr. and Mrs. Myron Baum
Leo Bauman
Mr. and Mrs. Robert J. Baumann
Mrs. Ferne P. Baumgardner
Ms. Marlene Bayard
Mr. George Baylacq
Mr. and Mrs. Eric Bayles
Mr. and Mrs. David Beadles
Ms. Elizabeth Beadling

David and Charlotte Sato Beales
Col. and Mrs. Rutland D. Beard
Ms. Elaine Beatson
Duane and Marsha Beck
Ms. Marsha Beck
Mr. and Mrs. Gilbert Beebe
Mr. Allan Beekman
Mr. and Mrs. Yoshiro Befu
Mr. and Mrs. Thad S. Beggaley
Ms. Shera Behram
Mr. and Mrs. John L. Belcher
Mr. David H. Belkin
Mr. and Mrs. Davis Bell
Dr. Michael Beller and Ms. Lesley Yamauchi
Ms. Nancy Hanada Bellin
Mr. Paul F. Bentrup
Mrs. Alice Beppu
Mr. Alvin T. Beppu
Ms. Elsie Bergamini
Mr. and Mrs. Briton Berglund
Mr. Jeffrey S. Berlin
Mr. Howard Bern
Mr. and Mrs. Jerry Berson
Mr. and Mrs. Victor P. Bertoni
Mr. and Mrs. John Beshoar
Mr. Marc Bessho
Ms. Lynn Hirabayashi Bettencourt
Mr. and Mrs. Willi Beusch
Mr. Brad C. Beutter
Dr. and Mrs. N. V. Bhagavan and Family
Mr. Jagdish J. Bhatt
Mr. and Mrs. James Bichsel
Mr. Kenneth B. Bielinski
Big Island Candies
Mr. David S. Billings
Ms. Nanci M. Billings
Mr. and Mrs. Thomas T. Bingo
Mr. and Mrs. Scott Birbeck
Rev. Betty Jo Birkhahn-Rommelfanger
Mr. and Mrs. Alex Bischoff
Mr. and Mrs. Dennis J. Bissell
Ms. Evelyn Black
Mr. and Mrs. John Black
Mr. and Mrs. Millard L. Black
Ms. Ruth S. Blanchard
Ms. Penny Blankenship-Buck
J.H. Blaustein
Mr. and Mrs. Jack Bleckman
Ms. Lucinda Blekas
Rev. Edgar G. Bletcher
Dr. Edward Blight
Ms. Nancy Blitz
Mr. Jack D. Blondell
Mr. and Mrs. Andrew Bloom
Mr. and Mrs. Gary Bloom
Dr. Richard A. Bloom
Mr. and Mrs. Ralph Bluthenthal
Mr. and Mrs. Charles A. Boch
Mr. Alfred Bodian
Mr. and Mrs. Leonard Boers
Mr. and Mrs. Leonard Bogaev
Ms. Dianne M. Bohmer
Mr. and Mrs. Vilhelm Bohr
Mr. and Mrs. George Bokios
Mr. and Mrs. Yoshinori Bokura
Mr. Edward E. Bollinger
Ms. Sadako Bolt
Bon Jour, Inc.
Bonbori Restaurant
Mr. Jack Bondell
Mr. Ormand A. Bontempo
Mr. and Mrs. Neil L. Borgert
Mrs. Diana Bottlemy
Mr. and Mrs. Arthur Boucher
Dr. Robert D. Boudreau
Mr. Faubion Bowers
Ms. Martha Belle Bowers
Ms. Alice S. Boyer
Mr. Ted Bradley
Bradley Hills Presbyterian Church
Mr. and Mrs. Charles L. Brady
Ms. Colleen A. Brady
Ms. Margaret U. Brady
Ms. Amy Bragdon
LTC Clarke Brandt
Ms. Akino Lorraine Brannen
Mr. and Mrs. Charles Braunstein
Ms. Shelia Tojo Bray
Mrs. Yaye Togasaki Breitenbach
Mr. and Mrs. Klaus Breitsameter
Mr. and Mrs. Barry Brennan
Ms. Kathleen Brennan
Ms. Elizabeth Ann Bresnahan
Robert J. Breuer
Mr. and Mrs. James P. Brickey
Mr. and Mrs. Herbert M. Bridge

Jonathan and Bobbe J. Bridge
Mr. Robert L. Bridge
Ms. Linda C. Brightfield
Mr. and Mrs. Harold Brinkama
Ms. Lillian Brinnon
Mr. Shawn Brinsfield
Mr. and Mrs. Jerry Briscoe
Ms. Ruth Britton
Mr. Stephen Broccoli
Mr. and Mrs. Horace Brooks
Mr. Isoroku Brooks
Ms. Meredith Maeyama Brooks
Ms. Julia Brossman
Mr. and Mrs. A. Broucaret
Dr. Bruce S. Brown
Mr. George Brown
Mr. Jack C. Brown
Ms. Judie Imoto Brown
Mr. and Mrs. Milford S. Brown
Ms. Miyoko Brown
Mrs. Peggy Kobayashi-Brown
Ms. Ruth E. Brown
Mr. and Mrs. Stephen Brown
Mr. Wesley H. Brown
Mr. and Mrs. William F. Brown
Mr. Joseph Browning
Mr. William Browning
Mr. Brent R. Broyles
Mr. and Mrs. David Bruce
Mr. Eugene Brudno
Ms. Jennifer Brugger
Mr. and Mrs. Q. Bryan
Ms. Judith Buckles
Mr. and Mrs. Emanuel Buckley
Ms. Helen A. Buckley
Mr. and Mrs. Robert Budoff
Mr. Ralph Buenaga
Mr. Wesley T. Buhrmester
Dr. and Dr. Stephen Bundra
Mr. and Mrs. Gordon Bundy
Mr. and Mrs. Edwin J. Bungo
Mr. and Mrs. Jim Bungo
Mr. and Mrs. James M. Bunting
Mr. Frank N. Bunya
Mr. George Bunya and Family
K. Bunya
Mr. and Mrs. Michael Burke
Ms. Debbie Burnell
Ms. Diane Burrows
Mr. Reynold L. Burrows
Mr. and Mrs. John Burwell
Mr. Dennis Busching
Allison I. Bush
Byakudo-kai Summer Fest
Ms. Ruth Byram
Mr. and Mrs. John K. Bywaters
CBO Staff
COSCOM, 311th Munemori Armory
Mr. and Mrs. Edmund Cababa
Ms. Miyeko Cabello
Mr. and Mr. Billy Cade
Mr. C. S. Caglia
Mr. and Mrs. Kevin Daniel Cahill
Dr. Michelle Sugiyama Caird
Ms. Martha Cairnie
Mr. Michael Caldare
Ms. Kathleen D. Caldwell
Mr. and Mrs. Alexander Calhoun
Ms. Kimiko Calhoun
Mr. and Mrs. Alfred Callan
Ms. J. Reiko Callner
Richard and Carolyn Callner
Calvary Presbyterian Church
Dr. and Mrs. John R. Campbell
Mrs. Miyoko S. Campbell
Mr. and Mrs. Robert P. Campbell
Mr. Tommie Campbell
Ms. Lisa A. Campobasso
Ms. June Campos
Mr. and Mrs. Clifton Canaday
Mr. Brown W. Cannon
Mr. and Mrs. Jim Cantwell
Ms. Haru Capewell
Capital Group Companies
Ms. Terese A. Caplan
Mr. and Mrs. Gerald Cardamone
Mr. and Mrs. Harvey Caren
Ms. Julianne A. Carlin
Ms. Cheron Carlson
Tomi Carlyle
Mr. Wann S. Caron
Mr. G. Carp
Ralph Carr Foundation
Carson City Clerk's Office Staff
Mr. and Mrs. Conway Carter, Jr.

Ms. Frances J. Carter
Mr. and Mrs. Horace Carter
Ms. JoAnn Carter
Mr. Paul Caruso and Mrs. Jocelyn Ishimaru
Mr. and Mrs. Vito Caruso
Ken Caryl Vet. Hospital, Inc.
Ms. Joyce Yamamoto Casso
Mr. John Castellano
Ms. Kelly Caulk
Mr. Richard A. Caulk
Mr. Louise Cavagnaro
Mr. and Mrs. Mike Cavalletto
Cental CA Independant Grocer's Association
Centech Group, Inc.
Ms. Susanne Cerrelli
Mr. and Mrs. Deano C. Cerri
Mr. and Mrs. John Cha
Mr. and Mrs. Rigo Chacon
Ms. Cathy M. Chagami
Mr. Henry Chagami
Mrs. Bonnie Chalvatsiotis
Mr. and Mrs. William J. Chambliss
Mrs. Michiko Y. Chamness
Ms. Cheryl Chan
Ms. Ikuko Chan
Ms. May S. Chan
Mr. and Mrs. Michael Chan
Ms. Nancy Chan
Paul Wah and Carmen Tsuboi Chan
Mr. and Mrs. Thomas K. Chan
Wai Ping Chan
Yen-Den A. Chan
Mr. and Mrs. Clayton Chang
Mr. and Mrs. Vincent Chang
Ms. Thelma Charen
Mrs. Irene F. Chau
Ms. Stacey Chee
Mr. and Mrs. Robert T. Chen
Mr. Stephen Chen and Ming Hsu
Mr. George G. Cherepes
Mr. Robert G. Cheshier
Dr. and Mrs. Alan Cheung
Chevy Chase Fencing Club
Ms. Eve Chewning
Mr. and Mrs. Patrick Chiamori
Ms. Elaine T. Chiao
Ms. Taeko Chiba
Mr. and Mrs. Takashi Chiba
Ms. Yurika Chiba
Chicago Japanese American Historical Society
Chicago Yamanashi Kyoyu-kai
Mrs. Fumi Chida
Mr. Takeshi Chida
Mr. Akino Chihara
Mr. Archie T. Chihara
Ms. Bonnie Chihara
Mr. and Mrs. Yozo Chihara
Mr. and Mrs. Shigeru Chikami
Mr. and Mrs. Roger Chikamura
Mr. and Mrs. Takeshi Chikamura
Ms. Chiyeko Chikaraishi
Dr. Dona Chikaraishi
Ms. Nancy Chikaraishi
Mr. Victor Chikasawa
Ms. Eleanor E. Chikasue
Mr. Albert Chikasuye
Mr. Kiyoshi Chikata
Ms. Faye Chikuma
Ms. Eva Y. Chikusa
Al and Nancy Chin
Mr. and Mrs. Ark Chin
Mr. and Mrs. Howard K. Chin
Mr. and Mrs. Stephen Chin
Mr. and Mrs. Ralph T. Chinaka
Ms. Diane Chinen
Mr. George M. Chinen
Mr. Kaname Chinen
Mrs. Karleen Chinen
Mr. Larry T. Chinen
Mr. and Mrs. Paul Chinen
Mr. Thomas K. Chinen
Mrs. Amy A. Ching
Ms. Jeannette F. Ching
Mr. and Mrs. Yick Chinn
Mr. and Mrs. Thomas Chino
Mr. Allan K. Chiogioji
Mr. Melvin Chiya
Mr. and Mrs. Raymond S. Chlapecka
Mr. and Mrs. Frank F. Cho
Mr. Richard Chogyoji
Mr. Eric S. Chon
Mr. Randolph Chono
Mr. and Mrs. Barney A. Chotzen-Tsuruda
Mr. Edward Chow
Ms. Sophia Chow

Koon Hin Choy
Sandra Christenson and Beth Minato
Chronicle Foundation of San Francisco
Mr. and Mrs. David Chu
Mr. and Mrs. Raymond Chun
Mr. and Mrs. Donald Chung
Mr. and Mrs. Edna Chung
Mr. and Mrs. Robert Chung
Church of Christ, Presbyterian
Mr. and Mrs. John R. Churchill
Ms. Esther C. Churchwell
Dr. and Mrs. Flavio Ciferri
Ms. Lucy Cifuentes
City Clerk's Office Staff
Mr. and Mrs. Harry Clancy
Dudley and Lori Clapp
Ms. Betty M. Clark
Mr. Dennis Clark
Ms. Kathryn Clark
Peter Yuichi and Amy A. Smith Clark
Robert and Nancy Yuriko Nakamura Clark
Mr. and Mrs. Samuel F. Clark
Mrs. Shirley Clark
Ms. Vera E. Clark
Ms. Mary M. Claytor
Ms. Margaret Cleary
Mr. Wayne Clem
Mr. and Mrs. Arthur Clerici
Ms. Barbara M. Clough
Matt and Carol Ichikawa Clouse
Mr. and Mrs. Lawrence Clovis
Clovis Buddhist Church
Clovis Community Church
Clovis Dharma School
Club Item -Hilo
Mrs. Marcia Clukey
Mr. Harry R. Coates
Mr. and Mrs. Selma Coble
Ms. Marjorie R. Cochran
Mr. Max Coddington
Ms. Sandy Codlin
Mrs. Evon G. Cody
Mr. Adam D. Cohen
Mrs. Frances Cohen
Mr. and Mrs. Les Cohen
Mr. and Mrs. Leslie B. Cohen
Mr. Sheldon S. Cohen
Stuart and Vivian Cohn
Edward H. Coker and Carol J. Schneider
Ms. Donna Fujimoto Cole
Cole Chemical
Chicago Mita-Kai
Clovis Dharma School
Ms. Marjorie D. Collins
Mr. and Mrs. Tom Collins
Mr. and Mrs. Wayne Collins
Ms Maria Comfort
Communicart
Community Youth Services
Como Inn
Mr. and Mrs. Charles P. Condon
Ms. Jane Condon
Ms. Agnes A. Conley
Mr. and Mrs. Michael W. Conlon
Mr. and Mrs. Charles F. Conner
Ms. Tomiko Conner
Dr. Joseph P. Connolly
Ms. Mary Y. Connolly
Ms. Mary E. Connor
Ms. Elva Bess Cook
Ms. Shirley I. Cook
Ms. Tsuyako Cook
Ms. Yayoi K. Cooke
Mr. and Mrs. Jack Coon
Mr. Edsel Cooper
Mr. and Mrs. Fred Cooper
Mr. and Mrs. Kenneth Cooper
Ms. Linda Cooper
Mr. James F. Corbett
Ms. Judy Okada Corbett
Mr. and Mrs. John Corbin
Mr. and Mrs. Vincent J. Corbo
Mr. John Corbridge
Ms. Betty Holman Corker
Mr. and Mrs. Bruce D. Corker
Ms. Carolyn Corker-Free
Mr. and Mrs. Robert Cormack
Mr. and Mrs. James Corning
Mr. Robert P. Coronado
Mr. and Mrs. William J. Corrigan
Cosmo Space of America Co.
Mr. Gordon Cotler
Dr. Maritza Cotto
Ms. Yuriko M. Cottom
Mr. and Mrs. Jerome Cottrell

Mr. and Mrs. Thomas Courneya
Ms. Joyce Cousin
Consulate General of Japan Staff
Mr. Dru Cox
Mr. and Mrs. Reginald K. Cox
Ms. Atsuko Craft
Mr. and Mrs. Jim Craig
Ms. Diane T. Cramer
Mr. and Mrs. Gustave Cramond
Mr. James D. Crampton
Mr. and Mrs. Alan Crawford
Mr. and Mrs. Bob Cree
Mr. Austin B. Creel
Mr. and Mrs. Edward R. Creighton
Mr. and Mrs. Charles Crigler
Mr. and Mrs. John Croft
Mr. Jose T. Croll
Ms. Donna J. Cross
Ms. Grace Victor Cross
Ms. Nance L. Crow
Dr. James Crowe
Diana M. Cull
Rev. Kathleen Cullinane
Izumi T. Cummings
Mrs. Yoshie Cummisky
Mr. and Mrs. Timothy A. Cunningham
Ms. Debra Curran and Charles Tittle
Mr. William Curtis
Mr. Jon E. Cushman
Ms. Emiko Hara Custer
Col. and Mrs. John R. Czerwinski
Mr. and Mrs. Matthew L. Daday
Mr. and Mrs. Tim Dagoberg
Mr. and Mrs. David Dahlgren
Mr. and Mrs. Clifford Daida
Mr. and Mrs. Hiroshi Daifuku
Mr. Greg A. Daijogo
Mr. Christopher W. Daikai
Y., J. and E. Daikoku
Mr. Herbert S. Daimonji
Mr. and Mrs. Masato Daimyo
Mr. and Mrs. George Dakuzaku
Ms. Florence M. Dalton
Mr. Michael J. Daly
Ms. Kathryn Danbara
Ms. Masue Danbara
Mr. and Mrs. John Daniels
Ms. Lorna T. Daniels
Ms. Megan H. Daniels
Waka Dannenhauer
Mr. and Mrs. Charles Dant
Mr. and Mrs. Robert R. Dardis
Dark Star Leather
Pat Darrows
Mr. and Mrs. Fernando DaSilva
Mr. and Mrs. Stanley Date
Ms. Barbara Daum
Ms. Akemi Davidson
Mr. and Mrs. David Davidson
Mr. and Mrs. Charles F. Davis
Mr. Dwight J. Davis
Mr. Herb Davis
Ms. Margaret Davis
Ms. Mary J. Davis
Mr. and Mrs. Michael E. Davis
Wayne Davis and Louise Hara
Ms. Susan Teiko De Garcia
Mr. and Mrs. Robert De Levie
Mr. and Mrs. Thomas De Loyd
Mr. and Mrs. Warren Dearstine
Mr. Tomonori Degawa
Ms. Traci Deguchi
Mr. and Mrs. Yash Y. Deguchi
Yasuhiro Deguchi
Mr. and Mrs. Donald Delcollo
Ms. Takako Okura Delizza
Mr. and Mrs. Thomas DeLoyd
Ms. Jean Dembo
Ms. Sue Dembo
Mr. Simon Demirjian
Mr. and Mrs. Ben Tsutomu Demise
Mr. and Mrs. Rick deMoya
Ms. Mary Ann Denham
Denver Art Museum
Denver Buddhist Temple Boy Scout Troop 169
Denver-Takayama Committee
Mr. and Mrs. Paul DePalma
Ms. Kristine Dequeiroz
Ms. Lucille A. Deretich
Mr. Anil DeSai
Dr. Stamatia Destounis
Ms. Setsu Detolla
Mr. and Mrs. Robert Dewa
Ms. Frances H. Diamond
Mr. and Mrs. Gregory Diamond

Mr. Margarito Mike Diaz
Mrs. Rose Dicerbo
Mr. Norman Dickens
Mr. Robert M. Dickover
Ms. Yuko N. Dierkes
Mr. and Mrs. Alfred Dilascia
Mr. and Mrs. Jackeline R. Din
Mr. and Mrs. Daniel Dinell
Diner & Associates
Ms. Bernice Dingley
Ms. Judy Dionzon
Mr. and Mrs. Leslie Dirks
Mrs. Kazuko Dishong
Ms. Kathleen DiTommaso
Ms. Kathy Doane
Ms. Ruby Dobana
Ms. Florence Dobashi
Mr. and Mrs. Mark Dobashi
Mr. and Mrs. Masami Dobashi
Mr. Wesley K. Dobashi
Mr. Matthew Dodge and Ms. Alisa Tanaka
Ms. Helen M. Doe
Mr. and Mrs. Thomas M. Doeblin
Ms. Hinako Dogen
Mr. Les Dogen
Ms. Toshiko Dogen
Ms. Kazuko Doherty
Mr. and Mrs. Paul Dohi
Ms. Sylvia Dohi
Mr. Jeffrey T. Dohzen
Mr. and Mrs. Arthur N. Doi
Dr. and Mrs. Bradley Doi
Mr. and Mrs. Carl K. Doi
Dr. Daryl A. Doi
Mr. and Mrs. David P. Doi
Ms. Dorothy M. Doi
Mr. Edward J. Doi
Mrs. Faye F. Doi
Mr. Frank S. Doi
Ms. Fumiye Doi
Mr. and Mrs. Geoffrey Doi
Ms. Helen H. Doi
Mr. Hideaki Doi
Mr. and Mrs. Ichiro Doi
Mr. and Mrs. James Y. Doi
Ms. Jane Doi
Ms. Janice Doi
Mr. and Mrs. Jerry Doi
Ms. Mary Y. Doi
Ms. Mary Louise Doi
Judge and Mrs. Masato Doi
Mr. Masato Doi
Mr. and Mrs. Mitsuru Doi
Mr. and Mrs. Peter Doi
Mr. and Mrs. Richard Doi and Family
Mr. and Mrs. S. Bill Doi
Mr. and Mrs. Stanley T. Doi
Mr. and Mrs. Steven Doi
Mr. and Mrs. Thomas Y. Doi
Mr. and Mrs. Wes Doi
Mr. and Mrs. Yoshio Doi
Mrs. Mae Doida
Mr. and Mrs. S. Doiwchi
Mr. Ronald Doizaki
Ms. Sandra Dolan
Ms. Lynne Dominguez
Mr. Bruce Domoto
Dr. and Mrs. Douglas Domoto
Mr. and Mrs. Ed Domoto
Mr. and Mrs. Hiroshi Domoto
Mr. Mo Domoto
Mr. and Mrs. Paul A. Domoto
Mr. William H. Domoto
Don Ellis & Associates
Ms. Faith T. Donaldson
Mr. and Mrs. Martin Donnelly
Mr. and Mrs. Merlin Dorfman
Mr. and Mrs. Arthur R. Dornheim
Ms. Grace Dote
Mr. and Mrs. Hiroaki Dote
Mr. Jack Dote
Ms. Tomiko Dote
Mrs. Tria Pell Dove
Mr. and Mrs. Willard F. Downer
Mr. and Mrs. David Downs
Ms. Julie Doyle
Ms. Karen Doyle and Mr. Patrick Cosgrove
Ms. Noreen Doyle
Ms. Patricia Dozen
Drapery Shack
Mr. and Mrs. Daniel Drechney
Ms. Michaelene Drechney
Ms. Sandra A. Drees
Mr. and Mrs. R. W. Drescher
Mr. and Mrs. Mark A. Dresser
Mr. Arnold Drooz

Mr. John Drotz and Ms. Beth Fujimoto
Charles S. Drum
Ms. Jennifer Dubon
Ms. Jacqueline H. Dudley
Mr. William S. Duffy
Ms. Jackie Duncan
Mr. Steven Dungan
Mr. Shige Dunmore
Mr. and Mrs. Jack Dunn
Ms. Joanne Dunn
Mr. and Mrs. Francis K. Durham
Mr. S. Isamu Dwyer
Mr. and Mrs. Tom Dwyer
LTC and Mrs. George J. Dydek
Mr. and Mrs. Robert Dye
ESGVJCC Leisure Club
Mr. and Mrs. Robert Eason
Ms. Dianna K. Eaton
Mr. and Mrs. Dan Eberly
Mr. Wallace T. Ebesu
Mr. Daniel D. Ebihara
Mrs. Nancy Ebihara
Mr. and Mrs. Roy Ebihara
Mr. William T. Ebihara
Mr. Tsuyoshi Ebina
Ms. Therese O'Connell Echeveste
Mr. Koeki Echigo
Ms. Sally J. Economon
Mr. and Mrs. Eddie Edamatsu
Mr. Fred J. Edamatsu
David and Tracy Edds Family
Mr. and Mrs. George Y. Egami
Mr. and Mrs. Ronald Egami
Ms. Alicia Egashira
Mr. George H. Egashira
Mr. and Mrs. Jerry Egashira
Mr. Ray Egashira
Mr. Scott Egashira
Mr. and Mrs. Ken K. Egawa
Dr. and Mrs. Michael Ego
Mr. and Mrs. Shiro Ego
Mr. Shunkichi Ego
Mr. and Mrs. Eugene M. Eguchi
Mr. Eugene Y. Eguchi
Mr. George K. Eguchi
Mrs. Miyoko Eguchi
Mr. and Mrs. Takaaki Eguchi
Mr. Gary Ehara
Paul and Alison Ehara
Mr. and Mrs. Tsutomu Ehara
Ms. Helen Sumida Ehrhardt
Mr. and Mrs. Akemi D. Ehrlich
Mr. and Mrs. Warren Eijima
Mr. Neal R. Eisenberg
Mr. and Mrs. Frank Eki
Ms. Eileen Ekinaka
Ms. Fumi Ekinaka
Mr. Kazuo Ekinaka
Mr. Raymond Elgin
Ms. Sarah Eller
Mr. and Mrs. Thomas Ellingsworth
Ms. Ann Ellis
Mr. and Mrs. Leo E. Ellis
Mr. Vincente A. Elmgren
Mrs. Jeanne K. Elyea
Mr. and Mrs. Arthur Emerson
Ms. Joan Yasui Emerson
Mr. and Mrs. Susumu Emori
Mr. John Emoto
Ms. Ada Otera Endo
Mrs. Aileen T. Endo
Ms. Alice A. Endo
Mr. Andrew I. Endo
Mr. and Mrs. Arthur Endo
Mr. David K. Endo
Ms. Doris S. Endo
Mr. Eugene Endo
Ms. F. Louise Endo
Mr. Frank Endo
Mr. and Mrs. Frank S. Endo
Mr. Frederick Y. Endo
Mr. and Mrs. Gene Endo
Mr. Goro Endo
Mr. and Mrs. Goro Endo
Mr. Herbert Y. Endo
Mr. and Mrs. Hichiro Endo
Mr. Ichiro Endo
Mr. and Mrs. Masaru Endo
Mr. and Mrs. Mike Endo
Mr. Minoru Endo
Mrs. Nellie Endo
Mr. and Mrs. Robert M. Endo
Mr. Robert T. Endo
Mr. Russell S. Endo
Mr. Samuel Endo
Mr. Toru Endo

Mr. and Mrs. Toshio Endo
Mr. Wallace Endo
Toake Endoh
Eric and Kimberly Endow
Mr. Henry Endow
Mr. and Mrs. Hideo Endow
Mr. and Mrs. Kazuo Endow
Ms. Lily Endow
Mr. Noboru Endow
Mr. Stephen Endow
Moy Eng
Ms. Nancy Engebretson
David and Janice Englebright
English Feedlots, Inc.
Mr. John Enkoji
Ms. June S. Enkoji
Ms. Yoshie Enkoji
Ms. Doris Enman
Mr. and Mrs. Hiroshi Enoki
Mr. and Mrs. Richard Enoki
Ms. Irene I. Enokida
Ms. Miyoko Enokida
Mr. John Enomoto
Mr. and Mrs. John Enomoto
Mr. John G. Enomoto
Mr. and Mrs. Kent Enomoto
Mr. Kii Enomoto
Mrs. Lorraine S. Enomoto
Ms. Mary H. Enomoto
Michiye Enomoto
Ms. Shirley Enomoto
Mr. and Mrs. Shirow Enomoto
Ms. Sumi Enomoto
Mr. Tom Enomoto
Mr. Frank Isao Enseki
Mr. Hiroshi Enseki
Mr. Kakuichi Enseki
Mr. Richard Katsuto Enseki
Mr. Ted Tetsuichi Enseki
Mr. Raymond F. Ensher
Mr. and Mrs. Chinoree T. Enta
Mr. and Mrs. Randy Erkson
Mr. Richard Ernst
Ms. Akiko Shinoda Erwin
Mr. and Mrs. Ralph L. Erwin
Mr. Kazuo Esaka
Mr. Godwin Esaki
Ms. M. Jean Esaki
Mr. Thomas Esaki
Mr. and Mrs. Will Escalante
Mr. Fernando Escobar
Mr. George Escobar and Family
Mr. Kenichi Eshima
Mr. Bijan H. Eskandani
Ms. Y. Keimi Espinoza
Ms. Le Rae Esterburg
Mr. and Mrs. Kay F. Etemad
Mr. and Mrs. David Eto
Mr. and Mrs. Frank Eto
Mr. and Mrs. Hiroshi Eto
Mr. John Eto
Mr. Robert Eto
Mr. Steven N. Eto
Mr. and Mrs. Taro Gene Eto
Mr. Toshiyuki Eto
Mr. Uta T. Eto
Mr. and Mrs. Yoshiaki Eto
Ms. Julia N. Eulenberg
Mr. Dale Evans
Mrs. Doreen Sugimoto Evans
Mr. and Mrs. Russell Evans
Ms. Katherine Everly
Mr. and Mrs. Keiso Eya
Mr. John D. Eyre
Mr. & Mrs. Dave Eytcheson and Russell Fukushima
Ms. Betty Ezaki
Mr. and Mrs. Edwin M. Ezaki
Mr. and Mrs. Mark D. Ezaki
Mr. and Mrs. Masami Ezaki
Mr. and Mrs. Tom Ezaki
Mr. Tom Ezaki, Jr.
FK Nursery
Mr. Ben Faber
Mr. and Mrs. Gerald R. Fahrney
Fahrney Automotive Group
Dr. and Mrs. Rodney Fair
Ms. Shirley M. Fairhart
Faith Bible Church
Ms. Shirley Falcon
Mr. and Mrs. John Fales
Mr. Stanley L. Falk
Mrs. Nancy Farinas
Mr. Yoshi Faris
Mr. and Mrs. Neil R. Farmer
Mr. and Mrs. Orlando Farnesi
Mrs. Karen Farquhar

Mr. and Mrs. Edward Farrell, Jr.
Mr. Patrick Fasang
Ms. Jenny Fauth
Ms. Susan Feagley
Mr. and Mrs. John E. Feeley
Ms. Sharon Fees
Ms. Joe Ann Feibusch
Feitler Family Fund
Dr. and Mrs. Horace Z. Feldman
Mrs. Mildred B. Fencl
Ms. Aeko Fenelon
Mr. and Mrs. William R. Fenton
Ms. Margaret A. Ferguson
Ms. Sherin K. Ferguson
Mr. and Mrs. Norman J. Ferin
Ms. Georgia Ferreri
Mr. and Mrs. Tom Ferris
Ms. Sue B. Ferron
Ms. Jane Fessenden
Ms. Anne E. Field
Ms. Billie M. Field
Mr. and Mrs. David Fields
Mr. and Mrs. Harold Paul Figueroa
Ms. Emily Filling
Mr. Jerrold Fink
Mr. Ed Finke
Mr. and Mrs. Rodger Finke
Ms. Dallas Finn
Ms. Esther S. Fireman
Ms. Janice Umezawa Fischer
Mr. and Mrs. Sy Fischer
Mr. and Mrs. Merton R. Fish
Mr. Henry D. Fisher
Ms. Linda A. Fisher
Ms. Masako Fisher
Mr. and Mrs. Ralph T. Fisher
Ray Fischer Pharmacy
Mr. Ryoko Fisher
Dr. Shirley A. Fiske
Mr. and Mrs. James E. Fitzgerald
J. Nicholas and Betty Fitzsimmons
Ms. Geraldine Flaherty
Flamm Funeral Home
Mr. Bernard Flashberg
Mr. and Mrs. Paul Flaten
Ms. Ruth Fleischman
Mr. Eric W. Fleisher
Ms. Mary L. Fleisher
Collete J. Flink
Mr. and Mrs. Curtis Follansbee
Mr. and Mrs. Bruce Fong
Ms. Mary K. Fong
Ms. Ina Takashima Forbes
Mr. Allen H. Ford
Mr. and Mrs. Richard Ford
Mr. and Mrs. Mark W. Forde
Dr. Richard Forman
Mr. Donald Forslund
Mr. and Mrs. Theodore Fotos
Peter Fowler and Katsuya Nishimori
Ms. Sadako Fowler
Mr. and Mrs. William Endo Fox
Ms. Mary Lou Foy
Mr. Douglas Frago
Mr. John Ed Francis
Franklin Templeton Group
Ms. Marie Franson
Mr. and Mrs. Ken Frantz
Ms. Edith Frederick
Mr. and Mrs. John Fredrickson
Mr. Brian Free
Mr. Tyler C. Free
Ms. Helen R. Freeman
Freestone Capital Management
Mr. Edward O. Freimuth
Mr. and Mrs. Luis Freire
Freitag Funeral Home
Mr. and Mrs. Robert Freitas
Mr. Ted French
Mr. Albert Friedman
Ms. Lisa Beth Friedman
Ms. Lucille W. Friedman
Mr. Edward A. Friend
Mr. and Mrs. Morton Friendman
Philip and Mindy Friess
Mr. Stuart Frisch
Mr. and Mrs. George E. Froelich
Mr. and Mrs. Robert Fuchigami
Mr. and Mrs. Walter Fuchigami
Mr. and Mrs. Joe Fuchino
Ms. Esther J. Fuchita
Ms. Lori G. Fuchiwaki
Mrs. Harold Fudenna
Mr. Keith Fudenna and Ms. Lorraine Iida
Mr. Paul M. Fugami
Ms. Midori Fugino

Mr. and Mrs. Stephen Fugita
Mr. Hiroshi Fuji
Mr. and Mrs. Kiyoshi Fujieda
Mr. and Mrs. Gary Fujihara
Mr. and Mrs. George Fujihara
Mr. Glenn A. Fujihara
Mr. Henry H. Fujihara
Mr. and Mrs. Herbie T. Fujihara
Mr. Mark Fujihara
Mr. Thomas Fujihara
Ms. Betty H. Fujihira
Mr. Arthur Fujii
Mr. and Mrs. Buddy H. Fujii
Calvin, Jeanne, Tiffany and Taryn Fujii
Mr. and Mrs. Carey Fujii
Ms. Christine Fujii
Dr. Cindy M. Fujii
Mr. and Mrs. Craig D. Fujii
Mr. and Mrs. Dewey Fujii
Mr. Dick H. Fujii
Dr. Donald Fujii
Ms. Donna Fujii
Mr. Eric Fujii
Mr. Fred Y. Fujii
Mr. Gerald N. Fujii
Mr. Gerald T. Fujii
Mr. and Mrs. Gilbert Y. Fujii
Mr. and Mrs. Harry Fujii
Mr. and Mrs. Harumi Fujii
Ms. Helen Fujii
Ms. Janet A. Fujii
Mr. and Mrs. Jim Fujii
Mr. Jinx Fujii
Mr. Kenji Fujii
Mr. and Mrs. Kenneth Fujii
Ms. Kimiko Fujii
Ms. Kiyo Fujii
Mr. and Mrs. Lester M. Fujii
Mrs. Mary F. Fujii
Mr. and Mrs. Masayuki Fujii
Mr. and Mrs. Masuto Fujii
Ms. Maureen Fujii
Mr. and Mrs. Mike Fujii
Mr. and Mrs. Minoru Fujii
Ms. Miyako May Fujii
Mrs. Natsuye Fujii
Ms. Patricia A. Fujii
Ms. Penny M. Fujii
Mr. Raymond Y. Fujii
Mr. and Mrs. Richard M. Fujii
Mr. and Mrs. Robert Fujii
Mr. Robert K. Fujii
Mr. and Mrs. Robin K. Fujii
Mr. Roger Fujii
Mr. Roger U. Fujii
Mr. Ryoji Fujii
Mr. and Mrs. Sid Fujii
Ms. Sono Fujii
Mr. and Mrs. Sueo Fujii
Mr. Takaaki Fujii
Mr. Takashi Fujii
Mr. Takeo Fujii
Mr. and Mrs. Thomas Fujii
Mr. Thomas T. Fujii
Ms. Tomiye Fujii
Mr. Wayne Fujii
Ms. Yoko Fujii
Mr. Yoshio Joe Fujii
Ms. Suyeko Fujikado
Toshi and Kei Fujikado
Dr. and Mrs. Bruce Fujikawa
Mr. Charles Fujikawa
Ms. Cynthia Y. Fujikawa
Mr. David K. Fujikawa
David, Yuri and Eric Fujikawa
Mr. and Mrs. Derek Fujikawa
Ms. Donna R. Fujikawa
Ms. Ellen K. Fujikawa
Mr. and Mrs. Frank Fujikawa
Mr. and Mrs. Fred Fujikawa
Mr. George Fujikawa
Mr. Goro Fujikawa
Mr. and Mrs. Hiroshi Fujikawa
Ms. Janet Fujikawa
Mr. Kenji Fujikawa
Mr. Louis Fujikawa
Margaret Fujikawa and Irving Chew
Mr. and Mrs. Mark A. Fujikawa
Mr. and Mrs. Masao Fujikawa
Mr. and Mrs. Nobus Fujikawa
Richard, Eileen, Russell and Wendy Fujikawa
Ms. Sachi Fujikawa
Mr. and Mrs. Sadayuki Fujikawa
Mr. Shigeru Fujikawa
Mr. Toshi Fujikawa
Ms. Wendy Y. Fujikawa

Ms. Kazuko Fujiki
Mr. and Mrs. Ken Fujikuni and Ms. Itsuko Furuta
Mr. Rik P. Fujikuni
Dr. and Mrs. Toshio Fujikura
Mr. Tyra Fujikura
Mr. Tadao Fujimatsu
Mrs. Akiko Fujimori
Mr. Edward Fujimori
Mr. George Fujimori
Mr. and Mrs. James S. Fujimori
Melody Fujimori and Justin Smith
Mr. Roy S. Fujimori
Mr. and Mrs. William S. Fujimori
Mrs. Agnes H. Fujimoto
Mr. Akira Fujimoto
Albert and Suzuko Fujimoto
Ms. Amy Fujimoto
Ms. Aya Fujimoto
Mr. and Mrs. Benjamin Fujimoto
Mr. and Mrs. Berg Fujimoto
Ms. Brenda Fujimoto
Mr. Charles Fujimoto
Mr. Clifford M. Fujimoto
Mr. and Mrs. Derek Fujimoto
Mr. and Mrs. Don Fujimoto
Mr. and Mrs. Elgen K. Fujimoto
Ms. Emiko Fujimoto
Mr. and Mrs. Frank S. Fujimoto
Mr. Fred Fujimoto
Mr. and Mrs. Frederick Fujimoto
Mr. and Mrs. George Fujimoto
Mr. and Mrs. George K. Fujimoto
Mr. and Mrs. George T. Fujimoto
Mr. Gordon M. Fujimoto
Mr. Harley T. Fujimoto
Mr. and Mrs. Harold K. Fujimoto
Mr. and Mrs. Hideaki Fujimoto
Mr. and Mrs. Hikaru Fujimoto
Mr. and Mrs. Hiro Fujimoto
Ms. Jean I. Fujimoto
Ms. Jodi M. Fujimoto
Mr. John Fujimoto
Mr. Jon K. Fujimoto
Mr. and Mrs. Kay Fujimoto
Mr. and Mrs. Kenneth Fujimoto
Mr. and Mrs. Kiyoshi Fujimoto
Mr. Kunio Fujimoto
Mr. Larry T. Fujimoto
Dr. and Mrs. Lloyd Fujimoto
Mrs. Mabel Y. Fujimoto
Mr. and Mrs. Martin Fujimoto
Mrs. Mary Fujimoto
Mrs. Midori Fujimoto
Mr. and Mrs. Mitsusuke Fujimoto
Mr. Nathan H. Fujimoto
Mr. and Mrs. Paul Fujimoto
Mr. Peter Fujimoto
Mr. Reginald Fujimoto
Mr. Richard M. Fujimoto
Mr. Robert F. Fujimoto
Mr. and Mrs. Robert K. Fujimoto
Mr. and Mrs. Roy Fujimoto
Dr. and Mrs. Royce Y. Fujimoto
Ms. Ruth K. Fujimoto
Ms. Ruth M. Fujimoto
Ms. Sachi Fujimoto
Ms. Sanae Fujimoto
Ms. Shizue Fujimoto
Miss Stacey K. Fujimoto
Mr. Stephen Fujimoto
Mr. Takao Fujimoto
Mr. and Mrs. Ted Fujimoto
Ms. Terrie M. Fujimoto
Mr. and Mrs. Thomas T. Fujimoto
Mr. and Mrs. Tom Y. Fujimoto
Mr. Tsugio Fujimoto
Mr. and Mrs. Tsugio Fujimoto
Mr. Tsutomu Fujimoto
Mr. Van Fujimoto
Ms. Wesleyann Fujimoto
Mr. and Mrs. Willaim Fujimoto
Mr. and Mrs. William K. Fujimoto
Mr. Y. Fujimoto
Mrs. Yaeko R. Fujimoto
Mr. Yoshimi Fujimoto
Mr. Yoshito Fujimoto
Mr. and Mrs. Yukio Fujimoto
Mrs. Donna Fujimoto-Saka
Ms. Dorothy Fujimura
Mr. Frank Fujimura
Mr. Guy Fujimura
Kay and Mary Jane S. Fujimura
Mr. and Mrs. Kent Fujimura
Mr. Robert Fujimura
Mr. and Mrs. Shigeru Fujimura
Mrs. Shizu Fujimura

Mr. Stanley F. Fujimura
Mr. Ted Fujimura
Mr. and Mrs. William S. Fujimura
Mr. Edward Fujinaka
Dr. and Mrs. Glenn Fujinaka
Mr. and Mrs. Goichi Fujinaka
Ms. S. May Fujinaka
Mr. George T. Fujinami
Mr. Kazuo Fujinami
Mr. Kiyoshi Fujinami
Ms. Loreen Fujinami-Okada
Ms. Alice M. Fujinari
Mr. Clifford R. Fujinari
Mr. Eugene M. Fujinari
Mr. and Mrs. Chester Fujino
Mr. and Mrs. Frank Fujino
Mr. and Mrs. George Y. Fujino
Mr. Harry Fujino
Mr. Harry H. Fujino
Mr. Kazutoshi Fujino
Mr. Manabu Fujino
Mr. and Mrs. Mikio Fujino
Mr. and Mrs. Patrick T. Fujino
Ms. Reiko Fujino
Mr. Yasuo Fujino
Mr. and Mrs. Yeaji Fujino
Mr. Rodney Fujio
Ms. Anne T. Fujioka
Mr. Art and Dr. JoAnn Fujioka
Mr. and Mrs. Bob T. Fujioka
Mr. Cary Fujioka
Mr. Frank S. Fujioka
Mr. Fred Fujioka
Mr. and Mrs. Harold Fujioka
Mr. and Mrs. Hiriyuki Fujioka
Mr. James Fujioka
Ms. Linda Fujioka
Mr. Mark Fujioka and Ms. Lori Ann Fujioka
Mr. Masao Fujioka
Mr. Mollie T. Fujioka
Mr. and Mrs. Robert S. Fujioka
Mr. and Mrs. Roy Y. Fujioka
Ms. Stella S. Fujioka
Mr. and Mrs. Steve I. Fujioka
Ms. Tracy and Robb Fujioka
Mr. William T. Fujioka
Ms. Yoshie Fujioka
Ms. Yukie T. Fujioka
Ms. Yukio Fujioka
Mr. Hiroshi Fujisaki
Mr. Takeshi J. Fujisaki
Mr. Arthur A. Fujise
Mr. and Mrs. Fred Fujishige
Ms. Julie T. Fujishige
Mr. Melvyn Fujishige
Mrs. T. Fujishige
Mr. Yukio Fujishige
Mr. and Mrs. Burt Fujishima
Ms. and Ms. Kay K. Fujishin
Mrs. Sam Fujishin
Mr. and Mrs. David Fujishiro
John and Shirley Fujishiro
Mr. K. Kenneth Fujishiro
Mr. Kenneth Fujishiro and Ms. Daisy Semling
Ms. Mary Y. Fujishiro
Mrs. Seda Fujishiro
Mr. Harold H. Fujisue
Mr. Norman S. Fujisue
Ms. Paige Fujisue
Ms. Ann S. Fujita
Bill and Dorothy Fujita
Mr. and Mrs. David Fujita
Mr. and Mrs. Dennis Fujita
Mrs. Dora Fujita
Mr. Edward K. Fujita
Frank and Satsuki Fujita
Ms. Fumiko Carole Fujita
Mr. George S. Fujita
Henry T. and Beverly T. Fujita
Mr. and Mrs. Jack Fujita
Mr. and Mrs. James T. Fujita
Mr. and Mrs. Joe Fujita
Mr. and Mrs. Joel Fujita
Mr. and Mrs. Kai Fujita
Ms. Kathy Fujita
Mr. Kaz Fujita
Mr. Kenneth S. Fujita
Mr. and Mrs. Kikuo Fujita
Mrs. Leslie Fujita
Mrs. Lillie E. Fujita
Ms. Lilly Fujita
Ms. Lilly T. Fujita
Ms. Margaret K. Fujita
Mr. and Mrs. Minoru Fujita
Mr. and Mrs. Mitsuo Fujita
Mr. and Mrs. Nagatoshi Fujita

Mr. and Mrs. Naoya Fujita
Mr. Noriharu Fujita
Mr. and Mrs. Norman K. Fujita
Mr. and Mrs. Paul Fujita
Mr. Robert E. Fujita
Mr. and Mrs. Robert K. Fujita
Mr. and Mrs. Roy E. Fujita
Mr. and Mrs. Roy M. Fujita
Mr. and Mrs. S. Neil Fujita
Mr. Samuel I. Fujita and Mrs. Audrey H. Mizokami
Ms. Sandra Fujita
Ms. Shirley Y. Fujita
Mr. Sidney T. Fujita
Mr. and Mrs. Tetsuo Fujita
Mr. and Mrs. Tokunori Fujita
Mr. Tom Fujita
Mr. Toshio Fujita
Mr. and Mrs. Tsuneo Fujita
Mr. and Mrs. Wayne Fujita
Mr. Wesley Fujita
Mr. and Mrs. Wilfred S. Fujita
Ms. Yasuko Fujita
Mr. Yoshio Fujita
Mr. and Mrs. Yutaka Fujita
Carrie Masako Fujita-Nijmeh
Mr. Shusuke Fujitake
Mr. and Mrs. Francis Fujitani
Mr. Harry A. Fujitani
Mr. Lloyd Fujitani
Mr. and Mrs. Ralph Fujitani
Ms. Sharon Fujitani
Ms. Judith S. Fujito
Mr. and Mrs. Wayne Fujito
Mr. and Mrs. Albert Fujitsubo
Wayne and Sylvia Fujitsubo
Ms. Jean M. Fujiu
Ms. Kiyoko K. Fujiu
Mrs. Gladys Fujiuchi
Mr. Ernest Fujiura
Mr. Howard Fujiura
Ms. Betty Fujiwara
Ms. Emma Fujiwara
Mr. Goro Fujiwara
Mr. Hiromi Fujiwara
Mr. Joel D. Fujiwara
Miss Junko Fujiwara
Mr. and Mrs. Kiyoshi Fujiwara
Mrs. Paula I. Fujiwara
Mr. Ronald Fujiwara
Mr. and Mrs. Roy Fujiwara
Ty K. Fujiwara and sons Christopher C. & Michael T.
Mr. Yoshimi Fujiwara
Mr. Yoshio Fujiwara
Ms. Margie M. Fujiyama
Mr. Show Fujiyama
Mr. and Mrs. Mike Fujizawa
Ms. Aiko Fukagawa
Mr. and Mrs. Sam Fukagawa
Mr. Frank T. Fukami
Ms. Joyce M. Fukami
Tesuya Fukami
Mr. Yohsuke Fukami
Mr. and Mrs. Fred T. Fukano
Mr. and Mrs. Henry Fukano
Mr. Fred K. Fukasawa
Mr. and Mrs. James Fukasawa
Ms. Joyce Y. Fukasawa
Mr. and Mrs. Peter Fukasawa
Mr. Tom Fukasawa
Mr. and Mrs. Jeff Fukawa
Mr. and Mrs. Ted Fukawa
Mr. George M. Fukayama
Ms. Susan L. Fukayama
Ms. Helen Fukaye
Mr. Mark Fukeda
Mr. Jerry Fukida
Mrs. Susan Fukida
Mr. and Mrs. Bruce Y. Fukuchi
Ms. Ruth Fukuchi
Ms. Aileen Fukuda
Allan and Susan Fukuda
Mr. Arthur S. Fukuda
Ms. Betty Fukuda
Mr. David Fukuda
Mr. David H. Fukuda
Mr. and Mrs. David M. Fukuda
Mr. David S. Fukuda
Mr. Dick Fukuda
Mr. Fumiyo Fukuda
Mr. Harry Fukuda
Ms. Helen Fukuda
Mr. Herbert A. Fukuda
Mr. Hiroshi Fukuda
Mr. Howard A. Fukuda
Mr. Howard Y. Fukuda
Mr. James M. Fukuda

Dr. James S. Fukuda
Mr. and Mrs. James T. Fukuda
Ms. Janice G. Fukuda
Mr. Jason B. Fukuda
Mr. John Y. Fukuda
Ms. Katsuko Fukuda
Mrs. Kay L. Fukuda
Mr. Ken C. Fukuda
Mr. and Mrs. Kenji Fukuda
Dr. Kevin Fukuda
Mr. and Mrs. Kevin Fukuda
Dr. Kiyoshi Fukuda
Mr. and Mrs. Koichi Fukuda
Ms. Lynn Fukuda
Mr. Minoru K. Fukuda
Mr. and Mrs. Mitsugi Fukuda
Ms. Rachel S. Fukuda
Mr. Richard I. Fukuda
Mr. Robert Fukuda
Mr. Saburo Fukuda
Ms. Shizuko Fukuda
Mr. and Mrs. Tatsuyuki Fukuda
Mr. Thomas A. Fukuda
Ms. Toni Fukuda
Mr. and Mrs. Toshiharu Fukuda
Ms. Toshiko Fukuda
Ms. Yaeko Fukuda
Ms. Yohko Fukuda
Mr. Yoneo Fukuda
Mr. and Mrs. Andy M. Fukudome
Mr. Roy Fukugawa
Mr. and Mrs. Earl H. Fukuhara
Mr. and Mrs. Francis Fukuhara
Mr. and Mrs. Frank Fukuhara
Mr. and Mrs. Frank K. Fukuhara
Dr. and Mrs. George Fukuhara
Ms. Hana Fukuhara
Mr. Henry Fukuhara
Ms. Himeko Fukuhara
Mr. and Mrs. James T. Fukuhara
Mr. and Mrs. Kenji Fukuhara
Ms. Linda H. Fukuhara
Mr. and Mrs. Michael James M. Fukuhara
Mr. Misao Fukuhara
Mr. Paul A. Fukuhara
Mr. and Mrs. Abe Fukui
Mr. Abraham Fukui
Mr. and Mrs. Ben Fukui
Mr. Billy S. Fukui
Mr. and Mrs. Chi Fukui
Ms. Cynthia Fukui
Mr. and Mrs. Frank Fukui
Mr. George M. Fukui
Mr. George T. Fukui
Mr. and Mrs. Henry Fukui
Ms. Jennifer Fukui
Ms. Kiku Fukui
Mr. Masaru Fukui
Mr. and Mrs. Ray Fukui
Mr. Rodney Fukui
Mr. Takashi Fukui
Mr. Edwin Fukuji
Mr. and Mrs. George Fukukai
F. Fukukaki
Mr. and Mrs. Gary Fukukawa
Mr. Marshall Fukuki
Mr. and Mrs. Donald Fukuma
Mrs. Karen Fukuma
Mr. Paul Fukuma
Mr. Ernest J. Fukumae
Mr. and Mrs. Bill T. Fukumitsu
Mr. and Mrs. Clifford Fukumitsu
Mr. Gregory S. Fukumitsu
Keith and Pamela Fukumitsu
Mr. Brian M. Fukumoto
Mr. Clarence N. Fukumoto
Dr. Dick Fukumoto
Mrs. Jeri A. Fukumoto
Mr. and Mrs. John Fukumoto
Mr. and Mrs. Kiyo Fukumoto
Mrs. Michiko Fukumoto
Ms. Misako Fukumoto
Mr. and Mrs. Ray Fukumoto
Mr. and Mrs. Richard Fukumoto
Mrs. Sue T. Fukumoto
Dr. and Mrs. Teruo Fukumoto
Ms. Yae Fukumoto
Mr. Alvin Fukunaga
Mr. and Mrs. Frank T. Fukunaga
Mr. and Mrs. Fred M. Fukunaga
Ms. Helene N. Fukunaga
Ms. Jean Fukunaga
Ms. Judy S. Fukunaga
Mr. and Mrs. Robert Fukunaga
Mr. Wayne Fukunaga
Mr. Chris Fukuoka

Mr. Ray Fukuoka
Mr. and Mrs. Ronnie Fukuoka
Fukuoka Nikkei-Jin Kai
Fukuoka Nikkeijin-Kai
Mr. and Mrs. Peter Fukusawa
Mrs. Betti Fukushima
Mr. Bob M. Fukushima
Mr. and Mrs. Dick H. Fukushima
Mr. and Mrs. Eiichi Fukushima
Mr. Fred Fukushima
Mr. and Mrs. Hisashi Fukushima
Mr. and Mrs. Isao Fukushima
Mr. and Mrs. Jun Fukushima
Mr. and Mrs. Ken Fukushima
Ms. Kiyomi Fukushima
Mr. and Mrs. Marvin Fukushima
Ms. Michiko Fukushima
Mrs. Nellie A. Fukushima
Mr. Ted Fukushima
Mr. and Mrs. Toshihei Percy Fukushima
Mr. Tsuruo Fukushima
Mr. Warren K. Fukushima
Mr. Yasutaka Fukushima
Mr. Yugo Fukushima
Mr. Frederick K. Fukutaki
Ms. Iris Fukutaki
Mr. and Mrs. Eugene T. Fukute
Mr. and Mrs. Morio L. Fukuto
Anne Kimi Fukutome and Robert Mithun
Mr. and Mrs. Ichiro Fukutome
Mr. and Mrs. Masatoshi Fukutomi
Shig and Koko Fukutomi
Mr. and Mrs. Craig Fukuyama
Mr. and Mrs. Dennis K. Fukuyama
Mr. and Mrs. Hiroshi Fukuyama
Mrs. Mitsuka Fukuyama
Nancy Fukuyama and Reiko Ohye
Mr. and Mrs. Walter Fukuyama
Mr. and Mrs. Ben Fukuzaki
Mr. Jimmie Fukuzaki
Ms. Toshiko Fukuzaki
Ms. Barbara Fukuzawa
Ms. May Fukuzawa
SSG Daniel Fuller
Mr. and Mrs. Max Fullner
Mr. David R. Funabashi
Mr. Walter Funabiki
Mr. and Mrs. George Funai
Ms. Hisako Funai
Ms. Ruth C. Funai
Mr. Yuji Funai
Mr. Brian K. Funaki
Dr. and Mrs. Clarence Funaki
Mr. James T. Funaki
Mr. Shinichi Funaki
Mr. Brent K. Funakoshi
Mrs. Elayne M. Funakoshi
Mr. Francis Funakoshi
Mr. and Mrs. Fred S. Funakoshi
Mr. and Mrs. Laurence H. Funakoshi
Mrs. Lori Ann Funakoshi
Mr. and Mrs. Sam Funakoshi
Mr. and Mrs. Sam S. Funakoshi
Mr. Edmund Funaku
Mr. and Mrs. Jack Funamura
Mr. and Mrs. Henry T. Funasaki
Dr. Bert K. Funatsu
Mr. Rodney Fung
Mr. and Mrs. Masuo Funo
Mr. Alex P.S. Furubayashi
Mr. and Mrs. Hugh Furubayashi
Mr. Kenji Furubayashi
Maliki and Reika Furubayashi
Mr. Richard Furuhashi
Mr. Yoshiki Furuhata
Mr. Clifford T. Furuichi
Ms. May Ann Furuichi
Mr. Haruo Furuike
Mr. Isamu Furuike
Dr. and Mrs. Tetsuo Furuike
Mr. Yoshio Furuike
Mr. and Mrs. Nobuo Furuiye
Mr. Ben Furukawa
Ms. Clara Furukawa
Edward, Aileen and Bruce Furukawa
Mr. Fred Y. Furukawa
Gary and Amy Furukawa
Mr. and Mrs. George S. Furukawa
Mr. Harold Furukawa
Harry Furukawa and Tina Sung
Mr. Helen O. Furukawa
Mr. and Mrs. Hiroshi Furukawa
Mr. and Mrs Jack Y. Furukawa
Mr. and Mrs. James T. Furukawa
Mr. Jim Y. Furukawa
Mr. and Mrs. Joseph Furukawa

LTC. and Mrs. Kenneth T. Furukawa
Kip and Diann Furukawa
Ms. Lois Y. Furukawa
Lynn and Georgette Furukawa
Mr. Mark W. Furukawa
Mr. and Mrs. Paul M. Furukawa
Mr. and Mrs. Richard Furukawa
Mr. and Mrs. Robert Furukawa
Mr. Roy H. Furukawa
Ms. Ruth Furukawa
Mr. Tamotsu Furukawa
Mr. Theodore Furukawa
Mr. Vance I. Furukawa
Mr. and Mrs. Walter Furukawa
Mr. Yoshio Furukawa
Mr. and Mrs. Charles T. Furumasu
Mr. and Mrs. Sam Furumasu
Mr. Roy Furumizo
Mr. and Mrs. Takeshi Furumoto
Dr. Yasuko Margie Furumoto-Sakimura
Mr. Glenn Furumura
Jack and Dorothy Furumura
Mr. Gary Furuno
Mr. Fred Y. Furusawa
Mr. Masao Furusawa
Mr. Alan Furushima
Mr. and Mrs. Henry Furushima
Ms. Maurine Furusho
Mr. and Mrs. Ralph Furusho
Mr. and Mrs. Yasuto Furusho
Mr. Chikara W. Furuta
Mr. and Mrs. Donald T. Furuta
Mr. Harry Furuta
Mr. Kiyoaki Furuta
Ms. Martha Furuta
Mr. and Mrs. Minobu Furuta
Ms Miyeko Midge Furuta
Mr. and Mrs. Soichi Furuta
Mr. Thomas T. Furuta
Ms. Carol Furutani
Ms. Mary Y. Furutani
Mr. Gordon T. Furuto
Mr. and Mrs. Minoru Furuto
Mr. Harry Furuya
Mr. and Mrs. Herbert K. Furuya
Mr. and Mrs. Howard J. Furuya
Mr. and Mrs. Isamu Furuya
J. H. and M. Furuya
Mr. and Mrs. Jack K. Furuya
Mr. Keizo Furuya
Mr. and Mrs. Mal Furuya
Mr. and Mrs. Monte Furuya and Mrs. Yasuko Furuya
Mr. Paul A. Furuya
Mr. and Mrs. Yas Furuya
Ms. Aileen T. Furuyama
Mr. and Mrs. Charles Furuyama
Mrs. Renee H. Furuyama
Mr. Don Furuzawa
Mr. and Mrs. Fred Furuzawa
Ms. May Furuzawa
Mr. and Mrs. David T. Fusato
Ms. Cay M. Fuse
Mr. and Mrs. Fred C. Fushimi
Ms. Janet Fushimi
Ms. Darlene Fuso
Mr. and Mrs. Sunao Futa
Mr. and Mrs. Walter Futa
Ms. Chiyo Futagaki
Futamachi Fund
Mr. Jiro Futamachi
Mr. and Mrs. Atsushi Futamase
Mr. and Mrs. Keiji Futamase
Ms. Ruth T. Futenma
Futron Corporation
Dr. Mitsuo Fuwa
Ms. Rosemarie A. Gaiduk
Mrs. V. Gajarian and Family
Mrs. Joyce Gallagher
Mr. and Mrs. William Galligan
Mr. and Mrs. James Galloway
Mr. and Mrs. Bill C. Gamble
Ms. Mitsuko Garcia
Garden Gate Elementary School
Gardena Sansei Baseball League
Mr. and Mrs. Wayne Gardner
Ms. Diane Gareen
Mr. and Mrs. Raymond Garrett
Charles B. and Lillian Garrigus
Mr. and Mrs. Merle Garten
Mr. and Mrs. Terence M. Garvey
Mr. Samuel Gary
Ms. Reiko K. Gaspar
Mr. and Mrs. Koichi Gatanaga
Ms. Anita K. Gates
Mr. and Mrs. George Gates
Ms. Eleanor R. Gebacz

Ms. Evelyn R. Geist
Mr. Richard Gelfand
Ms. Beverly Gelwick
Gemini Associates, Inc.
Ms. Kiyoe Genda
Ms. Celia Genishi
Mr. Daniel E. Genovaldi
Ms. Misako J. Gergurich
Mr. Frank Gerow
Mr. James Gerrity
Mr. Daryl W. Gerwin
Mr. and Mrs. Telemak G. Gharibian
Mr. Dominick M. Giampietro
Ms. Carrie Gibbany
Mr. Toshio Gibo
Mr. and Mrs. Frank Gibson
Mr. and Mrs. Richard Gibson
Mr. Edward Gilbert
Ms. Peggy Gilbert
Mr. and Mrs. Don S. Gilbertson
Ms. Linda Furuto Giles
Mr. George D. Gilmartin
Mr. and Mrs. George Gilmore
Col. Donald M. Gilner
Ms. Deloris Giltner
Mr. Johnnie Gim
Mr. and Mrs. Charles M. Gima
Mr. David S. Gima
Mr. Earl Gima
Mr. Gilbert A. Gima
I. M. Gima
Mr. and Mrs. Lance Gima
Dr. Masaichi Gima
Mr. and Mrs. Paul Gima
Mrs. Masa Gin
Dr. and Mrs. John C. Gingerich
Mr. and Mrs. Robert M. Ginn
Ms. Helen Ginoza
Ms. Jeannine Ginyard
Mrs. Martha Giovanelli
Ms. Janet Girdner
Ms. Rebekah Gisnet
Glassworks
Dr. Jerome Glazer
Mr. and Mrs. Hal Gnoske
Dr. and Mrs. Sumio Go
Go For Broke Nat'l Vets Association
Ms. Susan Goddard
Mr. and Mrs. Sanjay Godhwani
Ms. Annabelle Godwin
Mr. Gerald Goff
Ms. Kikuno M. Goh
Mr. and Mrs. Ted Gohata
Mr. and Mrs. Yasunori Gohata
Mr. and Mrs. George Goi
Mr. and Mrs. James Goichi
Mr. and Mrs. Henry Goishi
Mr. and Mrs. John Goka
Mr. Kenneth K. Goka
Ms. Anne Goldberg
Ms. June O. Goldberg
Mrs. Yoshiko M. Golden
Golden Gate Nisei Post 9879
Cdr. David Goldstein
Mr. and Mrs. Herbert Goldstein
Mr. Harry K. Gondo
Mr. Raymond T. Gondo
Mr. and Mrs. Suzuo Gondo
Mr. Tom Gondo
Mr. and Mrs. Peter K. Goo
Mr. Edward Goodlaw
Mr. Joseph Goodman
Mr. and Mrs. Mark S. Goodside
Ms. Miyuki Mabel Googins
Mr. and Mrs. Arthur S. Gorai
Ms. Dorothy Gorai
Ms. April S. Goral
Mr. William Gordon
Mr. and Mrs. James Gorman
Ms. Jeanne Gosho
Ms. Helen N. Gota
Mr. Steven Gotanda
Mr. and Mrs. Harvey Gotliffe
Arthur and Bow Chu Goto
Ms. Barbara Goto
Mr. Byron Goto
Ms. Clara Goto
Daniel, Patty and Allyson Goto
Mr. Denichi Goto
Mr. Edwin N. Goto
Ms. Esther M. Goto
Ms. Florence Goto
George and Midori Goto
Mr. and Mrs. George Goto
Mrs. Helen Goto
Mr. Herbert H. Goto

Ms. Hisae Y. Goto
Mr. and Mrs. Itsumi Goto
Ms. Kathleen T. Goto
Ms. Kay K. Goto
Mr. Kiyo K. Goto
Mr. Koji Goto
Mr. Leo T. Goto
Ms. Lily Goto
Mr. Lloyd Goto
Mr. Marc M. Goto
Mr. and Mrs. Masayoshi Goto
Misao Goto
Mr. and Mrs. Renji Goto
Mr. Robert Goto
Sam and Edna Goto
Mr. Shigeru Goto
Mr. Tad Goto
Mr. Thomas N. Goto
Ms. Tomoye Goto
Ms. Yoshiko Goto
Mr. and Mrs. Yoshio Goto
Mr. Gary Gotow Family
Dr. and Mrs. Keith Gottesdiener
Mr. and Mrs. Edwin Goya
Mr. Frank Goya
Mr. and Mrs. Hideo Goya
Mr. and Mrs. Shinsuke Goya
Mr. and Mrs. Takemi Goya
Yeiko and Jackie Goya
Dr. and Mrs. William F. Grace
Ms. Kay Graham
Mr. Norman Graham
Ms. Phoebe Grange
Mr. and Mrs. Scot Granger
Ms. Ruth Granick
Ms. Kay Grantham
Mr. and Mrs. Gerald T. Grassi
Mr. and Mrs. Jerry Graves
Mr. and Mrs. Richard Graves
Mr. and Mrs. Herbert Gray
Ms. Ruth T. Gray
Donald M. Graydon and Elaine Solomon
Mr. Othello Grayson
Mr. Bill A. Grazidi and Ms. Rose Zauner
Mr. and Mrs. Calvin Green
Mr. and Mrs. Ken Green
Mr. and Mrs. Stanford Green
Mr. and Mrs. Derek Greenberg
Mr. and Mrs. E. Greenberg
Mr. and Mrs. Norm Greenberg
Ms. Margaret Greenblatt
Mr. Roy Greene
Ms. Ann B. Gregory
Ms. Susan Gregory
Mr. William H. Gresham
Ms. Helen Grey
Ms. Carol Griffin
Mr. and Mrs. Charles Griffin
Mr. and Mrs. Richard Griffin
Ms. Virginia Griffin
Mr. and Mrs. Walter E. Griffin
Dr. and Mrs. Walter R. Grobelny
Mr. Keith W. Groebe
Ms. Betsy S. Grossman
Mr. David Gruba
Ms. Jane Grubb
Mr. and Mrs. David Gruenewald
Ms. Mary M. Gruenewald and Mr. Jack M. Aldrich
Raymond Gruenewald and James Bushnell
Ms. Jane Sanbuichi Guerin
Mr. and Mrs. John A. Guffey
Dr. and Mrs. Pedro Guinto
Mr. and Mrs. Eric Guion
Mr. Lewis Gulick
Gunnell Aviation Japan
Ms. Judy Das Gupta
Mr. and Mrs. Donald Gurewicz
Ms. Cynthia R. Gurey and Mr. Mark Yonchak
Mr. and Mrs. Richard Guro
Mr. Barney K. Gushiken
Mr. Henry Gushikuma
Mr. Gerald A. Gustafson
Mr. Richard T. Gyotoku
Mr. Walter Haas
Ms. Hatsue Habara
Mr. Donald T. Hachiya
Mrs. Gail Hachiya
Mr. Homer Hachiya
Dr. Kiyoshi George Hachiya
Takashi Hachiya
Mr. and Mrs. Ted Hachiya
Mr. Tomohara Hachiya
Mary D. Hacker and Steven Nishibayashi
Mr. and Mrs. George L. Hackett
Mr. and Mrs. Roger F. Hackett
Mr. and Mrs. Calvin Hada

Gerry Kay and Shizuye Hada
Hiroshima Kenjin Kai-James Hada
Mrs. Jane K. Hada
Kazuaki and Jacqueline Hada
Ms. Mae T. Hada
Mr. and Mrs. Sadaichi Hada
Mr. and Mrs. Michael Hadley
Ms. Tomiye K. Haertig
Mr. and Mrs. Thomas Haga
Mr. Francis J. Hagan
Mr. and Mrs. Karl Hagg, Jr.
Mrs. Alice S. Hagihara
Mr. and Mrs. Carl J. Hagihara
Ms. Joyce Hagihara
Isamu and Carol Hagino
Mr. Nobuyoshi Hagino
Mr. and Mrs. Allan Hagio
Mr. John Hagio
Mr. Leo N. Hagio
Mr. and Mrs. Roland Hagio
Mr. Alvin Hagiwara
Mr. Nobuo Hagiwara
Mr. and Mrs. Patrick K. Hagiwara
Mr. Raymond Hagiwara
Mr. and Mrs. Tsutomu Hagiwara
Mr. Yoshiyuki Hagiwara
Mr. Yutaka Hagiwara
Dr. and Mrs. Harlan Hague
Mr. and Mrs. Bruce Haines
Hairpro Salon
Mr. and Mrs. Gordon Haitsuka
Mr. and Mrs. Barney Hajiro
Mr. Tokuro Hajiro
Mr. and Mrs. Konao Hakoda
Mr. Tsutomu Hakoda
Mr. and Mrs. Charles J. Halevi
Christine Sato Hall
Mr. and Mrs. David Hall
Mrs. Keyko T. Hall
Ms. Kumiko Hall
Hall Charitable Foundation
Mr. and Mrs. James Hallowell
Ms. Joanne Hama
Mr. and Mrs. Take Hama
Mr. and Mrs. Kenichi Hamabe
Mr. Gordon T. Hamachi
Mr. and Mrs. John Hamachi
Ms. Kristina Hamachi
Mr. Mike Hamachi
Mr. and Mrs. R. Mike Hamachi
Ms. Cheryl Hamada
Chikato Hamada
Mr. Dennis Hamada
Mr. Dick Hamada
Mrs. H. Y. Hamada
Ms. Karen Hamada
Mr. and Mrs. Kiyoshi Hamada
Mrs. Masako Hamada
Ms. Masako Hamada
Ms. May Hamada
Ms. Michiko Hamada
Mr. and Mrs. Muneo Hamada
Ms. Teruko Hamada
Mr. Tetsuo K. Hamada
Mr. and Mrs. Wallace Y. Hamada
Mr. and Mrs. Yukio Hamada
Mr. Yuso Hamada
Mr. Joseph Hamade
Mr. and Mrs. Tommy Hamade
Mr. and Mrs. Gene Hamaguchi
Mr. and Mrs. Harry Hamaguchi
Mr. and Mrs. Ken Hamaguchi
Mr. Les R. Hamaguchi
Ms. Lily S. Hamaguchi
Mr. and Mrs. Robert Hamaguchi
Mr. Shoji G. Hamaguchi
Mr. Stephen Hamaguchi
Mr. Katsuyoshi Hamahashi
Mr. Tom Hamahashi
Mr. and Mrs. Albert T. Hamai
Mr. Daniel M. Hamai
Mr. Ernest O. Hamai
Mr. and Mrs. George Hamai
Mr. Junji Hamai
Ms. Karen Hamai
Mr. Shoichi Hamai
Mr. and Mrs. Walter K. Hamai
Ms. Wendy Hamai
Mr. and Mrs. Bill Hamakawa
Mr. Shigeyuki Hamamatsu
Mr. and Mrs. Ben Hamamoto
Ms. Edna S. Hamamoto
Mr. and Mrs. Glenn Hamamoto
Mr. and Mrs. Goichi Hamamoto
Mr. and Mrs. Kiyoshi Hamamoto
Ms. Linda Hamamoto

Mr. Max M. Hamamoto
Mr. Patrick Hamamoto
Mrs. Sumie Hamamoto
Ms. Susan T. Hamamoto
Mr. and Mrs. Thomas K. Hamamoto
Mr. Wataru Hamamoto
Mr. Henry Hamamura
Mr. and Mrs. Satoshi Hamamura
Mr. Stanley Hamamura
Ms. Yoko Hamamura
Mr. and Mrs. Hisao Hamanaka
Ms. Lionelle Hamanaka
Ms. Lucy Hamanaka
Mr. and Mrs. Alan Hamane
Mr. Gregory S. Hamane
Mr. and Mrs. Kimio Hamane
Mr. and Mrs. Andrew Hamano
Mr. Buck Hamano
Mr. and Mrs. Ehaku Hamano
Mr. Fumio Hamano
Mr. James Hamano
Mr. and Mrs. John H. Hamano
Mr. and Mrs. Miles Hamano
Mrs. Mitsy Hamano
Mr. and Mrs. S. John Hamano
Mr. Shoichi Hamano
Mr. Timothy Hamano
Mr. and Mrs. Wallace Y. Hamano
Mr. Robert T. Hamaoka
Mr. and Mrs. Akira Hamasaki
Mr. and Mrs. David Hamasaki
Mr. Dickey Hamasaki
Mr. Harrison Hamasaki
Mr. and Mrs. Hatsumasa Hamasaki
Mr. and Mrs. James S. Hamasaki
Mr. James Y. Hamasaki
Ms. Karen Hamasaki
Mr. Kiyoshi Hamasaki
Mr. Michael Hamasaki
Mr. and Mrs. Richard Hamasaki
Mr. Carl Hamashige
Mr. Kenneth Hamashige
Mr. and Mrs. Sean Hamashige
Mr. Takao Hamashima
Mrs. Teruko Hamashima
Mr. Joe Hamashita
Mr. and Mrs. Mitsuo Hamasu
Mr. Ron Hamataka
Ms. Sally Hamatake
Ms. Masako Hamatani
Mr. Robert Hambarian
Ms. Eileen Hambly
Mr. Michael Hambridge
Dawn M. Hamilton
Mr. and Mrs. Thomas C. Hamilton
Mr. Charles Hamori
Ms. Betsy Hamura
Mr. and Mrs. Gerald Hanabusa
Mr. Neil Hanabusa
Mr. Russell M. Hanabusa
Mr. and Mrs. George K. Hanada
Mr. Hisamaru Hanada
Mr. and Mrs. Roger Hanada
Mr. and Mrs. Steve Hanada
Mrs. Fumiko Hanaki
Mr. Ichiro L. Hanami
Mr. Jiro Hanami
Mr. and Mrs. Yoshimi Hanami
Ms. Mitsui M. Hanamoto
Ms. Namiye Hanamoto
Mr. and Mrs. Ric Hanamoto
Mr. Wataru Hanamoto
Mr. and Mrs. George Hanamura
Mr. and Mrs. Haruo Hanamura
Mr. and Mrs. Minoru Hanamura
Mr. and Mrs. Steve Hanamura
Mrs. Betty Hanaoka
Mr. Gary T. Hanaoka
Mr. James S. Hanaoka
Ms. Jane Hanaoka
Mr. Y. Hanaoka
Mr. and Mrs. Seijo Hanashiro
Mr. and Mrs. Seishin Hanashiro
Ms. Violet Hanashiro
Mr. and Mrs. George Hanasono
Mr. Donald Handa
Mr. and Mrs. Frank Handa
Mr. and Mrs. John Handa
Mr. Katsunori Handa
Mr. Peter Handa
Mr. Robert Handa
Mr. and Mrs. Tadao Handa
Mr. Takeo Handa
Mr. Gene M. Hane
Mr. and Mrs. Gerald Hane
Mr. Isao Hane

Mr. and Mrs. Mikiso Hane
Dr. Wayne S. Hane
Mr. and Mrs. H. Hanemoto
Mr. and Mrs. James Hanert
Mr. and Mrs. Noboru Hangai
Mr. A. Stuart Hanisch
Mr. and Mrs. Byron Hanke
Mr. and Mrs. Tom Hanlon
Mr. and Mrs. Dean A. Hanna
Mr. and Mrs. Richard E. Hannah
Mr. Jun I. Hano
Mr. and Mrs. Harley Hansen
Mrs. Tomoko T. Hanway
Mr. George Hanzawa
Mr. Masao Hanzawa
Mr. Ralph T. Hanzawa
Mr. and Mrs. Akira Hara
Dr. and Mrs. Ben Hara
Mr. Calvin Hara and Donalynn Owfook
Mr. Hawaii, Inc.
Ms. Debra Hara
Mr. and Mrs. Edward K. Hara
Eri Hara
Mr. Frank Hara
Mr. and Mrs. George F. Hara
Dr. and Mrs. George S. Hara
Mr. Gregory Hara
Mr. and Mrs. Henry Hara
Mr. J. Todd Hara
Mr. James H. Hara
Mr. and Mrs. James M. Hara, Jr.
Mr. and Mrs. Joe Hara
Mr. and Mrs. Kalvin K. Hara
Mr. Kaoru Hara
Ms. Karen K. Hara
Mr. and Mrs. Kent Hara
Ms. Kimi Hara
Mrs. Komayo Hara
Mr. and Mrs. Lawrence Hara
Ms. Linda M. Hara
Mr. and Mrs. Lloyd Hara
Ms. Lori Hara
Mr. Michael Hara
Mr. and Mrs. Minoru Hara
Ms. Philip S. Hara and Mr. Nancy Omi-Hara
Mr. and Mrs. Richard M. Hara
Mr. and Mrs. Richard T. Hara
Mr. and Mrs. Roderick Hara
Mrs. Rose Hara
Dr. and Mrs. S. Hara
Mr. Shinobu D. Hara
Ms. Taiko Hara
Mr. and Mrs. Thomas I. Hara
Mr. Toshimichi Hara
Mr. and Mrs. Yasuo Hara
Mr. Atsumu Harada
Ben T. Harada
Mrs. Chiaki Harada
Mr. Daisaku Harada
Mr. Dick T. Harada
Ms. Frances F. Harada
Mr. George S. Harada
Mr. and Mrs. Haruto Harada
Ms. Helen Harada
Mr. and Mrs. Henry Harada
Mr. and Mrs. Hideo Harada
Mr. and Mrs. Hideo H. Harada
Mr. and Mrs. Howard Harada
Mr. Jack K. Harada
Mr. and Mrs. James T. Harada
Jimmy E. and Toshiko Harada Family
Mr. and Mrs. Joe Harada
Ms. Josephine M. Harada
Ms. Karen T. Harada
Mr. and Mrs. Kay Y. Harada
Larrene Harada and Grant Nakayama
Mr. and Mrs. Luke Harada
Ms. Lynn H. Harada
Mr. Mack Harada
Ms. Marion Y. Harada
Ms. Mary Ann Kiyoye Harada
Mr. Masao Harada
Mr. and Mrs. Masato Harada
Mr. and Mrs. Masayoshi Harada
Ms. Melanie J. Harada
Mr. Michael Harada
Dr. Michael T. Harada
Dr. and Mrs. Michael Y. Harada
Mrs. Misao Kume Harada
Mr. and Mrs. Nobuyuki Harada
Mr. Paul Harada
Ms. Priscilla Harada
R. B. Harada
Mr. and Mrs. Raymond Harada
Mr. Richard Harada
Mr. Robert Harada

Mr. Rodney Harada
Mr. and Mrs. Ronald Harada
Mr. and Mrs. Roy Harada
Mr. and Mrs. Roy H. Harada
Dr. Russell N. Harada
Mrs. Saburo Harada
Mr. and Mrs. Scott Harada
Ms. Sharon J. Harada
Ms. Suzan M. Harada
Mr. Taneyuki Harada
Mr. and Mrs. Theodore Harada
Mr. and Mrs. Toshio Joe Harada
Mr. Tsutomu Harada
Mr. Yoshiaki G. Harada
Ms. Faye Haraguchi
Ms. Karol Haraguchi
Ms. Kazuko Haraguchi
Mr. Norman Haraguchi
Mr. Tatsue Haraguchi
Sayuri Harami
Mr. Larry Haramoto
Mr. and Mrs. Allen A. Harano
Ms. Chieko Harano
Mr. and Mrs. George Harano
Mr. Jerry Harano
Mr. Richard Harano
Mr. Richard K. Harano
Mr. Richard M. Harano
Mr. Ross Harano
Mr. Samuel T. Harano
Mr. and Mrs. Yoshio K. Harano
Mr. and Mrs. Donald Haratani
Mr. Joseph Haratani
Mrs. Robert Harder
Ms. Betty Hardy
Dr. Deane Y. Harimoto
Mr. and Mrs. Yoneji Harioka
Mrs. David R. Harman
Mr. Clyde E. Harmon
Mr. and Mrs. Terry Harms
Mrs. Joy Harper
Mr. and Mrs. Arthur L. Harris
Mrs. Dianne Harris
Ms. Mary T. Harris
Mr. and Mrs. Albert C. Harrison
Mr. and Mrs. Weymeth Harrison
Ms. Pam Konishi Harrold
Mr. Kyoshin J. B. Harrower
Ms. Erica Harth
Mr. and Mrs. Burne E. Hartsook
Mr. Norio Harui
Mrs. Barbara Haruki
Mr. Naoya Haruta
Mr. Jonathan Harveson
Lloyd C. and Christie Hosokawa Harveson
Mr. Matthew W. Harveson
Ms. Tiffany Harveson
Mr. and Mrs. George Hasabe
Mr. and Mrs. Icy Hasama
Mr. Albert A. Hasara
Mr. Tatsuo Hase
Ms. Amy Hasegawa
Ms. Ann Y. Hasegawa
Ms. Anne Hasegawa
Mr. Aylen I. Hasegawa
Carol Hasegawa
Mr. and Mrs. Charles Hasegawa
Mrs. Dorothy Hasegawa
Ms. Ethel N. Hasegawa
Mr. Francisco N. Hasegawa
Dr. Fred I. Hasegawa
Mr. Harry Hasegawa
Mr. Hiromi Hasegawa
Mr. and Mrs. Ichiro Hasegawa
Mr. James C. Hasegawa
Ms. Kathy H. Hasegawa
Rev. and Mrs. Kenneth Hasegawa
Mr. and Mrs. Kiyoshi Hasegawa
Mr. Leighton Hasegawa
Mr. Lester K. Hasegawa
Ms. Linnea Hasegawa
Ms. Lisa M. Hasegawa
Ms. Marjorie Hasegawa
Mr. Mitsuo Hasegawa
Mr. Paul Hasegawa
Mr. and Mrs. Robert A. Hasegawa
Mr. and Mrs. Robert K. Hasegawa
Mr. Saburo Hasegawa
Ms. Susan S. Hasegawa
Mr. and Mrs. Tetsuo T. Hasegawa
Mr. and Mrs. Tom Hasegawa
Mr. Tomio Hasegawa
Wataru Hasegawa
Y. Hasegawa
Mr. Hiroyasu Hasejima

Ms. Ayako Hashiba
Grace and Carolyn Hashiba
Mr. and Mrs. Grace K. Hashiguchi
Mr. and Mrs. Hachiro Hashiguchi
Mr. and Mrs. Henry Hashiguchi
Mr. and Mrs. James Hashiguchi
Mr. and Mrs. John Hashiguchi
Mr. and Mrs. Nobuo Hashiguchi
Mr. and Mrs. Scott K. Hashiguchi
Ms. Yuki Hashiguchi
Edie E. Hashima and Rodney H. Kubomoto
Mr. Ray Hashima
Alice T. Hashimoto and Elenor C. Niizawa
Ms. Bernice Hashimoto
Mr. Brandon T. Hashimoto
Mrs. Clara Hashimoto
Mr. and Mrs. Frank Hashimoto
Mr. Fred Hashimoto
Mr. and Mrs. George Hashimoto
Mr. George S. Hashimoto
Mr. Glen Hashimoto
Mr. Harlan Hashimoto
Mr. Harold A. Hashimoto
Mr. and Mrs. Harry H. Hashimoto
Mr. and Mrs. Hisao Hashimoto
Mr. and Mrs. Hitoshi Hashimoto
Mr. Ichiro Hashimoto
Mr. and Mrs. Isamu Hashimoto
Mr. Isao Hashimoto
Mr. James H. Hashimoto
Mr. James M. Hashimoto
Mr. and Mrs. Joe Hashimoto
Mr. and Mrs. Junichi Hashimoto
Mr. and Mrs. Katsumi Hashimoto
Mr. Katsumi G. Hashimoto
Mr. Kevin T. Hashimoto
Mr. and Mrs. Larry Hashimoto
Mr. Lawrence Hashimoto
Mr. and Mrs. Masateru H. Hashimoto
Mr. and Mrs. Masayuki Hashimoto
Mitsuhiko and Kazuko Hashimoto
Ms. Monica Fusaye Hashimoto
Nobuto and Masayo Hashimoto
Mr. and Mrs. Richard Hashimoto and Family
Mr. Robert H. Hashimoto
Ryan and Kelly Hashimoto
Ms. Sachiko Hashimoto
Ms. Sande Hashimoto
Mr. and Mrs. Shigemi Hashimoto
Ms. Stacie Hashimoto
Mr. and Mrs. Tom Hashimoto
Mr. Tsuyoshi Hashimoto
In Honor of Utaro and Natsu Hashimoto
Dr. Walter W. Hashimoto
Mr. William K. Hashimoto
Mr. William T. Hashimoto
In Memory of Yukiko Hashimoto
Mr. and Mrs. Henry Hashioka
Mr. and Mrs. James Hashisaka
Mr. and Mrs. Norman Y. Hashisaka
Mrs. Masako B. Hashizu
Ms. Arlene Hashizume
Mr. Robert Hashizume
Sato Hashizume
Mrs. Tokiyo Hasuko
Mr. Bob Hata
Mr. and Mrs. Eiji Hata
Mr. and Mrs. Joshua Hata
Ms. Judith Setsuko Hata
Mr. Makoto M. Hata
Ms. Margie T. Hata
Ms. Mari S. Hata
Mr. and Mrs. Misao Hata
Ms. Nancy R. Hata
Mr. and Mrs. Raymond Hata
Mrs. Richard Hata
Mr. Ron Hata
Mr. Tony Hata
Mr. and Mrs. Yoshimi Hata
Mr. James Hatada
Mr. Randall Hatada
Mr. and Mrs. Saburo Hatada
Mr. and Mrs. Masaji Hatae
Mr. and Mrs. Edward Hatago
Mr. Arnold Hatai
Mr. Shuso Hatai
Mr. Ariji Hatakeda
Mr. and Mrs. Ben T. Hatakeda
Mr. and Mrs. Duke Hatakeda
Mr. Harold Hatakeda
Jun Jimmy Hatakeda
Mr. and Mrs. Jesse H. Hatakenaka
Mr. Mamoru Hatakenaka
Mr. Jon Y. Hatakeyama
Mr. and Mrs. Kimio Hatakeyama

Mr. and Mrs. Lawrence Hatakeyama
Mr. and Mrs. Yoneo Hatakeyama
Ms. Leslie Hatamiya
Mr. and Mrs. Robert Hatamiya
Mr. Andrew T. Hatanaka
Ann Hatanaka and Dewey Horton
Mr. and Mrs. Ben Hatanaka
Mrs. Hanako Hatanaka Family
Ms. Hatsuyo Hatanaka
Mr. and Mrs. Isao Hatanaka
Mr. and Mrs. Jack Hatanaka
Ms. Jill K. Hatanaka
Mr. and Mrs. Ross Hatanaka
Mr. Roy Hatanaka
Mr. and Mrs. Roy Hatanaka
Mr. Daryl Hatano
Mrs. Grace Hataoka
Mr. and Mrs. Harry Hatasaka
Mr. and Mrs. Sam Hatasaka
Mr. Stanley Hatasaka
Ms. Helen Hatashita
Mr. Isao Hatashita
Ms. Marion Hatashita
Mr. and Mrs. Nob Hatashita
Ms. Irene E. Hatate
Mr. and Mrs. Raymond Hatate
Ms. Aiko Hatayama
Mr. Kiyoshi Hataye
Mr. and Mrs. Ike Hatchimonji
James and Abby Hatchimonji
Ms. P. Janine Hathaway and Mr. Steve Hunt
Ms. Amy Hatsukano
Ms. Patricia Hatten
Ms. Alice Hattori
Ms. Diane Hattori
Mrs. Florence M. Hattori
Mr. and Mrs. Fred Hattori
Mrs. Fumi Hattori
Mr. Hidefumi Hattori
Mr. and Mrs. Jack Hattori
Mr. James M. Hattori
Mr. and Mrs. John D. Hattori
Mr. Kiyoshi E. Hattori
Mr. and Mrs. Mike Hattori
Mr. Robert M. Hattori
Mr. Steven Hattori
Dr. Takashi Hattori
Mrs. Toshiko Hattori
Mr. and Mrs. Mike D. Hatzinger
Mr. Frank E. Hawk
Avis Hawkins
Ms. Carol Hayakawa
Mr. and Mrs. George Y. Hayakawa
Mr. Hisakazu Hayakawa
Mr. and Mrs. John Y. Hayakawa
Mr. and Mrs. Mark Hayakawa
Mr. Mark R. Hayakawa
Mr. and Mrs. Masami Hayakawa
Mr. Milton Hayakawa
Ms. Ruth Hayakawa
Mr. Takeshi Hayakawa
Mr. Thomas R. Hayakawa
Mr. Toshio Hayakawa
Mr. and Mrs. William Hayakawa
Kyle Hayama and Jena Hayama
Mr. Toshio Hayama
Mr. Arthur Hayame
Mr. and Mrs. Frank Hayami
Mr. and Mrs. Marvin Y. Hayami
Mr. and Mrs. Smith Y. Hayami
Mr. and Mrs. Stanley T. Hayami
Mr. and Mrs. Walter Hayami
Mr. and Mrs. David Hayasaka
Mrs. Mary Ann Hayase
Mr. and Mrs. Paul Hayase
Mrs. Agnes Hayashi
Mr. and Mrs. Albert Hayashi
Dr. and Mrs. Arthur K. Hayashi
Ms. Constance Hayashi
Mr. David Hayashi
Mr. Donald L. Hayashi
Ms. Doris Hayashi
Mrs. Flora M. Hayashi
Ms. Florence Hayashi
Mr. Frank Hayashi
Mr. Frank Y. Hayashi
Ms. Fumi M. Hayashi
Ms. Fumiye E. Hayashi
Mr. Garrett S. Hayashi
Mr. George Hayashi
Mr. and Mrs. George I. Hayashi
Mr. Glen Hayashi
Mr. and Mrs. Harold Hayashi
Mr. and Mrs. Harold T. Hayashi
Mr. and Mrs. Harry S. Hayashi

Ms. Haruye Hayashi
Mr. and Mrs. Hideo Hayashi
Mr. and Mrs. Ichiro Hayashi
Mr. and Mrs. James Hayashi
Ms. Jeanne Hayashi
Mr. and Mrs. John Hayashi
Ms. Joyce T. Hayashi
Mr. and Mrs. K. George Hayashi
Mr. and Mrs. Kazuo Hayashi
Keiko and Stephen Hayashi
Mr. Ken Hayashi
Mr. and Mrs. Ken Hayashi
Mr. Kenneth S. Hayashi
Mr. and Mrs. Kiyoto Hayashi
Ms. Marian M. Hayashi
Mr. and Mrs. Masami Hayashi
Mr. Michael Hayashi
Dr. Mie M. Hayashi
Mr. Minoru Hayashi
Ms. Pat M. Hayashi
Miss Patsy Hayashi
Mr. and Mrs. Paul H. Hayashi
Mr. Paul Y. Hayashi
Ms. Rae Hayashi
Mr. Richard J. Hayashi
Dr. Riley Hayashi
Mr. and Mrs. Robert S. Hayashi
Mr. Ronald S. Hayashi
Mr. Roy Hayashi
Sakaye and Emiko Hayashi
Ms. Sandra Hayashi
Mr. and Mrs. Satoshi T. Hayashi
Scott Hayashi Family
Mr. and Mrs. Shigeo Hayashi
Mr. Shigeru Hayashi
Mr. and Mrs. Shizuka Hayashi
Mr. Steve Hayashi
Mr. Steven Hayashi
Mr. Tadashi Hayashi
Ms. Tamae Hayashi
Mr. and Mrs. Tokio Hayashi
Dr. and Mrs. Will I. Hayashi
Yoko H. Hayashi
Mr. Yozo Hayashi
Mr. and Mrs. Yutaka Hayashi
Mr. Alan Hayashida
Mrs. Alice Hayashida
Amy and Sady Hayashida
Mrs. Annie L. Hayashida
Mr. Art Hayashida
Ms. Audrey Hayashida
Ms. Bette N. Hayashida
Mr. David Hayashida
Mrs. Doris H. Hayashida
Ms. Elsie E. Hayashida
Ms. Frances Hayashida
Mr. Frank Hayashida
Mr. and Mrs. Frank J. Hayashida
Mr. Frank M. Hayashida
Mr. Harry Hayashida
Mr. Henry Hayashida
Mr. Himeo Hayashida
Mr. Joel J. Hayashida
Mr. John Hayashida
Mr. Michihiko Hayashida
Mr. Nelson Hayashida
Mr. Ronald Y. Hayashida
Dr. Ted Hayashida
Mr. Shotaro F. Hayashigatani
Mr. Shujiro Hayashigatani
Ms. Allison Haydadi
Ms. Elaine Hayes
Mr. and Mrs. Timothy M. Hayes
Ms. Jane Hays
Ms. Catherine Hazama
Mr. and Mrs. Richard Hazama
Mr. and Mrs. Kazuo J. Hazeyama
Mr. and Mrs. William Heard
Heart Mountain Wyoming Foundation
Mrs. Lana S. Heck
Joseph Heco Society
Mr. and Mrs. Akira Hedani
Mr. and Mrs. Tokuji Hedani
Ms. Jeanne M. Heimann
Heinz, USA
Mr. and Mrs. Walter Heirakuji
Heiwa Terrace
Mr. and Mrs. Douglas Hellmer
Mr. Leo Helzel
Mr. Robert F. Hemphill, Sr.
Mr. and Mrs. Robert C. Hendel
Mr. and Mrs. Arden Henderson
Pat Henderson
Mr. Kenneth Hendree
Mr. and Mrs. Betty Hendricks

Bishop and Mrs. Daiyu Henjyoji
Mr. and Mrs. Daniel Henmi
Mr. and Mrs. Edward Henmi
Mr. Peter H. Henmi
Mr. Rod Henmi
Mr. and Mrs. Shigeo Henmi
Mr. Steven Henmi
Dr. Sumiko Hennessy
Mr. Donald G. Henry
Ms. Elizabeth R. Henry
Mr. and Mrs. Ted Henry
Mr. and Mrs. Ernest M. Hepler
Mr. and Mrs. James Herbert
Mr. and Mrs. James E. Herbert
Ms. Ava Herbrick
Mr. and Mrs. Raymond Herbrick
Ms. A. Herman
Mr. and Mrs. Norbert S. Herman
Ms. Bea Hernandez
Mr. Charles F. Hernandez
Mr. and Mrs. Phillip Herrera
Ms. Shizue A. Herron
Mr. Phillip Hesser
Dr. Ruth E. Hetland
Mr. Gerald J. Hewitt
Mr. and Mrs. George Heyamoto
Mr. and Mrs. Hiromu Heyamoto
Dr. and Mrs. Roland Heyne
Ms. Sharon Heyward
Mr. Satoshi Hibi
Mr. Sen Hibino
Mr. Tatsu Hibino
Mr. and Mrs. Yukio Hibino
Amy and Pamela Hidaka
Mr. and Mrs. Bill Hidaka
Mr. and Mrs. Carey Hidaka
Mr. and Mrs. Frank Hidaka
Mr. and Mrs. Fred Hidaka
Mr. George Hidaka
Ms. Naoko Hidaka
Mrs. Shizuko Hidaka
Mr. and Mrs. Susumi Hidaka
Mr. William Hidaka
Mr. and Mrs. Tom Hide
Mr. and Mrs. Hank Hidekawa
Ms. Akino Hideshima
Mr. and Mrs. Charles A. Higa
Mr. David I. Higa
Ms. Edith K. Higa
Mrs. Edith S. Higa
Mr. and Mrs. Edward I. Higa
Mr. and Mrs. Frank Higa
Mr. Gary S. Higa
Mr. George Higa
Ms. Grace F. Higa
Ms. Grace M. Higa
Mr. Hatsuyo M. Higa
Mr. and Mrs. Hideo Higa
Mr. James S. Higa
Mrs. Janet H. Higa
Ms. Jean Higa
Mr. Jinji Higa
Mr. and Mrs. Jinki Higa
Mr. and Mrs. Kenneth Higa
Mr. and Mrs. Lawrence Higa
Mrs. Margaret H. Higa
Ms. Mary Higa
Mr. and Mrs. Matsusuke Higa
Ms. Mitsuko Higa
Mr. and Mrs. Miyoshi Higa
Mr. and Mrs. Ramsay Higa
Mr. and Mrs. Richard Higa
Mr. and Mrs. Robert J. Higa
Mr. Ronald Higa
Mr. Roy Higa
Mr. Roy T. Higa
Roy Yoshihiko and Itsuko Higa
Mr. and Mrs. Sadaichi Higa
Mr. Samuel T. Higa
Mr. Seichi Higa
Mr. Sherwin H. Higa
Mr. and Mrs. Shigeo Higa
Mr. and Mrs. Shigeru Higa
Mr. Shinichiro Roy Higa
Mr. Stephen Higa
Mr. Stephen N. Higa
Mr. and Mrs. Steven Higa
Mrs. Sumie Higa
Mr. Takeichi Miles Higa
Mr. and Mrs. Takeo Higa
Mr. and Mrs. Tom T. Higa
Mr. Naomi Higaki
Mr. Robert T. Higaki
Mr. and Mrs. Shigeo Higaki
Mr. Shigeru Higaki
Mr. Shiro Higaki

Ms. Wanda Higaki
Mr. and Mrs. Akitoshi Higashi
Mr. Alfred K. Higashi
Ms. Chiwa Higashi
Ms. Donna T. Higashi
Ms. Edith T. Higashi
Mr. and Mrs. Eiichi Higashi
Elver and Mildred Higashi
Mrs. Evelyn K. Higashi
Ms. Gaile Higashi
Higashi Family
Mr. and Mrs. Henry Higashi
Mr. Hisao Higashi
Mrs. Iseko Higashi
Mr. Joseph Higashi
Ms. Kelly Ann Higashi
Mr. and Mrs. Kiyoshi Higashi
Ms. Mary Higashi
Mr. and Mrs. Masami Higashi
Mr. and Mrs. Michael Higashi
Mr. Raymond Higashi
Mr. Richard Higashi
Mr. Sanford Higashi
Mr. Shiro Higashi
Ms. Sueko Higashi
Mr. Toyohisa Higashi
Lt. Col. and Mrs. Yoshikazu Higashi
Mr. and Mrs. Ernest Higashida
Ms. Amy Higashihara
Ms. Betty Higashino
Mr. Dale Higashino
Mr. Glenn Higashioka
Mr. and Mrs. Patricia Higashioka
Ms. Leslie Higashiuchi
Mr. Shigeru Higashiura
Dr. and Mrs. Robert T. Higashiyama
Mr. Robert G. Higgins
Mr. Norman R. Higo
Ms. Patricia S. Higo
Mr. and Mrs. Albert Higuchi
Mr. and Mrs. Asa A. Higuchi
Lt. Col. and Mrs. Curtis Higuchi
Mr. and Mrs. George K. Higuchi
Mr. George S. Higuchi
Mr. and Mrs. Henry S. Higuchi
Mrs. Hideko Higuchi
Mr. and Mrs. James Higuchi
Mr. Jone H. Higuchi
Ms. Joyce Higuchi
Mr. and Mrs. Kakuto Higuchi
Mr. and Mrs. Kiyoshi Higuchi
Mrs. Mary Higuchi
Mr. Paul N. Higuchi
Mr. Ronny Higuchi
Mr. Roy Y. Higuchi
Mr. and Mrs. Tak Higuchi
Mr. and Mrs. William I. Higuchi
Mr. Norman S. Hihara
Ms. Barbie Hikawa
Mr. and Mrs. Richard K. Hikawa
Mrs. Agnes Hikida
Mr. and Mrs. Albert Hikida
Ms. Erlene H. Hikida
Ms. Marcy Lynn Hikida
Mr. Martin M. Hikida
Mr. and Mrs. Ray M. Hikida
Mr. and Mrs. Richard Hikida
Mr. and Mrs. Robert S. Hikida
Ms. Sadako Hikida
Mrs. Emily Hikido
Mr. and Mrs. Katsumi Hikido
Mr. and Mrs. Harold Hikiji
Ms. Helen Hikiji
Mr. and Mrs. Larry Hikiji
Mr. and Mrs. Allan Hikoyeda
Dr. Elizabeth Hill
Ms. Twyla Hill
Ms. Stephanie P. Hillard
Mr. and Mrs. Gregg Hillis
Lt. Col. and Mrs. Sam Hillis
Ms. Marilyn Himaka
Mr. Osao Himaka
Mr. and Mrs. William Himel
Mrs. Miyo Himeno
Mr. Robert Himoto
Mr. Samuel Himoto
Mr. George M. Hinaga
Ms. Lillian Y. Hinaga
Mr. and Mrs. Damond Hinatsu
Ms. Diana M. Hinatsu
Mrs. Alice H. Hino
Ms. Blanche K. Hino
Ms. Carolyn E. Hino
Ms. Elizabeth K. Hino
Mrs. Jayanne Hino
Mr. and Mrs. Mitsugi Hino

Mr. and Mrs. Terry Hino
Wendell and Jennifer, Chris, Adr Hino
Mr. Roy T. Hinokawa
Mr. Frank T. Hinoki
Mr. George Hinoki
Mr. Hiroyuki A. Hinoki
Mr. Koe Hinoki
Mr. and Mrs. David Hintermeister
Mr. Chris Hioki
Mr. Matthew C. Hipp
Mr. Clark K. Hirabara
Mr. and Mrs. Bill Y. Hirabayashi
Mr. and Mrs. Dean Hirabayashi
Donald and Judith Hirabayashi
Mr. and Mrs. George Hirabayashi
Ms. Hannah Hirabayashi
Mr. James Hirabayashi
Mr. and Mrs. Jonathan Hirabayashi
Ms. Kazuko Hirabayashi
M. James and Sharon Hirabayashi
Mr. and Mrs. Michael Hirabayashi
Mr. Osamu Hirabayashi
Mr. and Mrs. Roy Hirabayashi
Mr. and Mrs. Sam Hirabayashi
Mrs. Shizu Hirabayashi
Mr. and Mrs. Theodore Y. Hirabayashi
Mr. Timothy Hirabayashi
Mr. and Mrs. Tom Hirabayashi
Mr. and Mrs. Clement Hirae
Mr. Walter Hirae
Ms. Akiko S. Hiraga
Ms. Helen M. Hiraga
Mr. and Mrs. Kei Hiraga
Mikio H. Hiraga
Mr. Ronald K. Hiraga
Mr. and Mrs. Ted I. Hiraga
Mr. and Mrs. Tom Hiraga
Mr. and Mrs. William Hiraga
Ms. Alice Hirahara
Mr. Frank Hirahara
Mr. Howard K. Hirahara
Stan and Carol Hirahara
Ms. Alice Hirai
Mr. Bob I. Hirai
Mr. and Mrs. Craig Hirai
Ms. Evelyn S. Hirai
Mr. and Mrs. Frederick Hirai
Mr. George T. Hirai
Mr. George Y. Hirai
Mr. Gordon Hirai
Mr. and Mrs. Jack K. Hirai
Mr. and Mrs. John S. Hirai
Mr. Keizo Hirai
Mrs. Kiku Hirai
Mr. Koji Hirai
Mr. Michael Hirai
Mr. Richard Hirai
Ms. Rina Hirai
Mrs. Shigeko Hirai
Mr. and Mrs. Shunichi B. Hirai
Mr. and Mrs. Tom Hirai
Mr. Toshia E. Hirai
Mr. and Mrs. Toshiyuki Hirai
Mr. Wallace S. Hirai
Mr. West Y. Hirai
Mr. John Hiraishi
Mr. Ritsuro Hiraishi
Mr. and Mrs. Dave Hiraiwa
Mr. Gary Hiraiwa
Ms. Ruth Michiko Hiraiwa
Mr. and Mrs. Kenneth Hirakami
Ms. Carole Hirakawa
Mr. Fred Hirakawa
Ms. Kikuye Hirakawa
Mr. and Mrs. Louis Hirakawa
Ms. Ryoko Hirakawa
Ms. Debra Hiraki
Mr. and Mrs. Harry Hiraki
Mr. Julian T. Hiraki
Mr. Kenneth Hiraki
Mr. Richard M. Hiraki
Mr. and Mrs. Ronald T. Hiraki
Ms. Bette Hiramatsu
Mr. Charles Hiramatsu
Ms. Julie Hiramatsu
Sandra Hiramatsu and Michael Morishima
Mr. Akira Hirami
Ms. Yuri Hirami
Mr. Hiroshi Hiramoto
Mr. and Mrs. John J. Hiramoto
Mr. Kelly Hiramoto
Mr. and Mrs. Kiichi Hiramoto
Mr. and Mrs. Kinji Hiramoto
Mr. and Mrs. Richard Hiramoto
Mr. and Mrs. Tatsumi Hiramoto
Ms. Yuriko Hiramoto

Ms. Kinue L. Hiranaga
Mr. Tom Hiranaga
Mr. and Mrs. Robert Hiranaka
Mr. Albert K. Hirano
Ms. Alice H. Hirano
Mr. Clarence J. Hirano
Mr. Dick Hirano
Howard and Christine Hirano
Mr. Izumi Hirano
Ms. Kathryn G. Hirano
Mr. Kenneth K. Hirano
Kikuye and Michael Hirano
Ms. Kimiye Hirano
Mr. Kiyoshi Hirano
Mr. and Mrs. Kiyoshi Hirano
Mr. Mikito Hirano
Mr. Peter M. Hirano
Mr. Pierre Hirano
Mr. Raymond Hirano
Mr. Richard Hirano
Mr. and Mrs. Robert Y. Hirano
Mr. Tom Hirano
Mr. Yoshio Hirano
Mrs. Chiyeko Hiraoka
Mr. Joseph M. Hiraoka
Ms. Kiyoko Hiraoka
Mr. Stanley H. Hiraoka
Mr. and Ms. Stanley K. Hiraoka
Mr. Tsutomu Hiraoka
Mr. and Mrs. Yoshimi Hiraoka
Mr. and Mrs. George J. Hirasaki
Mr. Kitt N. Hirasaki
Mr. Toshiki F. Hirasawa
Mr. and Mrs. Kiyoshi Hirase
Mr. and Mrs. George Hirashiki
Mr. Dan T. Hirashima
Mr. John M. Hirashima
Mrs. Takeo Hirashima
Dr. and Mrs. Alan T. Hirasuna
Mr. and Mrs. Fred Y. Hirasuna
Dr. and Mrs. John Hirasuna
Mr. Jon Hirasuna
Ms. Kiyomi Hirasuna
Mr. Matsue Hirasuna
Mr. and Mrs. R. M. Hirasuna
Mr. Stuart Hirasuna
Mr. and Mrs. Akito Hirata
Ms. Alice Hirata
Ms. Anna K. Hirata
Mr. Bob M. Hirata
Mr. and Mrs. Bryan Hirata
Ms. Charlotte A. Hirata
Mr. Donald Hirata
Mr. Edward Y. Hirata
Mr. George Hirata
Mr. and Mrs. Hajime Hirata
Mr. Harry Hirata
Mr. Hideo Hirata
Mr. Jerry H. Hirata
Mr. Jerry N. Hirata
Ms. Jodel Hirata
K. Hirata
Ms. Katrine T. Hirata
Mr. and Mrs. Ken Hirata
Mr. Kenji Hirata
Ms. Lee Hirata and Mr. Tyrrell Norris
Ms. Mary C. Hirata
Ms. Mary T. Hirata
Ms. May Hirata
Ms. Meri Hirata
Ms. Mineko Hirata
Ms. Motoko Hirata
Mr. and Mrs. Patrick Hirata
Mr. and Mrs. Peter M. Hirata
Mr. and Mrs. Richard Hirata
Mr. and Mrs. Rodney A. Hirata
Mr. and Mrs. Sammie Hirata
Mr. Takeshi Hirata
Ted T. Hirata Family
Mr. and Mrs. Thomas Hirata
Mr. and Mrs. Toshio Hirata
Mrs. Toshiye Hirata
Mr. and Mrs. William Hirata
Mr. and Mrs. Willis M. Hirata
Cheryl Hirata-Dulas and Daniel Dulas
Mr. Isao Hiratani
Mr. and Mrs. Frank Hiratsuka
Ms. Josephine Hiratsuka
Mr. Takashi Hiratsuka
Mr. Charles Hiraya
Mr. and Mrs. Arthur Y. Hirayama
Mr. Bruce Hirayama
Mr. Charles Hirayama
Mr. Duane Hirayama
Mr. Glenn Hirayama
Mr. and Mrs. Harold S. Hirayama

Mr. and Mrs. Keith Hirayama
Mrs. Kiyome Hirayama
Mr. Noboru Hirayama
Mr. and Mrs. Robert M. Hirayama
Mr. Satoshi F. Hirayama
Mr. and Mrs. Tetsu Hirayama
Mr. Yasumasa Hirayama
Mr. Yukio Hirayama
Mr. Yoshihiro Hirayanagi
Mr. Hisao Hiro
Mr. Sean Hiro
Mr. Franklin M. Hiroe
Mr. and Mrs. Calvin Y. Hirohama
Mr. Bill Hirohata
Ms. Chiyoko Hirohata
Mr. George Hirohata
Mr. Herbert H. Hirohata
Mr. and Mrs. John K. Hirohata
Mr. and Mrs. John S. Hirohata
Mr. Larry Hirohata
Mr. and Mrs. George Hirokane
Mr. and Mrs. Ichiro Hirokane
Mr. and Mrs. Jerry Y. Hirokane
Ms. Yasuko Hirokane
Mr. George M. Hirokawa
Mr. Hiroshi Hirokawa
Mr. and Mrs. Ichiro Hirokawa
Mr. Jay S. Hirokawa
Mrs. Karen Hirokawa
Ms. Trooda Hirokawa
Mr. Howard Hiroki
Mr. and Mrs. George Hiromoto
Mr. and Mrs. Harry Hiromoto
Mr. and Mrs. Kazuo J. Hiromoto
Mr. and Mrs. Richard T. Hiromoto
Mr. Alan Hiromura
Mr. and Mrs. Kozo Hiromura
Mr. Henry Hironaga
Mr. Kazuo Hironaga
Mr. Alvin Hironaka
Ms. Cathy Hironaka
Mr. Dennis D. Hironaka
Mr. and Mrs. Hiram Hironaka
Mr. Hiroshi Hironaka
Mr. and Mrs. Jim Hironaka
Ms. Kazu S. Hironaka
Mr. Kenji Hironaka
Mr. and Mrs. Kuni Hironaka
Martha and Sam F. Hironaka
Mr. Minoru Hironaka
Mr. and Mrs. Mitsuji Hironaka
Mr. Paul S. Hironaka
Mr. and Mrs. Pete Hironaka
Mr. and Mrs. Sam S. Hironaka
Mr. Takashi Hironaka
Mrs. Tokie Hironaka
Mr. and Mrs. Wallace Hironaka
Mr. and Mrs. Miki M. Hiroo
Ms. Momoye M. Hirooka
Mr. and Mrs. Ronald Hirosawa
Ms. Adele P. Hirose
Ms. Charlotte Hirose
Mr. and Mrs. George T. Hirose
Mrs. Hanako Hirose
Mr. Henry Hirose
Mr. and Mrs. Henry I. Hirose
Dr. and Mrs. Hideo Hirose
Mr. Keiichi Hirose
Ms. Kimberly Hirose
Mr. Momoru Hirose
Mrs. Tamaye Hirose
Mr. Thomas Hirose
Mrs. Barbara Hiroshige
Mr. Cliff Hiroshige
Hon. Ernest Hiroshige
Mrs Fred Hiroshima
Mr. and Mrs. Howard Hiroshima
Ms. Barbara Hirota
Mr. Haruo Hirota
Mr. Joseph S. Hirota
Ms. Katsuko Hirota
Mr. Masahiro Hirota
Mrs. Murray Hirota
Mr. Sherry Hirota
Mr. and Mrs. Susumu Hirota
Mr. and Mrs. Takashi Hirota
Ms. Teresa Hirota
Mr. Tom Hirota
Mr. Yoshikazu Hirota
Mrs. Yukino Hirota
Mr. Edwin Hiroto
Mr. Roy Hirotsu
Mr. Tats Hirotsuka
Ms. Joan E. Hirozawa
Ms. Sharlene Hirsch
Mr. and Mrs. Juan E. Hisada

Margie T. Hisaka and Jean Terashita
Ms. Stacey Hisaka
Ms. Lorraine H. Hisamoto
Mr. and Mrs. Hiroshi Hisamune
Mr. and Mrs. Toshio Hisamune
Mrs. Ichiko M. Hisanaga
Mr. Yoshio Hisaoka
Mr. Yukio Hisaoka
Mr. and Mrs. Masashi Hisata
Mr. and Mrs. Kune Hisatomi
Mr. and Mrs. Setsuo Hisatomi
Mr. Jack Hisayasu
Mr. Hugh Hitchcock
Mr. Hisashi Hitomi
Ms. Myrna Hitomi
Ms. Mika Hiuga
Ms. Barbara Hiura
Mr. Gregory M. Hiura
Dr. Jerrold A. Hiura
Ms. Toshiye Hiura
Mr. Gerald N. Hiyakumoto
Ms. Laurie S. Hiyakumoto
Ms. Chiyeko Hiyama
Mr. and Mrs. Howard Hiyama
Ms. Midori F. Hiyama
Ms. Misao Hiyama
Mr. and Mrs. Paul S. Hiyama
Mr. Robert Hiyama
Stephen Hiyama and Sarah Zearfoss
Mr. and Mrs. Richard Hiyane
Mr. Howard Hiyoshida
Ms. Kendra K. Ho
Mr. and Mrs. Kenneth Ho
Mr. and Mrs. Paul Ho
Dr. and Mrs. Victor Ho
Mr. and Mrs. Martin Hoade
Mr. and Mrs. Lyle N. Hoag
Mr. Seichi Hoashi
Sister Jose Hobaay
Mr. and Mrs. James E. Hobbs
Ms. Mary E. Hobbs
Mr. and Mrs. Martin Hochi
Mr. and Mrs. Paul W. Hodler
Ms. Ashley Hoffar
Mr. and Mrs. Bruce Hoffman
Mr. John R. Hoffmaster
Ms. Hannah Hogan
Mr. and Mrs. John W. Hogan
Hoh Daiko Drummers
Mr. and Mrs. Thomas Hoisington
Mr. and Mrs. Ejitsu Hojo
Danny and Wayne N. Hokama
Mr. and Mrs. Edward Hokama
Mr. George Hokama
Mr. George T. Hokama
Mr. and Mrs. Harold H. Hokama
Mr. and Mrs. Shinsei Hokama
Mr. and Mrs. Stanley Hokama
Mr. Tom Y. Hokama
Mr. Walter C. Hokama
Mr. Yokichi Hokama
Mr. and Mrs. Yosh Hokama
Yoshitsugi Hokama
Mr. and Mrs. Samuel Y. Hokari
Mr. Masato Hokoda
Mr. and Mrs. John Hokoyama
Ms. Tsugiko Holdaway
Dr. and Mrs. James Holden
Mr. and Mrs. W. Douglas Holdren
Dr. Harrison Holland
Ms. Atsu Hollister
Ms. Ruth Hollman
Mr. and Mrs. C. James Holloway
Ms. Masako Hollowell
Hollywood Dodgers Parents Assoc.
Ms. Christine Holst
Ms. Michiko Holt
Mr. Michael A. Holubar and Ms. Karen C. Inaba
Holy Cross Health Staff
Holy Cross Medical and Dental Staff
Mr. and Mrs. Nathan A. Hom
Mr. and Mrs. Richard Hom
Mr. and Mrs. Sik Hom
Mr. Robert I. Homma
Ms. Teiko Homma
Dr. and Mrs. Wes Honbo
Mr. and Mrs. Akira Honda
Mr. and Mrs. Ben Honda
Messrs. Derek, Travis, Blake and Rex Honda
Dixie and Helene Honda
Mr. Earl Honda
Mr. and Mrs. Edward Honda
Mr. and Mrs. Edwin H. Honda
Ms. Eleanor H. Honda
Mr. Glen Honda
Mr. and Mrs. Gordon Honda

Mr. Harold H. Honda
Harry and Ada Honda
Mr. and Mrs. Harry J. Honda
Mr. and Mrs. Harry M. Honda
Helen and Eric Honda
Mr. Henry Honda
Mr. Hideo Honda
Ms. Ikuko Honda
Ms. Ikuyo Honda
Mr. Iwao Honda
Ms. Joyce F. Honda
Mr. and Mrs. Jun Honda
Ms. June E. Honda
Mr. and Mrs. Kay Honda
Mr. Kenneth S. Honda
Mr. Kenneth T. Honda
Mr. and Mrs. Larry Honda
Mr. Masao Honda
Mike M. and Jeanne M. Honda
Mr. and Mrs. Minoru Honda
Mr. and Mrs. Mitsuo Honda
Mr. Naoko Honda
Mr. and Mrs. Natsue Honda
Mr. and Mrs. Nobuo Honda
Ms. Norma Honda
Mr. and Mrs. Osamu Honda
Mr. and Mrs. Ralph Honda
Mr. Robert K. Honda
Mr. Robert S. Honda
Mr. Ryan Honda
Rev. and Mrs. Shojo Honda
Mr. Stanley Takeo Honda
Mr. and Mrs. Sunao Honda
Mr. and Mrs. Takashi Honda
Ms. Tamiko Honda
Mr. and Mrs. Tom T. Honda
Mr. and Mrs. Tomio Honda
Mr. Toshiaki Honda
Wari Honda and Hideko Okamura
Ms. Florence Hongo
Mr. and Mrs. Jimmy Hongo
Mr. and Mrs. Sandra Hongo
Mr. Sunao Hongo
Mr. George T. Honjiyo
Mrs. Mizue Honjiyo
Mr. Warren Honjiyo
Mr. and Mrs. Yoshi Honkawa
Ms. Melanie U. Honma
Mr. Robert K. Honma
Scott K. Honma and Family
Mr. Mas Honmyo
Mr. and Mrs. Yujiro Honmyo
Mr. Bob Hontani
Emo A. Honzaki and Jang-Harn Su
Ms. Harumi M. Hooker
Mr. Greg Hora
Ms. Karla Hora
Mr. and Mrs. Keith Hora
Mr. and Mrs. Scott H. Hora
Seiko Hora
Ms. Joann Horai
Ms. Betty T. Hori
Ms. Chikako M. Hori
Mr. Edward H. Hori
Mrs. Florence Hori
Ms. Frances K. Hori
Ms. Francine M. Hori
Dr. Frank Hori
Mr. Fukashi Hori
Ms. Helen Hori
Mrs. Hisa Hori
Mr. James Hori
Ms. Jeanette Hori
Mr. and Mrs. Kazuo Hori
Mr. and Mrs. Kei Hori
Mr. and Mrs. Kevin M. Hori
Kiyoaky Hori
Lester and Helen Hori
Mr. Mark Hori
Mr. Pamela A. Hori
Mr. Richard N. Hori
Ms. Ruby Hori
Mr. Satoko Hori
Mr. Soichiro Hori
Mr. Tashi Hori
Mr. and Mrs. Tatsu Hori
Mr. Tom N. Hori
Ms. Viola Hori
Mr. and Mrs. Kay Horiba
Mr. Masatake Horiba
Ms. Grace Horibe
Ms. Harue Horibe
Mr. Royden T. Horibe
Mr. and Mrs. Georph Horie
Mr. and Mrs. Mark Horie
Mr. Yueji Horie
Mr. Brian Horii

Mr. George F. Horii
Mr. Howard Horii
Mr. and Mrs. Jim Horii
Ms. Karen N. Horii
Mr. Samon Horii
Tak and Sumie Horii
Dr. and Mrs. Herbert J. Horikawa
Ms. Karen Horikawa
Ms. Kikue Horikawa
Mr. Mark Horikawa
Mr. and Mrs. N. Richard Horikawa
Mr. and Mrs. Takayuki Horikiri
Ms. Teruko Horikoshi
Mr. Gary Horimoto
Mr. and Mrs. Susumu Horimoto
Mr. Donald N. Horina
Mr. and Mrs. Frank G. Horino
Mr. Irene I. Horino
Ms. Niki Horino
Mr. Ernest M. Horinouchi
Mr. Ken Horio
Mr. Marion M. Horio
Mr. and Mrs. George R. Horishige
Ms. Bessie Horita
Mr. and Mrs. Shoji Horita
Mr. and Mrs. Tom Horita
Ms. Aiko Horiuchi
Mr. Akira Horiuchi
Mr. and Mrs. Ben Horiuchi
Mrs. Bernadette Horiuchi
Mr. David Horiuchi
Mr. Floyd Horiuchi
Mr. and Mrs. Fred Horiuchi
Mr. and Mrs Kenzo Horiuchi
Mr. Masaru Horiuchi
Mr. Masayuki Horiuchi
Mr. and Mrs. Mitsugi Horiuchi
Mr. and Mrs. Noboru Horiuchi
Mr. and Mrs. Paul M. Horiuchi
Mr. and Mrs. Paul Y. Horiuchi
Mr. Richard H. Horiuchi
Mr. Takeo Horiuchi
Mr. Tal R. Horiuchi
Horiuchi Family
Mr. and Mrs. Charlie M. Horiye
Mr. Gordon Horiye
Mr. Handy Horiye
Joseph M. Horiye
Nancy S. Horiye
Mr. Harold Horn
Mr. and Mrs. Robert Horn
Mr. and Mrs. David D. Horner
Ms. Cleora Y. Horton
Mr. and Mrs. George Hosaka
Mr. and Mrs. John Hosaka
Mr. Teruo Hosaka
Mr. L. M. Hose
Mr. Kenichi Hoshi
Mr. Paul Hoshi
Sono Hoshi
Mrs. Susan R. Hoshi-Castoro and
Mr. Anthony M. Castoro
Mr. Sutar G. Hoshida
Mr. and Mrs. Hideo Hoshide
Ms. Nori Oda Hoshijo
Ms. Taeko Hoshikawa
Mrs. Jean A. Hoshiko
Mr. and Mrs. Larry S. Hoshiko
Mr. William Hoshiko
Ms. Aiko M. Hoshino
Mr. and Mrs. Alan T. Hoshino
Mr. George Hoshino
Mr. Isamu Hoshino
Mrs. Keiji Hoshino
Mr. Noboru Hoshino
Mr. Seitaro Hoshino
Ms. Susan Hoshino
Mr. Yuichi Hoshino
Mr. and Mrs. George Hoshizaki
Mr. Hiroshi Hoshizaki
Ms. Kimiye Hoshizaki
Mr. Kotaro Hoshizaki
Mr. Reiji Hoshizaki
Dr. and Mrs. Takashi Hoshizaki
Tomi Hoshizaki
Mr. Leo H. Hosoda
Ms. Shirley Hosoi
Ms. Adrienne M. Hosokawa
Mr. and Mrs. Fred Hosokawa
Mr. Patrick W. Hosokawa
Ms. Satoko L. Hosokawa
Mr. Thomas S. Hosokawa
Mr. and Mrs. William T. Hosokawa
Mr. Tsutomu Hosomi
Mr. Erwin Hosono
Mr. Buro Hosoume
Mr. John Hosoume

Mr. and Mrs. Yo Hosozawa
Ms. Michi Hotta
Mr. and Mrs. Toshiharu Hotta
Ms. Suzanne Ninomiya Hough
Mr. and Mrs. Bruce H. Howard
Dr. Katsuyo Howard
Ms. Margaret K. Hayashi
Ms. Masako B. Howard
Ms. Stacy Howard
Mr. and Mrs. Tom Howarth
Ms. Cheri L. Howe
Mr. Frederick H. Howell
Mr. and Mrs. Joseph H. Howell
Ms. Rose C. Howell
Mr. Mitsuo Hozaki
Mr. Tamotsu Hozaki
Mr. Albert Hsu
Mr. Robert H. Hsu
Ms. Susan S. Htoo
Mr. Paul Huang
Mr. and Mrs. Wei-Chang Huang
Mr. and Mrs. Wen H. Huang
Mr. Gary Hubbard
Mr. Harry G. Huberth
Mr. Edward A. Hudson
Mr. and Mrs. Kay Hudson
Mr. and Mrs. Robert Hudson
Ms. Utako Hudson
Mr. and Mrs. Jose Huerta
Ms. Kazuko Huey
W. Huff
Mr. and Mrs. Walter Munemitsu Huff
Mr. Charles Hughes
Ms. Esther Hughes
Mr. and Mrs. Bruce Hull
Mr. and Mrs. Robert Hulse
Betty Hum and Sarah Schoppenhorst
Mr. and Mrs. Ming H. Hung
Mr. V. Stephen Hunt
Ms. Mitsue Kamikawa Hurlbert
Mr. and Mrs. Charles Hurley
Mrs. Haruko Hurt
Ms. Carolyn Hussey
Ms. Patricia Hutchings and Dr. Bill Costello
Ms. Randi Hutchinson
Mr. and Mrs. William E. Hutchinson
Mrs. Sachiko I. Huttenmann
Muoi Huynh
Mr. and Mrs. Samuel H. Hyman
Mr. Alfred M. Hyosaka
Ms. Jane S. Hyosaka
Mr. and Mrs. Edward T. Iba
Ms. Jennifer Iba
Ms. June Iba
Mr. Yojiro Iba
Mr. and Mrs. Dexter K. Ibara
Mr. Albert T. Ibaraki
Mr. and Mrs. Howard Ibaraki
Mr. Kevin T. Ibaraki
Mr. and Mrs. Thomas H. Ibaraki
Mr. and Mrs. Thomas T. Ibata
Mr. Lawrence K. Iboshi
Mr. and Mrs. Shinji Ichida
Mr. George M. Ichien
Mr. James E. Ichien
Mr. and Mr. Hiroshi Ichihara
Mr. Craig Ichiho
Mr. Daisuke D. Ichiho
Mr. Henry Ichiho
Dr. and Mrs. Ben Ichikawa
Mr. and Mrs. Buster K. Ichikawa
Mr. David Ichikawa
Mr. and Mrs. Grant Ichikawa
Ms. Janice H. Ichikawa
Ms. Kimiyo Ichikawa
Ms. Laura Ichikawa
Mrs. May S. Ichikawa
Mr. Robert Ichikawa
Mr. Ruth S. Ichikawa
Mr. Sam Ichikawa
Mr. Shoji Ichikawa
Mr. and Mrs. Takeo Ichikawa
Mr. Tom Ichikawa
Mr. Yasu Ichikawa
Mrs. Yayoko Ichikawa
Ms. Helen Ichiki
Ms. Kristine Ichiki
Mr. and Mrs. Stephen Ichiki
Mr. and Mrs. George Ichimoto
Ms. Akiko Ichimura
Mr. Elliott Ichimura
Mr. Gary H. Ichimura
Mr. and Mrs. Fred Ichinaga
Mr. and Mrs. Roy Ichinaga
Mr. and Mrs. Phillip Ichino
Ms. Tazuko Ichinobe

Mr. Arthur Ichinose
Mr. Calvin M. Ichinose
Mrs. June Ichinose
Mr. and Mrs. Sadami Ichinose
Mr. Toshio Ichinose
Mr. Gary K. Ichishita
Dr. T. Steven Ichishta
Mr. and Mrs. Jimmie Ichiuji
Ms. Mary M. Ichiuji
Dianne, Audrey and Francine Ida
Mr. Kanichi Ida
Mae and Lynne A. Ida
Ms. Mary Ida
Mr. T. Ida
Mr and Mrs. Tom Ida
Mr. and Mrs. Andrew J. Ide
Mr. and Mrs. Buster Ide
Mr. and Mrs. Kazuyoshi Ide
Mr. and Mrs. Michael M. Ide
Mr. Richard Ide
Mr. and Mrs. Robert Ide
Mr. Yukio Ide
Mr. Roy K. Idehara
Mr. Russell Ideishi
Ms. Judi Y. Idemoto
Mr. and Mrs. Kenneth Idemoto
Mr. and Mrs. Robert Idemoto
Ms. Helen Ideno
Mr. and Mrs. Yukichi Ido
Ms. Anna L. Idol and Mr. Michael Sugano
Mr. and Mrs. Richard Iga
Mr. and Mrs. Minoru Igarashi
Mr. and Mrs. Peter Igarashi
Ms. Portia K. Igarashi
Mr. Shigeru Igarashi
Mr. Yoshiya Igarashi
Ms. Grace K. Igasaki
Mr. Paul M. Igasaki
Ms. Asako Igawa
Mr. George Igawa
Mr. Hisashi K. Igawa
Mr. Stanley E. Igawa
Mr. and Mrs. Hiro Ige
Ms. Joyce F. Ige
Mr. and Mrs. Ken Ige
Ms. Kiyoko K. Ige
Ms. Patty Ige
Dr. and Mrs. Philip Ige
Mr. and Mrs. Seiichi Ige
Mr. and Mrs. Takeichi Ige
Mr. Tokucho Ige
Mr. Yukio Ige
Mr. and Ms. Morton Igelman
Mr. John Igoe
Mr. Ben Y. Iguchi
Mr. Gale S. Iguchi
Mr. George Iguchi
Ms. Mary Iguchi
Mr. Motohiko Iguchi
Ms. Tamiko Iguchi
Mr. and Mrs. Yoneo Iguchi
Mr. Darryl J. Iha
Mr. Fred S. Iha
Mr. Maurice Iha
Mr. and Mrs. Craig Ihara
Ms. Helene Ihara
Mr. and Mrs. Hideo Ihara
Mr. Phillip Ihara
Mr. Sheldon K. Ihara
Mr. and Mrs. Stephen Ihara
Mr. and Mrs. Toshio Ihara
Mr. Yutaka Ihara
Mr. and Mrs. Alvin S. Ihori
Mrs. Sue S. Ihori
Ms. Jane T. Iida
Mr. Jeffrey Iida
Mr. and Mrs. Joseph B. Iida
Mr. Sam I. Iida
Mr. Tetsuo Iida
Dr. and Mrs. Theodore M. Iida
Ms. Yasuko Iida
Ms. Grace Iijima
Mr. and Mrs. Issac Iijima
Mr. and Mrs. Yuichi Iikuto
Ms. Helen Iino
Ms. Alice Sumiye Iiyama
Ms. Carol A. Iizuka
Mr. T. J. Iizuka
Mr. John S. Ijichi
Mr. and Mrs. Charles T. Ijima
Ms. Sue A. Ikai
Ms. Lily Ikami
Dr. and Mrs. Norman S. Ikari
Mr. Robert N. Ikari
Mr. Stephen Ikari
Mr. Scott Ikata

Mrs. Sumiko Ikata
Mr. and Mrs. Jack Ikawa
Ikebana International Fresno Chapter
Mr. and Mrs. Tots Ikebe
Mr. and Mrs. Akihisa Ikeda
Mr. and Mrs. Albert B. Ikeda
Mr. and Mrs. Albert S. Ikeda
Mr. and Mrs. Craig Ikeda
Mr. David Ikeda
Mrs. Diann Ikeda
Mr. and Mrs. Don S. Ikeda
Mr. Donald H. Ikeda
Mr. and Mrs. Donald S. Ikeda
Ms. Donna Ikeda
Mrs. Dorothy I. Ikeda
Mr. and Mrs. Edmund Ikeda
Ms. Elizabeth R. Ikeda
Mr. and Mrs. Fumio Ikeda
Mr. and Mrs. George A. Ikeda
Mr. George J. Ikeda
Mr. and Mrs. George K. Ikeda
Mr. George R. Ikeda
Ms. Gladys Ikeda
Mr. Henry H. Ikeda
Mr. Henry S. Ikeda
Mrs. Hideko Ikeda
Mr. and Mrs. James Ikeda
Mr. James Ikeda, Mrs. Lynn and Grace K. Osako
Dr. Jane Y. Ikeda and Family
Mr. and Mrs. Joe Ikeda
Mr. John P. Ikeda
Mr. Katsunori Ikeda
Ms. Kazu Ikeda
Mr. Kazumasa Ikeda
Mr. and Mrs. Kazumi Ikeda
Mr. and Mrs. Kazuo Ikeda
Mr. Kazuyoshi Ikeda
Mr. Keiichi Ikeda
Mr. and Mrs. Kenneth Ikeda
Mr. Kevin G. Ikeda and Mrs. Patricia Ikeda
Ms. Landa Ikeda
Mr. Larry I. Ikeda
Ms. Lawrie J. Ikeda
Ms. Linda M. Ikeda
Ms. Margaret F. Ikeda
Ms. Margaret M. Ikeda
Ms. Marion Ikeda
Mr. Mark Ikeda
Ms. Mary Ikeda
Ms. Mary Jane Ikeda
Mr. and Mrs. Masumi Ikeda
Mr. Michael Ikeda
Ms. Michi Ikeda
Ms. Mildred Y. Ikeda
Mr. and Mrs. Minoru Ikeda
Mr. Minoru B. Ikeda
Ms. Misae Ikeda
Mr. and Mrs. Miyoshi Ikeda
Ms. Naomi Ikeda
Mr. and Mrs. Noboru Ikeda
Mr. and Mrs. Nobuaki Ikeda
Nona Ikeda and Akino Komazaki
Mr. and Mrs. Owen Ikeda
Ms. Peyton Ikeda
Mr. and Mrs. Richard Ikeda
Ronnie and Irene Ikeda
Ms. Ruth Ikeda
Mr. Saburo Ikeda
Mr. Sachio Ikeda
Dr. Sandra Ikeda
Ms. Sharon Ikeda
Mr. and Mrs. Shizuo Ikeda
Mr. and Mrs. Stanley Ikeda
Ms. Susan Ikeda
Mr. Takeo Ikeda
Ms. Thelma Ikeda
Ms. Thomas Ikeda
Mr. and Mrs. Thomas M. Ikeda
Mr. Tim L. Ikeda
Mr. and Mrs. Victor Ikeda
Mr. and Mrs. Yoshiaki Ikeda
Ms. Yoshimi Ikeda
Mr. Yoshitada Ikeda
Ms. Yukiko Ikeda
Ms. May E. Ikeda Cambra
Ms. Karen Ikefugi
Ms. Joan Ikefuji
Mr. Toshiaki Ikegami
Mr. and Mrs. Kazuo Ikehara
Mr. Kris Ikejiri
Ms. Carolyn A. Ikemiya
Mr. and Mrs. George Ikemiya
Dr. Daniel F. Ikemiyashiro
Ms. Diane Ikemiyashiro
Mr. and Mrs. Jorge Ikemiyashiro
Mr. Bill Ikemoto

Mr. Frank S. Ikemoto
Mrs. Harriet Ikemoto
Mr. and Mrs. Michael Ikemoto
Mr. and Mrs. Roger Ikemoto
Mrs. Sakae Ikemoto
Mr. Sam Ikemoto
Mr. Tadashi Ikemoto
Mr. Wilfred T. Ikemoto
Mr. and Mrs. Francis K. Ikenaga
Mr. George N. Ikenaga
Mr. and Mrs. Herbert Ikenaga
Mr. Kiyoshi Ikenaga
Scott A. Ikenaga, Ph.D.
Mr. Shigeru Ikenaga
Mr. James K. Ikeno
Hideo and Helen Ikenoyama
Mr. and Mrs. Teddy Ikeuchi
Mr. Wayne Hiroshi Ikeuchi
Ms. Margaret C. Ikeya
Betty, Wes and Warren Ikezoe
Mr. and Mrs. Jay Ikezoe
Mr. Quentin Ikezoe
Mr. and Mrs. Francis Ikezoye
Mr. Darrell Iki
Mr. and Mrs. Richard Ikkanda
Mr. Roy M. Ikkanda
Mr. and Mrs. Tom Ikkanda
Mr. Keiji Iko
Mr. and Mrs. Robert Ikoma
Mr. Arthur Ikuma
Mr. Edmond K. Ikuma
Ms. Mary Ikuma
Dr. and Mrs. Dennis Ikuta
Ms. Lily H. Ikuta
Ms. Louise S. Ikuta
Mr. Masayoshi Ikuta
Ms. Mutsuko Ikuta
Ms. Nancy M. Ikuta
Shizuko and Lynnette Ikuta
Mr. Yoichi Ikuta
Mr. and Mrs. Kenji Ima
Mr. and Mrs. Dave Imada
Mr. and Mrs. Gerald Imada
Mr. and Mrs. Howard Imada
Mr. Junichi Imada
Mr. and Mrs. Leonard S. Imada
Mr. Louie Imada
Mr. and Mrs. Vaughn Imada
Ms. Kueko Imaeda
Ms. Jane S. Imagawa
Mrs. Noriko Imagawa
Mr. and Mrs. Art Imagire
Ms. Fran E. Imahara
Mr. Walter M. Imahara
Dr. Shiro Imahori
Mr. and Mrs. Shiro Imahori
Mr. and Mrs. Akio Imai
Mr. and Mrs. Clifton Imai
Mr. Edward J. Imai
Mr. George E. Imai
Mr. Hiroshi Imai
Mr. and Mrs. James Imai
Ms. and Ms. Jane Imai
Mr. Joel Imai
Mr. Keiichiro Imai
Ms. Martha Imai
Ms. Mary H. Imai
Mrs. May Imai
Ms. Mikiko Imai
Mr. Nobuo Imai
Mr. Randy Imai
Mr. and Mrs. Roy Imai
Mr. Samuel O. Imai
Mr. Shige Imai
Mr. and Mrs. Shoichi Imai
Ms. Susan Imai
Mr. Takeo Imai
Mr. Terence Imai
Mr. and Mrs. Tom Imai
Mr. and Mrs. Yoshi T. Imai
Dr. Yosuke Imai
Ms. Chow Chow Imamoto
Mr. and Mrs. Edward Imamoto
Mr. Gary S. Imamoto
Ms. Jean R. Imamoto
Mr. Sam S. Imamoto
Mr. Akira Imamura
Mr. Albert M. Imamura
Ms. Alison Imamura
Ms Dale Lynne Imamura
Mr. and Mrs. Edwin Imamura
Mr. Frank Imamura
Mr. Gary Imamura
Mr. George I. Imamura
Mr. and Mrs. Guy G. Imamura
Mr. and Mrs. Ise Imamura

Mr. Jack Imamura
Mr. and Mrs. Ken Imamura
Ms. Lisa Imamura
Mr. and Mrs. Masatoshi Imamura
Mrs. May L. Imamura
Mr. Ray Imamura
Mr. Sam Imamura
Mr. Seigi Imamura
Mr. Terry N. Imamura
Mr. and Mrs. James Imanaka
Ms. May T. Imaoka
Mr. James Imatani
Mr. and Mrs. Denis Imazeki
Mr. and Mrs. Muneo Robert Imon
Mr. and Mrs. Akio Imori
Mr. and Mrs. Teruo Imori
Ms. Chiz Imoto
Ms. Hatsuye Imoto
Mr. and Mrs. Hiyoshi Imoto
Ms. Michie Imoto
Mr. and Mrs. Mike Imoto
Mr. Sam S. Imoto
Mr. Yoshio Imoto
Mr. and Mrs. Harry Imura
Mr. Michael K. Imura
Mr. and Mrs. Shigeo Imura
Mr. Todd Imura
Mr. and Mrs. Kenneth Ina
Dr. Satsuki Ina
Mr. Edward Inaba
Mr. Frank T. Inaba
Ms. Georgene S. Inaba
Mr. and Mrs. Goro Inaba
Mr. and Mrs. Ken Inaba
Mr. and Mrs. Lawrence A. Inaba
Mr. and Mrs. Leslie Gilbert Inaba
Mr. and Mrs. Lon Inaba
Mr. and Mrs. Mitsugi Inaba
Mr. and Mrs. Ralph Inaba
Sheane Inaba
Inaba Bros. A CA Limited
Mr. and Mrs. George Inabata
Mr. Paul K. Inabu
Hanako Inada
Mr. and Mrs. Kenneth Inada
Mr. and Mrs. Masao T. Inada
Mr. and Mrs. David Inadomi
Ms. Jennifer Inadomi
Mr. and Mrs. Minoru Inadomi
Mr. and Mrs. Francis Inafuku
Mr. and Mrs. George Inafuku
Mr. and Mrs. Harumi Inagaki
Mr. and Mrs. Saburo Inagaki
Mr. and Mrs. Shigeru Inagaki
Ms. Mary Inagami
Ms. Betty M. Inahara
Mr. and Mrs. Yosh Inahara
Mr. and Mrs. Robert Inai
Mr. and Mrs. Frank Inamasu
Dr. Melvin S. Inamasu
Mr. and Mrs. Harry Inami
Ms. Evelyn S. Inamine
Mr. John S. Inamine
Mrs. Mabel Inamine
Mr. Seizen Inamine
Mrs. Barbara Inamoto
Fumiko and Chiyeko Inashima
Mr. and Mrs. O. James Inashima
Mr. and Mrs. Kiyohiko Inatomi
Mr. and Mrs. Charles Inatsuka
Mr. and Mrs. Bruce Inenaga
Mr. George Inenaga
Ms. Jerita Ingle
Ms. Doris Ino
Mr. Jimmie Ino
Mr. Takao Ino
Ms. Miyuki Inoashi
Mr. Peter Inokoji-Kim
Mrs. Emiko Inokuchi
Mr. and Mrs. Takeo Inokuchi
Mr. Wes J. Inomoto
Dr. Arthur Inoshita
Mr. Marion S. Inoshita
Mr. and Mrs. Masaji Inoshita
Tadashi and Viola Inoshita
Ms. Terry Inoshita
Mr. Alvin M. Inoue
Mr. Jason Inoue
Mrs. Aiko Inouye
Mr. Allan T. Inouye
Mr. Andrew L. Inouye
Mr. and Mrs. Annette Inouye
Mr. and Mrs. Art Inouye
Ms. Barbara M. Inouye
Mr. and Mrs. Barry Inouye
Ms. Chiyo Inouye

Ms. Darlene Inouye
Mr. Darrel Inouye
Mr. and Mrs. David Inouye
Mr. and Mrs. Ed Inouye
Ms. Edith Inouye
Ms. Emi Inouye
Mr. and Mrs. Eric Inouye
Mr. Eric A. Inouye
Ms. Florence Inouye
Mr. Fred Inouye
Mr. Fusae Inouye
Miss Gale T. Inouye
Mr. and Mrs. George Inouye
Mr. George S. Inouye
Mr. George T. Inouye
Mrs. Grace Inouye
Mr. and Mrs. Harry Inouye
Ms. Haruko Ann Inouye
Mr. and Mrs. Herbert H. Inouye
Ms. Hester E. Inouye
Mr. and Mrs. Hiroshi Inouye
Hiroshi and Hilda N. Inouye
Mr. Hisao Inouye
Ms. Ida J. Inouye
Mr. and Mrs. Isamu Inouye
Mr. Jim Inouye
Mr. and Mrs. Jim M. Inouye
Ms. Joan Inouye
Mr. John W. Inouye
Ms. Julie Inouye
Mr. and Mrs. K. Reo Inouye
Ms. Katheryn M. Inouye
Dr. and Mrs. Kazuo Inouye
Mr. and Mrs. Kazuo Inouye
Mr. Kenneth K. Inouye
Mr. and Mrs. Kiichiro Inouye
Ms. Kikue Inouye
Mr. Kiyoshi Inouye
Mr. Lawrence G. Inouye
Ms. Margaret K. Inouye
Mrs. Margaret Y. Inouye
Ms. Marianne Inouye
Mrs. Mariko K. Inouye
Mrs. Martha Inouye
Ms. Martha M. Inouye
Ms. Mary H. Inouye
Mrs. Mary M. Inouye
Mr. Masao Inouye
Mr. Masao S. Inouye
Mr. Masato Inouye and Mrs. Veda Marsh-Inouye
Mr. Mike Inouye
Mr. Nancy N. Inouye
Ms. Nicole A. Inouye
Mr. Nobuo Inouye
Mr. Paul Inouye
Mr. Peter K. Inouye
Mr. Robert Inouye
Mr. Robert H. Inouye
Mr. Robert K. Inouye
Mr. and Mrs. Sadayuki Inouye
Mr. and Mrs. Sakae Pete Inouye
Mr. and Mrs. Sam Inouye
Mr. Samuel Inouye
Ms. Sandra Inouye
Mr. and Mrs. Shigeo Inouye
Mr. Shigeru Inouye
Mr. and Mrs. Shingo Inouye
Mr. Steve Inouye
Ms. Suma Inouye
Tadashi Inouye
Dr. and Mrs. Takashi Inouye
Mr. and Mrs. Takashi Inouye
Mr. Takuzo Inouye
Mr. Tatsuo Inouye
Mr. and Mrs. Theodore T. Inouye
Mr. and Mrs. Tom S. Inouye
Mr. and Mrs. Toshio Inouye
Mr. William Inouye
Mr. William K. Inouye
Mr. and Mrs. Yoshihiko Inouye
Mr. and Mrs. Yukio Inouye
Mr. and Mrs. Samuel Insolera
Interoffice System Division of CIS
Ms. Margaret Inui
Mr. Eichi Ioka
Ms. Helene C. Ioka
Mr. James Ioki
Ms. Katherine K. Irie
Ms. Peggy F. Iriguchi
Mr. Karl K. Irikura
Mr. Tex Irinaga
Mr. Todd M. Irinaga
Mr. and Mrs. Howard J. Irish
Dr. and Mrs. Craig A. Iriye
Ms. Dorothy Iriye
Ms. Shirley Iriye

Ms. Eiko Irokawa
Mr. and Mrs. Albert Isa
Mr. and Mrs. David Isa
Mr. and Mrs. Derrick Isa
Mr. Raymond Isa
Mr. and Mrs. Tooru Warren Isa
Mr. and Mrs. Wayne Isa
Mr. and Mrs. Hal Ise
Mr. Gerald Iseda
Mr. and Mrs. Keiko Iseda
Betty and Carl Iseki
Col. Arthur S. Iseri
Mr. Carl Iseri
Ms. Chie Iseri
Ms. Gail Iseri
Mr. and Mrs. George Iseri
Mr. George N. Iseri
Mr. James T. Iseri
Mr. and Mrs. Joe Iseri
Ms. Kathleen Iseri
Mr. and Mrs. Mike Iseri
Ms. Minnie Iseri
Dr. Oscar Iseri
Mr. and Mrs. Richard Iseri
Mr. Ron K. Iseri
Mr. and Mrs. Akira Ishibashi
Ms. Cecilia Ishibashi
Ms. Emiko Ishibashi
Mrs. Emiko A. Ishibashi
Ms. Fumiko Ishibashi
Mr. Harold M. Ishibashi
Ms. Jane M. Ishibashi
Mr. Jon Ishibashi
Rev. and Mrs. Samuel Ishibashi
Mr. and Mrs. Shigeo Ishibashi
Mrs. Shizuye Ishibashi
Mr. and Mrs. Toshi Ishibashi
Mr. Willam A. Ishibashi
Mr. William I. Ishibashi
Ms. Yolisa Ishibashi
Mrs. Akiye Ishida
Mrs. Barbara M. Ishida
Mr. and Mrs. Bill Ishida
Mr. Brian Y. Ishida
Miss Carol Ann Ishida
Ms. Dorothy Ishida
Mr. Edward H. Ishida
Ms. Elsie Ishida
Mrs. Florence Tama Ishida
Mr. Gary Ishida
Mr. Glenn Ishida
Ms. Hiroko Ishida
Dr. and Mrs. Itaru Ishida
Mr. James Ishida
Ms. Kaye K. Ishida
Ms. Kumiko Ishida
Mr. Larry F. Ishida
Mr. Masaru Ishida
Mr. Masato Ishida
Mr. Noboru Ishida
Mr. Nobu Ishida
Mr. and Mrs. Ralph Ishida
Mr. and Mrs. Robert Ishida
Ms. Sachi Y. Ishida
Mr. and Mrs. Sodatsu Ishida
Mr. Tad Ishida
Mr. and Mrs. Tom Ishida
Ms. Yaeko Ishida
Mr. Osamu Ishido
Mr. Douglas T. Ishigaki
Mr. Harry Ishigaki
Dr. Miles Ishigaki
Mr. Shigeru Ishigaki
Ms. Kei Ishigami
Masami and Merry Ishige
Ms. Hisae Ishigo
Ms. Susumu Ishigo
Ms. Aki S. Ishiguri
Mr. and Mrs. Kitoku Ishiguro
Mr. Tadao Ishiguro
Mr. and Mrs. Masao Ishihama
Ms. Coreen Ishihara
Mr. James Ishihara
Mr. and Mrs. James T. Ishihara
Mr. Joey T. Ishihara
Mr. Masayuki Ishihara
Mr. and Mrs. Mitsuo Ishihara
Ms. Miyeko Ishihara
Ms. Robbie Ishihara
Mr. Saburo Ishihara
Ms. Shizuko Ishihara
Mr. Tack Ishihara
Mr. and Mrs. Terry Ishihara
Mr. Tosh Ishihara
Yoshiharu and Fumie Ishihara
Yoshimara Ishihara

Ms. Yumi E. Ishihara
Mrs. Alice Ishii
Anthony, Jeanette, and Michael Ishii
Ms. Bernice Ishii
Mr. Chris K. Ishii
Mr. and Mrs. Christopher S. Ishii
Mr. Clayton M. Ishii
Mr. Curtis D. Ishii
Dr. and Mrs. Edward Ishii
Mr. Erick Ishii
Mr. and Mrs. George Ishii
Mr. and Mrs. George G. Ishii
Ms. Gloria Ishii
Ms. Hatsumi Ishii
Mr. Herbert Ishii
Mr. and Mrs. James Ishii
Jan K. and Barbara Ishii
Ms. Jayne Ishii and Mrs. Mary Ishii
Mr. and Mrs. Joe Ishii
Mr. and Mrs. John D. Ishii
Mr. K. Ishii
Dr. Kay Ishii
Mr. Kazuko Ishii
Ms. Kimi Ishii
Ms. Kiyome Ishii
Mr. and Mrs. Les Ishii
Ms. Mary Ishii
Mr. Masaharu Ishii
Ms. Mayumi M. Ishii
Mr. Michael A. Ishii
Mr. and Mrs. Michael E. Ishii
Mr. Motomu Ishii
Mr. Paul T. Ishii
Ms. Reiko Ishii
Mr. Robert Ishii
Mr. Russell Ishii
Ms. Sachi Ishii
Mrs. Sachiko T. Ishii
Mr. Seishi Ishii
Mr. and Mrs. Stanley Ishii
Mrs. Sue S. Ishii
Mr. and Mrs. Sueo Ishii
Mr. Teruo Ishii
Mr. and Mrs. Tom Ishii
Mr. and Mrs. Walter Ishii
Mr. Yoshio Ishii
Mr. and Mrs. Alan Ishikawa
Mrs. Bernice M. Ishikawa
Mr. Calvin Ishikawa
Ms. Carol Lee Ishikawa
Mr. Donald Ishikawa
Mr. Emerick Ishikawa
Ms. Emi Ishikawa
Ms. Emiko Ishikawa
Mr. George Ishikawa
Mr. John Ishikawa
Mrs. Keiko Ishikawa
Mr. Lawrence Ishikawa
Ms. Machiko Ishikawa
Mrs. Margaret Ishikawa
Mr. Mas Ishikawa
Ms. Michiko Ishikawa
Ms. Moffet Ishikawa
Mr. Paul J. Ishikawa
Mr. Robert T. Ishikawa
Ms. Ruby Ishikawa
Mr. Woodrow Ishikawa
Mr. and Mrs. Yoshiro Ishikawa
Ms. Yuri Ishikawa
Ms. Chiyoko Ishiki
Mr. James Ishiki
Mr. Takeo Ishiki
Mr. Thomas Ishiki
Ms. Amy M. Ishima
Mrs. Betty Ishima
Ms. Chizuko Mary Ishimaru
Mr. and Mrs. Gary K. Ishimaru
Mr. and Mrs. Kent Ishimaru
Mr. and Mrs. Kenzo Ishimaru
Mr. and Mrs. Lloyd Ishimaru
Mr. and Mrs. Mikio Ishimaru
Mr. and Mrs. Richard Ishimaru
Mr. Richard K. Ishimaru
Mr. Robert Ishimatsu
Mr. Warren Ishimi
Mr. Hideo Ishimine
Mrs. Kichio K. Ishimitsu
Mr. Michael Ishimitsu
Mr. and Mrs. Richard Ishimitsu
Mr. Bill Ishimoto
Ms. Diane M. Ishimoto
Ms. Doreen Ishimoto
Mr. Guy K. Ishimoto
Mr. Herbert Ishimoto
Ms. Janet L. Ishimoto
Dr. and Mrs. Kenneth S. Ishimoto

Ms. Kimiye Ishimoto
Mr. Masao Ishimoto
Ms. May Ishimoto
Mr. and Mrs. Roger A. Ishimoto
Mr. and Mrs. Stan Ishimoto
Mr. and Mrs. Stephen Ishimoto
Mr. Wade Y. Ishimoto
Mr. Craig Ishino
Mrs. Eleanor J. Ishino
Mr. and Mrs. Iwao Ishino
Mr. and Mrs. Jerry Ishino
Mr. Joe Ishino
Mr. Roy Y. Ishino
Mr. Tracy Ishino
Ms. Catherine S. Ishioka
Mr. George Ishioka
Mr. John Ishioka
Ms. Masako Ishioka
Mr. Rodney S. Ishioka
Mr. Denis Ishisaka
Mr. and Mrs. Giichi Ishisaka
Ms. Marge D. Ishisaka
Mr. Morris Ishisaka
Mr. Ted Ishisaka
Mr. Marc Ishisaka-Nolfi
J. T. Ishisaki
Ms. Denise Ishitani
Mr. Jack Ishitani
Mr. James Ishitani
Ms. Janis K. Ishitani
Mr. Ted Ishiwari
Haruko Ishiyama
Mr. Richard K. Ishiyama
Mr. and Mrs. Toaru Ishiyama
Mr. Gregory M. Ishizaki
Mr. and Mrs. Henry Ishizaki
Mr. Sean E. Ishizaki
Ms. Catherine Sakaye Ishizawa
Mr. James S. Ishizawa
Mr. Hachiro Ishizu
Mr. and Mrs. Sakae Ishizu
Ms. Shigeko Ishizu
Dr. and Mrs. Kenneth Ishizue
Dr. Kenneth K. Ishizue
Mr. and Mrs. Seiso Ishizue
Ms. Joanne Ishizuka
Mr. Mozart H. Ishizuka
Ms. Patricia Ishizuka
Mr. and Mrs. Tadayoshi Ishizuka
Mr. Yoshizo Ishizuka
Ms. Yuriko Ishizuka
Isla Vista Bookstore
Mrs. Tomiko Ismail
Mr. Kazuaki Iso
Mr. Craig T. Isobe
Mr. David M. Isobe
Mr. Gary G. Isobe
Mr. Henry U. Isobe
Mr. Robert N. Isobe
Mr. and Mrs. Sadashi Isoda
Mr. and Mrs. Seishi Isoda
Mr. Masaharu Isogai
Mr. Frank Isogawa
Mr. and Mrs. Hiroshi Isogawa
Mr. Robert K. Isokane
Mr. Leonard Isomura
Ms. Chito Isonaga
Mr. James Isono
Mr. and Mrs. Kay Isono
Mr. Larry Isono
Mr. Lawrence Isono
Dr. Steven S. Isono
Ms. Marjorie Isozaki
Mrs. Yukiko J. Israel
Mr. George M. Itagaki
Mr. and Mrs. John Itagaki
Mrs. Minnie Itaki
Mr. Yuuichi Itakura
Mr. Daniel Itami
Mr. Henry Itami
Mr. Jefferson Itami
Mr. Jim Itami
Mr. Alfred Y. Itamura
Mr. and Mrs. Roy Itamura
Mr. and Mrs. Sadao Itamura
Ms. Chiyoko S. Itanaga
Ms. Roberta T. Itani
Mr. David Itano
Mr. and Mrs. Frank Itano
Mr. and Mrs. Glenn Itano
Mr. T.D. Itano
Mr. and Mrs. Tak Itano
Mr. and Mrs. H. Itatani
Mr. Robert Itatani
Mr. Frank Y. Itaya
Mr. and Mrs. Yoshio Ted Itaya

Mr. Ben S. Ito
Mr. Bill Ito
Brian M. Ito and Laura K. Sameshima
Miss. Chiyeko Ito
Mr. and Mrs. Dan Ito
Mr. and Mrs. Donald Y. Ito
Ms. Frances Ito
Mr. and Mrs. Frank K. Ito
Ms. Fukiko Ito
Mrs. Fumiko Ito
Mr. and Mrs. George T. Ito
Mr. and Mrs. Gerald Ito
Mr. and Mrs. Gordon Ito
Mr. and Mrs. Harley Ito
Ms. Hazel Ito
Mr. Henry Ito
Mr. Hidemi Ito
Mr. Hiroshi Ito
Hisa Ito
Ichiro and Florence Ito
Mr. Ichiro Ito
Ms. Ikuko Ito
Mr. Isami Ito
Mr. James G. Ito
Mr. and Mrs. James O. Ito
Mr. James T. Ito
Mr. and Mrs. John K. Ito
Mr. Kenichi Ito
Mr. and Mrs. Kenji Ito
Mr. Kenji Ito
Ms. Kerry Ito
Dr. Kinko Ito
Ms. Kiyoshi Ito
Mr. and Mrs. Kow Ito
Mr. and Mrs. Lander Ito
Mr. and Mrs. Masaji Ito
Mr. and Mrs. Masaru Ito
Ms. Michiko Ito
Mr. Muneo Ito
Mr. and Mrs. Paul Ito
Mr. and Mrs. Robert Ito
Dr. Ron K. Ito
Mr. and Mrs. Sam I. Ito
Mr. Sam O. Ito
Mr. Satoshi Ito
Mr. and Mrs. Satoshi Ito
Dr. and Mrs. Setsuo Ito
Ms. Shelley Ito
Mr. and Mrs. Shigeo Ito
Mrs. Shigeto Ito
Mr. and Mrs. Shinji Ito
Ms. Shizue Ito
Mr. Shuichi Ito
Mr. Shunji Ito
Mr. Shuzi Ito
Mr. and Mrs. Steven Ito
Mr. and Mrs. Sueo Ito
Mr. and Mrs. Tadao Ito
Mr. and Mrs. Takao Ito
Takashi Ito
Mr. Tamotsu Tom Ito
Mr. and Mrs. Thomas Ito
Mr. Thomas I. Ito
Mr. and Mrs. Tomi Ito
Mr. and Mrs. Tomio Ito
Mr. Victor N. Ito
Ms. Violet Ito
Ms. Virginia Ito
Mr. and Mrs. Walter R. Ito
Mr. and Mrs. Y. Marvin Ito
Ms. Yaeko Ito
Ms. Yasuko Ito
Mr. and Mrs. Yasushi Ito
Mrs. Yone Ito
Mr. Yoshio Ito
Mr. and Mrs. John Y. Itoda
Mr. Harvey Itogawa
Ms. Eiko Itoh
Mr. and Mrs. Henry Itoi
Mrs. Lily Itokazu
Taeko Itokazu
Mr. and Mrs. Kenjo Itoku
Mr. and Mrs. Clifford Itomitsu
Mrs. Patricia Itomitus
Mrs. Lisa M. Itomura
Ms. Pauline Itow
Mrs. Yoneko J. Itow
Mr. and Mrs. Tadashi Iura
Mr. Iver R. Iversen
Mr. Richard P. Iverson
Mr. and Mrs. Katsutoshi Iwagoshi
Mr. and Mrs. Donald K. Iwahashi
Mr. George Iwahashi
Mr. and Mrs. Michio Iwahashi
Mr. and Mrs. Tom Iwahashi
Mr. Toshiyuki Iwahashi

Mr. and Mrs. Wayne S. Iwahashi
Mr. and Mrs. Michael K. Iwahiro
Mr. and Mrs. Shoji Iwahiro
Mr. Derek Iwai
Mr. Gary Y. Iwai
Mr. George Hitoshi Iwai
Mr. and Mrs. George Iwai
Mr. James K. Iwai
Mr. and Mrs. James Y. Iwai
Mr. John H. Iwai
Mr. and Mrs. Kaz Iwai
Mr. Michio Iwai
Mr. and Mrs. Robert Iwai
Mr. and Mrs. Shiro Iwai
Mr. Thomas Iwai
Mr. and Mrs. Tokuji Iwai
Mr. and Mrs. Wilfred Iwai
Dr. Margaret Iwai-Ey
Ms. Reiko Abby Iwaihara
Mr. and Mrs. Alan M. Iwaishi
Ms. Miyuki Iwaki
Mr. Mori M. Iwaki
Mr. Toshi J. Iwaki
Mr. Alfred Iwamasa
Dr. Gayle Y. Iwamasa
Mr. and Mrs. Gilbert H. Iwamasa
Mr. Craig Iwami
Mr. and Mrs. Hideo C. Iwami
Mr. and Mrs. Hisao Iwami
Mr. and Mrs. James Iwami
Mr. Wilbert S. Iwami
Mr. William D. Iwami
Ms. Cassandra Iwamiya
Mr. and Mrs. George Iwamiya
Mr. and Mrs. Tom Iwamiya
Mr. and Mrs. Akio Iwamoto
Mr. Bruce Iwamoto
Ms. Carrolyn Iwamoto
Mr. and Mrs. Charles M. Iwamoto
Mr. and Mrs. Daniel Iwamoto
Mr. Douglas Iwamoto
Rev. and Mrs. Edward Iwamoto
Ms. Florence N. Iwamoto
Mr. and Mrs. George Iwamoto
Mr. and Mrs. Harry Iwamoto
Mr. Hiroshi Iwamoto
Mr. James T. Iwamoto
Ms. Jani Iwamoto
Mr. Jerry Iwamoto
Mr. Kichiro Iwamoto
Kumiko Iwamoto
Mr. Lance K. Iwamoto
Ms. Lorraine Iwamoto
Ms. Lucille Iwamoto
Ms. Lynn Iwamoto
Mr. Masaru R. Iwamoto
Ms. Michiko Iwamoto
Mr. and Mrs. Raymond K. Iwamoto
Mr. Richard H. Iwamoto
Mr. and Mrs. Richard T. Iwamoto
Mr. Robert Iwamoto
Mr. Shigeru Iwamoto
Mr. and Mrs. Shigeru Iwamoto
Mr. and Mrs. Stanley Iwamoto
Mr. and Mrs. Takeo Iwamoto
Mr. and Mrs. Tomio Iwamoto
Mrs. Toshiko Iwamoto
Mr. and Mrs. Wallace Iwamoto
Mr. Yoshito Iwamoto
Mr. and Mrs. Akira Iwamura
Mr. James Iwamura
Mr. S. Iwamura
Ms. Sandra M. Iwamura
Mr. Warren Iwamura
Mr. Robert M. Iwamuro
Ms. Fumiye Iwana
Mr. and Mrs. Saburo Iwana
Mr. Shiro Iwana
Mr. Robert Hideo Iwanabe
Ms. Adrienne Reiko Iwanaga
Mr. and Mrs. Aki Iwanaga
Mr. Carl Iwanaga
Courtney and Ashley Iwanaga
Mr. and Mrs. Dan Iwanaga
Mr. Douglas G. Iwanaga
Dr. George Iwanaga
Mr. George S. Iwanaga
Mr. Henry Iwanaga
Mr. Michael Iwanaga
Mr. Paul Iwanaga
Ryan Iwanaga Family
Ms. Teri Iwanaga
Ms. Yoshie N. Iwanaga
Ms. Elizabeth Iwano
Mr. Joseph H. Iwano
Mr. Eddie Iwao

Mr. Kumiy Roy Iwao
Ms. Ellyn J. Iwaoka
Mr. and Mrs. Joe Iwaoka
Mr. John J. Iwaoka
Ms. Judy Iwaoka
Ms. Molly M. Iwaoka
Drs. Robert and Elizabeth Iwaoka
Mr. and Mrs. Tom Iwaoka
Mr. Dean H. Iwasa
Ms. Hisako Iwasa
Mr. and Mrs. Walter Iwasa
Ms. Yasuko Iwasa
Mr. and Mrs. Yoshio Iwasa
Mr. Ryan Iwasaka
Mr. Toshiyuki Iwasaka
Mr. and Mrs. Carl Iwasaki
Mrs. Christi Iwasaki
Mr. and Mrs. Dean Iwasaki
Ms. Dorothy Iwasaki
Ms. Ellen L. Iwasaki
George, Sylvia, Jennifer and Keith Iwasaki
Ms. Helen H. Iwasaki
Ms. Irene Iwasaki
Mr. and Mrs. Isamu Iwasaki
Ms. Joni Iwasaki
Ms. Joyce Iwasaki
Mr. Kenneth Iwasaki
Larry and Midori Iwasaki
Mrs. Marjorie S. Iwasaki
Mr. Mike Kojiro Iwasaki
Mr. and Mrs. Norman Iwasaki
Mrs. Pamela T. Iwasaki
Mr. and Mrs. Rich Iwasaki
Mr. and Mrs. Robert Iwasaki
Mr. Robert K. Iwasaki
Mr. Ronald Iwasaki
Mr. and Mrs. Satoru Iwasaki
Mr. Shig Iwasaki
Mr. Tadao Iwasaki
Mr. Tadashi Iwasaki
Mr. Thomas K. Iwasaki
Mr. Ken K. Iwashika
Mrs. Alice H. Iwashita
Mr. Harold T. Iwashita
Mr. Haruo Iwashita
Mr. John Iwashita
Mr. and Mrs. Tadashi Iwashita
Ms. Akiko Iwata
Mr. Akira Iwata
Mrs. Annita Iwata
Dr. Chris H. Iwata
Mrs. Doreen Iwata
Mr. Frank T. Iwata
Mr. and Mrs. Harry M. Iwata
Mr. Harry T. Iwata
Mr. and Mrs. Harvey Iwata
Mr. Hideo Iwata
Mr. Himeo Iwata
Mr. and Mrs. Ira G. Iwata
Mr. and Mrs. Jae Iwata
Ms. Jane S. Iwata
Mr. and Mrs. Masahiro Iwata
Mrs. Midori Iwata
Ms. Miki Iwata
Ms. Peggy S. Iwata
Mr. Rick Iwata
Mr. Rodney G. Iwata
Mr. Roy T. Iwata
Ms. Sami Iwata
Mr. Samuel H. Iwata
Mr. Samuel I. Iwata
Mr. and Mrs. Stephen Iwata
Mr. Tadao T. Iwata
Mr. Toshio Iwata
Mrs. Yoko B. Iwata
Ms. Carole Iwataki
Mr. Gregory M. Iwatani
Mr. Samson Iwatani
Ms. Kazue Iwatsubo
Mrs. Sophia Iwatsubo
Ms. Kimiye Iwawaki
Mr. and Mrs. Masao Iwawaki
Mr. and Mrs. Kuniyasu Iwazaki
Mr. Shoye Iwo
Mr. Shigeo Iwohara
Mr. and Mrs. Frank Iyama
Mr. and Mrs. Donald S. Iyeki
Mr. and Mrs. Kenneth N. Iyeki
Ms. Cathy Iyemura
Ms. Mary Funamura Iyemura
Mr. Kenneth Iyenaga
Mr. Junko Iyo
Mr. and Mrs. Kunio Iyoda
Ms. May Izuhara
Mr. and Mrs. Tom M. Izuhara
Mr. Charles Izui

Mr. and Mrs. George Izui
Takino Izuka
Mr. Calvin Izumi
Ms. Carol Izumi and Mr. Frank Wu
Mr. Clyde Izumi
Ms. Dora Izumi
Mr. Frederick S. Izumi
Mr. George I. Izumi
Mr. George K. Izumi
Mr. Gerald Izumi
Ms. Jane Izumi
Mr. and Mrs. Kenneth H. Izumi
Mr. M. H. Izumi
Mr. and Mrs. Richard Izumi
Mr. and Mrs. Rick H. Izumi
Ms. Sue Izumi
Ms. Joan Izumigawa
Mr. and Mrs. Stanley Izumigawa
Ms. Amy E. Izumizaki
Mr. and Mrs. James Y. Izumizaki
Mr. and Mrs. Hideo Izumo
Ms. P. K. Izumo
Mrs. Mary M. Izuno and Family
Mr. and Mrs. Masaru Izuno
Ms. Tamako Izuno
Mr. and Mrs. Victor Izuo
Ms. Eleanor Izutsu
Mr. and Mrs. Tadami Izutsu
J. Milano Co., Inc.
J. Morey Company
JA Fellowship Society
J.A.A.R.S
JACL Arkansas Valley Chapter
JACL Carson Chapter
JACL Chicago Chapter
JACL Delano Chapter
JACL Fremont Chapter
JACL Gilroy Chapter
JACL Greater LA Singles Chapter
JACL Headquarters
JACL Houston Chapter
JACL Lake Washington Chapter
JACL Las Vegas Chapter
JACL Livington-Merced Chapter
JACL Midwest Council District
JACL New Mexico Arts and Crafts Club
JACL Pacific Northwest District
JACL Parlier Chapter
JACL San Mateo Chapter
JACL Seabrook Chapter
JACL Selanoco Chapter
JACL Selma Chapter
JACL Solano County Chapter
JACL South Bay Chapter
JACL Tulare County Chapter
JACL Twin Cities Chapter
JACL Watsonville Chapter
JAE Awards
JAVA Washington, D.C.
JETRO San Francisco
Ms. Dianne Jablon
Ms. Carol B. Jackson
Ms. Kathy Jacob
Ms. Patricia C. Jacob
Mr. Leon A. Jacobian
Mr. Norman Jacobs
Ms. Jean Jahara
Mr. James
Ms. P. Evangeline Jamison
Ms. Kathryn T. Jan
Ms. Christine Jang
Mr. and Mrs. Jeff Janousek
Japan America Society
Japan Auto Mfr Assn, Inc.
Japan Development Bank
Japan Inn, Inc.
Japan Studies Institute
Japanese American Consultants
Japanese American Fellowship Society
Japanese American Resource Center/Museum
Japanese American Senior Citizens Club
Japanese American Service Committee
Japanese American Services of the East Bay
Japanese Americans for Political Action, Inc.
Japanese Children's Society
Mr. and Mrs. Bob Jarboe
Ms. Lynette M. Jarreau
Mr. and Mrs. Thomas Jee
Jefferson County Democratic Party
Cdr. and Mrs. Melody Jeffrey
Mr. and Mrs. Kay Jeneye
Mr. Edward W. Jenkins
Mr. and Mrs. Jeff Jenks
Dr. Gwenn M. Jensen
Ms. Jane Jensen
Mr. and Mrs. George Jernstedt

Jerome Reunion V Committee
Mr. Mike Jeziorski
Mr. Jaime Jimbo
Mr. and Mrs. Dennis Jinnohara
Mr. and Mrs. Shinji Jinyama
Mr. Allan Jio
Mr. Gary D. Jio and Jo Ann Okabe-Kubo
Mr. George Jitodai
A. Jitsumyo
Dr. Daniel D. Jo
Mr. Scott Jofuku
Mr. and Mrs. Shigeyuki Jofuku
Mr. Lansing K. Johansen
Ms. Carmen Johnson
Ms. Jeannette Goya Johnson and Mr. Ian Capps
Mr. Joseph F. Johnson
Ms. Karla Johnson and Ms. Judy Thomas
Ms. Kimi S. Johnson
Ms. Linda D. Johnson
Mr. Nick Johnson
Mr. Reuben Johnson
Ms. Wilda N. Johnson
Mr. Paul Joichi
Ms. Bessie Joko
Mr. and Mrs. Todd Joko
Mr. Yuri Joko
Ms. Eleanor M. Jones
Mrs. Jenn R. Jones
Mr. and Mrs. Phillip Jones
Mr. and Mrs. Stanley Jones
Ms. Suzy M. Jones
Ms. D. Misa Joo
Mr. and Mrs. Gary Joseff
Mr. Charles E. Joseph
Mr. Rose Jow
Ms. Rita Judd
Mr. Albert H. Jung
Mr. and Mrs. James W. Junker
Mr. and Mrs. Kunio Jyoda
Mr. Harry M. Jyono
K & K Mason Stone Supply, Inc.
KASHO (USA), Inc.
Mr. Masao Kabashima
Ms. Carol Kabat
Mrs. Shizuko O. Kabei
Kabuki Enterprise, Inc.
Mr. and Mrs. Jack Kabumoto
Ms. Cynthia Kada
Ms. Kiyoko Kadani
Mrs. Betty Kadekawa
Mr. and Mrs. Joseph Kado
Ms. Mildred Kado
Mr. Richard Kado
Mrs. Susan Y. Kado
Ayako and Kazuko Kadogawa
Mr. and Mrs. Hiroshi Kadogawa
Ms. Miyako N. Kadogawa
Ms. Motoyo Kadohata
Ms. Hatsune Kadoi
Mr. and Mrs. Hideo Kadokawa
Mr. Hiroshi Kadokura
Mr. Masao Kadomatsu
Mr. and Mrs. George Kadonaga
Dr. and Mrs. James Takuro Kadonaga
Mr. and Mrs. Shoichi Kadonaga
Dr. Tadashi Kadonaga
Mr. Tetsuo Kadonaga
Mr. and Mrs. Yuwao Kadonaga
Mr. and Mrs. Skip Kadooka
Mr. Gary Kadota
Mr. and Mrs. Harry S. Kadota
Mr. Kenneth K. Kadotani
Dr. and Mrs. Barry Kadowaki
Mr. and Mrs. James T. Kadowaki
Mr. Joe G. Kadowaki
Mr. and Mrs. Ken Kadowaki
Ms. Sally S. Kadowaki
Ms. Yuki Kadowaki
Sachiko Kagami
Mr. and Mrs. William Kagami
Mr. Doug Kagawa
Mr. and Mrs. Gary Kagawa
Mr. George M. Kagawa
George and Lily Kagawa
Mr. and Mrs. Henry Kagawa
Mr. Mark S. Kagawa
Ruben and Phyllis Kagawa
Mr. Seigo Kagawa
Mr. T. Kagawa
Mr. and Mrs. Tadashi Kagawa
Mr. Takeo Kagawa
Mr. Ted Kagawa
Mr. William Kagawa
Mr. William H. Kagawa
Yoshiki and June Kagawa
Mr. Kazuo Kage

Ms. Elsie Kagehiro
Mr. and Mrs. Goro Kagehiro
Mr. Mitsuo Kagehiro
Mr. and Mrs. Satoru Kagehiro
Mr. Yoshino Kagehiro
Mr. Herbert Kagemoto
Mr. Stuart H. Kageta
Ms. Michie Kageto
Mr. and Mrs. Russell H. Kageura
Ms. Adele Kageyama
Mr. Akira Kageyama
Mr. and Mrs. Chitose Kageyama
Dr. and Mrs. Colin Kageyama
Kageyama Properties, Ltd.
Mr. and Mrs. Ken Kageyama
Ms. Lily Kageyama
Ms. Norma Kageyama
Ms. Reiko Kageyama
Mr. and Mrs. Ronald Kageyama
Mr. Wynn Kageyama
Dr. Lynette E. Kagihara
Mr. Elton Kagimoto
Mr. and Mrs. Atsushi Kagiyama
Mr. Richard H. Kagiyama
Mr. Tom Kagohara
Mr. and Mrs. Mike Kagoshima
Mr. Jack Kaguni
Mr. and Mrs. Fred S. Kai
Mr. James Kai
Miwa Kai
Mr. and Mrs. Stanley Kai
Mr. Tak Kai
Mr. Bob Kaichi
Ms. Etsu Kaida
Mr. and Mrs. Katsumi Kaida
Mr. and Mrs. Robert Kaida
Mr. and Mrs. Tatsuo Kaida
Mr. Rusty Kaihara
Mr. Omar Kaihatsu
Ms. Taeko Kaili
Ms. Thelma Kailiwai
Mr. and Mrs. Philip Kain
Mr. Frank Kaino
Mr. and Mrs. Arthur Kaisaki
Mr. Edward Kaita
Mr. and Mrs. Noboru Kaita
Mr. Shigeru Kaita
Mr. Ben Kaito
Mr. and Mrs. Walter Kaiura
Mr. and Mrs. Carl K. Kaizawa
Mr. Stanley Kaizawa
Mr. Masaru Kaizu
Mr. and Mrs. Hubei Kaji
Mr. and Mrs. Hugo Kaji
Mr. Melvin Kaji
Mr. and Mrs. Henry Kajihara
Mr. and Mrs. Roy Kajihara
Mr. and Mrs. Clarence F. Kajikawa
Mr. Frank M. Kajikawa
Mr. Lloyd T. Kajikawa
Ms. Takemi Kajikawa
Mr. William Kajikawa
Mr. Darrell K. Kajioka
Ms. Hitoshi Kajioka
Ms. Grace Kajita
Ms. Grace M. Kajita
Ms. Janis H. Kajita
Mr. Akira Kajitani
Ms. Iko Kajitani
Mr. and Mrs. Buichi Kajiwara
Mr. and Mrs. Clifford Kajiwara
Mr. Douglas Kajiwara
Mr. Edward I. Kajiwara
Mr. and Mrs. Etsue Kajiwara
Mr. and Mrs. George Kajiwara
Mr. and Mrs. George S. Kajiwara
Mr. Glenn Kajiwara and
Mrs. Colette Miyamoto-Kajiwara
Mr. and Mrs. Kenneth Kajiwara
Mr. Ronald Kajiwara
Ms. Sachi Kajiwara
Mr. Takamasa Kajiwara
Mr. and Mrs. Ken Kajiya
Mr. Clifford K. Kajiyama
Mr. Joe Kakazu
Mr. Reginald S. Kakazu
Mr. Samuel Y. Kakazu
Ms. Stella Kakazu
Mr. Yoshio Kakehashi
Ms. Sayoko Kakehi
Ms. Toshiye Kakigi
Mr. Dale F. Kakimoto
Ms. Jenna Kakimoto
Mr. Paul Kakimoto
Ms. Dana Kakishita
Ms. Chiz C. Kakita

Mr. and Mrs. George Kakita
Mr. Kris T. Kakita
Mrs. Lilly Y. Kakita
Mr. and Mrs. Kazuo Kakiuchi
Ms. Kim Kakiuchi
Ms. Naomi W. Kakiuchi
Ms. Nobuko Kakiuchi
Mr. and Mrs. Robert Kakiuchi
Mr. and Mrs. Andrew F. Kaku
Ms. Esther Kaku
Mr. Haruo Kaku
Mr. and Mrs. Hideo D. Kaku
Mr. Isao Kaku
Mr. and Mrs. Keige Kaku
Mr. Leonard Kaku
Mr. Michio Kaku
Mr. Noboru M. Kaku
Stanley, Alice, Kimberlee and Shawn Kaku
Mr. Yoshio Kaku
Mrs. Yuriko Kaku
Mr. Joe Kakude
Mr. Keiichi Kakuda
Mr. Yutaka Kakugawa
Mr. and Mrs. Gene W. Kallsen
Ms. Allison M. Kaluza
Ms. Aiko Kamada
Mr. Carey K. Kamada
Mr. George Kamada
Mr. and Mrs. Herbert Kamada
Mrs. Mitsuye Kamada
Dr. Satoshi Kamada
Rev. Clarence K. Kamai
Mr. Kenneth A. Kamakura
Mr. Gary Kamatani
Mr. and Mrs. Masaru Kamatani
Mr. and Mrs. Edward Kamaura
Mr. Masayuki Kamaura
Mr. Wayne Kamaura
Dr. Andrew Kambara
Dr. George K. Kambara
Mr. George Kambe
Dr. and Mrs. Minao Kamegai
Dr. Asao Kamei
Mr. and Mrs. Hiroshi Kamei
Mr. Ichiro Kamei
Dr. and Mrs. Jerry Kamei
Ms. Midori Watanabe Kamei
Mr. and Mrs. Toshio Kamei
Mr. and Mrs. Yoshimi Kamei
Mr. Ed Kamemoto
Mr. and Mrs. H. Kamemoto
Dr. Lori E. Kamemoto
Mr. and Mrs. Stanley Y. Kamemoto
Mr. and Mrs. Bob Kameoka
Dr. and Mrs. Haruo Kameoka
Ms. Lynn Kameoka
Mr. Kazuya Kametani
Mr. Thomas Kametani
Mr. Andrew Kameya
Mr. and Mrs. Warren Kameyama
Mr. Dale K. Kamibayashi
Ms. Mary Kamidoi
Mr. Wayne Kamidoi
Mr. and Mrs. Carmel Kamigawachi
Ms. June S. Kamigawachi
Mr. and Mrs. James Kamihachi
Mr. and Mrs. Arthur Kamii
Ben and May Kamikawa
Ms. Emi Kamikawa
Mr. and Mrs. Harry Kamikawa
Mr. and Mrs. Joe Kamikawa
Mr. and Mrs. Joseph Kamikawa
Mr. Juichi Kamikawa
Mr. and Mrs. Masao Kamikawa
Ms. Melanie M. Kamikawa
Mr. Tommy K. Kamikawa
Mr. Yoshito Kamikawa
Ms. Lily Kamikihara
Mr. and Mrs. Jim Kamimoto
Mr. Koyuki Kamimoto
Mr. and Mrs. Sho Kamimoto
Ms. Carol M. Kamimura
Mr. Charles M. Kamimura
Mr. and Mrs. Charles S. Kamimura
Mr. and Mrs. Kenneth Kamimura
Kunito Kamimura
Mr. Frank Kamino
Mr. Ichiro Kamisako
Dr. Javier Kamisato
Ms. Toshiko Kamishita
Mr. and Mrs. Henry Kamisugi
Mrs. Judy Kamisugi
Dr. and Mrs. Michael Kamitsuka
Mr. and Mrs. Akira Kamiya
Mr. and Mrs. Eiichi Kamiya
Mr. George S. Kamiya

Mr. and Mrs. James K. Kamiya
Mr. Kenji Kamiya
Kenneth M. and Kristine M. Kamiya
Mr. Mark A. Kamiya
Mr. Tsukasa Kamiya
Mr. Yoshio Kamiya
Ms. Emi E. Kamiyama
Mr. and Mrs. Wesley Kamiyama
Mr. and Mrs. Roy Kamo
Ms. Julia Kamura
Mrs. June J. Kan
Dr. and Mrs. Daniel J. Kanada
Ms. Evelyn Kanada
Mr. Kay Kanagaki
Mr. and Mrs. Kin Kanagaki
Mr. and Mrs. Dallas Kanagawa
Mr. and Mrs. Wayne Y. Kanagawa
Ms. Grace Kanai
Jewel M. Kanai and Walter Zattera
Mr. Masao Kanai
Mr. and Mrs. Sam Kanai
Mr. Scott Kanai
Mrs. Shigeru Kanai
Mr. Minoru Kanaki
Ms. Katherine Kanamori
Ms. Mary Kanashiro
Mr. and Mrs. Douglas Kanaya
Mr. Duane Kanaya
Mr. Kimio Kanaya
Mr. and Mrs. Richard K. Kanayama
Mr. Richard T. Kanayama
Mr. Yoshimasa Kanayama
Mr. Clyde Kanazawa
Mr. and Mrs. Henry Kanazawa
Mr. Jay Kanazawa
Mr. and Mrs. Tooru Kanazawa
Ms. Teruko Kanba
Mr. Calvin Kanda
Mr. and Mrs. Craig Kanda
Mr. and Mrs. Harry Kanda
Mr. Harry K. Kanda
Mr. and Mrs. John Kanda
Mr. John S. Kanda
Master Justin-Thomas Shinkichi Kanda
Dr. and Mrs. Masami Kanda
Mr. Minoru Kanda
Ms. Miyoko Kanda
Ms. Phyllis M. Kanda
Ms. Rose Kanda
Mr. Shigeo Kanda
Dr. Tadahito Kanda
Mr. Tedi N. Kanda
Mr. Yukio Kanda
Mr. Yoshio Kanechika
Mr. Frank N. Kaneda
Mr. Kay K. Kaneda
Mr. Roy S. Kaneda
S. Kaneda
Mr. Thomas T. Kanegai
Mr. and Mrs. Hiroshi Kanegawa
Mr. Shuzo B. Kanegawa
Ms. Rosalie Kanehira
Mr. Charles Kanehiro
Mr. Raymond Kanehiro
Ms. Sayeko Kaneishi
Mr. and Mrs. Arthur M. Kaneko
Mr. Edwin T. Kaneko
Ms. Elizabeth M. Kaneko
Mrs. Emiko Kaneko
Mr. Frank M. Kaneko
Mr. George I. Kaneko
Mr. and Mrs. Jim Kaneko
Mr. and Mrs. John Kaneko
Ms. Judy Kaneko
Koichi Kaneko
Mr. and Mrs. Larry H. Kaneko
Mr. Masamitsu Kaneko
Dr. Maureen M. Kaneko
Mr. Michio Kaneko
Mr. Mike Kaneko
Mr. and Mrs. Paul T. Kaneko
Mr. and Mrs. Robert M. Kaneko
Mr. and Mrs. Robert Y. Kaneko
Ms. Sue Kaneko
Mr. and Mrs. Takeo Kaneko
Ms. Vickie Kaneko
Mr. Wayne Kaneko
Mr. and Mrs. Isamu Kanekuni
Mr. Morris S. Kanekuni
Mr. Arthur Kanemaru
Mr. Donald K. Kanemaru
Ms. Kimi Kanemasu
Russell and Jill Kanemasu and Family
Mr. Wayne T. Kanemasu
Mr. Edward Kanemori
Mr. and Mrs. James Kanemori

Dr. Scott F. Kanemori
Mr. and Mrs. Shoso Kanemori
Mrs. Yoshi Kanemori
Ms. Amy E. Kanemoto
Mr. Fumio Kanemoto
Mr. Gary Kanemoto
Mr. Gene K. Kanemoto
Ms. Hatsuko Kanemoto
Mr. and Mrs. Howard Kanemoto
Mr. and Mrs. Kenneth Kanemoto
Mr. Kenzo Kanemoto
Mr. and Mrs. Michael Kanemoto
Mr. Randall K. Kanemoto
Mrs. Sandra M. Kanemoto
Tadaji Kanemoto and Fred Katayama
Mr. and Mrs. Tadashi Kanemoto
Mr. and Mrs. Wayne Kanemoto
Mr. and Mrs. Yutaka Kanemoto
Mr. Gary K. Kanemura
Mr. and Mrs. Robert Kanemura
Mr. S. Kanenaka
Mr. Manabu Kanesaka
Mr. Byron Kaneshige
Mr. George T. Kaneshige
Mr. and Mrs. Hayami Kaneshige
Mr. John T. Kaneshige
Mr. and Mrs. Lloyd Kaneshige
Mr. and Mrs. Norman Kaneshige
Mr. and Mrs. Robert S. Kaneshige
Mr. Susumu Kaneshige
Ms. Emiko E. Kaneshiki
Mr. and Mrs. Roy Kaneshina
Mr. Calvin M. Kaneshiro
Mr. David Kaneshiro
Mr. Denko Kaneshiro
Mr. Duane K. Kaneshiro
Mr. Fred Kaneshiro
Mr. Harry Kaneshiro
Mr. Herbert S. Kaneshiro
Mr. Isamu Kaneshiro
Mr. and Mrs. Jerry Y. Kaneshiro
Mrs. Kazumi Kaneshiro
Mr. Kazuo R. Kaneshiro
Mr. Kenei Kaneshiro
Mr. and Mrs. Kenneth K. Kaneshiro
Mr. Kenneth M. Kaneshiro
Mr. Lance U. Kaneshiro
Mr. Leslie Y. Kaneshiro
Mr. Lincoln H. Kaneshiro
Mrs. Lorraine L. Kaneshiro
Ms. Masako Kaneshiro
Mr. Maurice M. Kaneshiro
Mr. Paul K. Kaneshiro
Mr. Paul M. Kaneshiro
Mr. Robert Kaneshiro
Mr. and Mrs. Roy Kaneshiro
Mr. Shigeru Kaneshiro
Mr. Stanley K. Kaneshiro
Mr. Tom I. Kaneshiro
Mr. Wesley Kaneshiro
Miss Miyoko Kaneta
Ms. May Y. Kaneta-Ikeda
Mr. and Mrs. Chester Kaneyuki
Mr. and Mrs. Paul Kaneyuki
Mr. and Mrs. John Kanki
Mr. and Mrs. John S. Kanno
Ms. Janet Kanno-Newton
Mr. Hiroyuki Kano
Mr. and Mrs. John Kano
Mr. and Mrs. Kent Kano
Mrs. Michiko Kano
Ms. Lori Kanogawa
Mrs. Agnes H. Kanow
Ms. Hisako Kanow
Ms. May Kanow
Mr. and Mrs. Miyoshi Kansaki
Mr. and Mrs. Albert Kanzaki
Mr. Frank Kanzaki
Mr. Stanley N. Kanzaki
Mr. and Mrs. Tsutomu Kanzaki
Ms. Yoneko Kanzaki
Higashi-Nihon Fresh Bakery Sys
Mr. Yukiya Kanzaki
Mr. Sanji Kanzawa
Mr. Alan M. Kaplan
Mr. and Mrs. David S. Kaplan
Mrs. Dolly Shimizu Kaplan
Mr. and Mrs. Elliot Kaplan
Mr. William T. Kaplan
Mr. and Mrs. Susumu Karaki
Chiemi Karasawa
Mr. and Mrs. Richard Y. Karasawa
Mr. and Mrs. George Karatsu
Dr. and Mrs. Hideo Karatsu
Ms. Jane Karatsu
Mr. Allan Karimoto

Mr. Roy S. Karimoto
Ms. Machiko Karino
Mr. Brian Kariya
Mr. Bruce Kariya
Ms. Cheryl S. Kariya
Mr. Hisashi Kariya
Mr. James P. Kariya
Mr. Kent S. Kariya
Mr. Kikuo Kariya
Ms. Laura Kariya
Mr. and Mrs. Minoru Kariya
Mr. Ray Kariya
Ms. Suzanne Kariya
Mr. and Mrs. Yoneo Kariya
Mr. and Mrs. Jisaburo Kasa
Ms. Susan Kasa
Mr. Akira Kasahara
Mr. Henry Kasahara
Mr. Kiyoshi Kasahara
Mr. and Mrs. Masahiro Kasahara
Ms. Noriko Kasahara
Ms. Shizuko R. Kasahara
Mr. and Mrs. George Kasai
Mr. and Mrs. George S. Kasai
Mr. and Mrs. Glenn K. Kasai
Mr. and Mrs. Haruo Kasai
Ms. Hideko Kasai
Mr. and Mrs. Hideo Kasai
Mr. and Mrs. Hugh Kasai
Ms. Kimi Kasai
Mr. Kiyoshi Kasai
Mr. and Mrs. Seiko Kasai
Mr. Taro Kasai
Mr. and Mrs. Tokio Kasai
Mr. and Mrs. Tosh Kasai
Mr. and Mrs. Yo Kasai
Mr. Felix S. Kasamatsu
Ms. Fumiko Kasamatsu
Mr. Takuji T. Kasamatsu
Ms. Alice Kase
Mr. and Mrs. Matthew Kaseda
Mr. and Mrs. Paul Kaseguma
Mr. Mack Kashaba
Mr. Tom T. Kashi
Mr. and Mrs. Jack Y. Kashihara
Mr. and Mrs. John Kashiki
Mrs. Eugenia Kashima
Mr. Henry M. Kashima
Mr. and Mrs. Hideyoshi Kashima
Mr. Kenn Kashima
Ms. Sara R. Kashima
Ms. Beverly Kashino
Mr. Paul S. Kashitani
Ms. Ann Kashiwa
Ms. Himeko Kashiwabara
Mr. Merrill Kashiwabara
Mr. and Mrs. Naomi Kashiwabara
Mr. Tadashi Kashiwabara
Mr. Thomas Kashiwabara
Mr. and Mrs. Harry Kashiwada
Mr. Richard B. Kashiwaeda
Mr. Alan S. Kashiwagi
Mr. and Mrs. Jim Kashiwagi
Mr. Masao Kashiwagi
Mr. and Mrs. Robert I. Kashiwagi
Ms. Tomoko E. Kashiwagi and Tadashi Sakuma
Mr. Fred Y. Kashiwahara
Mr. and Mrs. Earnest Kashiwase
Mr. and Mrs. Paul J. Kashiwase
Mr. and Mrs. William Kashiwase
Mr. Bill Kashiwazaki
Mr. John Kasubuchi
Mr. and Mrs. Joe Kasuga
Mr. Kazumi Kasuga
Mr. and Mrs. Ken Kasukabe
Mr. Tom H. Katada
Mr. and Mrs. Rodney H. Katagihara
Mr. Joe Katagiri
Mr. Joe M. Katagiri
Mr. and Mrs. Michael Katagiri
Ms. Nobu Katagiri
Mr. George Katahira
Ms. Grace Katahira
Mr. and Mrs. Ken Katahira
Mr. Russell Katahira and Ms. Claudette Rasmussen
Mr. George Katai
Mr. and Mrs. Frank Katakura
Ms. Dorothy Katano
Mr. and Mrs. Joe Katano
Ms. Kaneko Katano
Mr. Paul H. Katano
Dr. Sam Katano
Mr. George T. Kataoka
Mr. Jerry Kataoka
Mr. and Mrs. Jiro Kataoka
Mr. and Mrs. Joe K. Kataoka

Ms. Kiyoko Kataoka
Ms. Lily Kataoka
Mr. Masamichi Kataoka
Mrs. Nan Kataoka
Ms. Naoko Kataoka
Mr. Patrick Kataoka
Mr. Yoichi Kataoka
Mr. and Mrs. Satoshi Kataoko
Mr. and Mrs. Ben Katayama
Mr. and Mrs. Chester Katayama
Miss Fay S. Katayama
Mr. and Mrs. Fred Katayama
Mr. Jerry J. Katayama
Mr. John Katayama
Ms. Karen Katayama
Mr. and Mrs. Ken Katayama
Mr. and Mrs. Larry T. Katayama
Mr. Mits Katayama
Dr. Paul Katayama
Mr. Robert Katayama
Ms. Rosie Katayama
Mr. Roy Katayama
Mr. and Mrs. Roy H. Katayama
Mr. Sid Katayama
Mr. and Mrs. Tad Katayama
Mr. and Mrs. Takeo Katayama
Mr. and Mrs. Terry T. Katayama
Mr. and Mrs. Michael Katayanagi
Kato Brothers
Mr. Arthur Kato
Mr. and Mrs. Benny Kato
Mr. and Mrs. Carl Kato
Mr. Darin Kato
Mr. David Kato
Ms. Diane A. Kato
Mr. and Mrs. Edward Kato
Mr. and Mrs. Edward E. Kato
Mr. Edward T. Kato
Ms. Eiko Kato
Ms. Florence Kato
Mr. Fukuo Kato
Ms. Fumiko Kato
Mr. George Kato
Mr. and Mrs. George Kato
Mr. Glen T. Kato
Mr. Glenn R. J. Kato
Ms. Hana Kato
Miss Hannah K. Kato
Mr. and Mrs. Harry Kato
Mr. and Mrs. Hawley H. Kato
Mr. and Mrs. Henry Kato
Mr. and Mrs. Howard T. Kato
Mr. James K. Kato
Mr. and Mrs. Jiro Kato
Mr. and Mrs. Jon Kato
Mr. Junzo Kato
Mr. Kazuhiko Kato
Ms. Kazuko Kato
Mr. Kazuo Kato
Mr. and Mrs. Keith Kato
Mr. and Mrs. Keith M. Kato
Miss Kenly K. Kato
Ms. Kimiko Kato
Mr. Kiyomi Kato
Mrs. Lily Kato
Ms. Linda Kato
Ms. Louise Kato
Ms Mariko Kato
Mr. Mark Reed Kato
Ms. Mary Kato and Family
Mr. and Mrs. Mas Kato
Mr. and Mrs. Masao Kato
Mr. Masao G. Kato
Ms. Masaye Kato
Mr. Matthew A. Kato
Mr. Maurice S. Kato
Dr. Maya Kato
Mr. Mike Kato
Mr. Mineo Kato
Misao Kato
Mr. and Mrs. Mitsuto Kato
Ms. Patricia Kato
Ms. Phyllis Kato
Mr. and Mrs. Richard Kato
Mr. and Mrs. Robert B. Kato
Mr. Robert M. Kato
Mr. Robert Y. Kato
Sachie Kato
Mr. and Mrs. Sam F. Kato
Mr. Shigeyuki Kato
Ms. Susan K. Kato
Mr. and Mrs. Tadashi Kato
Mr. and Mrs. Taira Kato
Mr. and Mrs. Tak Kato
Mr. Takashi Kato
Mrs. Tama Kato

Mr. Teruaki Kato
Mr. Toshio Kato
Mr. Wade S. Kato
Mr. and Mrs. Wayne N. Kato
Ms. Waynna Kato
Mr. Yoshio Kato
Mr. and Mrs. Yoshio Kato
Mr. and Mrs. Yukio Kato
Mr. and Mrs. Yusei Kato
Dr. Jean Phyllis Katow
Takeyuki Katow
Ms. Lois Katsu
Ms. May Katsuda
Ms. Suzy S. Katsuda
Mr. and Mrs. Noboru Katsuhiro
George and Kim Katsuki
Ms. Thelma T. Katsuki
Mr. and Mrs. Ernest Katsumata
Mr. Wayne Katsumata
Mr. Hideo Katsumoto
Mr. Ken Katsumoto
Mr. and Mrs. Kiyoshi Katsumoto
Mr. Alan Katsura
Ms. April Katsura
Ms. Blanca S. Katsura
Mr. and Mrs. Roy Katsura
Mr. and Mrs. Yosh Katsura
Mr. and Mrs. Tetsuo Katsuren
Mr. and Mrs. Paul Katsuro
Mr. and Mrs. Ronald Katsuyama
Mr. Ernest Katsuyoshi
Mr. and Mrs. Howard Katzman
Mr. and Mrs. James Kaufman
Mrs. Yoshie O. Kaufmann
Mr. and Mrs. John Kauzlarich
Mr. Henry S. Kawa
Mr. and Mrs. Kenji Kawa
Mr. and Mrs. James Kawabata
Mrs. Mary M. Kawabata
Ms. Robbin R. Kawabata
Mr. Takeshi Kawabata
Mr. and Mrs. Taketo Kawabata
Dr. and Mrs. Milton Kawabe
Mrs. Irene K. Kawachi
Ms. Joyce Kawachi
Mr. and Mrs. Mitsuo Kawachi
Mr. Rick T. Kawachi
Mr. and Mrs. Ted Kawachi
Mr. Allan Kawada
Mr. Barney S. Kawada
Mr. Charles S. Kawada
G Kawada
Mr. and Mrs. Jitsuo Kawada
Mr. Richard Kawada
Wakao and Doris Kawada
Mr. and Mrs. Allan Kawafuchi
Mr. Kenneth Y. Kawafune
Mr. George Kawagoe
Ms. Toshiko Kawagoe
Mr. and Mrs. Dave T. Kawagoye
Mr. Mitsunori Kawagoye
Mr. and Mrs. Bobby Kawaguchi
Mr. Bruce Kawaguchi
Dr. Eugene Kawaguchi
Mr. Kazuto Kawaguchi
Mr. Keiji Kawaguchi
Mr. and Mrs. Kojiro Kawaguchi
Ms. Mae Kawaguchi
Ms. Martha Kawaguchi
Mr. Masaru Kawaguchi
Mr. Michael Kawaguchi
Ms. Mizuye Kawaguchi
Ms. Patricia Kawaguchi
Mr. and Mrs. Robert Kawaguchi
Mr. Scott A. Kawaguchi
Mr. and Mrs. Shim Kawaguchi
Ms. Taeko Kawaguchi
Mr. and Mrs. Takeyoshi Kawaguchi
Mr. Benjamin A. Kawahara
Mr. and Mrs. Bob Kawahara
Mr. and Mrs. Edward Kawahara
Mr. Edwin Kawahara
Mr. Frank Kawahara
Mr. Fred Kawahara
Mr. Gary F. Kawahara
Dr. Gayle Kawahara
Mr. George K. Kawahara
Mr. and Mrs. George M. Kawahara
Ms. Hatsuko F. Kawahara
Dr. and Mrs. Henry Y. Kawahara
Mr. and Mrs. Ikuro Kawahara
Mr. and Mrs. Isami Kawahara
Mr. and Mrs. John T. Kawahara
Mr. Karl Kawahara
Mr. Kent Kawahara
Ms. Lisa Kawahara

Mr. Mamoru Kawahara
Ms. Mary K. Kawahara
Mr. and Mrs. Masayuki Kawahara
Mr. and Mrs. Raymond Kawahara
Mr. Takashi Kawahara
Mr. and Mrs. Takayoshi Kawahara
Mr. and Mrs. Takeo Kawahara
Mr. Tom K. Kawahara
Mr. Toshiyuki Kawahara
Mr. and Mrs. Yoshio Kawahara
Mrs. Yukie Kawahara
Mr. Yukio Kawahara
Mr. Michael Kawaharada
Mr. Glenn M. Kawahata
Mr. James Kawahata
Mr. and Mrs. John Kawahata
Mr. Clarence Y. Kawahigashi
Mr. George Kawai
Mr. Harvey Y. Kawai
Mr. Masaru Kent Kawai
Mr. Masataka Kawai
Mr. and Mrs. Takeshi Kawai
Ms. Tomiko K. Kawai
Mr. and Mrs. William Kawai
Ms. Yukiko Kawai
Mr. David Kawajiri
Ms. Aki Kawakami
Mr. Alan Kawakami
Dr. Alan P. Kawakami
Mr. Albert Kawakami
Mr. Alvin Y. Kawakami
Mr. and Mrs. Charles Kawakami
Mr. and Mrs. Daniel T. Kawakami
Mr. and Mrs. David Kawakami
Mr. and Mrs. Hachi Kawakami
Mr. James H. Kawakami
Mrs. Jayne N. Kawakami
Mrs. Joan Kawakami
Mr. Karl Kawakami
Ms. Kathryn Kawakami
Mr. and Mrs. Keiji Kawakami
Mr. and Mrs. Kenneth N. Kawakami
Mr. Marc Kawakami
Mr. Mark Kawakami
Mr. Meiji Kawakami
Ms. Micki Kawakami
Mr. Nathan Kawakami
Mr. and Mrs. Paul Kawakami
Ms. Robin K. Kawakami
Mr. and Mrs. Sam Kawakami
Ms. Sheena Kawakami
Mr. Shigeto Kawakami
Mr. and Mrs. Thomas T. Kawakami
Ms. Tokie A. Kawakami
Mr. and Mrs. Toshiaki Kawakami
Ms. Vivien Kawakami
Wright and Grace Kawakami
Mr. Yasuo Kawakami
Mr. and Mrs. Kazuyuki Kawakita
Ms. Nancy C. Kawakita
Mr. and Mrs. Socky Kawakita
Mr. and Mrs. Yoneo Kawakita
Mr. Dennis Kawamata
Ms. Ann M. Kawamoto
Mr. Arthur N. Kawamoto
Mr. and Mrs. Atsuhiko Kawamoto
Mr. Casey A. Kawamoto
Ms. Chizuko Kawamoto
Mr. Craig Kawamoto
Mr. and Mrs. Dan Kawamoto
Mr. Edward K. Kawamoto
Mr. and Mrs. Glenn K. Kawamoto
Mr. Hiromu Kawamoto
Mrs. Hisako Kawamoto
Mr. and Mrs. Howard Kawamoto
Mr. Isamu Kawamoto
Mr. and Mrs. Isao Kawamoto
Mr. and Mrs. Jim Kawamoto
Mr. and Mrs. Jon Kawamoto
Mr. Jon J. Kawamoto
Ms. Joyce N. Kawamoto
Mr. and Mrs. Junichi Kawamoto
Ms. Kazuko Kawamoto
Mr. and Mrs. Keith Gary Kawamoto
Mr. Kenneth Kawamoto
Kiyoshi and Sue Kawamoto
Ms. Louise A. Kawamoto
Mr. and Mrs. Masayoshi Kawamoto
Ms. Michele Kawamoto
Mr. and Mrs. Michio M. Kawamoto
Mr. and Mrs. Mitsugi Kawamoto
Mr. Miyoji Kawamoto
Mr. and Mrs. Morris Kawamoto
Mr. and Mrs. Mutsuo Kawamoto
Mr. and Mrs. Noboru Kawamoto
Mr. Robert T. Kawamoto

Mr. Ronald Kawamoto
Mr. Roy Y. Kawamoto
Ruby and Pearl Kawamoto
Ms. Samiyo Kawamoto
Mr. Seikichi J. Kawamoto
Ms. Sharon Kawamoto
Mr. Shigio Kawamoto
Mr. Sho Kawamoto
Ms. Susan Y. Kawamoto
Mr. and Mrs. Susumu Kawamoto
Mr. Tom T. Kawamoto
Mr. and Mrs. Toshio Kawamoto
Mrs. Umeko Kawamoto
Mr. and Mrs. Yukio Kawamoto
Ms. Aiko A. Kawamura
Ms. Akiko Kawamura
Ms. Alice Kawamura
Ms. Asae Kawamura
Mr. and Mrs. George Kawamura
Mr. Jiro A. Kawamura
Mr. Jon T. Kawamura
Ms. June Kawamura
Mr. Kazuhiko Kawamura
Dr. Keith S. Kawamura
Mr. Kenneth Kawamura
Mr. and Mrs. Kodo Kawamura
Mr. and Mrs. Kuni Kawamura
Mrs. Nellie Kawamura
Mrs. Nellie S. Kawamura
Mr. and Mrs. Peter A. Kawamura
Dr. R. M. Kawamura
Mrs. Samuel Kawamura
Mr. and Mrs. Shigeo Kawamura
Mr. and Mrs. Shizuto Kawamura
Mr. Wilfred N. Kawamura
Mr. and Mrs. Teiji Kawana
Mr. Walter Kawana
Mr. and Mrs. Yuji Kawana
Mr. Kenzo Kawanabe
Mr. Naohiko Kawanabe
Mr. and Mrs. Henry Kawanaga
Mr. and Mrs. Richard T. Kawanaka
Mrs. Tokiko T. Kawanami
Mr. and Mrs. Hideki Kawanishi
Mr. David Kawano
Mr. and Mrs. Donald Kawano
Mr. Edward Kawano
Mr. and Mrs. James T. Kawano
Mr. Jerry M. Kawano
Mr. John Kawano
Mr. and Mrs. John M. Kawano
Ms. Kazuko Kawano
Ken, Lillian and Kreiton Kawano
Mr. and Mrs. Max Kawano
Ms. Nancy Kawano
Richard and Iris Kawano
Mr. Robert H. Kawano
Mr. and Mrs. Robert K. Kawano
Mr. and Mrs. Shoji Kawano
Mr. Thomas Kawano
Mr. and Mrs. Eddie Kawaoka
Ms. Rose C. Kawaoka
Mrs. Tatsumi Kawaoka
Mr. and Mrs. Shinichi Kawaratani
Mr. Tsutomu Kawaratani
Mr. and Mrs. Yukio Kawaratani
Mr. Charles M. Kawasaki
Mr. and Mrs. David Kawasaki
Mr. Elwell H. Kawasaki
Mr. Frank K. Kawasaki
Mr. Harold Kawasaki
Ms. Harumi Kawasaki
Mr. Hideki Kawasaki
Mr. and Mrs. Hiroshi Kawasaki
Mr. and Mrs. James Kawasaki
Mr. Kevin Kawasaki
Ms. Marsha Kawasaki
Masasuke and Sato Kawasaki
Ms. May C. Kawasaki
Mr. Michael A. Kawasaki
Mr. Osamu Kawasaki
Mr. and Mrs. Seiso Kawasaki
Mr. Takeru Kawasaki
Mr. Teruso Kawasaki
Mr. and Mrs. Thomas Kawasaki
Ms. Tomi J. Kawasaki
Mr. and Mrs. Trace Kawasaki
Mrs. Yasue Kawasaki
Ms. Carol Kawase
Mr. and Mrs. George T. Kawase
Mr. and Mrs. Jim Kawase
Mr. Ben Kawashima
Mr. and Mrs. Bob Kawashima
Ms. Christine Kawashima
Mr. and Mrs. David Kawashima
Diane M. Kawashima and Timm Morris

Mr. Fred H. Kawashima
Mr. Masao D. Kawashima
Ms. Shirley Kawashima
Dr. Steven Kawashima
Ms. Sue Kawashima
Ms. Yoshiko Kawashima
Dr. and Mrs. Zitsuo Kawashima
Sakae Kawashiri
Dr. Carol Kawata and Dr. Jon Kobashigawa
Mr. and Mrs. Hideo Kawata
Mr. and Mrs. Joe S. Kawata
Mr. and Mrs. Kaz Kawata
Dr. Kazuyoshi Kawata
Mr. and Mrs. Sam Kawata
Mr. Shig Kawata
Rev. Teruo Kawata
Mr. Wayne H. Kawata
Mr. and Mrs. Arthur Kawatachi
Mr. Richard K. Kawatani
Mr. and Mrs. Elwyn Kawate
Mr. Robert Kawate
Dr. Daniel Kawato
Mr. William M. Kawato
Ms. Emily Kawauchi
Mrs. Haruko Kawauchi
Mr. Scott Kawauchi
Mr. and Mrs. Y. Burt Kawauchi
Mr. Yasuhiko Kawawaki
Mr. and Mrs. David Kawayoshi
Mr. and Mrs. Harry T. Kawayoshi
Ms. Marilyn Kawazoe
Mr. and Mrs. Yutaka Kawazoye
Mr. and Mrs. Albert Kaya
Mr. and Mrs. Haruyoshi Kaya
Mr. and Mrs. Robert I. Kaya
Mr. Robert M. Kaya
Mr. Sumito Kaya
Ms. Hisae Kayahara
Mr. Steven E. Kayahara
Mr. Hugo Kayano
Mr. Isamu Sam Kayano
Ms. Penny Kayano
Ben and Rogee Kayashima
Mrs. Dorothy Y. Kayashima
Mr. Minoru Kayatani
Ms. Ayako Kazahaya
Ms. Sally Kazama
Mr. Jacob Kazanjian
Ms. Fusaye Kazaoka
Ms. Faye Kazato
Mr. and Mrs. Andris Kazmers
Mr. Larry T. Kazumura
Ms. Mieko T. Keating
Mr. Jon S. Kebo
Mr. John F. Keegan
Mr. and Mrs. Robert Keenan
Mr. and Mrs. David V. Keene
Mr. and Mrs. Janet Kishi Kehoe
Mrs. Gerald Keir
Mrs. Janiece Kelley-Kiteley
Ms. Helen Kellogg
Ms. Irene C. Kelly
Mr. Stewart Kelly
Mr. and Mrs. Richard S. Kelso
Mr. and Mrs. Russell Kemp
Capt. William E. Kenealy, USN
Mr. and Mrs. George J. Kenmotsu
Mr. Richard T. Kenmotsu
Mr. and Mrs. Raymond Kennair
Ms. Lois A. Kennedy
Mr. George Kent
Ms. Marian Kerr
Mr. and Mrs. Archie Keyser
Dr. M. Aqiq Khan
Ms. Miyo Kiba
Ms. Alice Kida
Mrs. Emi Kida
Mr. Haruo Kida
Mr. and Mrs. Leo K. Kida
Mr. Shuji Kida
Mr. Theodore Kida
Kida Farms
Mr. Chester Kido
Mr. Fred T. Kido
Mr. Fumio Kido
Mr. and Mrs. George J. Kido
Mr. and Mrs. Hiroshi Kido
Mr. James I. Kido
Ms. Mary Kido
Mrs. Miki Kido
Ms. Momoko Kido
Mr. Wallace T. Kido
Ms. Hiroko Kifune
Mr. Sam T. Kiguchi
Ms. Elaine Kihara
Mr. Gary Kihara

Mr. Harry Kihara
Mr. Henry H. Kihara
Mr. Mike Kihara
Mr. Morris Kihara
Mr. Robert Y. Kihara
Mr. and Mrs. Robert K.U. Kihune
Mr. Gerald Kika
Mr. Gary Y. Kikawa
Mr. and Mrs. Robert S. Kikawa
Mr. and Mrs. Tak T. Kikawa
Ms. Margaret S. Kikkawa
Mr. Robert O. Kikkawa
Mrs. Tomeko Kikkawa
Mrs. Chiyo Kikuchi
Mr. Danny Kikuchi
Mr. Darrell M. Kikuchi
Mr. Darren Kikuchi
Mr. David Kikuchi
Mrs. Ella Y. Kikuchi
Mr. and Mrs. Francis Kikuchi
Mr. and Mrs. George Kikuchi
Mrs. Hide Kikuchi
Dr. John F. Kikuchi
Mr. Joseph Kikuchi
Mr. Ken Kikuchi
Mr. and Mrs. Masao Kikuchi
Mr. Norman D. Kikuchi
Mr. and Mrs. Robert Kikuchi
Mr. Rod Kikuchi
Mr. Shinya L. Kikuchi
Shizue Kikuchi
Suwako Kikuchi
Mr. and Mrs. Tommy Kikuchi
Ms. Toyoko Kikuchi
Mr. Akira Kikugawa
Yushi Kikumoto
Mr. Sam Kikumoto
Ms. Akemi Kikumura
Mr. George M. Kikuta
Mr. Jerry M. Kikuta
Mr. and Mrs. Kunio Kikuta
Mr. and Mrs. Lawrence M. Kikuta
Mr. Noboru Kikuta
Mr. Seikatsu Kikuyama
Mr. and Mrs. Robert E. Kilian
Mr. Thomas Brock Killeen
Ms. Emi Killeri
Dr. and Mrs. James Kim
Ms. Linda L. Kim
Ms. Sally N. Kim
Mr. Soon Ja Kim
Mrs. Tsuyako Kim
Mr. Gerald I. Kimata
Mr. and Mrs. Francis Kimoto
Mr. and Mrs. Herbert M. Kimoto
Mr. Kenji Kimoto
Ms. Patricia Kimoto
Mr. and Mrs. Ralph T. Kimoto
Mr. Robert Kimoto
Mr. Sanji Kimoto
Ms. Satoko Kimoto
Mr. and Mrs. Tak Kimoto
Mr. and Mrs. William Kimoto
Ms. Chika Kimotsuki
Mr. Akiko Kimura
Mr. and Mrs. Akimichi Kimura
Mr. and Mrs. Alex K. Kimura
Ms. Amy Y. Kimura
Mr. Ben N. Kimura
Mr. Bryan Kimura
Mr. Clarence Kimura
Mr. Cliff N. Kimura
Mr. and Mrs. Clyde D. Kimura
Mr. David Kimura
Mr. David M. Kimura
Mr. and Mrs. David Y. Kimura
Ms. Eiko Kimura
Ms. Emiko Kimura
Mr. Ernest T. Kimura
Mr. and Mrs. Gary Kimura
George and Sets Kimura
Mr. and Mrs. George Kimura
Mr. George Y. Kimura
Mr. Gilbert Kimura
Mr. Goro Kimura
Ms. Grace Kimura
Mr. and Mrs. Grant Kimura
Mr. and Mrs. H. J. Kimura
Mr. and Mrs. Harry Y. Kimura
Ms. Haruko Kimura
Mr. and Mrs. Henry K. Kimura
Mr. Hidemi Kimura
Mr. and Mrs. Jack Yukio Kimura
Mr. and Mrs. James K. Kimura
Mr. James T. Kimura
Mr. and Mrs. James T. Kimura

Mrs. Jeanne Kimura
Ms. Jodi L. Kimura
Mr. John Kimura
Ms. Karen Kimura
Ms. Karen C. Kimura
Ms. Kay Kimura
Mr. and Mrs. Kazuo Kimura
Mr. and Mrs. Keith Kimura
Mr. Ken Kimura
Mr. Kenneth K. Kimura
Mr. Kenneth S. Kimura
Mr. Kevin Kimura
Mr. Kiyo Kimura
Mr. Koichi Kimura
Mr. Koshi Kimura
Ms. Lillian Y. Kimura
Mr. and Mrs. Lowell G. Kimura
Ms. Marci Kimura
Mr. Mark Kimura
Ms. Martha Kimura
Mr. Max J. Kimura
Mr. Michael Kimura
Mr. and Mrs. Michael M. Kimura
Ms. Natsuko Kimura
Mr. Norman N. Kimura
Mr. Paul Kimura
Mr. and Mrs. Paul Kimura
Mrs. Pearl Kimura
Ms. Renee R. Kimura
Mr. Robert Kimura
Robert and Aya Kimura
Mr. Robert S. Kimura
Mr. Robert T. Kimura
Mr. and Mrs. Robert T. Kimura
Mr. and Mrs. Robert Y. Kimura
Mr. Rocky Kimura
Mr. Ross Kimura
Mr. Roy Kimura
Mr. and Mrs. Royce Kimura
Mr. and Mrs. Sadao Kimura
Ms. Sandra Kimura
Mr. and Mrs. Shoichi Kimura
Mr. and Mrs. Shunichi Kimura
Mr. Stuart K. Kimura
Mr. Tad Kimura
Mr. and Mrs. Takayuki Kimura
Mr. and Mrs. Takeshi Kimura
Mr. and Mrs. Ted "Bo" Kimura
Mr. and Mrs. Terry K. Kimura
Mr. and Mrs. Tetsumi Kimura
Mr. and Mrs. Toshiaki Kimura
Ms. Toshiko Kimura
Mr. and Mrs. Toshio Kimura
Ms. Utako Kimura
Mr. and Mrs. Victor Kimura
Dr. and Mrs. Wayne Kimura
Wendell Kimura and Family
Mr. and Mrs. Wilfred Kimura
Mr. and Mrs. William Kimura
Ms. Yoshiko Kimura
Mr. Bruce Kina
Ms. Elaine Y. Kina
Mr. Karl Kinaga
Mr. Thomas Kinaga
Mr. David King
Ms. Jo Ann King
Mr. and Mrs. Rex King
Steve Kingswood and Arlene Kumamoto
Mr. and Mrs. Isamu Kinjo
Mr. and Mrs. Masuo Kino
Mr. Shoji Kino
Mr. and Mrs. Charles Kinoshita
Mr. Fukuo Kinoshita
Mr. and Mrs. George Kinoshita
Mr. and Mrs. H. James Kinoshita
Ms. Haruko Kinoshita
Mr. James F. Kinoshita
Ms. Janet Kinoshita
Mr. and Mrs. Jim Kinoshita
Ms. Karen N. Kinoshita
Mr. Kazuo Kinoshita
Mr. Kenneth E. Kinoshita
Mr. Kenneth K. Kinoshita
Mr. and Mrs. Kim Kinoshita
Kiyoko Kinoshita
Mr. Kiyoshi K. Kinoshita
Mr. Kyle Kinoshita
Mr. and Mrs. Leonard Kinoshita
Mr. and Mrs. Masaji Kinoshita
Mrs. Mitsuko Kinoshita
Mr. Noboru Kinoshita
Ms. Reiko Kinoshita
Dr. and Mrs. Robert Kinoshita
Mr. Robert S. Kinoshita
Mr. and Mrs. S. George Kinoshita
Mr. Sadao Kinoshita

Mr. and Mrs. Shigeru Kinoshita
Mr. Takeji Kinoshita
Ms. Tami Kinoshita
Mr. and Mrs. Ted Kinoshita
Ms. Terumi Kinoshita
Mr. and Mrs. Thomas Kinoshita
Mr. and Mrs. Tom Kinoshita
Ms. Yoe Kinoshita
Ms. Yukiye Kinoshita
Yumiko Kinoshita
Ms. Mary C. Kinsella
Anne Kinzel and Lou Cathcart
Mr. and Mrs. Eric S. Kira
Mr. Richard M. Kira
Mr. and Mrs. Stanley Kira
Mr. and Mrs. James Kirihara
Mr. and Mrs. John Kirihara
Ms. Sakaye Kirita
Ms. Amy Kiritani
Mr. and Mrs. George Kiriyama
Mr. Michael Kirk
Clara Kirkman and Samuel Bogorad
Ms. Kay L. Kirkpatrick
Mrs. Nagiko Kiser
Mr. and Mrs. Harold Kishaba
Mr. and Mrs. Kunihiro Kishaba
Mr. Mack Kishaba
Ms. Seiko Boris Kishaba
Mr. and Mrs. Arthur Kishi
Ms. Betty Kishi
Mr. Bill Kishi
Ms. Carolyn T. Kishi
Cynthia Kishi and Larry Robinson
Mr. and Mrs. Dan M. Kishi
Mr. Francis Kishi
Mr. and Mrs. Frank M. Kishi
Mr. and Mrs. Frank R. Kishi
Mr. and Mrs. Hajime Kishi
Ms. Helen S. Kishi
Mr. and Mrs. Henry Kishi
Ms. Kimberly Kishi
Kimiye Kishi
Ms. Louise Kishi
Ms. Patricia K. Kishi
Ruth Ann Kishi and Michael Woodring
Mr. and Mrs. Tetsuo Kishi
Mr. William Kishi
Dr. and Mrs. Gary Kishida
Ms. Kikuye Kishida
Mr. Ralph Kishida
Mr. Mike M. Kishihara
Mr. Charles Kishimoto
Mr. Donald Kishimoto
Mr. George Kishimoto
Mr. Kiyoshi Kishimoto
Mr. Nobuo Kishimoto
Ms. Noreen Kishimoto
Mr. Richard N. Kishimoto
Mr. and Mrs. Sadao Kishimoto
Ms. Terri T. Kishimoto
Mr. and Mrs. Torao Kishimoto
Mr. Yoneji Kishimoto
Mr. Paul Y. Kishinami
Mr. and Mrs. Akira Kishishita
Ms. Lucy Kishiue
Mr. and Mrs. N. Kishiue
Mr. Albert Kishiyama
Mr. and Mrs. Arthur Kishiyama
Mr. and Mrs. Keith Kishiyama
Mr. and Mrs. Ken Kishiyama
Mr. and Mrs. Larry Kishiyama
Mr. and Mrs. Michi Kishiyama
Mr. and Mrs. Min R. Kishiyama
Mr. Gerald K. Kita
Ms. Kim Kita
Mr. Roy Kita
Mr. Yasunori Kita
Mr. and Mrs. Jim Kitabayashi
Mr. and Mrs. Sam Kitabayashi
Mr. Eli Kitade
Mr. Wayne Kitade
Mrs. Antoinette F. Kitagawa
Mr. Arthur S. Kitagawa
Miss Chieko Kitagawa
Ms. Evelyn Kitagawa
Ms. Frances Kitagawa
Mrs. Fujiko S. Kitagawa
Mr. George Kitagawa
Mr. and Mrs. George H. Kitagawa
Mr. and Mrs. Jack Kitagawa
Mr. Joe K. Kitagawa
Rev. and Mrs John Kitagawa
Ms. June Kitagawa
Mr. and Mrs. Manuel Kitagawa
Mr. Martin A. Kitagawa
Mr. and Mrs. Mutsuo Kitagawa

Mr. Naotaka Kitagawa
Mr. Richard Kitagawa
Mr. Seiki Kitagawa
Mr. Teruo Kitagawa
Mr. Richard N. Kitaguchi
Dr. and Mrs. Akio Kitahama
Ms. Carol Kitahara
Mr. Larry Kitahara
Mr. and Mrs. Jack A. Kitahata
Mr. and Mrs. Thomas Kitahata
Ms. Helen H. Kitaji
Mr. Akira Kitajima
Mr. Hideshi Kitajima
Ms. Mitsuye Kitajima
Mr. Robert Kitajima
Ms. Katherine Kitamura
Mr. and Mrs. Masuo Kitamura
Mr. Shozo Kitamura
Mr. Yoko Kitamura
Mr. Ben Kitani
Mr. and Mrs. Kazuo Kitani
Mr. Gary Kitano
Mr. and Mrs. Joseph Kitano
Masami Kitano
Mr. and Mrs. Tom Kitano
Mr. Harvey N. Kitaoka
Mr. Roy Kitaoka
Mr. Shoso Kitaoka
Mr. Takashi Kitaoka
Mr. Takeshi T. Kitaoka
Mr. Yasuki Kitaoka
Mr. and Mrs. Utaro Kitasaki
Mr. Geary J. Kitashima
Mrs. Mary Kitashima
Mr. and Mrs. Richard Kitashima
Mr. and Mrs. Sox (Tsuyako) Kitashima
Ms. Kimi Kitasoe
Ms. Hifumi Kitayama
Iku Kitayama
Ms. Naomi Kitayama
Mr. and Mrs. Ray Kitayama
Mr. and Mrs. Ted S. Kitayama
Mr. and Mrs. Yoichi Kitayama
Mr. and Mrs. John Kitazaki
Ms. Mixie Kitazaki
Dr. and Mrs. Gary N. Kitazawa
Mr. George Kitazawa
Mr. Thomas Kitazawa
Mrs. Yoshitaka Kitazawa
Mr. Nelson Kitsuse
Dr. George Kittaka
Mr. Martin Kittaka
Mr. Robert S. Kittaka
Ms. Amy Kiuchi
Mr. and Mrs. Atsushi Kiuchi
Mr. and Mrs. Ken Kiwata
Mr. and Mrs. Harry S. Kiyabu
Mr. Tadashi D. Kiyabu
Mrs. Claire Kiyama
Mr. Kevin J. Kiyan
Mrs. Satsuki Kiyan
Mr. John Y. Kiyasu
Ms. Stacy Kiyasu
Mr. and Mrs. David Kiyohara
Mr. and Mrs. Ed Kiyohara
Mr. Isao Kiyohara
Mr. Takeshi Kiyohara
Mr. Tetsutaro Kiyohara
Mr. and Mrs. Tom Kiyohara
Mr. and Mrs. Leo Kiyohiro
Mr. George Kiyoi
Mr. and Mrs. Jack Kiyoi
Mr. Jaren R. Kiyokawa
Mr. Tatsu Kiyokawa
Mr. Seyichi Kiyomoto
Mr. Harry Kiyomura
Mr. Henry Kiyomura
Dr. and Mrs. Ira Kiyomura
Mr. Kazuo Kiyomura
Bina C. Kiyonaga
Mr. and Mrs. Stanley Kiyonaga
Mr. and Mrs. Buster I. Kiyono
Mr. Ronald Kiyono
Mr. and Mrs. Wayne S. Kiyosaki
Mr. and Mrs. Henry Kiyota
Mr. and Mrs. John H. Kiyota
Ms. Myra Yoshiko Kiyota
Mr. Ronald Kiyota
Ms. Tsugi Kiyota
Ms. Mildred F. Kiyotake
Mr. and Mrs. Myron Kiyotake
Paul and May Kiyotoki
Mr. Kenneth Kiyotsuka
Mr. Fred M. Kiyuna
Mr. and Mrs. Mark J. Kizior
Mr. Frank L. Klapperich

Ms. Barbara Klassen
Mr. and Mrs. Robert Klaus
Mr. Arthur E. Klauser
Mr. Richard P. Kleeman
Kimi Klein and Warren Harada
Mr. and Mrs. Horst Kleinschmidt
Mr. and Mrs. Erskine W. Klyce
Ms. Cathy D. Knepper
Ms. Stacey Kniff
Mr. Robert Knisely
Mr. and Mrs. Brian A. Knollenberg
Mr. Fumi Knox
Mr. Harold E. Knuckles
Mr. Roy Ko
Mr. and Mrs. Frank Koba
K. K. Koba
Mr. and Mrs. Kenneth Koba
Mr. and Mrs. Mitsuro Koba
Mr. Teruo Koba
Mr. Mitchell L. Kobara
Mr. and Mrs. Rod Kobara
Ms. Jean Kobashi
Mr. Kay Kobashi
Ms. Kimi S. Kobashi
Mr. Philip K. Kobashi
Mr. Richard Kobashi
Mr. Atsuyoshi Kobashigawa
Mr. Dean Kobashigawa
Mr. Harry Kobashigawa
Mr. and Mrs. Kiichi Kobashigawa
Mr. and Mrs. Masaichi Kobashigawa
Mr. Masashi Kobashigawa
Mr. Edward A. Kobata
Mr. and Mrs. Harold S. Kobata
Mr. and Mrs. Harold T. Kobata
Mr. and Mrs. Isamu Kobata
Mr. J. Kobata
Mr. Kaz Kobata
Ms. Rose Kobata
Ms. Sumi Kobata
Mr. and Mrs. Ted T. Kobata
Mr. and Mrs. Toshio Kobata
Ms. Yoshiko Kobata
Mr. Gilbert Kobatake
Ms. Ann H. Kobayashi
Ms. Anne M. Kobayashi
Mr. Bert Kobayashi, Jr.
Mr. Charles Kobayashi
Ms. Chizuko I. Kobayashi
Mr. Clifford K. Kobayashi
Ms. Constance M. Kobayashi
Mr. David K. Kobayashi
Mr. and Mrs. Don Kobayashi
Mr. and Mrs. Eddie M. Kobayashi
Mr. and Mrs. Edward S. Kobayashi
Mr. and Mrs. Eiichi Kobayashi
Mr. and Mrs. Eizo Kobayashi
Ms. Emily Kobayashi
Mr. and Mrs. Fred Kobayashi
Ms. Gene Kobayashi
Ms. Haruko Kobayashi
Ms. Helen Kobayashi
Mr. and Mrs. Henry E. Kobayashi
Mr. Hester A. Kobayashi
Mr. Hiromu Kobayashi
Mr. Hisato Kobayashi
Mr. and Mrs. Hitoshi Kobayashi
Mr. and Mrs. Jack Kobayashi
Mr. James Kobayashi
Mr. Jeff Kobayashi
Jim and Chisato Kobayashi
Mr. Joseph Kobayashi
Mr. and Mrs. Kazuo Kobayashi
Mr. and Mrs. Keichi Kobayashi
Mr. and Mrs. Kenge Kobayashi
Mr. and Mrs. Kiyo Kobayashi
Leslie E. Kobayashi
Mr. and Mrs. Manabu Kobayashi
Mr and Mrs. Mark Kobayashi
Mr. Mark M. Kobayashi
Ms. Masako Kobayashi
Mr. Micheal Kobayashi
Mr. Minoru Kobayashi
Mr. and Mrs. Noboru Kobayashi
Mr. Peter N. Kobayashi
Mr. Richard Kobayashi
Mr. Richard M. Kobayashi
Mr. Richard S. Kobayashi
Mr. and Mrs. Richard T. Kobayashi
Mr. and Mrs. Robert Kobayashi
Mr. Rodger Kobayashi
Gen. and Mrs. Rodney Kobayashi
Drs. Roger H. and Ai Lan D. Kobayashi
Ms. Ryoko Kobayashi
Shizuo and Mary Kobayashi
Mr. Tadashi Kobayashi

Ms. Tae Kobayashi
Mr. and Mrs. Takao Kobayashi
Mr. and Mrs. Takashi Kobayashi
Mr. Tamotsu Kobayashi
Messers Thomas E. and William Kobayashi
Mr. Thomas T. Kobayashi
Prof. and Mrs. Tohru Kobayashi
Mr. and Mrs. Tom Kobayashi
Mr. and Mrs. Yuji Kobayashi
Mrs. Yukimi Kobayashi
Mr. and Mrs. Yutaka Kobayashi
Yutaka and Maureen Kobayashi
Mr. and Mrs. George T. Kobori
Mr. and Mrs. Yutaka Kobori
Ms. Henrietta B. Koch
Mr. and Mrs. James Kochi
Mr. and Mrs. Kikuo C. Kochi
Ms. Nancy S. Kochi
Ms. Mitsuye Kocker
Mr. and Mrs. George Koda
Ms. Haruye Koda
Ms. Jean Y. Koda
Mr. Kenji Koda
Mr. and Mrs. Kenneth M. Koda
Ms. Paula Koda
Mrs. Kikuyo Kodakari
Kodama Orchid Nursery Ltd.
Benjamin and Florence Kodama
Ms. Beverly Kodama
Ms. Cathy Kodama
Mr. and Mrs. David A. Kodama
Mr. David N. Kodama
Mr. and Mrs. Eric W. Kodama
Mr. and Mrs. George Kodama
Ms. Grace M. Kodama
Mr. Hugh Kodama
Mr. Ikuo Kodama
Mr. and Mrs. Jiro Kodama
Mr. Jon Kodama
Ms. Julie Kodama
Mr. Kazuo Kodama
Mr. Kelly Kodama
Kevin, Haruko and Andrew Kodama
Ms. Lori Kodama
Mr. Mitsuhiro J. Kodama
Mr. and Mrs. Mitsuo Kodama
Ms. Miyoko Kodama
Mr. Ronald A. Kodama
Mr. and Mrs. Saburo Kodama
Mr. Sadao Kodama
Ms. Takeko Kodama
Mr. and Mrs. Tatateru Kodama
Ms. Traci Kodama
Mr. Y. George Kodama
Mr. Dick Kodani
Mr. and Mrs. Eugene Kodani
Mr. and Mrs. George Kodani
Mr. Harold Masao Kodani
Mr. and Mrs. Kei Kodani
Ms. Kuniko Kodani
Mr. and Mrs. Powell T. Kodani
Mr. Raymond Kodani
Dr. Miyako N. Kodogawa
Mr. and Mrs. Richard Koeppe
Mr. and Mrs. Ronald A. Koetz
Mr. and Mrs. Ben Koga
Mr. Frank Koga
Mr. and Mrs. James Koga
Mr. and Mrs. Kei K. Koga
Mr. Kevin Koga
Ms. Lalaine K. Koga
Mr. and Mrs. Makoto Koga
Ms. Marie Koga
Ms. Peggie Koga
Mr. and Mrs. Peter Koga
Mr. and Mrs. Robert Koga
Mr. and Mrs. Robert K. Koga
Mrs. Ruth Koga
Ms. Sharon M. Koga
Ms. Shizuko S. Koga
Mr. Stanley S. Koga
Mrs. Sue Koga
Rev. and Mrs. Sumio Koga
Mr. and Mrs. Tom Koga
Mr. Wayne Koga
Mr. Yuji Koga
Mr. Ronald Kogen
Ms. Mary K. Kogiku
Ms. Shirley Kogoma
Mr. and Mrs. Tadao Kogura
Mr. Jackson Kohagura
Mr. and Mrs. Ankichi Kohama
Mr. and Mrs. Wataru Kohashi
Mr. Ernie Kohatsu
Ms. June Kohatsu
Mr. and Mrs. Takeshi Kohatsu

Ms. Mae Y. Kohaya
Ms. Laurie Kohli
Mr. Fred Kohno
Mr. and Mrs. Shuntatsu Kohno
Mr. and Mrs. Peter Tadashi Koida
Mr. William Koida
Mr. Den Koide
Mr. and Mrs. Douglas Koide
Mr. Eric Koide
Mr. and Mrs. George Koide
Mr. and Mrs. Henry Koide
Mr. and Mrs. Jimmy Koide
Mr. and Mrs. Minoru Koide
Ms. Ritzuko Koide
Mr. Wayne Y. Koide
Mr. and Mrs. Glenn Koike
Kazuhiko and Suzanne Koike
Dr. Kimberly Koike
Mr. Kiyomichi Koike
Ms. Linda Koike
Ms. Louise Koike
Mr. Masao Koike
Ms. Miyoko Koike
Mr. Pierson Koike
Mr. Roy Koike
Mr. and Mrs. Toshikazu Koike
Mr. Wayne Koike
Mr. Noboru Koito
Ms. Chiyoko Koiwai
Mr. Mark Koiwai
Dr. Kiyomi Koizumi
Mr. and Mrs. Koin Koizumi
Mr. Roy Koizumi
Mr. and Mrs. Tom T. Koizumi
Mr. and Mrs. Jiro Koja
Mr. and Mrs. George Kojaku
Kiyoshi Kojaku
Mr. Craig Kojima
Mr. Fred Kojima
Mr. and Mrs. Hiroshi Kojima
Ms. Iris Kojima
Ms. Karen Kojima
Mr. Kenn Kojima
Mrs. Lily Kojima
Mrs. Mary Kojima
Ms. Mieko Kojima
Ms. Nancy S. Kojima
Mr. and Mrs. Richard Kojima
Mr. Ryoichi Kojima
Mr. Seichi Kojima
Ms. Sharon Kojima
Mr. Shoji Kojima
Mr. Takeshi Kojima
Ms. Yasuko E. Kojima
Mr. Yasunobu Kojima
Ms. Yuriko L. Kojima
Dr. and Mrs. Gregg Kokame
Mr. Nick Kokame
Mr. and Mrs. Miwao Kokami
Ms. Irene Kokawa
Mr. and Mrs. Minoru Kokawa
Mr. Masao Koketsu
Mr. Neil T. Koketsu
Ms. Nancy S. Koki
Mr. Henry Kokka
Mr. Henry Kokubun
Mr. Morita Kokubun
Mr. Paul Kokubun
Mr. Laurence L. Kolber
Mr. Karl Koles
Mr. and Mrs. Roger Koll
Ms. Dolores Koller
Dan and Shizuye Komai
Mr. Neil M. Komai
Mr. and Mrs. Ray Komai
Mr. and Mrs. Ted Komaki
Ms. Mary Komaru
Mr. and Mrs. Ben Komatsu
Mr. Gene Komatsu
Mr. and Mrs. Harold Y. Komatsu
Ms. Rose Komatsu
Mr. and Mrs. Thomas Komatsu
Mr. Toru Komatsu
Mrs. Carol M. Komatsuka
Mr. and Mrs. Kelvin Komeiji
Mr. and Mrs. Toshio Komeiji
Ms. Ruriko Komine
Ms. Bernice Komoda
Mr. Shinichi Komoda
Mr. and Mrs. Hisashi Komori
Ms. Vivian Komori
Mr. and Mrs. Brian Komoto

Mr. and Mrs. Frank Komoto
Mr. and Mrs. Kazuo Komoto
Mr. Kiyoshi Komoto
Mr. Masao Komoto
Mr. and Mrs. Robert G. Komoto
Mr. and Mrs. Tech Komoto
Mr. and Mrs. Yasuro Komoto
Mr. and Mrs. Kay Komura
Mr. Robert M. Komura
Mr. Arito Komure
Ms. Kathryn Komure
Mr. S. Ted Komure
Ms. Teruko Komure
Ms. Margaret Komuro
Mr. and Mrs. Paul Komuro
Mr. and Mrs. Herman S. Kon
Mr. Masao Kon
Ms. Nancy H. Kon
Mrs. Betty L. Konatsu
Mr. Mas H. Konatsu
Mr. and Mrs. Barry Kondo
Mr. and Mrs. Barry Y. Kondo
Mr. Bill M. Kondo
Ms. Chie Kondo
Mr. and Mrs. Fred Kondo
Frederick and Pualani Kondo
Mr. Gordon Kondo
Mr. and Mrs. Harry Kondo
Mr. and Mrs. Hideo Kondo
Mr. Hiroshi Kondo
Ms. Kazuyo I. Kondo
Mr. Kenneth J. Kondo
Mr. and Mrs. Lance Kondo
Dr. Mark Kondo
Michi Kondo
Ms. Nancy M. Kondo
Ms. Nancy N. Kondo
Dr. and Mrs. Norman S. Kondo
Mr. and Mrs. Shizuo Kondo
Mr. and Mrs. Sueo Kondo
Mr. and Mrs. Takeo Kondo
Ms. and Ms. Tracy Kondo
Ms. Yoko Kondo
Mr. and Mrs. Yoshio Kondo
Bessie and Maurice Kong
Mr. Alban H. Konishi
Mr. and Mrs. Daijiro Konishi
Mr. and Mrs. Donald M. Konishi
Mr. and Mrs. Gary Konishi
Mr. Harry H. Konishi
Mr. and Mrs. Henry Konishi
Mr. and Mrs. James Konishi
Mr. and Mrs. James T. Konishi
Mr. Joe Konishi
Mrs. Margaret Konishi
Mr. Muneaki Konishi
Ms. Reiko Konishi
Mr. Seishiro Konishi
Konko Mission of Hawaii
Mr. and Mrs. Akira Konno
Mr. Jimmy Konno
Mr. John Konno
Ms. Miyo V. Konno
Mr. Rex H. Konno
Mr. and Mrs. Allan Kono
Mr. Andrew S. Kono
Ms. Carol Kono
Ms. Cheryl Kono
Derek Kono, Jaryn Kono
Devin Kono, Kaela Kono, Kara Kono
Ms. Donna Kono
Mr. Edward S. Kono
Mr. and Mrs. Eugene Kono
Mr. Gale P. Kono
Mr. and Mrs. Gary R. Kono
Mr. George M. Kono
Mrs. Grace Y. Kono
Ms. Haruyo Kono
Ms. Heather Kono
Mr. and Mrs. Henry M. Kono
Mr. and Mrs. Kazuo Kono
Mrs. Keiko Kono
Ms. Keiko F. Kono
Mr. and Mrs. Kern Kono
Ms. Kikue Kono
Ms. Marlene Kono
Ms. Maya Kono
Mrs. Patricia H. Kono
Ms. Patricia R. Kono
Mr. Ronald T. Kono
Mr. Roy Kono and Mrs. Judith Roy
Mr. and Mrs. Russell K. Kono
Mr. and Mrs. Stephen Kono
Mr. and Mrs. Susumu Kono
Mr. Takashi Kono
Mr. and Mrs. Takashi Kono

Mr. Tom M. Kono
Mr. Akio Konoshima
Mr. Kiyokazu Konoya
Mr. and Mrs. Takashi Kora
Ms. Jackie L. Korbholz
Mr. and Mrs. Edward Korin
Mr. and Mrs. Shoji Korin
Mr. and Mrs. Frank Korn
Mr. and Mrs. Tom Kornelly
Mr. Phil Kornstein
Mrs. Rosemarie DeLuca-Korphage
Mr. Kenneth Kosai
Mr. Akira Kosaka
Mr. Alan Kosaka
Ms. Debra A. Kosaka
Ms. Karen K. Kosaka
Mr. LeRoy M. Kosaka
Mr. Minoru Kosaka
Mr. Roberto B. Kosaka
Mr. Roger Kosaka
Mr. and Mrs. Roy Kosaka
Mr. Terry T. Kosaka
Mr. and Mrs. Richard H. Kosaki
Mr. and Mrs. Morris Kosakura
Mr. Paul Koschara
Mr. Calvin Koseki
Ms. Jane N. Koseki
Mr. and Mrs. Donald M. Koshi
Mr. and Mrs. George Koshi
Mr. Jerry T. Koshi
Mr. Joe Koshi
Mr. Leslie Y. Koshi
Mr. Samuel Koshi
Mr. David A. Koshiba
Makoto and Shizuko Koshimizu
Ms. Gloria M. Koshio
Mrs. Katy S. Koshio
Mr. and Mrs. Tom Koshio
Mr. and Mrs. Masayoshi Koshiro
Mr. Calvin Koshiyama
Ms. Teri Koshiyama
Ms. Gladys J. Kosobayashi
Mr. and Mrs. Tomo Kosobayashi
Dr. and Dr. F. V. Kostelnik
Mr. Yoshihisa Kosugi
Mr. Shoichi Kotaka
Mr. Kingo Kotake
Mr. Masao Kotake
Ms. Mona Kotake
Mr. and Mrs. Ben Kotani
Mr. and Mrs. Randy Koto
Mr. Alfred Kotomori
Mr. and Mrs. Jim Kotsubo
Ms. Amy H. Kouchi
Mr. and Mrs. Roger Kouchi
Mr. Ronald Kouchi
Mr. Toshio Kouchi
Mr. and Mrs. Arthur Y. Koura
Mr. and Mrs. Nob Koura
Mr. and Mrs. Rudy Kovacic
Mr. and Mrs. Glenn Nobuo Kowaki
Ms. Hiroko Kowta
Mr. and Mrs. Tadashi Kowta
Mr. and Mrs. Asa Koyama
Mr. Barry Koyama
Miss Eimee Koyamam and Miss Beau Mitsuko Koyama
Mr. and Mrs. F. K. Koyama
Ms. Hiromi Koyama
Mr. and Mrs. Jerry Koyama
Ms. Leslie Asagi Koyama
Mrs. Mabel Koyama
Ms. Margaret Koyama
Mr. Masatoshi Koyama
Mr. Nobuhiko Koyama
Mr. Ray Koyama
Mr. and Mrs. Richard Koyama
Mr. Richard Y. Koyama
Col. and Mrs. Spady A. Koyama
Mr. Takashi Koyama
Mrs. Tsuneko Koyama
Ms. Kristi Koyamatsu
Mr. and Mrs. Shig Koyamatsu
Mr. and Mrs. Takeo J. Koyamatsu
Ms. Christine Koyanagi
Mrs. Rose Koyanagi
Mr. and Mrs. Suenari Koyasako
Mr. Kenny Kozaiku
Mr. Matsunori Kozawa
Ms. Ima Kozen
Mr. Robert Kozen
Ms. Colleen Kozohara
Mr. and Mrs. I. Sam Kozu
Mr. and Mrs. Shig Kozu
Mr. and Mrs. Yeichi Kozu
Kozuki Bros.
Mr. and Mrs. Gary Kozuki

Ms.Irene Kozuki
Ms. Irene T. Kozuki
Ms. Kari Y. Kozuki
Ms. Miwa L. Kozuki
Mr. and Mrs. Tadashi Kozuki
Mr. Tim Kozuki
Mr. Todd G. Kozuki
Mr. Douglas Y. Kozuma
Mr. Frank T. Kozuma
Mr. Maurice H. Kraines
Mr. Michiko Krell
Mr. and Mrs. William Kresin
Mr. and Mrs. James Krick
Mr. and Mrs. Tad Krupa
Mr. Galen M. Kuba
Ms. Sally Shinobu Kuba
Mr. and Mrs. Toshio Kuba
Mr. and Mrs. Yoshio Kuba
Mr. Aki Kubo
Mrs. Aki T. Kubo
Mr. and Mrs. Calvin J. Kubo
Mr. Chisato Kubo
Mr. and Mrs. David Kubo
Mr. and Mrs. Edward Kubo
Mr. and Mrs. Eiichi Kubo
Mrs. Elsie Kubo
Mr. and Mrs. Frank Kubo
Mr. and Mrs. George J. Kubo
Mr. and Mrs. George T. Kubo
Mr. and Mrs. George Y. Kubo
Mr. Greg Dennis Kubo
Mr. and Mrs. Harry Kubo
Mr. and Mrs. James J. Kubo
Mr. and Mrs. Karl Kubo
Ms. Patricia Kubo
Mr. Ralph Kubo
Mr. and Mrs. Richard T. Kubo
Ms. Sakae Kubo
Ms. Sue Y. Kubo
Dr. and Mrs. Sumio Kubo
Mr. Yone Kubo
Mr. and Mrs. Don A. Kubose
Rev. and Mrs. Koyo Kubose
Mr. Fred Kuboshima
Ms. Alma A. Kubota
Mr. and Mrs. Barney Kubota
Mr. Charles Kubota
Mr. and Mrs. Duke Kubota
Mr. Edward Y. Kubota
Mr. Frank F. Kubota
Dr. Frederick Kubota
Dr. Glenn T. Kubota
Mr. Hideo Kubota
Mr. and Mrs. James Kubota
Mr. Joseph Kubota
Mr. Kazuo Kubota
Mr. and Mrs. Ken Kubota
Mr. Kenneth Kubota
Mr. Larry I. Kubota
Ms. Marlene Kubota
Ms. Mary Kubota
Mr. and Mrs. Mike Kubota
Ms. Miyeko Kubota
Ms. Momoyo Jane Kubota
Mr. Randall K. Kubota
Mr. Ryo Kubota
Mr. and Mrs. Sadaichi Kubota
Ms. Sadako Kubota
Ms. Sadie S. Kubota
Mr. and Mrs. Ted T. Kubota
Ms. Teiko Kubota
Mr. and Mrs. Toshio Kubota
Mr. and Mrs. Tsugio Kubota
Mr. and Mrs. Tsuneyuki Kubota
Ms. Yoshiko Kubota
Mr. and Mrs. Setsuo Kuboyama
Mr. and Mrs. Terry Kuckenbaker
Mr. Cliff M. Kudo
Ms. Kay T. Kudo
Mr. Kazuo Kudo
Mr. and Mrs. Kazuyuki Kudo
Mr. Chosei Kuge
Ms. June H. Kuge
Kuida AG Supply
Mr. and Mrs. Alton Kuioka
Ms. Evelyn Kuioka
Dr. Dean A. Kujubu
Mr. Herbert Y. Kujubu
Mr. and Mrs. Atsuo Kuki
Mr. and Mrs. Toshio Kumabe
Mr. and Mrs. Arthur Kumada
Mr. Katsuhiro Kumagai
Mr. Kazuo Kumagai
Mr. and Mrs. Ken Kumagai
Kiyoshi Kumagai
Ms. May Kumagai

Mr. Mitchell C. Kumagai
Mr. and Mrs. Rikio Kumagai
Mr. Roland N. Kumagai
Mr. and Mrs. Ross Kumagai
Ms. Ruth K. Kumagai
Mr. and Mrs. Satoru Kumagai
Mr. and Mrs. Teruo Kumagai
Mr. and Mrs. Yoshinori Kumagai
Mrs. Denice Kumagai-Hoy
Mr. and Mrs. James Kumaki
Mr. Robert Kumaki
Mr. David Kumamoto
Mr. Howard J. Kumamoto
Mr. Masahiro Kumamoto
Mr. and Mrs. Mitsuru Kumamoto
Kumamoto Kyoyu Kai
Kumamoto-Kenjinkai
Mr. and Mrs. Chiaki Kumano
Ms. Motoko Kumano
Mr. Ralph F. Kumano
Mr. Thomas Kumano
Mr. Archie M. Kumasaka
Dr. and Mrs. Brian Kumasaka and Family
Mr. and Mrs. Haruo Kumasaka
Mr. Kaneo Kumasaka
Mr. Robert Kumasaka
Dr. and Mrs. Roland Kumasaka
Mr. Roy Kumasaka
Dr. and Mrs. Donn Kumasaki
Mr. Joseph Y. Kumasaki
Doris and Frances Kumashiro
Mr. Kenneth K. Kumashiro
Mr. and Mrs. Tommy Kumashiro
Ms. Lillian Kumata
Ms. Ruth K. Kumata
Mr. James Kumpel
Mr. and Mrs. Ben Kunibe
Mr. and Mrs. Thomas Kunibe
Mr. Ritchie K. Kunichika
Mr. Clyde Kunieda
Ms. Mary C. Kunihiro
Mr. and Mrs. Mitsuo Kunihiro
Mr. and Mrs. Ted Kunihiro
Mrs. Fujie Kunimoto
Mr. Richard K. Kunimoto
Mr. and Mrs. Tadashi Kunimoto
Mr. and Mrs. Takao Kunimoto
Mr. and Mrs. Walter Kunimoto
Ms. Karen A. Kunimura
Mr. and Mrs. Masaru Kunimura
Mr. and Mrs. Seichi Kunioka
Mr. Todd T. Kunioka
Mr. Gordon Kunisaki
Mr. Masashi Kunisaki
Mr. and Mrs. Rodney Kunisaki
Mr. Thomas H. Kunisaki
Mr. Alvin T. Kunishi
Ms. Marilyn M. Kunishi
Mrs. Dora Y. Kunishige
Mr. Grant W. Kunishige
Ms. Jill Kunishige
Mr. Melvin A. Kunishige
Mr. and Mrs. Takeo Kunishige
Mr. and Mrs. Dennis Kunishima
Ms. Isako Kunishima
Mr. George Kunitake
Mr. and Mrs. George Kunitake
Ms. Grace T. Kunitake
Mr. and Mrs. Saburo Kunitake
Mr. Stanley Kunitake
Mr. Mich Kunitani
Mr. Y. Jack Kunitomi
Mr. and Mrs. Hiroshi Kunitsugu
Mr. Ted Kunitsugu
Mr. and Mrs. Robert Kuniyoki
Charles and Cathleen Kuniyoshi
Mr. and Mrs. George Kuniyoshi
Ms. Lisa Kuniyoshi
Mr. Masao Kuniyoshi
Mr. and Mrs. Patrick Kuniyoshi
Mr. Frank Kuniyuki
Mr. and Mrs. Henry Kuniyuki
Mrs. Irene Kuniyuki
Mr. Kenneth K. Kuniyuki
Mr. and Mrs. Robert Kuniyuki
Ms. Miho Kunzer
Ms. Cynthia Kuokos
Mrs. Jeanette Kuperman
Mr. Yuzo Kura
Mr. and Mrs. Edward Kurachi
Mr. George M. Kurachi
Mr. and Mrs. William S. Kurachi
Mr. Conrad Kurahara and Family
Ms. Mitsuko Kurahara
Mr. and Mrs. Tom Kurahara
Mr. and Mrs. Koichi Kurahashi

Ms. Korinne R. Kurakake
Mr. and Mrs. Melvin Y. Kurakake
Ms. Yukiko K. Kurakata
Mara Kurakazu
Mrs. Natsuko Kurakazu
Ms. Reiko Kurakazu
Mr. and Mrs. Hideo Kurakusu
Mrs. Toshi Kuramatsu
Yayoe Kuramitsu
Mr. Akira Bob Kuramoto
Mr. and Mrs. Arthur Kuramoto
Ms. Eimi Kuramoto
Ms. Eunice Kuramoto
Mr. Jack Kuramoto
Mr. and Mrs. Kikaku Kuramoto
Mr. and Mrs. Richard Kuramoto
Mr. Simpey Kuramoto
Mr. Toby S. Kuramoto
Mr. and Mrs. Tom Y. Kuramoto
Dr. and Mrs. Masatake Kuranishi
Frances and Elaine S. Kuraoka
Mr. James Kuraoka
Mr. Melvin Kuraoka
Ms. Jean Kurasaki
Ms. Elsie Kurashige
Mr. Isamu Kurashige
Mr. and Mrs. James T. Kurashige
Mr. Stanley S. Kurashige
Ms. Diana M. Kurashima
Dr. Masaru Kurashima
Ms. Mitzi Kurashita
Kurata's Auto Services
Mr. and Mrs. Edwin Kurata
Mr. and Mrs. James H. Kurata
Ms. Miyo Kurata
Ms. Esther Kuratani
Ms. Akiko Kuratomi
Mr. Reed Kuratomi
Ms. Ruby M. Kuratomi
Mr. S. R. Kuratomi
Mr. and Mrs. Allan M. Kurihara
Mr. Carl Kurihara
Rev. and Mrs. Don Kurihara
Mrs. Fusae Kurihara
Mr. George Kurihara
Mr. Jack Kurihara and Ms. Carol Inge
Mr. James Y. Kurihara
Mr. and Mrs. John Kurihara
Mr. Kei Kurihara
Mr. and Mrs. Kenneth K. Kurihara
Mr. and Mrs. Lawrence Kurihara
Mrs. Masami Kurihara
Mr. and Mrs. Raymond Kurihara
Mr. and Mrs. Rokuro Kurihara
Mr. and Mrs. Saburo Kurihara
Mr. and Mrs. Sam Kurihara
Mr. Thomas Kurihara
Mr. Thomas M. Kurihara
Mr. Velma Kurihara
Mr. Wally Kurihara
Ms. Nancy Kuriki
Mr. Ronald Kuriki
Mr. and Mrs. Dick Kurima
Mr. and Mrs. Glenn Kurimoto
Ms. Peggy Kurimoto
Mr. and Mrs. Takumi Kurimoto
Mr. and Mrs. Terry Kurimura
Ms. Ayako Kurio
Mr. George Kurisu
Ms. Lily Kurisu
Mr. and Mrs. Robert Kurisu
Mr. and Mrs. Sam Kurisu
Ms. Debra Kurita
Mr. and Mrs. Robert T. Kurita
Mr. Toshio Kurita
Mrs. Janis Kuritsubo
Ruby Kuritsubo
Mr. Daniel Kuriyama
Ms. Sally Kuriyama
Mr. Frank Kuroda
Mr. and Mrs. Frank T. Kuroda
Mr. Joseph Kuroda
Dr. Koson Kuroda
Ms. Linda K. Kuroda
Mr. Paul K. Kuroda
Mr. and Mrs. Stanford Kuroda
Ms. Ruth K. Kuroishi
Mr. G. M. Kuroiwa
Mrs. Hideko Kuroiwa
Ms. Aiko Kurokawa
Mr. and Mrs. Akemi Kurokawa
Mrs. Bette Kurokawa
Mr. Byron Kurokawa
Hiromi Kurokawa
Dr. and Mrs. K. M. Kurokawa
Ms. Karen H. Kurokawa

Mr. Kiichi Kurokawa
Mr. Masahiro Kurokawa
Mr. Philip K. Kurokawa
Mr. Ben Kuroki
Mr. and Mrs. George Kuroki
Ms. Shari Kuroki
Mr. Takeshi Kuroki
Ms. Aiko Kurosaka
Mrs. Mikiko Kurosaka
Mr. and Mrs. Terry Kurosaka
Mr. Randolph Kurosaki
Mr. and Mrs. Satoshi Kurosaki
Mr. Frank Kurose
Mr. and Mrs. Thomas Kurose
Mr. Robert N. Kurosu
Mr. Harry Kurotori
Tom and Alice Kurotori
Dr. and Mrs. Roy Y. Kurotsuchi
Mr. and Mrs. Tom Kurowski
Gary and Lily Kuroyama
Mr. and Mrs. Nori Kuroyama
Mr. and Mrs. Shigeo Kuroye
Ms. Rachel Kuruma
Dr. and Mrs. Stephen K. Kurumada
Mr. and Mrs. Tim Kurumaji
Mr. Jack Kusaba
Ms. Margaret I. Kusaba
Mr. and Mrs. George Kusaka
Mrs. Mitsuko Kusaka
Mr. and Mrs. Hiroshi Kusakai
Mr. Hirotsugu Kusakawa
Ms. Ruth Kusamura
Mr. Kiyoshi Kusano
Mr. and Mrs. Shigeo Kusano
Mr. Clyde Kusatsu
Mr. and Mrs. Clyde Kusatsu
Ms. Dorothy Kuse
Mr. Ronald Kuse
Mr. Devin Kushi
Mr. and Mrs. Shigeru Kushi
Mr. and Mrs. Akito Kushida
Mr. Toshimoto Kushida
Ms. Elise K. Kushino
Ms. June Kushino
Ms. Marcia L. Kushino
Dr. Norman Kushino
Mr. Richard T. Kushino
Mr. and Mrs. Thomas Kushino
Mr. and Mrs. Yurie Kushino
Mr. and Mrs. Mitch Kushner and Jessica & Stephen
Ms. Hiroko Kusuda
Ms. Misao M. Kusuda
Ms. Shigeko Kusuda
Mr. Ted Kusudo
Mr. and Mrs. Katsumi Kusumi
Mr. Nobuo Kusumi
Mr. and Mrs. Satoshi Kusumi
Mr. Shogo Kusumi
Mr. Kajizo Kusumoto
Mr. and Mrs. Lee Kusumoto
Mrs. Lily Kusumoto
Mr. and Mrs. Sadahei Kusumoto
Mrs. Florence Kusunoki
Mr. and Mrs. George S. Kusunoki
Ms. Harriet Kusunoki
Mr. and Mrs. Jim Kusunoki
Mr. and Mrs. Robert Kusunoki
Mr. Sid H. Kusunoki
Susan A. Kusunoki
Dr. Richard L. Kusunose
Mr. Roland S. Kutaka
Mrs. Tomi Kutaka
Mr. and Mrs. Alvin M. Kutara
Mr. Morris L. Kutcher
Mr. Andrew H. Kutsunai
Ms. Pamela Kutsunai
Mr. Hajime Kuwabara
Mr. and Mrs. Kenichi Kuwabara
Mr. Shizuo Frank Kuwabara
Mr. and Mrs. Edward A. Kuwada
Ms. Florence M. Kuwada
Mr. Harry Kuwada
Mr. Henry Kuwada
Mr. James T. Kuwada
Mr. John Kuwada
Mrs. June Kuwada
Mr. and Mrs. Paul Y. Kuwada
Mr. Buddy Kuwahara
Ms. Cathy Kuwahara
Mr. Ernest Kuwahara
Ms. Florice Kuwahara
Mr. Gary S. Kuwahara
Mr. George Kuwahara
Ms. Joanne Kuwahara
Mr. and Mrs. Joe Kuwahara
Dr. and Mrs. Joseph D. Kuwahara

Mr. and Mrs. Kenji Kuwahara
Mr. Masayuki Kuwahara
Ms. May Kuwahara
Mr. Melvin Den Kuwahara
Mr. Shigeo Kuwahara
Mr. Tak Kuwahara
Mr. Terry Kuwahara
Ms. Helen Kuwamoto
Mr. and Mrs. Yasuyuki Kuwamoto
Mr. and Mrs. Michael Kuwana
Rysosuke Kuwana
Mr. Douglas Kuwano
Mr. and Mrs. Fujio Kuwano
Mr. Iwao O. Kuwano
Ms. Helen Kuwashima
Frank and Patsy Kuwata
Ms. Lillian Y. Kuwata
Ms. Amy E. Kuwatani
Mr. and Mrs. Danny Kuwatani
Ms. Yaeko J. Kuwatani
Ms. Tomi Kuwayama
Mr. Charles Kuwaye
Mrs. Dorothy Kuwaye
Mr. Henry K. Kuwaye
Ms. Janet K. Kuwaye
Mr. and Mrs. Richard Y. Kuwaye
Ms. Daphne Kwok
Mr. Momo Nagano Kwong
Mr. and Mrs. Allan Kydd
Brian, Lisa and Brandon Kyono
Ms. Janice Kyono
Mr. and Mrs. Leslie P. Kyono
Ms. Marianne Yuki Kyono
Mr. and Mrs. Masatoki Kyono
Mr. Ray Kyono
Mr. and Mrs. William Y. Kyono
Mr. and Mrs. Kahei J. Kyutoku
Kyutoku Nursery, Inc.
L.I.Q. Investors
L.T. Food Service
Mr. and Mrs. Russell G. La Borde
Mr. and Mrs. W. M. Lachowitzer
Mr. and Mrs. Louise Lackey
Ms. Mary M. Lain
Mr. William Lam
Lam Research
Mr. and Mrs. Jack Lamb
Dr. Robert G. Lamb
Ms. Bonnie Lambert
Ms. Meri Lane
Susan Kay Lang and Robert Levenson
Mr. and Mrs. Peter Langowski
Spring Intl. Lang. Center
Dr. and Mrs. Robert C. Laning
Ms. Jill Lansing
Dr. and Mrs. Edward Lanson
Mr. Marvin E. Lantz
Mr. S. Lao
Mr. and Mrs. Claude E. Larouche
Ms. Carol Larson
Pamela J. Larson
Mr. and Mrs. Dennis Lastrapes
Mr. and Mrs. David Latwesen
Mr. Chester Lau
Mr. and Mrs. Fredrick L. Lau
John and Dianne Laumann
Lautman & Company
Mrs. Lynne and Mr. George T. Lavigne
Ms. Barbara M. LaVilleta
Ms. Eileen Lavin
Ms. Sumi Lavin
Mr. and Mrs. Stephen Law
Mr. and Mrs. Roger Lazarus
Ms. Dominique Le Bihan
Kerry Leber
Mr. Richard Lebrecht
Ms. Anna Lee
Ms. Annabelle M. Lee
Mr. C. Lee
Mr. and Mrs. David K. Lee
Ms. Elaine Y. Lee
Mr. and Mrs. James Lee
Mr. John Lee
Ms. Katherine Lee
Ms. Lahoma Lee
Ms. Linda Lee
Ms. Mary Lee
Mr. and Mrs. Richard Lee
Mr. and Mrs. Thomas Lee
Ms. Valorie Lee
Mr. and Mrs. William Lee
Ms. Yoshiko Lee
Mr. Walter Leech
Mr. and Mrs. Nelson B. Leenhouts
Mr. David Lefever
Mr. Richard Lefever

Ms. Janine LeFrois
Mr. Richard LeFrois
Ms. Margaret D. Legath
Ms. Janice Lehman
Mr. and Mrs. David E. Lehr
Mr. Howard P. Leibow
Mr. Ian Leibowitz
Mr. and Mrs. Albert Leighton
Mr. and Mrs. Herman Lemke
Mr. Michael C. Lemke
Mr. and Mrs. Dudley P. Leonard
Mr. and Mrs. David Leong
Mr. and Mrs. Edward Leong
Ms. Aida LeRoy
Ms. Gay Lester
Ms. Margaret R. Lester
Eldean and Dolores Letto
W. Bing and Susan Kamei Leung
Mr. Ed Levine
Dr. and Mrs. Stephen Levine
Mr. and Mrs. Peter F. Levonowich
Mr. and Mrs. Joseph W. Levy
Ms. Doreen Lew
Ms. Etsuko Lew
Mr. and Mrs. Leonard Lew
Ms. Lillie Lew
Mr. and Mrs. Troy Lew
Mr. and Mrs. David Leong
Ms. Alice M. Lewis
Mr. and Mrs. C. Randel Lewis
Mr. and Mrs. Christopher E. Lewis
Dr. Eloise Lewis
Ms. Sharon L. Lewis
Ms. Sonoe Lewis
Ms. Nannette Lichliter
Ms. Natalie G. Lichtenstein
Dr. and Mrs. Edwin Liebner
Life Force, LLC
Mrs. Mary Lilley-Thompson
Mrs. Teru Lincoln
Mr. Fred Lindeman
David and Candice Linder
Mr. Eric Lindquist
Mrs. Emiko A. Lindsay
Mr. and Mrs. Howard Lindsay
Mrs. Kyoko Honda Linehan
Ms. Janet M. Linfoot
Ms. Barbara D. Linney
Mr. John Lipsett
Mr. Doug Little
Mr. and Mrs. Edward A. Livingstone
Mr. and Mrs. David Lloyd
Ms. Femma Lo
A. Lock & Assoc.
Lockheed Missiles & Space Co. Inc.
Mr. and Mrs. Robert F. Lockman
Mr. and Mrs. M. Ayako Loder
Mr. and Mrs. Joan K. Loew
Nathan and Sue Lofton
Mr. Lucian J. Loguirato
J. Paul Lomio and Sharon Inouye
Mr. William London
Ms. Ann K. Long
Ms. Kimiye Long
Mr. and Mrs. Randall Long
Mr. and Mrs. Lawrence E. Looby
Mr. Rich Lopez
Dr. and Mrs. Mortimer Lorber
Ms. Mitsuko M. Loret
Mr. and Mrs. Gerald Lotenberg
Mr. Herbert Lotz
Mr. Charles S. Loucks
Mr. and Mrs. Dean Louie
Mr. and Mrs. Dick E. Louie
Mr. and Mrs. Paul Louie
Mr. and Mrs. Gerald Love
Ms. Vicky Lovell
Ms. Cinda L. Low
Ms. Harumi Low
Dr. and Mrs. Niels Low
Ms. Ann Lowe
Ms. Greg Lowe
Ms. Nobu Nakayama Lowe
Mr. and Mrs. Karen Tanaka Lucas
Ms. Rosemary Lucey
Ms. Lynn Lueck
Ms. Amy H. Lum
Ms. Catherine K. Lum
Ms. Pauline B. Lum
Mr. and Mrs. Robert Lumby
Ms. Margaret Lumoden
Mr. Tomoko S. Lumpkin
Mark and Cheryl Lund
Ms. Florence L. Lundquist
Dr. and Mrs. Sven B. Lundstedt
Mr. Roy Lundstrom

Mr. Frances Lust
Mr. Stanford Lyman
Ms. Phyllis Lyons
Col. William M. Lyons
Ms. Hilda A. Mabe
Ms. Emily MacDougall
Ms. Frances Maceachron
Mrs. Masako A. MacFarlane
Mr. Kevin MacGregor
Mr. Raymond Machesney
Mr. and Mrs. Calvin Machida
Ms. Carrie K. Machida
Miss Joyce Machida
Mr. and Mrs. Michael S. Machida
Mr. and Mrs. Mike T. Machida
Mrs. Sandra Machida
Mr. Steven J. Machida
Ms. Ellen A. Machikawa
Ms. Christyne Macho
Mr. Norman Macleod
Ms. Kiyoko S. Macrina
Mr. Sumio Madokoro
Mrs. Amelia T. Maeda
Mr. and Mrs. Arnold Maeda
Mr. Daren Maeda
Mr. Fumio Maeda
Mr. Futami Maeda
Mr. George Maeda
Ms. Helen H. Maeda
Mr. Hiroshi Sam Maeda
Mr. and Mrs. James S. Maeda
Mr. Jon V. Maeda
Mr. and Mrs. Kazuo Maeda
Mr. Kenneth Maeda
Ms. Lillian S. Maeda
Mr. Lincoln Maeda
Mr. Manabu Maeda
Ms. Marcy M. Maeda
Ms. Marian H. Maeda
Mr. Minoru Maeda
Mr. and Mrs. Peter Maeda
Mr. and Mrs. Ralph Maeda
Mr. Robert Maeda
Mr. Ronald Y. Maeda
Mr. and Mrs. Roy Maeda
Mr. Sachio Maeda
Mr. and Mrs. Samuel Maeda
Ms. Shizue Maeda
Ms. Sue Maeda
Mr. Takeyoshi Maeda
Mr. Wayne Maeda
Ms. Yaeko Maeda
Mr. Yoshimi Maeda
Mr. and Mrs. Yoshitsugu Maeda
Mr. Alan Maedo
Mr. and Mrs. Patrick Maehara
Ms. Romola S. Maehara
Mr. Sam Maehara
Mr. and Mrs. Don Maekawa
Mr. and Mrs. Hiram Maekawa
Mr. and Mrs. James Maekawa
Mr. Kiyoshi Maekawa
Mr. Koh Maekawa
Mr. and Mrs. William Maekawa
Mr. Yasunori Maekawa
Mr. Hatsuo Maemura
Ms. Betsy T. Maesaka
Mr. Theodore T. Maesaki
Ms. Betty M. Maeshiro
Ms. Helen K. Maeshiro
Ms. Mieko Maeshiro
Mr. and Mrs. Jun Maeyama
Mr. Ronald E. Magden
Mr. and Mrs. Charles Magneson
Mr. Margaret H. Magness
Mr. Shuji Magota
Mr. and Mrs. Phillip Mah
Ms. Maryann Mahaffey
Ms. Meriko Maida
Mr. Vito Maida
Ms. Marjorie White Main
Mr. Marshall M. Mainaga
Mr. Bharat K. Mainali
Mainichi Newspapers
Mr. Haruyuki Majima
Mr. Wilson Makabe
Ms. Tsugi Makeshima
Ms. Diane Maki
Mrs. Edna L. Maki
Ms. Haruye Maki
Mrs. John Y. Maki
Mr. and Mrs. Ralph Maki
Ms. Yuri Makino
Mr. and Mrs. Takashi Makinodan
Mr. and Mrs. Mitsuo Makishi
Mr. and Mrs. Craig S. Makishima

Mr. and Mrs. Harvey Makishima
Mr. Lawrence Makishima
Mr. and Mrs. Takeo Makishima
Mr. Takeshi Makishima
Ms. Arlene Makita-Acuna
Mr. and Mrs. Fumio Makiuchi
Mr. M. Denis Makiya
Mr. David Makiyama
Mr. Marvin Malk
Total Living Construction, Inc.
Ms. Miyoshi Mametsuka
Mr. Jonathan D. Mamiya
Mr. Lawrence S. Mamiya
Mr. Masami Mamiya
Mrs. Yoshi Mamiya
Mr. and Mrs. M. Benjamin Manabe
Mr. Samuel K. Manabe
Morton and Barbara Mandel Family Foundation
Jennifer Mandell
Mr. and Mrs. David Maney
Dana Manfredi and Michael Masuda
Mr. Billy Manji
Mr. and Mrs. Robert M. Manji
Mr. and Mrs. S. M. Manley
Mr. and Mrs. Lewis Mann
Mr. David J. Manner
Mr. and Mrs. George Mano
Mr. and Mrs. Kyuma Mano
Mr. Shuri Mano
Mr. and Mrs. Mitsuo Mansho
Dr. Terry T. Maoki
Mr. Nicholas S. Marcellos
Ms. C. Emi Marcus
Pamela M. Marcus
Ms. Margaret B. Maree
Ms. Emily Margulis
Mr. and Mrs. L. J. Marietti
Mr. Francis M. Marino
Mr. and Mrs. Holland Marks
Ms. Charlotte K. Marmaros
Ms. Bonnie S. Marquardt
Mr. Fred Carl Marra
Amy Marschilok and Lisa Szczepura
Mr. and Mrs. Timothy J. Marsh
Ms. Cecilia S. Marshall
Ms. Kazue Y. Marshall
Ms. Alice S. Martin
Mr. and Mrs. Arnold Martin
Mr. and Mrs. David Martin
Ms. Grace Martin
Ms. Laine Lorenzini Martin
Ms. Mildred O. Martin
Mr. Peter C. Martin
Mr. James V. Martin, Jr.
Ms. Luz J. Martinez-Miranda
Mr. Stanley H. Marubayashi
Mr. Allan Maruji
Maruka U.S.A., Inc.
Ms. Jennie Maruki
Mr. and Mrs. Eiji Maruko
Mr. Teruo Maruko
Mr. Albert Marumoto
Mr. Bill M. Marumoto
Mr. John K. Marumoto
Mr. Shigeki Marumoto
Ms. Susan K. Marumoto
Mr. Todd E. Marumoto
Mr. and Mrs. Tsuneshi Maruo
Mr. and Mrs. Yoshikatsu Maruo
Mr. and Mrs. Frank Maruoka
Mr. Kazuo R. Maruoka
Mr. and Mrs. Robert Maruoka
Mr. and Mrs. Ikuto Maruta
Mr. Joel K. Marutani
Mr. Marcus D. Marutani
Mr. Matthew D. Marutani
Mr. Wesley A. Marutani
Mr. and Mrs. George Maruya
Mr. Harvey Maruya
Mey and Junko Maruya
Mr. Akira George Maruyama
Mr. Alan Maruyama
Mr. and Mrs. Allen Maruyama
Ms. Christal K. Maruyama
Mr. Edwin Maruyama
Mrs. Florence T. Maruyama
Mr. Frank Maruyama
Dr. and Mrs. Frank S. Maruyama
Mr. and Mrs. George M. Maruyama
Mr. and Mrs. George N. Maruyama
Ms. Grace Maruyama
Mr. Henry Maruyama
Mr. and Mrs. Joseph Maruyama
Mr. Joseph K. Maruyama
Ms. Karen A. Maruyama
Mr. and Mrs. Ken K. Maruyama

Mr. and Mrs. Ken T. Maruyama
Ms. Kimiko and Yukiko Maruyama
Ms. Kiyoko Maruyama
Mr. Kiyoshi Maruyama
Ms. Laurie Maruyama
Ms. Marilynn M. Maruyama
Mr. Martin Maruyama
Masami and Midori Maruyama
Mr. and Mrs. Masaru Maruyama
Mr. and Mrs. Michael Maruyama
Dr. and Mrs. Michael M. Maruyama
Mr. and Mrs. Paul K. Maruyama
Mr. Richard Maruyama
Mr. and Mrs. Robert T. Maruyama
Mr. Saburo Maruyama
Ms. Shizue Maruyama
Mr. Thomas Maruyama
Mr. and Mrs William Maruyama
Mr. Yoneo Maruyama
Mr. and Mrs. Yoshimi Maruyama
Mr. Yukio Maruyama
Miss Barbara Marvin
Mr. and Mrs. George Masada
Ms. Judy Masada
Mr. and Mrs. Kats Masada
Rev. and Mrs. Saburo Masada
Ms. Yoshiko Masada
Mr. John Masai
Mr. Akira Masaki
Akito and Emi Masaki
Dr. H. S. Masaki
Mrs. Hideko Masaki
Mr. Melvin Masaki
Ms. Nobuko Masaki
Mr. and Mrs. Richard Masaki
Mr. and Mrs. Thomas Y. Masaki
Mrs. Jane Masamitsu
Mr. and Mrs. Kenneth Masamitsu
Ms. Mary Masaoka
Mr. Robert Masaoka
Mr. and Mrs. Tad T. Masaoka
Mr. and Mrs. Toshio Masaoka
Mr. and Mrs. Ben Masatani
Mr. and Mrs. Koji Masatani
Mr. and Mrs. Ralph Masatani
Mr. Richard Masatani
Mr. and Mrs. Nobuichi Masatsugu
Mr. and Mrs. Dan Mashihara
Mr. and Mrs. Lionel K. Mashima
Dr. and Mrs. J. Malcolm Masten
Mr. Arthur Masuda
Mr. and Mrs. Barry T. Masuda
Ms. Diane L.and Mr. Benjamin K. Masuda
Mr. Don K. Masuda
Ms. Evelyn Masuda
Ms. Grace N. Masuda
Mr. and Mrs. Hayden Masuda
Mr. and Mrs. Hiroshi Masuda
Dr. Ikuko Masuda
Mr. Itsuo Masuda
Mr. and Mrs. Katsuyoshi Masuda
Ms. Marjorie Masuda
Ms. Mary Masuda
Ms. Masako Masuda
Mr. and Mrs. Masao Masuda
Mr. and Mrs. Michael T. Masuda
Salinas Young Buddhist Association
Mr. Mike Masuda
Mr. Raymond Masuda
Mr. Robert Masuda
Mr. and Mrs. Ronald Masuda
Mr. and Mrs. Satoshi Masuda
Shirley Masuda and Susan Furutani
Mr. and Mrs. Takao Masuda
Mr. Tokuo Masuda
Mr. and Mrs. Toshiaki Masuda
Mr. Toshio Masuda
Rev. and Mrs. William Masuda
Mr. Yasumasa Masuda
Mr. and Mrs. Yoshio Masuda
Ms. Yuriko Masuda
Ms. Genevieve C. Masuhara
Ms. Shizuko Masuhara
Mr. Donald Masui
Mr. Eddie Masui
Mr. Hiromitsu Masui
Ms. Joan Y. Masui
Mr. and Mrs. Ray Masui
Mr. and Mrs. Tamotsu Masui
Asami and Aiko Masumiya
Masumoto Family
Mr. and Mrs. George Masumoto
Jack and Teruko Masumoto
Mr. James Masumoto
Dr. Kenneth S. Masumoto
Ms. Mary Masumoto

Mr. Mas Masumoto
Mrs. Myrtle H. Masumoto
Mr. Samuel T. Masumoto
Mr. Takashi Masumoto
Ms. Stephanie Masumura
Mr. and Mrs. Jess Masunaga
Mr. John T. Masunaga
Mr. Kazuo Masunaga
Mr. and Mrs. Keith Y. Masunaga
Ms. Laura J. Masunaga and Mr. Arthur Kameda
Mr. and Mrs. Michael Masunaga
Mr. Rose T. Masunaga
Ms. Sachiko Masunaga
Ms. Irene Masunaka
Mr. and Mrs. Mareo Masunaka
Ms. Tomi G. Masunaka
Mr. David Masuo
Mr. Robert Masuo
Ms. Connie L. Masuoka
Mr. Edward J. Masuoka
Mrs. Elaine Masuoka
Mr. and Mrs. Hiro Masuoka
Mr. Kayoshi Masuoka
Dr. Lorianne K. Masuoka
Mr. Shozo Masuoka
Mr. and Mrs. George Masushige
Gail Masutani and Tracy Nishikawa
Ms. Tsugiye F. Masuto
Mr. and Mrs. Ben Masutomi
Mr. and Mrs. Patrick Masutomi
Ms. Etsuko Masuzumi
Mr. Paul Masuzumi
Mr. and Mrs. Yosh Mataga
Mr. and Mrs. Albert H. Matano
Ms. Florence Hiroko Matano
Mrs. Yoshino Matano
Mr. and Mrs. Brian Matayoshi
Mr. Edmund D. Matayoshi
Mr. and Mrs. Edward Matayoshi
Dr. and Mrs. James K. Matayoshi
Mr. and Mrs. Rocky S. Matayoshi
Mr. Shintaro Matayoshi
Toyoko and Deborah Matayoshi
Beth Mathews and Burt Gilmer
Mr. and Mrs. Donald L. Mathews
Ms. Celia R. Matlin
Mr. Richard Noboru Mato
Mrs. Alice Y. Matoba
Mr. and Mrs. Frank Matoba
Mr. Kaname Matoi
Mr. Susumu Matoi
Mr. Tadashi T. Matoi
Mr. Howard M. Matsuba
Mr. and Mrs. Charlie Matsubara
Dale and Tammy Matsubara
Mr. Frank T. Matsubara
Mr. and Mrs. Greg Matsubara
Jean and Kiyoko Matsubara
Mr. Leslie S. Matsubara
Mr. and Mrs. Ray Matsubara
Mr. and Mrs. Roy Matsubara
Mr. and Mrs. Tetsuo Matsubara
Mr. Alfred Matsuda
Ms. Bessie M. Matsuda
Bob and Janet Matsuda
Mr. Bryon Matsuda
Mr. and Mrs. Dale Matsuda
Mr. Don Matsuda
Mr. and Mrs. Donald Matsuda
Ms. Doris M. Matsuda
Ms. Fannie Matsuda
Ms. Florence Matsuda
Frances and Susan Matsuda
Mr. George K. Matsuda
Mr. and Mrs. Hisashi Matsuda
Mr. Ikuo Matsuda
Mr. and Mrs. Irvin S. Matsuda
Mr. and Mrs. John Matsuda
Mr. Justin Matsuda
Mr. Kaoru Matsuda
Mr. and Mrs. Kenji Matsuda
Mr. Kent M. Matsuda
Mr. and Mrs. Kiyoshi Matsuda
Mr. and Mrs. Mamoru Matsuda
Ms. Mary T. Matsuda
Mr. Mas Matsuda
Mr. Matt Matsuda
Mr. Michael Matsuda
Mr. and Mrs. Minoru Matsuda
Mr. and Mrs. Morley Matsuda
Mr. Morris Matsuda
Mr. Nobuo Matsuda
Mr. Patrick Matsuda
Mr. Rie Matsuda
Mr. Sakae Matsuda
Mr. Sam Matsuda

Mr. Seiyei S. Matsuda
Mr. and Mrs. Shinobu Matsuda
Ms. Shizumi Matsuda
Mr. and Mrs. Sumio Matsuda
Mr. Takeshi Matsuda
Mr. Thomas T. Matsuda
Mr. Tsutomu Matsuda
Mr. Walter H. Matsuda
Mr. and Mrs. Walter S. Matsuda
Mr. Yasuo Matsuda
Mr. and Mrs. Joe Matsudaira
Mr. Paul Matsudaira
Mr. and Mrs. Peter Matsudaira
Ms. Ruth M. Matsudaira
Mr. and Mrs. Tebo Matsudaira
Mr. and Mrs. Theophane Matsudaira
Mr. and Mrs. Gary Matsueda
Mr. Jim Matsueda
Ms. June Matsueda
Mr. and Mrs. Denny Matsufuji
Mr. and Mrs. Shig Matsufuji
Mr. and Mrs. Howard Matsuhara
Mr. and Mrs. Yoshiro Matsuhara
Mr. and Mrs. Bob Matsui
Mr. and Mrs. Dick G. Matsui
Mr. Eric Matsui
Mr. Eugene Matsui
Mr. and Mrs. Everett Matsui
Ms. Florence N. Matsui
Ms. Gail Matsui
Mr. George J. Matsui
Mr. and Mrs. George M. Matsui
Mr. George T. Matsui
Ms. Georgia Matsui
Mr. Glenn T. Matsui
Ms. Helen Matsui
Mr. Henry K. Matsui
Mr. Kenichi Matsui
Ms. Kimie Matsui
Ms. Margaret Yaeko Matsui
Mr. and Mrs. Nobu Matsui
Mr. and Mrs. Richard G. Matsui
Mr. and Mrs. Takanobu Matsui
Mr. Takashi Matsui
Mr. and Mrs. Takashi Matsui
Mr. Tetsuo Matsui
Mr. and Mrs. Victor M. Matsui
Dr. Wesley Matsui
Yeiki Matsui
Mr. and Mrs. Edes M. Matsukado
Mr. William M. Matsukado
Ms. Fay M. Matsukage
Mr. and Mrs. Charles Matsukawa
Mr. Harushige Matsukawa
Mr. and Mrs. Hidehiro Matsukawa
Lori L. Matsukawa and Larry Blackstock
Mr. Matsuki Matsukawa
Mr. Stephen Matsukawa
Mr. T. Matsukawa
Mr. Wayne Matsukawa
Mr. and Mrs. Harry N. Matsuki
Mr. Mike Matsumiya
Ms. Sherri Matsumiya
Mr. Shigeru Matsumiya
Mr. and Mrs. Ikera Matsumonji
Mr. and Mrs. Sauce Matsumori
Ms. Akemi Matsumoto
Mr. and Mrs. Akio Matsumoto
Mr. and Mrs. Alan Matsumoto
Mr. Albert Matsumoto
Mr. and Mrs. Allen T. Matsumoto
Ms. Amiko Matsumoto
Ms. Amy E. Matsumoto
Ms. Ayako Matsumoto
Ms. Barbara R. Matsumoto
Mr. and Mrs. Ben M. Matsumoto
Mr. and Mrs. Ben T. Matsumoto
Ms. Betty Y. Matsumoto
Mr. and Mrs. Bob Matsumoto
Mr. Calvin Matsumoto
Mr. and Mrs. Charles Matsumoto
Ms. Chizuko M. Matsumoto
Mr. Clarence Matsumoto
Mr. and Mrs. Dan Matsumoto
Mr. Dan E. Matsumoto
Mr. and Mrs. Dan T. Matsumoto
Ms. Diane Matsumoto
Mr. Donald I. Matsumoto
Mr. Donald M. Matsumoto
Ms. Earlynn A. Matsumoto
Mr. Edwin Matsumoto
Mrs. Elsie Matsumoto
Mr. Eugene Matsumoto
Mr. and Mrs. Frank M. Matsumoto
Mr. Frank S. Matsumoto
Ms. Fumiko Matsumoto

Dr. Gary H. Matsumoto
George and Kimi Matsumoto
George and Asano Matsumoto
Mr. George A. Matsumoto
Mr. and Mrs. George H. Matsumoto
Mr. George M. Matsumoto
Mr. and Mrs. George N. Matsumoto
Mr. George S. Matsumoto
Mr. and Mrs. George S. Matsumoto
Mr. and Mrs. George Y. Matsumoto
Ms. Georgia Matsumoto
Mr. Herb S. Matsumoto
Mr. and Mrs. Howard M. Matsumoto
Mr. and Mrs. Itsuto Matsumoto
Mr. James I. Matsumoto
Ms. Jean A. Matsumoto
Mr. and Mrs. Jesse Matsumoto
Mr. Jimmy Matsumoto
John and Akie Matsumoto
John and Sadako Matsumoto
Ms. Kazuko Matsumoto
Mr. and Mrs. Keith Matsumoto
Mr. Keith T. Matsumoto
Ken and Yas Matsumoto
Mr. and Mrs. Ken Matsumoto
Mr. Kevin Matsumoto
Ms. Kikuko Matsumoto
Ms. Kiyoko Matsumoto
Kosei and June Matsumoto
Mr. and Mrs. Larry Matsumoto
Ms. Lillian I. Matsumoto
Mrs. Lillian S. Matsumoto
Mr. and Mrs. Mark M. Matsumoto
Mr. and Mrs. Masao Matsumoto
Masao and Karen Matsumoto
Mr. Mason M. Matsumoto
Mrs. Matsuko K. Matsumoto
Michiyo Matsumoto and Jane M. Iwashita
Mr. and Mrs. Mickey Matsumoto
Mr. and Mrs. Mitsuo Matsumoto
Mr. and Mrs. Neal Hichiro Matsumoto
Mr. Neil M. Matsumoto
Ms. Pat H. Matsumoto
Mr. Paul Matsumoto
Mr. Ralph Matsumoto
Mr. Ray M. Matsumoto
Mr. Raymond Matsumoto
Ms. Reiko Matsumoto
Mr. Richard A. Matsumoto
Mr. Richard J. Matsumoto
Mr. and Mrs. Ricky A. Matsumoto
Mr. and Mrs. Robert K. Matsumoto
Mr. and Mrs. Robert S. Matsumoto
Mr. Roy A. Matsumoto
Mr. and Mrs. Roy S. Matsumoto
Mr. Roy T. Matsumoto
Ms. Sally Matsumoto
Mr. Satoshi Matsumoto
Mrs. Sharie Matsumoto
Mr. Shig Matsumoto
Mr. and Mrs. Shigeru Matsumoto
Shimako Matsumoto
Mr. and Mrs. Stanley Matsumoto
Mr. Stephen Matsumoto
Mr. Steven Matsumoto
Mr. and Mrs. Sumio Matsumoto
Susumu Matsumoto
Ms. Suyemi Matsumoto
Terry and Sachi Matsumoto
Mr. and Mrs. Terry T. Matsumoto
Mr. Tom Matsumoto
Tom M. Matsumoto and Linda Ogawa
Ms. Virginia Matsumoto
William and Rainbow Matsumoto
Mr. Yoshio Matsumoto
Mr. Yosuke Matsumoto
Mr. and Mrs. Yukio Matsumoto
Mr. and Mrs. Yutaka Matsumoto
Ms. Hisaye Matsumune
Ms. Betsy C. Matsumura
Mr. Calvin Matsumura
Ms. Donna Matsumura
Ms. Florence S. Matsumura
Mr. Fred M. Matsumura
Mr. George U. Matsumura
Mr. and Mrs. Isamu Matsumura
Ms. Janice Matsumura
Mr. Jon Matsumura
Mr. and Mrs. Kazuo Matsumura
Mr. and Mrs. Kenneth T. Matsumura
Mr. and Mrs. Paul T. Matsumura
Mr. Philip Matsumura
Mr. and Mrs. Robert Matsumura
Mrs. Sue Matsumura
Ms. Sue S. Matsumura

Mr. and Mrs. Thomas Matsumura
Ms. Yukiye Matsumura
Mr. Henry Matsumuro
Mr. Arlon Matsunaga
Mr. and Mrs. Ben Matsunaga
Mr. and Mrs. Douglas S. Matsunaga
Mr. Ernest Matsunaga
Mr. and Mrs. George Matsunaga
Mr. and Mrs. George H. Matsunaga
Mr. and Mrs. Haruo Matsunaga
Mr. Henry Matsunaga
Mr. and Mrs. Hideo Matsunaga
Mr. Ivan Matsunaga
Dr. and Mrs. Jon S. Matsunaga
Ms. Kim Matsunaga
Mrs. Margaret Matsunaga
Matsunaga Charitable Foundation
Mr. and Mrs. Mitsuki Matsunaga
Mr. and Mrs. Phillip Matsunaga
Mr. Richard Matsunaga
Mr. and Mrs. Susumu Matsunaga
Mr. Tom Matsunaga
Mr. Yoshimi Matsunaga
Mr. Yutaka Matsunaga
Mr. Arthur Matsunami
Mr. and Mrs. Manabu Matsunami
Dr. Lance Matsune and Dr. Paul Teranishi
Mr. and Mrs. Les Matsune
Mr. and Mrs. Alvin Matsuno
Mr. and Mrs. Frank Matsuno
Mr. and Mrs. George Matsuno
Mr. Harry H. Matsuno
Mr. and Mrs. John Y. Matsuno
Ms. Masae Matsuno
Mr. Mike H. Matsuno
Mr. and Mrs. Takatow S. Matsuno
Mr. and Mrs. Anthony T. Matsuo
Mr. and Mrs. David Matsuo
Hanayo B. Matsuo
Mr. and Mrs. Hideo Matsuo
Mr. Joseph Matsuo
Mr. Kenichi Matsuo
Mr. and Mrs. Kirk Matsuo
Mr. and Mrs. Masami Matsuo
Mr. and Mrs. Mitsuo Matsuo
Mr. and Mrs. Roy Matsuo
Mr. Shigeru T. Matsuo
Mr. Ted Matsuo
Ms. Teiko I. Matsuo
Ms. Audrey Matsuoka
Mr. Dale Matsuoka
Mr. and Mrs. David Matsuoka
Mr. David K. Matsuoka
Mr. Douglas Matsuoka
Mr. and Mrs. Edward Matsuoka
Ms. Emi Matsuoka
Mr. and Mrs. Eric Matsuoka
Mr. Fred E. Matsuoka
Ms. Grace Matsuoka
Mr. and Mrs. James T. Matsuoka
Mr. and Mrs. Jimmy Matsuoka
Ms. Joan L. Matsuoka
Mr. John Matsuoka
Mr. Keith Matsuoka and Ms. Kathryn Obana
Mr. Kenneth H. Matsuoka
Mr. Matsuo Matsuoka
Ms. Miyoko Matsuoka
Mr. and Mrs. Norio Matsuoka
Paul Matsuoka and Janis Honkawa
Mr. Richard T. Matsuoka
Mr. Samuel Matsuoka
Mr. and Mrs. Shinya Matsuoka
Mr. Soichi Matsuoka
Mr. and Mrs. Takawo Matsuoka
Mr. Tats Matsuoka
Mr. Thomas T. Matsuoka
Mr. and Mrs. Toru Matsuoka
Mr. Yoneo Matsuoka
Mr. Dennis K. Matsura
Ms. Mariko Matsura
Mr. Edwin Matsusaka
Mr. and Mrs. Isaac Matsushige
Mr. Richard Matsushige
Mr. Vivian Matsushige
Mr. Alan Matsushima
Mr. and Mrs. David Matsushima
Ms. Eileen Matsushima
Ms. Harriet H. Matsushima
Ms. Jody Matsushima
Mr. Masashi Matsushima
Ms. Okiko Matsushima
Ms. Robin Matsushima
Mr. and Mrs. Akira Matsushita
Mr. David D. Matsushita
Mr. and Mrs. Dick K. Matsushita

Mr. and Mrs. George Matsushita
Mr. John T. Matsushita
Mrs. Mae K. Matsushita
Ms. Mary Matsushita
Dr. Masahiko Matsushita
Mr. Masaru Matsushita
Mr. and Mrs. Mike Matsushita
Mrs. Mitsu S. Matsushita
Mr. and Mrs. Mitsuo Matsushita
Mr. Norman Matsushita
Ms. Rose Y. Matsushita
Ms. Tadzuyo M. Matsushita
Mr. Wakao Matsushita
Ms. Yurika Matsushita
Mr. Bruce Matsutsuyu
Mr. and Mrs. Toshiro Matsutsuyu
Mr. Yuzo Matsutsuyu
Ms. Alyce Matsuuchi
Mr. and Mrs. Art Matsuura
Dr. and Mrs. Don T. Matsuura
Mr. and Mrs. Frank Matsuura
Ms. Fumie Matsuura
Mr. Harold Matsuura
Ms. Harriet Matsuura
Mr. Henry T. Matsuura
Mr. Hiroshi Matsuura
Mr. Kaz Matsuura
Mr. Kenneth R. Matsuura
Mr. Motoaki Matsuura
Dr. Peter A. Matsuura
Mr. and Mrs. Richard Matsuura
Mrs. Rosie Matsuura
Ms. Shirley Matsuura
Mr. and Mrs. Tommy Matsuura
Mr. and Mrs. Tosh Matsuura
Mr. Toshio Matsuura
Ms. Faith A. Matsuwaka
Mr. Akito Matsuyama
Mr. and Mrs. Arthur M. Matsuyama
Earl and Brenda Matsuyama
Mr. Hideo Matsuyama
Ms. Karen Matsuyama
Ms. Kazuko Matsuyama
Mr. Theo Matsuyama
Ms. Tracey Seki Matsuyama
Mr. and Mrs. Hirozo Matsuzaka
Mr. Colin K. Matsuzaki
Mr. and Mrs. Edwin Matsuzaki
Mr. and Mrs. Joseph Matsuzaki
Mr. Saburo Matsuzaki
Mr. Takao Matsuzaki
Ms. Amy E. Matsuzawa
Deen and Toshiko Matsuzawa
Mr. Roy Matsuzawa
Mrs. Audrey Matzen
Ms. Emily Mau
Ms. Lillian H. Mau
Mr. and Mrs. Ralph Maurer
Ms. Shizue Mauyama
Mr. Robert Maxon
Mr. and Mrs. Bob Maxwell
May Dept. Stores Co.
Mr. and Mrs. Thomas Mayahara
Fuki Mayaji
Mr. Ben Mayeda
Dr. and Mrs. Bryan Mayeda
Mr. and Mrs. Cary S. Mayeda
Mr. and Mrs. Charles Mayeda
Daniel M. Mayeda and Susan I. Rosales
Mr. Dave K. Mayeda
Mr. Dennis Mayeda
Mr. Donald Mayeda
Mr. and Mrs. Edward Mayeda
Mrs. Eileen Mayeda
Ms. Fumiyo Mayeda
Mrs. Fusaye Mayeda
Mr. and Mrs. Henry S. Mayeda
Mr. and Mrs. Hiroshi Mayeda
Mr. Joel Mayeda
Mr. John Mayeda
Mrs. Josephine Mayeda
Ms. Kathy C. Mayeda
Dr. and Mrs. Kaz Mayeda
Mr. and Mrs. Kenzo Mayeda
Mr. Mack Mayeda
Mr. Michael M. Mayeda
Mr. and Mrs. Minoru Mayeda
Mr. and Mrs. Ray Mayeda
Mr. Shoji Mayeda
Mr. and Mrs. Stephen Mayeda
Mr. Steven E. Mayeda
Mr. and Mrs. Takashi Mayeda
Mr. Tamiki Mayeda
Mr. and Mrs. Ted Mayeda
Mr. Terry T. Mayeda

Mr. and Mrs. Tony Mayeda
Mr. and Mrs. Toshio Mayeda
Mr. and Mrs. Toyone Mayeda
Mr. Victor Mayeda
Ms. Yaeko Mayeda
Yoshikatsu Mayeda
Mr. Joseph Mayekawa
Mr. Roy Mayemura
Ms. Nancy Mayeno
Ms. Jean Mayer
Mr. and Mrs. Andrew Mayeshiba
Mr. Albert S. Mayeshiro
Mr. George Mayeske
Mr. and Mrs. Bradley McCague
Ms. Lorraine McCall
Jim and Gale Awaya McCallum
Mr. and Mrs. W. L. McCamey
Mr. David J. McCarty
Ms. Kazuyo McCleer
Mr. and Mrs. David McClure
Ms. Debra N. McCollom
Ms. Evelyn W. McCool
Mr. and Mrs. John McCue
Ms. Barbara McCullough
Mr. and Mrs. Donald McDonald
Mr. and Mrs. Jack W. McDowell
Mrs. Harriet A. McFarlane
Mr. and Mrs. R. McGee
Mr. and Mrs. William McGovern
Ms. Yuriko M. McGowan
Mr. Richard E. McGrath
Mr. and Mrs. Rob R. McGregor
Mr. David A. McGuire
Ms. Tomoko K. McGuire
Mr. and Mrs. Primo McHugh
Mr. Bill McJohn
Ms. Ayanna McKay
Dr. William G. McKechnie
Mr. William S. Mckee
Ms. Kathleen M. McKenna
Mr. and Dr. Andrew McKinley
Mr. and Mrs. Alexis McKinney
Ms. Barbara Amazaki McLaughlin
Mr. Michael S. McLaughlin
Mr. and Mrs. Andrew McLean
Mr. Thomas McMenamin
Mrs. Wanda A. McMullin
Ms. Sylvia McNair
Ms. Aime McNamara
Ms. Jane McNeely
Mr. and Mrs. Richard B. McNees
Ms. Janice K. Mead
Mr. Robert E. Meadows
Mr. and Mrs. Eric W. Measles
Mr. Lawrence F. Mecklenburg
Mr. and Mrs. Rick A. Medlen
Nelder and Mariagnes Medrud
Mr. Richard N. Meginnity
Mr. Leo Meguro
Mr. and Mrs. Stanley Mehr
Dr. Mohini Mehra
Mr. Mitsuo H. Menda
Kruse Mennillo & Company
Mr. and Mrs. Koichi Mera
Mr. and Mrs. Michael Merlander
Merrill Lynch
Merrill's Marauders Assoc.
Ms. Coleen Merritt
Mr. John Hays Mershon
Ms. Barbara Meyer
Mr. Robert H. Meyer
Mr. Arthur Meyers
Mr. Howard Meyers
Ms. Marilyn Namba Meyers
Mrs. Janis H. Meza
Mr. and Mrs. Osami S. Mibu
Michi Japanese Restaurant
Mr. Kazuo Michihara
Mr. Rokuichiro Michii
Mr. Henry I. Michisaki
Mr. and Mrs. James K. Michiuye
Ms. Louise Mickelsen
Mr. and Mrs. Ken Migaki
Mr. and Mrs. Mas Migaki
Ms. Sueno Migaki
Mr. and Mrs. Ted Migaki
Mr. and Mrs. Tom Migaki
Mr. Tadao Migimoto
Mr. Arthur Mihara
Ms. Helen Mihara
Mr. and Mrs. Lawrence Mihara
Mr. Mike O. Mihara
Mr. and Mrs. Mitsuru Mihara
Mr. and Mrs. James Mihori
Ms. Jean Miike

Mr. and Mrs. William J. Mika
Ms. Claire Kimi Mikami
Dr. and Mrs. Donald Mikami
Ms. Fusa Mikami
Mr. and Mrs. H. C. Mikami
Mr. Isao Mikami
Mr. Kuni Mikami
Ms. Mae M. Mikami
Mr. and Mrs. Richard Mikami
Mr. and Mrs. Richard N. Mikami
Mr. and Mrs. Satoshi M. Mikami
Mr. and Mrs. Takayuki Mikami
Mr. and Mrs. Takumi Mikami
Ms. Yaeko Mikami
Ms. Yoshie Mikami
Mr. and Mrs. Akira M. Mikasa
Mr. Clifford T. Mikasa
Ms. Emiko A. Mikasa
Mr. Glenn Mikasa
Mr. Haruo Mikasa
Mr. Kenneth K. Mikasa
Mr. Tadayoshi Mikasa
Mr. and Mrs. Yasuhiro Mikasa
Mr. Francis Mikawa
Mr. and Mrs. Hiroshi T. Mikawa
Mr. and Mrs. Osame Miki
Mrs. Sachi Miki
Mr. and Mrs. Ubukinokami Miki
Mr. Alan M. Mikuni
Mr. and Mrs. Donald S. Mikuni
Mr. and Mrs. Fred Mikuni
Mr. Gary S. Mikuni
Mr. Jimmy I. Mikuni
Mr. and Mrs. John Mikuni
Mr. and Mrs. Kei Mikuriya
Ms. Mary Jane Mikuriya
Military Order of the World Wars
Mr. Don W. Millard
Mr. and Mrs. Curtis Miller
Mr. John M. Miller
Mr. and Mrs. Joseph H. Miller
Dr. June Miller
Mrs. Misono I. Miller
Mr. and Mrs. Richard Miller
Mr. Richard A. Miller
Rev. Robert Miller
Mr. and Mrs. Randolph B. Mills
Mr. and Mrs. Roy C. Milton
Mrs. Donna L. Mimaki
Mr. James Mimaki
Ms. Betty J. Mimura
Mr. James Mimura
Mr. Walter N. Minaai
Mr. Shiro Minabe
Ms. Yoshiye B. Minabe
Mr. and Mrs. Yuki Minaga
Mr. Arthur Minagawa
Mr. and Mrs. Calvin Minakata
Ms. Leticia Minakawa
Ms. Betty Minami
Carol Minami
Mrs. Claire F. Minami
Mr. Dale Minami
Mr. Don M. Minami
Mr. and Mrs. Henry Minami
Ms. Lynne Minami
Mrs. Mabel M. Minami
Mr. and Mrs. Manabu Minami
Mr. and Mrs. Philip Minami
Mr. Robert Y. Minami
Mr. and Mrs. Tatsuo Minami
Ms. Terri Minami
W. Minami
Mr. Wesley (Denny) Minami
Mr. Yaichiro Minami
Mr. Yasuji Minami
Mr. Yoshio Minami
Mr. and Mrs. Akira Minamide
Ms. Asako Minamide
Mr. Jerry Minamide
Mrs. Harue Minamoto
Mr. James Minamoto
Ms. Lou Minamoto
Ms. Mary Minamoto
Mr. Tsuyoshi Minamoto
Mr. and Mrs. George Minata
Mr. and Mrs. Alan K. Minato
Mr. and Mrs. Curtis Minato
Mr. and Mrs. Michael H. Minato
Mr. and Mrs. Paul Minato
Mr. Robert Minatoya
Mr. and Mrs. Bill Mine
Mr. and Mrs. Jumpei Mine
Mr. and Mrs. Michimasa Mine
Mr. and Mrs. Masaki Minei
Mr. Takefumi Mineishi

Mr. and Mrs. Katsumi Minemoto
Mr. and Mrs. Robert M. Minemoto
Ms. Peggy Miner
Minidoka Reunion Committee - 2001
Ms. Sandra Hayashi Minner
Ms. Hisako Minobe
Ms. Lillian Dina Mintz
Mr. and Mrs. George Mio
Mrs. Marjorie Y. Mio
Mr. Ronald Mirikitani
Y. Mirikitani and M. Tanaka
Ms. Jeanette Misaka
Hisaye Misaki
Ms. Laurie Misaki
Mr. and Mrs. Takami Misaki
Ms. Yoriko Misaki
Mr. and Mrs. Misawa
Mr. Leo F. Mishige
Mr. David Mishima
Mr. and Mrs. David Mishima
Ms. Helen Y. Mishima
Mr. Henry Mishima
Mr. and Mrs. James Mishima
Mr. and Mrs. Tom Mishima
Ms. Kathryn Misna
Mr. Calvin Misono
Ms. June Misono
Mr. and Mrs. Kunio S. Misono
Misumi Family
Mr. and Mrs. Donald Misumi
Ms. Haruko Misumi
Mr. and Mrs. James Misumi
Mr. Rodney J. Misumi
Mr. and Mrs. Donald Mita
Ms. Doris Mita
Mr. Enge Mita
Mr. and Mrs. Kay Mita
Mr. Satomi Mita
Mr. and Mrs. Yoshio Mita
Mr. and Mrs. Charles Mitamura
Mr. and Mrs. Don Mitani
Ms. Janet Mitani
Ms. Kiyoko Mitani
Mr. and Mrs. Mark Mitani
Ms. Mary Mitani
Mr. and Mrs. Masatoshi Mitani
Mr. and Mrs. Mike Mitani
Mr. Clifford J. Mitchell
Mr. and Mrs. David Mitchell
Ms. Lynn Mitchell
Ms. Helen Mito
Mr. Yasuo Mito
Mr. Larry Mitobe
Mr. and Mrs. Chozo Mitoma
Mr. Edwin Y. Mitoma
Mr. T. F. Mitoma
Mr. George Mitsuda
Mr. and Mrs. George Mitsuda
Ms. Marie M. Mitsuda
Mr. Robert M. Mitsueda
Ms. Janie Mitsuhashi
Mr. and Mrs. George Mitsuhata
Ms. Jeanette Mitsuhata
Mr. Akira Mitsui
Mr. Edward Mitsui
Mr. and Mrs. James H. Mitsui
Mr. and Mrs. Pete Mitsui
Mr. Yasunari Mitsui
Ms. Violet Mitsumori
Ms. Betty Mitsunaga
Mr. Edwin Mitsunaga
Mr. Gary Y. Mitsunaga
Ms. Kay Mitsunaga
Ms. Mae K. Mitsunaga
Mr. and Mrs. Richard Mitsunaga
Ms. Miyoko Ann Mitsuoka
Mr. and Mrs. Norio Mitsuoka
Ms. Pearl Mitsushima
Mr. Yasukichi Mitsuta
Ms. Amy Mitsuuchi
Mr. Hisashi Mitsuuchi
Mr. Masao Mitsuyasu
Ms. Carol L. Mitsuyoshi
Mr. and Mrs. Cary T. Mitsuyoshi
Mr. Earl Mitsuyoshi
Mr. Howard Mitsuyoshi
Ms. Meri Mitsuyoshi
Mr. and Mrs. T. J. Mitsuyoshi
Ms. Ann Y. Miura
Mr. Benjamin Miura
Dr. C. Ken Miura
Mr. Christopher Miura
Mr. and Mrs. Dan Y. Miura
Mr. Jeffrey Miura
Mr. and Mrs. Kazuo Miura
Ms. Kiyoko Miura

Dr. Masako K. Miura
Mrs. Michiko Miura
Mr. and Mrs. Neal Miura
Mr. Norman Miura
Mr. and Mrs. Randal S. Miura
Mr. Richard Miura
Rin Miura
Ms. Ruri Miura
Ms. Stacy M. Miura
Mr. and Mrs. Taro Miura
Mr. Thomas Miura
Mr. Fred Miwa
Mr. Jack L. Miwa
Mr. Masao D. Miwa
Mr. Robert Miwa
Ms. Yoshiko Miwa
Ms. Marlene Mixell
Mr. Darrell H. Miya
Ms. Grace Miya
Harry and Nancy Miya
Mr. and Mrs. Hisa Miya
Mr. Hitoshi Miya
Mr. and Mrs. Ken Miya
Mr. Marcus Miya
Mitsue, Lindsay, Keiko and Darron Miya
Ms. Miwako M. Miya
Mr. and Mrs. Shig Miya
Mr. and Mrs. Tom Miya
Mr. Tomio Miya
Ms. Joyce Miyabe
Mr. Henry Y. Miyachi
Ms. Julie N. Miyachi
Mr. and Mrs. Charles Miyada
Mr. and Mrs. Akira Miyade
Mr. Robert Miyade
Mr. Jon H. Miyade, II
Mr. John T. Miyagawa
Mr. Malcolm D. Miyagawa
Mr. Starr T. Miyagawa
Mr. and Mrs. Earl M. Miyagi
Mr. and Mrs. Genji Miyagi
Mr. and Mrs. Takamori Miyagi
Mrs. William Miyagi
Ms. Yoko Miyagi
Mrs. Lillie Miyagishima
Mr. Mike Miyagishima
Mr. and Mrs. Roland Miyagishima
Mr. Yuji Miyagishima
Mr. Hisao Miyaguchi
Mr. Allen Miyahara
Mr. and Mrs. Fumitaka Miyahara
Mr. Gary T. Miyahara
Mr. and Mrs. Harry H. Miyahara
Ms. Jane F. Miyahara
Rev. John M. Miyahara
Kazumi Miyahara
Mr. and Mrs. Peony Miyahara
Mr. Peter Miyahara
Ms. Sandra G. Miyahara
Mrs. Setsuko Miyahara
Ms. Yae Miyahata
Mr. Abel Miyahira
Mr. and Mrs. Calvin I. Miyahira
Mr. Harry Miyahira
Ms. Marian Miyahira
Mr. Wallace Miyahira
Mr. and Mrs. Wallace S. Miyahira
Mr. Wayne Miyahira
Dr. and Dr. Willard Miyahira
Mr. and Mrs. Yoshinobu Miyahira
Mr. Yoshihito Miyairi
Mr. Hiroshi Miyaji
Mrs. Mary Miyaji
Miyawo Co. Ltd.
Ms. Tamae Miyajima
Mr. Edward T. Miyakawa
Mr. and Mrs. Isao G. Miyakawa
Mr. and Mrs. Jimmie S. Miyakawa
Mr. Jon Miyakawa
Mr. and Mrs. Kelvin Miyakawa
Mr. and Mrs. Mitsugi Miyakawa
Mr. and Mrs. Richard Y. Miyakawa
Ms. Rinko I. Miyakawa
Mr. Robert H. Miyakawa
Mr. and Mrs. Seiichi Miyakawa
Ms. Dorothy Miyake
Ms. Frances Miyake
Mr. Garrett Miyake
Mr. George Miyake
Mr. and Mrs. George C. Miyake
Mr. George T. Miyake
Mr. and Mrs. Gregory Miyake
Mrs. H. Helen Miyake
Ms. Helen Miyake
Mr. Hiroshi Miyake
Mr. Jack Miyake

Mr. and Mrs. James Miyake
Ms. Jan Miyake
Mr. and Mrs. Kazuo Miyake
Mr. Kenneth Miyake
Mr. Kevin K. Miyake
Mr. and Mrs. Kuni Miyake
Ms. Laura Miyake
Ms. Lillian Miyake
M. Miyake
Mr. Masaji Miyake
Mr. Masato Miyake
Mr. and Mrs. Mike Miyake
Ms. Ocean Miyake
Mr. and Mrs. Perry Miyake
Mr. and Mrs. Roy Miyake
Mr. and Mrs. Sanae Miyake
Mr. and Mrs. Shawn Miyake
Mr. and Mrs. Shinpei Miyake
Mr. Tetsuo Miyake
Ms. Laraine Miyake-Combs
Revs. Robert and Nobuko Miyake-Stoner
Mrs. Amy A. Miyaki
Ms. Colleen K. Miyaki
Ms. Doris Miyamae
Mr. Ben Miyamoto
Mr. Carl T. Miyamoto
Mr. Dan T. Miyamoto
Mr. and Mrs. Dave Miyamoto
Mr. Edwin T. Miyamoto
Ms. Emiko Miyamoto
Dr. and Mrs. Eric K. Miyamoto
Mr. Frank K. Miyamoto
Mr. and Mrs. Fred J. Miyamoto
Mr. Fujio Miyamoto
Mrs. Fusae Miyamoto
Mr. Gary Miyamoto
Mr. and Mrs. Genji Miyamoto
Mr. and Mrs. George Miyamoto
Dr. Glenn Miyamoto
Mr. and Mrs. Grant S. Miyamoto
Mr. and Mrs. Harry James Miyamoto
Mr. Henry Miyamoto
Mr. Herbert Miyamoto
Mr. Hisao Miyamoto
Mr. John M. Miyamoto
Mr. and Mrs. Joseph Miyamoto
Mrs. Judy N. Miyamoto
Mr. Kameso Kay Miyamoto
Mr. Kaname Miyamoto
Mr. and Mrs. Ken Miyamoto
Mr. and Mrs. Kenneth Miyamoto
Ms. Kise S. Miyamoto
Ms. Kiyoka Kawai Miyamoto
Kyle and Susan Miyamoto
Mr. and Mrs. Lou Miyamoto
Ms. Lynne Miyamoto
M. Miyamoto
Ms. Margie K. Miyamoto
Ms. Martha M. Miyamoto
Mr. Masao M. Miyamoto
Ms. May Miyamoto
Maya and Gladyce Miyamoto
Mr. and Mrs. Michio Miyamoto
Mr. Mickey Miyamoto
Mr. and Mrs. Mikio Miyamoto
Ms. Mitsue Miyamoto
Mr. and Mrs. Nobuo Miyamoto
Mr. Ray Miyamoto
Mr. and Mrs. Ronald Miyamoto
Mr. and Mrs. Roy Miyamoto
Mr. Sadao Miyamoto
Mr. and Mrs. Sam Miyamoto
Mr. and Mrs. San Miyamoto
Ms. Sharon Miyamoto
Mr. and Mrs. Shigeo Miyamoto
Mr. Shigeru D. Miyamoto
Mrs. Shirley Miyamoto
Mr. Steven K. Miyamoto
Tadashi and Florence Miyamoto
Mr. and Mrs. Ted Miyamoto
Ms. Tomiko Miyamoto
Mr. Wayne Miyamoto
Mrs. Wendy Miyamoto
Dr. William Miyamoto
Mr. Yoshiaki W. Miyamoto
Ms. Anne Miyamura
Dr. Candace Miyamura
Mrs. Marjorie F. Miyamura
Ms. Martha Miyamura
Mr. and Mrs. Tadayuki Miyamura
Mr. Frank Miyanaga
Ms. Jean Miyano
Mr. and Mrs. Sam Miyano
Mr. and Mrs. George H. Miyao
Mr. and Mrs. George M. Miyao

Ms. Mary Ann S. Miyao
Mr. and Mrs. Sid Miyao
Mr. and Mrs. Clifford Miyaoi
Ms. Mary Jane Miyaoka
Mr. Masashi M. Miyaoka
Ms. Vickie L. Miyaoka
Ms. Candice Miyasaki
Mr. and Mrs. George Miyasaki
Mr. and Mrs. George T. Miyasaki
Ms. Mabel T. Miyasaki
Ms. Maryann Miyasaki
Mr. Roy Miyasaki
Mr. and Mrs. Shuji Miyasaki
Mr. and Mrs. Tom Miyasaki
Mr. and Mrs. Von C. Miyasaki
Warren and Jane Miyasaki
Mr. Randy Miyasako
Mr. Albert Miyasato
Ms. Frances N. Miyasato
Miyasato Orchids
Mr. Jack Miyasato
Mr. Michael Miyasato
Mr. Robert Miyasato
Mr. Robert S. Miyasato
Mr. Ronald S. Miyasato
Mr. Stuart R. Miyasato
Mr. Toshio Miyasato
Mr. Toshiro Miyasato
Mr. Wayne Miyasato
Mr. Wilbert Miyasato
Mr. Yasuo Miyasato
Mr. Akiho Miyashiro
Mr. Calvin Miyashiro
Mr. and Mrs. Clarence S. Miyashiro
Mr. Donald Miyashiro
Mrs. Florence Miyashiro
Mr. Gary H. Miyashiro
Mr. George I. Miyashiro
Mr. Harold Miyashiro
Mr. and Mrs. Henry Miyashiro
Mr. Herbert S. Miyashiro
Mr. and Mrs. Isami Miyashiro
Mr. and Mrs. Isamu Miyashiro
Mr. James J. Miyashiro
Mr. James S. Miyashiro
Mr. and Mrs. James T. Miyashiro
Mr. and Mrs. Jintoku Miyashiro
Ms. Kimiyo Miyashiro
Mr. and Mrs. Kotoku Miyashiro
Mr. and Mrs. Larry Miyashiro
Mrs. Melody K. Miyashiro
Mr. Melvin S. Miyashiro
Ms. Norma A. Miyashiro
Ms. Patsy Miyashiro
Mr. Ralph T. Miyashiro
Mr. and Mrs. Richard Miyashiro
Mr. Robert T. Miyashiro
Mr. Robert Y. Miyashiro
Mr. and Mrs. Ronald H. Miyashiro
Mr. Roy J. Miyashiro
Mr. Susumu Miyashiro
Mr. and Mrs. Takeichi Miyashiro
Mr. Thomas K. Miyashiro
Mr. and Mrs. William Miyashiro
Mr. Yoshio Miyashiro
Mr. and Mrs. Yoshio Miyashiro
Yoshito and Emiko Miyashiro
Mrs. Doris H. Miyashita
Mr. and Mrs. John Miyashita
Mr. Kazuaki J. Miyashita
Mr. and Mrs. Kazuo Miyashita
Mr. and Mrs. Charles Miyata
Mr. and Mrs. Chieko Miyata
Mr. George Miyata
Ms. Helen S. Miyata
Mr. Katsuo Miyata
Mr. and Mrs. Masao Miyata
Ms. Peggy K. Miyata
Mr. and Mrs. Sam Miyata
Mr. and Mrs. Satoshi M. Miyata
Mr. Shig Miyata
Mr. and Mrs. Shoichi Miyata
Mr. Ted I. Miyata
Dr. Thomas Miyata
Mr. and Mrs. Tommy H. Miyata
Mr. Wayne T. Miyata
Ms. Lynne H. Miyatake
Ms. Mari C. Miyatake
Mr. and Mrs. Robert Miyatake
Ms. Tokimi M. Miyatake
Ms. Hatsuye Miyauchi
Mr. Perry Miyauchi
Mr. Richard Miyauchi
Mr. Richard Miyauchi
Ms. Grace M. Miyawaki
Mr. Harumi Miyawaki

Mr. and Mrs. Ichiro Miyawaki
Ms. Masami Marion Miyaya
Dr. and Mrs. Fred S. Miyazaki
Mr. Kevin J. Miyazaki
Kurt Miyazaki and Ruth Hoff
Mr. Richard T. Miyazaki
Mr. Shigekazu Miyazaki
Mr. Tsuyoshi Miyazaki
Mr. James Y. Miyazawa
Mr. and Mrs. Akira Miyoda
Mr. Edward M. Miyoda
Evelyn Miyose and Jay Tomokiyo
Mr. and Mrs. Alex Miyoshi
Mr. Allan M. Miyoshi
Mr. and Mrs. George Miyoshi
Mr. Kenneth S. Miyoshi
Mr. Kenneth T. Miyoshi
Ms. Marcia Miyoshi
Mr. and Mrs. Masaru Miyoshi
Ms. Nobu Miyoshi
Mr. and Mrs. Russell Miyoshi
Mrs. Viola S. Miyoshi
Mr. and Mrs. Yuji Miyoshi
Mr. and Mrs. A. B. Mizoguchi
Ms. Chiami Mizoguchi
Mr. J. Mizoguchi
Mr. and Mrs. Audrey Mizokami
Mr. Mark Mizokami
Mr. and Mrs. Mike Mizokami
Mrs. Tomiko Mizokami
Ms. Yoneko Mizokani
Mr. and Mrs. George A. Mizono
Mr. and Mrs. Jack K. Mizono
Ms. Diane K. Mizota
Mr. Kyoji Mizota
Ms. Louise K. Mizota
Mr. and Mrs. Frank Mizote
Dr. Hisashi E. Mizote
Mrs. Taka Mizote
Mr. Ty N. Mizote
Mr. and Mrs. Walt Mizote
Ms. Kazuko Mizoue
Mr. and Mrs. Jack Mizuhara
Ms. Teri R. Mizuhara
Mr. Kiyoshi Mizuhata
Mr. and Mrs. Masami Mizuiri
Ms. Kit Mizukami
Mr. and Mrs. Robert Mizukami
Mr. Takeshi Mizukami
Ms. Frances Mizuki
Mr. Hiroshi Mizuki
Mr. and Mrs. Howard Mizuki
Mr. and Mrs. Jim Mizuki
Mr. Roger K. Mizumori
Mr. Allen Mizumoto
Mr. Eiichi Mizumoto
Mr. and Mrs. Katsutoshi H. Mizumoto
Ms. Kazuko Mizumoto
Linda, Kiyomi, Reiko Mizumoto and Kevin Gardiner
Ms. Lisa Y. Mizumoto
Mrs. Margaret M. Mizumoto
Mr. and Mrs. Robert Mizumoto
Ms. Jessie Mizunaka
Ms. Amy Hiratzka Mizuno
Mr. and Mrs. Bill Mizuno
Ms. Fumi Mizuno
Mr. Harry Y. Mizuno
Mr. and Mrs. Jiro Mizuno
Mrs. Michiko Mizuno
Ms. Natsuko Mizuno
Robert H. and Michie Mizuno
Mr. and Mrs. William T. Mizuno
Mrs. Masako Mizunoue
Mr. Lenard A. Mizusaka
William and Teri Mizusaka
Mr. Susumu Mizusaki
Mr. Tom Mizusaki
Mr. and Mrs. Bert Mizusawa
Mr. George T. Mizusawa
Ms. Mie Mizusawa
Ms. Tomoko Mizusawa
Mr. Toshio Mizusawa
Mr. George Mizushima
Mr. Gregory Mizushima
Mr. Hiroki Mizushima
Ms. Joy Mizushima
Mr. Marcus Mizushima
Mr. Masataka Mizushima
Mrs. Sumi Mizushima
Ms. Carla R. Mizuta
Mr. Fred Mizuta
Mr. and Mrs. Jim Mizuta
Mr. and Mrs. Takanori Mizuta
Mr. and Mrs. Edwin Mizutani
Mr. and Mrs. Ted Mizutani
Mr. and Mrs. Yoshiharu Mizutani

Mr. and Mrs. Michiro Mizutari
Mr. and Mrs. Toshiyuki Mizutari
Mr. and Mrs. Yasuo Mizuuchi
Mr. James Moceri
Mr. and Mrs. Roy Moceri
Mrs. Yukie Mochida
Mr. and Mrs. Sadao Mochidome
Thomas and Chisato Mochimaru
Mr. and Mrs. Bernard Y. Mochizuki
Ms. Carmen Y. Mochizuki
Mr. and Mrs. Eugene Mochizuki
Mr. and Mrs. Gilbert Mochizuki
Ms. Hideko O. Mochizuki
Mr. Joseph Mochizuki
Judy Mochizuki and Buck Oakes
Mr. Masaru Mochizuki
Mr. and Mrs. Mike Mochizuki
Dr. Ronald Mochizuki and Dr. Shelly Halper
Mr. and Mrs. S. R. Mochizuki
Ms. Tara K. Mochizuki and Mr. Jeffrey M. Chu
Dr. and Mrs. William J. Mochizuki
Mr. Yukio Mochizuki
Mr. and Mrs. Walter Mock
Mr. and Mrs. Robert Mogg
Mr. James F. Mohan
Ms. Judy Mohizuki
Ms. Jennifer N. Mohr
Mr. Iris Yasui Moinat
Mr. Richard Molina
Mr. and Mrs. Dick Momii
Mr. and Mrs. Isamu Momii
Ms. Mary U. Momii
Mr. and Mrs. Rikito Momii
Mr. Jerry Momoda
Mr. and Mrs. Gary Momohara
Momotaro Sushi Japanese Restaurant
Ms. Anne Horikawa Monari
Kimie and Alice Monden
Mrs. Shigeko Monden
Ms. Diane Mondschein
Mr. and Mrs. Irving Mondschein
Mr. Dan S. Monji
Mr. David Monji
Mr. Haruo Monji
Ms. Kay Monma
Mr. Laurence Monson
Mr. Ricardo Montejano
Mr. and Mrs. Charles Moon
Mr. John T. Moon
Mr. Michie M. Moon
Mr. and Mrs. Thomas Moon
Al C. and Yuki Moore
Mr. and Mrs. James M. Moore
Mr. and Mrs. John Moore
Ms. Meg Moore
Ms. Pauline Moore
Mr. David C. Moore, II
Mr. Robert T. Moori
Ms. Sara A. Moran
Mr. and Mrs. Samuel Moreno
Mr. Tom Morgan
Ms. Alice Mori
Ms. Barbara L. Mori
Mr. and Mrs. Bob Mori
Mr. and Mrs. Bruce S. Mori
Mr. Darryl Mori
Mr. David Mori
Ms. Emma Mori
Mr. and Mrs. Frank S. Mori
Ms. Fumie Mori
Mr. and Mrs. George Mori
Mr. George K. Mori
Mr. Giichiro Mori
Mr. and Mrs. Gilbert Mori
Mrs. Hatsuyo Mori
Mrs. Helene Mori
Dr. and Mrs. Hironobu Mori
Mr. and Mrs. Jack Mori
Mr. James Mori
Ms. Janice Mori
Mr. and Mrs. Jeffrey K. Mori
Jim Mori and Martha Fushimi
Mr. and Mrs. Jiro Mori
Mr. and Mrs. John Y. Mori
Mrs. June K. Mori
Ms. Katherine K. Mori
Ms. Kay Mori
Mr. Kenneth Mori
Mr. and Mrs. Lawrence Mori
Mr. Masao Mori
Mr. and Mrs. Masao Mori
Ms. Mayumi Mori
Ms. Meriko Mori
Mr. Mikio Mori
Mr. and Mrs. Nobuo Mori
Mr. and Mrs. Osamu Mori

Mr. and Mrs. Richard T. Mori
Jerome Reunion V Committee
S. F. Mori
Mr. Shigeru Mori
Mr. and Mrs. Stanley Mori
Ms. Susanne Mori and Mr. Chris Souleles
Mr. Susumu Mori
Mr. and Mrs. T. Peter Mori
Mr. Tom Mori
Ms. Toshiko Mori
Dr. and Mrs. Victor Mori
Ms. Yoshiko Mori
Mr. and Mrs. Yoshio Mori
Mr. and Mrs. Yuki Mori
Mr. and Mrs. Lee Moribe
Mr. Robert K. Moribe
Mr. Paul Morichika
Mr. David Moriguchi
Ms. Denise Moriguchi
Mr. and Mrs. George S. Moriguchi
Mr. Joe Moriguchi
Mr. Kenneth Moriguchi
Mr. and Mrs. Mark S. Moriguchi
Ms. Susan Moriguchi
Mrs. Tayeko Moriguchi
Mr. Pat Morihata
Mr. George Morihiro
Mr. Mike Y. Morihiro
Mr. and Mrs. Shoji G. Morihisa
Dr. Kent Morikado
Mr. Ken T. Morikami
Morikami Museum and Japanese Garden
Mr. Bill Morikawa
Mr. and Mrs. Frank Morikawa
Mr. and Mrs. Frank T. Morikawa
Mr. Gary Morikawa
Mr. George Morikawa
Mr. and Mrs. Harry Morikawa
Mr. and Mrs. Henry Morikawa
Mrs. Janice Morikawa
Mr. and Mrs. Jim Morikawa
Dr. Jon H. Morikawa
Mr. Kazuo Morikawa
Mr. and Mrs. Samuel Morikawa
Mr. Thomas M. Morikawa
Mr. and Mrs. Tom Morikawa
Mr. Treasure Morikawa
Mr. and Mrs. Wilfred Morikawa
Mr. James I. Moriki
Mr. Tsuneo T. Moriki
Mr. Yukio Morikubo
Mr. and Mrs. Jack Morimitsu
Mr. Sam Morimitsu
Mr. Alan Morimizu
Mr. Andrew S. Morimoto
Ms. Ayako Morimoto
Charles and Naurie Morimoto
Mr. Daniel Morimoto
Mr. David Morimoto
Mr. and Mrs. Edward Morimoto
Mr. Frank Y. Morimoto
Mr. and Mrs. Gordon Morimoto
Mr. Hiroshi Morimoto
Mr. and Mrs. Isamu Morimoto
Mr. Kan Morimoto
Mr. and Mrs. Karen Ann Morimoto
Mr. Kiyoshi Morimoto
Mrs. Lois Morimoto
Mrs. Masako Morimoto
Mr. Michael H. Morimoto
Mr. Minoru Morimoto
Mr. and Mrs. Munaki Morimoto
Mrs. Noriko Morimoto
Dr. Paul Morimoto
Mr. and Mrs. Pete M. Morimoto
Mr. and Mrs. Richard I. Morimoto
Mr. Richard Y. Morimoto
Ms. Risa Morimoto
Mr. and Mrs. Robert Morimoto
Mr. Robert A. Morimoto
Rev. and Mrs. Roger V. Morimoto
Mr. and Mrs. Stan Morimoto
Mr. and Mrs. Stanley S. Morimoto
Mr. and Mrs. Tom T. Morimoto
Ms. Tsurue Morimoto
Ms. Valerie Morimoto
Mr. and Mrs. Walter G. Morimoto
Mr. Yosh Morimoto
Ms. Yoshie D. Morimoto
Mr. and Mrs. Harry Morimune
Mr. Helen K. Morimune
Mr. and Mrs. Akiko Morinaga
Mr. and Mrs. Lloyd Morinaga
Mr. and Mrs. Samuel Morinaga
Mr. Sueo Morinaga
Mr. Teichi T. Morinaga

Mr. Yoshinori Morinaga
Mr. and Mrs. Jerry Morino
Mr. William Morino
Ms. Hiroko Morio
Mr. and Mrs. Noboro Morio
Ms. Betty Morioka
Mr. and Mrs. Dennis Morioka
Mr. and Mrs. Eddie T. Morioka
Ms. Frances Morioka
Mr. and Mrs. Fred Morioka
Y. and Mrs. James Morioka
Mr. and Mrs. James T. Morioka
Mr. Katsuto Morioka
Leslie Morioka
Mr. and Mrs. Takashi Morioka
Mr. and Mrs. Wilfred Morioka
Mrs. Dorothy Morisaki
Mr. and Mrs. John Morisaki
Mrs. Yukie T. Morisaki
Nowa Morisaku
Mr. Edward H. Morishige
Ms. Fumiko Morishige
Ms. Himi Morishige
Mrs. Ida Morishige
Ms. Jacqueline Morishige
Jerry and Mutsue Morishige
Mr. Jim Morishige
Ms. Maxine T. Morishige
Ms. Mutsue Morishige
Mrs. Yuki Morishige
Mr. Akira E. Morishima
Ms. Amy Morishima
Mrs. Helen K. Morishita and Friends
Ms. Janet S. Morishita
Mr. and Mrs. Jon Morishita
Ms. Joyce C. Morishita
Mr. and Mrs. Jundo Morishita
Mr. and Mrs. Leroy Morishita
Ms. Mary Morishita
Mr. R. J. Morishita
Mr. and Mrs. Ray J. Morishita
Mrs. Shigeko Morishita
Ms. Susan F. Morishita
Mr. and Mrs. William Morishita
Ms. Amy Morita
Asayo S. Morita
Mr. Ben T. Morita
Mr. Calvin Morita
Ms. Chiyoko Morita
Ms. Denise N. Morita
Mr. Dennis D. Morita
Mr. Dennis T. Morita
Mr. and Mrs. Donald Morita
Mrs. Flora Morita
Mr. Frank Morita
Mr. and Mrs. Fred Morita
Mr. and Mrs. Fujio Morita
Mr. Gary Morita
Mr. and Mrs. George Morita
Mr. and Mrs. George S. Morita
Ms. Gloria H. Morita
Mr. Harry Morita
Ms. Helen H. Morita
Mr. Hiroshi Y. Morita
Mr. and Mrs. Jim Morita
Mrs. Juliet Morita
Ms. Karen Morita
Ms. Karen M. Morita
Mr. and Mrs. Karl K. Morita
Mr. Kazuo Morita
Mr. and Mrs. Ken Morita
Ms. Kimi Morita
Ms. Linda Morita
Mr. Lloyd Morita
Mr. Makoto M. Morita
Mr. Mamoru Morita
Ms. Mary Morita
Mr. and Mrs. Masaji Morita
Mr. and Mrs. Michio Morita
Ms. Mizue Morita
Mr. Mototsugu M. Morita
Ms. Nobuko C. Morita
Dr. and Mrs. Paul Morita
Mr. Ray Morita
Mr. and Mrs. Raymond Morita
Mr. and Mrs. Richard Y. Morita
Mr. Roy S. Morita
Mrs. Sada A. Morita
Mr. and Mrs. Stanley Morita
Mr. Yuji Morita
Ms. Yumiko Morita
Mrs. Aiko Moriuchi
Ms. Atsuko Moriuchi
Mr. Toshio Moriuchi
Mr. Kiyoto Moriwake
Mr. and Mrs. Edwin Moriwaki

Mr. George G. Moriwaki
Mr. Howard M. Moriwaki
Mr. Masuo Moriwaki
Mr. Arthur K. Moriya
Mr. Stanley Moriya
Mr. and Mrs. Walter Moriya
Mr. George B. Moriyama
Mr. and Mrs. Kenneth Moriyama
Mr. and Mrs. Roberto Moriyama
Mr. Rodney Moriyama
Mrs. Tom Moriyama
Mr. Henry M. Moriyasu
Ms. Katherine Moriyasu
Mr. Roy Moriyasu
Ms. Sharon A. Moriyasu
Ms. Teriko Moriyasu
Ms. Grace Morizawa
Mr. Yoshimi Morizawa
Mr. and Mrs. Kiyoshi Morodomi
Mr. and Mrs. Doug Moromisato
Mr. Jorge Moromisato
Ms. Martha M. Morooka
Ms. Geanne R. Moroye
Mr. and Mrs. Ray Moroye
Mr. John I. Morozumi
Mr. and Mrs. George J. Morris
Mrs. Mary I. Morris
Mr. and Mrs. Phillip J. Morris
Mr. and Mrs. B. Ross Morrison
Mr. and Mrs. Charles Morrison
Ms. Nancy Jane Morrow
Mr. and Mrs. Walter Morton
Mr. and Mrs. David L. Moseley
Mr. and Mrs. Rasin Moser
Mr. Michael H. Moss
Mr. and Mrs. Eugene D. Mossner
Mr. and Mrs. Robert Moteki
Mr. Raymond T. Motoda
Mr. Takeyasu Motoi
Mrs. Aya Motoike
Ms. Beverly M. Motokane
Mr. Jay H. Motokawa
Mr. and Mrs. Shigeru Motoki
Mr. Jerry S. Motomura
Mr. Takeshi Motomura
Mr. Bert T. Motonaga
Mr. Neal Motonaga
Mr. Dan Motooka
Ms. Etsuko N. Motooka
Ms. Grace Motooka
Mr. and Mrs. Sam Motooka
Mr. Eiichi Motoshige
Mr. Ben Motoyama
Mr. and Mrs. Hayao Motoyama
Mr. and Mrs. Masaru Motoyama
Mr. and Mrs. Ray S. Motoyama
Mr. Robert S. Motoyama
Ms. Teruko T. Motoyama
Ms. Violet S. Motoyama
Mr. Steven K. Motoyasu
Mr. Y. Motoyoshi
Mr. Richard M. Mowbray
Ms. Jean Y. Moy
Mr. and Mrs. Lawrence M. Moy
Mr. Rocky Moy
Mr. and Mrs. Thomas Moy
Mr. and Mrs. Tow H. Moy
Ms. Marnie Mueller
Mr. and Mrs. Paul Mueller
Mr. Masashi Mueoka
Mr. Akira Mukai
Mr. Chieto Mukai
Mr. and Mrs. Dennis Mukai
Mr. Don T. Mukai
Mr. and Mrs. Douglas Mukai
Mr. Eugene S. Mukai
Mr. and Mrs. Francis Mukai
Ms. Gail Mukai
Mr. and Mrs. George Mukai
Mr. and Mrs. George T. Mukai
Mr. and Mrs. Gerrold Mukai
Mr. and Mrs. Greg Mukai
Ms. Hatsuko Mukai
Mr. and Mrs. Henry Mukai
Mr. and Mrs. Joe Y. Mukai
Mr. Larry Mukai
Ms. Margret Mukai
Mr. and Mrs. Mark Mukai
Mr. and Mrs. Michael Mukai
Mr. Richard S. Mukai
Mr. Robert Mukai
Mr. and Mrs. Robert Mukai
Mr. and Mrs. Roy Mukai
Mr. and Mrs. Shinichi Mukai
Mr. Taro Mukai
Mr. and Mrs. Tomeo Mukai

Mr. and Mrs. Tommy Mukai
Mr. Wayne Mukai
Mr. Donald Mukaida
Mr. Kaz Mukaida
Mr. and Mrs. Ikuo Mukasa
Mr. Thomas Mukasa
Mr. and Mrs. Robert Mukoda
Mr. and Mrs. Howard Mukoyama
Mr. and Mrs. John H. Mukoyama
Mr. and Mrs. W. K. Mukoyama
Mr. Shunji W. Mukozaka
Mr. and Mrs. Hisashi Mukumoto
Ms. Marcia Mullins
Ms. Nomi Lee Mummert
Mr. Kenneth K. L. Mun
Mr. and Mrs. Donald Munakata
Mr. and Mrs. Charles E. Munat
Ms. Hisako Mune
Dr. Ken K. Munechika
Mr. and Mrs. Henry Munehiro
Mr. Marian Munekata
Ms. Fumi Munekiyo
Dr. Saylo Munemitsu
Ms. Yone Munemitsu
Ms. Mary Munemura
Mr. and Mrs. Thomas Muneno
Mrs. Tomiye Muneno
Mr. Masashi Muneoka
Ms. Anita Muneta
Mr. Edward Munoz
Mr. and Mrs. Hideo Mura
Mr. and Mrs. Masao Mura
Ms. Sayoko Kay Mura
Mr. Richard Murabayashi
Mr. and Mrs. Larry Murahashi
Mr. and Mrs. Sueki Murahata
Ms. Dawn M. Murai
Ms. Gladys S. Murai
Mr. Karl Murai
Mr. and Mrs. Katsumi Murai
Mr. Kazuo Murai
Mr. Mark Murai
Mr. Masakazu Murai
Mr. Michael A. Murai
Mr. Robert R. Murai
Mr. Akira Murakami
Mr. and Mrs. Chester M. Murakami
Mr. and Mrs. Daniel Murakami
Mr. Denny Murakami
Ms. Dorothy Y. Murakami
Mr. Douglas Murakami
Mr. and Mrs. Eddie Murakami
Ms. Emi Murakami
Mr. Eric D. Murakami
Mr. and Mrs. Eugene Murakami
Mr. Fuji Murakami
Mr. George Murakami
Mr. and Mrs. George Murakami
Mr. Glen M. Murakami
Mrs. Grace Murakami
Mr. and Mrs. Henry M. Murakami
Mr. Howard Murakami
Mr. and Mrs. Isamu Murakami
Mr. and Mrs. James Murakami
Ms. Jean Murakami
Mr. and Mrs. Joe Murakami
Mr. John Murakami
Mr. and Mrs. John S. Murakami
Mr. Kameki Murakami
Mr. Ken Murakami
Rev. Ken Murakami
Ms. Kimi Murakami
Mr. Koichi Murakami
Mr. and Mrs. Larry Murakami
Mr. Masaru Murakami
Ms. Masaye Murakami
Mr. and Mrs. Masayoshi Murakami
Mr. Melvin K. Murakami
Mr. and Mrs. Mitsuharu Murakami
Mrs. Mitsuko Murakami
Mr. and Mrs. Mitsuo Murakami
Mr. Noboru Murakami
Mr. Ralph Murakami
Mr. Rick Murakami
Mr. Robert D. Murakami
Mr. and Mrs. Roy Murakami
Mr. Roy L. Murakami
Mr. Roy M. Murakami
Mr. and Mrs. Roy S. Murakami
Mr. and Mrs. Saburo Murakami
Mr. and Mrs. Satoru Murakami
Shigemi Murakami
Ms. Shizuye Murakami
Mr. Tadao Murakami
Mr. and Mrs. Takashi Murakami
Mr. Thomas Murakami

Mr. Timothy Murakami
Mr. and Mrs. Tokuo Murakami
Mr. and Mrs. Tom Murakami
Dr. and Mrs. Tomomi Murakami
Mr. Toshio Murakami
Mrs. Toshiye Murakami
Mrs. Tsui Murakami
Mr. Tsukasa Murakami
Ms. Tsutaye Murakami
Mr. and Mrs. Tsuyoshi Murakami
Mr. Walter Murakami
Mr. William Murakami
Mr. and Mrs. William Murakami
Mr. and Mrs. Yoshito Murakami
Mr. Yuji Murakami
Dr. Fay Murakawa
Mr. and Mrs. Galen S. Murakawa
Mr. Hugh Murakawa
Mr. Teruko Muraki
Mr. Tom Muraki
Mr. and Mrs. Robert Murakoshi
Ms. Suzen Murakoshi
Mr. Tsuneo Muramaru
Mr. and Mrs. Frank Muramatsu
Ms. Masae Muramatsu
Mr. and Mrs. Richard Muramatsu
Mrs. Barbara N. Muramoto
Mr. and Mrs. Daniel Muramoto
Mr. Dennis Muramoto
Ms. Eliese Y. Muramoto
Mr. George Muramoto
Dr. and Mrs. George G. Muramoto
Ms. Helen K. Muramoto
Mr. Keith Muramoto
Mrs. and Ms. Muramoto
Mr. Michael Muramoto
Mr. and Mrs. Tsukasa Muramoto
Mrs. Wendy Muramoto
Mrs. Eiko Muranaka
Ms. Gwen Muranaka
Mr. and Mrs. Hugh T. Muranaka
Ms. Margaret Muranaka
Mr. and Mrs. Tadashi Muranaka
Mr. and Mrs. Terry Muranaka
Mr. Tomio Muranaka
Mr. Joseph Murano
Mr. and Mrs. Roy Y. Murano
Mr. Ted H. Murano
Mr. Peter Murao
Mr. Clarence K. Muraoka
Mr. and Mrs. Clifford Muraoka
Mr. David F. Muraoka
Mr. Ernest Muraoka
Mr. and Mrs. Frank Muraoka
Mr. and Mrs. George Muraoka
Ms. Haruko Muraoka
Mr. and Mrs. James Muraoka
Mr. and Mrs. John J. Muraoka
Mr. Katsuyuki Muraoka
Mr. and Mrs. Kenneth H. Muraoka
Mr. Leighton T. Muraoka
Mr. Miles C. Muraoka
Mr. Miles Y. Muraoka
Mr. Seiji Muraoka
Ms. Sueaki Muraoka
Mr. Tad Muraoka
Mr. Takashi Muraoka
Mr. and Mrs. Tom Muraoka
Ms. Vivian Muraoka
Mr. and Mrs. William Muraoka
Mr. Zenichi Muraoka
Ms. Emily Murase and Mr. Neal Taniguchi
Mrs. Hannah Murase
Mr. and Mrs. Kenji Murase
Ms. Kimi Murase
Mr. and Mrs. Takashi R. Murase
Mr. and Mrs. Yoshio Murase
Mr. Allen Murashige
Mr. Alvin Murashige
Mr. Bert Y. Murashige
Mr. Calvin Murashige
Mr. Dennis Murashige
Mr. and Mrs. Hiroshi Murashige
Mr. Masaru Murashige
Mr. Michael Murashige
Mr. and Mrs. Richard S. Murashige
Mr. Rickey S. Murashige
Mr. Frederick Murashima
Mr. and Mrs. Harry G. Murashima
Mitsuo Murashima
Mr. Akira Murata
Mr. Brent T. Murata
Mr. and Mrs. George Murata
Mr. Henry Murata
Mr. and Mrs. James Murata
Mr. and Mrs. Jiro Murata

Ms. Kikuye Murata
Mr. and Mrs. Koji Murata
Ms. Mary Murata
Mr. Ronald Murata
Mrs. Ruth H. Murata
Sadane Murata
Ms. Susan Murata
Mr. and Mrs. Tetsuo Murata
Mr. Victor Murata
Ms. Yorie Murata
Mr. Yoshinori Murata
Mr. and Mrs. Yoshio Murata
Mr. Jiro Muratsuchi
Mrs. Atsuko Murayama
Mr. Dennis Murayama
Ms. Fumiko Murayama
Mr. Herbert Murayama
Ms. Ruth Murayama
Mr. and Mrs. Takashi Murayama
Ms. Gail E. Murdock
Mr. Jesse Murga
Ms. Gerda Muri
Mr. and Mrs. Kim Muromoto
Mr. Kenneth R. Muronaka
Ms. Tsuyuko Muronaka
Mr. and Mrs. Kako Murosako
Mrs. Amy Muroshige
Ms. Tama Murotani
Mr. and Mrs. Alfred J. Murphy
Mr. and Mrs. Cecil Murphy
Ms. Debbra M. Murphy
Mr. and Mrs. Paul Murphy
Mr. WIlliam Murphy
Mr. Douglas E. Murray
Ms. Ester J. Murray
Mr. and Mrs. Charles Murrell
Mr. and Mrs. Susumu Musashi
Mr. Jack Mushiake
Ms. Cheryl L. Muszynski
Art and Ann Muto
Mr. Ernest Muto
Mr. Lawrence C. Myers
Mr. Dennis Myose and Family
NAFSA
NHK- Associated Spring Suspension Component
Mr. Harry Nabeshima
Mr. and Mrs. Henry T. Nabeshima
Satoko Nabeta
Ms. Laurie J. Nadamoto
Mr. and Mrs. Yoshiaki Nadaoka
Y. Nadashim
Mr. and Mrs. Ray Naegele
Ms. Lorraine Nagae
Mr. and Mrs. Dabo Nagafuchi
Rev. Gyosei Nagafuji
Mr. Shion Nagahara
Mr. and Mrs. Edwin S. Nagahashi
Ms. Sally A. Nagahashi
Mr. and Mrs. Stanley Nagahashi
Ms. Grace S. Nagahiro
Ms. Sherri L. Nagahiro
Mr. David Nagai
Mrs. Dorothy Y. Nagai
Mr. Edward H. Nagai
Mr. and Mrs. Ernest Nagai
Mr. Hisashi Nagai
Ms. Ida A. Nagai
Mr. and Mrs. Ikuo Nagai
Mr. M. Donald Nagai
Mr. and Mrs. Mas Nagai
Mrs. Matsuko A. Nagai
Mr. Mineo D. Nagai
Mr. and Mrs. Nelson Nagai
Ms. Patricia Nagai
Mr. and Mrs. Roy Nagai and Family
Mr. Shuichi Nagai
Ms. Therese M. Nagai
Mr. Yosh Nagai
Ms. Chiseko Nagaishi
Ms. Haruko Nagaishi
Ms. Patricia Nagaishi
Mr. and Mrs. Akira Nagaki
Ms. Alice Nagaki
Mr. and Mrs. Mitsuo Nagaki
Mrs. Martha S. Nagakura
Mr. Jaime A. Nagal
Mr. Glenn Nagamatsu
Mr. and Mrs. Henry Nagamatsu
Mr. and Mrs. Jun Nagamatsu
Mr. and Mrs. Tom Nagamatsu
Mr. and Mrs. Henry Nagami
Mas and Setsuko Nagami
Mr. and Mrs. Willis Nagami
Ms. Betty Nagamine
Mr. Harry Nagamine
Mr. and Mrs. Kazuo Nagamine

Ms. Nannette Nagamine
Ms. Reeko Nagamine
Mr. and Mrs. Sadao Nagamoto
Mrs. Yasuko K. Nagamoto
Mr. Hideo Naganawa
Ms. Anne M. Nagano
Mr. George K. Nagano
Mr. James Nagano
Mr. and Mrs. Kiminori Nagano
Ms. Momo Nagano
Mr. and Mrs. Paul M. Nagano
Mr. Raymond Nagano
Mr. and Mrs. Steve Nagano
Mr. Henry Naganuma
Ms. Nancy A. Naganuma
Mr. Tony Naganuma
Mr. Charles T. Nagao
Mr. and Mrs. David Nagao
Mr. Dennis Nagao
Mr. and Mrs. Dennis H. Nagao
Mr. Edward Nagao
Ms. Esther F. Nagao
Mr. and Mrs. Fred Nagao
Mr. and Mrs. Fred T. Nagao
Mr. and Mrs. Hikaru Nagao
Mr. and Mrs. Norito Nagao
Mr. Norman K. Nagao
Mr. and Mrs. Wallace Nagao
Ms. Aileen S. Nagaoka
Mr. and Mrs. Harry Nagaoka
Mr. Joe Nagaoka
Mr. Minoru Nagaoka
Mr. Richard T. Nagaoka
Ms. Barbara Nagareda
Ms. C. Nancy Nagareda
Mr. and Mrs. Neil Nagareda
Mr. Richard Nagareda
Mr. Peter J. Nagaro
Mr. Bruce Nagasaka
Ms. Corrin Nagasaka
Mr. and Mrs. George Nagasaka
Ms. Yoko Nagasaka
Mr. and Mrs. Kengo Nagasako
Mr. and Mrs. Minoru Nagasako
Ms. Emi Nagasawa
Mr. Gary T. Nagasawa
Ms. Grace Nagasawa
Mr. and Mrs. Hiro Nagasawa
Ms. Mary Nagasawa
Mr. Shigeo Nagasawa
Goro and Takako Nagase
Mr. Satoshi Nagase
Mr. and Mrs. John Nagashiki
Mr. and Mrs. Ken Nagashima
Mr. and Mrs. Nobuo Nagashima
Ms. Amy Nagata
Mr. and Mrs. Barton Nagata
Mr. Brian Nagata
Mr. Carl Nagata
Mr. and Mrs. Ed H. Nagata
Ms. Florence Nagata
Mr. George J. Nagata and Ms. Sally S. Nagata
Mr. and Mrs. Gerald D. Nagata
Mr. and Mrs. Gordon Nagata
Ms. Grace Nagata
Mrs. Gwen T. Nagata
Mr. and Mrs. Harry M. Nagata
Mr. Harry W. Nagata
Mr. Herbert Nagata
Ms. Joyce J. Nagata
Kevin and Michelle Nagata and Family
Mr. and Mrs. Masaaki Nagata
Mr. and Mrs. Masaru Nagata
Mr. and Mrs. Masayuki Nagata
Mrs. Pamela S. Nagata
Mr. Rick T. Nagata
Mr. Robert T. Nagata
Mr. Roger Nagata
Mr. and Mrs. Stanley Nagata
Mr. Steven C. Nagata
Mr. Terrell T. Nagata
Mr. and Mrs. Tom Nagata
Mr. and Mrs. Tsutomu Nagata
Mr. Walter S. Nagata
Yukio and Edna Nagata
Nagata-Yamauchi Educational Fund
Mr. and Mrs. Ben Nagatani
Mr. and Mrs. Edward Nagatani
Mr. and Mrs. John L. Nagatani
Mr. and Mrs. Kiyoshi Nagatani
Dr. and Mrs. Ronald Nagatani
Mr. Ronald Nagatani
Rosie K. Nagatani
Mr. and Mrs. Tsutomu Nagatani
Mr. Gary K. Nagatoishi
Ms. Jean S. Nagatomi

Mr. and Mrs. Glenn T. Nagatori
Mr. Roy K. Nagatoshi
Mr. and Mrs. Tom T. Nagatoshi
Mr. James Nagatsuka
Mr. Sig Nagayama
Mr. and Mrs. Takashi Nagayama
Ms. Ruth K. Nagler
Mr. Yoshio Nago
Mr. and Mrs. Jack Nagoshi
Mr. and Mrs. Kenro Nagoshi
Mr. Mark Nagumo
Ms. Tsuruko Naguwa
Mr. Harry Nahiro
Mr. Carl S. Naito
Ms. Fumiko Naito and Mr. Chris Naito
Mr. and Mrs. Hiroshi Naito
Mrs. Hisaye Naito
Mr. and Mrs. Ken Naito
Mr. and Mrs. Kiyoshi Naito
Mr. and Mrs. Motoi Naito
Ms. Stephanie A. Naito
Mr. Tadami Naito
Mr. and Mrs. Tak Naito
Ms. Jennifer Najima-Mohr
Mr. and Mrs. Frank Naka
Mr. Terry Y. Naka
Mr. and Mrs. Frank T. Nakaba
Mr. Kenneth S. Nakaba
Mrs. Jane I. Nakabayashi
Mr. and Mrs. Kazuo Nakabayashi
Mr. and Mrs. Robin H. Nakabayashi
Mr. W. K. Nakabayashi
Mr. Harry Nakabe
Mr. Paul S. Nakachi
Mrs. Ann H. Nakada
Mr. Harry M. Nakada
Ms. Haruko Nakada
Mr. and Mrs. Hiro Nakada
Mr. James H. Nakada
Ms. Joyce Nakada
Mrs. Kiyo Nakada
Ms. Laura Nakada
Ms. Linda Nakada
Mr. Michael S. Nakada
Mr. Mike Nakada
Mr. Minoru P. Nakada
Ms. Patricia Nakada
Mr. Steven V. Nakada
Mr. James R. Nakada
Dr. and Mrs. Katsumi Nakadate
Ms. Marie Nakade
Mr. and Mrs. Mike Nakade
Mr. and Mrs. Takuro Nakae
Mr. Tatsuo Nakae
Mr. Tomo T. Nakae
Ms. Fumiye Nakagaki
Ms. Nora Nakagama
Mr. Jason Nakagami
Mr. and Mrs. Wally Nakagami
Mr. and Mrs. Akira Nakagawa
Mr. and Mrs. August T. Nakagawa
Mr. and Mrs. Bill I. Nakagawa
Mr. Bob Nakagawa
Mr. and Mrs. Bob H. Nakagawa
Mr. Brian J. Nakagawa
Dr. and Mrs. Bunzo Nakagawa
Mr. Charles N. Nakagawa
Ms. Chiyo Nakagawa
Mr. Craig K. Nakagawa
Mr. and Mrs. Dean T. Nakagawa
Mrs. Diane T. Nakagawa
Ms. Dorothy Nakagawa
Mr. and Mrs. Eiki Nakagawa
Mrs. Ethel K. Nakagawa
Francis S. and Marian F. Nakagawa
Mr. Fred T. Nakagawa
Mr. and Mrs. George Nakagawa
Capt. and Mrs. Gordon R. Nakagawa
Mr. Harry M. Nakagawa
Mr. Hideo Nakagawa
Mr. James Y. Nakagawa
Dr. Janice Y. Nakagawa
Mr. and Mrs. John Nakagawa
Ms. Katsuko T. Nakagawa
Mr. and Mrs. Ken Nakagawa
Mr. Kenny K. Nakagawa
Mr. and Mrs. Kerry Y. Nakagawa
Ms. Kylan Nakagawa
Mr. and Mrs. Lawrence T. Nakagawa
Mrs. Lynne H. Nakagawa
Miss M. M. Nakagawa
Mr. Mamoru Nakagawa
Mr. Marcos F. Nakagawa
Ms. Martha Nakagawa
Ms. Mary K. Nakagawa
Mr. Masato Nakagawa

Ms. May M. Nakagawa
Ms. Nadine Nakagawa
Mr. Noboru Nakagawa
Mr. Raymond Nakagawa
Mr. and Mrs. Richard M. Nakagawa
Mr. Ron Nakagawa
Mr. and Mrs. Rusty Nakagawa
Mr. and Mrs. Sammy Nakagawa
Ms. Shimeyo Nakagawa
Mr. and Mrs. Shiro Nakagawa
Ms. Susie Nakagawa
Mr. Susumu Nakagawa
Mr. Takeshi Nakagawa
Dr. and Mrs. Thomas A. Nakagawa
Mr. Thomas H. Nakagawa
Mr. and Mrs. Tom T. Nakagawa
Mr. William S. Nakagawa
Mrs. Yoshie Nakagawa
Mr. and Mrs. Yoshio Nakagawa
Ms. Yoshiye Nakagawa
Mr. and Mrs. Hiroshi Nakagawara
Mr. and Mrs. Minoru Nakagawara
Daniel and Nancy Nakagiri
Mr. and Mrs. Jim Nakagiri
Mrs. Kay Nakagiri
Mr. and Mrs. Neal E. Nakagiri
Ms. Sonoye Nakagiri
Mr. Thomas Nakagiri
Mr. and Mrs. Wakamatsu Nakagiri
Mr. and Mrs. Glenn M. Nakaguchi
Mr. Peter M. Nakaguchi
Mr. and Mrs. Richard Nakaguchi
Ms. Clarisse Nakahama
Ms. Elizabeth Nakahama
Mr. Yves Nakahama
Mr. Akio Nakahara
Mr. Arthur Y. Nakahara
Mr. and Mrs. Ben Nakahara
Mr. and Mrs. George J. Nakahara
Mr. and Mrs. Ichiro Nakahara
Mr. James Nakahara
Mr. James T. Nakahara
Ms. Jennifer Nakahara
Ms. Judy A. Nakahara
Ms. Kim C. Nakahara
Mr. Larry Y. Nakahara
Ms. Lucille H. Nakahara
Ms. Lynda E. Nakahara
Mr. and Mrs. Masaru Nakahara
Mr. and Mrs. Midori Nakahara
Ms. Nancy Nakahara
Mr. and Mrs. Norio Nakahara
Mr. and Mrs. Peter Nakahara
Mr. Peter M. Nakahara
Mr. and Mrs. Saburo Nakahara
Mrs. Sumiko Nakahara
Mr. and Mrs. Toshio Nakahara
Mr. W. Nakahara
Ms. Yasuko Nakahara
Mr. Andrew S. Nakahata
Dr. and Mrs. Donald T. Nakahata
John T. Nakahata and Pamela Smith
Mr. Yutaka Nakahata
Mr. Suzuto Nakahira
Mr. Yasuo Nakahira
Mr. Yukio Nakahira
Ms. Emiko Nakahiro
Mr. and Mrs. William T. Nakahiro
Ms. Cynthia Nakai
Mr. George S. Nakai
Mr. Hideaki Nakai
Ms. Janet Nakai
Mrs. Miyoko Nakai
Mr. and Mrs. Raymond T. Nakai
Mr. and Mrs. Roy Nakai
Mr. Ryo Nakai
Dr. and Mrs. Thomas T. Nakai
Mr. Ernest M. Nakaji
Ms. Makiko Nakaji
Ms. Marjorie S. Nakaji
Mr. Norman K. Nakaji
Ms. Susan H. Nakaji
Mr. and Mrs. Akira Nakajima
Kunio Nakajima and Family
Mr. Jurai Nakajima
Mr. Martin M. Nakajima
Dr. Yasuko Nakajima
Mr. Masashiro Nakajo
Ms. June K. Nakaki
Mrs. Peggy K. Nakaki
Mr. and Mrs. Thomas Nakaki
Mr. and Mrs. Tosh Nakakiro
Mr. and Mrs. Kenneth Nakakura
Ms. Akiko Nakama
Mr. and Mrs. Albert K. Nakama
Mr. and Mrs. Donald Nakama

Mr. George Y. Nakama
Mr. and Mrs. James K. Nakama
Mr. and Mrs. Thomas Nakama
Mr. Wallace I. Nakama
Mr. Akihito Nakamachi
Mrs. Lillian Nakamaru
Mr. and Mrs. Mark Nakamaru
Mr. Henry Y. Nakamatsu
Mr. Jon Nakamatsu
Ms. Judith A. Nakamatsu
Leslie Nakamatsu and Richard Sakai Nakamatsu
Mr. and Mrs. Sam Nakamatsu
Mr. Masatada Nakamichi
Mr. Hideo Nakamine
Mr. Tom T. Nakamine
Mr. and Mrs. Terry Nakamitsu
Mr. Allan S. Nakamori
Mr. and Mrs. Albert K. Nakamoto
Mr. and Mrs. Ben I. Nakamoto
Mr. Bob M. Nakamoto
Ms. Carolyn S. Nakamoto
Mr. and Mrs. Clark H. Nakamoto
Mr. Corey K. Nakamoto
Mr. and Mrs. David Nakamoto
Mr. Dennis S. Nakamoto
Mrs. Doreen A. Nakamoto
Ms. Dorothy K. Nakamoto
Edwin M. and Fay N. Nakamoto
Mr. Francis M. Nakamoto
Mr. Gary G. Nakamoto
Mr. and Mrs. George Nakamoto
Mr. Haruo Nakamoto
Mr. and Mrs. Herman Nakamoto
Ms. Hisako Nakamoto
Mr. Jim Nakamoto
Mr. Joel S. Nakamoto
Mr. and Mrs. Jon M. Nakamoto
Mrs. Marianne F. Nakamoto
Ms. Norie Nakamoto
Mr. Richard R. Nakamoto
Mr. Robert Nakamoto
Ms. Sharon Nakamoto
Dr. and Mrs. Stanley K. Nakamoto
Mr. and Mrs. Stanley Y. Nakamoto
Mr. Takeo Nakamoto
Dr. and Mrs. Tetsuo Nakamoto
Dr. and Mrs. Tokumasa Nakamoto
Mr. Warren K. Nakamoto
Mr. and Mrs. Yasuo Nakamoto
Mr. and Mrs. Yoriyoshi Nakamoto
Mr. Yoshinori H. Nakamoto
The Nakamura Family
Ms. Aileen S. Nakamura
Mr. and Mrs. Akira Nakamura
Mr. Albert A. Nakamura
Mr. and Mrs. Allan Nakamura
Ms. Amy I. Nakamura
Mrs. Anna M. Nakamura
Mr. and Mrs. Asaharu Nakamura
Mr. Ben M. Nakamura
Ms. Bette F. Nakamura
Ms. Betty H. Nakamura
Mr. Bob M. Nakamura
Mr. Bruce R. Nakamura
Ms. Carolyn K. Nakamura
Mr. Cayleen R. Nakamura
Mr. Charles Y. Nakamura
Mr. Clarence K. Nakamura
Mr. and Mrs. Clark S. Nakamura
Mrs. Claudia Y. Nakamura
Mr. Cliff S. Nakamura
Mr. Colin Y. Nakamura
Mr. David Nakamura
Mr. and Mrs. David T. Nakamura
Mr. Dennis M. Nakamura
Mr. Don Nakamura
Mr. and Mrs. Donald Nakamura
Mr. Donald F. Nakamura
Ms. Doris Nakamura
Mrs. Dorothy Nakamura
Mr. Douglas K. Nakamura
Mr. and Mrs. Ed Nakamura
Mr. Edward Nakamura
Mr. and Mrs. Edward H. Nakamura
Mr. Edward K. Nakamura
Mr. Edward Y. Nakamura
Mr. Eugene Nakamura
Mr. and Mrs. Frank Nakamura
Mr. and Mrs. Frank A. Nakamura
Mr. and Mrs. Frank Y. Nakamura
Ms. Fujiye Nakamura
Mr. and Mrs. Fumio Nakamura
Mr. Garry T. Nakamura
Mr. and Mrs. Gary M. Nakamura
Mr. and Mrs. George S. Nakamura
Mr. George S. Nakamura

Ms. Gladys Y. Nakamura
Mr. Glenn A. Nakamura
Mr. Harold M. Nakamura
Mr. Harry M. Nakamura
Mr. and Mrs. Harry T. Nakamura
Mrs. Harumi Nakamura
Mr. and Mrs. Henry Nakamura
Mr. Henry Z. Nakamura
Mr. and Mrs. Hideki Nakamura
Mr. and Mrs. Hiomi Nakamura
Mr. and Mrs. Howard K. Nakamura
Mr. Irene R. Nakamura
Mr. and Mrs. Isamu Sam Nakamura
Mr. Jack M. Nakamura
Mr. and Mrs. Jake K. Nakamura
Mr. and Mrs. James A. Nakamura
Mr. James E. Nakamura
Mr. and Mrs. James I. Nakamura
Mr. James S. Nakamura
Ms. Janet F. Nakamura
Mr. Jerry Nakamura
Mr. and Mrs. Jim Nakamura
Mr. Jim H. Nakamura
Mr. Joe J. Nakamura
Mr. John H. Nakamura
Mr. John K. Nakamura
Mr. John T. Nakamura
Mr. and Mrs. Joseph Nakamura
Ms. Judith Nakamura
Ms. Julia V. Nakamura
Mr. K. Nakamura
Mr. and Mrs. Kaname Nakamura
Mr. Karl K. Nakamura
Ms. Kay K. Nakamura
Ms. Kayo I. Nakamura
Ms. Kazumi Nakamura
Mr. Kenjiro Nakamura
Mr. and Mrs. Kenneth T. Nakamura
Ms. Kim Nakamura
Mr. and Mrs. Kiyoyuki Nakamura
Dr. and Mrs. Lawrence Nakamura
Mrs. Manny Nakamura
Ms. Marie M. Nakamura
Mr. and Mrs. Mark M. Nakamura
Mr. and Mrs. Mark S. Nakamura
Mrs. Mary Nakamura
Ms. Mary J. Nakamura
Mr. Masaaki Nakamura
Mr. and Mrs. Masao Nakamura
Mr. Masao Nakamura
Mr. and Mrs. Masao Nakamura
Mr. and Mrs. Masashi Nakamura
Mr. and Mrs. Masayoshi Nakamura
Mr. Mataro Nakamura
Dr. and Dr. Michael Nakamura
Mr. and Mrs. Michael O. Nakamura
Mr. Michiyuki Nakamura
Ms. Mildred S. Nakamura
Mr. and Mrs. Minoru Nakamura
Ms. Mona Nakamura
Morio Nakamura
Ms. Mutsuko Nakamura
Ms. Nancy Nakamura
Mr. Norman K. Nakamura
Mrs. Patricia S. Nakamura
Mr. Patrick E. Nakamura
Mr. Paul S. Nakamura
Ms. Peggy Nakamura
Mr. and Mrs. Phil Nakamura
Dr. and Mrs. R. M. Nakamura
Mr. and Mrs. Ralph K. Nakamura
Mr. and Mrs. Ray K. Nakamura
Mr. Ray T. Nakamura
Mr. and Mrs. Raymond S. Nakamura
Mr. Richard H. Nakamura
Mr. and Mrs. Richard I. Nakamura
Mr. Richard K. Nakamura
Mr. Richard O. Nakamura
Mr. Richard T. Nakamura
Mr. and Mrs. Richard T. Nakamura
Mr. Robert Nakamura
Mr. and Mrs. Robert Nakamura
Mr. and Mrs. Ronald A. Nakamura
Mrs. Rose K. Nakamura
Mrs. Sade S. Nakamura
Mr. Satoru Nakamura
Mr. Satoshi Nakamura
Mr. Shigeharu Nakamura
Mr. and Mrs. Shigeo Nakamura
Mr. and Mrs. Shigeru Nakamura
Mr. and Mrs. Shiro Nakamura
Mr. Shoichi Nakamura
Mr. Shuichi H. Nakamura
Mr. Stanley S. Nakamura
Mr. and Mrs. Stanley T. Nakamura
Steven Nakamura and Sally Provow

Mr. and Mrs. Steven T. Nakamura
Mr. and Mrs. Sto Nakamura
Ms. Sunako Nakamura
Mr. Suyeichi Nakamura
Mr. and Mrs. Tak Nakamura
Mr. Taka O. Nakamura
Mr. and Mrs. Takeshi Nakamura
Mrs. Tamaye Nakamura
Mr. Ted T. Nakamura
Mr. Theodore M. Nakamura
Dr. Theodore T. Nakamura
Mr. and Mrs. Thomas Nakamura
Mr. and Mrs. Todd T. Nakamura
Mr. Tom I. Nakamura
Mr. Tom K. Nakamura
Ms. Toshiko Nakamura
Mr. Toshio Nakamura
Mr. and Mrs. Toshio Nakamura
Mr. and Mrs. Wallace I. Nakamura
Mr. and Mrs. Wilfred M. Nakamura
Mr. and Mrs. William Nakamura
Mr. Wynn M. Nakamura
Mrs. Yae Nakamura
Mrs. Yaeko K. Nakamura
Mrs. Yo Nakamura
Mr. and Mrs. Yoshio Nakamura
Mr. and Mrs. Yoshito Nakamura
Mr. Yutaka Nakamura
Mr. and Mrs. Jitsuyoshi Nakandakare
Ms. Karen M. Nakandakare
Mrs. Ann Sachiko Nakanishi
Arline M. Nakanishi
Ms. Arline M. Nakanishi and Mr. Michael Mizutani
Mr. Cory S. Nakanishi
Dr. Don Nakanishi
Mr. and Mrs. Donald Nakanishi
Mr. and Mrs. Donald T. Nakanishi
Mr. Eddie K. Nakanishi
Mr. and Mrs. Edward T. Nakanishi
Miss Fusaye Nakanishi
Mr. George Nakanishi
Mr. and Mrs. George Nakanishi
Mr. Ikutaro Nakanishi
Mr. Joe Nakanishi
Mr. Joe M. Nakanishi
Mr. Joe Y. Nakanishi
Ms. Kaneko Nakanishi
Mr. Kazuo Nakanishi
Ms. Kimi V. Nakanishi
Mr. Kiyoshi Nakanishi
Mr. Masaru Nakanishi
Mr. and Mrs. Mitsuo Nakanishi
Mr. Robert Y. Nakanishi
Dr. Roger Nakanishi and Dr. Teresa Yagi
Mr. and Mrs. Ronald Nakanishi
Mr. and Mrs. Shigeo Nakanishi
Mr. Tosaku Nakanishi
Mr. Toshio Nakanishi
Mr. and Mrs. Toshio Nakanishi
Mr. Zenkichi Nakanishi
Ms. Arleen T. Nakano
Ms. Barbara S. Nakano
Ms. Chiyo Nakano
Mrs. Clara K. Nakano
Mr. David H. Nakano
Ms. Donna Nakano
Mr. Douglas G. Nakano
Mr. Edward Nakano
Mr. Edward H. Nakano
Mr. Edwin H. Nakano
Dr. Francis K. Nakano
Mr. Frank D. Nakano
Dr. Frank H. Nakano
Mr. and Mrs. George Nakano
Mr. George Nakano
Mr. and Mrs. George Nakano
Mr. Glen S. Nakano
Ms. Helen Nakano
Mr. Henry Nakano
Mr. and Mrs. Jack Nakano
Mr. James K. Nakano
Mr. John Y. Nakano
Ms. Joyce M. Nakano
Ms. Joyce M. Morinaka Nakano
Katsumi F. Nakano
Mr. and Mrs. Kazuki Nakano
Mr. and Mrs. Ken (Akira) Nakano
Mr. Kenichi Nakano
Mr. Kenny K. Nakano
Mr. and Mrs. Lane Nakano
Mr. and Mrs. Mark K. Nakano
Mr. and Mrs. Otto Nakano
Ms. Patsy L. Nakano
Mr. Randall A. Nakano
Ms. Reiko Nakano
Mrs. Rosie S. Nakano

Dr. Russell L. Nakano
Mr. Sam M. Nakano
Mr. and Mrs. Shiro Nakano
Mr. Stephen K. Nakano
Mr. Steve H. Nakano
Tad T. and Katherine Nakano
Mr. Terry T. Nakano
Mr. and Mrs. Tokuichi Nakano
Mr. Tom Nakano
Mr. Tosh Nakano
Mr. Toshiaki Nakano
Mr. and Mrs. Walter S. Nakano
Mr. and Mrs. William Nakano
Mr. Yosh Nakano
Mr. and Mrs. Yoshio Nakano
Mr. Yoshio U. Nakano
Mrs. Chizuko Nakao
Ms. Ellen T. Nakao
Mr. Emil Mas Nakao
Mrs. Esther K. Nakao
Mr. George S. Nakao
Mr. Hideaki Nakao
Mr. Iwao Nakao
Mr. and Mrs. Jack Nakao
Mr. and Mrs. John J. Nakao
Mr. Masami B. Nakao
Miyeko Nakao
Misses Miyeko and Janice M. Nakao
Ms. Naomi A. Nakao
Mr. and Mrs. Richard M. Nakao
Mr. Robert Nakao
Mr. Scott K. Nakao
Mrs. Teruko M. Nakao
Mr. and Mrs. Tetsuo Nakao
Mr. Thomas Nakao
Mrs. Violet M. Nakao
Mrs. Leslie Nakao-Edman
Mr. Grant J. Nakaoka
Mr. Harold Nakaoka
Mr. and Mrs. Isao Nakaoka
Ms. Susan Nakaoka
Mr. and Mrs. Tom Nakaoka
Mr. and Mrs. William T. Nakaoka
Mr. and Mrs. Joe M. Nakaoki
Mr. Keisuke Nakasaki
Mr. Les Nakasaki
Mrs. Doreen Nakasako
Ms. Helen Nakasako
Mr. and Mrs. Tsutomu Nakasako
Ms. Violet S. Nakasako
Mr. George M. Nakasato
Ms. S. Ethel Nakasato
Mr. and Mrs. John Nakashige
Mr. and Mrs. Yoshio Nakashige
Ms. Akira Nakashima
Mr. and Mrs. Alan S. Nakashima
Ms. Aradith T. Nakashima
Ms. Ayako Nakashima
Mr. and Mrs. Bud Nakashima
Dr. Carol L. Nakashima
Ms. Connie Nakashima
Mr. and Mrs. Daniel T. Nakashima
Ms. Donna R. Nakashima
Mr. Douglas T. Nakashima
Mr. and Mrs. Eddie T. Nakashima
Mr. and Mrs. Edwin Nakashima
Mr. Frank Y. Nakashima
Mr. George Nakashima
Mr. George H. Nakashima
Mr. and Mrs. George H. Nakashima
Mr. Harry T. Nakashima
Mr. and Mrs. Hidemi Nakashima
Mr. Isao Nakashima
Mr. James Nakashima
Ms. Janice R. Nakashima
Mr. and Mrs. John S. Nakashima
Ms. Joyce R. Nakashima
Mr. Lance S. Nakashima
Ms. Laura T. Nakashima
Ms. Leslie K. Nakashima
Ms. Lois K. Nakashima
Mr. and Mrs. Masao Nakashima
Mr. Michael Nakashima
Ms. Michiko Nakashima
Mr. Mike Nakashima
Mr. Miles Nakashima
Mr. Mitchell Nakashima
Ms. Naomi Nakashima
Ms. Patricia Nakashima
Mr. and Mrs. Percy Nakashima
Mr. and Mrs. Renny Nakashima
Mr. and Mrs. Richard Y. Nakashima
Mr. and Mrs. Robert H. Nakashima
Mr. and Mrs. Roger Nakashima
Mr. Roy S. Nakashima
Ms. Sherri Nakashima

Mr. Shigeki Nakashima
Mr. and Mrs. Shoji Nakashima
Ms. Sumiko Nakashima
Mr. Tad Nakashima
Mr. and Mrs. Takashi Nakashima
Mr. and Mrs. Toichi Nakashima
Mr. Walter Nakashima
Mr. and Mrs. Walter H. Nakashima
Mr. and Mrs. Will Nakashima
Mr. and Mrs. Yoshiharu Nakashima
Mrs. Yoshio F. Nakashima
Mr. Kenichi Nakashioya
Mr. Michael K. Nakashoji
Ms. Judy Nakaso
Ms. Aiko Nakasone
Ms. Charlotte H. Nakasone
Mr. and Mrs. Edwin M. Nakasone
Mr. George Nakasone
Mr. George J. Nakasone
Mr. and Mrs. Glenn H. Nakasone
Mr. Herbert I. Nakasone
Ms. Ione C. Nakasone
Ms. Kris Nakasone
Ms. Laurie L. Nakasone
Mr. and Mrs. Richard Y. Nakasone
Mr. Robert T. Nakasone
Ms. Seiko Nakasone
Mr. Stanley Nakasone
Mr. and Mrs. Warren Nakasone
Ms. Yoshi Nakasone
Mr. and Mrs. Hisao Nakasuji
Ms. Lauren K. Nakasuji
Mr. and Mrs. Richard Nakasuji
Mr. Albert Y. Nakata
Ms. Ann Nakata
Mr. and Mrs. Bill T. Nakata
Mr. Bob M. Nakata
Mr. Clifford Y. Nakata
Mr. Colbert K. Nakata
Mr. David Nakata
Dr. and Mrs. Dennis A. Nakata
Mr. Edward M. Nakata
Mr. Eric M. Nakata
Mr. and Mrs. Ernest Nakata
Mr. and Mrs. Francis H. Nakata
Mr. and Mrs. Frank W. Nakata
Mr. George Nakata
Mr. Harry Nakata
Mr. and Mrs. Harry H. Nakata
Mr. and Mrs. Harry Y. Nakata
Ms. Haruko Nakata
Mr. and Mrs. Henry Nakata
Mr. and Mrs. Herbert M. Nakata
Mr. and Mrs. Isaac Nakata
Mr. Isao Nakata
Mr. James Nakata
Ms. Janae S. Nakata
Mr. Jerry S. Nakata
Ms. Joanne S. Nakata
Mr. and Mrs. Joe Nakata
Ms. Julie A. Nakata
Mrs. Smith Nakata
Ms. Kathleen C. Nakata
Mr. and Mrs. Kenzie Nakata
Mr. Kiyo Nakata
Mr. and Mrs. Larry Nakata
Ms. Leslie A. Nakata
Mrs. Marion S. Nakata
Ms. Mildred Nakata
Mrs. Misao Nakata
Mr. Osamu W. Nakata
Mr. Paul Nakata
Mr. Rick D. Nakata
Mr. Robert K. Nakata
Mr. Sharon Nakata
Mr. Thomas Y. Nakata
Mr. and Mrs. Tom Nakata
Mrs. Toshiko Nakata
Mr. Walter Nakata
Mr. and Mrs. William Nakata
Mr. Alan I. Nakatani
Ms. Christine H. Nakatani
Mr. and Mrs. David Nakatani
Mr. and Mrs. George Nakatani
Mr. and Mrs. Harry Nakatani
Ms. Laura K. Nakatani
Ms. Misae Nakatani
Mrs. Nancy Nakatani
Mr. Nancy K. Nakatani
Mr. and Mrs. Norrie N. Nakatani
Mr. and Mrs. Sam Nakatani
Mr. Shinichi Nakatani
Mr. Teruko Nakatani
Mr. Yasuo Nakatani
Mr. and Mrs. Kinjiro K. Nakatogawa
Ms. Toyoko Nakatogawa

Mr. and Mrs. George Y. Nakatsu
Mr. and Mrs. Joseph D. Nakatsu
Mr. and Mrs. Lorry M. Nakatsu
Ms. Nancy Nakatsu
Ms. Ruth Nakatsu
Mr. Yasuaki Nakatsu
Mr. Ronald M. Nakatsuji
Mr. and Mrs. Keiji Nakatsuka
Mr. Lester S. Nakatsuka
Ms. Louise Nakatsuka
Mr. and Mrs. Neal M. Nakatsuka
Mr. and Mrs. Sam Nakatsuka
Mr. and Mrs. Tom Nakatsuka
Mr. and Mrs. Walter Nakatsukasa
Mr. and Mrs. Edward M. Nakauchi
Mr. and Mrs. Mark Nakauchi
Mr. Aki Nakauye
Mr. and Mrs. Fushio Nakawaki
Mr. and Mrs. Tad Nakawaki
Mrs. Aiko Nakawatase
Ms. Betty T. Nakawatase
Mr. and Mrs. Richard Nakawatase
Dr. and Mrs. Roy S. Nakawatase
Mrs. Sachiko Nakawatase
Mr. and Mrs. Shizuo Nakawatase
Mr. and Mrs. Ben Nakaya
Mr. and Mrs. Harvey Nakaya
Mr. Morey M. Nakaya
Mr. Todd C. Nakaya
Mr. Alan Nakayama
Mr. and Mrs. Arling A. Nakayama
Mr. Curtis Nakayama
Mr. and Mrs. David I. Nakayama
Col. David T. Nakayama
Dr. Denny Nakayama
Mr. Eugene Nakayama
Ms. Fumi Nakayama
Mr. and Mrs. Harry M. Nakayama
Mr. Harry S. Nakayama
Mr. Haruo Nakayama
Mr. Herbert E. Nakayama
Mr. Hideo Nakayama
Mr. and Mrs. Izumi Nakayama
Dr. and Mrs. Leo Nakayama
Ms. Lois Nakayama
Ms. Lynn Nakayama
Ms. Marie Nakayama
Mr. Masao Nakayama
Ms. Paula Nakayama
Mr. and Mrs. Pete Nakayama
Mr. and Mrs. Randy Nakayama
Mr. and Mrs. Richard H. Nakayama
Mr. Ronald J. Nakayama
Mr. and Mrs. Roy S. Nakayama
Mrs. Setsuko Nakayama
Shige and Nancy Nakayama
Mr. and Mrs. Shun Nakayama
Mr. and Mrs. Stuart Nakayama
Ms. Sue Nakayama
Mr. Terry Nakayama
Mr. Thomas K. Nakayama
Mr. and Mrs. Tosh Nakayama
Mr. and Mrs. Wayne N. Nakayama
Mrs. Yoneko Nakayama
Mr. and Mrs. Yosh Nakayama
Mr. Yukio Nakayama
Mr. and Mrs. Susumu Nakazato
Ms. Teiko Nakazato
Ms. Florence M. Nakazawa
Mr. and Mrs. Harumi Nakazawa
Mr. and Mrs. Jun Nakazawa
Mr. Kango Nakazawa
Mr. and Mrs. Kazuo Nakazawa
Mr. and Mrs. Keito Nakazawa
Mr. Kiyoshi Nakazawa
Ms. Mary Nakazawa
Mr. and Mrs. Masao Nakazawa
Mrs. Motoko Murayama Nakazawa
Ms. Noriko Nakazawa
Mr. and Mrs. Robert T. Nakazawa
LCDR Shin Nakazawa
Mr. T. G. Nakazawa
Mr. and Mrs. Tadashi Nakazawa
Lt. and Mrs. Takeshi Nakazawa
Mr. and Mrs. Harry Nakazono
Ms. Sami Nakazono
Mr. and Mrs. Minoru Nakumura
Mr. and Mrs. Frank Nam
Mr. and Mrs. Bob Namba
Mr. and Mrs. Earl Namba
Mr. and Mrs. Gary Namba
Mr. Harry T. Namba
Kenneth and Charlotte F. Namba
Mr. and Mrs. Mas Namba
Ms. May Y. Namba
Mr. and Mrs. Richard Namba

Mr. Richard H. Namba
Mr. and Mrs. Sam Namba
Mr. and Mrs. Tadashi Namba
Mr. and Mrs. Takeshi Namba
NAMBACO
Mr. Hugh Namekawa
Mr. David Namimoto
Ms. Joyce Namimoto
Ms. Mollie M. Namimoto
Mr. and Mrs. Emory Namura
Mr. Glenn Namura
Mr. and Mrs. Michael Namura
Mr. Jeffrey Nanbara
Mr. George T. Nanbu
Mr. James Nanbu
Mr. and Mrs. Kiyoshi Nanbu
Ms. Yumi Nang
Kay and Carolyn K. Naples
Mr. and Mrs. Allan Nara
Mrs. Mitsuko and Taro Nara
Mrs. Dorothy Narahara
Dr. and Mrs. Hiromichi Narahara
Mrs. Hisako Narasaki
Mr. and Mrs. Joseph Narasaki
Ms. Karen K. Narasaki
Mr. Richard Narasaki
Ms. Kiyoko Narikawa
Mr. Randal Narike
Mr. Brion H. Narimatsu
Mr. Galen M. Narimatsu
Mr. Layne H. Narimatsu
Mrs. Nancy K. Narimatsu
Tom Narimatsu and Rosie Yamamoto
Miss Eiko Narita
Mr. and Mrs. Kenneth K. Narita
Mr. Wesley N. Narita
Mr. Yoshio Narita
Mr. Lawrence S. Naritomi
Mr. Stanley T. Naritomi
Ms. Chiyoko Naruko
Mr. and Mrs. George Naruo
Mr. and Mrs. Taka Naruo
Mr. and Mrs. William Naruo
Mr. Raymond Narusawa
Mr. Walter M. Narusawa
Mr. Steven B. Nasatir
Mr. James E. Nash
Mr. Harry M. Nashiro
Mr. Ken Nasu
Mieko and Yuko Nasu
Mr. Tak Nasu
Mr. Yoshio Nasu
Mr. Francis Natori
Mr. Jack Y. Natsuhara
Sharon, Bonnie, Kathryn, Jean and Charles Natsuhara
Mr. and Mrs. Tom Natsuhara
Mr. Yasukichi Natsuhara
Mr. and Mrs. Yoshio Natsuhara
Jack and Dirce Natsuhori
Mr. Larry Natsume
Ms. Margaret M. Natsume
Ms. Joann B. Naugle
Ms. Arlene Navarro
Michael and Shirley Navarro
Ms. Aoi Nawashiro
Ms. Susan Ah Nee
Ms. Lillian Neeno
Mrs. Clara B. Negoro
Ms. Jane T. Negoro
Ms. Yukiko Negoro
Mr. Gregg S. Neiman
Mr. and Mrs. Ken Neishi
Ms. Lynne M. Neishi
Ms. Barbara H. Neisser
Mr. and Mrs. Jeff Nekoba
Mr. and Mrs. Bruce W. Nelan
Mr. Ralph E. Nelson
Ms. Beverly Nemec
Ms. Ellen Nemoto
Mrs. Tokie Nerio
Dr. Teruko S. Neuwalder
New York Buddhist Church
Ms. Carroll Newberry
Mr. and Mrs. Donald Newbold
Mr. and Mrs. Ben Newcomb
Mr. and Mrs. George Neyama
Mr. Jim Shig Nezu
Mr. Franklin Ng
Mr. and Mrs. Kenneth W. Ng
Ms. May Ng
Hanh Van Nguyen
Ms. Hisae Nicewonger
Nichi Bei Bussan, Inc.
Mr. and Mrs. Eric Nichols
Mr. and Mrs. Michael J. Nichols
Mr. and Mrs. Charles Nicholson

Mr. and Mrs. David Nieda
Ms. Helen P. Niederfrank
Ms. Jayne-Lei C. Nielsen
Ms. Yayoi Nigo
Mr. Satoshi Nihashi
Mr. Albert T. Nihei
Ms. Ethel F. Nihei
Mr. and Mrs. Henry Shoichi Nihei
Mr. Richard C. Nihei
Mr. Kazuo Nihira
Mr. and Mrs. Frank Nii
Mr. and Mrs. George Nii
Mr. and Mrs. Ivor Nii
Ms. Janice A. Nii
Mr. Jeffrey C. Nii
Mrs. Marna M. Nii
Dr. and Mrs. Scott Nii
Mr. and Mrs. Ted Nii
Ms. Teri Nii
Mr. Yutaka Nii
Mr. Kiyomi Niigata
Mr. George Niimi
Ms. Amy K. Niino
Mr. and Mrs. Jackson Niino
Mr. and Mrs. Nobuhisa Niino
Mr. Steven Niino
Mr. and Mrs. Yutaka Niisato
Mr. Charles S. Niitani
Mr. and Mrs. Michio Niiya
Mr. and Mrs. Jerry Niiyama
Mr. and Mrs. Min Niiyama
Mr. and Mrs. Bennet Niizawa
Mr. and Mrs. Johnny C. Niizawa
Mrs. Lillian Niizawa
Ms. Mae Momoyo Niizawa
Mr. Misao Niizawa
Ms. Natsu Niizawa
Mr. and Mrs. Richard Niizawa
Mr. Stanley T. Niizawa
Ms. Sumi L. Niizawa
Mr. T. N. Niizawa
Mr. Arthur S. Nikaido
Ms. Jane Y. Nikaido
Nikkei Widowed Group
Mr. David B. Nikuni
Mr. and Mrs. Benjamin Nimer
Mrs. Kiyoko J. Nimi
Mr. and Mrs. Frank Ninokawa
Mr. and Mrs. Calvin Ninomiya
Mr. Clyde K. Ninomiya
Dr. Eifuku Ninomiya
Mr. and Mrs. George Ninomiya
Mrs. Harue Mae Ninomiya
Mr. Jack Ninomiya
Mr. and Mrs. Kazuo Ninomiya
Mr. William Nisbet
Nisei VFW Auxiliary Post #8985
Ms. Alice Nishi
Mr. and Mrs. Carl B. Nishi
Ms. Cindy Nishi
Mr. Clarence Nishi
Mr. Harold H. Nishi
Mr. and Mrs. Hatsuo Nishi
Mr. Hiro Nishi
Mr. and Mrs. Hiromu Nishi
Mr. and Mrs. Hito Nishi
Mr. James S. Nishi
Ms. Joanne C. Nishi
Mr. and Mrs. John C. Nishi
Mr. and Mrs. Katsuhisa Nishi
Ms. Mie Nishi
Mr. Mitsuru Nishi
Ms. Naomi Nishi
Mr. Ron Nishi
Mr. Sachio Nishi
Mr. and Mrs. Takahisa Nishi
Mr. and Mrs. Travis Nishi
Mrs. Yoshiko Nishi
Mr. and Mrs. Yoshio Nishi
Mr. and Mrs. Mas Nishibayashi
Mr. Tsunetake Nishibayashi
Mr. and Mrs. Wallace Nishibayashi
Mr. Walter Nishibayashi
Miss Akiyo Nishida
Mr. Charles M. Nishida
Mr. David Nishida
Mr. Floyd M. Nishida
Mr. and Mrs. Frank Nishida
Mr. and Mrs. Fred Nishida
Mr. Genzo J. Nishida
Dr. and Mrs. George T. Nishida
Mr. and Mrs. Hiroshi Nishida
Mr. and Mrs. Joel Nishida
Mr. John Y. Nishida
Mr. Jon Nishida
Mr. Kaoru Nishida

Mrs. Kathleen C. Nishida
Mr. and Mrs. Larry Nishida
Mr. and Mrs. Masayuki Nishida
Mr. and Mrs. Mel Nishida
Ms. Nanako Nishida
Mr. Robert A. Nishida
Mr. Robert Y. Nishida
Mr. and Mrs. Roger S. Nishida
Mrs. Ruth Nishida
Ms. Sarah H. Nishida
Ms. Sumiye Nishida
Mr. and Mrs. Tom Nishida
Mr. Toshiaki Nishida
Mr. Dennis Nishiguchi
Mr. Masahiro Nishihama
Ms. Alice Nishihara
Mr. and Mrs. Harry Nishihara
Ms. Julie Nishihara
Mr. Keith Nishihara
Mr. and Mrs. Kenneth Y. Nishihara
Mrs. Lila K. Nishihara
Ms. Monica L. Nishihara
Mr. and Mrs. Robert Nishihara
Mr. Takeo L. Nishihara
Mr. Dick S. Nishihira
Mr. and Mrs. Kikuo Nishii
Miss Louise Nishii
Mr. and Mrs. William Nishii
Mr. and Mrs. Edward Nishiie
Ms. Kazuma Nishiie
Mr. and Mrs. Kanji Nishijama
Mr. and Mrs. Dean Nishijima
Mr. Teruo Nishijima
Mr. Albert K. Nishikawa
Bronwen Nishikawa and Robert C. Glass
Mr. Dennis Y. Nishikawa
Ms. Evelyn Yoshiko Nishikawa
Mr. and Mrs. Frank S. Nishikawa
Ms. Fukuko Nishikawa
Ms. Fusako M. Nishikawa
Rev. and Mrs. George Nishikawa
Mr. and Mrs. George J. Nishikawa
Mr. George K. Nishikawa
Mr. and Mrs. George T. Nishikawa
Mr. and Mrs. Haru Nishikawa
Ms. Hattie H. Nishikawa
Mr. and Mrs. Jay Nishikawa
Mrs. Jean Nishikawa
Ms. Jeannette Nishikawa
Mr. and Mrs. Joe Nishikawa
Ms. June Nishikawa
K. Nishikawa
Katsumi Nishikawa
Katsuya Nishikawa
Ms. Kimiko Nishikawa
Ms. Kyoko Nishikawa
Mr. and Mrs. Masato Nishikawa
Mr. Philip Nishikawa
Ms. Sue Nishikawa
Mr. Tetsuji Nishikawa
Mr. Thomas Nishikawa
Mr. and Mrs. Yukio Nishikawa
Mr. Gordon Nishiki
Ms. Miyona L. Nishikibo
Mr. and Mrs. Ben Nishikubo
Ms. Carol Nishikubo
Mr. and Mrs. Hiroshi Nishikubo
Mr. and Mrs. Shigeo Nishikuni
Ms. Fusaye Nishima
Mr. and Mrs. William Nishimatsu
Mr. and Mrs. Jiro Nishime
Mr. Saburo Nishime
Mr. and Mrs. Gilbert Nishimi
Mr. Jimmie Nishimi
Mr. John T. Nishimi
Mr. and Mrs. Ralph H. Nishimi
Mr. and Mrs. Jinobu Nishimori
Mr. Roy I. Nishimori
Mr. and Mrs. T. Nishimori
Mr. Bill T. Nishimoto
Ms. Carol Nishimoto
Ms. Cindy Nishimoto
Mrs. Clara Nishimoto
Mr. Clifford Nishimoto
Mr. Dick Nishimoto
Mr. Edgar I. Nishimoto
Mr. Egan K. Nishimoto
Mr. Francis Nishimoto
Mr. Frank S. Nishimoto
Mr. George Nishimoto
Dr. and Mrs. Gordon Nishimoto
Harry and Frances Nishimoto
Mrs. Hisako Nishimoto
Mr. and Mrs. Jerry Nishimoto
Mr. John Nishimoto
Mr. John T. Nishimoto

Dr. and Mrs. Joseph Nishimoto
Mr. and Mrs. Kanoye Nishimoto
Mr. Karl Nishimoto
Mr. Katsumi Nishimoto
Kazuhiko and Miyoko Nishimoto
Mr. and Mrs. Keith Nishimoto
Ms. Kiyoko Nishimoto
Ms. Kiyono Nishimoto
Mr. Kiyoto Nishimoto
Mr. and Mrs. Mac Nishimoto
Mr. Merrick Nishimoto
Mr. and Mrs. Michael Y. Nishimoto
Mr. Motomi Nishimoto
Mr. Rei Nishimoto
Mr. Richard Nishimoto
Mr. and Mrs. Robert K. Nishimoto
Mr. and Mrs. Ronald S. Nishimoto
Mr. Stephen J. Nishimoto
Mr. and Mrs. Steve T. Nishimoto
Mr. and Mrs. Sunny Nishimoto
Mr. Tom H. Nishimoto
Mr. Toshio Nishimoto
Mr. Toshio J. Nishimoto
Mr. and Mrs. Wallace Nishimoto
Mr. Yukio Nishimoto
Dr. and Mrs. Akira Nishimura
Mr. Buddy Nishimura
Dr. Clyde E. Nishimura
Ms. Constance Nishimura
Ms. Deborah Nishimura
Ms. Diana H. Nishimura
Ms. Donna R. Nishimura
Ms. Elizabeth Nishimura
Mr. George Nishimura
Mr. and Mrs. George H. Nishimura
Mr. and Mrs. George K. Nishimura
Mr. Gerald F. Nishimura
Mr. Glenn S. Nishimura
Mr. and Mrs. Hank Nishimura
Mr. Hatsue Nishimura
Ms. Hazel Nishimura
Mr. Henry M. Nishimura
Mr. Herman Nishimura
Mr. Hiro Nishimura
Mr. Hiroaki Nishimura
Mr. and Mrs. Ichiro Nishimura
Mrs. Ida Nishimura
Mr. and Mrs. Irwin G. Nishimura
Mr. and Mrs. Iso Nishimura
Ms. Janet Nishimura
Mr. and Mrs. Joe Nishimura
Mr. Joe Y. Nishimura
Mr. and Mrs. John T. Nishimura
Mr. and Mrs. John Y. Nishimura
Ms. Karen Nishimura
Mr. Karl K. Nishimura
Mr. and Mrs. Katsumi Nishimura
Mr. Kiyoto Nishimura
Mr. Lyn Nishimura
Mr. and Mrs. Masami Nishimura
Ms. Merry Nishimura
Mr. Miles Nishimura
Mr. and Mrs. Norman Nishimura
Mr. and Mrs. Oliver Nishimura
Paul and Margaret K. Nishimura
Mr. Raymond Nishimura
Mr. Richard Nishimura
Mr. Robert Nishimura
Mr. Robert H. Nishimura
Mr. and Mrs. Roy Nishimura
Dr. and Mrs. Russell Nishimura
Mr. and Mrs. Shizuo Nishimura
Mr. and Mrs. Steve Nishimura
Mr. and Mrs. Tadao George Nishimura
Mr. Tatsumi Nishimura
Mr. and Mrs. Ted Nishimura
Mr. and Mrs. Tom Nishimura
Ms. Tsuyako K. Nishimura
Valerie Nishimura and Michael P. Nagan
Ms. Violet O. Nishimura
Mr. Walter M. Nishimura
Mr. and Mrs. William Y. Nishimura
Rev. and Mrs. William Y. Nishimura
Ms. Yoshiko Nishimura
Mr. and Mrs. Yoshio Nishimura
Ms. Yuriko Nishimura
Mr. Earl Nishina
Mr. and Mrs. Harold Nishina
Mr. Howard T. Nishina
Mr. Todd T. Nishina
Mr. Walter T. Nishina
Mr. Angel K. Nishinaka
Mr. and Mrs. Robert S. Nishinaka
Mr. and Mrs. Ronald Nishinaka
Ms. Sumako Nishinaka
Mr. and Mrs. Andrew Nishino

Ms. Julie Nishino
Mr. and Mrs. Kei Nishino
Mr. Yoshinori Nishino
Ms. Chiharu Nishio
Sister Eleanor Nishio
Mr. George Nishio
Mr. and Mrs. James K. Nishio
Mrs. Jane M. Nishio
Ms. Karen Nishio
Mr. Kaz Nishio
Mr. and Mrs. Mike Nishio
Mr. and Mrs. Roy Nishio
Mr. and Mrs. Akira Nishioka
Ms. Annabelle I. Nishioka
Mr. and Mrs. Arthur Nishioka
Mr. and Mrs. Atsuo Nishioka
Mrs. Charlene K. Nishioka
Mr. Charles K. Nishioka
Mr. David J. Nishioka
Mr. Forrest Nishioka
Mr. James T. Nishioka
Ms. Joyce S. Nishioka
Mrs. Kazumi Nishioka
Mr. Kenji Nishioka
Mr. Mikio Nishioka
Rev. and Mrs. Richard T. Nishioka
Mr. Walter Nishioka
Ms. April Nishioka-Joke
Mr. and Mrs. Ben Nishioki
Mr. and Mrs. Norman Nishioki
Mr. Joe Nishisaki
Mr. Don Nishita
Mr. and Mrs. Frank Nishita
Mr. and Mrs. Jerry Nishita
Mr. Kevin F. Nishita
Mr. Peter Nishita
Mr. Brian Nishitani
Mr. and Mrs. James Nishitsuji
Ms. Diana Nishiura
Mr. George T. Nishiura
Ms. Lori Nishiura
Mr. and Mrs. Bruce Nishiwaki
Mr. and Mrs. Ace Nishiyama
Ms. Akiko Nishiyama
Mr. Earl Nishiyama
Mr. Jimmy Nishiyama
Mr. and Mrs. Kinichi Nishiyama
Mr. and Mrs. Massey Nishiyama
Mrs. Mildred K. Nishiyama
Mr. Robert Nishiyama
Ms. Sally S. Nishiyama
Mr. and Mrs. Sidney Y. Nishiyama
Mr. Thomas Nishiyama
Mr. Toby Nishiyama
Mr. John M. Nishizaka
Mr. and Mrs. James G. Nishizaki
Ms. Sharon Nishizaki and Mr. Michael Billiel
Mr. and Mrs. Terumi Nishizaki
Ms. Beatrice K. Nishizawa
Mr. Eric Nishizawa
Mr. and Mrs. Fred Nishizawa
Mr. Nobuhiro Nishizawa
Akira Nishizono
Mr. Masaaki Nishizu
Mr. and Mrs. Carlos Nisi
Mr. Sart S. Nitahara
Mr. and Mrs. Harry Nitake
Mr. and Mrs. Michael Nitake
Mr. Akio Nitta
Mr. and Mrs. Alfred Nitta
Mr. Clarence Nitta
Ms. Denise M. Nitta
Mr. George H. Nitta
Gordon and Tatsuko Nitta
Ms. Hiroko Nitta
Mr. Hitoshi Nitta
Mr. and Mrs. John Nitta
Katharine C. Nitta
Ms. Kathleen J. Nitta
Mr. Kenneth Nitta
Mr. Mark Nitta
Mr. and Mrs. Masato Nitta
Mr. and Mrs. Minoru Nitta
Mr. Reiji Nitta
Mr. and Mrs. Satoru Nitta
Ms. Teruko T. Nitta
Mr. Thomas A. Nitta
Mr. Toshimi Nitta
Mrs. Trudy Nitta
Niu Valley Middle School 8th Grade Class Team
Ms. Florence Niwa
Ms. Marie M. Niwa
Mr. and Mrs. Thomas Niwa
Nix of America
Mr. and Mrs. Curtis Nixholm
Ms. Catherine Nobe

Ms. Antonette Chambers Noble
Mr. Dean Nobori
Ms. Mariko Nobori
Mr. and Mrs. Richard Nobori
Mr. and Mrs. Wayne Nobori
Mr. Masao Noborikawa
Mr. Ben Nobuhiro
Mr. and Mrs. Naoya Nobuhiro
Mr. Tetsuo Nobuku
Mrs. Yemi Nobusada
Mr. Nobuo Nobusawa
Mr. and Mrs. Masaru Nobuto
Ms. Eleanor Nobuye
Mr. and Mrs. Steven C. Nock
Ms. Akiko Noda
Mr. Bruce Noda
Mr. and Mrs. Dave Noda
Mr. Dean Noda
Mrs. Grace Noda
Ms. June A. Noda
Mr. Kenji K. Noda
Mr. Kirk T. Noda
Mr. and Mrs. Masaaki Noda
Ms. Masuye Noda
Mrs. Mizuye Noda
Mr. and Mrs. Robert Noda
Mr. Yasuo Noda
Mr. Yoshio Noda
Ms. Esther Noda-Toyoda
Mr. Eugene K. Nodohara
Ms. Anne M. Nogaki
Mr. Kurt Nogaki
Ms. Amy E. Nogami
Mr. Darryl I. Nogami
Mr. Robert Nogami
Ms. Yukiye Nogami
Ms. Yuriko Nogami
Ms. Susan Nogas and Dave Godwin
Mr. Ben Nogawa
Mr. James Nogawa
Mr. Alfred Noguchi
Mr. and Mrs. David H. Noguchi
Mr. George Noguchi
Mr. Harold Noguchi
Mr. and Mrs. Hiroshi Noguchi
Ms. Irene Noguchi
Ms. Iris K. Noguchi
Ms. Jean Noguchi
Mr. and Mrs. John T. Noguchi
Mr. and Mrs. Kinya Noguchi
Mr. Masashi Noguchi
Mrs. Nellie H. Noguchi
Mrs. Sayeko Noguchi
Mr. Ted T. Noguchi
Mr. Albert Nohara
Mr. Shinko T. Nohara
Fumi Noji
Mr. and Mrs. Harold Noji
Mr. Mamoru Noji
Mr. and Mrs. Thomas T. Noji
Mrs. Betty Nojima
Ms. Hannah Nojima
Mr. N. Nojima
Dr. Williams S. Nojima
Mr. Masao Nojiri
Ms. Carol W. Nolan
Ms. Keiko Noma
Norimitsu T. Noma
Mr. William K. Noma
Kaori Nomi
Mr. and Mrs. Taichi Nomi
Ms. Takeko Nomiya
Mr. Ken N. Nomiyama
Nomura Enterprise Inc.
Mr. and Mrs. Al Nomura
Ms. Ann Nomura
Ms. Bernice S. Nomura
Ms. Carolyn M. Nomura
Mr. Clifford S. Nomura
Ms. Dorothy Y. Nomura
Ms. Emi Nomura
Mr. Francis Nomura
Mr. and Mrs. Frank Nomura
Gail M. Nomura, Emi N. and Stephen H. Sumida
Mr. and Mrs. George Nomura
Mr. and Mrs. Hiromi Nomura
Mr. Jack Nomura
Mr. Ken Nomura
Ms. Lori Nomura
Ms. Mary Nomura
Mrs. Masa Nomura
Ms. Mitsu R. Nomura
Ms. Mitsuye Nomura
Mr. Paul N. Nomura
Mr. and Mrs. Paul T. Nomura

Mr. Philip H. Nomura
Mr. Ronald Nomura
Roy and Yvonne Nomura
Mr. Samuel Nomura
Mr. Steven Nomura
Ms. Sylvia Nomura
Mr. and Mrs. Tak Nomura
Mr. and Mrs. Tokuo Nomura and Family (Carrie, Darryl, Greg, Jeff and Nikki)
Mr. and Mrs. Tom Nomura
Ms. Wakako Nomura
Walter and Chieko Nomura
Mr. and Mrs. Frank S. Nonaka
Mr. and Mrs. Fred S. Nonaka
Ms. Masami Nonaka
Mr. Masatoshi Nonaka
Mr. Scot J. Nonaka
Mr. Yutaka Nonaka
Mr. Charles A. Nordhausen
Mr. and Mrs. Koji Norikane
Mr. and Mrs. Mas Norikane
Mr. Akira Norimoto
Mr. Masanobu Norimoto
Mr. Joe Norisada
Mr. and Mrs. Joe O. Noritake
Mr. and Mrs. Gram Noriyuki
Mr. and Mrs. Samuel Noriyuki
Ms. Kimberly Norman
Mr. Don H. Noro
H. Noro
Norwalk Karaoke Club
Mr. Fred K. Nosaka
Mr. and Mrs. William M. Nosaka
Ms. Matsuyo Nose'
Dr. Peter S. Nose'
Mr. Steven K. Nose'
Mr. and Mrs. John H. Nosse
Ms. Laraine Noto
Ms. Hana M. Notomi
Mr. and Mrs. Stephen Nowatzki
Mr. and Mrs. Albert Nozaki
Mr. and Mrs. Arthur Nozaki
Mr. David N. Nozaki
Ms. Haruko Nozaki
Mr. Melvin Nozaki
Mr. Michael Nozaki
Mr. and Mrs. Roger Nozaki
Donald and Arlene Nozawa
Mr. and Mrs. Eddie I. Nozawa
Mr. and Mrs. Masao Nozawa
Mr. Tsuneyoshi Nozoe
Mr. Samuel O. Nukazawa
Mr. William R. Nunn
Mr. Mark Nunokawa
Mr. Robert F. Nunokawa
Dr. Walter Nunokawa
Mr. Daniel Nunotani
Mr. Jack M. O'Brien
Mr. and Mrs. John O'Brien
Ms. Polly O'Brien
Mr. and Mrs. Kenneth O'Dea
Ms. Alva O'Donoghue
Mr. and Mrs. Don O'Hara
Mr. James M. O'Neill
Mrs. June O'Neill and Ms. Akemi Wakishita
Ms. Maria F. O'Reilly
Mr. Frank A. O'Toole
Mr. Kirby G. Oak
Ms. Shirley L. Oakes
Mr. and Mrs. Thomas Oakley
Mr. Calvin Oba
Mr. George Oba
Mr. Harold Oba
Mr. and Mrs. Harold Oba
Mr. Kenneth Oba
Ms. Michiko Oba
Ms. Mildred C. Oba
Mr. and Mrs. Ronald Oba
Ms. Sakaye Oba
Ms. Edna Obata
Fusae Obata
Mr. and Mrs. Jack Obata
Ms. Kiyoko E. Obata
Ms. Mae Obata
Ms. Mary M. Obata
Mrs. Shinko Obata
Mr. Shuichi Obata
Mr. Wesley Obata
Mr. and Mrs. William M. Obata
Dr. and Mrs. Paul Obatake
Mr. Henry Obayashi
Mr. and Mrs. Joseph H. Obayashi
Mrs. June T. Obayashi
Ms. Linda Toyo Obayashi
Mr. and Mrs. Mikihiko Obayashi
Mr. and Mrs. Norman T. Obayashi

Mr. Teruo Obayashi
Mr. Walter H. Obayashi
Mr. Ray H. Obazawa
Mr. and Mrs. Hideo Ochi
Mr. Howard M. Ochi
Mr. and Mrs. Jerry Ochi
Mr. Lane Ochi
Mr. Michel Ochi
Mr. and Mrs. Mickie Ochi
Mr. and Mrs. Raymond T. Ochi
Mr. Seichi Ochi
Mr. and Mrs. Somao Ochi
Mr. Steve Ochi
Kazuo Ochiai
Dr. and Mrs. Tadashi Ochiai
Mr. Clark G. Ochikubo
Ms. Ariye Oda
Mr. and Mrs. Arthur Oda
Ms. Beverly Oda
Mr. Carl Oda
Mr. Charles Oda
Mr. Dane Oda
Mr. Dwight Oda
Ms. Ethel Aiko Oda
Mr. and Mrs. Fred U. Oda
Mr. and Mrs. Harold Oda
Ms. Harua Oda
Mr. and Mrs. Jack Oda
Mr. James Oda
Mr. and Mrs. John Oda
Ms. Kathy Oda
Ms. Linda K. Oda
Ms. Lucy A. Oda
Mr. and Mrs. Macoto Oda
Mr. Mark S. Oda
Ms. Nancy Oda
Mr. and Mrs. Nobuo Oda
Mr. Nobuyuki Robert Oda
Mr. and Mrs. Richard M. Oda
Mr. and Mrs. Robert N. Oda
Ms. Ruth Oda
Mr. S. Russell Oda
Sets and Kimi Oda
Mr. Stanley S. Oda
Mr. and Mrs. Stephen Oda
Mr. Tak Oda
Mr. and Mrs. Takashi Oda
Mr. Ted Oda
Mr. Terry N. Oda
Mr. Thomas Oda
Mr. Tom I. Oda
Mr. Toshio Oda and sons
Mr. Tsuneo L. Oda
Mr. Vincent M. Oda
Mr. and Mrs. William S. Oda
Mr. and Mrs. Yoshio Ping Oda
Ms. Katsuko Odanaka
Ms. Julia B. Odenbach
Mr. and Mrs. Franklin Odo
Mr. and Mrs. Kenji Odo
Mr. Marcus K. Odo
Mr. Tetsuo Odo
Ms. Nori Ann Odoi
Mr. and Mrs. Steve Odum
Mr. Harry Oga
Ms. June F. Oga
Ms. Emmy E. Ogami
Dr. Noboru Ogami
Bill and Shelia Ogasawara
Mr. Edwin T. Ogasawara
Mr. and Mrs. Paul W. Ogasawara
Mr. and Mrs. Roy Ogasawara
Mr. Stome T. Ogasawara
Mr. and Mrs. Akira Ogata
Mr. and Mrs. Charles M. Ogata
Mr. Dudley Ogata
Dr. Edward S. Ogata
Mr. George Ogata
Mr. and Mrs. Gerald Ogata
Mr. and Mrs. Hal T. Ogata
Ms. Hatsumi Ogata
Mr. Henry K. Ogata
Mr. and Mrs. Herbert Ogata
Hisayo Ogata
Ms. Isabell M. Ogata
Mr. Jerry Ogata
Mr. Jun S. Ogata
Mr. Kasuke Ogata
Mr. Kazuma Ogata
Mr. M. Ogata
Ms. Mae Ogata
Mr. Maui F. Ogata
Mr. Mitsunari Ogata
Mr. Mitsuo Ogata
Mr. Raymond M. Ogata
Mr. Richard K. Ogata

Mr. and Mrs. Robert Ogata
Mr. Sakae Bert Ogata
Mr. and Mrs. Tabo Ogata
Mr. Tetsuo Ogata
Mr. Wayne M. Ogata
Mr. Yasuo Ogata
Mr. Yoshito J. Ogata
Ms. Alice Ogawa
Mr. Arthur E. Ogawa
Mr. and Mrs. David Ogawa
Mr. and Mrs. Eary Ogawa
Mr. and Mrs. Ed Ogawa
Ms. Elsie I. Ogawa
Mr. and Mrs. Francis Ogawa
Mr. Gary S. Ogawa
Mr. and Mrs. Gerald F. Ogawa
Mr. Glen K. Ogawa
Ms. Grace S. Ogawa
Ms. Haru Ogawa
Ms. Helen T. Ogawa
Mr. Henry K. Ogawa
Mr. Herbert F. Ogawa
Mr. and Mrs. Hoichi Ogawa
Mr. Jerry Ogawa
Mr. and Mrs. Jerry G. Ogawa
Mr. and Mrs. Jiro Ogawa
Jonathan and Kyoko Ogawa
Ms. Julee Ogawa
Mr. Kazuo Ogawa
Ms. Keio Ogawa
Mrs. Kiyoko Ogawa
Mr. Kiyoshi Ogawa
Mrs. Lillian S. Ogawa
Ms. Lilly Ogawa
Ms. Mae Mie Ogawa
Mr. Marcus Ogawa
Ms. Margie Ogawa
Mr. and Mrs. Masashi Ogawa
Mr. Norman N. Ogawa
Mr. Richard Ogawa
Mr. and Mrs. Roy Ogawa
Mr. and Mrs. Seido Ogawa
Ms. Shizuko Ogawa
Mr. and Mrs. Shuichi Ogawa
Mr. and Mrs. Steve Ogawa
Mr. Takashi Ogawa
Mr. Tamotsu Ogawa
Mr. Wayne Ogawa
Mr. and Mrs. Wesley Ogawa
Mr. Yasushi Ogawa
Mr. and Mrs. Robert E. Ogi
Mr. and Mrs. Stanley Ogi
Mr. Yoshio Ogi
Mrs. Diana T. Ogimi
Ms. Frances S. and Ms. Maxine J. Ogino
Ms. Teresa M. Ogino
Mr. and Mrs. Toshio Ogino
Ms. June Ogisaka
Ms. Toshiko Ogita
Ms. Asenath Oglesby
Mr. Joseph Oglesby
Ms. Shizue S. Ogomori
Mr. Susumu Ogomori
Ms. Donna N. Ogura
Mr. Hidetake T. Ogura
Mr. James R. Ogura
Mrs. Richard Ogura
Mr. Ruth M. Ogura
Mr. Ben Ohama
Mr. and Mrs. George Ohama
Mr. Paul Ohama
Richard Ohama and Linda Basham
Ms. Robin L. Ohama
Ms. Sadako R. Ohama
Ms. Chisato Ohara
Mr. and Mrs. George Ohara
Mr. and Mrs. Haruo Ohara
Ms. Hilda Ohara
Mr. and Mrs. Hitoshi Ohara
Ms. June Ohara
Mr. Masami Ohara
Mr. and Mrs. Masanobu Ohara
Mrs. Miyo Ohara
Mr. Ronald Ohara
Mr. and Mrs. Sam Ohara
Ms. Sandra Ohara
Mr. and Mrs. Susumi Ohara
Mr. Tadashi Ohara
Mr. and Mrs. Toshio Ohara
Mr. Wichi Ohara
Ms. Yukie Ohara
Ms. Yuri Ohara
Mr. Arnold Ohashi
Mr. and Mrs. Bunjiro Ohashi
Ms. Cheryl L. Ohashi
Mr. Edward Ohashi

Mr. and Mrs. James T. Ohashi
Ms. Leslie A. Ohashi
Ms. Lisa Ohashi
Ms. Michiko Ohashi
Mr. and Mrs. Taro Ohashi
Mrs. Terry Ohashi
Mr. Wayne K. Ohashi
Mr. Tasuka Ohazama
Mr. Kazuo Ohde
Mr. Frank Ohgi
Mr. and Mrs. Paul Ohi
Mr. Jack Ohigashi
Ms. Jane S. Ohigashi
Ms. Christine Ohira
Mr. John M. Ohira
Mr. John T. Ohira
Mr. and Mrs. Masao Ohira
Mr. Steve H. Ohira
Ms. Janet Ohka
Ms. Anne A. Ohki
Mr. and Mrs. Robert Ohki
Mrs. Kiyono M. Ohmura
Mr. Akira Ohno
Ms. Iku Ohno
Mr. Joe Ohno
Mr. and Mrs. Joe Ohno
Mr. Robert K. Ohno
Ms. Bessie S. Ohnoki
Ms. Takako Ohori
Ms. Hitomi A. Ohsawa
Kazuko and Miyuki Ohshita
Mr. Francis Ohta
Mr. Gerald Ohta
Ms. Hilda Ohta
Mr. and Mrs. Hiram Ohta
Mr. John Ohta
Ms. Leslie C. Ohta
Mr. and Mrs. Roy Ohta
Mr. Roy Y. Ohta
Mr. and Mrs. Shuhei Ohta
Mr. Wallace Ohta
Mrs. Rose T. Ohtaki
Ms. Michi Ohtani
Ms. Alma A. Ohtomo
Ms. Mary Tachiko Oi
Mr. and Mrs. Oliver K. Oi
Mr. Takatsugu Oi
Mr. and Mrs. Shizuo Oide
Mr. Kenneth E. Oie
Dr. and Mrs. Y. Oikawa
Mr. Dale H. Oishi
Mr. David S. Oishi
Mr. and Mrs. Donald Oishi
Ms. Elsie J. Oishi
Mrs. Ethel S. Oishi
Mr. Hideo Oishi
Ms. Jeanette C. Oishi
Mr. and Mrs. Jiro Oishi
Ms. Joyce H. Oishi
Miss Julie J. Oishi
Mr. and Mrs. Kazuo Oishi
Mr. and Mrs. M. K. Oishi
Ms. May Oishi
Ms. Mayumi Oishi
Mr. and Mrs. Roy T. Oishi
Mr. Takanori Oishi
Mr. Takashi Oishi
Ms. Toshiko Oishi
Helen Oji and Charles Luce
Ms. Mitsue Oji
Mr. Masuo Ojima
Ms. Donna Ojiri
Satoshi Ojiri
Mr. Alan Oka
Mr. and Mrs. Alexander J. Oka
Mr. Arthur A. Oka
Ms. Asako Oka
Mr. Don C. Oka
Mr. Harry Oka
Mr. and Mrs. Hidekazu Oka
Mr. and Mrs. Isamu Oka
Mr. James H. Oka
K. Oka
Mr. and Mrs. Kayji Oka
Mr. and Mrs. Keith Oka
Mr. and Mrs. Kiyoshi Oka
Mr. and Mrs. Michael L. Oka
Mr. Michio Oka
Mr. Naoto Oka
Mr. Nobuo Oka
Mr. Rick Oka
Mr. and Mrs. Robert Oka
Mr. Robert M. Oka
Mr. and Mrs. Robert M. Oka
Ms. Shigeko B. Oka
Mr. Shizuo Oka

Mr. Sumio Okabayashi
Mrs. Yoshiko Okabayashi
Mr. Craig Okabe
Mr. and Mrs. Martin Okabe
Ms. Patrice S. Okabe
Mr. Thomas M. Okabe
Mr. and Mrs. Thomas S. Okabe
Mrs. Akiko Okada
Ms. Amy M. Okada
Ms. Barbara Okada
Ms. Bessie K. Okada
Ms. Beverly A. Okada
Dr. and Mrs. Donald Okada
Mr. and Mrs. Edward Okada
Mr. and Mrs. Elvis K. Okada
Ms. Emiko Okada
Mr. and Mrs. Enro Okada
Mr. Eric J. Okada
Mrs. Fujino Okada
Mr. George M. Okada
Mr. Glenn H. Okada
Mr. & Mrs. Harold I. Okada
Mr. and Mrs. Harry Okada
Mrs. Hazuki Okada
Mrs. Helen Okada
Mr. Herbert Okada
Ms. Jane Okada
Ms. Jean C. Okada
Mrs. Jean K. Okada
Mr. John C. Okada
Mr. John T. Okada
Mr. Kengo Okada
Mr. Lawrence H. Okada
Mr. and Mrs. Mako Okada
Mr. and Mrs. Manabu Okada
Ms. Michiko Okada
Mr. Minoru Okada
Mr. Minoru M. Okada
Ms. Misao Okada
Ms. Nancy T. Okada
Mr. Nat Okada
Mr. and Mrs. Nobi Okada
Mr. Philip Okada
Mr. Robert Okada
Mr. and Mrs. Robert H. Okada
Ms. Sandie S. Okada
Ms. Sandra Okada
Mr. and Mrs. Shig Okada
Ms. Shigeko Okada
Mr. and Mrs. Shigeo Okada
Mr. Susumu Okada
Mr. Takeshi Okada
Mr. and Mrs. Tetsunobu Okada
Ms. Toni D. Okada
Mr. William M. Okada
Ms. Yukiko Okada
Mr. Gary R. Okafuji
Ms. Ruby Okafuji
Mr. Sadao Okafuji
Ms. Amy Okagaki
Ms. Janet Okagaki
Mr. and Mrs. Warren J. Okagaki
Mr. and Mrs. John Okagawa
Mr. Tsuru Okagawa
Ms. Dorothy Okahira-Chang
Mr. and Mrs. George Okajima
Ms. Kimiko Okajima
Ms. Aiko Okamoto
Ms. Akiko Okamoto
Mr. Albert Y. Okamoto
Mr. and Mrs. Allen H. Okamoto
Mr. and Mrs. Clifford Okamoto
Mr. David Okamoto
Mr. and Mrs. Dennis I. Okamoto
Ms. Dianne Okamoto
Mrs. Donna L. Okamoto
Mr. Edward G. Okamoto
Mr. and Mrs. Eiichi Okamoto
Ms. Frances F. Okamoto
Mr. Fred K. Okamoto
Ms. Fumie Okamoto
Dr. and Mrs. Gary A. Okamoto
Mr. and Mrs. George Okamoto
Mr. George A. Okamoto
Mr. and Mrs. Hiroharu Okamoto
Mrs. Jean Okamoto
Mr. Jeffrey A. Okamoto
Mr. John M. Okamoto
Mr. K. Keith Okamoto
Mr. Kaname Okamoto
Rev. and Mrs. Kanya Okamoto
Ms. Kay Okamoto and Ms. Yoshiko Nakagawa
Mr. and Mrs. Kazumi Okamoto
Mrs. Kelly A. Okamoto
Mr. Kenneth M. Okamoto
Ms. Kimiko Y. Okamoto

Mr. Kosuke Okamoto
Ms. Kumi and Mrs. Hatsuko Okamoto
Mr. Kurt Okamoto
Kyo Okamoto
Ms. Lily T. Okamoto
Mr. and Mrs. Louis Okamoto
Mrs. Mary Okamoto
Mr. and Mrs. Masami Okamoto
Mr. Matthew Okamoto
Mr. Melvin Okamoto
Mr. Melvin M. Okamoto
Ms. Mitsuko Okamoto
Mr. Mitsuo Okamoto
Mr. and Mrs. Mitsuru Okamoto
Ms. Nancy Okamoto
Mr. Paul Okamoto
Mr. and Mrs. Peter Okamoto
Mr. Quinn Okamoto
Mr. and Mrs. Richard Okamoto
Mr. Richard Y. Okamoto
Mr. and Mrs. Robert Okamoto
Mr. and Mrs. Samuel Okamoto
Mr. and Mrs. Shizuo Okamoto
Mrs. Sumi Okamoto
Ms. Susan Okamoto
Mr. Takashi Okamoto
Mr. and Mrs. Takeru Okamoto
Mr. Takumi Okamoto
Mr. Tetsuo Okamoto
Mr. Tsuguo Okamoto
Mr. and Mrs. William K. Okamoto
Mr. and Mrs. William S. Okamoto
Ms. Yuri Okamoto
Ms. Aisaku Okamura
Mr. Alan Okamura
Ms. Ann Okamura
Mr. and Mrs. Bob Okamura
Mr. Dennis I. Okamura
Mr. Edward Okamura
Mr. and Mrs. Eugene Okamura
Mr. and Mrs. F. Okamura
Mr. George Okamura
Ms. Hazel Okamura
Mr. Hirofumi Okamura
Dr. and Mrs. Ichiro Okamura
Ms. Jan Okamura
Kimiko and Kinuko Okamura
Ms. Lynn A. Okamura
Mr. Michael Okamura
Mr. and Mrs. Mike Okamura
Minoru and Naomi Okamura
Mr. and Mrs. Paul Okamura
Mr. and Mrs. Ray Okamura
Mr. Sakaye Okamura
Mrs. Sanaye Okamura
Mr. and Mrs. Shinji Okamura
Stanley A. and Martha E. Okamura
Mr. and Mrs. Stanley Y. Okamura
Mr. Stuart Okamura
Ms. Sue Okamura
Mr. Thomas Okamura
Mr. and Mrs. Toshio Okamura
Mr. Van T. Okamura
Mrs. Sabrina E. Okamura-Johnson
Mr. and Mrs. Carl Okaneko
Mr. Hideo Okanishi
Mrs. Yoneko Okanishi
Mr. David Okano
Mrs. Dorothy M. Okano
Ms. Elaine Okano
Mr. G. Bruce Okano
Mr. and Mrs. Hiroshi H. Okano
Mr. Kenneth T. Okano
Mr. Mark K. Okano
Mr. and Mrs. Mel Okano
Mr. Minoru Okano
Mr. Richard Okano
Mr. and Mrs. Robert T. Okano
Mr. Yuji Okano
Mr. and Mrs. David Okasaki
Mr. and Mrs. Frank Okasaki
Mr. and Mrs. George K. Okasaki
Mrs. Agnes N. Okasako
Mr. Edward Okasako
Mrs. Elsie T. Okata
Mr. and Mrs. Roy Okata
Col. and Mrs. Earl K. Okawa
Ms. Laura M. Okawa
Mrs. Marcelle Okawa
Ms. Sumi W. Okawa
Ms. Teru Okawa
Mr. and Mrs. Kimio Okawachi
Mr. and Mrs. Tsuneo Okawachi
Mr. Arthur K. Okawauchi
Mr. Jack Okayama
Mr. and Mrs. Ron Okayama

Mr. and Mrs. Alan Okazaki
Ms. Alice Okazaki
Mr. and Mrs. Buzzy T. Okazaki
Ms. Carolyn Okazaki
Mr. and Mrs. Charles Okazaki
Ms. Chieko Okazaki
Ms. Chieko N. Okazaki
Mr. and Mrs. Clyde Y. Okazaki
Mr. and Mrs. David Okazaki
Mr. Dennis Okazaki
Ms. Donna S. Okazaki
Mrs. Eric T. Okazaki
Mr. and Mrs. Frank Okazaki
Mr. and Mrs. Fumio Okazaki
Mr. Gary L. Okazaki
Mr. and Mrs. Guy Okazaki
Mr. and Mrs. Harry Okazaki
Ms. Harue Okazaki
Mr. James M. Okazaki
Mr. James Y. Okazaki
Mr. Jeffrey H. Okazaki
Mr. and Mrs. John Okazaki
Ms. Joyce Okazaki
Mr. Kaichi H. Okazaki
Ms. Katherine Okazaki
Mr. Ken Okazaki
Mrs. Lillian Okazaki
Mr. Mark Okazaki
Mr. Marlon Okazaki
Mr. Masahiko Okazaki
Mr. and Mrs. Masayuki Okazaki
Mr. Michael Okazaki
Mr. Mits Okazaki
Mr. and Mrs. Mitsuo Okazaki
Mr. and Mrs. Nabo Okazaki
Mr. and Mrs. Noboru Okazaki
Mrs. Rosy S. Okazaki
Mr. and Mrs. Roy Okazaki
Ms. Ryoko S. Okazaki
Ms. Shizue A. Okazaki
Mr. Thomas Okazaki
Mr. Tokuo Okazaki
Ms. Yumiko Okazaki
Mr. and Mrs. Takashi Okemura
Mr. Masateru Oketani
Mr. and Mrs. Albert Y. Oki
Ms. Arlene T. Oki
Ms. Dianne C. Oki
Mr. and Mrs. Frank Oki
Mr. Fred Oki
Ms. Hisako Oki
Ms. Mieko Oki
Mr. Newton Oki
Mr. and Mrs. Sadao Oki
Mr. and Mrs. Takashi Oki
Ms. Yayoi Oki
Mr. Joel M. Okida
Ms. Alice Okihara
Mr. and Mrs. Craig T. Okihara
Mr. and Mrs. Toshio Okihara
Mr. George Okihiro
Mr. and Mrs. Scott Okiishi
Mr. and Mrs. Harold T. Okikawa
Mr. Mikito Okimi
Mr. Alexander Okimoto
Mr. Anson T. Okimoto
Mr. and Mrs. Charles T. Okimoto
Dr. Daniel Okimoto
Mr. and Mrs. Frank Okimoto
Mr. Frank S. Okimoto
Mr. Fred Okimoto
Ms. Jan Okimoto
Mr. Joe Okimoto
Dr. Joseph Okimoto
Ms. R. Yoshiko Okimoto
Dr. and Mrs. Ray Okimoto
Mr. and Mrs. Roy Okimoto
Mr. Steven Okimoto
Okimoto's Auto Center, Inc.
Mr. and Mrs. George Okimura
Ms. Georgina M. Okimura
Ms. Hazel H. Okimura
Ms. Kay Okimura
Mr. and Mrs. Michael Okimura
Mr. Ronny T. Okimura
Mr. Shig Okimura
Mr. Stanley S. Okimura
Mr. Tom I. Okimura
Mrs. Chieko Okinaga
Mr. Harold Okinaka
Mr. and Mrs. Kunitaka Okinaka
Mr. Mark Okinaka
Mr. and Mrs. Yasuo Okinaka
Ms. Agnes Okino
Mr. Haruo Okino
Mr. and Mrs. Masaru Okino

Mr. and Mrs. Minoru Okino
Mr. and Mrs. Roy Okino
Mr. Saburo Okino
Mr. Tamotsu Okino
Mr. and Mrs. Todd Okino
Mr. and Mrs. Wilfred Okino
Mr. Bret T. Okita
Mr. George 'Taka' Okita
Mr. and Mrs. George Okita
Ms. Kiyo Okita
Mr. Masao Okita
Mrs. Teresita Okita
Mr. Jon Okitsu
Mr. Jou Okitsu
Ms. Gail Okiyama
Mrs. June H. Okizaki
Mr. Mark M. Okohira
Mr. Richard S. Okouchi
Ms. Alice Y. Oku
Mr. and Mrs. Edward Oku
Ms. Kimberly J. Oku
Mr. Masao Oku
Ms. Miye M. Oku
Mr. and Mrs. Makoto Okubara
Ms. Donna K. Okubo
Mr. and Mrs. Floyd Okubo
Mr. and Mrs. George Okubo
Ms. Grace Okubo
Ms. Haruye Okubo
Mr. and Mrs. Henry Okubo
Mr. Herbert N. Okubo
Mr. and Mrs. Hikaru Okubo
Mr. and Mrs. Hiram Okubo
Ms. Jane K. Okubo
Ms. Janet M. Okubo
Mr. and Mrs. Kenneth K. Okubo
Mr. Kiyoto G. Okubo
Mr. Michael H. Okubo
Mr. Milton Okubo
Mr. and Mrs. Minoru Okubo
Ms. Mitsuye Okubo
Mrs. Nobuyo Okubo
Mr. Roy Okubo
Ms. Ruby Okubo
Ms. Shigeko Okubo
Mrs. Sumiko Okubo
Mr. and Mrs. Tom M. Okubo
Mr. Tom T. Okubo
Mr. and Mrs. William Okubo
Mrs. Alice Okuda
Mr. Bob Okuda
Mrs. Elsa Okuda
Mr. Harris Okuda
Mrs. Hiroko Okuda
Mr. and Mrs. Jim S. Okuda
Mr. Kazunobu Okuda
M. Okuda
Ms. Michi S. Okuda
Mr. and Mrs. Michio Okuda
Mrs. Mitsuye Okuda
Mr. and Mrs. Noboru R. Okuda
Mr. and Mrs. Richard Okuda
Mr. and Mrs. Robert Okuda
Mr. and Mrs. Teiji Okuda
Mr. and Mrs. Yasuyori Okuda
Ms. Kazuko Okudaira
Mrs. Janice Okudara
Mr. and Mrs. Jimmie Okugawa
Mr. and Mrs. Albert Okuhara
Ms. Heidi S. Okuhara
Mr. Takashi Okuhara
Mr. Kunio Okui
Mr. and Mrs. Michio Okui
Mr. Toshio Okui
Mr. and Mrs. David Okuji
Ms. Haru Okuma
Mr. and Mrs. Kenneth Okuma
Mrs. Nancy F. Okuma
Mr. and Mrs. Ryotoku Okuma
Mr. William Okuma
Ms. Yoshie Okuma
Mr. and Mrs. Matsuo Okumoto
Mr. and Mrs. Ted Okumoto
Mr. Victor Okumoto
George and Helen Okumura
Mrs. Helen H. Okumura
Mr. John T. Okumura
Mr. Kazuma Okumura
Mr. Minoru Okumura
Mr. Randy Okumura
Mr. and Mrs. Takeo Okumura
Mr. and Mrs. Takeshi Okumura
Ms. Toyoko Okumura
Mr. Hideo Okunami
Mr. Albert Okuno
Ms. Hope E. Okuno

Mr. Joe Okuno
Mr. and Mrs. Katsumi Okuno
Mr. and Mrs. Makoto Okuno
Ms. Frances Okura
Mrs. Takako Okura
Mr. and Mrs. Ted Okura
Drs. Mark and Diane Okusa
Mr. Harry Okusako
Mr. Art Okusu
Mr. Ben Okusu
Ms. Nora Okusu
Mr. Anthony T. Okutsu
Mr. John Okutsu
Mr. and Mrs. Ben Okuye
Mr. and Mrs. Paul Okuye
Ms. Susan S. Oldham
Mr. and Mrs. Bob Olson
Mr. and Mrs. Rodney Omachi
Mr. and Mrs. Shigeru Omae
Ms. Sonia Omahen
Mr. Richard J. Omata
Mr. Harold T. Omatsu
Mr. Paul T. Omatsu
Mr. and Mrs. Takeo Omatsu
Mr. Thomas Omaye
Mr. and Mrs. Eugene Omi
Mr. and Mrs. George Omi
Mr. and Mrs. Kotaro Omine
Mr. Tetsuo Omine
Mr. Bruce H. Omiya
Ms. Jane A. Omiya
Mr. Kazuo Omiya
Mr. and Mrs. Masayuki Omiya
Ms. Jean A. Omokawa
Mr. Dean M. Omori
Ms. Deborah Jean Omori
Mr. Gary Omori and Ms. Lisa K. Nakata
Mr. and Mrs. George Omori
Mr. and Mrs. Hideo Omori
Mr. and Mrs. James H. Omori
Mr. John Omori
Mr. Kazuo J. Omori
Ms. Lydia Omori
Mr. Masahiro Omori
Mr. Patrick Omori
Ms. Rachel Omori
Mr. and Mrs. Richard T. Omori
Mr. and Mrs. Shigeru Omori
Mrs. Shirley Yoshiko Omori
Mr. Thomas Omori
Mr. and Mrs. Tsutomu Omori
Mr. David Omoto
Ms. Jennifer Omoto
Mr. Milton Omoto
Mr. and Mrs. Mits Omoto
Mrs. Pat Omoto
Mr. Russell T. Omoto
Mr. Sadayoshi Omoto
Mr. William H. Omoto
Anne Tamiko Omura and Whitty Somvichian
Mr. Daniel M. Omura
Mrs. Emiko Omura
Mr. George A. Omura
Mr. Hisanori Omura
Mr. Jim K. Omura
Mr. and Mrs. Jimmy A. Omura
Mr. and Mrs. Masayoshi Omura
Mr. and Mrs. Mits Omura
Mrs. Mitsuko Omura
Mr. Richard Omura
Mr. and Mrs. Tsurumato Omura
Ms. Velma Omura
Mr. Eric Omuro
Mr. Masahito Omuro
Mr. Dexter Onaga
Ms. Eiko Onaga
Mr. George Onaga
Mr. Herbert H. Onaga
Mr. Edward Onaka
Mr. Howard M. Onchi
Mr. and Mrs. Joe M. Onchi
Mr. Bob One
Mr. and Mrs. Dick One
Ms. Gladys Oniki
Mr. and Mrs. Thomas Oniki
Ms. Alice S. Onishi
Mr. and Mrs. Donald T. Onishi
Mr. and Mrs. Harold H. Onishi
Mr. and Mrs. Harold M. Onishi
Mrs. Ida Onishi
Mr. and Mrs. Ken Onishi
Mr. and Mrs. Kenji Onishi
Ms. Mary M. Onishi
Mr. and Mrs. Masato Onishi
Mr. Noboru Onishi
Mr. and Mrs. Randall Onishi

Mr. and Mrs. Raymond K. Onishi
Ms. Reiko Onishi
Ms. Tomoko Onishi
Mr. L. K. Onitsuka
Mr. and Mrs. Lawrence H. Onitsuka
Mr. and Mrs. Ryoji Onitsuka
Dr. and Mrs. Richard Onizuka
Mr. and Mrs. Akio Ono
Ms. Amy E. Ono
Mr. Cary Ono
Mr. and Mrs. Charles N. Ono
Mr. Christoph Y. Ono
Dr. and Mrs. Clyde Ono
Ms. Edith S. Ono
Mr. Ernest S. Ono
Mr. Fred Ono
Mr. and Mrs. Goichiro Ono
Ms. Hanaes H. Ono
Mr. and Mrs. Harry H. Ono
Mr. and Mrs. Harry T. Ono
Mr. and Mrs. Henry M. Ono
Mr. Isao Ono
Mr. and Mrs. Joseph Ono
Ms. Joyce Ono
Mr. Junya Ono
Mr. Katsumi Ono
Ms. Kay Ono
Mr. and Mrs. Kazuo Ono
Ms. Linda Ono
Ms. Lynne Ono
Mrs. Mariko Ono
Mary and Robert Ono
Mr. and Mrs. Mas Ono
Mr. and Mrs. Mason Ono
Mr. Miles M. Ono
Mr. Patrick Ono
Mr. Robert Ono and Ms. Betty Masuoka
Mr. Rodney T. Ono
Mr. Roy Ono
Mr. Sam H. Ono
Mr. Samuel K. Ono
Mr. Stuart Ono
Mr. Sukeichi Ono
Mr. Susumu Ono
Mrs. Tami Ono
Mr. Theodore K. Ono
Mr. and Mrs. Tsuyoshi Ono
Mr. and Mrs. Yoshi Ono
Ms. Carol Onoda
Mr. and Mrs. Tom Onoda
Mr. and Mrs. Dilford Onodera
Mr. and Mrs. Joe M. Onodera
Mr. Ken Onodera
Ms. Shirley D. Onodera
Ms. Sumi Onodera
Mr. Ernest Onomoto
Mr. Hiroshi Onomoto
Mr. and Mrs. Lionel Onomura
Mr. Eddie Onouye
Mr. and Mrs. Isao Onuki
Mr. and Mrs. Darel Onuma
Mr. Tom T. Onuma
Mrs. Barbara Ooka
Mr. and Mrs. Masaaki Ooka
Mr. Walter Oppenheimer
Orange County Nikkei Jr. Golf
Orange County Widows and Widowers
Organization of Chinese Americans, Inc.
Organization of Chinese Americans - Washington
DC Chapter
Mr. Wayne Oride
Mr. and Mrs. Norio Origuchi
Ms. Fusaye Orimoto
Mr. George Orite
Mr. Ray Orite
Mr. and Mrs. Vincent Oritz
Mr. and Mrs. Bob Orlandi
Ms. Patricia Orr
Ms. Megumi Osa
Mr. and Mrs. Stanley H. Osada
Mr. William Osada
Mr. Glenn R. Osaka
Michi Osaka
Mr. Carl H. Osaki
Mr. and Mrs. Charles Osaki
Mr. and Mrs. Edward Osaki
Mrs. Haruye Osaki
Mr. Henry I. Osaki
Mr. and Mrs. Herbert Osaki
Ms. Kazuye Osaki
Mr. and Mrs. Kenji Osaki
Ms. Mary E. Osaki
Mr. Masao Osaki
Mr. Wayne Osaki
Mr. Suzushi Osako
Mr. and Mrs. Takanobu Osako

Ms. Yoshiko F. Osako
Mrs. Karen Osato
Mr. Roy Osato
Mr. George Osawa
Ms. Helen K. Oshiba
Mr. Otto Oshida
Mrs. Sue R. Oshida
Ms. Teruye H. Oshidari
Mr. David T. Oshige
Ms. Nellie T. Oshige
Mr. and Mrs. Noboru Oshige
Mrs. Beatrice T. Oshika
Ms. Tsugiye Oshika
Mr. Alan Y. Oshima
Ms. Chiyoko Oshima
Mr. and Mrs. Elmer S. Oshima
Mr. and Mrs. Fred K. Oshima
Mr. Gary Oshima
Mr. and Mrs. George M. Oshima
Mr. George T. Oshima
Mr. Harry H. Oshima
Mr. and Mrs. Haruto Oshima
Mr. Hiromu Oshima
Mr. and Mrs. Hiroyuki Oshima
Mr. Joe Oshima
Ms. Kathy Oshima
Mr. Katsu Oshima
Mr. Kaz Oshima
Mr. and Mrs. Keiji Oshima
Mr. Kiyomi Oshima
Ms. Kristie M. Oshima
Ms. Lily Oshima
Mr. Martin M. Oshima
Mr. Moses Oshima
Mr. and Mrs. Raymond M. Oshima
Mr. Richard Oshima
Mr. Rita M. Oshima
Mr. Roy Oshima
Mr. and Mrs. Thomas Oshima
Mr. Charles M. Oshiro
Mr. Clifton Y. Oshiro
Mr. and Mrs. Dennis Oshiro
Mr. Edward M. Oshiro
Ms. Eva Oshiro
Mr. and Mrs. Francis Oshiro
Mr. and Mrs. Harry Oshiro
Ms. Joan S. Oshiro
Mr. and Mrs. John K. Oshiro
Mr. John T. Oshiro
Mr. and Mrs. Joseph Oshiro
Mr. Kaname Oshiro
Dr. Karen N. Oshiro
Mr. Ken T. Oshiro
Mr. Kerry Oshiro
Kiyoshi and Jeanne Oshiro
Ms. Lisa M. Oshiro
Mr. and Mrs. Lyndon S. Oshiro
Mr. and Mrs. Masaki Oshiro
Mr. Masanobu Oshiro
Mr. and Mrs. Masaru Oshiro
Mrs. Myrtle Oshiro
Mr. and Mrs. Paul I. Oshiro
Mr. Paul N. Oshiro
Mr. and Mrs. R. Oshiro
Mr. Richard E. Oshiro
Mr. Richard Y. Oshiro
Mr. and Mrs. Robert Oshiro
Mr. Robert T. Oshiro
Mr. Roger K. Oshiro
Mr. Ross Y. Oshiro
Mr. and Mrs. Roy M. Oshiro
Mr. Ryosei Oshiro
Mr. and Mrs. Sam Oshiro
Mr. and Mrs. Seiji Oshiro
Mr. Seiki Oshiro
Mr. Seishun Oshiro
Mr. Seizen Oshiro
Mr. Stanley M. Oshiro
Mr. and Mrs. Steve Oshiro
Mr. Sydney Oshiro
Mr. Takehiro Oshiro
Mr. and Mrs. Takeo Oshiro
Mr. Tomatsu Oshiro
Mr. Tsugio Oshiro
Mrs. Tsurue N. Oshiro
Mr. Walter N. Oshiro
Mr. Walter T. Oshiro
Mr. Wilfred S. Oshiro
Mr. William Oshiro
Mr. and Mrs. Yoshinobu Oshiro
Mr. Yoshio F. Oshiro
Mr. Yukisada Oshiro
Ms. Aiko Oshita
Mr. Ben Oshita
Ms. Edith Oshita
Mr. and Mrs. George I. Oshita

Mr. and Mrs. George N. Oshita
Dr. and Mrs. Gordon H. Oshita
Ms. Helen Oshita
Mr. Hideo Oshita
Mr. Howard Oshita
Mr. Jack Oshita
Mr. and Mrs. Jack H. Oshita
Dr. Leslie Oshita
Ms. Miyuki Oshita
Mr. and Mrs. Saburo Oshita
Mr. and Mrs. Teruyuki Oshita
Mr. and Mrs. Tom Oshita
Ms. Irene Osuga
Ms. Jane A. Osuga
Mr. and Mrs. Paul M. Osuga
Dr. and Mrs. Stephen K. Osuga
Mr. George Osumi
Mr. Harry M. Osumi
Mr. and Mrs. Henry D. Osumi
Mr. Kazuo Osumi
Ms. Kiyo Osumi
Mr. and Mrs. Norman Osumi
Mr. William Osumi
Mr. and Mrs. Alan Ota
Mr. Arao Ota
Mr. and Mrs. Buster M. Ota
Mr. Clem Z. Ota
Ms. Colleen Ota
Mr. Francis Ota
Mr. and Mrs. Frank S. Ota
Mr. and Mrs. Franklin K. Ota
Mr. and Mrs. Fred T. Ota
Mrs. Fujiko Ota
Geri M. Ota
Mr. and Mrs. Glenn A. Ota
Mr. H. Harold Ota
Mr. Herbert Ota
Mr. Hitoshi Ota
Mr. Isao Ota
Mr. and Mrs. Jack Ota
Ms. Jacqueline K. Ota
Mr. Jeffrey Ota
Mr. and Mrs. Johnny S. Ota
Miss Kay K. Ota
Mr. Kenso Ota
Mr. and Mrs. Kikuji Ota
Mr. and Mrs. Larry Ota
Mr. Lawrence H. Ota
Ms. Mabel T. Ota
Ms. Marjorie F. Ota
Ms. Mary H. Ota
Ms. Masae Ota
Mr. and Mrs. Masaru Ota
Mr. and Mrs. Minoru Ota
Mr. Minoru J. Ota
Mr. Richard Ota
Mr. Roy N. Ota
Mr. and Mrs. Roy W. Ota
Mr. S. John Ota
Ms. Sue T. Ota
Mr. and Mrs. Susumu Ota
Mr. and Mrs. Tad Ota
Mr. Takeshi Ota
Mr. and Mrs. Terry Ota
Mr. and Mrs. Thomas Ota
Mr. Tsutomu Ota
Mr. and Mrs. Zen Ota
Mr. and Mrs. Curtis Otaguro
Debra and Roy N. Otaguro
Ms. Geraldine M. Otaguro
Ms. Janice M. Otaguro
Ms. Susan D. Otaguro
Mr. and Mrs. Eugene Otake
Mr. Hiroshi Otake
Mr. and Mrs. Mike Otake
Mr. Toshiro Otake
Mr. and Mrs. Howard K. Otamura
Mr. Roy M. Otamura
Mr. and Mrs. Akira Otani
Mr. and Mrs. Allen Otani
Mr. Chester H. Otani
Ms. Chisato Otani
Mrs. Gloria Otani
Mr. and Mrs. Hideo Otani
Ms. Keiko Otani
Mr. Ken Otani
Mr. and Mrs. Kenneth S. Otani
Mr. Mitsuru Otani and Ms. Lin-Lin Tsou
Ms. Patti Otani
Mr. and Mrs. Robert T. Otani
Mr. Ronald M. Otani
Mr. Stan Otani
Mr. and Mrs. Theodore Otani
Mr. and Mrs. William Otani
Mr. and Mrs. John M. Otera
Dr. Paul Y. Otera

Mr. Duane Oto
Mr. Earl K. Oto
Ms. Edith K. Oto
Mr. Hiroshi Oto
Mr. Robert N. Oto
Mr. and Mrs. Shigeru Oto
Mr. and Mrs. Yoshio G. Oto
Ms. Aiko Otomo
Mr. and Mrs. John Otomo
Ms. Joan Otomo-Corgel
Col. and Mrs. Gary Otoshi
Mr. and Mrs. Tom Y. Otoshi
Ms. Helen Otow
Mr. and Mrs. Fumio Otsu
Mr. and Mrs. Tamio Otsu
Mr. George J. Otsubo
Mr. Harry R. Otsubo
Ms. Chiyo Otsuji
Mr. and Mrs. Richard Otsuji
Otsuka Farms, Inc.
Mr. Akira Otsuka
Mr. Brad Otsuka
Mr. and Mrs. Charles Otsuka
Mr. Clarence K. Otsuka
Mr. and Mrs. Hideyuki Otsuka
Mr. and Mrs. Kameo Otsuka
Ms. Kimberly Otsuka
Mr. and Mrs. Kiyoshi Otsuka
Ms. Lucinda Otsuka
Dr. Mervyn Otsuka
Mr. and Mrs. Osamu Otsuka
Mr. and Mrs. Ray Otsuka
Mr. Ronald Y. Otsuka
Mr. Warren Otsuka
Mr. Yukio Otsuka
Mr. Henry H. Otsuki
Mr. Hideo Otsuki
Mr. and Mrs. Isamu Otsuki
Mr. Isawo Otsuki
Mr. Julius Otsuki
Mrs. Misao Otsuki
Ms. Noriko Otsuki
Mr. Richard L. Ott
Ms. Adeline R. Otto
Mr. and Mrs. James Otto
Ms. Sachiko Otto
Mr. Albert Y. Ouchi
Ms. Chizue Ouchi
Mr. and Mrs. Edward Ouchi
Mr. and Mrs. George Y. Ouchi
Ms. Janet Ouchi
Mr. Kazuo Ouchi
Ms. Margaret M. Ouchi
Mr. and Mrs. Saburo Ouchi
Mr. Takeshi Ouchi
Ms. Joan Ouchida
Mr. and Mrs. Lester Ouchida
Mr. Takashi Ouchida
Ms. Tereza Ouchida
Mr. and Mrs. Tommy Ouchida
Mr. and Mrs. Raymond Oumi
Mr. Donald Oura
Mr. and Mrs. James S. Oura
Mr. and Mrs. Carnegie Ouye
Mr. Fred M. Ouye
Ms. Grace M. Ouye
Mr. James Ouye
Mr. and Mrs. Minoru Ouye
Mr. and Mrs. Neal N. Ouye
Mr. and Mrs. Wesley Ouye
Mr. and Mrs. Brian Owada
Mr. John Owada
Mr. Clyde T. Owan
Mr. Thomas C. Owan
Mr. Vernon Owara
Mrs. Aiko Owashi
Mr. Norman Owashi
Mr and Mrs. Allen Owyang
Ms. Frieda Oxman
Ms. Caroline S. Oya
Mr. George S. Oya
Mr. and Mrs. Ken Oya
Ms. Merry Oya
Mr. Michael Oya
Mr. Paul T. Oya
Mr. Thomas Oya
Mr. Tsuyoshi Oyabu
Mr. George Oyadomari
Mr. James Oyadomari
Mr. and Mrs. Harry H. Oyafuso
Rev. and Mrs. E. Michio Oyakawa
Ms. Lyla Oyakawa
Ms. Agnes T. Oyama
Mr. and Mrs. Chris Oyama
Mr. David Oyama
Mr. and Mrs. David Y. Oyama

Mr. and Mrs. Harry T. Oyama
Mr. and Mrs. James N. Oyama
Ms. Janet T. Oyama
Mr. and Mrs. Kenneth Oyama
Ms. Louise Oyama
Mr. and Mrs. Michael Oyama
Mr. Nobuaki Oyama
Mr. and Mrs. Paul Oyama
Mr. Rodney T. Oyama
Mr. and Mrs. Roy Oyama
Mr. and Mrs. Seichi Oyama
Mr. Shigenori Oyama
Mr. and Mrs. Tom Oyama
Ms. Violet Oyama
Mr. Seiji Oyamada
Mr. and Mrs. Waichi Oyanagi
Mr. and Mrs. Chisei Oyasato
Mr. Seiji Oyasu
Mr. and Mrs. George I. Oye
Mr. and Mrs. George M. Oye
Mr. Hiromu Oye
Mr. and Mrs. Joe Oye
Mrs. Kazue T. Oye
Mr. Kevin Oye and June Y. Hsiao
Ms. Patricia Oye
Ms. Rose Miyoko Oye
Mr. Thomas Asa Oye
Mr. Toshimi Oye
Mr. and Mrs. John H. Oyenoki
Mr. Norio Ozai
Mr. and Mrs. Charles Ozaki
Dr. Charles T. Ozaki
Mr. and Mrs. George Ozaki
Mr. and Mrs. George T. Ozaki
Mr. and Mrs. Henry Y. Ozaki
Mr. and Mrs. Joe Ozaki
Mr. Joe K. Ozaki
Mr. and Mrs. John Ozaki
Mr. and Mrs. Masato Ozaki
Mrs. Mitzy O. Ozaki
Mr. and Mrs. Reid Ozaki
Mr. Ronald Y. Ozaki
Mr. and Mrs. Roy A. Ozaki
Mr. and Mrs. Sam S. Ozaki
Ms. Teruko Sophy Ozaki
Mr. and Mrs. Tom Ozaki
Mr. Wayne H. Ozaki
Mr. and Mrs. Yoji Ozaki
Ms. Diane Ozasa
Mr. Isamu Ozasa
Ms. Karen Ozasa-Crandall
Ozawa & Associates, Inc.
Dr. Carol L. Ozawa and Dr. Robert Burns
Ms. Connie Ozawa
Mr. Galen Ozawa
Mr. George Y. Ozawa
Mr. and Mrs. Kei Ozawa
Mr. Ken Ozawa
Mr. and Mrs. Spencer Ozawa
Mr. Takao Ozawa
Dr. William Ozawa
Mr. Makoto Ozeki
Ms. Ellen Ozima
Ms. Ruby Ozima
Mr. and Mrs. Shigenobu Ozima
Mr. and Mrs. Charles Pace
Mr. and Mrs. Ord Pace
Ms. Chieko Pacelli
Pacific County Democrats
Ms. Masako Packard
Mrs. Kikuko M. Packness
Ms. Tomoko Page
Mr. George G. Pagonis
Col. Donald E. Painter
Mr. and Mrs. John Painter
Mr. Christopher J. Paisano
Mr. Frances S. Palk
Mr. and Mrs. M. T. Palmer
Mrs. Ryoko Palmer
Mr. and Mrs. Gerald Pang
Ms. Linda J. Panko
Mr. and Mrs. Joseph Papalia
Mr. Don Park
Mr. and Mrs. Woonsun Park
Mrs. Charlene Parker
Parker Services, Inc.
Dr. Linda S. Parlin
Mr. Francis R. Partridge
Mr. and Mrs. Richard Pascual
June and Jerry Pater
Ms. Patricia A. Paton
Mr. Donald E. Patrick
Mrs. Christina M. Patterson
Mrs. Kaye C. Patterson
Mrs. Mary Pattishall and Ms. Brooke Garrett
Dr. and Mrs. Gordon L. Pattison

Mr. Allan Paul
Mr. and Mrs. N. V. Paul
Mr. and Mrs. Gary Paulson
Mr. and Mrs. Richard Paulson
Mrs. Jean Pavela
Mr. Edward Pawlowski
Ms. Lenore Pearlman
Mrs. Junko Pecht
Pediatric Medical Services Co.
Mr. and Mrs. Robert W. Pedlow
Mrs. D. C. Pedrini
Mr. K. C. Peer
Mr. and Mrs. John G. Peetz
Mr. and Mrs. Howard A. Pellett
Mr. Thomas E. Penn
William Penn Foundation
Ms. Kiyoko Penso
Pepper Tree Mobile Home Park
Ms. Stacey Perino
Mr. and Mrs. Bob Perkins
Maj. Norris H. Perkins
Vanessa Perry and Bryan Yagi
Mr. Mark A. Peters
Mr. and Mrs. Carl A. Petersen
Mr. and Mrs. Robert B. Petersen
Mr. and Mrs. Bruce T. Peterson
Dr. Carole Peterson
Mr. John Peterson
Ms. Kazuko Peterson
Ms. Teiko Peterson
Mr. and Mrs. Walfred Peterson
Ms. Monica Petit
Mr. and Mrs. Charles E. Petot
Mr. and Mrs. Allen J. Pfaff
Rev. Jessica J. Phelps
Ms. Amy M. Phillips
Mr. Bertrand D. Phillips
Jill and Keith Phinney
Mr. Jack H. Pickup
Mr. Darold D. Pieper
Ms. Lynne Yamaguchi Pieper and Mr. Paul Pieper
Mr. Pat Pierce
Pine United Methodist Church
Ms. Alice Wang Ping
Cindy Ping, Parvin Norwrasteh and Toni Adsit-Wilson
Mr. and Mrs. Ernest Piron
Pitney Bowes
Ms. Laura Plaskett
Dr. and Mrs. Martin J. Plax
Ms. Thelma T. Poland
Mr. and Mrs. George Politis
Mr. Thomas Pollack and Ms. Jayne Higo
Dr. and Mrs. Curtis Pon
Mr. Leighton R. Pong
Ms. Ione M. Pope
Dr. Nadine Popham
Ms. Suki Ports
Poston Memorial Monument Fund
Ms. Jeanette R. Potter
Mr. Thomas Potter
Mr. Donald G. Potts
Ms. Barbara Azeka Powell
Mr. Arlette A. Pratscher
Mr. Joseph L. Price
Ms. Karen Price
Ms. Alvera Pritchard
Mr. Stephen M. Proctor
Mr. and Mrs. Mark Proper
Mr. and Mrs. Clifford A. Prout
Ms. Carol B. Prussia
Ms. Tonya Pulanco
Ms. Shirley Fukuda-Pullston
Pulmonologists, PC
Mr. and Mrs. Alan L. Pultz
Mrs. Helen K. Purcell
Ms. Kiyo Quashen
Ms. Kayeko Quinlan
Ms. Jennifer Quinn
Mr. and Mrs. T. Anthony Quinn
Mr. Chung W. Quock
Mr. and Mrs. Wing Quon
Jason and Frieda Rabinovitz
Rabison Family
Mr. Senge Rabten and Mrs. Cynthia Tanaka
Mr. and Mrs. Terence Rabun
Mr. and Mrs. Guillermo I. Racines
Mr. and Mrs. David Radmore
Mrs. Irene Rafael
Ms. Haruko I. Rainsberry
Mrs. Fumi Raith
Ms. Amanda Kimiyo Rajabzadeh
Ms. Adel M. Rajscok
Mr. and Mrs. David Ramos
Mr. H. Richard Randall
Ms. Rose L. Randolph
Rank Family Foundation

Ms. Gail Ransom
Panganamamula Rao
Mr. and Mrs. John T. Rapp
Mrs. Jayne Muraki Rasmussen
Mr. and Mrs. Bruce M. Rathbun
Ms. Marie R. Rattenbury
Mr. Eino J. Rauman
Mr. and Mrs. Henry F. Reavey
Ms. Jean T. Reavey
Mrs. Trudy T. Rebollo
Mrs. Dorothy Rector
Mr. and Mrs. Kenneth Redden
Mr. and Mrs. Dean Redemer
Mr. Chuck Reed
Ms. Susan Yaeko Reed
Reed & Roth
Ms. Susan Reeve
Ms. Sheree Reeves
Mr. and Mrs. Dave Reilly
Mr. and Mrs. Stanley Reines
Reliance Insurance Company
Mr. and Mrs. Nobuo Renge
Mr. Helmuth H. Renken
Ms. Bebe Toshiko Reschke
Ms. Sumiko Resetarits
Mr. Thomas Reunion
Ms. Linda A. Revilla
Ms. Katherine M. Reyes
Ms. Chidori O. Reynolds
Ms. Katherine Reynolds
Ms. Linda G. Reynolds
Carol, Cliff and Ryan Rhee
Mr. and Mrs. Robley Rhine
Mr. Chester T. Rice
Ms. Joan J. Rice
Mr. and Mrs. Stanley Richard
Mr. and Mrs. Gene Richards
Mr. and Mrs. William S. Richards
Mr. and Mrs. Donald Richardson
Ms. Laura C. Richter
Mr. and Mrs. William P. Riddle
Ms. Elizabeth Ridout
Ms. Dawn K. Riedy
Ms. Pam Rifenberg
Riken of America, Inc.
Ms. Annette M. Rikimaru
Mr. and Mrs. S. Arthur Rikimaru
Mr. Donald Rindler
Mr. William H. Risteen
Mr. and Mrs. Steven Ritter
Mr. and Mrs. Greg Rivera
Mr. and Mrs. Dennis Roach
Mr. Sean P. Roach
Ms. Michiyo Robbs
Mr. and Mrs. Charles Roberts
Dr. and Mrs. David Roberts
Mr. Frank Roberts
Mr. Glenn Eric Roberts
Mrs. JoAnne Roberts
Mrs. Leslie Roberts
Mr. Michael Roberts
Mr. A. C. Robertson
Ms. Mitsuko Robertson
Mr. James Robinett and
Mrs. Hideko Nishimura Robinett
Ms. Debra Robins
Mr. and Mrs. Clayton Robinson
Mr. and Mrs. Keith L. Robinson
Dr. William A. Robinson
Mr. Eric R. Rock
Ms. Anita Rodgers
Mr. and Mrs. George W. Rodgers
Mr. and Mrs. Stephen Rodgers
Mrs. Beverly Rodley
Mr. and Mrs. Daniel Rodriguez
Mr. and Mrs. Eduardo Rodriguez
Ms. Linda Takahashi Rodriguez
Mr. Carl Roebuck
Mr. and Mrs. Ralph Roen
Ms. Ruth L. Roettinger
Ms. Elizabeth Rogacz
Ms. Lillie Rogers
MSgt. Ret. Michael L. and Shizue Rogers
Ms. Mary Jo Rohlfing
Mr. George Rokuhara
Mr. and Mrs. Stan Rollins
Mr. and Mrs. Jack Rollo
Mr. and Mrs. Jay Romyn
Ms. Masako Roscoe
Mr. and Mrs. Herbert Rose
Dr. Michi Rose
Ms. Miriam Rosen
Ms. Nancy P. Rosenberger
Dr. and Mrs. Saul Rosenfeld
Mr. Harold Rosenn
Paul A. Rosensteil and Jan Masaoka

Mr. Robert F. Rosensteil
Ms. Joyce Rosensteil
Mr. Robert I. Ross
Mr. and Mrs. P. L. Rothchild
Mr. and Mrs. William Rothschild
Mr. G. F. Rothwell
Ms. Junko Rothwell
Ms. Jennifer Rott
Dr. Susan Roux
Ms. Kazuko Y. Rowe
Mr. and Mrs. Russell Royston
Dr. Robert Rubenstein
Dr. G. Theodore Ruckert
Robert Rudasill and Miriam Sohn
Mr. Richard W. Rudden
Rudolf Ranches
Mr. Harmon H. Rulifson
Mr. and Mrs. Morton M. Rumberg
Mr. Shanon S. Russell
Russell Realty Enterprises
Ms. Dorothy Rutkin
Ms. Laura M. Ryan
Mr. and Mrs. Richard Ryer
Alan and Teri Hirasuna Ryo
Dr. C. Robert Ryono
Katsumi Ryono
Mr. and Mrs. Takashi Ryono
Mr. Takeshi Ryono
Mr. and Mrs. Kay Ryugo
Mr. and Mrs. Kikuji Ryugo
Mr. and Mrs. Morris Ryusaki
Mr. and Mrs. Masaru Ryuto
Mr. Michiko M. Ryuto
Mr. Takeshi Ryuto
STT Farms LLC
Mr. and Mrs. Dan Sabo
Mr. and Mrs. Robert W. Sackett
Sacramento Japanese Seventh Day Adventist Church
Sacramento Nikkei Singles Corporation
Mr. and Mrs. Suyeyoshi Sada
Mrs. Janice Sadahiro
Mr. and Mrs. Nozomu Sadakane
Mr. George Sadamoto
Mr. and Mrs. Kiyoshi Sadanaga
Mrs. Irene Sadler
Ms. Helene H. Saeda
Ms. Jan Saga
Mr. and Mrs. Arthur Sagami
Mrs. Edith Sagami
Mr. and Mrs. Douglas Sagara
Mr. Stanley M. Sagara
Mr. and Mrs. Walter Sagara
Ms. Yoshie Sagara
Sagara Trucking, Inc.
Mr. and Mrs. Juro Sagata
Ms. Amy Sagawa
Mr. and Mrs. Makoto P. Sagawa
Mr. and Mrs. Scott Satoru Sagawa
Mr. Sherwin Sagawa
Mr. and Mrs. John Sager
Mr. and Mrs. Donald Saguchi
Mr. and Mrs. Robert Sahara
Mr. and Mrs. William Saiget
Ms. Dorothy S. Saika
Mr. and Mrs. Dick Saiki
Mr. Donald Saiki
Mr. Ernest O. Saiki
Mr. and Mrs. George Saiki
Mr. and Mrs. George R. Saiki
Mr. Glen Saiki
Mrs. Helen Saiki
Mr. Hideyo Beck Saiki
Mr. James Y. Saiki
Mr. Joe Saiki
Kay and Misako Saiki
Mr. Kazutaka Saiki
Ms. Patsy S. Saiki
Mr. Ralph M. Saiki
Dr. Richard R. Saiki
Mr. Ronald S. Saiki
Mr. and Mrs. Teddy Saiki
Mr. and Mrs. Joseph Sailus
Mr. Kiyoto Saisho
Mr. Taro E. Saisho
Mr. and Mrs. Masaru Saita
Mr. and Mrs. Albert Saito
Ms. Ann C. Saito
Mr. Atsushi Saito
Ms. Candice Saito
Mr. Charles Saito
Mr. Colin T. Saito
Ms. Connie Saito
Ms. Connie Y. Saito
Ms. Deborah Saito
Ms. Diane Saito
Mr. Frank Saito

Mr. Fred S. Saito
Mr. Fujio Saito
Mr. and Mrs. Fumio Saito
Mr. George Saito
Mr. and Mrs. George Y. Saito
Mr. Harry Saito
Mr. Henry T. Saito
Mr. and Mrs. Herbert I. Saito
Mr. Hiroshi Saito
Ms. Hisako Saito
Mr. and Mrs. Itsuo Saito
Mr. Jason H. Saito
Ms. Jeri Saito
Mr. and Mrs. Joe Y. Saito
John Saito Family
Mr. Jon Saito
Ms. Kaoru R. Saito
Ms. Katherine Saito
Mr. and Mrs. Kay Saito
Mr. and Mrs. Kazuo Saito
Mr. and Mrs. Larry Y. Saito
Ms. Leslie Saito
Leslie K. Saito
M. Saito
Mr. Makoto Saito
Mrs. Margaret T. Saito
Ms. Margaret T. Saito
Ms. Margie Saito
Mrs. Martha Saito
Mr. and Mrs. Masaharu Saito
Mr. and Mrs. Masaji Saito
Mrs. Masako Saito
Ms. Masako Saito
Ms. Matsuyo Saito
Mr. Matthew Saito
Mr. and Mrs. Michael A. Saito
Ms. Michiko Saito
Mr. and Mrs. Mitsuo Saito
Ms. Miyoko K. Saito
Mr. Naoki Saito
Ms. Nobie Saito
Mr. Norman Saito
Mr. P.A. Saito
Pat Saito
Mr. Paul S. Saito
Mr. and Mrs. R. M. Saito
Mr. Ralph Saito
Mr. and Mrs. Richard Saito
Mr. Richard K. Saito
Mr. and Mrs. Robert Saito
Ms. Ruby Saito
Mr. and Mrs. Shiro Saito
Mrs. Sumiko Saito
Mr. and Mrs. Tak Saito
Mr. Tatsuo Saito
Mr. Tetsuo Saito
Mr. and Mrs. Thomas Saito
Mr. Tim Saito
Mr. Tim T. Saito
Mr. and Mrs. Toichi Saito
Mrs. Ukie Saito
Walter and Elsie Saito
Mr. and Mrs. Yasuo Saito
Mr. Yoshimasa Saito
Ms. Jennifer K. Saito-Fukai
Ms. Yoshiko Saji
Mr. S. T. Saka
Ms. Rachael M. Sakado
Mr. Matsuda Sakae
Mr. and Mrs. Roy K. Sakae
Mr. and Mrs. Spencer M. Sakae
Mr. Wayne Sakae
Mr. and Mrs. Gary Sakagawa
Mr. Guarrin Sakagawa
Mr. Norman T. Sakagawa
Mr. Allan Y. Sakaguchi
Ms. Bettye L. Sakaguchi
Mr. and Mrs. Douglas Sakaguchi
Mrs. Frances Sakaguchi
Mr. George Sakaguchi
Ms. Mae Sakaguchi
Mr. and Mrs. Minoru Sakaguchi
Mr. Noboru Sakaguchi
Mr. and Mrs. Noboru Sakaguchi
Mr. and Mrs. Ross Sakaguchi
Ms. Ruth Y. Sakaguchi
Mrs. Sandra E. Sakaguchi
Mrs. Shirley C. Sakaguchi
Mr. Steve Sakaguchi
Mr. Thomas Sakaguchi
Mr. Tom T. Sakaguchi
Ms. Tomiko Sakaguchi
Mr. and Mrs. Yeichi Sakaguchi
Mrs. Grace Sakahara
Mr. Hiroshi Sakahara
Ms. Karin Sakahara

Mr. Michael Sakahara
Mr. Timothy J. Sakahara
Mr. and Mrs. William Sakahara
Mrs. Alice W. Sakai
Ms. Betty Sakai
Ms. Carol Sakai and Mr. Ted Hochstadt
Mr. Charles Sakai
Mr. and Mrs. Charles D. Sakai
Ms. Cora Sakai
Mr. Craig Sakai
Mr. Dale T. Sakai
Mr. and Mrs. Damon H. Sakai
Mr. David A. Sakai
Mr. David I. Sakai
Mr. and Mrs. David M. Sakai
Mr. and Mrs. David T. Sakai
Ms. Debbie A. Sakai
Mr. Dennis Sakai
Mr. Don Sakai
Ms. Fusako Sakai
Mr. Garrett Sakai
Mr. George Sasaki
Mr. and Mrs. Gordon Sakai
Mr. and Mrs. Henry Sakai
Mr. and Mrs. Henry S. Sakai
Ms. Hide I. Sakai
Dr. and Mrs. Hisaji Q. Sakai
Mr. and Mrs. Howard Sakai
Mr. and Mrs. Jack Sakai
Mr. and Mrs. Jay Sakai
Mr. Jonathan L. Sakai
Ms. Josephine Sakai
Mr. and Mrs. K. Sakai
Mr. Kadushi Sakai
Ms. Karen P. Sakai
Mr. Kazuo S. Sakai
Mr. and Mrs. Kenneth Sakai
Mr. Kiyoto Sakai
Mr. and Mrs. Larry Sakai
Ms. Lili S. Sakai
Ms. Linda J. Sakai
Ms. Linda S. Sakai
Michi Sakai
Mr. Milton Sakai
Mr. and Mrs. Mineo Min Sakai
Mr. Mitsuru Sakai
Mr. Paul Andrew Sakai
Mr. Peter Sakai
Mr. Richard Sakai
Mr. Richard T. Sakai
Mr. Robert Sakai
Mr. and Mrs. Robert Sakai
Mr. and Mrs. Robert K. Sakai
Mrs. Robert S. Sakai
Mr. Robert T. Sakai
Mr. Ronald K. Sakai
Mr. and Mrs. Ronald T. Sakai
Ms. Rose Sakai
Mr. Russell H. Sakai
Mrs. Shigeko Sakai
Shizuye and Kay Sakai
Mr. and Mrs. Sterling K. Sakai
Mr. and Mrs. Steven Sakai
Mr. Takashi Sakai
Mr. Tatsuya Sakai
Mr. Tessi Sakai
Mr. and Mrs. Thomas S. Sakai
Mr. Thomas T. Sakai
Tom and Kathleen Sakai
Mr. and Mrs. Tom Sakai
Mr. Toshiyuki G. Sakai
Mr. and Mrs. Tsugio Sakai
Mr. and Mrs. Walter Sakai
Mr. Wayne Sakai
Mr. William I. Sakai
Mr. and Mrs. William K. Sakai
Mr. William T. Sakai
Mr. and Mrs. Yoshio Sakai
Mr. and Mrs. Yoshitaro Sakai
Ms. Yukiko Sakai
Mr. and Mrs. Brent S. Sakaida
Mr. and Mrs. Seichi Sakaida
Dr. Irene Sakaishi
Mr. and Mrs. Haruo Sakaji
Mr. and Mrs. Donald Sakaki
Ms. Judy Sakaki
Mr. and Mrs. Joseph Sakakibara
Mr. Lloyd Sakakihara
Ms. Margaret Sakakihara
Mr. and Mrs. Philip Sakakihara
Mr. and Mrs. Tom Sakakihara
Mr. and Mrs. Ted Sakakuchi
Mr. and Mrs. Arthur Sakakura
Mr. and Mrs. Arthur Y. Sakakura
Mr. and Mrs. Waterloo Sakakura
Mr. and Mrs. William Sakakura

Mr. and Mrs. Timothy Sakamaki
Dr. Walter Sakamaki
Mr. Allen Sakamoto
Mr. Arthur Sakamoto
Ms. Ayako Sakamoto
Ms. Barbara C. Sakamoto
Ms. Barbara J. Sakamoto
Mr. Brian Sakamoto
Mr. and Mrs. Calvin Sakamoto
Ms. Chiyeko J. Sakamoto
Ms. Chiyoko Sakamoto
Mr. David Sakamoto
Mr. and Mrs. Donald Sakamoto
Ms. Dorothy K. Sakamoto
Ms. Edna K. Sakamoto
Mr. Edward I. Sakamoto
Mr. Edward K. Sakamoto
Ms. Elsie Sakamoto
Mrs. Elton Sakamoto
Ms. Emi Sakamoto
Mr. Ernest Y. Sakamoto
Mr. Frank M. Sakamoto
Mr. and Mrs. Gary Sakamoto
Mr. and Mrs. George Sakamoto
Mr. and Mrs. Gerald Sakamoto
Dr. Glenn D. Sakamoto
Mr. and Mrs. Harry Sakomato
Ms. Helen Sakamoto
Mr. and Mrs. Henry Sakamoto
Mr. and Mrs. Ikumi Sakamoto
Mr. and Mrs. James N. Sakamoto
Mr. James R. Sakamoto
Mr. and Mrs. Jerry Sakamoto
Mr. and Mrs. Jiro Sakamoto
Mr. and Mrs. John Sakamoto
Ms. Julie A. Sakamoto
Mr. Ken S. Sakamoto
Mr. Kiyoshi Sakamoto
Kurt and Laura Sakamoto
Mr. Larry S. Sakamoto
Mr. Lee A. Sakamoto
Mrs. Lisa Sakamoto
Ms. Lorene F. Sakamoto
Ms. Louise Sakamoto
Mr. and Mrs. M. Karry Sakamoto
Ms. Mae F. Sakamoto
Ms. Mary A. Sakamoto
Mrs. Merry T. Sakamoto
Ms. Mildred T. Sakamoto
Mr. and Mrs. Misao Sakamoto
Ms. Mitsuko Sakamoto
Mr. and Mrs. Mitsuru Sakamoto
Ms. Miyoko Sakamoto
Ms. Miyoshi Sakamoto
Ms. Molly Sakamoto
Ms. Mutsumi Sakamoto
Mr. and Mrs. Norman Sakamoto
Mr. Norman L. Sakamoto
Mr. Oscar Sakamoto
Mr. P. Scott Sakamoto
Mr. Randall G. Sakamoto
Mr. Randall L. Sakamoto
Mrs. George N. Sakamoto
Mr. and Ms. Roy Sakamoto
Mr. Ryan T. Sakamoto
Mr. S. Joe Sakamoto
Mr. and Mrs. Sadayoshi Sakamoto
Ms. Sandra K. Sakamoto
Mr. and Mrs. Satoshi Sakamoto
Ms. Sherry A. Sakamoto
Mr. Shinichi Sakamoto
Mr. and Mrs. Shoji Sakamoto
Mr. Steve M. Sakamoto
Mr. Sueo Sakamoto
Mr. Sunao Sakamoto
Mr. and Mrs. Tadao Sakamoto
Mr. and Mrs. Thomas Sakamoto
Ms. Tillie A. Sakamoto
Mr. and Mrs. Tom Sakamoto
Mr. Torao Sakamoto
Mr. Tsuruo Sakamoto
Mr. Val Sakamoto
Mr. Wilfred Sakamoto
Mr. William Sakamoto
Ms. Yachiyo Sakamoto
Mr. and Mrs. Yoshiaki Sakamoto
Mr. and Mrs. Yoshimi Sakamoto
Mr. and Mrs. Sidney S. Sakane
Mr. Theodore Sakano
Mr. Takao Sakase
Mr. and Mrs. Dean Sakasegawa
Mr. and Mrs. Harry K. Sakasegawa
Mr. Phillip I. Sakashita
Ms. Sheila Sakashita
Mr. B. Sakata
Ms. Chizuyo Sakata

Mr. and Mrs. Edward Sakata
Mr. Frank Sakata
Mr. and Mrs. Frank S. Sakata
Mr. and Mrs. Gary Sakata
Mr. George Sakata
Mr. Hiroshi Sakata
Mr. Ken Sakata
Mr. and Mrs. Ken Sakata
Mr. Kiichi Sakata
Ms. Mae Mitsuye Sakata
Ms. Margaret H. Sakata
Dr. and Mrs. Marlin K. Sakata
Mr. Matthew Sakata
Mr. Merritt Sakata
Mr. Michael D. Sakata
Mr. and Mrs. Norman Sakata
Mr. Robert M. Sakata
Miss Rose A. Sakata
Mr. Spencer Sakata
Mr. Thomas Sakata
Mr. Thomas S. Sakata
Mr. and Mrs. Tom M. Sakata
Mrs. Fumiko Sakato
Mr. John T. Sakato
Ms. Sumiye Sakato
Ms. Marlene Sakaue
Ms. Naoko Sakaue
Mr. Robert S. Sakaue
Mr. and Mrs. Yoshio Sakaue
Ms. Fumi Sakauye
Dr. and Mrs. Kenneth Sakauye
Minoru and Toshihiko Sakauye
Mr. and Mrs. Steve Sakauye
Mrs. Ruby Sakawye
Mr. and Mrs. William Sakayama
Ms. Heidi Hideko Sakazaki
Ms. Miyako Sakazaki
Mr. and Mrs. Shoya Sakazaki
Ms. Tomiko Sakazume
Mrs. Sueko Saki
Mr. Thomas N. Sakihama
Ms. Cindy Y. Sakihara
Mr. and Mrs. Raymond Sakihara
Akira and Jane Sakima
Mr. Edward Sakima
Dr. Richard Sakimoto
Mr. and Mrs. Frank A. Sakioka
Ms. Mary Sakioka
Masaru and Melinda Sakioka
Mr. Susumu Sakiyama
Mr. Edward Sako
Mr. and Mrs. Fumio Sako
Mr. Harvey N. Sako
Mr. and Mrs. Hiroshi Sako
Ms. Mie Sako
Mr. and Mrs. Rekiso Sako
Ms. Tsuyoko Sako
Mr. and Mrs. Duane Sakoda
Mr. George T. Sakoda
Mr. Isamu Sam Sakoda
Mr. and Mrs. Jerry H. Sakoda
Mr. Shigeru Sakoda
Mr. and Mrs. Tom Sakoda
Mr. Michi Sakohira
Mr. and Mrs. Kazuo Sakomoto
Mr. Kunio Sakomoto
Mr. Gerald K. Sakuda
Ms. Nancy S. Sakuda
Mr. Rick Sakuda
Mr. Tetsuo Sakuda
Mr. Walter T. Sakuda
Ms. Chizuko Sakuma
Mr. and Mrs. Edward Sakuma
Ms. Fumi Sakuma
Ms. Grace H. Sakuma
Ms. Hana Sakuma
Dr. Karen Sakuma
Mr. and Mrs. Katsuji Sakuma
Mr. Masanobu Sakuma
Mr. and Mrs. Nolan Sakuma
Ms. Patsy N. Sakuma
Mr. Paul S. Sakuma
Mr. Roy Sakuma
Mr. and Mrs. Steven M. Sakuma
Mr. and Mrs. Tad T. Sakuma
Tadashi Sakuma and Tomoko Kashiwagi
Mr. and Mrs. Teruo Sakuma
Mr. Toshio Sakuma
Mr. Yoshizaku Sakuma
Mrs. Ayako Sakumoto
Mr. and Mrs. Kenichi Sakumoto
Ms. Catherine K. Sakura
Dr. Chester Y. Sakura
Sakura Gifts
Sakura Kai
Sakura Woodfield, Inc.

Mr. Hideaki Sakuraba
Hirao Sakurada and Alyce Hong
Ms. Phyllis F. Sakurada
Mr. Bill Sakurai
Mr. Darren M. Sakurai
Mr. Giichi Sakurai
Dr. and Mrs. Hideki Sakurai
Mr. Joe Sakurai
Mr. Mark D. Sakurai
Mr. Richard Sakurai
Mr. and Mrs. Robert Y. Sakurai
Ms. Shizu Sakurai
Mr. Shuzo Sakurai
Mr. Hideo Sakurauchi
Mr. and Mrs. Fred Salador
Ms. Silvia Astorga Salcido
Ms. Gladys Sallas
Dr. and Mrs. Arthur Saltz
Anne and John Salwach
Mr. and Mrs. John Salzberg
LTC. Henry J. Samborski
Mr. Akio Sameshima
Ms. Chihiro Sameshima
Mr. Glenn Sameshima
Mr. and Mrs. K. Jack Sameshima
Mr. Ko Sameshima
Mr. Steven T. Sameshima
Mr. and Mrs. Robert Sammons
San Jose Contributors
San Jose Nikkei Singles
Mr. George Sanada
Mr. and Mrs. Fred Sanbongi
Ms. Marjorie Sanbongi
Mr. Yoshiro Sanbonmatsu
Ms. Shirlee Sanda
Mr. Vasant T. Sande
Mr. Alan J. Sanders
Mr. and Mrs. Edward H. Sanders
Mr. Maurice S. Sanders
Ms. Pat Sanders
Mr. Edmund M. Sanehira
Mrs. Lily Sanehira
Ms. Satomi Saneto
Mr. and Mrs. Satoshi Saneto
Mr. and Mrs. Tsukasa Saneto
Mrs. Anita Mitsuko Sankey
Mr. and Mrs. Bruce W. Sano
Ms. Doris Sano
Ms. Georgia Sano
Mr. and Mrs. Ishizo Sano
Mrs. Kikue L. Sano
Ms. Mari Sano
Mrs. Patti Sano
Mr. Robert S. Sano
Mr. Shigeru Sano
Mr. Stephen M. Sano
Mr. and Mrs. Toshio Sano
Mr. and Mrs. Tsugio Sano
Sansei Basketball Association
Ms. Chiyo Sansone
Mr. and Mrs. Anthony Santarelli
Ms. S. Grace Santistevan
Mr. and Mrs. Raiji Santo
Mr. Daniel Santos
Ms. Dorothy T. Santos
Mr. Hisashi Sanui
Mr. and Mrs. Aaron Sanwo
Mr. Ichika Sanwo
Mr. and Mrs. Norman Sapiro
Ms. Lana S. Sappa
Ms. Takako Sarai
Mr. Kenneth M. Sargent
Mr. Clifford Saruwatari
Mr. Jonn Saruwatari
Mr. and Mrs. Kaz Saruwatari
Mr. and Mrs. Takaaki Saruwatari
Mr. and Mrs. Thomas Saruwatari
Mr. and Mr. Saruwatari
Dr. and Mrs. Paul Sasa
Mr. and Mrs. George F. Sasabuchi
Ms. Lucy Sasada
Mr. and Mrs. Susie Sasagawa
Dr. Arthur A. Sasahara
Mr. Ed Sasahara
Mr. James Sasahara
Ms. Yoshiko Sasahara
Dr. and Mrs. Taro Sasai
Ms. Masu Sasajima
Mr. Hideki Sasakawa
Mr. and Mrs. Akira Sasaki
Mr. Alan G.C. Sasaki
Mr. Alvin T. Sasaki
Ms. Ann K. Sasaki
Mr. and Mrs. Art Sasaki
Mr. and Mrs. Barton H. Sasaki
Mr. Ben Sasaki

Mr. and Mrs. Bernard Y. Sasaki
Mr. Byron Sasaki
Mr. and Mrs. Carl Sasaki
Mr. and Mrs. Charles Sasaki
Ms. Chiyo Sasaki
Mr. Clifford M. Sasaki
Mr. Conrad Sasaki
Mr. and Mrs. Dick Sasaki
Mr. Don R. Sasaki
Mr. Donald J. Sasaki
Mr. Douglas S. Sasaki
Mr. and Mrs. Ed Sasaki
Mr. Edwin H. Sasaki
Mr. Eli Sasaki
Mr. Eric Sasaki
Mr. Ernest Sasaki
Mr. Ernest J. Sasaki
Mr. Ewao Sasaki
Ms. Frances Sasaki
Mr. Fred Sasaki
Mr. and Mrs. Fred Y. Sasaki
Mrs. Fujie V. Sasaki
Mr. and Mrs. George Sasaki
Mr. George A. Sasaki
Dr. and Mrs. Go Sasaki
Greg, Randall, Jason and Kimberly Sasaki
Mr. Harold Sasaki
Mr. and Mrs. Herbert M. Sasaki
Mr. Hide Sasaki
Mrs. Hideko Sasaki
Mr. and Mrs. Hideo Sasaki
Ms. Hisako Sasaki
Ms. Irene A. Sasaki
Mr. Irvin K. Sasaki
Mr. Jim Sasaki
Mr. Joe Sasaki
Mr. John Sasaki
Mr. and Mrs. John Sasaki
Ms. Joyce Sasaki
Ms. Joyce F. Sasaki
Ms. Julie L. Sasaki
Ms. June J. Sasaki
Mr. and Mrs. Kay Sasaki
Mr. and Mrs. Kazuto Sasaki
Mr. Ken Sasaki
Mr. and Mrs. Kiyoshi Sasaki
Mr. and Mrs. Leo Sasaki
Ms. Lili Sasaki
Mr. and Mrs. Louis Sasaki
Makoto and Haru Sasaki
Ms. Mary Sasaki
Mr. Masakazu Sasaki
Ms. May S. Sasaki
Mrs. Mazie Sasaki
Mrs. Midori Sasaki
Mr. and Mrs. Minoru Sasaki
Mr. Nobuichi Sasaki
Ms. Pauline E. Sasaki
Ms. Rakumi Sasaki
Mr. and Mrs. Randy Sasaki
Mr. and Mrs. Raymond Sasaki
Mr. Raymond G. Sasaki
Mr. Richard M. Sasaki
Mr. and Mrs. Robert Sasaki
Mr. and Mrs. Robert K. Sasaki
Mr. and Mrs. Robert M. Sasaki
Mr. and Mrs. Robert S. Sasaki
Mr. Ron Sasaki
Mr. and Mrs. Roy Sasaki
Mr. Sadayoshi Sasaki
Mr. and Mrs. Satori Sasaki
Ms. Sharon K. Sasaki
Mr. and Mrs. Shigeru Sasaki
Dr. Shirow Sasaki
Mr. Shoken Sasaki
Mr. Sus Sasaki
Mr. and Mrs. Tad Sasaki
Mr. and Mrs. Takayuki Chilly Sasaki
Mr. and Mrs. Teruo Sasaki
Phyllis, Cynthia and Thomas Sasaki
Mr. Thomas H. Sasaki
Mr. and Mrs. Thomas T. Sasaki
Mr. and Mrs. Tomiko Sasaki
Ms. Toshiko Sasaki
Mr. and Mrs. Walter Sasaki
Mr. and Mrs. Yasuo Sasaki
Mrs. Pamela Sasaki-Powers
Mr. Albert Y. Sasamoto
Mr. Hiroaki Sasamoto
Mr. Ned Sasamoto
Mr. and Mrs. Tad Sasamoto
Mrs. Suzanne Sasano
Mr. Miyohiro Sasao
Ms. T. Alice Sasao
Mrs. Jeanne R. Sasaran
Mr. and Mrs. Toshihiro Sasaya

Mr. Hugo V. Sase
Mr. Mark Sashihara
Mr. and Mrs. Thomas Sashihara
Dr. Witold Saski
Mrs. Ellen M. Sass
Mr. and Mrs. Frank Sata
Mr. and Mrs. Gregory P. Sata
Dr. William and Ms. Shizuka Sata
Mr. and Mrs. Yasuo Sata
Mr. and Mrs. Al Satake
Mr. and Mrs. Edwin Satake
Vikram Sathineni
Mr. A. Stanley Sato
Mr. and Mrs. Akira Sato
Mr. Alan H. Sato
Ms. Amy Y. Sato
Mr. Andrew Sato
Mr. and Mrs. Atsu Sato
Mr. and Mrs. Atuo Sato
Mr. and Mrs. C. K. Sato
Mr. Charles T. Sato
Mr. Clarence Sato
Mr. Conrad Sato
Mr. and Mrs. Denichi Sato
Mr. and Mrs. Douglas Sato
Mr. Earl Sato
Mr. and Mrs. Eddie Sato
Mr. Edward H. Sato
Mr. Edwin H. Sato
Mr. Edwin M. Sato
Mr. and Mrs. Fred A. Sato
Mr. and Mrs. Fred T. Sato
Ms. Fumiko Sato
Mr. George Sato
Mr. and Mrs. George Sato
Mr. George F. Sato
Mr. and Mrs. George K. Sato
Mrs. Gladys T. Sato
Mr. Glenn Sato
Mr. Gregg Sato
Mr. and Mrs. Hajime Sato
Ms. Hamayo Sato
Mr. and Mrs. Harry H. Sato
Mr. Harry I. Sato
Mr. Haruo Sato
Mr. Henry Sato
Mr. and Mrs. Henry Sato
Mr. and Mrs. Hideo Sato
Mr. and Mrs. Irving Sato
Mr. James Sato
Mr. and Mrs. James T. Sato
Mr. Jay Sato
Mrs. Jean Sato
Mr. Jeffrey Sato
Mr. Jerry S. Sato
Mr. and Mrs. Joe Sato
Mr. and Mrs. Joseph Sato
Mr. and Mrs. Junji Sato
Mr. Katsumi Sato
Mr. Kazuo Sato
Mr. Keiichi Sato
Mr. Kenneth Sato
Mr. and Mrs. Kenneth H. Sato
Mr. Kenzo Sato
Ms. Kimi Sato
Mrs. Kimi M. Sato
Miss Kisoko D. Sato
Mr. Kiyomi O. Sato
Mr. Louie S. Sato
Ms. Lury Sato
Mr. Lyle H. Sato
Mr. Mamoru Sato
Ms. Margaret Sato
Mr. and Mrs. Masao Sato
Mr. Masuko Sato
Mr. Melvin Sato
Mr. Mitchell H. Sato
Mrs. Miyo Sato
Mr. Nobuo Sato
Mr. Norman Sato
Mr. and Mrs. Norman K. Sato
Mr. and Mrs. Osao Sato
Mr. Ralph I. Sato
Mr. and Mrs. Randolph Sato
Mr. and Mrs. Ray Sato
Mr. Robert Sato
Mrs. Rose Sato
Mrs. Rosemary S. Sato
Mr. and Mrs. Roy Sato
Mr. and Mrs. Ryuichi Sato
Ms. Sanaye Sato
Ms. Sandra L. Sato
Mrs. Sharlene S. Sato
Ms. Sharon R. Sato
Mr. and Mrs. Shuji Sato
Mr. and Mrs. Skip Sato

Mr. Steve Sato
Mr. Steve S. Sato
Mr. and Mrs. Susumu Sato
Dr. and Mrs. Tada Sato
Mr. and Mrs. Tadashi Sato
Mr. and Mrs. Takami Sato
Mr. Takayuki Sato
Ms. Teruko Sato
Mr. Tetsuo Sato
Mr. Todd Sato
Mr. and Mrs. Tommy M. Sato
Mr. Toshiko Sato
Mr. and Mrs. Victor Sato
Mr. Virginia Sato
Ms. Vivienne Y. Sato
Mr. and Mrs. William Sato
Mr. William Sato
Mr. William H. Sato
Mr. William K. Sato
Ms. Yaeko Sato
Ms. Yasuhiko Sato
Mr. and Mrs. Yasuo Sato
Mr. Yasutomo Sato
Ms. Yoko Sato
Mrs. Yukiko Sato
Ms. Yumi Sato
Ms. Kiyo Sato-Viacrucis
Mr. David Satoda
Ms. Nancy Satoda
Mr. and Mrs. Yozo Satoda
Ms. Mitsuhiko Satoh
Satoru Satoh
Mr. and Mrs. Yoshiharu Satoh
Mr. and Mrs. Bruce W. Satow
Mr. and Mrs. Fumio P. Satow
Ms. Hannah Satow
Mr. and Mrs. Hideo Satow
Mrs. Midori Satow
Mr. Susumu Satow
Ms. Toshiko Satow
Mr. Ken Satoyoshi
Mr. and Mrs. Preston H. Satsuma
Ms. Kim Saucier
Dr. Allan F. Saunders
Ms. Marion Grace Saunders
Ms. Jean C. Sawa
Ms. Patsy M. Sawa
Mr. and Mrs. Paul Sawabe
Ms. Ruth M. Sawabe
Mr. and Mrs. Akio Sawada
Mr. and Mrs. Harry H. Sawada
Mrs. Joy H. Sawada
Mr. Makoto Sawada
Ms. Sachiko Sawada
Ms. Suzanne Sawada and Mr. Leonard Joy
Ms. Georgiana Sawahata
Mr. Bruce Y. Sawai
Mr. and Mrs. Masayoshi Sawai
Mr. and Mrs. Steve Sawai
Mr. Stanley Sawamoto
Mr. and Mrs. Lucky Sawamura
Mr. Steven Sawamura
Mr. and Mrs. Yuji Sawamura
Ms. Mary Sawasaki
Mr. Bill and Dr. Lisa Sax
Mr. and Mrs. David Sayama
Mr. Howard Sayegusa
Mr. Joshua Sayegusa
Mr. and Mrs. Yukiharu Sazaki
Ms. Emi M. Scala
Ms. Jetta L. Scalzitti
Ms. Jean Naomi Scandlyn
Ms. Vincenza Scarpaci
Ms. Marrie Y. Schaefer
Mr. and Mrs. Elizabeth N. Schaffer
Mr. and Mrs. John M. Schaffer
Mr. Mutsuko S. Schaffer
Dr. and Mrs. Robert Scharf
Josephine S. Schifano
Mrs. Dorothy A. Schiff
Ms. Marilyn and Mr. Don Schlief
Ms. Susan Schmid
Ms. Mary Jo Schmit
Ms. Ida Nakashima Schneck
Mrs. Karen Hiyama Schodowski
Ms. Joanne Scholin
Ms. Alice Ikuta Scholz
Mr. and Mrs. Jeff Schriber
Ms. Allison Schroeder
Ms. Margaret K. Schultz
Mr. Robert A. Schutt
Mr. David Schwartz
Mr. and Mrs. Jack M. Schwartz
Mr. and Mrs. Robert C. Schwartz
Mr. Seymour Schwartzberg
Ms. Marjorie Schweiger

Ms. Feikje B. Scott
Ms. Ramona Scott
Mr. and Mrs. Stephen W. Scott
Mr. and Mrs. Thomas H. Scott
Ms. Leatrice Scow
Seabrook Buddhist Temple
Seabrook Educational and Cultural Center
Seabrook Minyo Dancers
Mr. Michael Seagal
Meryl Shader and Paul Seave
Mr. LaRoy E. Seaver
Ms. Rie H. Seaver
Mr. and Mrs. Randal Seech
Ms. Ruby Seehaas
Dr. and Mrs. Scott Segars
Mr. and Mrs. David Segawa
Mrs. Hiroko Segawa
Mr. and Mrs. Mike Segawa
Mr. Randall Segawa
Mr. Stanley Segawa
Mr. David L. Segel
Mr. Arthur K. Segimoto
Mr. Masaru Segimoto
Ms. Carol Shizue Seigel
Ms. Sai K. Seigel
Ms. Sathya D. Seigel
Ms. Shanti Gabriel Seigel
Mr. and Mrs. Hideo R. Seiji
Mr. William Seiji
Ms. Elaine Seike
Ms. Iris Seiki
Mr. and Mrs. Sim S. Seiki
Seinan Golf Club
Dr. James K. Seino
Ms. Midori Seino
Mr. Robert Seino
Mr. Craig Seki
Ms. Fukiko Seki
Mr. and Mrs. Kunihiro Seki
Mr. Steven Seki
Mr. Toshio Seki
Mr. William Seki
Mrs. Yaeko Seki
Mr. and Mrs. Satoshi Sekigahama
Ms. Amy E. Sekiguchi
Mr. and Mrs. George Sekiguchi
Mr. Joh Sekiguchi
Ms. Robin Sekiguchi
Mr. and Mrs. Tadashi Sekiguchi
Ms. Tochiko Sekiguchi
Mr. and Mrs. H. Sekijima
Mr. and Mrs. Sam Sekikawa
Mr. and Mrs. Ted Sekikawa
Ms. Masako Sekimoto
Mr. and Mrs. Rodney Sekimoto
Mr. Carl T. Sekimura
Mr. and Mrs. Gerald Sekimura
Mr. and Mrs. Tom Sekimura
Ms. Anne Sekino
Ms. Lillian S. Sekino
Mr. and Mrs. Ben Sekishiro
Mr. and Mrs. John Sekishiro
Mr. and Mrs. Kenji Sekishiro
Mr. and Mrs. Etsuro Sekiya
Mr. and Mrs. Takeki Sekiya
Mr. Walter Sekiya
Mr. and Mrs. John Sekiyama
Mr. Craig Y. Seko
Ms. Joan T. Seko
Ms. Joyce Seko
Mr. and Mrs. Robert Seko
Mr. and Mrs. Roy T. Seko
Mr. and Mrs. Roy Y. Seko
Mr. Ryan Seko
Mr. and Mrs. Albert L. Seligmann
Ms. Brenda Sell
Ms. Mabelle M. Selland
Mr. Anthony F. Sellitto
Mr. and Mrs. Albert Sells
Selma Japanese Mission Church
Ms. Yoshiko A. Seltzer
Dorothy Seman and Linda Peterson
Ms. Flora M. Senda
Mr. and Mrs. Kazuo Senda
Mr. Randy J. Senescall
Mr. and Mrs. Masashi Seno
Mr. Shugo Seno
Ms. Miyo M. Senzaki
Mr. and Mrs. Akio Seo
Mr. and Mrs. Robert A. Seo
Mr. Setsuko Seo
Mr. and Mrs. Tadao Seo
Mr. Takayuki Seo
Mr. and Mrs. George Sera
Mr. and Mrs. Kimihiro Sera
Mr. and Mrs. Shunso Sera

Mr. Tako Y. Sera
Mr. and Mrs. Walter Serata
Mr. and Mrs. Paul Serber
Mr. and Mrs. George T. Seriguchi
Mr. David Y. Serikawa
Mr. and Mrs. Michael Serikaku
Mr. and Mrs. Seisuke Serikaku
Mr. Stanley S. Serikaku
Mr. Fumio Serikawa
Mr. and Mrs. Michael Serisawa
Mr. and Mrs. Akio Serizawa
Mr. and Mrs. Michael D. Serlin
Ms. Ruth Serrano
Mr. and Mrs. Aram Serverian
Mr. and Mrs. Melvin Seshiki
Mr. and Mrs. Brad Seto
Mr. Frank Seto
Mr. and Mrs. George T. Seto
Ms. H. Deki Seto
Mr. Masao Seto
Mr. Paul S. Seto
Mr. Steven Seto
Mr. and Mrs. Robert Setoguchi
Mr. and Mrs. Yoshio Setoguchi
Mr. and Mrs. Steven C. Setsuda
Ms. Grace Settsu
Mr. Patrick S. Settsu
Mr. and Mrs. James A. Sewrey
Ms. Grace M. Sgambati
Ms. Sue Izumi Shackelford
Drs. Joel A. and Ann R. Shamaskin
Shapiro Family
Mr. and Mrs. Larry J. Shapiro
Ms. Frances Sharma
Mr. Richard H. Shay
Mr. and Mrs. Donald Sheehan
Ms. Sarah Shelly
Mr. William C. Sherman
Dr. and Mrs. William K. Sherwin
Mr. and Mrs. Natalie Shew
Mr. and Mrs. David Shiba
Mr. Frank Y. Shiba
Ms. Gayle Shiba
Mr. and Mrs. Harry N. Shiba
Ms. Hisa Shiba
Ms. Kathie Shiba
Mr. and Mrs. Katsuumi Shiba
Ms. Kay Shiba
Mr. and Mrs. Roy R. Shiba
Dr. and Mrs. Seiji Shiba
Mr. and Mrs. Sus Shiba
William and Marie Shiba
Mr. and Mrs. Haratsuna Shibao
Mr. and Mrs. Henry Shibao
Mr. and Mrs. Michael Shibao
Mr. Patrick Shibao
Ms. Rose Y. Shibao
Mr. Shuya Shibasaki
Mr. Dean Shibata
Ms. Dora C. Shibata
Ms. Eileen A. Shibata
Rev. and Mrs. George E. Shibata
Mr. and Mrs. Henry Shibata
Mr. and Mrs. Jason Shibata
Mr. and Mrs. Kaoru Shibata
Mr. and Mrs. Kay Shibata
Mr. Lloyd Shibata
Mr. Minoru Shibata
Mr. and Mrs. Myrtle Shibata
Ms. Phyllis A. Shibata
Ms. Reiko Shibata
Mr. and Mrs. Roy Shibata
Mr. and Mrs. Tad Shibata
Mr. and Mrs. Victor Shibata
Mr. Walter Shibata Family
Ms. Yoshiko Shibata
Ms. Yoshio Shibata
Ms. Yukiko Shibata
Ms. Yuriko M. Shibata
Ms. Yutaka T. Shibata
Mr. and Mrs. Takeshi Shibayama
Mr. Todd Shibayama
Mr. Yoshiaki Shibusawa
Dr. Kinichi Shibutani
Ms. Alice R. Shibuya
Mr. Edward Shibuya
Ms. Fusako Shibuya
Mr. and Mrs. Henry Shibuya
Mr. Mark Shibuya
Mr. Patrick Shibuya
Mr. and Mrs. Yoshio Shibuya
Mr. and Mrs. Hitoshi Shichi
Mr. Kevin Shida
Mr. and Mrs. Koji Shida
Ms. Miho M. Shida
Ms. Rosemary Shieh

Mr. and Mrs. James W. Shields
Mrs. Fern Shigaki
Mr. and Mrs. Harry Shigaki
Mr. James Shigaki
Ms. Gwynn Shigaya
Mr. and Mrs. Harry Shigaya
Mr. and Mrs. Ken K. Shigaya
Mr. and Mrs. Steven Shigaya
Ms. Susan K. Shigaya
Mr. Kiyoshi Shigefuji
Mr. and Mrs. Ken Shigehara
Mr. Herbert Y. Shigekane
Mrs. Joanne Shigekane
Mr. and Mrs. Fred Shigekawa
Mr. and Mrs. John Shigekawa
Ms. Jane H. Shigemasa
Mr. and Mrs. Thomas Shigemasa
Mr. Conrad Shigematsu
Mr. Dayne Shigematsu
Mr. Fred Shigematsu
Mr. and Mrs. George Shigematsu
Mr. and Mrs. Ray Shigematsu
Dr. Ronald Shigematsu
Ms. Yumiko Shigematsu
Mr. Allan H. Shigemitsu
Mr. and Mrs. Thomas M. Shigemitsu
Mr. Alan K. Shigemoto
Mr. and Mrs. Iwao Shigemoto
Mr. Barton Y. Shigemura
Ms. Jessica Shigemura
Mr. and Mrs. Jitsuo Shigemura
Mr. Kaname Shigemura
Mrs. Ann M. Shigemura-Hildebrand
Mr. and Mrs. Raymond Shigenaga
Mr. and Mrs. Winston T. Shigenaga
Mr. and Mrs. Bob Shigenaka
Mr. James Shigenaka
Ms. Grace Shigeno
Mr. and Mrs. Ted Shigeno
Ms. Dorothy F. Shigeoka
Ms. Sho Shigeoka and Mr. Darrell K. Hosaka
Mr. and Mrs. Daniel Shigeta
Mr. Earl T. Shigeta
Mr. James Shigeta
Mr. Stanley Shigeta
Mr. Tsutomu Shigeta
Mr. Jack H. Shigetomi
Mr. Kenji K. Shigetomi
Mr. Reiko Shigetomi
Ms. Doris M. Shigihara
Mr. Don T. Shigio
Mr. Frank M. Shigio
Mr. and Mrs. Thomas Shigio
Mr. Tetsuo Shigyo
Mr. Ernest Cesar Shih
Mr. Arthur I. Shiigi
Mr. and Mrs. Lawrence Shiigi
Mr. Hideo Shiine
Mrs. Michiko Shiino
Mrs. Muroko Shijo
Shika, Inc.
Mr. and Mrs. James Y. Shikami
Mr. and Mrs. Joe Shikami
Mr. and Mrs. Bert Shikasho
Mr. Satoru Shikasho
Mr. and Mrs. Gregory Shikata
Ms. Chiyeko Shikuma
Mr. Frank Shikuma
Ms. Hiroko Shikuma
Ms. Jeri Shikuma
Mr. Lawrence Shikuma
Mr. Andrew Shima
Mr. and Mrs. Bill Shima
Mr. and Mrs. Clarence Shima
Mr. and Mrs. George Shima
Mr. Miles Shima
Ms. Sueko Shima
Mrs. Helen F. Shima-Imamura
Mr. Daniel M. Shimabuku
Mr. and Mrs. Ray Y. Shimabuku
Ms. Annie S. Shimabukuro
Ms. Betty Shimabukuro
Ms. Betty Y. Shimabukuro
Mr. and Mrs. Edwin K. Shimabukuro
Mr. and Mrs. Edwin N. Shimabukuro
Mr. and Mrs. Gary Shimabukuro
Mrs. Gladys Shimabukuro
Mr. and Mrs. Glenn M. Shimabukuro
Mr. and Mrs. Haruko Shimabukuro
Ms. Hisako Shimabukuro
Mrs. Joyce Shimabukuro
Mr. Kaoru Shimabukuro
Mr. Kenny Shimabukuro
Mr. and Mrs. Kikuji Shimabukuro
Ms. Kiyoko Shimabukuro
Mr. Larry Shimabukuro

Mr. Mitchell Shimabukuro
Mr. and Mrs. Paul Shimabukuro
Mr. and Mrs. Reynold Y. Shimabukuro
Ms. Sally S. Shimabukuro
Mr. Sam Shimabukuro
Mr. and Mrs. Tarusuke Shimabukuro
Mr. Yukichi Shimabukuro
Mr. Allen Shimada
Mrs. Amy E. Shimada
Ms. Ann Shimada
Mr. Ben Shimada
Mr. and Mrs. Cary Shimada
Mr. and Mrs. Dick Shimada
Ms. Ellen Shimada
Ms. Fumiko Shimada
Mr. Glenn A. Shimada
Mrs. Ikuko Shimada
Ms. Mikiko Shimada
Mr. and Mrs. Mitsuyoshi Shimada
Ms. Nadyne Shimada
Mr. Paul Shimada
Mr. Paul H. Shimada
Mr. Roger Shimada
Mr. and Mrs. Shige Shimada
Ms. Toshie Shimada
Mr. and Ms. David Shimahara
Mr. and Mrs. Tatsuo Shimahara
Gene, Nobuko and Mark Shimaji
Mr. Chris T. Shimamoto
Mr. Ed Shimamoto
Ms. Faith Y. Shimamoto
Mr. and Mrs. Gene Shimamoto
Mr. George Shimamoto
Mrs. Harry Shimamoto
Mr. and Mrs. Mark Shimamoto
Mr. and Mrs. Rodney A. Shimamoto
Mr. and Mrs. Roy S. Shimamoto
Ms. Dayle Shimamura
Mr. Takeshi Shimana
Mr. and Mrs. Sam Shimane
Mr. and Mrs. Bruce Shimano
Mr. Ida I. Shimanouchi
Mr. Goichi Shimanuki
Mr. and Mrs. Thomas Shimaoka
Mr. and Mrs. Fred F. Shimasaki
Mr. Gary Shimasaki
Mr. Jack Shimasaki
Mr. and Mrs. Kyser Shimasaki
Mr. Lynn Shimasaki
Mr. and Mrs. Masaharu Shimasaki
Mr. and Mrs. Robert Shimasaki
Mr. and Mrs. Sam Shimasaki
Mr. and Mrs. William Shimasaki
Mr. and Mrs. John Shimashita
Ms. Alice Shimatsu
Mr. and Mrs. Mas Shimatsu
Mr. and Mrs. Rokuro Shimatsu
Ms. Bertha Y. Shimazu
Mr. and Mrs. Fred Shimazu
Mr. and Mrs. Glen Shimazu
Mr. Hal S. Shimazu
Mr. Harry S. Shimazu
Mr. Harumi Shimazu
Mr. Hiroshi Shimazu
Mr. John Shimazu
Mr. and Mrs. Katsuki Shimazu
Mr. Kazuo S. Shimazu
Ms. Kiyoko Shimazu
Mr. Nobuo Shimazu
Mr. and Mrs. Shigeru H. Shimazu
Mr. Wesley D. Shimazu
Mr. Robert T. Shimida
Mr. and Mrs. Allen B. Shimizu
Mr. and Mrs. Asayuki A. Shimizu
Mr. and Mrs. Ben Shimizu
Ms. Carolyn K. Shimizu
Mrs. Chieko Shimizu
Mr. and Mrs. Craig Shimizu
Mrs. Emi H. Shimizu
Ms. Emiko H. Shimizu
Mr. and Mrs. Frank Shimizu
Mr. and Mrs. Franklin Shimizu
Mr. and Mrs. Gary K. Shimizu
Mr. and Mrs. George Shimizu
Dr. and Mrs. George K. Shimizu
Dr. and Mrs. Grant Shimizu
Mr. Harry Shimizu
Mr. Henry Shimizu
Mr. and Mrs. Hideo Shimizu
Mr. and Mrs. Hiroshi Shimizu
Mr. and Mrs. James Shimizu
Mr. and Mrs. James K. Shimizu
Ms. Joann K. Shimizu
Mr. and Mrs. John H. Shimizu
Ms. Karen Shimizu
Mr. and Mrs. Kazuto Shimizu

Mr. and Mrs. Keichi Shimizu
Mr. Keiji Shimizu
Ms. Kimi Shimizu
Ms. Kiyomi Shimizu
Mr. Ko Shimizu
Ms. Kristina M. Shimizu
Mr. Lawrence D. Shimizu
Mr. Mark Y. Shimizu
Mr. and Mrs. Martin Shimizu
Ms. Mary J. Shimizu
Mr. Mas Shimizu
Ms. Masako Shimizu
Mr. and Mrs. Masao Shimizu
Ms. Masaye G. Shimizu
Mr. and Mrs. Melvin Shimizu
Mr. Michael D. Shimizu
Dr. and Mrs. Paul Shimizu
Mr. Richard Shimizu
Mr. Richard E. Shimizu
Mr. and Mrs. Robert Shimizu
Mr. and Mrs. Ronald K. Shimizu
Mr. Roy Shimizu
Mr. Ruth Shimizu
Mr. and Mrs. Sato Shimizu
Ms. Shirley Shimizu
Mr. and Mrs. Stanley Shimizu
Mr. and Mrs. Tad Shimizu
Mr. and Mrs. Takeo Shimizu
Mr. and Mrs. Tameo Shimizu
Mr. Ted Shimizu
Mr. Ted T. Shimizu
Ms. Tokuko Shimizu
Mr. Tomio Shimizu
Mr. Toshiechi Shimizu
Ms. Toyoko Shimizu
Treva (Bell) Shimizu
Mr. and Mrs. Tsutomu Shimizu
Mr. William H. Shimizu
Mr. Yoshiaki Shimizu
Ms. Sandra S. Shimko
Mr. and Mrs. Cedrick M. Shimo
Mr. Fred Shimo
Mr. Craig Shimoda
Ms. Ethel S. Shimoda
Mr. Gary Shimoda
Ms. Jane H. Shimoda
Mr. and Mrs. Jiro Shimoda
Ms. Judy H. Shimoda
Ms. Kathleen Shimoda
Mr. and Mrs. Mark K. Shimoda
Mr. Masaru Shimoda
Mrs. Misao Shimoda
Mr. and Mrs. Sam Shimoda
Mr. Sam M. Shimoda
Mr. Satoru Shimoda
Mr. and Mrs. Steven K. Shimoda
Mr. and Mrs. Todd H. Shimoda
Mr. and Mrs. Frank M. Shimogawa
Ms. Kiyoshi Shimogawa
Mr. and Mrs. Yasuo Shimoguchi
Mrs. Ellen Shimohara
Mr. and Mrs. Kaoru Shimoide
Mr. John Shimoji
Ms. Anne L. Shimojima
Ms. Connie and Ms. Gloria Shimojima
Mr. and Mrs. Henry Shimojima
Mr. and Mrs. Tomi Shimojima
Mr. and Mrs. Kiyoshi Shimokaji
Mr. and Mrs. Gary Shimokawa
Mr. Ralph T. Shimokawa
Mr. Masao Shimoki
Mr. Mark Shimokochi
Mr. Nobu Shimokochi
Mr. and Mrs. Paul Shimokochi
Ms. Toshiye Shimokon
Mr. Larry Shimomi
Ms. Alice N. Shimomura
Mr. David S. Shimomura
Ms. Edith Shimomura
Mr. Floyd D. Shimomura
Mr. Hiromu Shimomura
Ms. Masako Shimomura
Dr. Sam K. Shimomura
Dr. and Mrs. Seiichi Shimomura
Mr. and Mrs. Warren S. Shimonishi
Mr. and Mrs Donald Shimono
Mr. Mike S. Shimooka
Mr. David Shimotakahara
Ms. Amy Shimotsu
Mr. Gary W. Shimotsu
Mr. and Mrs. Kenneth Shimotsu
Ms. Nancy N. Shimotsu
Mr. Wilfred Y. Shimotsu
Mr. and Mrs. T. Shimotsuka
Dr. and Mrs. Kenneth Shimozaki
Mr. and Mrs. Samuel Shimozaki

Mr. Norio Shimozono
Ms. Helen Akiko Shimura
Ms. Yumi Shimura
Ms. Mia U. Shin
Shin Zen Friendship Garden
Ms. Irene Shinagawa
Mr. and Mrs. John T. Shinagawa
Dr. and Mrs. Larry Shinagawa
Ms. Lil Shinagawa
Mr. and Mrs. Tsutomu Shinagawa
Mr. and Mrs. Jim M. Shinbara
Mr. Joe M. Shinbara
Mr. and Mrs. Tadao Shinbo
Dr. and Mrs. Dennis D. Shinbori
Mr. and Mrs. George Shindo
Ms. Grace M. Shindo
Mr. and Mrs. Richard Shindo
Ms. Vera Shindo
Mr. and Mrs. Isamu S. Shingai
Ms. Matsuye Shingai
Mr. Sam Shingai
Mr. and Mrs. Yukio Shingai
Mr. Fred T. Shingu
Shinju Pearl, Ltd.
Mr. and Mrs. Jack Shinkawa
Dr. Austin T. Shinkoda
Mr. Jim M. Shinmachi
Ms. Alyce M. Shinmoto
Ms. Betty Shinmoto
Mr. and Mrs. Hiroshi Shinmoto
Mr. and Mrs. Minoru Shinmoto
Ms. Priscilla Shinmoto
Mr. Scott S. Shinmoto
Ms. Teru Shinn
Ms. Yasu Shinn
Ms. Tat Shinno
Mr. Bill Shino
Ms. Beatrice S. Shinoda
Mr. and Mrs. Daniel Shinoda
Mr. and Mrs. Frank J. Shinoda
Mr. and Mrs. Fred M. Shinoda
Mr. James Shinoda
Mr. and Mrs. Kiyoshi Shinoda
Mr. and Mrs. Minoru Shinoda
Mr. Paul Shinoda
Mr. and Mrs. Robert Shinoda
Mr. Yoshimi Shinoda
Mr. and Mrs. Bruce Shinohara
Mr. and Mrs. Koichiro Shinohara
Mr. Leo S. Shinohara
Ms. Yoko Shinohara
Mr. Craig M. Shinozaki
Mr. and Mrs. Kaye Shinozaki
Mr. and Mrs. Faith Shinsato
Mr. Fred H. Shinsato
Mr. Hisao Shinsato
Mr. Kenneth Shinsato
Ms. Leinette Shinsato
Mr. Lloyd Shinsato
Mr. Roy T. Shinsato
Wayne Shinsato and Yvonne Puttler
Mr. and Mrs. Yasuhiko Shinsato
Gen. and Mrs. Eric K. Shinseki
Mr. Kyle F. Shinseki
Ms. Michelle Shinseki
Mr. Kinito Shinta
Mr. and Mrs. Asa Shintaku
Mr. Fumiko Shintaku
Mr. Glenn Shintaku
Mr. Gordon H. Shintaku
Ms. Haruko Shintaku
Mr. Kikuo Shintaku
Mrs. Mary Shintaku
Mr. Misao Shintaku
Ms. Miyo Shintaku
Mr Robert Shintaku
Mr. and Mrs. Robert M. Shintaku
Mr. Steven Shintaku
Ms. Doris C. Shintani
Ms. Haruyo Shintani
Mr. and Mrs. Kazumi Shintani
Ms. Lily Shintani
Ms. Mary Shintani
Ms. Mas Shintani
Mrs. Miye Shintani
Mr. and Mrs. Takao Shintani
Dr. and Mrs. Y. Ron Shintani
Ms. Yoshie Shintani
Mr. and Mrs. Jim Y. Shinto
Mr. and Mrs. Richard U. Shinto
Mrs. Chizuko Shinzaki
George and Karen Shinzaki Family
Mr. and Mrs. Fudge Shiogi
Ms. Elayne Shiohama
Mr. Masa Shiohira
Mrs. Masako Shioji

Mr. and Mrs. Tokio Shiomichi
Mr. and Mrs. Sam S. Shiomoto
Mr. and Mrs. Henry Shiosaka
Mr. and Mrs. Fred A. Shiosaki
Mr. Gregg N. Shiosaki
Mr. and Mrs. Rodney Shiosaki
Ms. Masako Shiota
Ms. Yuriko Shiota
Ms. Betty Y. Shiotani
Ms. Tami Shiotani
Mr. and Mrs. E. Sam Shiotsuka
Mr. Ko Shioya
Mr. and Mrs. Akira Shiozaki
Ms. Alice F. Shiozaki
Mr. Dale Shiozaki
Mr. and Mrs. Harry Shiozaki
Mr. and Mrs. Masaru Shiozaki
Mr. and Mrs. Mitz Shiozaki
Mr. and Mrs. Ronald Shiozaki
Ms. Shelia D. Shiozaki
Mr. Takashi Shiozaki
Mr. and Mrs. Toshio Shiozaki
Mr. Hiroyuki Shiozawa
Ms. May Shiozawa
Ms. Sam Shiozawa
Mr. and Mrs. Joseph B. Shipley
Mrs. Geneva Shira
Mr. Martin L. Shira
Mr. and Mrs. William Shirachi
Ms. Fumiko Shirado
Ms. Grace Shirado
Ms. Sharon L. Shiraga
Ms. Akiko M. Shirai
Ms. Eucaly Shirai
Mr. and Mrs. Makoto Shirai
Mr. Curtis I. Shiraishi
Mr. Leroy Shiraishi
Mr. and Mrs. Michael M. Shiraishi
Ms. Mollie M. Shiraishi
Ms. Nora S. Shiraishi
Mr. Richard A. Shiraishi
Mr. and Mrs. Shigeo Shiraishi
Ms. Shizuko Shiraishi
Mrs. Spencer S. Shiraishi
Mr. and Mrs. Yutaka Shiraishi
Mr. and Mrs. David Shiraiwa
Mr. Harris Shirakawa
Mr. John Shirakawa
Mr. and Mrs. Tom Shirakawa
Dr. and Mrs. Fred A. Shiraki
Mr. George Shiraki
Mr. and Mrs. Phil Shiraki
Mr. Spud Shiraki
Ms. Michele Shirakura
Mr. and Mrs. Hiromi Shiramizu
Mr. Melvin Shiramizu
Mrs. Virginia Shiras
Mr. and Mrs. Fred Shirasago
Ms. Michele Shirasu
Mr. Takeshi Shiratori
Mr. and Mrs. Misao Shiratsuki
Mr. Thomas Shiratsuki
Ms. Misako Mogi Shirk
Mr. Orville Shirley
Mr. George Shiro
Mr. Joji Shiro
Mr. and Mrs. Randy Shiroi
Mr. and Mrs. Allen Lane Shiroishi
Ms. Debra Shiroishi
Mr. Masaru Shiroishi
Mr. and Mrs. Robert Shiroishi
Mr. and Mrs. Scott Shiroishi
Mr. and Mrs. David S. Shiroma
Mr. Ernest Shiroma
Ms. Genevieve A. Shiroma
Ms. Grace S. Shiroma
Mr. and Mrs. Joseph Shiroma
Ms. Kay K. Shiroma
Mr. Kenneth S. Shiroma
Mr. and Mrs. Lionel T. Shiroma
Mrs. Lynette Y. Shiroma
Mr. Masaichi Shiroma
Mr. and Mrs. Shuichi Shiroma
Mr. Stanley Shiroma
Ms. Beth J. Shironaka
Mr. and Mrs. Jon Shirota
Mr. Dean Shiroyama
Mr. and Mrs. Mits Shiroyama
Mr. and Mrs. Samuel Shiroyama
Mr. Thomas Shiroyama
Mr. and Mrs. Charles H. Shishida
Mr. and Mrs. Ben Shishido
Mr. Dan K. Shishido
Mr. Glenn Shishido
Mr. and Mrs. Harry Shishido
Mr. and Mrs. Hiroshi Shishido

Mr. and Mrs. Kiyotaka Shishido
Mr. and Mrs. Melvyn T. Shishido
Mr. and Mrs. Ralph Shishido
Ms. Sandra Shishido
Mr. and Mrs. Seigi Shishido
Ms. Shirley Shishido
Ms. Thelma Shishido
Mr. and Mrs. Tomio Shishido
Mr. and Mrs. Toru Shishido
Mr. Toshio Shishido
Mr. and Mrs. Bill Shishima
Mr. and Mrs. Paul Shishima
Mr. R. T. Shishima
Mr. Tony Shishima
Mr. and Mrs. Hayao Shishino
Ms. Karen Shishino
Ms. Kimiko Shitanishi
Mr. and Mrs. Tom Shitanishi
Mr. Ford Shiu
Ms. Bess Shiyomura
Mr. James J. Shizuru
Ms. Kathleen Shizuru and Mr. Robert Moulenbelt
Mr. and Mrs. Saburo Shizuru
Mr. Charles Shoda
Mr. Fred Y. Shoga
Mr. and Mrs. Sei Shohara
Mr. Russell K. Shoho
Mr. and Mrs. Yasunobu Shoho
Mrs. Alice Shoji
Mr. and Mrs. Arthur A. Shoji
Mr. Arthur J. Shoji
Mr. and Mrs. Carroll Shoji
Mr. and Mrs. Chiseo Shoji
Mr. Ernest Shoji
Mr. and Mrs. Frank Shoji
Ms. Julie D. Shoji
Dr. Nancy E. Shoji
Mr. and Mrs. Samuel J. Shoji
Mr. Sergio Shoji
Ms. Umeko Shoji
Mr. and Mrs. William J. Shoji
Mr. and Mrs. Raymond A. Sholes
Mr. and Mrs. Jeffery Sholian
Mr. and Mrs. Howard Shono
Mr. and Mrs. Masao Shono
Showa Jusetsu Kabushikigaisha
Mr. Howard W. Shriver
Mr. and Mrs. Scott Shropshire
Ms. Geraldine Shu
Mr. and Mrs. Henry Shu
Ms. Renu Shukla
Mr. Allen K. Shultz
Mr. and Mrs. Ralph Sibert
Mr. Caden Jackson Side
Mr. Daniel Blake Side
Mr. and Mrs. Eugene Side
Mr. Alex Sidorovsky
Ms. Barbara Siebertz
Dr. Elliot J. Siegal
Mr. Dan Siegel and Ms. Marianne O'Malley
Ms. Harrie Siegel
Mr. Winifred W. Siegel
Mr. and Mrs. Richard Simko
Ms. Kathryn Simmons
Mr. Donald M. Simonds
Mr. and Mrs. David Simpson
Ms. Elizabeth Simpson
Mr. and Mrs. Richard P. Simpson
Simpson United Methodist Church
Mr. John D. Sims
Mr. and Mrs. Robert Sinclair
Mr. and Mrs. Allyn Sing
Mrs. Haruko Singh
Mr. and Mrs. James F. Singleton
Ms. Frances Sivak
Mr. and Mrs. Thomas Skinner
Mr. Joseph Skolnick
Mr. John L. Slade
Ms. Jane Slater
Amy Slonkier Family
Ms. Patricia Slovinac
Mr. and Mrs. Larry Small
Mr. and Mrs. Russ Smedley
Mrs. James Smee
Ms. Abigail Smith
Ms. Cheryl Smith
Ms. Christine A. Smith
Mr. David B. Smith
Ms. Etsuko Y. Smith
Cmdr. and Mrs. Eugene Smith
Maj. Gen. Foster L. Smith, USAF Ret.
Mr. Harold K. Smith
Mrs. Jean Sekiguchi Smith
Mr. and Mrs. Merlin G. Smith
Ms. Patricia J. Smith
Mr. Robert J. Smith

Ms. Stefania Smith
Mr. and Mrs. Philip L. Snyder
Ms. Susan Soares
Mr. Anthony Soda
Ms. Norine M. Soda
Mr. Takushi Sodetani
Mr. and Mrs. Toshimi Sodetani
Mr. Noboru Soeda
Mr. Ben J. Soejima
Mr. Clem Soga
Mr. and Mrs. Glenn Soga
Mr. and Mrs. Michitoshi Soga
Mr. Donald T. Sogioka
Ms. Helen Sogioka
Ms. Ruth S. Sogioka
Ms. Carolyn K. Sokugawa
Mr. Raymond Sokugawa
Ms. Lois A. Solberg
Ms. Marjorie Z. Solenberger
Mr. and Mrs. Ibrahim M. Soliman
Mr. and Mrs. Paul J. Solnick
Mr. and Mrs. Thomas Solomon
Mr. Roy Soltoff
Mr. and Mrs. Ken Somberg
Ms. Emi Somekawa
Somerset Ladies
Mr. Herman F. Son
Mr. and Mrs. David M. Sone
Mr. and Mrs. Geary M. Sone
Mr. Philips Sone
Mr. and Mrs. Shinji Soneda
Dr. Selvin Sonken
Ms. Suzanne Sonnergren
Mr. Faye Emiko Sono
Ms. May Sono
Mr. and Mrs. Toshiro Sono
Mr. and Mrs. George S. Sonoda
Mr. and Mrs. Howell Sonoda
Ms. Janelle Sonoda
Mr. and Mrs. Ken Sonoda
Ms. Midori Sonoda
Mr. Pearl M. Sonoda
Mr. Sueo Sonoda
Ms. Taka I. Sonoda
Mr. and Mrs. Toji Sonoda
Mr. Yuki Sonoda
Mr. and Mrs. Albert Sora
Mr. and Mrs. Hiroshi Sorakubo
Mr. Manabu Sorakubo
Mr. and Mrs. Shigeo Sorakubo
Mr. Peter Soraoka
Mr. and Mrs. Kenneth S. Sorayama
Ms. Nancy Soreide
Mr. and Mrs. Everett A. Sorensen
Ms. Gloria C. Soriano
Mr. Frank Sorrel
Ms. Sachiko T. Sorrell
So. Alameda County Buddhist Church Dharma School
So. California Nisei Women's Golf Association
So. County Veterinary Hospital
Mr. Bohdan S. Sowa
Mr. Ichiro Sowa
Mr. and Mrs. William Soyejima
Ms. Christine Sparks and Mr. Scott Furushia
Mr. and Mrs. Robert L. Spear
Warren Speckhart Farms
Ms. Theodora Speer
Mr. Elmer L. Spencer
Mrs. Virginia P. Spencer
Mr. and Mrs. Leonard D. Speyer
Mr. and Mrs. Steven P. Spiegel
Ms. Tamio Spiegel
Mr. David Spokely
Ms. Janis Ann Sposato and Mr. Marco Bonvillian
Mrs. Ko Hanamura Stanley
Mr. James Stansfield
Mr. and Mrs. Edwin Stanton
Mr. Milton Stanzler
Mr. Daniel Stapleton
Mr. and Mrs. Harold B. Stark
Mr. and Mrs. Michael Stark
Mr. and Mrs. Ken Staton
Mrs. Mary Stauss
Ms. Michiko Stavert
Ms. Marsha S. Steffen
Mr. and Mrs. Alan Stein
Mr. and Mrs. Kathleen Stein
Mr. and Mrs. John Steiner
Mr. Kurt Steiner
Ms. Momoko O. Steiner
Mr. and Mrs. Frank Stelwagon
Ms. Donita Stepan
Mrs. Y. Jean Stephens
Ms. Elizabeth L. Stephenson
Mr. Mason W. Stephenson
Mr. Thomas Stern

Mr. and Mrs. Harry Sternberg
Drs. Lawrence and Karin Redden Sternberg
Dr. and Mrs. David Stevenson
Mr. Donald Stewart
Mrs. Paula Nishibayashi Stewart
Mr. and Mrs. Terry Stewart
Mr. and Mrs. Mark E. Stickel
Mr. John R. Stock
Ms. Claudia A. Stoecker
Mrs. Kathy Stogbauer
Mr. Petra Stoick
Mr. and Mrs. Paul Stokes
Ms. Charlotte Stolmaker
Mr. and Mrs. Craig Stoner
Mr. Joseph E. Storer
Mr. C. Mitchell Stork
Mr. and Mrs. Ryan Stoutenborough
Ms. Patricia Strang
Mr. and Mrs. Leroy Strate
Mr. Ulrich A. Straus
Dr. Armar A. Strauss
Ms. Katherine Strehl
Mr. Christopher W. Strobel
Mr. Steven W. Stroker
Ms. Virginia Struhsaker
Ms. Kathleen Stuart
Mr. Gordon Stukenboeker
Mr. and Mrs. Bengiro Suda
Ms. Frances Suda
Mr. George R. Suda
Mr. and Mrs. Jack Suda
Mr. Stanley Suda
Mr. and Mrs. Toshio Suda
Mr. and Mrs. Willy Suda
Mr. and Mrs. Roger Suddith
Mr. and Mrs. Ben Suechika
Ms. Joanne Suechika and Mr. Bill Bennett
Mr. Bert Sueda
Mr. Jerry T. Sueda
Mr. Mamoru Sueda
Mr. and Mrs. Masamichi Sueda
Mr. and Mrs. Minori Sueda
Mr. and Mrs. Robert Sueda
Mr. and Mrs. Goichi Suehiro
Mr. Harold S. Suehiro
Mr. and Mrs. Hiromi Suehiro
Mr. and Mrs. Robert Suehiro
Mr. Roger Suekama
Mr. and Mrs. Sam Suekama
Ms. Tiffany C. Suekama
Mr. Arthur Suekawa
Mr. and Mrs. Michio Suekawa
Mr. Robert T. Suekawa
Mr. George Sueki
Ms. Lisa T. Sueki
Ms. B. Suemori
Ms. Emiko Suemori
Mr. Garrett H. Suemori
Mr. Jay Suemori
Mrs. Lois Suemori
Mr. and Mrs. James Suenaga
Ms. Mary Suenaga
Mr. Bill A. Sueoka
Mr. George H. Sueoka
Mr. George S. Sueoka
Mrs. Sarah S. Sueoka
Mr. James Sueyoshi
Mr. Alvin Suezaki
Mr. Richard H. Suezaki
Mr. Dave Suga
Dr. Steven H. Suga
Mr. Yasuo Suga
Mr. and Mrs. James Sugahara
Mr. and Mrs. Edwin Sugai
Mr. and Mrs. Francis Sugai
Mr. and Mrs. Gerald Sugai
Mr. and Mrs. Kit Sugai
Mr. Lee Sugai
Mr. and Mrs. Michael Sugai
Mr. Stanley Y. Sugai
Mr. Susumi Sugai
Mr. Takao Sugai
Mr. Wilfred Sugai and Mr. Sheryl Mosbarger
Ms. Kimiko Sugamura
Mr. and Mrs. Mark Sugamura
Mr. Douglas Sugano
Mrs. Edith Sugano
Mrs. Fusa Sugano Family
Mr. and Mrs. James Y. Sugano
Mr. Seiichi Sugano
Mr. Shoichi Sugano
Mr. and Mrs. Edwin Suganuma
Mr. and Mrs. Henry Y. Suganuma
Mr. A. W. Sugasawara
Mr. Daryl J. Sugasawara
Mr. Richard M. Sugasawara

Mr. and Mrs. Roy Sugasawara
Mrs. Tod W. Sugasawara
Mr. Hisashi Sugawara
Mr. and Mrs. Keith Sugawara
Mr. and Mrs. Ken F. Sugawara
Mr. and Mrs. Peter M. Sugawara
Mr. and Mrs. Robert H. Sugawara
Mr. and Mrs. Seiji Sugawara
Mr. Yutaka Sugawara
Mr. Henry H. Sugeno
Ms. Alice Y. Sugi
Mr. Fusako Sugi
Ms. Helen D. Sugi
Mrs. Tei Sugi
Mr. and Mrs. Ichiro Sam Sugidono
Ms. Eiko Sugihara
Ms. Fumi Sugihara
Ms. Fumiko Sugihara
Mr. Karenemi G. Sugihara
Mr. and Mrs. Larry Sugihara
Mr. and Mrs. Mas Sugihara
Mr. Masao Sugihara
Mr. Masato Sugihara
Mr. and Mrs. Paul Sugihara
Mr. and Mrs. Stanley Sugihara
Mr. and Mrs. T. Frank Sugihara
Mr. and Mrs. Thomas I. Sugihara
Mr. Toshiye Sugi
Mr. and Mrs. Kazuo Sugiki
Mr. and Mrs. Jacob Sugiman
Mr. and Mrs. Bruce Sugimoto
Mr. and Mrs. Dan S. Sugimoto
Mr. David Sugimoto
Mr. and Mrs. Frank Sugimoto
Mr. and Mrs. Fred Sugimoto
Mr. and Mrs. Hisashi Sugimoto
Mr. Isamu Sugimoto
Mr. Jack S. Sugimoto
Ms. Jayne C. Sugimoto
Mr. Jun Sugimoto
Ms. Katherine Sugimoto
Mr. Kazuo Fred Sugimoto
Mr. Lee Sugimoto
Ms. Lillian T. Sugimoto
Mrs. Mary S. Sugimoto
Mr. Melvin T. Sugimoto
Mr. Michael Sugimoto
Mrs. Midori Sugimoto
Ms. Nancy M. Sugimoto
Mr. and Mrs. Ralph Sugimoto
Mr. and Mrs. Richard K. Sugimoto
Mr. Rick Sugimoto
Mr. and Mrs. Robert M. Sugimoto
Mr. and Mrs. Robert T. Sugimoto
Mr. Ron Sugimoto
Mr. Ronald Sugimoto
Mr. and Mrs. Roy Sugimoto
Mr. Sam Sugimoto
Mr. Sam S. Sugimoto
Ms. Sarah Sugimoto
Mr. Scott T. Sugimoto
Mr. Spencer R. Sugimoto
Mr. and Mrs. Stanley T. Sugimoto
Ms. Sumire C. Sugimoto
Mr. T. Sugimoto
Ms. Thelma T. Sugimoto
Ms. Tina Sugimoto
Mr. Benjamin Sugimura
Mrs. Cynthia Sugimura
Mr. Gordon Sugimura
Mr. Marian Sugimura
Mr. Robert T. Sugimura
Mr. Scott Isao Sugimura
Ms. Yuriko and Ms. Masako Sugimura
Mr. Sam Sugine, Jr.
Mr. Junichi Sugino
Mr. Ken Sugino
Mr. and Mrs. Kameo Sugioka
Ms. Minnie Sugioka
Mr. and Mrs. Shoshi Sugioka
Mr. Tamotsu Sugioka
Mr. and Mrs. Shigematsu Sugisaki
Mr. David M. Sugishita
Mr. Gary Sugita
Mr. and Mrs. Koichi Sugita
Mr. Richard A. Sugita
Ms. Susan Y. Sugita
Mr. and Mrs. Toyoji Sugita
Mr. Wayne Sugita
Mrs. Chiemi Sugitani
Mr. David Sugiura
Ms. Masako Sugiura
Mr. Seichiro Sugiura
Mr. Takashi Sugiura
Miss Christine Sugiyama
Mr. Dean T. Sugiyama

Ms. Frances Sugiyama
Mr. Gary H. Sugiyama
Dr. and Mrs. George Sugiyama
Ms. Grace Sugiyama
Mr. and Mrs. Harry Sugiyama
Mr. John I. Sugiyama
Ms. Judith A. Sugiyama
Ms. Marie M. Sugiyama
Mr. and Mrs. Masao Sugiyama
Ms. Nancy Sugiyama
Ms. Naoko Sugiyama
Dr. and Mrs. Raymond M. Sugiyama
Mr. Shin Sugiyama
Ms. Shizue Sugiyama
Ms. Shunichi Sugiyama
Mr. and Mrs. Tadyoshi Sugiyama
Mr. and Mrs. Toshitada Sugiyama
Ms. Yumi Sugiyama
Mr. Yuriko Sugiyama
Mr. James M. Sugjihara
Mr. Jiro Suguro
Ms. Toshiko Suguro
Mr. and Mrs. Shohei Sukegawa
Mr. Timothy Sukimoto
Mr. and Mrs. Mitsuru Suko
Mr. Shoji Suko
Ms. Elizabeth Sullivan
Mr. and Mrs. Mitsugu Sumada
Mr. Howard Sumi
Mr. Joseph Sumi
Mrs. Lillie Sumi
Mr. Randall Sumi
Ms. Shizuko Sumi
Mr. and Mrs. Takashi Sumi
Mr. and Mrs. William Sumi
Mr. Alexander Sumida
Mr. Ben Sumida
Mr. Calvin Sumida
Ms. Dorothy Sumida
Mrs. Fujiko Sumida
Mr. and Mrs. Harry S. Sumida
Mr. and Mrs. Jack K. Sumida
Mr. Jeff Sumida
Mr. Jiro Sumida
Mr. and Mrs. Joey Sumida
Mr. and Mrs. Kunio Ace Sumida
Ms. Mabel Sumida
Mr. and Mrs. Marshall Sumida
Ms. Mary Sumida
Mr. and Mrs. Merwyn Sumida
Mr. Michael Sumida
Ms. Misao Sumida
Mr. and Mrs. Paul Sumida
Mr. Raymond Sumida
Mr. Richard Sumida
Mr. Robert K. Sumida
Ms. Sue Sumida
Mrs. Terry Sumida
Mr. and Mrs. Theodore Sumida
Mr. Wallace S. Sumida
Mr. Walter Sumida
Mr. William Sumida
Mr. and Mrs. Yukio Sumida
Sumiden Wire Products Corp.
Mr. and Mrs. Don C. Sumihiro
Ms. Florence M. Sumile
Ms. Keiko Sumitani
Mr. Masaharu Sumiuchi
Mr. Hiroaki Sumomogi
Mr. Yoshio Sumomogi
Mr. Donald Sunada
Mr. Frank K. Sunada
Mr. and Mrs. Glenn Sunada
Mr. and Mrs. John Sunada
Ms. Maxine A. Sunada
Mr. Paul Sunada
Mr. Robert Sunada
Mr. Roy Sunada
Mr. and Mrs. Thomas Sunada
Mr. and Mrs. Donald Sunahara
Mr. Keith Sunahara
Ms. Marilyn M. Sunahara
Mrs. Midori Sunahara
Mr. and Mrs. Tomoe Sunahara
Ms. Suyeko Sue Sunami
Mr. and Mrs. Katsumi Sunamoto
Mr. and Mrs. Kenichi Sunamoto
Mr. Robert H. Sunamoto
Mr. Takashi Sunata
Ms. Gloria M. Sundaresan
Mr. and Mrs. Walter Sunderland
Mr. and Mrs. David Sundius
Mr. Kemper Sundstrom
Mr. and Mrs. Russell Sung
Ms. Joann Suravech

Dr. Coral L. Surgeon
Mr. Ryoji Suruki
Sushi Kappo Kawasaki
Mr. John Suskey
Mr. and Mrs. Joe C. Suski
Ms. Christine Susumi-Hastings
Ms. Mary Sutow
Mr. Shizuo Sutow
Ms. Joan H. Sutter
Mr. and Mrs. Daniel Suttner
Mr. and Mrs. Alan Sutton
Ms. Mitsuko Suwa
Mr. and Mrs. Steven M. Suwabe
Mr. Brian Suyama
Mr. Paul Suyama
Ms. Toshiko Suyama
Ms. Tsuyuko Sallie Suyama
Ms. Stacey Suyat
Mr. George Suyehara
Ms. Lisbeth A. Suyehira
Mr. Rich Suyehira
Ms. Evelyn Suyehira
Mr. and Mrs. George Suyehiro
Mr. Tadao P. Suyeishi
Mr. Gerry Suyematsu
Mr. Lee Suyemoto
Mrs. Thelma T. Suyenaga
Mr. and Mrs. Hiroshi Suyeoka
Ms. Yoshiko Suyetsugu
Mr. William Suyeyasu
Mr. Kazuo Suyeyasu
Ms. Traci M. Suyeyasu
Mr. Eugene K. Suzaka
Ms. Amy K. Suzaki
Mr. Gilbert Suzawa
Mr. Richard Suzawa
Ms. Carole S. Suzui
Ms. Carolyn Suzukawa
Mr. Henry H. Suzukawa, Jr.
Mr. and Mrs. Akio Suzuki
Mr. and Mrs. Akira Suzuki
Alice, Florence and Edna Suzuki
Mrs. Bridget K. Suzuki
Mr. and Mrs. Chester Suzuki
Mr. and Mrs. Cory Suzuki
Mr. and Mrs. David Suzuki
Ms. Dorothy Suzuki
Mr. Eiji Suzuki
Ms. Ellen Suzuki
Ms. Florence Suzuki
Mr. and Mrs. Frank T. Suzuki
Mr. and Mrs. Fred Suzuki
Mr. George Suzuki
Mr. George E. Suzuki
Mr. and Mrs. George K. Suzuki Family
Mr. and Mrs. Gregory T. Suzuki
Mr. and Mrs. Harry Suzuki
Mr. and Mrs. Haruyuki Suzuki
Mr. and Mrs. Henry Suzuki
Mr. and Mrs. Hiroshi Suzuki
Mr. and Mrs. Hisashi Suzuki
Mr. Hitoshi Suzuki
Mr. and Mrs. Howard K. Suzuki
Mr. Isao Suzuki
Dr. and Mrs. Jon Suzuki Family
Mr. Joseph J. Suzuki
Mr. Joseph T. Suzuki
Ms. Julia Suzuki
Mr. and Mrs. Katsuo Suzuki
Mr. Kazuo Suzuki
Ms. Lena T. Suzuki
Ms. Lois Suzuki
Mr. Louis S. Suzuki
M. Suzuki
Mr. Makoto Suzuki
Mr. Manaji Suzuki
Mr. and Mrs. Mark Suzuki
Ms. Mary Suzuki
Mr. Masaharu Suzuki
Mr. Matthew J. Suzuki
Mr. Michael Koji Suzuki
Mr. and Mrs. Morris Suzuki
Ms. Namiko Suzuki
Ms. Naoko Suzuki
Mr. and Mrs. Naoye Suzuki
Ms. Natasha Suzuki
Mr. Nobuyuki Suzuki
Mr. Norihasa Suzuki
Mr. Paul T. Suzuki
Mr. R. T. Suzuki
Mr. Ralph M. Suzuki
Mrs. Reyeko Suzuki
Mr. Robert Suzuki
Mr. and Mrs. Ronald Suzuki
Ms. Ruth Suzuki
Mr. and Mrs. Sheik Suzuki

Mr. Shinichi S. Suzuki
Mr. Stephen Suzuki Family
Mr. and Mrs. Stephen Suzuki
Mr. and Mrs. Stimson S. Suzuki
Dr. and Mrs. Tadao Suzuki
Mr. and Mrs. Tadayoshi Suzuki
Mr. and Mrs. Takashi Suzuki
Mr. Tetsuro Suzuki
Mr. and Mrs. Tomokazu Suzuki
Mr. Toshi T. Suzuki
Mr. Toshihiro Suzuki
Mr. and Mrs. Warren M. Suzuki
Mr. and Mrs. Warren N. Suzuki
Mr. and Mrs. Wendell Suzuki
Ms. Wendy Suzuki
Mr. Yasutomo Suzuki
Ms. Yoshie Suzuki
Ms. Yoshiko Suzuki
Dr. and Mrs. Yugo Suzuki
Suzuki, Myers & Assoc., Ltd.
Mrs. Chiyo Suzukida
Ms. Linda E. Swanson
Mr. and Mrs. Robert C. Swanson
Mr. Sherwin Swartz
Luke and Anne Gilliland-Swetland
Ms. Marilynn Swinger
Mr. and Mrs. Robert Switzer
Ms. Kathleen E. Sykes
Ms. Mary O. Szanto
Mr. and Mrs. Clarence Taba
Mr. Dean K. Taba
Mr. and Mrs. Clarence Tabata
Mrs. Hiroko Tabata
Mr. and Mrs. J. Tabata
Mr. and Mrs. Jim Tabata
Mr. and Mrs. Mack Tabata
Mr. Mark Tabata
Mrs. Miyoko Tabata
Mr. Takeshi Tabata
Mr. and Mrs. Warren K. Tabata
Mr. and Mrs. Yoshio Tabata
Mr. and Mrs. Tadashi Tabe
Ms. Ruth M. Tabrah
Mr. and Mrs. Bob Tabuchi
Mr. and Mrs. Don Tabuchi
Mr. and Mrs. Douglas Tachi
Mr. and Mrs. Sadayoshi Tachi
Tachibana Restaurant
Ms. A. Janice Tachibana
Mr. and Mrs. Bob M. Tachibana
Mr. Hideo Tachibana
Mr. Kaoru Tachibana
Mr. and Mrs. Mas Tachibana
Mr. Mitsuo Tachibana
Mr. and Mrs. Richard Tachibana
Mr. and Mrs. Shigeru Tachibana
Mr. and Mrs. Toru Tachibana
Mr. Walter S. Tachibana
Mr. and Mrs.Yasuro Tachibana
Mr. and Mrs. Yoshinobu Tachibana
Mrs. Maria M. Tachihara
Ms. Ann Tachikawa
Mr. Martin Tachiki
Mr. William K. Tachiki
Mr. and Mrs. Kaz Tachino
Ms. Cheryl Tack
Ms. Anna Tackett
Mr. and Mrs. Ben Tada
Mrs. Joe Tada
Mr. and Mrs. Koji Tada
Mr. Satoru Tada
Mr. Spencer Tada
Mr. and Mrs. Tets Tada
Mr. Calvin Tadaki
Mrs. Barbara N. Tadakuma
Mr. and Mrs. Hiroshi Tadakuma
Mr. Larry Tadakuma
Mr. Ben Tadano
Ms. Mary M. Tadano
Ms. Michiko Tadano
Mr. William K. Tadano
Mr. and Mrs. Justin Taddeo
Mr. and Mrs. Raymond J. Taddeo, Jr.
Mrs. Yaeko Tademaru
Mrs. Haruko Tademoto
Mr. Cedric S. Tadokoro
Mr. and Mrs. Toshi Taenaka
Mr. Toshikuni Taenaka
Mr. and Mrs. Frank T. Taga
Mr. Hiroyuki Taga
Mrs. Morie Taga
Mr. Bert Tagami
Mr. and Mrs. Chiharu Tagami
Mr. and Mrs. Kenneth Tagami
Mr. and Mrs. Sam Tagami
Ms. Marsha Tagami-Tao

Mr. Sho Tagashira
Mr. and Mrs. Craig K. Tagawa
Dr. and Mrs. Derrick T. Tagawa
Mr. and Mrs. Gary Tagawa
Ira and Marilyn Tagawa
Messrs. Jack and Rick Tagawa
Mr. Jack T. Tagawa
Mr. Kenneth T. Tagawa
Mr. Michael Tagawa
Ms. Naomi Tagawa
Mr. Shoichiro Tagawa
Mr. Yasuji Tagaya
Mr. Masaharu Tage
Mr. Cal S. Taggart
Mr. and Mrs. Thomas D. Taggart
Mr. John Taguchi
Mr. Kenneth Taguchi
Mr. Kevin Taguchi
T. Taguchi
Mr. Toru Taguchi
Mr. Yutaka Taguchi
Mr. and Mrs. Craig K. Taguma
Mr. Victor Taguma
Mr. and Mrs. Yoshio Taguma
Ms. Alice Tahara
Mr. and Mrs. Harvey Tahara
Mr. and Mrs. Masaru Tahara
Ms. Mildred M. Tahara
Mr. Randi S. Tahara
Mr. Richard Tahara
Mr. and Mrs. Shiro Tahara
Mr. Robert H. Tai and Ms. Amy S. Lee
Taiga International Temari Japanese Café
Mr. and Mrs. Hiroshi Taiji
Mr. Albert H. Taira
Ms. Betty Taira
Dr. Calvin S. Taira
Mr. Eric M. Taira
Ms. Gay N. Taira
Mr. and Mrs. Jason Taira
Ms. Kay Taira
Ms. Keiko Taira
Mr. Koji Taira
Mr. and Mrs. Melvin Taira
Ms. Nadine Taira
Mr. Paul Taira
Mr. Robert Taira
Mr. Steven E. Taira
Dr. Susan Taira
Mr. Tim Taira
Mr. Victor Y. Taira
Mr. and Mrs. Walter Taira
Mr. and Mrs. Yoshinori Taira
Mr. and Mrs. Gengo Tajii
Mrs. Bernice A. Tajima
Mr. and Mrs. Calvin Tajima
Mr. and Mrs. Edmund Tajima
Mrs. Elaine Tajima
Mr. Harry A. Tajima
Mr. Michael S. Tajima
Ms. Sueyo Tajima
Mr. Taz Tajima
Mr. and Mrs. Ted Tajima
Dr. and Mrs. Akira Tajiri
Mr. Dennis Tajiri
Mr. and Mrs. Edward Tajiri
Mr. Harold M. Tajiri
Mr. James M. Tajiri
Mr. Steven K. Tajiri
TAK Petroleum
Ms. Florence Takaaze
Mr. and Mrs. Douglas T. Takaba
Mr. Roger Takabayashi
Ms. Sakaye Takabayashi
Mr. and Mrs. Susumu Takabayashi
Ms. Teru Takabayashi
Mr. and Mrs. David Takada
Ms. Janice Takada
Mr. and Mrs. Michael Takada
Mr. and Mrs. Michio Takade
Mr. and Mrs. Richard Takae
Mr. and Mrs. Paul M. Takaezu
Col. and Mrs. Ernest T. Takafuji
Mr. Kie Takagaki
Mr. Akira Takagi
Mr. Alpha Takagi
Ms. Asaye Ashizawa Takagi
Mr. and Mrs. David M. Takagi
Mr. Eiichi T. Takagi
Mr. Jon G. Takagi
Mr. and Mrs. Robert S. Takagi
Ms. Rose Y. Takagi
Mr. and Mrs. Satoru Takagi
Ms. Sumi Takagi
Ms. Susan Takagi
Mrs. Yoshiko Takagi

Mr. Craig Takagishi
Mr. and Mrs. Jonathan Takagishi
Ms. Kay Takagishi
Mrs. Lilyan Takaha
Ms. Tato Takahama
Mr. and Mrs. Kenjiro Takahara
Mr. Larry Takahara
Mr. and Mrs. Seiichi Takahara
Ms. Yuki Takahara and Mr. Aki T. Kubo
Mr. Aaron Takahashi
Mr. and Mrs. Alden Takahashi
Mr. Brandt Akio Takahashi
Mr. Byron Kei Takahashi
Mr. and Mrs. Charles Takahashi
Mr. and Mrs. Dean Takahashi
Mr. Delbert H. Takahashi
Mr. Duane K. Takahashi
Mr. Edward T. Takahashi
Mr. and Mrs. Eric Takahashi
Ms. Eva S. Takahashi
Mr. Frank Y. Takahashi
Frank and Hannah Takahashi Charitable Fund
Ms. Fumiko Takahashi
Mr. George Takahashi
Mr. and Mrs. George A. Takahashi
Mr. and Mrs. George E. Takahashi
Mr. George M. Takahashi
amd Mrs. George T. Takahashi
Mr. and Mrs. Gilbert Takahashi
Ginger and Tadashi Takahashi
Mr. Glenn Takahashi
Mr. and Mrs. Harlan Takahashi
Mr. Hideo Takahashi
Mr. and Mrs. Hiroki Takahashi
Mr. Homer Takahashi
Mr. and Mrs. James Takahashi
Mr. and Mrs. Joseph J. Takahashi
Ms. Joy Takahashi
Ms. Joyce N. Takahashi
Ms. June Takahashi
Ms. Karen Takahashi
Mr. Kay T. Takahashi
Mr. Kaz Takahashi
Mr. and Mrs. Kazue Takahashi
Mr. Kazumi Takahashi
Hon. Kazuo Takahashi
Mr. and Mrs. Kazuyoshi Takahashi
Mr. Kei J. Takahashi
Mr. Keith Takahashi
Mr. and Mrs. Ken Takahashi
Mr. and Mrs. Kenichi Takahashi
Mr. Kenji Takahashi
Mr. Kenneth Takahashi
Mr. Kenneth Y. Takahashi
Mr. Kiichi Takahashi
Mr. Kikuo Takahashi
Mr. Kiyo Takahashi
Mr. Larry F. Takahashi
Ms. Linda Y. Takahashi
Mr. and Mrs. Lloyd Takahashi
Ms. Lynn Takahashi
Ms. Mari Takahashi
Mr. Mark T. Takahashi
Mr. Mary K. Takahashi
Mr. and Mrs. Mas Takahashi
Mr. and Mrs. Masao Takahashi
Mr. Masato M. Takahashi
Ms. Michiko Takahashi
Mr. Michio Takahashi
Mrs. Mieko Takahashi
Ms. Mikiko Takahashi
Mr. Miles T. Takahashi
Mr. and Mrs. Mitsuru Takahashi
Mr. and Mrs. Moto Takahashi
Ms. Nancy A. Takahashi
Mr. Patricia Takahashi
Mr. Paul Y. Takahashi
Dr. Raymond M. Takahashi
Cdr. and Mrs. Rex Takahashi
Mr. and Mrs. Richard Takahashi
Mr. Richard M. Takahashi
Ms. Roberta Takahashi
Mr. Russell Takahashi
Mrs. Ruth T. Takahashi
Mr. and Mrs. Samuel Takahashi
Mr. and Mrs. Scott Takahashi
Ms. Sharon Takahashi
Mr. and Mrs. Shig Takahashi
Ms. Shizuye Takahashi
Mr. Sho Takahashi
Mr. Shuko Takahashi
Mr. Sugi Takahashi
Mr. and Mrs. Terry Takahashi
Mr. Thomas K. Takahashi
Mr. and Mrs. Tom Takahashi

Mr. Tom M. Takahashi
Ms. Tomiko T. Takahashi
Mr. and Mrs. Tommy Takahashi
Mr. and Mrs. Toshio Takahashi
Ms. Toshiye Takahashi
Mr. and Mrs. Tsuyoshi Takahashi
Mr. Wataru Takahashi
Mr. and Mrs. Wayne Takahashi
Mr. Wesley Takahashi
Mr. and Mrs. William S. Takahashi
Mrs. Yoshi Takahashi
Ms. Yoshie Takahashi
Ms. Yoshiko G. Takahashi
Mr. and Mrs. Saburo Takahata
Ms. Suzuko Takahata
Mr. and Mrs. Tsutomu Takahata
Mr. and Mrs. Akio Takai
Mrs. Barbara Takai
Mr. William Takai
Mr. Oliver H. Takaichi
Mr. Chris Takaishi
Dr. Arlene Takaki
Mr. and Mrs. Frank Takaki
Mr. and Mrs. George Takaki
Mr. Henry M. Takaki
Mr. and Mrs. Kenichi Takaki
Mr. Kiyoshi Takaki
Ms. Lillian K. Takaki
Ms. LuAnn Takaki
Mr. Masaru Takaki
Mr. Maxwell F. Takaki
Mr. McLean Takaki
Mr. and Mrs. Minoru Takaki
Mr. and Mrs. Mitsuru Takaki
Ms. Natsuko Takaki
Mr. and Mrs. Noboru Takaki
Mr. Nobuko Takaki
Dr. Norman K. Takaki
Mr. Paul T. Takaki
Mr. Reginald Takaki
Dr. and Mrs. Ronald Takaki
Mr. Russell H. Takaki
Mrs. Sachiko Takaki
Ms. Sadako A. Takaki
Mr. Steve Takaki
Ms. Momoye Takakoshi
Mr. and Mrs. William K. Takakoshi
Mr. and Mrs. William A. Takakuwa
Mr. Daniel I. Takamatsu
Mr. Gary Takamatsu
Mr. Toshio Takamatsu
Mr. Benson Takami
Ms. Hisako Takami
Ms. Jeanne Takami
Mary and Debra Takami
Mr. Roland D. Takami
Mr. and Mrs. Shigeo Takami
Mr. Shuichi Takami
Mr. Winston Takami
Ms. Doris Takamiya
Mr. George Takamiya
Ms. Genevieve Takamiyashiro
Mr. Thomas Takamiyashiro
Mr. and Mrs. Glen Takamori
Mr. and Mrs. Hideyuki Takamori
Mr. Kenta Takamori
Mr. Kevin Takamori
Mr. Adam M. Takamoto
Mr. and Mrs. Ernest Takamoto
Mr. Grant T. Takamoto
Mr. and Mrs. Iwao Takamoto
Ms. Janis Takamoto
Mr. and Mrs. Norito R. Takamoto
Mr. and Mrs. Robert N. Takamoto
Mr. Tokio Takamoto
Mr. and Mrs. Roy Takamune
Mr. and Mrs. Naoki Takamura
Mr. Sojiro Takamura
Mr. Ted J. Takamura
Ms. Fumie Takane
Mr. and Mrs. Harry Takane
Mr. Ken I. Takano
Takao Nursery
Mrs. Doris Y. Takao
Mr. and Mrs. Frank T. Takao
Ms. Fumiko Takao
Ms. Karen Takao
Mr. Lloyd H. Takao
Ms. Marlene Takao
Mr. and Mrs. Troy Takao
Ms. Chizu Takaoka
Mr. Hiroshi Takaoka
Mrs. Keiko Takaoka
Mr. Mike Takaoka
Ms. Utahna Takaoka
Mr. David M. Takara

Mr. Edwin I. Takara and Mrs. Joyce Curry-Takara
Mr. George T. Takara
Mr. Joe Takara
Mr. and Mrs. Lawrence Takara
Mr. Mitsuhide Takara
Mr. Richard Y. Takara
Mr. and Mrs. Ronald Takara
Mr. and Mrs. Seiichi Takara
Mr. and Mrs. Shinichi Takara
Mr. and Mrs. Yukio Takara
Mr. and Mrs. Heihachiro Takarabe
Mr. and Mrs. Dennis Takasaki
Mr. George Y. Takasaki
Ms. June Takasaki
Mr. and Mrs. Richard Takasaki
Mr. Robert Takasaki
Dr. and Mrs. Allan Takase
Mr. and Mrs. Charles T. Takase
Mr. Hayahiko Takase
Mr. Hayao Takashige
Mr. Setsu Takashige
Mr. Gary Takashima
Mr. Mamoru Takashima
Ms. May Takashima
Mr. and Mrs. Noboru Takashima
Mr. and Mrs. Tom Takashima
Ms. Mariko Takasu
Mr. Abraham Takasugi
Mr. George J. Takasugi
Ms. Karen K. Takasugi
Mr. Kingo Takasugi
Mr. Nao Takasugi
Robert and Dorothy M. Takasugi
Mr. and Mrs. Ronald Takasugi
Mr. and Mrs. Takeshi Takasugi
Mr. and Mrs. Kazuo Takasuka
Mr. and Mrs. Fred N. Takasumi
Mr. Albert Takata
Bruce H. Takata and Linda J. Novenski
Ms. Chiyoko Takata
Mr. and Mrs. Clarence Takata
Mr. and Mrs. Daniel T. Takata
Mr. and Mrs. Dennis Takata
Ms. Elsie T. Takata
Mr. George Takata
Mr. and Mrs. Jiro Takata
Ms. Joan M. Takata
Ms. Katsuko Takata
Mr. Keith A. Takata
Mr. and Mrs. Kenneth Takata
Ms. Lisa D. Takata
Ms. May Itsuko Takata
Mr. and Mrs. Michael Takata
Mr. Michio Takata
Mr. Mitsugi Takata
Mr. and Mrs. Rodney D. Takata
Mr. Roy T. Takata
Miss Setsu Takata
Mr. and Mrs. Shogi Takata
Mr. Stanley W. Takata
Mrs. Suzie Takata
Mr. and Mrs. Takanari Takata
Mrs. Thelma T. Takata
Mr. Theodore S. Takata
Mr. Thomas Takata
Mr. and Mrs. Timothy C. Takata
Tom and Rose S. Takata
Mr. and Mrs. Toshio Takata
Mr. and Mrs. Tsuruo Takata
Mr. Wallace K. Takata
Mr. Yoshihiro Takata
Mr. and Mrs. Yoshio Takata
Ms. Yoshiye Takata
Mrs. Yuki Takata
Ms. Yuriko Takata
Ms. Georgene Takato
Mr. Jake Takato
Mrs. Sadako Takato
Ms. Celine Y. Takatsuka
Ms. Ruth Takatsuki
Mr. and Mrs. Donald M. Takayama
Mr. and Mrs. Fred Takayama
Mr. and Mrs. Herbert Takayama
Mr. and Mrs. Kazuto Takayama
Mr. Kenneth Takayama
Mr. and Mrs. Kenneth Takayama
Mr. Mark T. Takayama
Mr. Mits Takayama
Mr. and Mrs. Shizuo Takayama
Mr. Thomas T. Takayama
Mr. and Mrs. Yoshio Takayama
Ms. Masako Takayanagi and Mr. Donald Wooten
Mr. Tadao Takayanagi
Megumi and Yoshiko Takayasu
Mr. and Mrs. Isamu Takayesu
Ms. Sandra S. Takayesu

Mr. Andrew Takayoshi
Ms. Masako Takayoshi
Mr. Futoshi Takazawa
Ms. Hatsuko Takechi
Mr. Soy S. Takechi
Mr. Akenori Takeda
Mr. and Mrs. Bill Takeda
Doc H. and Lucy S. Takeda
Mr. Don Takeda
Mr. and Mrs. Edward K. Takeda
Mr. and Mrs. Ernest Takeda
Mr. and Mrs. George Takeda
Mr. and Mrs. Hiroshi Takeda
Mr. and Mrs. James K. Takeda
Mr. and Mrs. Ken Takeda
Mr. and Mrs. Kent Takeda
Mr. and Mrs. Makoto Takeda
Mr. and Mrs. Masato Takeda
Mr. Michio N. Takeda
Mr. and Mrs. Robert Takeda
Mr. and Mrs. Roy Takeda
Mr. and Mrs. Sachio Takeda
Messers. Shin and Hiroshi Takeda
Mrs. Shinako Takeda
Ms. Shizue Takeda
Mr. Shozi N. Takeda
Ms. Tanja Takeda
Ms. Tomiko Takeda
Mr. and Mrs. Tonky Takeda
Mr. and Mrs. Walter Takeda
Mr. Warren K. Takeda
Dr. Yasuhiko Takeda
Mr. Kanoe and Yong Sun Takefuji
Mr. and Mrs. David Takegami
Mr. and Mrs. Milton Takeguchi
Mr. H Takeguma
Dr. Shigeru Takehana
Mr. Ichiro Takehara
Mr. Keo K. Takehara
Mr. Mark Takehara
Ms. Yohko Takehara
Mr. and Mrs. Gene Takei
Mr. and Mrs. Robert Takei
Mr. and Mrs. Roy A. Takei
Mr. Claude Takekawa
Mr. John A. Takekawa
Ms. Lisa M. Takekawa
Mr. and Mrs. James Takemori
Rev. and Mrs. A. Arthur Takemoto
Mr. Akira Takemoto
Mr. Arthur Takemoto, Jr.
Mr. Bob Takemoto
Ms. Chiyoko Takemoto
Mr. Cliff H. Takemoto
Mr. Eddie H. Takemoto
Mr. Eugene H. Takemoto
Mr. and Mrs. George Takemoto
Mr. Glenn H. Takemoto
Mr. Gordon Takemoto
Hitoshi and Yoshiko (Shindo) Takemoto
Mr. and Mrs. Joel S. Takemoto
Mr. John Takemoto
Mr. and Mrs. John Takemoto
Ms. Judy Takemoto
Ms. Julie Takemoto
Ms. June Takemoto
Mr. and Mrs. Kenneth K. Takemoto
Mr. and Mrs. Koichi Takemoto
Mr. and Mrs. Koso Takemoto
Mr. and Mrs. Mac Takemoto
Mrs. Mary Takemoto
Mr. Ryan Takemoto
Ms. Sakiko Takemoto
Mr. Steven E. Takemoto
Mr. Takeshi Takemoto
Mr. and Mrs. Thomas T. Takemoto
Ms. Toshiko Takemoto
Mr. Tsuneo Takemoto
Mr. and Mrs. Waichi Takemoto
Ms. Yasuko Takemoto
Mr. and Mrs. Arthur K. Takemura
Mr. and Mrs. Herbert Takemura
Ms. Janis Takemura
Ken and Marion Takei Takemura
Ms. Tokie Takemura
Mr. and Mrs. Eugene T. Takenaga
Mr. and Mrs. Frank Takenaka
Mr. Fred T. Takenaka
Ms. Hisae Takenaka
Dr. Jean Takenaka
Mr. John Takenaka
Ms. Kay Takenaka
Mr. Kerry T. Takenaka
Ms. Yuriko Takenaka
Mr. and Mrs. Roy M. Takeno
Mrs. Dorothy Takenouchi

Mr. and Mrs. Yasuo Takenouchi
Mr. Kazuo Takeo
Mr. Stanley Takeo
Mr. Daniel D. Takeoka
Mr. Glenn Takeoka
Mr. and Mrs. Mikio Takeoka
Mr. Noboru Takesaka
Mr. and Mrs. Akira Takeshita
Mr. and Mrs. Ben Takeshita
Ms. Bette N. Takeshita
Ms. Esther Takeshita
Kim and Arthur H. Takeshita
Mr. and Mrs. Masao Takeshita
Mr. and Mrs. Mickey Takeshita
Mr. Paul Takeshita
Mr. Reuben T. Takeshita
Dr. Richard T. Takeshita
Mr. Roy Takeshita
Dr. Saburo Takeshita
Mr. and Mrs. Shigeo Takeshita
Shiro Takeshita
Mr. Suzuo I. Takeshita
Mr. and Mrs. Ted Takeshita
Ms. Allyson Taketa
Ms. Ann Taketa
Mr. and Mrs. Bill Taketa
Mr. David Taketa
Mr. David J. Taketa
Mrs. Elaine Taketa
Mr. Glenn M. Taketa
Mr. Happy S. Taketa
Ms. Hideko Taketa
Mr. John G. Taketa
Mr. and Mrs. Keith M. Taketa
Ms. Lori Taketa
Ms. Mary S. Taketa
Mrs. Misae Taketa
Ms. Phyllis Taketa
Mr. Richard Y. Taketa
Mrs. Sally Taketa
Mr. Tatsuo Taketa
Mr. Terry Taketa
Teru Taketa
Ms. Emiko Taketomo
Mr. and Mrs. Shuji Taketomo
Dr. and Mrs. Yasuhiko Taketomo
Mr. and Mrs. Kiki Taketoshi
Mr. Arthur S. Takeuchi
Ms. Barbara G. Takeuchi
Mr. and Mrs. Clarence Takeuchi
Mr. David Takeuchi
Mr. David W. Takeuchi
Ms. Esther K. Takeuchi
Mrs. Florence Ahn Takeuchi
Mr. Floyd T. Takeuchi
Mr. Frank S. Takeuchi
Mr. George Takeuchi
Mr. and Mrs. Harry Takeuchi
Mr. and Mrs. Hideo Takeuchi
Mr. and Mrs. Hiro Takeuchi
Mr. and Mrs. James Takeuchi
Mr. and Mrs. Jeffrey Takeuchi
Mr. Jiro J. Takeuchi
Mr. and Mrs. John F. Takeuchi
Mr. John M. Takeuchi
Ms. and Mrs. Kay Takeuchi
Mr. Ken Takeuchi
Mr. and Mrs. Ken Takeuchi
Mr. and Mrs. Kenji Takeuchi
Mr. Kenneth Takeuchi
Mr. Kenneth A. Takeuchi
Drs. Kenneth J. and Esther Takeuchi
Mr. Kiyoshi Takeuchi
Ms. Laura Takeuchi
Ms. Lisa M. Takeuchi
Ms. Lucy Takeuchi
Mark and Marion Takeuchi
Mr. and Mrs. Mark Takeuchi
Mr. and Mrs. Masaru Takeuchi
Mrs. Masumi Takeuchi
Mr. and Mrs. Minoru Takeuchi
Ms. Misako Takeuchi
Ms. Mitsuru Louise Takeuchi
Mr. and Mrs. Nathan H. Takeuchi
Mr. Richard Y. Takeuchi
Mr. and Mrs. Robert Takeuchi
Mr. Robert H. Takeuchi
Robert S. and Yukio Takeuchi
Mr. Roy Takeuchi
Dr. Roy T. Takeuchi
Ms. Ruth Takeuchi
Ms. Sachi Takeuchi
Mr. and Mrs. Sam Takeuchi
Mr. and Mrs. Saturo Takeuchi
Mr. and Mrs. Steve Takeuchi
Mr. Stewart M. Takeuchi

Mr. Takao D. Takeuchi
Mr. Tom Takeuchi
Mr. and Mrs. Vic Takeuchi
Mr. and Mrs. William Takeuchi
Ms. Florence Takeyama
Mr. Roy Takeyama
Mr. Motoi Takeyasu
Mr. Howard Takiff
Mr. and Ms. Junichiro Takigayama
Ms. Alyce C. Takiguchi
Mr. Fred K. Takiguchi
Mr. and Mrs. Gary K. Takiguchi
Ms. Joyce Takiguchi
Mr. Mark Takiguchi
Mrs. Masako Takiguchi
Mr. Walter Takiguchi
Ms. Yoshiko Takiguchi
Ms. Yukie Takiguchi
Mr. Yasuhiro Takikawa
Mr. Glenn Takimoto
Mr. and Mrs. Hideyo Takimoto
Mr. Naoaki Takimoto
Mr. James T. Takisaki
Mr. Tsugiyo Takiuchi
Mr. and Mrs. Raymond Takiue
Ms. Hagumi Takizawa
Ms. Asako Takusagawa
Mr. and Mrs. Mike Takusagawa
Mr. and Mrs. Ancho Takushi
Ms. Bernice Takushi
Mr. and Mrs. James Takushi
Mr. Jaryd Takushi
Mr. and Mrs. Seichi Takushi
Mr. Charles S. Tamabayashi
Ms. Tomiko Tamae
Ms. Shizue Tamagawa
Ms. Shizue K. Tamagawa
Mr. Hoshiro Tamai
Mr. and Mrs. Kunimitsu Tamai
Mr. and Mrs. Michael J. Tamai
Mr. and Mrs. Stanley Tamai
Donald Tamaki and Suzanne Ah-Tye
Mr. Francis Tamaki
Jean and Lil Tamaki
Minoru and Iyo Tamaki
Mr. Sumiji Jim Tamaki
Mr. Conrad Tamanaha
Mr. Dennis Tamanaha
Mr. Edward M. Tamanaha
Ms. Ellen T. Tamanaha
Ms. June Tamanaha
Mr. Keichi Tamanaha
Mr. and Mrs. Kenneth Tamanaha
Ms. Lynn Tamanaha
Mr. Masaru Tamanaha
Mr. and Mrs. Rikio Tamanaha
Mr. and Mrs. Seichi Tamanaha
Mr. and Mrs. Seisuke Tamanaha
Mr. Shigeru Tamanaha
Ms. Flory J. Tamanini
Mr. Alvin K. Tamaribuchi
Mr. Michael Tamaru
Mr. and Mrs. Tom Tamaru
Mr. Naoshi Tamasaka
Mr. and Mrs. Alan Tamashiro
Mr. Alberto Tamashiro
Mr. and Mrs. Ben Tamashiro
Mr. and Mrs. Charlie T. Tamashiro
Ms. Hatsuko Tamashiro
Mr. Jitsuichi Tamashiro
Mr. and Mrs. Koki Tamashiro
Mr. and Mrs. Lawrence Tamashiro
Mr. and Mrs. Masato Tamashiro
Ms. May Tamashiro
Mr. Melvin S. Tamashiro
Mr. and Mrs. Susumu Tamashiro
Mr. and Mrs. T. R. Tamashiro
Mr. Warren Tamashiro
Mr. Yoshio Tamashiro
Mrs. Kris D. Tamashiro-Leon and Mr. Dennis R. Leon
Mr. Randolph R. Tamaye
Mr. Clarence Tamayori
Ms. Lucille A. Tamayori
Mr. Patrick S. Tamayori
Mr. E. Tamayose
Mr. Masanobu Tamayose
Mr. and Mrs. Yasunobu Tamayose
Mr. Dennis S. Tamayoshi
Dr. Wade A. Tambara
Mr. Bob O. Tamehiro
Ms. Nancy Tamehiro
Mr. Eric H. Tamichi
Mrs. Hisako Tamiya
Ms. Jeanne Tamizato
Mrs. Coleen M. Tamny
Mr. Bob Tamori

Mr. Akira Tamura
Ms. Amy Tamura
Miss April A. Tamura
Dr. and Mrs. Brian Tamura
Cary and Denise Tamura
Mr. Daniel M. Tamura
Mr. and Mrs. Douglas T. Tamura
Mr. Eddie T. Tamura
Mr. and Mrs. Elaine G. Tamura
Mr. Fred Y. Tamura
Mr. George Tamura
Mr. and Mrs. George K. Tamura
Mr. George M. Tamura
Mr. and Mrs. H. H. Tamura
Mr. Henry Tamura
Mr. Henry K. Tamura
Mrs. Isoye Tamura
Mr. and Mrs. James Tamura
Mr. Joe Tamura
Mr. John Tamura
Mr. John K. Tamura
Mr. and Mrs. John T. Tamura
Mr. Kaz Tamura
Mr. and Mrs. Kaz Tamura
Mr. Ken Tamura
Ms. Linda G. Tamura
Ms. Lynne Tamura
M. Tamura
Mrs. Marie S. Tamura
Masako Tamura and Eric Yap
Mr. Mits Tamura
Mrs. Nancy Tamura
Ms. Naomi Tamura
Ms. Patsy Tamura
Paul and Laura Tamura
Mr. and Mrs. Randall A. Tamura
Mr. Rey Tamura
Mr. and Mrs. Richard Tamura
Mr. and Mrs. Robert C. Tamura
Miss Robyn Tamura
Mrs. Ruth M. Tamura
Ms. Sachiko Tamura
Mr. Sam Tamura
Mr. Steve Tamura
Mr. Thomas T. Tamura
Mr. Tom Tamura
Mr. and Mrs. Tooru Tamura
Mr. Toshio Tamura
Mr. Warren Tamura
Mr. Yoshiaki Tamura
Mr. Yoshito V. Tamura
Ms. Diane M. Tan
Ms. Ann Tanabe
Mr. and Mrs. Arthur Y. Tanabe
Mr. Charles Tanabe
Mr. and Mrs. Don Tanabe
Ms. Dorothy G. Tanabe
Mr. Edward S. Tanabe
Mr. and Mrs. Elton Tanabe
Ms. Eru Tanabe
Ms. Fumiye Tanabe
Mr. Gilfred Tanabe
Mr. and Mrs. Hiroshi Tanabe
Mr. Jack Tanabe
Mr. Martin Tanabe
Mr. and Mrs. Masami Tanabe
Mr. Nicholas Tanabe
Mr. and Mrs. Patrick Tanabe
Mr. and Mrs. Paul Tanabe
Mr. and Mrs. Richard Tanabe
Mr. Richard S. Tanabe
Mr. Robert Tanabe
Mr. Roy Tanabe
Mrs. Ruby Tanabe
Mr. Sakaye Tanabe
Mr. T. Y. Tanabe
Mr. T. J. Tanabe
Ms. Tami Tanabe
Ms. Tina Tanabe
Yone Tanabe
Ms. Yoshiko Tanabe
Mr. Yoshinobu Tanabe
Mr. Takuma Tanada
Mr. and Mrs. Frank S. Tanagi
Mr. and Mrs. Rick M. Tanagi
A. Tanaka
Ms. Adele Tanaka and Mr. Roy Kanemoto
Mr. and Mrs. Alan Tanaka
Ms. Amy Tanaka
Ms. Anne Tanaka
Mr. and Mrs. Arthur Tanaka
Mr. Asa K. Tanaka
Ms. Ayako Tanaka
Ms. Barbara W. Tanaka
Mr. and Mrs. Bert M. Tanaka, Jr.
Ms. C. Tanaka

Mr. Carl Tanaka
Ms. Carolyn Tanaka
Mr. Chad W. Tanaka
Mr. Charles Tanaka
Mrs. Chester Tanaka
Mr. and Mrs. David Tanaka
Mr. and Mrs. Dean Tanaka
Ms. Diana Tanaka
Ms. Diane Tanaka
Ms. Diane C. Tanaka
Ms. Donna Tanaka
Ms. Dorothy Y. Tanaka
Mr. Duane Y. Tanaka
Mr. and Mrs. Eddy Tanaka
Ms. Edith A. Tanaka
Mr. and Mrs. Edward Tanaka
Mr. Edwin Tanaka
Ms. Emmy Tanaka
Ms. Florence Tanaka
Ms. Florence S. Tanaka
Dr. Francis I. Tanaka
Mr. and Mrs. Frank Tanaka
Mr. Frank K. Tanaka
Mr. Frank M. Tanaka
Mr. and Mrs. Frank N. Tanaka
Mr. Frank S. Tanaka
Mr. and Mrs. Frank Y. Tanaka
Mr. and Mrs. Fred Tanaka
Ms. Fusae Tanaka
Mr. and Mrs. Gary Tanaka
Mr. George Tanaka
Mr. George H. Tanaka
Mr. and Mrs. George H. Tanaka
Mr. and Mrs. George J. Tanaka
Mr. and Mrs. George M. Tanaka
Mr. George R. Tanaka
Mr. Goro Tanaka
Mr. and Mrs. Haruo Tanaka
Hayato Tanaka
Mr. and Mrs. Henry Tanaka
Mr. Hisaki Tanaka
Ms. Hisako Tanaka
Mr. Hitoshi Tanaka
Mrs. Humie Tanaka
Ms. Isabelle Tanaka
Mr. Isamu Tanaka
Mr. and Mrs. Jack Tanaka
Mr. James Tanaka
Mrs. Janet Tanaka
Ms. Jean E. Tanaka
Mr. and Mrs. Jim M. Tanaka
Mr. Jiro Tanaka
Ms. Joan Tanaka
Ms. Joan Y. Tanaka
Ms. JoAnne Tanaka
Mr. and Mrs. Joe J. Tanaka
Mr. Joe K. Tanaka
Mr. John Tanaka
Mr. John S. Tanaka
Ms. June H. Tanaka
Mr. Junji Tanaka
Mr. Kameo Tanaka
Ms. Kathleen K. Tanaka
Kathryn Tanaka and Michael Balogh
Ms. Kathryn F. Tanaka
Mrs. Kazuko Tanaka
Mr. and Mrs. Kazumi Tanaka
Mr. Keith Tanaka
Mr. and Mrs. Ken Tanaka
Ms. Kimi Tanaka
Mr. King K. Tanaka
Kiyo and June Tanaka
Ms. Kiyoko Tanaka
Ms. Komatsu Tanaka
Ms. Koto Tanaka
Ms. Kumiko Tanaka
Ms. Leila C. Tanaka
Ms. Lily Tanaka
Ms. Lorraine N. Tanaka
Mr. Louis M. Tanaka
Ms. Lynette Tanaka
Ms. Marilyn Tanaka
Ms. Marna A. Tanaka
Ms. Mary H. Tanaka
Ms. Mary Y. Tanaka
Ms. Mary Ann Tanaka
Mrs. Masako Tanaka
Masami Tanaka
Mr. and Mrs. Masao K. Tanaka
Mr. Masato Tanaka
Mr. and Mrs. Masato M. Tanaka
Ms. Masuyo Tanaka
Mr. Maurice Tanaka
Ms. May H. Tanaka
Ms. Mikiko Tanaka
Ms. Misao S. Tanaka

Mitsuyo and Val Tanaka
Ms. Mitzi H. Tanaka
Ms. Miyuki Tanaka
Ms. Momoye Tanaka
Ms. Mona Tanaka
Ms. Nancy Tanaka
Mrs. Nancy A. Tanaka
Ms. Nancy F. Tanaka
Mr. and Mrs. Noboru Tanaka
Mr. and Mrs. Nobuichi Tanaka
Mr. and Mrs. Norio Tanaka
Mr. Norman Tanaka
The Norman Katsuo Tanaka Family
Ms. Olive Sueko Tanaka
Mr. and Mrs. Pat Tanaka
Mr. Patrick Y. Tanaka
Mr. Paul Tanaka
Mr. Paul S. Tanaka
Mrs. Peg Tanaka
Mr. and Mrs. Peter Tanaka
Mr. and Mrs. Ralph Tanaka
Mr. Randall R. Tanaka
Mr. and Mrs. Ray Tanaka
Mr. and Mrs. Ray S. Tanaka
Mr. and Mrs. Raymond H. Tanaka
Mr. and Mrs. Richard T. Tanaka
Mr. Robert Tanaka
Mr. and Mrs. Robert Tanaka
Mr. and Mrs. Robert K. Tanaka
Mr. Robert T. Tanaka
Mr. and Mrs. Rodney G. Tanaka
Mr. Ronald A. Tanaka
Ms. Rose Tanaka
Mr. and Mrs. Roy E. Tanaka
Mr. and Mrs. Roy S. Tanaka
Mr. and Mrs. Roy T. Tanaka
Mr. Russell Tanaka
Mr. and Mrs. Russell I. Tanaka
Ms. Sadako Tanaka
Ms. Sadami Tanaka
Mr. and Mrs. Sam Tanaka
Mr. Sam M. Tanaka
Mr. and Mrs. Satoru M. Tanaka
Mr. Scott K. Tanaka
Mr. Shigeo Tanaka
Mr. and Mrs. Shigeo Tanaka
Ms. Shinayo Tanaka
Mr. Shinya Tanaka
Mrs. Shizuko Tanaka
Mr. and Mrs. Shizuo Tanaka
Mr. and Mrs. Shoji Tanaka
Mr. and Mrs. Stanley Tanaka
Ms. Sumiye Tanaka
Ms. Susan Tanaka
Mr. Tadashi Tanaka
Mr. Tadayuki Tanaka
Mr. and Mrs. Takayuki Tanaka
Takuji and Yachiyo J.S. Tanaka
Ms. Tami R. Tanaka
Mr. and Mrs. Tatsuo Tanaka
Ted and Darlene Tanaka
Mr. and Mrs. Ted K. Tanaka
Mr. Tek Tanaka
Mrs. Thomas Tanaka
Mr. Thomas T. Tanaka
Mr. Tomio Tanaka
Mr. Tommy H. Tanaka
Mrs. Toshiko Tanaka
Mr. Tsuyuo Tanaka
Mr. and Mrs. Tyler Tanaka
Mr. and Mrs. Val Tanaka
Mr. Wallace W. Tanaka
Mr. Wayne Tanaka
Mr. Wayne H. Tanaka
Col. and Mrs. Wayne K. Tanaka
Mr. Wesley Tanaka
Wibur and Grace Tanaka
Mr. William A. Tanaka
Mr. William H. Tanaka
Mr. and Mrs. William S. Tanaka
Mr. and Mrs. Winfred Tanaka
Mr. Winston T. Tanaka
Mrs. Y.M. Jane Tanaka
Mrs. Yasuko Tanaka
Yosh and Laura Tanaka
Mr. Yoshiaki Tanaka
Mr. and Mrs. Yoshinori Tanaka
Mr. Yuichiro Tanaka
Mr. Yukio T. Tanaka
Ms. Yumika Tanaka
Ms. Linda H. Tanaka-Esparrago
Mrs. Gladys Y. Tanamachi
Mr. James C. Tanamachi
Mrs. Kikuko Tanamachi
Ms. Yuriko Tanamachi
Ms. Lea Tanasale

Mrs. Ruth N. Tanbara
Ms. Sabrina Tanbara
Mr. and Mrs. Sharyl Tanck
Mr. and Mrs. Henry Tanda
Mr. and Mrs. Wayne Tanda
Mrs. Francine Tando
Mrs. Setsue Tando
Ms. Nobuhiko Tane
Mr. Takashi Tanezaki
Ms. Katsuko H. Tang
Mr. and Mrs. Calvin K. Tange
Mr. Cecil Tange
Mr. and Mrs. Kiichi Tange
Ms. Genevieve Tango
Mr. Benjamin Tani
Mr. and Mrs. Calvin Tani
Mr. Carl Tani
Ms. Carolyn S. Tani
Mr. Dennis M. Tani
Mr. Fred Tani
Dr. and Mrs. George Tani
Mr. Gordon K. Tani
Mrs. Kiyo Tani
Mr. Marion S. Tani
Ms. Midori Tani
Ms. Nancy L. Tani
Mr. Paul Tani
Mrs. Rose S. Tani
Mrs. Roxanne L. Tani
Mr. Shigemi Tani
Dr. T. Miriam Tani
Ms. Yoshi Tani
Mr. and Mrs. Yukio Tani
Mr. and Mrs. Barney Tanida
Ms. Jennifer Tanida
Mr. Clifford N. Tanigawa
Mrs. Edna Tanigawa
Ms. Katsumi Tanigawa
Ms. Nancy Tanigawa
Ms. Ayami Taniguchi
Mr. and Mrs. Baker Taniguchi
Mr. Brian Taniguchi
Mr. Eisei Taniguchi
Ms. Elsie Taniguchi
Mr. Emiko Taniguchi
Mr. Fred Taniguchi
Ms. Fusako M. Taniguchi
Mr. and Mrs. George Taniguchi
Mr. and Mrs. Harry Taniguchi
Mrs. Harumi Taniguchi
Ms. Ikuko Taniguchi
Dr. and Mrs. Izumi Taniguchi
Mr. Jerry Taniguchi
Mr. Jim Taniguchi
Mr. and Mrs. Jim Taniguchi
Mrs. Kinuko K. Taniguchi
Mr. Larry T. Taniguchi
Ms. Mari Taniguchi
Ms. Marie Taniguchi
Mr. Masami Taniguchi
Mr. Masayuki Taniguchi
Ms. Merrily Taniguchi
Ms. Nellie Taniguchi
Mr. Noboru Taniguchi
Ms. Pat Mari Taniguchi
Mr. Reagan Taniguchi
Mr. and Mrs. Robert I. Taniguchi
Mr. and Mrs. Shigeru Taniguchi
Mr. Shigiki Taniguchi
Taeko Taniguchi
Ms. Teri T. Taniguchi
Mr. and Mrs. Tetsuo Taniguchi
Mr. and Mrs. Tokuso Taniguchi
Mr. and Mrs. Yoshio Taniguchi
Mrs. Yuriko Taniguchi
Mr. and Mrs. Eddie Tanijiri
Mr. Wesley Tanijiri
Mr. Charles S. Tanikawa
Mr. Craig Tanikawa
Mr. Harry Tanikawa
Ms. Ruby S. Tanikawa
Mr. and Mrs. T. George Tanimasa
Ms. Alice F. Tanimoto
Ms. Beatrice Tanimoto
Mr. Craig Tanimoto
Mr. Dick Tanimoto
Ms. Doris Y. Tanimoto
Mr. Edward Tanimoto
Eri Tanimoto and Frank J. Del Barto
Mr. and Mrs. Itaru Tanimoto
Mr. and Mrs. James I. Tanimoto
Mr. Lawrence J. Tanimoto
Ms. Lorraine A. Tanimoto
Mr. Rockee Tanimoto
Ms. Sharon K. Tanimoto
Mr. and Mrs. Shikuo Tanimoto

Mr. Ted S. Tanimoto
Ms. Teruko T. Tanimoto
Mr. and Mrs. Albert T. Tanimura
Mr. and Mrs. Charles Tanimura
Mr. and Mrs. George M. Tanimura
Mr. Harold Tanimura
Mr. and Mrs. Masakazu Tanimura
Ms. May H. Tanimura
Mr. Robert Tanino
Mr. and Mrs. Ryomi Tanino
Mr. and Mrs. James Tanioka
Mr. and Mrs. Sakae Tanioka
Mr. and Mrs. Masato Tanisaki
Mr. and Mrs. Seichi Tanisawa
Mr. and Mrs. Ted Tanisawa
Dr. Daniel S. Tanita
Ms. Haruko Tanita
Mr. and Mrs. Stome Tanita
Ms. Gladys S. Taniwaki
Mr. Michio X. Taniwaki
Mr. and Mrs. David S. Tanizaki
Mr. and Mrs. Gary Tanizaki
Ms. Kimiye Tanizaki
Mr. and Mrs. Kaz Tanizawa
Mr. and Mrs. Milton T. Tanizawa
Mr. and Mrs. Richard Tanizawa
Mr. and Mrs. Samson Tanizawa
Mr. and Mrs. Dave Tanji
Ms. Flora M. Tanji
Mr. Frances Tanji
Mr. Gilbert T. Tanji
Ms. Joyce Tanji
Ms. Mary Tanji
Mr. and Mrs. Satoru Tanji
Mr. Shinami Tanji
Ms. Thelma T. Tanji
Mr. Walter Tanji
Mrs. William T. Tanji
Mr. George M. Tanna
Mr. and Mrs. Robert Y. Tanna
Mr. Masayoshi Tanno
Mr. Noboru Tanoue
Mr. Thomas T. Tanoura
Mr. and Mrs. Chic Tanouye
Mr. Harold Tanouye
Mr. and Mrs. James Tanouye
Mr. Jim T. Tanouye
Mr. John Tanouye
Mr. and Mrs. Nicholas Tanouye
Mr. Raymond H. Tanouye
Mr. Tokinori Tanouye
Mr. and Mrs. Tom Tanouye
Mrs. Toshi Tanouye
Ms. Tomoko Ikuma Tao
George and Jane Taoka
TAP Business Services, LLC
Ms. Janice L. Tarumoto
Ms. Mayko Tarumoto
Mr. Derrick Tasaka
Mr. Gene M. Tasaka
Ms. Grace Tasaka
Mr. and Mrs. Masaichi Tasaka
Mr. and Mrs. Wallace I. Tasaka
Ms. Carole Hiroshige-Tasaki
Mrs. Elaine M. Tasato
Mr. Armen Tashdinian
Mr. Alan Tashima
Ms. Alice Tashima
Mr. and Mrs. Eugene Tashima
Mr. Hiro Tashima
Mr. and Mrs. Irland L. Tashima
Mr. Mamoru Tashima
Ms. Midori Tashima
Ms. Mikiye Tashima
R. Tashima
Mrs. Yoshiko R. Tashima
Ms. Ethel Tashiro
Ms. Fujiyo Tashiro
Mr. and Mrs. Fukuo Tashiro
Gladys Y. and Ora A. Tashiro
Mr. and Mrs. Herbert R. Tashiro
Ms. Hisako Tashiro
Mr. and Mrs. Jack Tashiro
Ms. Jean Tashiro
Mr. and Mrs. John Tashiro
Mr. and Mrs. Joseph Tashiro
Mr. Kenji Tashiro
Mr. and Mrs. Kenneth A. Tashiro
Ms. Mimi Tashiro
Mr. and Mrs. Robert Tashiro
Mr. Shigeru Tashiro
Ms. Susan Tashiro
Mr. and Mrs. Yeiki Tashiro
Yoshihiko Tatami
Ms. Akiko Tateishi
Mr. and Mrs. Craig T. Tateishi

Mr. Hiroshi Tateishi
Mr. and Mrs. John Tateishi
Mr. and Mrs. Kiyoshi Tateishi
Mr. and Mrs. Masanori Tateishi
Mr. Richard Tateishi
Mr. and Mrs. Stanley Tateishi
Mr. Tom Tateishi
Mrs. Yuri Tateishi
Mr. David L. Tateya
Mr. Noboru K. Tateyama
Mr. and Mrs. Ted Tateyama
Barbara and Isamu Tatsuguchi
Mr. Reid G. Tatsuguchi
Ms. Sumi Tatsui
Mr. Tadashi Tatsui
Ms. Susan Tatsui-D'Arcy
Mrs. Cindy Tatsumi
Mr. and Mrs. Harry Tatsumi
Mr. and Mrs. Jack M. Tatsumi
Mr. Kaoru Tatsumi
Mr. and Mrs. Kaz Tatsumi
Mrs. Kazumi Tatsumi
Mr. Masato Tatsumi
Ms. Ryoko Tatsumi
Mr. Beau A.H. Tatsumura
Mr. and Mrs. Albert K. Tatsuno
Ms. Carol M. Tatsuno
Mr. and Mrs. Kenzo Tatsuno
Mr. and Mrs. Minoru Tatsuno
Mr. and Mrs. Walter N. Tatsuno
Ms. Irene T. Tatsuta
Mr. Owen Tatsuta
Ms. Kiyoko T. Taubkin
Mr. Hiroshi J. Tauchi
Ms. Jane Taura
Mr. Joe Taura
Mr. and Mrs. Masayasu Taura
Mrs. Mitzi M. Tawa
Mr. and Mrs. Bruce Tawara
Mr. and Mrs. Daryl Tawara
Ms. Karen S. Tawara
Ms. Mary Tawara
Mrs. Betty Y. Tawata
Mrs. Ellen Tay-Sakaye
Mr. Ty H. Tayama
Mr. and Mrs. Mitsugi Tayasu
Mr. and Mrs. Roger Tayasu
Ms. Lydia Taylor
Mr. and Mrs. Thurman M. Taylor
Mr. Wesley Taylor
Mr. and Mrs. Donald Taynton
Ms. Gail Tazawa
Mr. and Mrs. Harry Tazawa
Ms. Mary Tazawa
Mr. Edwin J. Tazoi
Ms. Norma Shimada Tazoi
Mr. and Mrs. Yukio Tazuma
Ms. Frances Tazumi
Mrs. Hisano Tazumi
Mr. Masashi Tazumi
Mrs. Naomi Tazumi
Mr. and Mrs. Tatsuo Tazumi
Mr. Marsh Tekawa
Ms. Peggy K.S. Teng
Mrs. Diane K. Tengan
Ms. Doris S. Tengan
Ms. Lillian Y. Tengan
Mr. Richard Tengan
Ms. Sadako Tengan
Mrs. Pearl Y. Tenma
Debbie Tenma-Perry Family
Mr. and Mrs. Francis B. Tenny
Ms. Alison G. Tennyson
Dr. Jonathan Tepper
Ms. Ailyn Terada
Mr. and Mrs. Albert Terada
Ms. Dianne Terada
Mr. Eric Terada
George and Yuko Terada
Mr. and Mrs. Henry Terada
Mr. Kazuji Terada
Mr. Keiju Terada
Mr. and Mrs. Masamitsu Terada
Mr. and Mrs. Roy Terada
Mrs. Shirley K. Terada
Ms. Sonoe Terada
Mr. Kenneth T. Teragawachi
Mr. and Mrs. Roy Teragouchi
Mr. James Terai
Ms. Barbara A. Teraji
Mr. and Mrs. Henry Teraji
Dr. and Mrs. James Teraji
Mr. Stephen Terakami
Mr. Alan K. Terakawa
Ms. Kiyoko Teramaye
Mr. and Mrs. Kenso Teramoto

Mr. Raymond Teramoto
Ms. Sumiko Teramoto and
Mr. and Mrs. George Rokutani
Ms. Aya Teramura
Mr. and Mrs. Kay Teramura
Mr. Steve Teranishi
Mr. Donald Terao
Ms. Ruth Kitayama Terao
Denise L. Teraoka, Hisashi and Keijiro Imura
Mr. and Mrs. George Teraoka
Mr. and Mrs. Henry Teraoka
Mrs. Jane K. Teraoka
Ms. Janice Teraoka
Mr. Masao Teraoka
Mr. Moriso Teraoka
Mr. Muneo K. Teraoka
Mr. and Mrs. Sakae Teraoka
Mr. and Mrs. David Teraoku
Mr. Carey Terasaki
Ms. Melanie Terasaki
Mr. Richard Terasaki
Mr. Sam Terasaki
Dr. Shigeo Terasaki
Mr. and Mrs. Shozoro Terasaki
Ms. Tomiye Terasaki
Dr. Robert Terashima
Mr. and Mrs. Toshio Terashita
Mrs. Mildred Terauchi
Sye S. Terauchi
Ms. Kunimi Terawaki
Mr. Dennis Terazawa
Ms. Fusaye Terazawa
Mr. and Mrs. Yoshio Terazawa
Mr. Anthony Terrulli
Ms. Sylvia Terry
Ms. Sandra T. Terui
Ms. Mary M. Terusaki
Mr. Edwin T. Teruya
Mrs. Judith S. Teruya
Mr. and Mrs. Ken Teruya
Mr. Kenneth H. Teruya
Mr. Masaru Teruya
Mr. and Mrs. Minoru Teruya
Ms. Nancy N. Teruya
Mr. Peter Teruya
Mr. Ralph Teruya
Mr. Stanley Teruya
Mr. Tommy Teruya
Mr. and Mrs. Wallace Teruya
Mr. and Mrs. Yoshio Teruya
Mr. Allen Teshima
Mr. Glen Teshima
Mr. and Mrs. Hubert S. Teshima
Mr. and Mrs. Ronald Teshima
Mr. and Mrs. Hiroshi Teshirogi
Ms. Bertha Theofane
Dr. and Mrs. Andrew J. Thibodeaux
Ms. Cindy Yamada Thomas
Mr. and Mrs. Ralph Thomas
Mr. and Mrs. Warren Thomas
Mr. Wayne H. Thomas, Jr.
Ms. Yayoi Thomas
Mr. Fred Thompson
Mr. and Mrs. Jeffrey W. Thompson
Mr. William Y. Thompson
Mr. and Mrs. Ivan Thoms
Mr. C. H. Thornburg
Ms. Cecelia M. Thornburg
Mr. and Mrs. Robert Y. Thornton
Ms. Julie Thukral
Mr. Guy W. Thurber
Mr. Stanley M. Thurman
Ms. Betty J. Ticho
Mr. Arthur E. Tiedemann
Tiger Management L.L.C.
Ms. Sandra P. Timmer
Mr. and Mrs. James B. Tingstrom
Mr. John Tinpe
Mr. Akiko Toba
Mr. Garry Toba
Mr. Goro Toba
Mr. Ichiro Toba
Dr. and Mrs. Richard E. Tobin
Mr. and Mrs. Henry Tobo
Mr. and Mrs. Richard Tocci
Mr. Allen Y. Tochihara
Mr. and Mrs. Richard Tochihara
Mr. Glenn R. Tochioka
Mr. and Mrs. Mikio M. Tochioka
Ms. Akira Toda
Mr. and Mrs. George Toda
Mr. Harry Toda
Mr. and Mrs. James Toda
Mr. Joesuke Toda
Mr. Katashi K. Toda
Messers. Kumao and Josuke Toda

Mr. Lloyd Toda
Mr. and Mrs. Seichi Toda
Mr. Takashi Toda
Ms. Yoko Toda
Mr. Robert H. Todani
Ann Yurie Todd
Mr. and Mrs. Jiro Todo
Dr. and Mrs. Mamoru Tofukuji
Ms. Evelyn Togami
Mr. and Mrs. George Togami
Henry and Chiyeko Togami
Mr. Paul Togami
Mr. Gordon Togasaki
Mr. and Mrs. Satoru Togashi
Mr. and Mrs. Satoru Togashi
Mr. Theodore Togashi
Mr. and Mrs. Fred Togawa
Mr. and Mrs. Johnnie Togioka
Ms. Mitsuko Togioka
Mr. and Mrs. Noboru Togioka
Alvin and Bonnie Togo
Ms. Satomi Togo
Mr. Adam Toguchi
Ms. Alice Toguchi
Ms. Betty Toguchi
Mr. and Mrs. Edward Toguchi
Mrs. Elizabeth Toguchi
Mr. Kiyoshi Toguchi
Ms. Naomi K. Toguchi
Mr. Richard M. Toguchi
Mr. and Mrs. Roy Toguchi
Mrs. and Ms. Miyeko Toguri
Mr. Alvin J. Tohara
Ms. Joanne Kiyoko Tohei
Tohokujin Shinwakai
Ms. Ikuko K. Toizumi
Toji Family
Mr. Michio Tojima
Mr. David P. Tojo
Mr. Frances Tojo
Mr. Tadashi Tojo
Mr. Janet I. Tokashiki
Ms. Tsuyako Tokashiki
Mr. and Mrs. Ed Tokeshi
Mr. and Mrs. Joseph Tokeshi
Mr. and Mrs. Philip Tokeshi
Mr. and Mrs. Robert Tokeshi
Mr. Roberto Tokeshi
Mr. Thomas Tokeshi
Mr. and Mrs. Akira Toki
Mr. and Mrs. Masaji Toki
Mr. and Mrs. Masato Toki
Ms. Debbie Tokimoto
Mr. and Mrs. Brent Tokita
Ms. Eileen Tokita
Mr. and Mrs. Joseph Tokita
Mr. and Mrs. Shokichi Tokita
Mr. and Mrs. Turk Tokita
Ms. Cheryl Tokiwa
Mr. and Mrs. Duke T. Tokiwa
Ms. Mary S. Tokiwa
Mr. and Mrs. Ken Tokiyama
Mr. and Mrs. Mas Tokiyama
Mr. and Mrs. Allan R. Tokuda
Mr. and Mrs. Craig Tokuda
Mr. Lee I. Tokuda
Mr. Robert Tokuda
Mr. Tadd T. Tokuda
Ms. Tama Tokuda
Mr. and Mrs. Yukio Tokuda
Ms. Toshiko Tokudomi
Ms. Vivian Tokuhama
Ms. Mary Nakamura Tokuhisa
Mr. Toru Tokuhisa
Aidrain Tokuhoshi
Maj. William Tokumoto
Mr. Harry Tokumura
Mrs. Aileen Tokunaga
Mr. and Mrs. Alan Tokunaga
Ms. Carolyn Tokunaga
Mr. and Mrs. Clark Tokunaga
Mr. and Mrs. Frank Tokunaga
Mr. Henry Tokunaga
Mrs. Iku Tokunaga
Mr. Keisuke Tokunaga
Ms. Lillian Tokunaga
Ms. Lorna Tokunaga
Mr. and Mrs. Michael Tokunaga
Mr. Mitsuo Tokunaga
Ms. Mitsuye Nomura Tokunaga
Ms. Molly Tokunaga
Mr. Nelson Tokunaga
Mr. and Mrs. Robert Tokunaga
Mr. and Mrs. Roger Tokunaga
Mr. and Mrs. Sueo Tokunaga
Mr. and Mrs. Toshio Tokunaga

Mr. Wayne T. Tokunaga
Mr. Anthony Tokuno
Mrs. Mary Tokuno
Mr. Tom Tokunow
Mr. Paul Tokusato
Mr. Bert T. Tokushige and Ms. Jane H. Okabe
Mr. and Mrs. H. V. Tokushige
Koichi Tokushige
Mr. E. Ken Tokutomi
Lt. and Mrs. Greg Tokuyama
Mr. and Mrs. Samuel Tokuyama
Mr. and Mrs. Arthur Tom
Baldwin and Madeline Nobori Tom
Mr. and Mrs. Michael Tom
LTC. and Mrs. Richard Tom
Ms. Shirley Tom
Mr. Bill M. Toma
Mr. Gilbert T. Toma
Ms. Haruko Toma
Mrs. Helen Toma
Mr. Herman T. Toma and Mrs. Penny Garrett-Toma
Mr. and Mrs. Masayuki Toma
Mr. and Mrs. Ronald Toma
Mr. and Mrs. Roy Toma
Mr. and Mrs. Seiko Toma
Dr. Takeyuki Toma
Mr. Walter K. Toma
Mrs. Setsuko Tomasu
Ms. Jean Tomatani
Mr. and Mrs. Takeshige Tomatani
Mr. Harold Tome
Ms. Maryann Tomecek
Mr. and Mrs. Doson Tomei
Mr. and Mrs. Ralph Tomei
Mr. Koji Tomikawa
Mr. and Mrs. Edward Tomikoshi
Ms. Amy E. Tominaga
Mr. and Mrs. Francis Tominaga
Mr. George M. Tominaga
Mr. George T. Tominaga
Grant and Alison Tominaga
Mr. and Mrs. Henry Tominaga
Mr. and Mrs. James Tominaga
Mr. Jim Tominaga
Ms. Nancy Y. Tominaga
Mr. and Mrs. Norio Tominaga
Mr. and Mrs. Robert Tominaga
Mr. and Mrs. Roy Tominaga
Mr. Yasuhiko Tominaga
Mr. and Mrs. Susumu Tomine
Mr. George T. Tomio
Mr. Takashi Tomioka
Mr. and Mrs. Art Tomita
Mr. and Mrs. Arthur K. Tomita
Mrs. Cynthia Mitsuyo Tomita
Ms. Dianne Tomita
Mr. and Mrs. Frank Tomita
Mr. and Mrs. George S. Tomita
Mr. Haruto Tomita
Mr. and Mrs. Hisao Tomita
Mr. and Mrs. James Tomita
Mr. John Tomita
Mr. Jun Tomita
Mr. and Mrs. Kazuo Tomita
Mr. and Mrs. Kenji Tomita
Ms. Kikue H. Tomita
Mr. and Mrs. Lewis Tomita
Mr. Louie Tomita
Mr. Mas Tomita
Ms. Masako Tomita
Mr. and Mrs. Masao Tomita
Mr. Michael Tomita
Ms. Midori Tomita and Eiko Koga
Dr. and Mrs. Mitsuo Tomita
Mr. Nagao Tomita
Mr. Nob Tomita
Mr. Ronald Tomita
Mr. and Mrs. Roy Tomita
Mr. and Mrs. Stanley Tomita
Mr. Taylor Tomita
Miss Tomiko Tomita
Mr. Ty Tomita
Mr. and Mrs. Walter Tomita
Mr. and Mrs. I. T. Tomiyama
Mr. Michael Tomizawa
Tomo No Kai
Mr. Stanley Tomono
Fred and Ayako H. Tomooka
Mr. and Mrs. James Tomooka
Lt. Col. Kazuto Tomoyasu
Mr. and Mrs. Mervin Tomoyasu
Mr. and Mrs. George Tomura
Ms. Mary Tonai
Mr. and Mrs. Yutaka Tonai
Mr. Francis Tonaki
Mrs. Betsy S. Tonda

Mr. and Mrs. Richard Tonda
Mr. and Mrs. Joe Tondo
Ms. Doris U. Tono
Mr. and Mrs. Masayoshi Tonokawa
Mr. Michio Tonokawa
Mrs. Alyson Tonomura
Mr. and Mrs. Keith Tonooka
Mr. Sunao Torakawa
Ms. Debora A. Toran
Dr. Ted Toribara
Mr. Harry Torigoe
Mr. Charles Torii
Mr. Charles S. Torii
Mr. and Mrs. Mike Torii
Mr. Ronald G. Torii
Mrs. Jane M. Torikai
Ms. Renee Toriumi
Mrs. Sophie Toriumi
Mr. and Mrs. William Toriumi
Ms. May Torizawa
Nicholas Torno and Joyce Horikawa
Ms. June D. Tosaya
Ms. Mabel K. Tosaya
Mrs. Miyeko Toshima
Ms. Suzuko Toshimitsu
Mr. John Y. Toshiyuki
Mr. Richard G. Towata
Ms. Marlania Town
Mr. Kazuo M. Townsend
Col. C. Stuart Townshend
Ms. Helen L. Toy
Mr. and Mrs. Wes Toy
Mr. and Mrs. Fumio Toya
Greg Toya and Jill Yoshikawa
Mr. Toshi D. Toya
Mrs. Amy M. Toyama
Mr. Daniel M. Toyama
Mr. and Mrs. David K. Toyama
Mr. and Mrs. Frederick Toyama
Mr. George Toyama
Mr. and Mrs. Henry Toyama
Mr. and Mrs. Henry I. Toyama
Mr. and Mrs. Hiro Toyama
Mr. and Mrs. Kenneth Toyama
Mr. Kenny Toyama
Mr. and Mrs. Kime Toyama
Mrs. Leo Toyama
Ms. Nikki Toyama
Mr. and Mrs. Peter Toyama
Mr. Ralph Toyama
Mr. and Mrs. Roy Toyama
Mrs. Ruth Toyama
Mr. and Mrs. Stan Toyama
Mr. Timothy M. Toyama
Mr. Fred Toye
Mr. and Mrs. Bob Toyoda
Ms. Kathleen L. Toyoda
Mr. and Mrs. Susumu Toyoda
Ms. Maria Toyofuku
Ms. Sachiko Toyofuku
Mr. and Mrs. Hiroshi Toyohara
Mr. Ketch Toyohara
Mr. and Mrs. Harry H. Toyomura
Mr. and Mrs. Calvin T. Toyooka
Mr. and Mrs. Jim Toyooka
Mr. Ronald Toyooka
Mr. Shizuo P. Toyoshima
Mr. and Mrs. Yoshi Toyota
Mr. and Mrs. Yoshito Toyota
Mr. and Mrs. Mike Toyota
Ms. Sharon Trader
Ms. Nobue K. Trafton
Mr. and Mrs. Donald Travis
Mr. and Mrs. Dan Treadwell
Mr. and Mrs. Loris M. Trice
Mr. and Mrs. Jeffery Trinca
Mr. Werner Franklin Trost
Mr. Henry Trowbridge
Mr. Lee Trucker
Mr. and Mrs. Raphael T. Tshibangu
Mr. and Mrs. John Tsu
Mr. Yachiyo Tsubaki
Mr. Shigeru Tsubakitani
Mr. and Mrs. Hiroshi Tsubakiya
Mr. Senryu Tsubame
Ms. Frances Tsubata
Mr. Anthoni Tsuboi
Mr. and Mrs. Ben Tsuboi
Ms. Dahni K. Tsuboi
Mr. and Mrs. Dennis Tsuboi
Mr. Don Tsuboi
Mr. Frank Louis Tsuboi
Mr. and Mrs. Hal Tsuboi
Mrs. Haruko Tsuboi
Mr. Henry Y. Tsuboi
Ms. Hiroko Tsuboi

Mr. Ken Tsuboi
Ms. Norma Tsuboi
Mr. Ossie Tsuboi
Mr. and Mrs. Tom Tsuboi
Ms. Yoshiye S. Tsuboi
Ms. Amy Tsubokawa
Ms. Sadako Tsubokawa
Mr. Bill Tsubota
Mr. and Mrs. Robert Tsubota
Mr. and Mrs. Shigeru Tsubota
Mr. and Mrs. Thomas K. Tsubota
Mr. and Mrs. Ernest Tsuchida
Mr. George Tsuchida
Mr. Jack Y. Tsuchida
Mr. John N. Tsuchida
Mr. and Mrs. Katsumi Tsuchida
Mr. Kiwamu Tsuchida
Mr. Sam Tsuchida
Mr. Satoshi Tsuchida
Mr. Steve Tsuchida
Mr. and Mrs. Tak Tsuchida
Mr. and Mrs. Robert Tsuchidana
Ms. Elizabeth Tsuchihashi
Mr. Kiyoshi Tsuchii
Mr. and Mrs. Osamu Tsuchikawa
Mr. Minoru Tsuchimochi
Mr. and Mrs. Donn S. Tsuchimoto
Chiyeko Tsuchitani
Mr. Brian Tsuchiya
D. Tsuchiya
Mr. Dennis H. Tsuchiya
Mrs. Helen Tsuchiya
Mr. and Mrs. Henry Tsuchiya
Mr. and Mrs. Herbert M. Tsuchiya
Ms. Jean H. Tsuchiya
Ms. Mary M. Tsuchiya
Ms. Mieko Tsuchiya
Mr. and Mrs. Robert Tsuchiya
Mrs. Setsu Tsuchiya
Mr. Takenori Tsuchiya
Mr. and Mrs. Todd Tsuchiya
Mr. and Mrs. Jimmie Tsuchiyama
Mr. Minoru Tsuchiyama
Mr. Ronald Tsuchiyama
Mr. and Mrs. Thomas Tsuchiyama
Mr. Yasuo Tsuchiyama
Mr. Tadao J. Tsuchiyose
Ms. Dani Tsuda
Mrs. Ethel Tsuda
Mr. Hal Tsuda
Mr. and Mrs. Hideya Tsuda
Ms. Kiyoko Tsuda
Mrs. Lila N. Tsuda
Ms. Mariko Tsuda
Mr. Neil A. Tsuda
Mr. and Mrs. Ralph S. Tsuda
Mr. and Mrs. Rikio Tsuda
Mr. Robert C. Tsuda
Mr. and Mrs. Takao Tsuda
Mr. and Mrs. Tom Tsuda
Mr. and Mrs. Yoshio Tsuda
Ms. Susie Tsudama
Mr. and Mrs. Ted Tsue
Mr. and Mrs. Satoru Tsufura
Mr. and Mrs. Tadashi Tsufura
Mr. and Mrs. Blaine Tsugawa
Mr. and Mrs. Ernest K. Tsugawa
Dr. and Mrs. James Tsugawa
Ms. Janis L. Tsugawa
Ms. Karen E. Tsugawa
Mr. Lloyd Y. Tsugawa
Mr. and Mrs. Roy S. Tsugawa
Mr. Stanley M. Tsugawa
Mr. and Mrs. Terumi Tsugawa
Mr. and Mrs. Tom Tsugawa
Mr. and Mrs. Wataru Tsugawa
Mr. and Mrs. Ralph S. Tsuha
Mr. Keiji Tsuhako
Mr. and Mrs. Takashi Tsuhako
Mr. and Mrs. Charles Tsuhara
Mr. and Ms. Bill H. Tsuji
Mr. and Mrs. Bill Z. Tsuji
Ms. Chiyoko Tsuji
Ms. Dorothy Akiyama Tsuji
Ms. Dorothy Tsuji
Mr. Fred Y. Tsuji
Mr. and Mrs. Frederick Tsuji
Mr. and Mrs. George Tsuji
Mr. Isami Tsuji
Isamu Tsuji and Ann Miyahira
Mr. Isao Tsuji
Mr. Kazuo Tsuji
Mr. and Mrs. Kenryu Tsuji
Mr. and Mrs. Kiyoshi Tsuji
Mr. Koichi Tsuji
Dr. Michael Tsuji

Mr. and Mrs. Miles Tsuji
Mr. and Mrs. Seiyo Tsuji
Mrs. Sumiye Tsuji
Mr. Takeo Tsuji
Mr. and Mrs. Mitsuo Tsujihara
Mr. and Mrs. Frank Tsujii
Mr. and Mrs. Ernest Tsujimoto
Mr. and Mrs. Eugene Tsujimoto
Mrs. Fumi Tsujimoto
Ms. Judy M. Tsujimoto
Ms. June Tsujimoto
Ms. Karen L. Tsujimoto
Ms. Marsha Tsujimoto
Mr. and Mrs. Richard Tsujimoto
Mr. and Mrs. Richard K. Tsujimoto
Mrs. Sharon E. Tsujimoto
Mr. Ted Tsujimoto
Ms. Trude Tsujimoto
Mrs. Sumiko Tsujimura
Ms. Terry G. Tsujioka
Mr. and Mrs. Takashi Tsujita
Dr. Yoshiaki Tsukada
Mrs. Yuriko Tsukada
Ms. Alice M. Tsukahara
Mr. and Mrs. Yoshinari Tsukahara
Ms. Ruth Tsukahira
Mr. Stanley K. Tsukahira
Mr. George Tsukamaki
Mr. Joe Tsukamaki
Mr. and Mrs. Bill T. Tsukamoto
E. E. Tsukamoto
Dr. and Mrs. Gene Tsukamoto
Mr. George Tsukamoto
Mr. Isami Tsukamoto
Mr. James Tsukamoto
Ms. Judith Tsukamoto
Mr. Kent Tsukamoto
Mr. Masako Tsukamoto
Ms. Midori Tsukamoto
Mrs. Miyoko Tsukamoto
Mr. and Mrs. Percy H. Tsukamoto
Mr. Stan Tsukamoto
Mr. and Mrs. Tetsuo Tsukamoto
Mr. Walter Tsukamoto
Mr. and Mrs. Wilfred Tsukamoto
Mr. and Mrs. Will Tsukamoto
Mr. and Mrs. Yoshio Tsukamoto
John and Judy T. Tsukano
Col. (Ret.) Mas Tsukasaki
Mr. George Tsukashima
Mr. and Mrs. Albert T. Tsukayama
Mr. Dean T. Tsukayama
Mr. John E. Tsukayama
Mr. John K. Tsukayama
Mr. Neil W. Tsukayama
Mr. Takeshi Tsukayama
Ms. Helen A. Tsukida
Mr. and Mrs. Jim Tsukida
Ms. Chiyeko Tsukiji
Mr. and Mrs. Howard Tsukiji
Mr. and Mrs. John S. Tsukiji
Mr. Akira Tsukimoto
Ms. Mary Tsukimura
Ms. Natsuyo Tsukimura
Mr. and Mrs. Robert Tsukui
Mr. Richard Tsukushi
Mr. Toby Tsuma
Mr. Eimo Tsumori
Mr. and Mrs. Mitsuo Tsumori
Mr. Eddy Tsumura
Mr. and Mrs. Masashi Tsumura
Mr. and Mrs. Paul Tsumura
Mr. Ronald Tsumura and Elaine T. Chiao
Mr. and Mrs. Ted Tsumura
Mr. and Mrs. Don C. Tsunawaki
Mr. Hidenori Tsunehisa
Ms. Alice E. Tsunekawa
Mr. and Mrs. Toshio Tsunekawa
Mr. Travis Tsunemori
Mr. Harry M. Tsuneta
Ms. Miki Tsuneyoshi
Mr. and Mrs. Motoo Tsuneyoshi
Mr. Yoshinori Tsuno
Mr. Gary H. Tsunoda
Mr. James Tsunoda
Mr. Kenneth Tsunoda
Mr. Lawrence Tsunoda
Mr. and Mrs. Tom Tsunoda
Thelma Tsunokai and Minoru Okumura
Mr. and Mrs. Donald Tsuru
Ms. Nancy Tsuru
Mr. Rick Tsuru
Mr. Takashi Tsuru
Mr. and Mrs. Alan Tsuruda
Mr. and Mrs. Dave Tsuruda
Mr. and Mrs. Ronald Tsuruda

Mr. Shigeto Tsuruda
Mr. and Mrs. Yo Tsuruda
Mr. and Mrs. Jimmie Tsurudome
Mr. and Mrs. Fred T. Tsurui
Mr. Hiroshi Tsurui
Mrs. Joy Tsurui
Mr. and Mrs. William Tsuruma
Dr. Toshi Tsurumaki
Mr. Ronald S. Tsurumoto
Mr. George Tsuruoka
Mr. and Mrs. Chikaji Tsurusaki
Ms. Jeri Tsurusaki
Mr. Koji Tsurusaki
Mr. Hiro Tsuruta
Mr. Willie Tsusaki
Mr. and Mrs. George Tsushima
Mr. and Mrs. Harry Tsushima
Mr. Mark S. Tsushima
Mrs. Ayame Tsutakawa
Mr. and Mrs. Edward Tsutakawa
Mr. and Mrs. Thomas S. Tsutakawa
Mr. James E. Tsutsui
Ms. Julie M. Tsutsui
Mr. and Mrs. Ken Tsutsui
Mr. and Mrs. Sam Tsutsui
Mr. and Mrs. Satoru Tsutsui
Mr. and Mrs. Takashi Tsutsui
Mr. Takashi T. Tsutsui
Ms. Thelma Tsutsui
Ms. Agnes Tsutsumi
Mr. Edward L. Tsutsumi
Mr. Hardy H. Tsutsumi
Mr. Haruo Tsutsumi
Mr. and Mrs. Masato Tsutsumi
Mr. Raymond Tsutsumi
Mr. and Mrs. Shig Tsutsumi
Ms. Toshiko Tsutsumi
Mr. and Mrs. Ben C. Tsutsumoto
Guy Y. Tsutsumoto and Katheryn Kozu
Mr. and Mrs. Isami Tsutumi
Mr. Roy Tsuya
Mr. Gary M. Tsuyuki
Mr. Lawrence R. Tsuyuki
Dr. and Mrs. Theodore Tsuyuki
Dr. and Mrs. Junji Tsuzuki
Mr. Robert Y. Tsuzuki
Mr. and Mrs. Alan K. Tu
Mr. Samson Tu
Mr. and Mrs. John Tubbs
Ms. Laura M. Tuck
Ms. Laura Tucker
Ted Tukloff and Wendy Sakazaki
Tule Lake Cemetery
Mr. and Mrs. Willis Clayton Tull, Jr.
Mr. and Mrs. Andrew T. Tun
Ms. Susan Tunkel
Mr. John J. Turley
Turlock Japanese American Club
Mr. and Mrs. Al Turner
Mr. and Mrs. Franklin Turner
Mr. and Mrs. Jack W. Turner
Ms. Joyce Turner
Ms. Kathleen Owyang Turner
Mr. and Mrs. Roy W. Turner
Twenty & Five Club
Mr. Paul Twitchell
Mr. and Mrs. Tom Tyner
Mr. Frederick S. Tyrrell, USN (retired)
Ms. Florence C. Uba
Mr. and Mrs. Hideo Uba
Ms. Laura Uba
Mr. and Mrs. Tosh Uba
Mrs. Joyce Mochizuki Ucci
Uchida Travel
Mr. and Mrs. Akira Uchida
Mr. Arthur Uchida
Mr. and Mrs. Bob Uchida
Dr. and Mrs. Bruce A. Uchida
Ms. Connie M. Uchida
Dr. Craig D. Uchida
Mr. Derek Uchida
Ms. Dorothy A. Uchida
Ms. Ellen K. Uchida
Mr. Elmer Uchida
Mr. and Mrs. Frank Uchida
Mr. and Mrs. Gary K. Uchida
Mr. and Mrs. George Uchida
Mr. Haruo Uchida
Mr. Henry S. Uchida
Mr. Hideo Uchida
Mr. Hiroshi Uchida
Mr. and Mrs. Hiroshi Uchida
Mr. Isamu Uchida
Mr. and Mrs. Jeff Uchida
Mr. and Mrs. Joe Uchida
Mr. Kenneth Y. Uchida

Ms. Kiyoko Uchida
Mr. and Mrs. Leo Uchida
Ms. Linda Uchida
Ms. Lois Uchida
Ms. Marian K. Uchida
Ms. Mary Uchida
Ms. Michiko F. Uchida
Mr. and Mrs. Min Uchida
Mr. and Mrs. Mitsuo Uchida
Mr. and Mrs. Prentiss S. Uchida
Mr. Robert Uchida
Mr. and Mrs. Ronald D. Uchida
Shizuko Uchida
Mr. and Mrs. Shunichi Uchida
Mr. Terry Uchida
Dr. Thomas K. Uchida
Mr. and Mrs. Tom Uchida
Dr. Toru Uchida
Ms. Toshiye Uchida
Mr. Toshiyuki Uchida
Mr. and Mrs. Yoshihiro Uchida
Ms. Yuka Uchida
Mrs. Alice S. Uchigakiuchi
Mr. Edward T. Uchihara
Mr. Ronn Uchihara
Mr. and Mrs. Donald S. Uchikura
Mr. and Mrs. Ansho Uchima
Mr. Clyde Uchima
Mr. Ray F. Uchima
Mr. Wayne Y. Uchima
Mrs. Mitsu Uchimoto
Mr. Gregory S. Uchimura
Capt. Kristin Uchimura
Mr. Lane Uchimura
Mr. and Mrs. Aiji Uchiyama
Ms. Alice S. Uchiyama
Mr. Don T. Uchiyama
Mrs. Dorothy Uchiyama
Mr. and Mrs. Fusao Uchiyama
Mr. Paul K. Uchiyama
Mr. and Mrs. Shiro Alfred Uchizono
Ms. Kiyomi Uda
Rev. Lowell M. Uda
Ms. Clara C. Uechi
Ms. Harue Uechi
Mr. Akio Ueda
Ms. Karen Ueda
Mr. Martha M. Ueda
Mr. and Mrs. Minoru Ueda
Steven and Tracy Ueda
Mr. Takashi Ueda
Mr. and Mrs. Tom Ueda
Mr. Yoshihisa Ueda
Mr. and Mrs Yoshio Ueda
Ms. Tammy Uedoi
Mr. and Mrs. Charles Uehara
Mr. and Mrs. Eugene Uehara
Mr. Henri Uehara
Mrs. Jane A. Uehara
Mr. and Mrs. John T. Uehara
Mrs. Kiyoko Uehara
Mr. Miyoshi Uehara
Ms. Susan H. Uehara
Mr. and Mrs. Walter D. Uehara
Uehara Accounting Service, LLC
Mr. Deni Y. Uejima and Ms. Annette R. Corio
Mr. Wilfred T. Uekawa
Mr. Blake T. Ueki and Ms. Lori K. Napier
Mr. and Mrs. Kenji Ueki
Mr. and Mrs. Masuo Ueki
Mr. and Mrs. Randy Ueki
Ms. Toshiko Ueki
Mr. and Mrs. William Ueki
Ms. Betty Ann Uematsu
Mr. and Mrs. Ray Uematsu
Mrs. Sue S. Uematsu
Ms. Karen T. Uemoto
Ms. Candice Uemura
Ms. Carole S. Uemura
Mr. and Mrs. Dean Uemura
Mr. and Mrs. Roy K. Uemura
Mr. T. Bob Uemura
Mr. and Mrs. Wataru Uemura
Mr. Gerald Uenaka
Mr. Clayton T. Ueno
Mr. and Mrs. Henry Ueno
Mr. and Mrs. Hideo Ueno
Mr. Joe Ueno
Ms. Mieko Ueno
Takemi Ueno
Ms. Tomiko Ueno
Mrs. Evelyn H. Ueoka
Mr. and Mrs. Alan T. Uesato
Mr. and Mrs. Toshi Uesato
Mr. Heiji Ueshima
Mr. and Mrs. Harry H. Ueshiro

Mr. George Uesugi
Mr. and Mrs. Isao Uesugi
Mr. William T. Uesugi
Mr. David Y. Ueunten
Mr. Mark M. Ueunten
Dr. Sensuke Ueunten
Mr. Jack S. Ugaki
Mrs. Esther M. Ujifusa
Mr. George Ujifusa
Howell and Jean Ujifusa
Mr. Robert Ujifusa
Mr. Albert Ujiie
Mr. and Mrs. Art Ujiiye
Mr. and Mrs. George I. Ujiiye
Mr. and Mrs. William Ujiiye
Mr. Kevin Ujita
Mrs. Fumiko Ukai
Mr. and Mrs. James Ukegawa
Mr. Joe Ukegawa
Ms. Colleen Ukita
Mr. and Mrs. Donald Ulander
Mr. and Mrs. Marc S. Ullman
Mr. and Mrs. Richard Ullman
Ms. Yasuko Ulm
Mr. George M. Umamoto
Mr. and Mrs. Daniel Umeda
Mr. and Mrs. Hebert Umeda
Mr. and Mrs. Isami Umeda
Mr. Joe Umeda
Mr. John Umeda
Mr. Kunio Umeda
Mr. Marc M. Umeda
Mr. and Mrs. Perry Umeda
Mr. and Mrs. Ren Umeda
Mr. Shin Umeda
Mr. Toshio T. Umeda
Mr. and Mrs. Howard T. Umehira
Mr. Russell Umeki
Mr. Tsutomu Umekubo
Mr. and Mrs. Akira Umemoto
Mr. and Mrs. David Umemoto
Mr. and Mrs. Dean Umemoto
Mr. and Mrs. Ernest M. Umemoto
Mr. Fred Umemoto
Mr. and Mrs. Gordon Umemoto
Mr. Hiro Umemoto
Mr. Hisato Umemoto
Ms. Kay Umemoto
Mrs. Ruth A. Umemoto
Ms. Shizuyo Umemoto
Mr. Teruo Umemoto
Mr. Thomas Umemoto
Mr. Toshio Umemoto
Ms. Yasuko Umemoto
Ms. Sharon H. Umene
Ms. Alice Y. Umetsu
Mr. Gary Umetsu
Mr. and Mrs. Harry Umetsu
Mr. James Umetsu
Ms. Lisa I. Umezawa
Mr. and Mrs. Yasuo Umezu
Al and Meri Umino
Mr. and Mrs. Jim M. Umino
Mr. Warren Unemori
United Methodist Women of Faith -
United Methodist Church
Ms. Gail Unno
Mr. Garrett Unno
Mr. James Unno
Mr. and Mrs. Taitetsu Unno
Mr. Tomio Unno
Mr. and Mrs. Dick U. Uno
Ms. Dorothy Uno
Mr. Frederic K. Uno
Ms. Helene M. Uno
Hiromu Uno
Judge and Mrs. Raymond Uno
Ms. Rosalind K. Uno
Mrs. S. Lorna Uno
Ms. Shigeko Uno
Mr. Thomas W. Uno
Mr. David Unoura
Mr. Dick Unten
Mr. H. Unterberger
Mr. Lon Unterseher
Mr. Mark Uomoto
Mr. and Mrs. Hiroshi Uota
Ms. Itsuko Uota
Mr. David M. Uozumi
Ms. Fumiko Upton
Uptown Service Station
Ms. Esther Ura
Mr. and Mrs. George M. Ura
Mr. Jack Ura
Jennifer and Maili Ura
Mr. Ted Ura

Mr. Ken Urabe
Mr. Scott Urabe
Ms. Dorothy Urada
Mr. James O. Uragami
Ms. Kumiko Uragami
Mr. Robert K. Uragami
Ms. Yoshiko Anne Uragami
Mr. and Mrs. Monty Urakami
Mr. and Mrs. Tak Urakawa
Mr. Takeshi Urakawa
Mr. and Mrs. Henry Urano
Mr. and Mrs. Craig Urasaki
Mr. Dennis H. Urasaki
Mr. and Mrs. Edward Urasaki
Ms. Lillie Urasaki
Mr. Taro Urasaki
Ms. Anna F. Urata
Mr. Greg Urata
Mr. Harry Urata
Mr. James T. Urata
Ms. Jane Urata
Mr. and Mrs. Masuye Urata
Mr. Raymond T. Urata
Ms. Shizu E. Urata
Mr. Wallace T. Urata
Mr. and Mrs. John Urauchi
Mr. and Mrs. Kiyoto Uriu
Ms. Miyeko Uriu
Mr. and Mrs. Scott D. Uriu
Uriu Associates
Ms. Sumiko M. Urquhart
Mr. and Mrs. Ray Urushima
US West Foundation
Mr. Shunichi Usami
Mr. and Mrs. Arthur Ushijima
Mr. and Mrs. James Ushijima
Mr. John Ushijima
Mr. and Mrs. Paul K. Ushijima
Mr. and Mrs. Richard Ushijima
Mr. and Mrs. Stanley S. Ushijima
Mr. W. Matthew Ushijima
Mr. Masahiko Mike Ushio
Mr. Masumi J. Ushio
Mr. Shigeki Ushio
Mr. and Mrs. Masaru Ushiro
Mr. and Mrs. Shigeo Ushiro
Mrs. Sueko Konishi Ushiro
Mrs. Aki Ushiyama
Mr. Garrett Ushiyama
Mr. Tomonori Usuda
Mr. and Mrs. James S. Usui
Mr. John Y. Usui
Mr. and Mrs. Roy Usui
Mr. Shigenari Usui
Mr. Yoichi Usui
Ms. Barbara Utsumi
Ms. Diane Utsumi
Mr. and Mrs. Donald N. Utsumi
Mrs. Chris Utsumi-Puryear
Tei Utsumiya
Ms. Ai Utsunomiya
San Utsunomiya
Ms. Tei Utsunomiya
Mrs. Michiye Uttal
Mr. Tak Uyechi
Mr. Thomas H. Uyechi
Mr. Akito Uyeda
Mr. and Mrs. Alice Uyeda
Mr. and Mrs. Arthur Uyeda
Ms. Carolyn Uyeda
Mr. and Mrs. Charles M. Uyeda
Mr. and Mrs. Chester K. Uyeda
Ms. Daisy Uyeda
Mr. Davis K. Uyeda
Mr. Don K. Uyeda
Mr. Donald M. Uyeda
Mr. Francis Y. Uyeda
Mr. and Mrs. Frank Uyeda
Mr. and Mrs. George Y. Uyeda
Mr. Harry Uyeda
Mr. Harry K. Uyeda
Mr. Harry M. Uyeda
Mr. and Mrs. Henry Uyeda
Hiromi Uyeda
Mr. Howard Uyeda
Mr. James N. Uyeda
Ms. Jeannie Uyeda
Mr. and Mrs. Jeff Uyeda
Mr. and Mrs. Joe Uyeda
Mr. and Mrs. John Uyeda
Dr. Kath Uyeda
Mr. and Mrs. Kei Uyeda
Mr. Ken Uyeda
Mr. and Mrs. Ken Uyeda
Kendrick A. Uyeda
Mr. Kenneth Uyeda

Mr. Kenneth K. Uyeda
Mr. Kevin C. Uyeda
Ms. Lily Y. Uyeda
Ms. Mary Y. Uyeda
Ms. Masako Uyeda
Mrs. Nora S. Uyeda
Mr. Randall T. Uyeda
Mr. and Mrs. Richard S. Uyeda
Mr. Robert Uyeda
Mr. and Mrs. Roy Uyeda
Mr. Saburo Uyeda
Mr. and Mrs. Samuel Uyeda
Mr. Susumu Uyeda
Mr. and Mrs. Thomas S. Uyeda
Mr. and Mrs. Tomochika Uyeda
Mr. Toshio Uyeda
Ms. Yasuko Uyeda
Mr. and Mrs. Yoneichi Uyeda
Mr. Aleric C. Uyehara and Family
Mrs. Amelia Uyehara
Mr. and Mrs. Cecil H. Uyehara
Mr. Dennis Uyehara
Mr. Dick M. Uyehara
Ms. Eiko Uyehara
Ms. Emi Uyehara
Mr. Geoffrey Uyehara
Mr. and Mrs. Harry Uyehara
Dr. Harry Y. Uyehara
Mr. Henry K. Uyehara
Mr. Hiroaki Uyehara
Mr. and Mrs. James Uyehara
Mr. James Y. Uyehara
Mr. Kazuo Uyehara
Mr. and Mrs. Kenneth Uyehara
Mr. Kenneth H. Uyehara
Mr. Laurence K. Uyehara
Mr. and Mrs. Lawrence Uyehara
Ms. Lisa Y. Uyehara
Mr. Logan S. Uyehara
Mr. Masao Uyehara
Paul M. Uyehara and Mary Yee
Mr. Paul Y. Uyehara
Mr. Peter M. Uyehara
Mr. and Mrs. Robert K. Uyehara
Mr. Roy T. Uyehara
Mr. and Mrs. Sam Y. Uyehara
Mr. and Mrs. Steven M. Uyehara
Mr. and Mrs. Takeo Uyehara
Mr. William S. Uyehara
Ms. Donna Uyehata
Mr. Douglas Uyehata
Maj. and Mrs. Stephen G. Uyehata
Mr. and Mrs. Magotsugu Uyeji
Mr. and Mrs. Minoru Uyeji
Mr. Saburo Uyeji
Mr. and Mrs. Victor Uyeji
Mr. Takashi Uyejo
Mr. and Mrs. Doug Uyeki
Mr. and Mrs. Edwin M. Uyeki
Mr. and Mrs. Eugene Uyeki
Mr. and Mrs. Mike A. Uyeki
Mr. William K. Uyeki
Mr. Aaron Y. Uyema
Blanche, Russell, Wesley and Garrett Uyema
Mr. Herman T. Uyema
Mr. Dennis Uyematsu
Mr. Harrison Uyematsu
Mr. and Mrs. Samuel M. Uyematsu
Mr. and Mrs. Jimmy Uyemoto
Ms. Michiko Uyemoto
Mr. Steve Uyemoto
Mr. Douglas Uyemura
Mrs. Fuyuko Uyemura
Ms. Hana S. Uyemura
Mr. James Uyemura
Tama Uyemura, Patricia Weber Uyemura and Martha Strain
Mr. Todd Uyemura
Mrs. Toshiye M. Uyemura
Mr. Wesley Uyemura
Ms. Dorothy Uyenishi and Family
Mrs. Frank Y. Uyenishi
Mr. Iwao P. Uyenishi
Mr. Al Uyeno
Mr. Alan Uyeno
Mr. Ben T. Uyeno
Mr. George Uyeno
Mr. and Mrs. George S. Uyeno
K. Francis Uyeno
Keiso Uyeno
Ms. Kiyoko Uyeno
Mr. and Mrs. Kiyoshi Uyeno
Mr. and Mrs. Koichi G. Uyeno
Mr. and Mrs. Masato Uyeno
Mr. Sadao Uyeno
Ms. Setsuko Uyeno

Mr. and Mrs. Tsukasa Uyeno
Mrs. Virginia Uyeno-Bridy
Ms. Cheryl Uyenoyama
Mr. Hidesuke Uyenoyama
Mr. Marcy K. Uyenoyama
Mr. Charles Uyeoka
Mr. and Mrs. Tom Uyeoka
Mr. Yoshio Uyeoka
Mr. and Mrs. Frank Uyesaka
Mr. and Mrs. Robert Uyesaka
Mr. Robert S. Uyesaka
Mr. Roy Uyesaka
Ms. Alice Y. Uyesato
Mr. and Mrs. Arthur Uyesato
Mr. Gerald Uyesato
Mr. Hikoharu Uyesato
Ms. Kitty K. Uyeshima
Mr. and Mrs. Allan Uyesugi
Mr. and Mrs. George S. Uyesugi
Mr. and Mrs. Jack Uyesugi
Ms. Kay Uyesugi
Dr. Kazuya Uyesugi
Mr. and Mrs. Ken Uyesugi
Mr. and Mrs. Kenji Uyesugi
Mrs. Mary M. Uyesugi
Ms. Sy Uyesugi
Mr. Edwin T. Uyeta
Uyeta's Nursery, Inc.
Mr. Richard T. Uyeunten
Mr. and Mrs. Jack Uyeyama
Ms. Miyoko Uzaki
Mr. and Mrs. Peter Vajda
Tanaka and Mitsuyo Val
Ms. Linda S. Valauskas
Ms. Suzanne Leonard Vallez
Mr. and Mrs. Aart Van Beek
Ms. Virginia M. Van Maanen
Hanh Van Nguyen and Hue Ky Tran
Mr. and Mrs. David H. Vance
Mr. Laduel Vance
Mr. Franklin Vansant
Ms. Betty Varga
Ms. Deborah Vasquez
Ms. Louise Vavrik
Dr. Balkrishna Venkatesh
LTC and Mrs. C. David Vesley
Ms. Catalina Vial
Ms. Jacqueline R. Vidourek
Mr. and Mrs. Robert F. Villaflor
Mr. and Mrs. Jorge Villegas
Mr. and Mrs. Stephen A. Vines
Visas For Life Foundation
Mr. Trung Vo
Mr. and Mrs. Raymond Vodopest
Voiture Locale 265 Inc. 40-8 of MD
Mr. and Mrs. Robert B. Vokac
Mr. and Mrs. Joe Volk
Ms. Alexandra Vu
W/Dance Class
W/W Group
Mr. Takahiro Wachi
Mrs. Ellen Wachtershause
Ms. Ada Wada
Mr. Albert Wada
Mrs. Ayako Wada
Mr. Ben K. Wada
Mr. Carl Wada
Mr. and Mrs. Dean Wada
Mr. and Mrs. Edward Wada
Mr. and Mrs. Frank M. Wada
Mr. and Mrs. George Wada
Mr. and Mrs. Glen N. Wada
Mr. Gregg H. Wada
Mr. Hide Wada
Ms. Honey T. Wada
Mr. Ichiro Wada
Mr. Irwin Wada
Jack I. Wada Family Trust
Mr. and Mrs. Jacob Wada
Ms. Jennifer Wada
Mr. Johnny M. Wada
Ms. Julia Wada
Mr. Kaoru Wada
Ms. Kayoko Wada
Mr. Kenneth M. Wada
Mr. Kennie Wada
Ms. Lillian M. Wada
Ms. Lucy Wada
Mrs. M. Wada
Mr. and Mrs. Mamoru Wada
Mr. Mikey Wada
Ms. Patricia Kay Wada
Mr. Robert M. Wada
Messrs. Ryo Wada and Tom Fujita
Mr. Steve Wada
Mr. and Mrs. Sumihiro Wada

Mr. and Mrs. Tad Wada
Mr. Ted Wada
Mr. Toru Wada
Mr. Wesley Wada
Mr. and Mrs. Yasuo Wada
Ms. Yoshie Wada
Mr. and Mrs. Yukio Wada
Mr. and Mrs. Henry H. Wadahara
Ms. Alice Wade
Ms. Mary Jo Wade
Mr. Robert B. Wade
Ms. Ellen Ogawa Waechterohaeuser
Mr. Jack Wagatsuma
Mr. Wallace Wagatsuma
Mr. Elliot Wager
Ms. Elizabeth Waggener
Ms. Esther O. Wagner
Ms. Mary Waite
Mr. and Mrs. Satoshi Waite
Mr. Takeshi Wajima
Mr. William Waka
Mr. Benjamin Wakabayashi
Mr. Dennis Wakabayashi
Mr. Hiro Wakabayashi
Mr. and Mrs. Roy Wakabayashi
Sachi Wakabayashi and Lillian Oka
Mr. Tsuneo Wakabayashi
Ms. Yemiko Wakahara
Mr. William Wakahiro
Mr. and Mrs. Harry Wakai
Mr. Ross H. Wakai
Mr. Theodore Wakai
Satoru and Janet Wakakuwa
Mr. and Mrs. Stanley Wakakuwa
Ms. Betty H. Wakamatsu
Dr. and Mrs. Harold T. Wakamatsu
Mr. and Mrs. James Wakamatsu
Mr. Leland Wakamatsu
Ms. Mary E. Wakamatsu
Ms. May Wakamatsu
Mr. Peter Wakamatsu
Mr. and Mrs. Shigeo Wakamatsu
Mr. Charles Wakamoto
Ms. Wendy Wakamoto
Mr. Akira Wakamura
Mr. Brian Wakano
Roy and Jane Wakasa
Mr. Kiyoshi Wakatani
Mr. and Mrs. Greg Wakatsuki
Dr. and Mrs. Walter Wakatsuki
Bruce Wakayama and Nancy Yamane
Mr. and Mrs. George Wakayama
Mr. and Mrs. Jack Wakayama
Mr. and Mrs. Jimmie Wakayama
Kyo and Bryon Wakayama
Mr. and Mrs. Kyuichi I. Wakayama
Wakayama Kenjin-Kai
Rev. Amy C. Wake and Mr. C. Kent Coarsey
Mr. Edward Wake
Mr. and Mrs. William Wake
Mr. Guy P. Wakefield
Ms. Jean Wakefield
Ms. Betty Waki
Mr. George H. Waki
Mr. and Mrs. Louis Y. Waki
Mr. Russell Waki
Mr. and Mrs. Ted Waki
Mr. Yasushi Waki
Mr. Edward Wakida
Mr. Shigeto Wakida
Ms. Kaoru Wakiji
Jon Wakimoto and Karen Bunya
Mr. Nelson K. Wakimoto
Mrs. Viola S. Wakimura
Mr. and Mrs. Asa Wakinaka
Mr. Fred K. Wakita
Ms. Kayoko Wakita
Mrs. Toshie Wakita
Ms. Sharon R. Wakiyama
Ms. Irene Wakumoto
Mrs. Clara Wakuzawa
Ms. Janice D. Waldorf
Mr. Henry A. Walker
Ms. Mary C. Walker
Mr. and Mrs. Warren Walker
Ms. Margaret Wallhagen
Mr. and Mrs. Gary Walloch
Mr. Gerald R. Walsh
Mr. Jesse P. Walsh
Ms. Susan Ozaki Walsh
Ms. Miki Walter
Mr. Don R. Walters
Mr. and Mrs. William E. Walters
Ms. Linda V. Waltz
Mr. and Mrs. John P. Walz
Ms. Vani Oye Wampler

Mr. and Mrs. Jimmy Wang
Mrs. Sumi S. Wanifuchi
Ms. Aiko Warashina
Ms. Peggy Ward
Mr. and Mrs. Robert E. Ward
Mrs. Sanae Ward
George and Sharon Warren
Ms. Leola Warren
Mr. and Mrs. Ronald J. Warren
Ms. Samantha Y. Warren
Washington State Democratic Central Committee
Mr. and Mrs. William Waste
Mr. and Mrs. Thomas T. Watabayashi
Mr. and Mrs. Masasue Watabe
Mr. Michael M. Watabe
Mr. Takao Watabe
Dr. and Mrs. Alley E. Watada
Mr. Everett Watada
Mr. and Mrs. Richard Watada
Mr. Robert Watada
Ms. Shizuyo Watahira
Mr. and Mrs. George Watai
Mrs. Rose Y. Watamura
Mr. and Mrs. Shogo Watamura
Mr. Akira Watanabe
Ms. Ann M. Watanabe
Mr. and Mrs. Arnold K. Watanabe
C. Y. Watanabe
Mrs. Carol M. Watanabe
Mr. and Mrs. Charles Watanabe
Mrs. Chiye Watanabe
Mr. Clyde Watanabe
Ms. Deborah Watanabe
Ms. Diana Watanabe
Mr. and Mrs. Donald Watanabe
Ms. Donnie S. Watanabe
Mr. and Mrs. Eay Watanabe
Ms. Ellen E. Watanabe
Mrs. Frances Watanabe
Mr. Gary I. Watanabe
Mr. and Mrs. Gary S. Watanabe
Mr. and Mrs. Geary Watanabe
Mr. George Watanabe
Mr. and Mrs. George Watanabe
Mr. George H. Watanabe
Mr. George M. Watanabe
Mr. George M. Watanabe
Mr. and Mrs. Gerald Watanabe
Mr. Glenn Watanabe
Ms. Haru Watanabe
Ms. Helen K. Watanabe
Ms. Helen T. Watanabe
Mr. and Mrs. Henry Watanabe
Mr. Hirohisa Watanabe
Mr. and Mrs. Hisashi Watanabe
Mr. and Mrs. Howard K. Watanabe
Mr. and Mrs. Isao Watanabe
Mr. Jack Watanabe
Mr. and Mrs. James H. Watanabe
Mr. Jessie Watanabe
Mr. and Mrs. John Watanabe
Miss Joyce Sachiko Watanabe
Ms. June K. Watanabe
Mr. and Mrs. Kaoru Watanabe
Ms. Karen T. Watanabe
Mr. and Mrs. Katsuo Watanabe
Mr. and Mrs. Kay Watanabe
Mr. and Mrs. Kay R. Watanabe
Mr. Kazumi Watanabe
Mr. Kazuo Watanabe
Mr. Keiji Watanabe
Mr. Kenneth Watanabe
Mr. and Mrs. Kiyoji Watanabe
Mr. Koichi Watanabe
Mr. Kozo Watanabe
Mr. and Mrs. Lewis Watanabe
Ms. Louise C. Watanabe
Ms. Martha M. Watanabe
Mr. and Mrs. Marvin Watanabe
Mr. Mary Watanabe
Ms. Mary R. Watanabe and Mr. Ralph J. Commiso
Ms. Masako Watanabe
Mr. Michiko Watanabe
Mr. Mitsuo Watanabe
Mr. Mitsuru Watanabe and Mrs. June Atsuko Watanabe
Ms. Noriko Watanabe
Ms. Patricia Watanabe
Mr. and Mrs. Paul Watanabe
Mr. Paul S. Watanabe
Mr. and Mrs. Reynold Watanabe
Dr. Richard Watanabe
Mr. Richard S. Watanabe
Mr. and Mrs. Robert S. Watanabe
Mr. Robert T. Watanabe
Mr. and Mrs. Ron Watanabe
Mr. Ronald Watanabe

Ms. Rose A. Watanabe
Mr. Roy Watanabe
Ms. Sachiye Watanabe
Ms. Sakaye Watanabe
Ms. Sally S. Watanabe
Mr. and Mrs. Sam Watanabe
Sheri Fujita and Scott Watanabe
Mr. Seichi Watanabe
Ms. Stacy Watanabe
Mr. Stanley Watanabe
Mr. and Mrs. Tak Watanabe
Mr. Takashi Watanabe
Mr. and Mrs. Ted Watanabe
Mr. and Mrs. Terry Watanabe
Mr. and Mrs. Thomas Watanabe
Mr. Thomas T. Watanabe
Mr. Togo Watanabe
Mr. Tom Watanabe
Mr. Tommy Watanabe
Mrs. Tomoye Watanabe
Ms. Toshiko T. Watanabe
Mr. Toshio Watanabe
Ms. Toyoko Watanabe
Ms. Tsugie Watanabe
Ms. Tsuruye Watanabe
Ms. Vicky Watanabe
Mr. Wayne Watanabe
Mr. Wayne S. Watanabe
Mr. Wesley K. Watanabe
Ms. Yayoi Watanabe
Mr. and Mrs. Yoshio Watanabe
Mr. and Mrs. Yutaka Watanabe
Ms. Ann Aiko Watanabe-Rocco
Mrs. Dorothy Watanuki
Mr. Thomas T. Watanuki
Mr. Fred Watari
Mr. and Mrs. Hideo Watari
Mr. and Mrs. Jack Watari
Lily Watari and Family
Mr. James S. Wataru
Mr. John Wataru
Mr. Harold J. Watase
Mr. Yachiyo Wataya
LTC (Ret.) Junius Watlington
Douglas and Evelyn Watson
Ms. Elaine S. Watson
Mr. Glenn R. Watson
Mr. and Mrs. John E. Watson
Mr. Leland S. Watson
Ms. Naomi Watson
Ms. Kathleen B. Wax
Mrs. Tonya Weaver
Mr. and Mrs. Leroy J. Weberg
Mr. Edward Webman
Webster Health Center
Ms. Joanne Webster
Ms. Joy Wegman
Mr. Howard L. Weinberger
Ms. Lily Y. Weiss
Mr. and Mrs. Raymond Weitzman
Mr. and Mrs. James Welch
Mr. and Mrs. Donn J. Wells
Mr. Williams Wells
Ms. Nancy Welsh
Mr. and Mrs. Richard Wentworth
Mr. George C. Werth
Mr. and Mrs. Derek West
Ms. Elsie E. West
Mr. Jaton West
Ms. Naomi Westcott
Western Asset
Peter and Lisa M. Westley
Mr. and Mrs. Eugene Weyland
Ms. Kiyoko Wheat
Wheaton Kiwanis Foundation
Mr. Charlie Wheeler
Mr. Thomas J. White
Ms. Kazuko S. Whitman
Mr. and Mrs. Jimmy Whittall
Ms. Lynn Whitted
Knute R. Wiegand
Mr. and Mrs. Albert Wienbarg
Mr. and Mrs. Allan Wiggans
Mr. and Mrs. Bruce Wilcox
Mr. and Mrs. Charles T. Wilcox
Mr. and Mrs. George Wilcox
Mr. James H. Wildman
Mr. and Mrs. Joseph Wiley
Ms. Liliane Willens
Ms. Betty M.S. Williams
Bob and Kay Williams, & Ricky and Kerry Albright
Mr. Charles Williams
Jack Williams Ranches, Inc.
Mr. and Mrs. Robert Williams
Kay Willis
David A. and Aileen Hanai-Wills

Melanie Willis and Asayo Sakahara
Ms. Mary Willmarth
Ms. Ann K.H. Wilson
Ms. Cathy Wilson
Ms. Katherine M. Wilson
Ms. Loretta Wilson
Ms. Tanya T. Wilson
Wimmer Yamada and Caughey
Mr. and Mrs. John Winans
Mr. and Mrs. Mike Winebarger
Messrs. Glenn Wing and Eric Herrera
Mr. John B. Winter
Ms. Kiyoko A. Wittenburg
Mr. and Mrs. Hermann H. Wittje
Mr. and Mrs. Eric Wolf
Ms. Beatrice Wolfe
Ms. Brenda M. Wolfe
Ms. Elizabeth Wolfe
Mr. George T. Wollschlaeger
Ms. Amy K. Wong
Mr. and Mrs. Brian Wong
Ms. Carolyn D. Wong
Ms. Gail Wong
Mr. and Mrs. Gene Wong
Mr. and Mrs. Guillermo Wong
Mr. and Mrs. Herbert S. Wong
Ms. Jane H. Wong
Mr. and Mrs. John Wong
Ms. June Wong
Ms. Kazuko Wong
Mr. Michael Wong
Mr. and Mrs. Rodney K. Wong
Ms. Ruth S. Wong
Mr. Victor Wong
Mr. and Mrs. Wallace S. Wong
Dr. and Mrs. Willard Wong
Mr. and Mrs. William Y. Wong
Mr. and Mrs. Darryl Wong-Sing
Mr. and Mrs. Benjamin Woo
Ms. Chung Soon Woo
Mr. and Mrs. Duncan J. Woo
The Print Network
Mr. and Mrs. Leon Wood
Ms. Ruby Wood
Mr. and Mrs. Stephen D. Wood
Ms. Joyce Woods
Mr. and Mrs. Charles F. Woodward
Mr. Richard G. Woodward
K. Workcuff
Mr. and Mrs. Don Workman
Mr. and Mrs. Kevin Worrall
Dr. and Mrs. David Wright
Ms. Elizabeth A. Wright
Mr. and Mrs. Garland Wright
Ms. Jackie Bong Wright
Mr. and Mrs. Chester Wu
Mr. Hai-jui Wu
Mr. and Mrs. Kenneth Wurtzel
Mr. and Mrs. Richard Wyles
Ms. Fumi Yabe
Mr. and Mrs. Yasuhiro Yabe
Mr. and Mrs. Ben Yabu
Mr. and Mrs. Jon D. Yabu
Mr. Takashi Yabu
Mr. Thomas Yabu
Mr. Alan H. Yabuki
Mr. and Mrs. Glenn T. Yabuki
Mrs. Edna Yabuno
Mr. George Yabusaki
Ms. Kikkuko Yabushita
Mr. Frank Yada
Mr. and Mrs. Jeffrey Yada
Mr. Ryujiro Yagasaki
Mrs. Akiko Yagi
Mr. Alan Yagi
Mr. and Mrs. Ben Yagi
Ms. Chiyoko Yagi
Frank and Hiro Yagi
Fumio Yagi
Mr. and Mrs. George Yagi
Mr. Herbert S. Yagi
Mr. Koichi Yagi
Mrs. Lenora Yagi
Mr. Lester S. Yagi
Mr. Masaichi Yagi
Ms. Miako K. Yagi
Mr. Michael K. Yagi
Mr. and Mrs. Peter Yagi
Mr. Sadayoshi Yagi
Mr. and Mrs. Tommy Yagi
Mr. Toshio Yagi
Mr. Victor Yagi
Mr. and Mrs. Clifton K. Yaguchi
Mr. and Mrs. Edward Yaguchi
Harko Yaguchi
Mr. Masaharu Yaguchi

Mr. and Mrs. Ralph R. Yaguchi
Ms. Chiyeko Anne Yagura
Mr. Hiroshi Yagura and Mrs. Mitsuko Yagura
Mr. Katsumi Yagura
Ms. Yukiko Yagyu
Mr. Alfred Yahanda
Mr. and Mrs. Mitsuo Yahata
Yasuko and Karl Yahiku
Mr. Mark H. Yahiro
Mr. Michael G. Yahiro
Mr. and Mrs. Robert Yahiro
Willie Yahiro Insurance
Mr. Steven Yaka
Mr. Glenn S. Yakabi
Mr. Brian T. Yakata
Mr. and Mrs. Larry Yakata
Mr. Tae J. Yaki
Mr. and Mrs. Michael Yakura
Mr. and Mrs. Susumu Yakura
Mr. and Mrs. Charles T. Yakushiji
Mr. and Mrs. Craig Masumi Yama
Mr. Gilbert Y. Yamabayashi
Mr. and Mrs. Nobuhiko T. Yamabe
Ms. Mary Y. Yamachi
Mr. Ronald Yamachi
Fumiko and Nancy Yamachika
Mr. Roddy M. Yamachika
Mr. and Mrs. Akira Yamada
Mr. Alan H. Yamada
Mrs. Alice A. Yamada
Mr. Alvin T. Yamada
Ms. Audrey T. Yamada
Ms. Ayako Yamada
Mr. Benny T. Yamada
Mr. and Mrs. Bill M. Yamada
Mr. Brian A. Yamada
Ms. Chiyoko Yamada
Ms. Colleen Yamada
Ms. Constance Yamada
Mr. Craig S. Yamada and Ms. Monice J. Kwok
Mr. Dan S. Yamada
Mr. David Yamada
Ms. Deborah Yamada
Mrs. Diana Yamada
Mr. and Mrs. Edward Yamada
Mr. and Mrs. Edwin A. Yamada
Mr. and Mrs. Edwin Y. Yamada
Mrs. Eiko Yamada
Mr. and Mrs. Eiro Yamada
Ms. Emiko Yamada
Ms. Faye Yamada
G. Yamada
Rev. and Mrs. Garett Yamada
Gayle Yamada and David Hosley
Mr. and Mrs. George R. Yamada
Mr. and Mrs. George T. Yamada
Mr. George Y. Yamada
Mr. and Mrs. Glenn Yamada
Mr. and Mrs. Gregory J. Yamada
Mr. and Mrs. Harry Yamada
Mr. Hatsuki Yamada
Mr. and Mrs. Henry Yamada
Mr. and Mrs. Henry T. Yamada
Mr. and Mrs. Hideo Yamada
Mr. and Mrs. Hideo J. Yamada
Mr. Hiroshi Yamada
Mr. Hiroyuki Yamada
Mr. James S. Yamada
Ms. Janet Yamada
Ms. Jill Yamada
Ms. JoAnn Yamada
Dr. Joyce Yamada
Mrs. June Yamada
Mr. Junichiro J. Yamada
Ms. Karen K. Yamada
Mr. Kazuhiko Yamada
Mr. Kenneth K. Yamada
Mr. Kenneth S. Yamada
Mr. and Mrs. Kent Yamada
Mr. Kerry T. Yamada
Mr. Kevin Yamada
Ms. Kikuko Yamada
Ms. Leslie Yamada
Mr. and Mrs. Leslie K. Yamada
Mr. and Mrs. Lloyd M. Yamada
Ms. Lorraine Yamada
Ms. Mae Yamada
Ms. Masako M. Yamada
Dr. Merilynn Yamada
Mr. Michael Yamada
Mr. and Mrs. Mitsuo Yamada
Mr. and Mrs. Mitsuru Yamada
Mrs. Miyoko Yamada
Ms. Naomi Yamada
Mr. Naoto Yamada
Mr. and Mrs. Noboru Yamada

Mr. Noriyasu Yamada
Ms. Peggy S. Yamada
Mr. and Mrs. Ray Y. Yamada
Mr. Richard Yamada
Dr. and Mrs. Richard H. Yamada
Mr. and Mrs. Richard S. Yamada
Mr. Ronald K. Yamada
Mr. and Mrs. Roy H. Yamada
Mr. and Mrs. Roy M. Yamada
Mr. and Mrs. Ryan K. Yamada and Family
Sachiko Yamada
Ms. Sachiko Yamada
Mr. Sam Yamada
Mr. Samuel T. Yamada
Yamada Electronics
Mrs. Sayuri Yamada and Mr. Preston Matthew
Shizuye A. Yamada
Mr. Shoji Yamada
Mr. Shuji Yamada
Mr. Shuji M. Yamada
Mr. and Mrs. Stanley U. Yamada
Ms. Susan Yamada
Mr. Takahiro Yamada
Mr. Takamasa Yamada
Mr. and Mrs. Takeo Yamada
Mr. and Mrs. Taro Yamada
Mr. and Mrs. Tatsuji H. Yamada
Mr. Ted Yamada
Dr. Ted K. Yamada
Mr. Teichi Yamada
Mr. and Mrs. Tetsuji Yamada
Mr. Thomas T. Yamada
Mr. Tom Yamada
Mr. Tsutomu Yamada
Mr. Yoshio Yamada
Mr. and Mrs. Yoshito Yamada
Mr. Yoshiyuki John Yamada
Mr. Yozo Yamada
Mr. and Mrs. Yuji Yamada
Ms. Dorothy Yamaga
Mr. and Mrs. Lucky Yamaga
Mr. Motoyuki Yamaga
Mr. and Mrs. Masao Yamagami
Mr. and Mrs. Ronald Yamagami
Mr. Yon Yamagami
Mr. and Mrs. Brian F. Yamagata
Mr. and Mrs. Howard Yamagata
Mr. Howard K. Yamagata
Mr. and Mrs. Isaac Yamagata
Ms. Joan M. Yamagata
Mr. Leslie C. Yamagata
Mr. Thomas Yamagata
Ms. Valerie Yamagata
Mr. Yoshio Yamagata
Yusaku Yamagata
Mr. Joe Yamagawa
Mr. Frederick Yamagishi
Hisashi Yamagishi
Mr. and Mrs. Ray Yamagishi
Mr. and Mrs. Shoichi Yamagishi
Mr. and Mrs. Ben Yamagiwa
Mr. Ben T. Yamagiwa
Mrs. Denise Yamagiwa
Ms. Gay Yamagiwa
Mr. George Yamagiwa
Mr. Kay Yamagiwa
Ms. Mary Yamagiwa
Mr. Terry Yamagiwa
Mr. and Mrs. Yoshiharu Yamagiwa
Ms. Yoshiye Yamagiwa
Mrs. Barbara Yamaguchi
Mr. Brian K. Yamaguchi
Mr. and Mrs. Charlie Yamaguchi
Mrs. Chiyoko Yamaguchi
Mrs. Clara M. Yamaguchi
Mr. David S. Yamaguchi
Ms. Dharma Yamaguchi
Mr. and Mrs. Ed Yamaguchi
Mr. and Mrs. Eugene Yamaguchi
Dr. Eugene T. Yamaguchi
Mr. and Mrs. Fred Yamaguchi
Mr. and Mrs. George Yamaguchi
Mr. George S. Yamaguchi
Ms. Grace Y. Yamaguchi
Mr. Herbert E. Yamaguchi
Mr. James S. Yamaguchi
Mr. Jim Yamaguchi
Jinko Yamaguchi
Mr. Jogi Yamaguchi
Mr. and Mrs. John Yamaguchi
Ms. Julie Yamaguchi
Mr. Kaoru Yamaguchi
Dr. Kathleen Yamaguchi
Mr. and Mrs. Kay Yamaguchi
Mr. and Mrs. Kei Yamaguchi
Mr. and Mrs. Ken Yamaguchi

Mr. and Mrs. Kirk Yamaguchi
Ms. Lois R. Yamaguchi
Dr. and Mrs. M. Lincoln Yamaguchi
Mr. and Mrs. Mack Yamaguchi
Ms. Marianne Yamaguchi
Mr. Mas Yamaguchi
Mr. and Mrs. Minoru Yamaguchi
Mr. and Mrs. Mitomu Yamaguchi
Ms. Nancy Yamaguchi
Mr. Peter Yamaguchi
Mr. Richard Yamaguchi
Mr. Rose Yamaguchi
Ms. Ruth Yamaguchi
Ms. Ruth S. Yamaguchi
Mrs. Shigeko Yamaguchi
Mr. Shogo Yamaguchi
Mrs. Sumiko Yamaguchi
Ms. Susan Yamaguchi
Mr. Tadashi Yamaguchi
Mrs. Tomoe Yamaguchi
Mr. and Mrs. Toru Yamaguchi
Mr. Walter Yamaguchi
Mr. Wayne Yamaguchi
Mr. Yoshiko W. Yamaguchi
Ms. Yuriko M. Yamaguchi
Mr. and Mrs. Joe Yamaguma
Ms. Shigeko Yamaguma
Mr. Yoshiyuki Yamahira
Mr. Glenn Yamahiro
Dr. and Mrs. Harry Yamahiro
Ms. Jacqueline C. Yamahiro
Mr. and Mrs. George Yamaichi
Mr. and Mrs. Jimi Yamaichi
Mr. and Mrs. Masaru Yamaichi
Mr. and Mrs. Richard Yamaichi
Mr. Russell J. Yamaichi
Mr. and Mrs. Stanley Yamaichi
Mr. George J. Yamaka
Mr. and Mrs. Woodrow Yamaka
Mr. and Ms. F. J. Yamakawa
Mr. George H. Yamakawa
Mr. and Mrs. Jimmy Yamakawa
Mr. and Mrs. Kunihiko Yamakawa
Ms. Mitsuko Yamakawa
Mr. Shinei Yamakawa
Mr. Thomas Yamakawa
Mr. and Mrs. Joe Yamaki
Mr. and Mrs. Yoshiwo Yamaki
Ms. Laureen A. Yamakido
Mr. and Mrs. Tadao Yamakido
Mr. and Mrs. Frank Yamakoshi
Mr. and Mrs. James T. Yamakoshi
Ms. Lois Yamakoshi
Mr. and Mrs. Tsugio Yamami
Mr. and Mrs. Hiro Yamamisaka
Ms. Aiko Yamamoto
Mr. and Mrs. Akimutsu Yamamoto
Mr. Akira Yamamoto
Mr. and Mrs. Albert Yamamoto
Mr. Alfred M. Yamamoto
Ms. Alice Yamamoto
Mr. and Mrs. Andrew Yamamoto
Mrs. Ann F. Yamamoto
Mrs. Anna S. Yamamoto
Dr. and Mrs. Arthur S. Yamamoto
Ms. Asako and Ms. Teresa Yamamoto
Ms. Barbara Yamamoto
Barbara and Kurt Yamamoto
Beans, Ruth, Alan and Doreen Yamamoto
Mr. Ben Yamamoto
Mr. and Mrs. Ben Yamamoto
Ms. Betty Yamamoto
Mr. and Mrs. Bob M. Yamamoto
Mr. and Mrs. Calvin T. Yamamoto
Mrs. Carol Yamamoto
Ms. Caroline Yamamoto
Ms. Catherine Yamamoto
Ms. Chieko Yamamoto
Ms. Chiyoko Yamamoto
Mr. Chris Yamamoto
Ms. Christine M. Yamamoto
Mr. and Mrs. Clarence A. Yamamoto
Mr. and Mrs. Clarence Y. Yamamoto
Ms. Claudia Yamamoto
Ms. Cynthia A. Yamamoto
Mr. and Mrs. Dave S. Yamamoto
Mr. and Mrs. David Yamamoto
Mrs. Debi Yamamoto
Mr. and Mrs. Dennis Yamamoto
Mr. and Mrs. Dick Yamamoto
Mr. Dick K. Yamamoto
Mr. and Mrs. Donald Yamamoto
Mr. Donald Y. Yamamoto
Ms. Doris Y. Yamamoto
Mr. Douglas Yamamoto
Mr. and Mrs. Edward Yamamoto

Mr. Eric R. Yamamoto
Mr. and Mrs. Ernest Yamamoto
Mr. Eugene Yamamoto
Mr. and Mrs. Francis S. Yamamoto
Mr. and Mrs. Frank Yamamoto
Mr. Frank S. Yamamoto
Mr. Fred T. Yamamoto
Mr. Fujio Yamamoto
Mr. and Mrs. Fumio Yamamoto
Ms. Fusaye Yamamoto
Mr. Gary Mikio Yamamoto
Mr. Gary Yamamoto
Mr. and Mrs. Gary D. Yamamoto
Mr. George K. Yamamoto
Mr. and Mrs. George M. Yamamoto
Mr. George S. Yamamoto
Mr. and Mrs. George S. Yamamoto
Mr. George T. Yamamoto
Mr. and Mrs. George T. Yamamoto
Mr. Gordon Yamamoto
Mr. Gordon Y. Yamamoto
Mr. and Mrs. Goro Yamamoto
Mr. and Mrs. Greg Yamamoto
Mr. and Mrs. Hajime Yamamoto
Mrs. Hanako Yamamoto
Mr. and Mrs. Harry Yamamoto
Ms. Hatsu Yamamoto
Helen and Kathy F. Yamamoto
Mr. Herbert S. Yamamoto
Mr. Hideo B. Yamamoto
Mr. Hiroshi Yamamoto
Mr. Hiroshi E. Yamamoto
Mr. Hisashi Yamamoto
Mr. and Mrs. Howard Yamamoto
Mr. and Mrs. Ikuo Yamamoto
Mr. and Mrs. Isao Yamamoto
Mr. Jack Yamamoto
Mr. and Mrs. Jack T. Yamamoto
Mr. James Yamamoto
Mr. and Mrs. James Yamamoto
Mr. Jeffrey K. Yamamoto
Mr. and Mrs. Joe Yamamoto
Ms. Joyce Yamamoto
Dr. Joyce S. Yamamoto
Mr. Jun Yamamoto
Mr. and Mrs. Jun W. Yamamoto
Ms. June Yamamoto
Ms. June C. Yamamoto
Mrs. June F. Yamamoto
Ms. June S. Yamamoto
Mr. Junichi Yamamoto
Mr. and Mrs. Junji Yamamoto
Mr. Kaoru Yamamoto
Ms. Kathryn Yamamoto
Mr. and Mrs. Katsumi Yamamoto
Ms. Kazuye Yamamoto
Mr. and Mrs. Kei Yamamoto
Ms. Kelly M. Yamamoto
Mr. and Mrs. Ken Yamamoto
Mr. and Mrs. Ken K. Yamamoto
Mr. Kenneth K. Yamamoto
Mr. and Mrs. Kevin Yamamoto
Mr. Kiyo Kay Yamamoto
Mr. Kiyomi Yamamoto
Mr. and Mrs. Kiyoo Yamamoto
Mr. Kiyoshi Yamamoto
Mr. and Mrs. Kiyoshi Yamamoto
Mr. Ko Yamamoto
Mr. Koichi Yamamoto
Mr. L Yamamoto
Ms. Laura Yamamoto
Mr. and Mrs. Leonard Yamamoto
Mr. Les Yamamoto
Ms. Lily Yamamoto
Ms. Linda Yamamoto
Margaret Yamamoto and Mark Hopkins
Mr. and Mrs. Mark A. Yamamoto
Dr. Mark Z. Yamamoto
Dr. and Mrs. Masa Yamamoto
Mr. Masahiro Yamamoto
Ms. Masako Yamamoto
Dr. and Mrs. Masao Yamamoto
Mr. and Mrs. Masaru W. Yamamoto
Mr. Masayoshi Yamamoto
Ms. Matsuye Yamamoto
Mr. Matthew T. Yamamoto
Ms. May Yamamoto
Ms. Michiaki Yamamoto
Ms. Michiko Yamamoto and Mr. John F. Okita
Mr. and Mrs. Michio Yamamoto
Ms. Midori Yamamoto
Mr. and Mrs. Miles Yamamoto
Mr. and Mrs. Mitchel Yamamoto
Mr. and Mrs. Mitsuo Yamamoto
Ms. Mitsuye Yamamoto

Mr. Motomu Yamamoto
Mrs. Nancy M. Yamamoto
Ms. Nobuko Yamamoto
Mr. Noriyuki Yamamoto
Mrs. Okuni Yamamoto
Mr. Paul Yamamoto
Mr. Paul Y. Yamamoto
Mrs. Penelope Yamamoto
Mr. and Mrs. Ray Yamamoto
Dr. Richard Yamamoto
Dr. and Mrs. Richard Yamamoto
Mr. Richard D. Yamamoto
Mr. Richard G. Yamamoto
Mr. and Mrs. Richard S. Yamamoto
Mr. Robert Yamamoto
Mr. Robert G. Yamamoto
Mr. and Mrs. Robert K. Yamamoto
Mr. and Mrs. Robert M. Yamamoto
Mr. Robert S. Yamamoto
Mr. Ron Yamamoto
Mr. Ronald Yamamoto
Mrs. Rose Yamamoto
Ms. Rose F. Yamamoto
Mr. and Mrs. Roy H. Yamamoto
Mr. and Mrs. Roy M. Yamamoto
Mrs. Sakai Yamamoto
Mr. Sam Yamamoto
Mr. and Mrs. Satoshi Yamamoto
Mr. Scott Yamamoto
Mr. Seichi Yamamoto
Mr. Shirley Yamamoto
Mr. and Mrs. Shogo Yamamoto
Mr. Shoji Yamamoto
Mr. and Mrs. Shuichi Yamamoto
Mr. Stanley Yamamoto
Mr. Steven K. Yamamoto
Mr. and Mrs. Stuart Yamamoto
Mr. Sueki Yamamoto
Mrs. Suyemi Yamamoto
Mr. Tadashi Yamamoto
Mr. and Mrs. Takeshi Yamamoto
Teruji Yamamoto
Mr. and Mrs. Tetsuo Yamamoto
Mr. Thomas Y. Yamamoto
Mr. Thomi J. Yamamoto
Mr. Tim Yamamoto
Mr. Tom M. Yamamoto
Mr. and Mrs. Tom T. Yamamoto
Mr. Tsuneaki Yamamoto
Mr. Victor M. Yamamoto
Mr. and Mrs. Wayne Yamamoto
Mr. and Mrs. William C. Yamamoto
Mr. and Mrs. William T. Yamamoto
Mr. Yoichi Yamamoto
Ms. Yoshiko J. Yamamoto
Mr. Yukio Yamamoto
Mr. and Mrs. Yukio Yamamoto
Mr. and Mrs. Yutaka Yamamoto
Mr. Gregory B. Yamamura
Mr. Kenneth I. Yamamura
Mr. Lawrence Yamamura
Mr. Mariko Yamamura
Mr. Norman K. Yamamura
Mr. and Mrs. Ron Yamamura
Mr. and Mrs. Yoshito Yamamura
Mr. Robert Yamanaga
Mr. Benjamin E. Yamanaka
Mr. Bill T. Yamanaka
Mr. Dale Yamanaka
Mr. Dean Yamanaka
Mr. Frank Yamanaka
Ms. Gail S. Yamanaka
Mr. Harold K. Yamanaka
Mr. Haruyuki Yamanaka
Mr. and Mrs. Iwao Yamanaka
Mr. Jiro Yamanaka
Ms. Kazue K. Yamanaka
Mr. and Mrs. Kazumasa Yamanaka
Ms. Lillian A. Yamanaka
Lynn Yamanaka and Tim Thompson
Mrs. Marjorie H. Yamanaka
Mr. Mark Y. Yamanaka
Mr. Masao Yamanaka
Mr. Sam Yamanaka
Ms. Susan Yamanaka
Ms. Terue Yamanaka
Mr. Thomas T. Yamanaka
Mr. Tohru Yamanaka
Ms. Yuriko Yamanaka
Ms. Kim Yamanaka Brayfield
Ms. Amy Yamane
Mr. and Mrs. Arthur Yamane
Mr. and Mrs. Bennie Yamane
Curt and Juliette Yamane
Mr. and Mrs. Daniel Yamane
Mr. David M. Yamane

Mr. and Mrs. David T. Yamane
Dawn, Karen and Erik Yamane
Mr. Dick H. Yamane
Mr. George T. Yamane
Mr. Glenn Yamane
Mr. Henry Yamane
Mr. Hideo Yamane
Mr. James Yamane
Ms. Janet K. Yamane
Mr. Jimmie Yamane
Mr. Katsumi Yamane
Mr. Kei Yamane
Mr. Kenji Yamane
Mr. and Mrs. Kenneth Yamane
Ms. Kimiko Yamane
Mr. and Mrs. Masaye Yamane
Mr. and Mrs. Mitsuzo Yamane
Ms. Patricia K. Yamane
Mr. Raymond Yamane
Mr. and Mrs. Roger Yamane
Mr. Takayuki Yamane
Mr. Terry Y. Yamane
Mr. and Mrs. Tonney Yamane
Mrs. Tora Yamane
William Yamane and Sharon A. Kumagai
Mr. Alan Yamani
Mr. and Mrs. Akiji Yamanishi
Mr. Herbert Yamanishi
Mr. Joseph Yamanishi
Mr. Louie Yamanishi
Mr. and Mrs. Fred Yamano
Mr. William Yamano
Mr. and Mrs. Allen Yamanoha
Ms. Carol Yamanuha
Ms. Chizuko Yamaoka
Mr. Clifford Yamaoka
Mr. and Mrs. Don Yamaoka
Mr. and Mrs. Don H. Yamaoka
Mr. George T. Yamaoka
Mr. Jim Yamaoka
Mr. Joseph Yamaoka
Mrs. Mas Yamaoka
Mrs. Ruby Yamaoka
Mr. Takaji Yamaoka
Mr. and Mrs. Ted Y. Yamaoka
Mr. Akira Yamasaki
Ms. Alice Yamasaki
Mr. Arthur Yamasaki
Mr. Brent B. Yamasaki
Mr. Bryan Yamasaki
Ms. Christine Yamasaki
Mr. Dean Yamasaki
Mr. and Mrs. Dennis Yamasaki
Mr. and Mrs. Frank Yamasaki
George and Sumiko Yamasaki
Mr. George Yamasaki
Mrs. Grace I. Yamasaki
Mr. and Mrs. Hideo Ray Yamasaki
Mrs. Hiromi Elizabeth Yamasaki
Mr. Hiroshi Yamasaki
Mr. and Mrs. Hiroshi Yamasaki
Mr. and Mrs. James N. Yamasaki
Mrs. Jane A. Yamasaki
Ms. Janet N. Yamasaki
Dr. and Mrs. Jun Yamasaki and Family
Mr. and Mrs. Kenneth Yamasaki
Mr. Kent Yamasaki
Ms. Kiyoko Yamasaki
Ms. Mary Yamasaki
Mrs. Mary M. Yamasaki
Mr. and Mrs. Mas Yamasaki
Mr. Masao Yamasaki
Mr. and Mrs. Morton Yamasaki
Mr. Moto Yamasaki
Mr. and Mrs. Noboru Yamasaki
Mr. Peter Yamasaki
Mr. and Mrs. Raymond Yamasaki
Richard and Fumi Yamasaki
Mr. Rick Yamasaki
Mr. and Mrs. Robert Yamasaki
Mr. and Mrs. Ryoichi Yamasaki
Mr. and Mrs. Sam Yamasaki
Mr. and Mrs. Scott Yamasaki
Mr. and Mrs. Shigeo Yamasaki
Mr. Steve H. Yamasaki
Ms. Sue Yamasaki
Mr. and Mrs. Suenobu Yamasaki
Mr. Takato Yamasaki
Mr. and Mrs. Thomas S. Yamasaki
Mr. Tom Yamasaki
Mr. and Mrs. Tsuneo Yamasaki
Mr. Vincent Yamasaki
Mr. Wesly Yamasaki
Mr. William Yamasaki
Ms. Y. Betty Yamasaki
Ms. Yoshiko Yamasaki

Ms. Youko Yamasaki
Mr. and Mrs. Yutaka Yamasaki
Mr. and Mrs. Yuzuru Yamasaki
Ms. Tomoko Yamasata
Mr. James Yamashige
Ms. Yukiko Yamashina
Dr. and Mrs. Alan Yamashiro
Mr. Allan K. Yamashiro
Ms. Alyce Yamashiro
Mr. and Mrs. Dean Yamashiro
Mr. and Mrs. Dennis T. Yamashiro
Mr. Donald Yamashiro
Mr. Edwin S. Yamashiro
Mr. Fred Yamashiro
Mr. George Yamashiro
Mr. and Mrs. Jack Yamashiro
Ms. Judy J. Yamashiro
Mr. Lance Yamashiro
Mr. Larry Yamashiro
Mr. and Mrs. Masao Yamashiro
Ms. Rachael Yamashiro
Mr. and Mrs. Rodney Yamashiro
Ms. Sandy T. Yamashiro
Mr. and Mrs. Setsuzo Yamashiro
Ms. Shizue Yamashiro
Mr. Shoei Yamashiro
Mr. Stephen K. Yamashiro
Mr. and Mrs. Tadao Yamashiro
Mr. Takeshi Yamashiro
Mr. and Mrs. Yasuo Yamashiro
Mrs. Yoshiyuki Yamashiro
Mr. Aichi Yamashiroya
Mr. and Mrs. Herbert Yamashiroya
Mr. and Mrs. Roy Yamashiroya
Mrs. Asako S. Yamashita
Bobby Yamashita and Ida Shimada
Mr. Bruce I. Yamashita
Byrnes K. Yamashita
Ms. Cheryl N. Yamashita
Ms. Dana Yamashita
Mr. David Yamashita
Mr. Duane Yamashita
Mr. and Mrs. Gary A. Yamashita
Mr. and Mrs. George Yamashita
Mr. and Mrs. George H. Yamashita
Mr. Glen Yamashita
Mr. and Mrs. H. H. Yamashita
Mr. Harry Yamashita and Ms. Kimberly J. Anderson
Ms. Haruka Yamashita
Mrs. Haruno Yamashita
Mr. and Mrs. Haruo Yamashita
Mr. and Mrs. Henry Yamashita
Mr. Henry H. Yamashita
Mr. Hisako Yamashita
Mr. and Mrs. Isami Yamashita
Mr. and Mrs. Isamu Sam Yamashita
Mr. and Mrs. Iwao Yamashita
Ms. Jane Yamashita
Mr. John H. Yamashita
Mr. and Mrs. Johnny Yamashita
Mr. and Mrs. Kaname Yamashita
Mrs. Kay K. Yamashita
Ms. Kazuyo Yamashita
Ms. Kelly A. Yamashita
Mr. Kenneth Yamashita
Mr. Kenneth K. Yamashita
Ms. Lily Yamashita
Ms. M. Barbara Yamashita
Ms. Margaret Yamashita
Mr. Masato Yamashita
Yamashita Flower Farm, Inc.
Ms. Pauline Yamashita
Mr. and Mrs. Robert Yamashita
Mr. and Mrs. Ruichi Yamashita
Mr. Sam Yamashita
Mrs. Saye Yamashita
Mr. Scot Yamashita
Mr. and Mrs. Shigeru Yamashita
Ms. Shizuho Yamashita
Mr. Sueo Yamashita
Ms. Sumika Yamashita
Ms. Susan Yamashita
Mr. and Mrs. Tak Yamashita
Mr. Takeshi Yamashita
Mr. Tokio Yamashita
Mrs. Tomoe Yamashita
Mr. and Mrs. Tsuneo Yamashita
Mr. and Mrs. Yoshio Yamashita
Mr. and Mrs. Mas Yamatani
Ms. Nancy Yamatani
Ms. Aileen Yamate
Mr. and Mrs. Henry T. Yamate
Kiyoto and Mitsuko Yamate
Ms. Tamiko Yamate
Mr. and Mrs. Lance Yamato
Mr. Ronald M. Yamato

Mr. Takeo Yamato
Mr. and Mrs. Tetsuo Yamato
Yamauchi Family
Mr. and Mrs. Akira Yamauchi
Mr. Bradley Yamauchi
Mr. Bud S. Yamauchi
Mr. and Mrs. Carl Yamauchi
Mr. and Mrs. Cary S. Yamauchi
Mr. and Mrs. Craig Yamauchi
Mr. Danny Yamauchi
Mr. Fujio Yamauchi
Mr. Gary Yamauchi
Mr. George M. Yamauchi
Ms. Gloria Yamauchi
Mr. Harry H. Yamauchi
Mr. and Mrs. Hiroshi Yamauchi
Ms. Joanne S. Yamauchi
Mr. Jonathan Yamauchi
Mr. and Mrs. Kenbo Yamauchi
Mrs. Kimi Yamauchi
Ms. Lisa M. Yamauchi
Ms. Lucy Yamauchi
Mr. and Mrs. Nancy Yamauchi
Mr. Richard Z. Yamauchi
Ms. Ruth S. Yamauchi
Mr. and Mrs. Samuel Yamauchi
Ms. Shizuko Yamauchi
Mr. and Mrs. Victor Yamauchi
Mr. George Yamayoshi
Mr. Tom Yamayoshi
Ms. Deborah Yamazaki
Dr. and Mrs. Francis Yamazaki
Mr. Genichi Yamazaki
Ms. Louise Hana Yamazaki
Dr. and Mrs. Mark W. Yamazaki
Mr. and Mrs. Peter Yamazaki
Mr. and Mrs. Russell Yamazaki
Mr. and Mrs. Scott K. Yamazaki
Mr. and Mrs. William T. Yamazaki
Mr. and Mrs. Hiroaki Yamoto
Mr. and Mrs. David Yanaga
Mr. Dwight Yanaga
Ms. Judy H. Yanaga
Mr. Oliver Yanaga
Mr. Carlton M. Yanagi
Ms. Dorothy Yanagi
Ms. Noriko Yanagi
Mr. Norio Yanagi
Mrs. Pius K. Yanagi
Mr. Sanford Yanagi
Mr. and Mrs. Tad Yanagi
Dr. Tom Yanagi
Mr. Gary S. Yanagida
Mr. and Mrs. Roy Yanagida
Mrs. Shizuye Yanagida
Mr. and Mrs. Tetsuo Yanagida
Mr. and Mrs. Yoshio Yanagida
Ms. Christine Yanagidate
Mr. Frederick T. Yanagihara
Mrs. Kaworu Yanagihara
Ms. Keiko Yanagihara
Mr. Alan R. Yanagimachi
Mr. and Mrs. Frank S. Yanagimachi
Mr. Harry Yanagimachi
Mr. and Mrs. Harry I. Yanagimachi
Mr. David Yanagisawa
Mackay Yanagisawa
Mr. and Mrs. Ronald Yanagisawa
Ms. Elizabeth Yanagitani
Mr. Noboru Yanagitani
Mr. H. Steve Yanai
Mr. and Mrs. Roy Yanai
Amb. Shunji Yanai
Miwako Yanamoto
Mr. and Mrs. Franklin Yanamura
Mr. Haines Yanamura
Mr. and Mrs. Carl Yanari
Mr. Dean M. Yanari
Mr. and Mrs. Frank Yanari
Mr. and Mrs. Ralph Yanari
Mr. and Mrs. Sam Yanari
Mr. and Mrs. Kazuo Yanase
Mr. Stanley H. Yanase
Ms. Beatrice Y. Yanehiro
Ms. Caroline Matano Yang
Ms. Roberta M. Yang and Jeffrey Chop
Ms. Tina Yang
Mr. Gregory A. Yankovsky
Mr. George A. Yankura
Ms. Alice Yano
Ms. Cheryl Yano
Mr. and Mrs. Edward H. Yano
Fumiko Yano
Mr. and Mrs. George Yano
Ms. Helen Yano
Mr. Hiroshi Yano

Mr. and Mrs. Katoshi Yano
Mr. and Mrs. Kiyoshi Yano
Mr. Lester Yano
Ms. Marcella T. Yano
Mr. and Mrs. Max W. Yano
Ms. Mutsuko Yano
Mrs. Pauline A. Yano
Mr. and Mrs. Ronald Yano
Mr. Satoji Yano
Seiichi Yano
Stella Yano and Family
Mr. and Mrs. Ted Yano
Mr. Toyo Yano
Ms. Yoshie Yano
Ms. Yuko Yano
Ms. Mary S. Yanokawa
Mr. David Y. Yao
Mrs. Naomi H. Yap
Ms. Mae E. Yaplee
Mr. and Mrs. Edward Yasaki
Mr. and Mrs. Masao Yasaki
Mr. and Mrs. N. Yasaki
Mr. Paul T. Yasaki
Mr. Philip Yasaki
Mr. David Y. Yasuda
Mr. Edward T. Yasuda
Mr. and Mrs. Henry Yasuda
Hirono and Kendo Yasuda
Isao and Marian Yasuda
Mr. and Mrs. Joseph Yasuda
Ms. Marion Yasuda
Mr. and Mrs. Masami Yasuda
Mr. and Mrs. Minoru Yasuda
Mr. Richard Y. Yasuda
Ms. Rosalie Y. Yasuda
Mrs. Sumiko Yasuda
Toni Yasuda
Ms. Yuriko Yasuda
Mr. Allan T. Yasue
Mr. Haruhiko Yasuhara
Mr. Herbert M. Yasuhara
Mr. Ted Yasuhara
Mr. Thomas Yasuhara
Mr. and Mrs. Shinsato Yasuhiko
Mr. Robert Yasuhira
Mrs. Lucy E. Yasuhiro
Mr. Arthur Yasui
Ms. Barbara Yasui
Mr. Bertram Yasui
Mr. and Mrs. Earl T. Yasui
Mr. and Mrs. Edward Y. Yasui
Mr. Hisashi Yasui
Ms. Holly Yasui
Ms. Kazuye Yasui
Ms. Laurel D. Yasui
Lise Yasui and David Haas
Dr. and Mrs. Robert S. Yasui
Mr. Tommy T. Yasui
Mrs. True S. Yasui
Mr. Fred Yasukawa
Mr. and Mrs. Leo I. Yasukawa
Mr. and Mrs. Ernest Yasukochi
Mr. and Mrs. Fred M. Yasukochi
Mr. and Mrs. George Yasukochi
George, Bess and Valerie Yasukochi and James Duff
Ms. Jennifer S. Yasukochi
Ms. Miyo Yasukochi
Ms. Peggy Yasukochi
Mr. Tasuke Yasukochi
Mr. Harry Yasumoto
Mr. and Mrs. John Yasumoto
Mr. and Mrs. Shyun Yasumoto
Mr. Walter Yasumoto
Ms. Yuriye Yasumoto
Mrs. Alice Yasumura
Mr. and Mrs. Kengi Yasumura
Mr. and Mrs. Roy Yasumura
Ms. Tomoe Yasumura
Ms. Ellen Yasunaga
Ms. Linda Yasunaga
Mrs. Sally Y. Yasunaga
Mr. Rodney Yasunari
Mr. Masahiro Yasuoka
Mrs. Eiko Yasutake
Mr. Gary H. Yasutake
Mr. and Mrs. Jim Yasutake
Ms. Joan T. Yasutake
Dr. and Mrs. Joseph Yasutake
Misao and Atsushi Yasutake
Mr. and Mrs. Tom Yasutake
Mr. Dennis Yasutomi
Mrs. Noriko Yasutomi
Mr. Wayne Yasutomi
Ms. Autumn Yatabe
Mr. and Mrs. Joseph Yatabe
Mr. and Mrs. Michael Yatabe

Mr. Sadao Yatabe
Mr. Robert M. Yatagai
Mr. Crail E. Yates
Mr. Harvey Y. Yatogo
Mr. and Mrs. Koji Yatogo
Mr. and Mrs. Charles Yatsu
Ms. Miyo Yatsu
Ms. Kikuye Yatsuhashi
Mr. Yasuo Yatsushiro
Ms. Maile Yawata
Mr. Eugene Yayoshi
Mr. and Mrs. Melvin Yazawa
Mr. and Mrs. Hisao W. Yebisu
Mr. and Mrs. Walter S. Yeda
Mr. Jimmie Yee
Ms. Lois K. Yee
Ms. Lucille A. Yee
Mr. Michael Yee
Mr. and Mrs. Richard F. Yee
Mr. and Mrs. Richard S. Yee
Mr. and Mrs. Shubert Yee
Ms. Sylvia M. Yee
Mr. Slim Yei
Mr. and Mrs. Elliott Yellin
Ms. Jane Yemoto
Mr. Misaki Yemoto
Mr. and Mrs. Russell Yemoto
Mr. Ralph Yempuku
Ms. Janice Yen
Dr. Midori Yenari
Mr. and Mrs. George Yenoki
Ms. Kikuko Yeto
Ms. Mary Yeto
Ms. Setsuko Faith Yim
Mr. and Mrs. William Yim
Mr. and Mrs. John Yockey
Mr. Shuji Yoda
Mr. Hiranori Yogi
Mr. Masayoshi Yogi
Mr. Tadashi Yogi
Ms. Toyoko Yogi
T. Yoketani
Mrs. Tamotsu Yokobata
Mr. Robert Yokobe
Mr. and Mrs. Charles Yokochi
Ms. Lance Yokochi
Mr. and Mrs. John M. Yokoe
Mr. and Mrs. Yukio Yokoe
Ms. Grace Yokogawa
Mr. and Mrs. Nobuyuki Yokogawa
Mr. and Mrs. Tadashi Yokogawa
Ms. Yoshimi Yokohari
Ms. Ellen H. Yokoi
Mr. and Mrs. Fred Yokoi
Mr. and Mrs. Henry K. Yokoi
Mr. Hiromasa Yokoi
Mr. Morio Yokoi
Mr. and Mrs. Paul H. Yokoi
Mr. Steven K. Yokoi
Ms. Amy Yokomi
Ms. Ann M. Yokomi
Ms. Jean M. Yokomi
Mr. and Mrs. Ben Yokomizo
Mr. and Mrs. Grant H. Yokomizo
Mr. and Mrs. Motomi Yokomizo
Mr. and Mrs. Shichiro Yokomizo
Ms. Tarynn N. Yokomizo
Ms. Yoshiko Yokomizo
Mr. and Mrs. Hidejiro Yokoo
Mr. and Mrs. Iwao Yokooji
Ms. June T. Yokooji
Ms. Lynn Yokooji
Ms. Shizuye Yokoro
Ms. Ai Yokota
Ms. Ann Yokota
Ms. Doris Yokota
Mrs. Frances M. Yokota
Ms. Fumi Yokota
Mr. Hideaki Yokota
Mr. Hiroshi Yokota
Ms. Irene Yokota
Mr. and Mrs. Itsuo Yokota
Mr. and Mrs. James M. Yokota
Ken, Fran and Todd Yokota
Mr. and Mrs. Ken Yokota
Ms. Laura Yokota
Mr. and Mrs. Minoru Yokota
Mr. Paul Yokota
Mr. Richard Yokota
Mr. and Mrs. Ronald Yokota
Mr. and Mrs. Seiken Yokota
Mr. and Mrs. Shigeo Yokota
Toshiye Yokota
Mrs. Yuriko Yokota
Mr. and Mrs. Eric Yokote
Mr. Royce Yokote

Mr. and Mrs. Shigeo Yokote
Ms. Ayako Alice Yokoyama
Mr. David R. Yokoyama
Mr. Don Yokoyama
Ms. Fusaye Yokoyama
Mr. and Mrs. George Yokoyama
Mr. and Mrs. George H. Yokoyama
Mr. and Mrs. Harold H. Yokoyama
Mrs. Hisako Yokoyama
Mr. and Mrs. Japo I. Yokoyama
Mr. and Mrs. Ken T. Yokoyama
Masami Yokoyama
Ms. Miyeko Yokoyama
Mr. Moto Yokoyama
Mr. Noboru Yokoyama
Mr. and Mrs. Norman K. Yokoyama
Mr. Ralph Yokoyama
Mr. and Mrs. Robert Yokoyama
Mr. and Mrs. Robert I. Yokoyama
Mr. Roy Yokoyama
Mr. Ryuji Yokoyama
Mr. Shigeru Yokoyama
Mr. and Mrs. Taro Yokoyama
Mr. and Mrs. Terry Yokoyama
Thomas and Francisca Yokoyama
Mr. Thomas W. Yokoyama
Mr. and Mrs. Tokuo Yokoyama
Mr. and Mrs. Torao Yokoyama
Mr. and Mrs. Wako Yokoyama
Mrs. Yaeko Yokoyama
Ms. Yasue Yokoyama
Mrs. Glenn Yomogida
Mr. and Mrs. Edward Yomogida
Mr. Lane Yonago
Mr. and Mrs. Lloyd Yonago
Ms. Lury Yonago
Mr. S. Yonaki
Mr. and Mrs. Sada Yonaki
Mr. Calvin Yonamine
Mr. Eikichi Yonamine
Mr. Henry K. Yonamine
Wally Yonamine Pearl Co.
Ms. Patsy Yonamine
Mr. Stanley S. Yonamine
Ms. Wendy Yonamine
Mrs. Edna Yonaoshi
Mr. Akira Yoneda
Mr. Garrett Yoneda
Ms. Grace Yoneda
Mr. and Mrs. Hiromi Yoneda
Mr. John Yoneda
Mr. and Mrs. Kazuo Yoneda
Mr. and Mrs. Minoru Yoneda
Mr. Ruth M. Yoneda
Mr. T. Ted Yoneda
Mr. Bruce L. Yonehiro
Mr. Grant Yonehiro
Mr. Donald Yoneji
Mr. and Mrs. Mitsuo Yoneji
Ms. Alice Yonekura
Mr. and Mrs. Iwao Yonemitsu
Mr. Ray Yonemitsu
Asa Yonemori
Ms. Aileen C. Yonemori
Mr. and Mrs. Hide Yonemoto
Mr. and Mrs. James Yonemoto
Ms. Marcia Yonemoto
Ms. Mary Yonemoto
Mr. and Mrs. Robert Yonemoto
Ronald M. Yonemoto
Ms. Ann Yonemura
Mr. Fred Y. Yonemura
Mr. and Mrs. George Yonemura
Mr. Jerry Yonemura
Mr. Joe Yonemura
Mr. and Mrs. Kenneth Y. Yonemura
Mr. Mark M. Yonemura
Ms. Mary S. Yonemura
Mr. Paul Yonemura
Mr. and Mrs. Raymond Yonemura
Mr. Susumu Yonemura
Mr. Tom Yonemura
Mrs. Yayeko Yonesawa
Mr. Frank Yoneshige
Mr. Hiroshi Yoneshige
Mr. and Mrs. Roy Yoneshige
Mr. and Mrs. Shoji Yoneshige
Ms. Nina Yonetani
Mr. Craig Yoneyama
Mr. and Mrs. George Yoneyama
Mr. and Mrs. Isamu Yoneyama
Ms. Linda Yoneyama
Mrs. Mary Yoneyama
Mr. and Mrs. Takao T. Yoneyama
Mr. Richard Yonezaki
Mr. Kengo Yorioka

Dr. George Yorita
Mr. James H. Yorita
Mr. and Mrs. Matao L. Yorita
Ms. Miwako Yorita
Ms. Sharon Yorita
Ms. Tomiko Yorita
Mr. Yasutomo Yoritaka
Mr. and Mrs. Kent T. Yoritomo
Mr. Henry K. Yorozu
Miss Aki Yosheda
Akiko Yoshida and Brian Bentel
Ms. Arlene Y. Yoshida
Mr. Ben T. Yoshida
Ms. Betty Yoshida
Mr. and Mrs. Byron Yoshida
Ms. Carol Yoshida
Ms. Carole Yoshida
Mr. and Mrs. Charles Yoshida
Mr. Clayton Yoshida
Mr. Dan Yoshida
Mr. David M. Yoshida
Mr. and Mrs. Don K. Yoshida
Mr. Douglas K. Yoshida
Mr. Douglas M. Yoshida
Mr. and Mrs. Douglas T. Yoshida
Mr. Edward T. Yoshida
Mr. Gary K. Yoshida
Ms. Gayle Yoshida
Mr. and Mrs. George Yoshida
Mr. and Mrs. George S. Yoshida
Mr. Harold Yoshida
Mr. and Mrs. Harry S. Yoshida
Mr. Irene R. Yoshida
Mr. and Mrs. James Yoshida
Mr. James M. Yoshida
Ms. Jessie C. Yoshida
Mr. Jitsuo Yoshida
Mr. Junko Yoshida
Ms. Kay Yoshida
Mr. Kazuto Yoshida
Mr. Kenneth K. Yoshida
Mr. and Mrs. Kiyoshi Yoshida
Mr. and Mrs. Kiyoto Yoshida
Mr. Korekazu Yoshida
Mr. and Mrs. Lester Yoshida
Mr. Mako Yoshida
Ms. Martha M. Yoshida
Ms. Mary T. Yoshida
Mr. Mas Yoshida
Mr. Masao Yoshida
Mr. and Mrs. Masaru Yoshida
Mr. and Mrs. Masayuki Yoshida
Mr. Matt Yoshida
Mrs. May Yoshida
Ms. Midori Yoshida
Ms. Miyako Yoshida
Mr. Mizuho David Yoshida
Mr. Norman E. Yoshida
Mr. and Mrs. Paul H. Yoshida
Mr. Paul M. Yoshida
Mr. Ray Yoshida
Mr. Richard Yoshida
Mr. Robert Yoshida
Mr. Robert Y. Yoshida
Ms. Roberta Yoshida
Mr. Rodney Yoshida
Mr. and Mrs. Ronald M. Yoshida
Mr. and Mrs. Ronald S. Yoshida
Mr. and Mrs. Scott Yoshida
Ms. Selma E. Yoshida
Ms. Sharon Yoshida
Mr. Shigeru Yoshida
Mr. and Mrs. Sho Yoshida
Mr. and Mrs. Stanley N. Yoshida
Ms. Susan Yoshida
Ms. Susan K. Yoshida
Dr. Takashi Yoshida
Mr. Takashi Yoshida
Mr. and Mrs. Takeshi Yoshida
Mr. Terence Yoshida
Mr. Thomas M. Yoshida
Mr. and Mrs. Thomas S. Yoshida
Mr. and Mrs. Warren S. Yoshida
Mr. and Mrs. Yasuo Yoshida
Ms. Yoko Yoshida
Mrs. Yone Yoshida
Mr. and Mrs. Yoshiichi Yoshida
Mr. Yoshitaka Yoshida
Mr. Yuji Yoshida
Yutaka and Sachi Yoshida
Mr. and Mrs. Yuzo Yoshida
Mr. and Mrs. Ben Yoshihara
Ms. Chiyoko Yoshihara
Mr. Dale Yoshihara
Mr. and Mrs. Harry M. Yoshihara
Mr. and Mrs. Koichi Yoshihara

Ms. Lucy Yoshihara
Mr. and Mrs. Robert Yoshihara
Mr. and Mrs. Taro Yoshihara
Mr. and Mrs. Yukio Bob Yoshihara
Dr. Ann Yoshihashi
Mr. Ichiro Yoshihashi
Mr. and Mrs. Taro Yoshihashi
Mr. and Mrs. Tokuji Yoshihashi
Mr. Robert M. Yoshihiro
Mr. and Mrs. Kiyoshi Yoshii
Ms. Mariko Yoshii
Mr. and Mrs. Michio Yoshii
Mr. T. L. Yoshii
Mrs. Thelma Yoshii
Mr. Yoshio Yoshii
Mr. Edward Yoshikado
Mr. and Mrs. Henry Yoshikai
Ms. Doris K. Yoshikami
Mr. and Mrs. Melvin Yoshikami
Dr. and Mrs. Shuko Yoshikami
Mr. Derek Yoshikane
Mr. Roy Yoshikane
Mr. and Mrs. Toma Yoshikane
Dr. and Mrs. Agness Yoshikawa
Mr. Albert S. Yoshikawa
Mr. Benjamin Yoshikawa
Ed and Aiko Yoshikawa
Mr. and Mrs. Edward Yoshikawa
Mrs. Elaine Y. Yoshikawa
Mr. Frank T. Yoshikawa
Mr. and Mrs. Gordon Yoshikawa
Mr. Harry Yoshikawa
Mr. and Mrs. Herbert Yoshikawa
Mr. Kenneth Yoshikawa
Ms. Kristi A. Yoshikawa
Ms. Lorraine Yoshikawa
Ms. Pamela Yoshikawa
Mr. and Mrs. Richard Yoshikawa
Mr. and Mrs. Robert M. Yoshikawa
Mr. and Mrs. Shiro Yoshikawa
Ms. Yoshio Yoshikawa
Mr. and Mrs. Yukio Yoshikawa
Ms. Teruko R. Yoshiki
Molly and Russell K. Yoshimaru
Mr. and Mrs. George Yoshimi
Mr. and Mrs. Henry Yoshimi
Mr. and Mrs. Carl Yoshimine
Dr. and Mrs. Masao Yoshimine
Mr. and Mrs. Mike Yoshimine
Mr. Gary N. Yoshimiya
Mr. Tim Yoshimiya
Herbert and Jeannette Yoshimori
Ms. Beatrice Yoshimoto
Mr. Carlos Yoshimoto
Mr. Cedric K. Yoshimoto
Dr. Cedric M. Yoshimoto
Mr. and Mrs. Craig Yoshimoto
Mrs. Edith Yoshimoto
Mr. and Mrs. Evan Yoshimoto
Ms. Gail N. Yoshimoto
Mr. George Yoshimoto
Mr. Herbert M. Yoshimoto
Ms. Irene H. Yoshimoto
Mr. Jack Yoshimoto
Ms. Jan E. Yoshimoto
Mr. and Mrs. Kazumi Yoshimoto
Mr. and Mrs. Kazuo Yoshimoto
Mr. Mike Yoshimoto
Mr. Miles M. Yoshimoto
Mr. Richard K. Yoshimoto
Mr. Ronald K. Yoshimoto
Mr. Satoru Yoshimoto

Mr. Shawn Yoshimoto
Mr. and Mrs. Shig Yoshimoto
Mr. and Mrs. Stanley Yoshimoto
Mr. and Mrs. Steven Yoshimoto
Mr. Tadao Yoshimoto
Mr. Watson T. Yoshimoto
Mr. Wayne T. Yoshimoto
Mr. and Mrs. William Yoshimoto
Mr. and Mrs. Tom M. Yoshimune
Mrs. Amy Y. Yoshimura
Ms. Arlene Yoshimura
Mrs. Betty M. Yoshimura
Mr. Charles Yoshimura
Mr. Clyde M. Yoshimura
Mr. David Yoshimura
Ms. Dawn Yoshimura
Ms. Dorothy H. Yoshimura
Mr. and Mrs. Elsie Yoshimura
Mr. Harold S. Yoshimura
Mr. and Mrs. Ichiro Yoshimura
Ms. Isako Yoshimura
Mr. and Mrs. James Yoshimura
Ms. Jayne Yoshimura
Ms. Jeaneatte Yoshimura
Mr. and Mrs. Kenji Yoshimura
Mr. and Mrs. Masaru M. Yoshimura
Ms. Michiko Yoshimura
Mr. and Mrs. Noboru Yoshimura
Mr. and Mrs. Roy Yoshimura
Mr. and Mrs. Samuel M. Yoshimura
Mr. Terry Yoshimura
Mrs. Thelma Yoshimura
Mr. Torajiro Yoshimura
Mr. and Mrs. Tosh Yoshimura
Mr. and Mrs. Toshio Yoshimura
Mr. Tsuyoshi Yoshimura
Dr. Valerie Yoshimura and Mr. William Shay
Mr. and Mrs. William K. Yoshimura
Mr. Yoneo Yoshimura
Ms. Yoshiko Yoshimura
Mr. and Mrs. Yoshimasa Yoshimura
Ms. Yosie Yoshimura
Mr. Yukio Yoshimura
Mr. Shigemi Yoshina
Mrs. Shizue M. Yoshina
Mr. and Mrs. Thurston Yoshina
Mr. and Mrs. Derrick Yoshinaga
Ms. Hime Yoshinaga
Mr. Robert S. Yoshinaga
Mr. Steven Yoshinaga
Mr. Tsugio Yoshinaga
K. A. Yoshinari
Mr. and Mrs. Masami Samuel Yoshinari
Mr. Melvin Yoshinari
Mr. Roger Yoshinari
Ms. Aileen Yoshino
Ms. Alyce M. Yoshino
Ms. Denise L. Yoshino
Mr. Donald Yoshino
Mr. and Mrs. Elmer Yoshino
Mr. Fred H. Yoshino
Mr. George M. Yoshino
Mr. George S. Yoshino
Mr. and Mrs. Hikaru Yoshino
Mr. John Yoshino
Mr. and Mrs. Kenneth K. Yoshino
Mr. Mark Yoshino
Ms. Mary Louise Yoshino
Ms. Nanaye Nina Yoshino
Ms. Patty Yoshino
Ms. Taeko Yoshino
Mr. and Mrs. William J. Yoshino

Ms. Betty Lou Yoshinobu
Mr. Stephen K. Yoshinobu
Mr. and Mrs. Arthur H. Yoshioka
Frank and Agnes Yoshioka
Mr. and Mrs. George Yoshioka
Mr. George S. Yoshioka
Mr. and Mrs. Harry M. Yoshioka
Dr. Howard Yoshioka
Mr. Howard H. Yoshioka
Mr. Jeffrey Yoshioka
Mr. and Mrs. Jitsuo Yoshioka
Ms. Joann Yoshioka
Ms. Karen L. Yoshioka
Mr. Koichiro Yoshioka
Dr. Larry M. Yoshioka
Mr. and Mrs. Lloyd Yoshioka
Ms. Lois Yoshioka
Mr. and Ms. Yoshioka
Mr. Masuo Yoshioka
Mr. and Mrs. Minoru Yoshioka
Ms. Namiye Yoshioka
Mr. Nobuo Yoshioka
Mr. and Mrs. Ralph H. Yoshioka
Mr. Richard H. Yoshioka
Mr. and Mrs. Robert Yoshioka
Mrs. Ruby M. Yoshioka
Mr. Russell Yoshioka
Mr. Takashi Yoshioka
Mr. and Mrs. Thomas Yoshioka
Mr. Toshie Yoshioka
Mr. and Mrs. Vernon T. Yoshioka
Mr. and Mrs. Wayne Yoshioka
Ms. Lois Yoshishige
Ms. Betty Yoshitake
Ms. Doris Yoshitake
Mrs. Miye Yoshitake
Mr. and Mrs. Shige Yoshitake
Mr. Bernard M. Yoshitani
Ms. Karen Yoshitomi
Mr. and Mrs. Michael S. Yoshitomi
Mr. and Mrs. Robert Yoshitomi
Mr. and Mrs. Kenneth T. Yoshiura
Ms. Sue Yoshiura
Ms. Frances Yoshiwara
Mr. Joe Yoshiwara
Ms. Tomiyo Tee Yoshiwara
Mr. Clayton Yoshiyama
Mr. and Mrs. James M. Yoshiyama
Mr. James S. Yoshiyama
Ms. Joan Yoshiyama
Ms. Kerri Yoshiyama
Mr. Kevin Yoshiyama
Mrs. Mary M. Yoshiyama
Mr. and Mrs. Takeo Yoshiyama
Mr. Wallace T. Yoshiyama
Ms. Fumi Yoshizaki
Grace Yoshizaki
Mr. Satoru Yoshizato
Mr. Edwin Yoshizawa
Ms. Ellen Yoshizawa
Mr. Saburo Yoshizawa
Mr. Ernest Yoshizuka
Mr. Homer Yoshizuka
Mr. Richard K. Yoshizuka
Ms. Dawn Yoshizumi
Mr. and Mrs. Gary Yoshizumi
Mrs. Peggy Yost
Ms. Toshiko Yotori
Mr. and Mrs. Aki Yotsuuye
Mr. and Mrs. David S. Yotsuuye
Mr. and Mrs. Roy Yotsuuye
Mr. and Mrs. Arthur Yotsuya

Mr. Marvin Yotsuya
Ms. Matsuko I. Youden
Ms. Chieko Young
Mr. and Mrs. Clay Young
Mr. and Mrs. David W. Young
Ms. Ruth Young
Dr. Wende W. Young
Mr. and Mrs. Harold Youngquist
Mr. and Mrs. Philip Yount
Ms. Mary Youssef
Mr. and Mrs. Hideo Yoza
Mr. Minoru Yoza
Ms. Yoneko Yu
Ms. Margarida Yuan
Mr. James Yuasa
Rev. and Mrs. Michihiro Yuasa
Mr. Takashi Yuasa
Teruyo Yuasa
Mr. and Mrs. Kenneth Yuen
Mrs. Fumiko Yuge
Mr. Isao Yuge
Mr. and Mrs. Shigeo Yuge
Ms. Irene A. Yuguchi
Mrs. Dorothy M. Yuhara
Mr. and Mrs. N. Henry Yui
Mr. and Mrs. John Yukawa
Mr. Rob Yukawa
Mr. and Mrs. Sumio Yukawa
Mr. and Mrs. Gary Yuki
Mr. and Mrs. Harvard Yuki
Ms. Margaret Yuki
Mr. Mike Yuki
Mr. and Mrs. Sadonori Yuki
Mr. Calvin M. Yukihiro
Mr. and Mrs. George Yukihiro
Mr. Robert Yukihiro
Mr. and Mrs. Yoshio Yukinaga
Mr. and Mrs. Paul Yukumoto
Mr. George Yumibe
Ms. Kiyoko Yumibe
Mr. and Mrs. Ben Yumori
Ms. Yukiko Yumori
Ms. Vickie Yumoto
Ms. Atsuko Sue Yusa
Dr. Frederick M. Yutani
Mrs. Jennifer K. Yutani
Mr. and Mrs. Nobuo Yutani
Mr. and Mrs. John Yuyama
Mr. Gene K. Yuzawa
Mr. and Mrs. George K. Yuzawa
Ms. Patricia Yuzawa-Rubin
Ms. Kimiyo Zaima
Mr. and Mrs. Stephen Zaima
Mr. William Zaima
Mr. and Mrs. Bratislav Zak
Mr. and Mrs. Christopher Zanette
Ms. Janet Zarchen
Mr. and Mrs. Richard M. Zarnowitz
Mr. and Mrs. Jonathan R. Zeko
Zen-Noh Unico America Corporation
Mr. Clint T. Zenigami
Mr. and Mrs. Kenso Zenimura
Hoyt Zia and Leigh-Ann Miyasato
Mr. and Mrs. Neal Zierler
Mr. and Mrs. Howard Zink
Ms. Ronnie Zuckerberg
Dr. Jacqueline Zuckerbrod
Ms. Sylvia Zuckerbrod
Mr. Richard Zuercher
Mr. and Mrs. Lester C. Zukeran

Our Supporters Proudly Made Donations In Honor of the Following Individuals and Organizations

100th and 442nd Battalions
100th and 442nd Infantryman
100th and 442nd Veterans
100th Battalion C Company
100th Battalion of Honolulu HI
1399 Veterans Club
176 Language Detachment (Japanese),
   11th Airborne Division
222nd Combat Team
232nd Engineer Combat Team
442 Infantry Regiment
442 RCT
442nd RCT: Anti-tank Company
442nd RCT: Deceased Veterans
442nd RCT: I Company KIAs
442nd RCT: K Company
442nd RCT: L Company
442nd RCT: M Company
Fusako N. Abe
George Y. Abe
Joe K. Abe
Masao Abe
Paul and Toshiko Abe
Mr. & Mrs. Sakichi Abe
Shizu Abe
Yasuaki Abe
Chiyeko T. Abo
Edward H. Aburamen
Sgt. Hiro Adachi
Shizuo R. Adachi
Eiko Aihara
Ben and Sumako Aihara Kaneda
AIJLS Ft. Snelling '45
Chidori Aiso
John Aiso
Paul J. Aiso
Phil C. Ajari
Nae Aka
Helen Akahori
Mr. & Mrs. Mitsuo Akahori
Kunisaburo and Toyo Akahoshi
Rev. & Mrs. Shigetsu and Fusako Akahoshi
Rev. Alfred S. Akamatsu
James T. Akamine
Isoko Akasaki
Tsuyoshi Akazawa
Victor and John Akimoto
Kiyoshi Akita
Kinuye Akiyama
Zentaro G. Akiyama
Mitchy Akiyoshi
Naoji and Hisayo Akune
Jim H. Akutsu
Mary and Jim Akutsu
All 442 Veterans
All Japanese American Servicemen
All Japanese American Soldiers
All Japanese Americans
All Japanese Americans wounded in service
All Nisei soldiers in WWII
All Nisei Vets
All Niseis
All the Isseis
All the People Past! Present! Future!
All those interned during WWII
All those who sacrificed their lives for the cause
All those who were relocated
All Veterans
All war casualties
All who gave their lives for our country
Nobutoshi Amemiya
Frank S. and Kiku Ando
Senkichi and Orae Ando
Enrique, Paul, Angel and Jose Andow
Andow Family
Fusataro and Kishiko Aoki
Jiro E. Aoki
Joseph S. Aoki
Shiro Aoki
Shigeo Aoyagi
Shun and Teru Aoyagi
Bud Aoyama
Sunichi J. and Chiyo R. Aoyama
Col. Toshio Dusty Aoyogi
Glen T. Arai
Harold S. Arai
Masayuki Arai
Junichi Arakaki
Kishin Arakaki
Eizo A. Arakawa
Masaki Araki
Masashi Araki
Robert N. Arao
Taisuke Arao
Violet Arase
Mr. & Mrs. George T. Aratani
Steve Arie
Jim and Asa Ariki
Toru and June Arisumi
Sokichi and Toshiko Arita
Tadashi Arita
Toichi, Yoshino and Takeshi Ariyoshi
Dix T. Asai
Mr. & Mrs. Masuji T. Asaki
Thomas S. Asaki
Shoichi and Shizu Asami
Ken Asamoto

Ryuemon and Mashie Asano
David Asao
Julie Asaoka
Henry Asato
Yeikichi Asato
Henry S. Asato, 442nd Veteran
Kiyoshi and Namiko Aso
Taketaro and Tokiwa Azeka
Mr. & Mrs. George K. Baba
Mitzi Baba
Yoshitaro and Toyo Baba
Sidney Barrows
Joe N. Benson
Sgt. Tadao Beppu
Masaaki Bokura
Shirley Bolinger
John O. Borunda
Broadway HS Nisei Veterans
Pearl S. Buck
Floyd Cambra
Margaret Chang
Taketoshi Chigawa
Chikahisa Family
Kaiji J. Chikamura
Thomas T. Chikaraishi
Iho Chiyoko
Matthew Chung
Mei Cobb
Joyce Y. Cooper
Judy Corbett Family
Charles E. Corker
Lyn Crost
Julie L. Cushman
Carl S. and Eiko Daikai
Taro and Kame Dakuzaku
Mr. Shiro Date
Deceased Parents
Yash Deguchi
William Dietz
Fred Dobana
Marjorie S. Doe
Albert Dohi
Arthur N. Doi
Manjiro and Uta Doi
Osame H. Doi
Thomas and May Doi
William M. Doi
Richard Dungar
Robert and Michi Eejima
Reysaku and Kikuno Egashira
Miyogi and Masa Egawa
Bunkichi Eguchi
Masako and George H. Eji
Chiyoko Eller
Aiji Endo
Den and Hiroshi Endo
Hiroko Endo
Kimio Endo
Neil T. Endo
Isaac and May Endow
Shohei and Tei Endow
Sho Endow, Jr.
Toshio Enokida
Kei Enomoto
Marvin Enomoto
Mas Enomoto
George Enosaki
George S. Eto
Ed Ezaki
James Ezaki
Edward Ezaki and Family
Fahrney Automotive Group
Fallen members of the 442
Father, Mother and their children
Fellow Japanese friends
Warren E. Fencl
Earl M. Finch
Mr. & Mrs. Royal H. Fisher
Keith W. Fiske
John L. Fitzgerald
Maria M. Flores
Friends who served in WWII, Korean
   and Vietnam Wars
Yuki Fuji
Mr. & Mrs. Kaichi Fujihara
Julius Y. Fujihira
Mr. & Mrs. Eikichi Fujii
Hideo H. Fujii
Kaneko, Shizuma, and George Shoji Fujii
Kinji and Midori Fujii
Takao and Kiku Fujii
Ted Fujii
Yoshito Fujii
Yukiko Fujii
Albert H. Fujikawa
Frank Y. and Sueko M. Fujikawa
Yuka Fujikura
Kenzo Fujimori
Fred Y. Fujimoto
George K. Fujimoto
Niozo, Ikuno and Masayuki Fujimoto
Walter L. Fujimoto
Susumu Fujimura
Pete Y. Fujino
Victor Fujio
Doris Fujioka
George, Sam and Curtis Fujioka

Ted Fujioka
PFC Teruo Fujioka
Tracey and Robb Fujioka
George S. Fujioka, PhD
Dr. & Mrs. Charles Fujisaki
June J. Fujisaki
Junji and Yaeno Fujishige
Toshiyuki Fujishige
Burt Fujishima
Mr. & Mrs. Kazzie Fujishima
Mr. & Mrs. Mits Fujishima
Rev. Shuey Fujishiro
Carl and Rosa Fujita
Charles and Keiko Fujita
Harold H. Fujita
Haru Fujita
Katsuichi and Shizue Fujita
Kawaru and Rosa Fujita
Mikiye Fujita
Monte M. Fujita
Yae Fujita
Guy Y. Fujiuchi
Itashiro and Osano Fujiura
PFC Shigeo T. Fukuba
Kozo Fukuda
Seiji and Shima Fukuda
Shigeo Fukuda
Tom Fukuda
Harry Fukuhara
Larry H. Fukuhara
Misayo Fukuhara
Shichi Fukuhara
Yukiye Fukuhara
Fukuhara Family
Yuri K. Fukui
Terumi Fukukawa
Sunshine Fukunaga
Mr. Charles S. Fukutaki
Edward T. Fukutaki
Amy E. Fukuyama
George Fukuyama
Carolyn Funai
Kametaro and Kane Funai
Mitsuko Funai
Hirokichi and Tatsu Funakoshi
Willie Funakoshi
Isamu, Minoru, Masao and James Funamura
Takaichi Furuhashi
Margaret and Sam Furuichi
Ukio Furuike
Jack Y. Furukawa
Sally S. Furukawa
Terumi Furukawa
Janette H. Furukawa-Boudreau
PFC Hank Furushiro
Henry T. Furushiro
Louis Furushiro
Kaz Furusho
Pete A. Furuta
Mr. & Mrs. Charles Furuyama
Kiyoshi and Hisao Furuzawa
Shigeo Futagaki
Daniel J. Garvey
John Gerrity
Gila River Relocation Center
Henry H. Gosho
George T. Goto
Kenneth K. Goto
Nobuaki Goto
Toshio L. Goto
George Yama Goya
Ushigi and Sandra Goya
Taki Greenberg
Harold Gresham
Robert Griffiths
Mr. & Mrs. M. Gyotoku
Mr. & Mrs. Shiroku Hachisuka
Frank T. Hachiya
Mr. & Mrs. Hisata Hachiya
Kimiyo Hachiya
Victor Hada
Noriko Hagan
Tom S. Haji
Anne Hall
Harry Hamada
Mr. & Mrs. Hachizo Hamaguchi
Lester M. Hamai
Robert Hamashige
Tona and Shinkichi Hamashige
Tsuru and Tokuji Hamasu
Toshio Hamataka
Hiroshi, Joe, Howard and David Hamaguchi
Kazumi Hanada
Mr. & Mrs. Masata Hanada
Masa Hanamura
Tamotsu Hanida
Harry N. Hara
Hikobe and Yoshino Hara
Minoru Hara
Mr. & Mrs. Tonakichi Hara
Dr. & Mrs. Harold Harada
Hideo Harada
Kiyomi Harada
Nobuko Harada
Saburo Harada
Takino F. Harada
Sgt. John Harano

Mrs. M. Harano
Yoshito Haratani
Junko Harui
Hiroshi R. Haruki
Roscoe Haruki
Andrew and Chiyoko Hasegawa
Helen and Ray Hasegawa
Hid Hasegawa
Margaret Hasegawa
Peter K. Hasegawa
Tomio Hasegawa
Mr. & Mrs. Hasegawa
Mr. & Mrs. Chokichi Hashiguchi
Chosaku and Riku Hashiguchi
Hachiro Hashiguchi
Nasuo Hashiguchi
Dick T. Hashimoto
James Hashimoto
Mr. & Mrs. Juichi Hashimoto
Mas Hashimoto
Mr. & Mrs. Masamori Hashimoto
Nobuto and Masayo Hashimoto
Reiko Hashimoto
Shigezu, Mizuye, Tamari Hashimoto
Shizuko and Hank Hashimoto
Skyler Hasuike
Harry Z. Hasuko
Jack Hata
Jack H. Hata
Richard H. Hata
Sakuji Hatada
Guy T. Hatago
Roy T. Hatakenaka
Tom and Kazue Hatanaka
Harry Hatasaka, DDS
Kim Hatashita
Kozo and Masaki Hattori
Harry M. Hayakawa
Kenneth Hayakawa
Dr. Samuel I. Hayakawa
Alice Hayama
PFC Stanley Hayami
Charles Hayase
Ryoichi and Satoko Hayase
Ei Hayashi
Futami Hayashi
Jack M. Hayashi
James and Alice Hayashi
Joan K. Hayashi
S/SGT Joe Hayashi
Katsuko Hayashi
Mr. & Mrs. Kiyoko Hayashi
Richard Hayashi
Richard and Donald Hayashi
Shigeo and Harumi Hayashi
Yukishige and Chiyoko Hayashi
Henry Y. Hayashida
Shige Hayashida
Misato K. Heard
Raymond P. Herbrick III
Frank K. Hibino
Nobu Hibino
Howard and Hide Hida
Hideo Higa
Terry S. Higa
Donald T. Higaki
Jiro B. Higaki
Gozaemon and Iso Higashi
Louis Higashi
Mike and Esther Higashi
Lt. Col. Roy Higashi
Mr. Ray Higo
Tatsumi (Ray) Higo
Kenneth I. Hino
Esther Hirabayashi
Grant J. Hirabayashi
Toby Hirabayashi
Tomosu Hirahara
Ronald Hiramatsu
Roy Y. Hiramatsu
Ben Hirano
Dick Hirano
Shig and Kikuye Hirano
Robert Hirasuna
Tatsushi Hirasuna
Akira Hirata
Betty K. Hirata
Mr. Kaname Hirata
Taka Hirata
Mrs. Toshio Hirata
Toshiye Hirata
Kotaro and Toku Hirohata
Wallace T. Hironaka
Steve Hirono
Eiki and Shigeno Hirose
Kana and Frank Hirose
Kiku Hirose
Mrs. Kinu H. Hirose
Mr. & Mrs. Shikuchiki and Sono Hirose
Toro Hirose
Tadashi T. Hirota
Minoru Hirozawa
Roy Hirozo
D. Hisaichi
Kazuma Hisanaga
Fumiyo Hisaoka
Dr. Thomas A. Hiura

Addie Hiura-Lawler
Kazuo Hiyama
Yeiichi Hiyama
Tom Homma
Frank S. Honda
Hiroshi Honda
Mary Fusako Honda
Satoru Honda
Tatsuo Honda
Sunao Hongo
Tatsuye and Minoru Honzaki
Bryan Hopkins
Anne Hori
Earl Hori
Hiroshi Hori
Minokichi and Mito Hori
Yasuki and Masaye Hori
Mr. & Mrs. Shojiro Horikawa
Frank G. Horino
Akira D. Hoshide
Chiyoko D. Hoshide
Dean A. Hoshide
Kimio Hoshide
Toshio Hoshide
Paul Hoshiko, Jr.
Robert S. Hoshino
Suematsu and Fuki Hoshiyama
William K. and Alice T. Hosokawa
Yoshi Hosokawa
Kihachiro Hotta
Mr. & Mrs. Rishiro Hotta
Toshio and Teruo Hozaki
Ray Hruska
Chia-Jung Hsu
George S. Hubbard
Masae Ibara
Mitsuko Ibara
LTC Benjamin T. Ibata
Muraichi and Sugi Ichiba
Rose and Joyce Ichihara
Stanley T. Ichikawa
Yonezo and Chiyo Ichikawa
Joe and Susie Ichiuji
Mickey Ichiuji
Ichiuji Family
Donald H. Ida
Harry Y. Ida
Mr. & Mrs. Sadamatsu Idemoto
Ruby Igarashi
Alfred J. Ige
Mr. & Mrs. Masakuni Iguchi
Nova and Keith Iida
Mr. & Mrs. Shiro Iida
Riuzo and En Iijima
Yae and Kaichi Iijima
Haruo Ikari
Hitoshi Ikata
Fumi A. Ike
Lionel Ikebe
Albert H. Ikeda
Albert S. Ikeda
Chiyoki Ikeda
Fly Ikeda
Hitumi Ikeda
Kazuo and Masano Ikeda
Kazuto Ikeda
Kichishiro and Kimiko Ikeda
May K. Ikeda
Shizuko Ikeda
Tsugio Ikeda
Tsuykuko Ikeda
Lloyd Ikefugi
Naoichi Ikegami
Lt.Col. Jospeh Ikeguchi
Charlotte S. Ikehara
Kazuo Ikehara
Koyo and Kumeta Ikemoto
Masayuki Ikemoto
Quentin and Betty Ikezoe
Jack S. and Aiko Ikuta
Joe and Lily Ikuta
Yasutaro and Shizuyo Ikuta
John Ikuzo
Tatsuo Imada
Ida H. Imai
Lucy K. Imai
Shuji Imai
Mr. & Mrs. T. Imai
Larry M. Imamura
Toro Imamura
Immigrants from Wakayama Ken, Japan
Yae I. Imon
Yaohachi and Sami Imoto
Yosh Imoto
Shizuko Ina
Tatsuno Inada
Yoshiko P. Inada
Yosh Inadomi
Dr. & Mrs. Toshio Inahara
Samuel Inai
Ben Inakazu
Thomas Inamasu
Charles T. Inatomi
Parents of James and Peggy Inatomi
Inokoji Family
Shigeru Inokuma
Mr. & Mrs. Maruji Inoshita

Calvin Inouye
Senator Daniel K. Inouye
Grandpa Inouye
Mr. & Mrs. Hanji Inouye
Hikotaro and Yae Inouye
Masato Inouye
Ryoko M. Inouye
Sadako Inouye
Takaji D. Inouye
Mr. & Mrs. Y. Inouye
Yoshiko Inouye
Internees of Poston, Arizona
Iwahei and Taki Inui
Lola Inui
Tom I. Ioka
George Ireda
Fumie Irihara
Saichi and Chitose Iritani
Louie Iriye
Robert T. Iseri
Ruth Iseri
Edward H. Ishibashi
Edward Hiroshi Ishibashi
Frank K. Ishida
Iwao Ishida
Joseph and Chiyoko Ishiguchi
Ivan Ishiguri
Ted and Shizuyo Ishihara
Charles Ishii
George F. Ishii
Jhn D. Ishii
Hanako R. Ishikawa
Herbert Y. Ishikawa
Kurataro and Hatsuno Ishikawa
Dr. Tokio Ishikawa
S.W. Ishiki
Kurahiko J. Ishimaru
Shoichi Ishimaru
Kelly Ishimoto
Paul I. Ishimoto
Earl Ishino
Parents of Col. Phil S. Ishio
Col. S. Phil Ishio
Roy and Aiko Ishiwari
Maruko Ishiyama
Tsuyo Ishiyama
Kunisaburo Ishizuka
Matsujiro Isokane
Issei Parents
Issei Pioneers
Isseis
Isseis and Niseis
Terry T. Itaki
Richard Itanaga
Mr. & Mrs. Itaro
Fred H. Ito
Mr. & Mrs. Gonsaku Ito
Hisano and Kamejiro Ito
Jack S. Ito
Kazuo and Isao Ito
Kiyoshi and Junko Ito
Mr. & Mrs. Mitsuyuki Ito
Tom T. Ito
Yoshiro Ito
Nui Itokawa
Yoshiko K. Iwahashi
Teruichi and Teruko Iwamiya
George Iwamoto
Shizuo Iwamoto
Sam, Tsugio, and Nob Iwanaga
Sam Iwaoka
James M. Iwasa
Arthur Iwasaki
K. Edward Iwasaki
Ruth S. Iwasaki
Yasukichi and Ito Iwasaki
Minoru Iwashika, PFC, 442nd RCT
Akiko J. Iwata
George T. Iwata
Harvey S. Iwata
Noboru and Kikuyo Iwata
Iwata Family
Peter O. and David K. Iwatsu
Mike Iwatsubo
Tad Izuhara
Michi Izui
Edward Izumi
Kazuto R. Izumi
Misao I. Izumi
Mrs. Izumi
Carol Izumi's father
Henry Izumizaki
James Izumizaki
George Izuta
Judith E. Jaeger
Japanese American Patriots
Japanese American Soldiers
Japanese American Vietnam Veterans
Japanese Americans of WWII
Japanese Americans who came to
    Chicago after internment
Japanese Immigrants and Japanese Americans
    of Florin, CA
Taeko S. Jenkins
Katsui and Kiyoshi Jinnohara
Dorothy Joseph-Yoshioka
William M. Jow

Toshio Kabutan
Kazo and Hide Kadokawa
Kenji Kadonaga
Walter S. Kadota, 100th Bn.
Kenji and Takao Kadowaki
Kathryn Kagawa
James and Robert Kagehiro
Isaac Kageyama
James Kagihara
Harry Y. and Helen K. Kagiwada
Kunimatsu and Tomi Kaji
Margaret Kajikawa
Mr. & Mrs. Yoshiharu Kajimura
Pvt. Nobuo Kajiwara
Mr. Seiichi Kakigi
Mr. Mike Kakiuchi
Yorio and Hifumi Kakiuchi
Chorge Kaku
Mr. & Mrs. Sakuji Kamachi
W. Kameda Family
Sgt. Yoichi Kamehawa
Masuichi and Kazu Kamikawa
Ray and Ben Kamikawa
May Kamo
May M. Kanatani
S/Sgt. John Kanazawa
Robert H., Bud M. and Henry K. Kanazawa
George R. Kaneda
George T. Kaneda
Kei Kaneda
Tome Kaneda
George M. Kaneko
May K. Kaneko
Mr. Kaneko
Shigetada F. Kanemori
Jean E. Kanemoto
Tahei and Dai Kanemoto
Kazuichi Kanemura
Mitsuko Funai Kaneshige
Harry Y. Kaneshiro
Keith Kaneshiro
Shinobu Kanetani
Mr. & Mrs. Kyuma Kanno
Kima Kanotsu
PFC Akira Kanzaki
Martin Karaki
Shig Kariya
Iyo NIshimi Kasai
Shizu Kasai
Tetsuyo Kashima
T. Kashima and family
Mr. Shiro Kashino
Henry Kashiwase
Tanemi and Miyo Katagiri
Hama Kataguri
Takio Kataoka
Tok Kataoka
Yasuki Kataoka
Taro Katayama
Yo Katayama
Katsumi Kato
Dr. Tsujio Kato
Unmitsu and Hatsu Kato
Wayne M. Kato
Victor Katsuchiyo
Tsunemi Katsuno
Ted U. Katsura
Harry and Yoshiye Kawabata
Mitsuye and Choji Kawada
Tom Kawaguchi
Kawaguchi-Sakihora Family
Parents of Dr. and Mrs. Henry Y. Kawahara
Shigeno Kawai
Fred M. Kawakami
Doc and Mary Kawamoto
George I. and Shigeko I. Kawamoto
Haruo Kawamoto
Jack Kawamoto
Mr. & Mrs. Yukio Kawamoto
Mr. & Mrs. Dentaro Kawamura
George R. Kawamura
Tom Kawamura
Otoichi and Kume Kawana Family
Akira Kawanabe
Cike C. Kawano
George U. Kawano
PFC George Y. Kawano
Aiko and Mataki Kawasaki
Jack Kawasaki
Nora and Seiso Kawasaki
Sgt. & Mrs. Ted D. Kawasaki
Kathryn Kawaye
Tsurukichi and Tani Kayashima
Dr. Harry Kazato
Stanley Kazuo
Johnson S. Kebo
Ryoichi R. Keikoan
Mitsutaro and Tomiye Kenmotsu
Eu-Eng Khan
Ed S. Kiba
Jack and Sumi Kiba
Shigeru Kiba
Fumiko Kida
Isaku Kida
Mr. & Mrs. Sadahiko Kihara
Sam I. Kihara
Isamu Kikuchi

Yoshiko Jane Kikuchi
Rev. & Mrs. Kenji Kikuchi
John F. Kikuchi, M.D.
Killed In Action
Thomas V. Killeen
Edward C.S. Kim
Herbert M. Kimoto
Onobu and Jirokichi Kimoto
Sadao and Joan Kimoto
Giichi and Hisayo Kimura
Grace Kimura
Harry K. Kimura
Mr. & Mrs. Kozo Kimura
Kimura Family
Nami Tsukamoto King
Babo Kinoshita
Mr. & Mrs. Kanetaro Kinoshita
Konosuke and Aya Kinoshita
Mamoru Kinoshita
Robert A. Kinoshita
Sadao Kinoshita
Mary Kirihara
Mitsunobu Kiritani
Mitsunobu G. Kiritani
Kazuo Kiritani
Virgil Kiser
Susumu Kishaba
Chiyoko Kishi
Fred Kishi
Hachiro Kita
Mr. & Mrs. Paul Kitagaki
Rev. Daisuke Kitagawa
Frances Kitagawa
Joseph Kitagawa
Sumie M. Kitagawa
Evelyn T. Kitahara
Allen Kitajima
Saburo Kitamura
Mr. & Mrs. Motoji Kitano
Teruo Kitashima
Tsuyako Kitashima
Tetsuo Kitayama
Tatsuye Y. Kitazaki
Jun Kito
Sadako and Kunisada Kiyasa
Dr. & Mrs. Robert K. Kiyasu
Masako Y. Kiyoi
Betty Kiyomoto
Takashi Kizu
Yeiki Kobashigawa
Yoshio Kobata
Key Kobayashi
Louie Kobayashi
Capt. Ray Kobayashi
Col. Thomas M. Kobayashi
Bill Kochiyama
William Kochiyama
Richard Koga
Ethel Kohashi, Sr.
Harry Kohaya
Dorothy Koide
Arthur, Lyman, Pierson and Will Koike
Kazue Koike
Sadamu Koito
Robert T. Koizumi
Yutaka Koizumi
Taizo Kokubo
George Komachi
Sakaye Kometani
Koji Komishi
James Komura
Mitsunori Komure
Kima Konatsu
Tom T. Kondo
Yoneko and Raymond Kondo
Tomoko Konishi
Harry and Chiyeko Kono
Kono Family
Isaku Konoshima
George Kosaka
Neil K. Kosasa
Ai Koshi
Mieko Kosobayashi
Mr. & Mrs. Yaokichi Kosobayashi
Charles T. Koto
Hideo Kouchi
Yas Kowashima
Mr. & Mrs. Einaga Koyama
Spady Koyama
Kenneth B.K. Kozai
S/Sgt. Ard A. Kozono
Chuichi George and Hisaye Kozuki
Kozuma Family
Sgt. Shigeo Kuba
Tom and Eleanor Kubo
James Kubokawa
Itaru and Koharu Kubota
John and Momoyo J. Kubota
Tommy S. Kubota
Takao Kubota, SSG 100 Inf.Bn.F Co.
Donald M. Kuge
George Kuge
Thomas T. Kuge
Toshiaki Kuge
Tomiko T. Kujubu
Frank Kumagai
Harry Kumagai

Henry M. Kumagai
Minoru and Mae Kumagai
Tomoye T. Kumagai
Dr. & Mrs. Koki Kumamoto
Thomas K. Kumano
George Kumasaka
Masaki Kunimoto
Kazuo, Kakusaburo and Kasumi Kunitake
Pvt. Tetsuo Kunitomi
Yoshimi Kunitsugu
Denji Kuniyoshi
Akia Kuniyuki
Mrs. Ichiyo Kuramoto
Fred S. Kurata
Masso Kurata
Momoye Kurihara
George S. Kurio
Andrew and Julia Kuroda
S/Sgt. Robert T. Kuroda, KIA
Aki Kurose
Sam Kurotani
Saburo and Tokie Kuroyama
Shig Kuroye
Seiji and Yoshiye Kusanagi
Tatsuo Kushida
Paul and Atsuko Kusuda
Kiyoko Kusudo
Masa Kutaka
Ronald Kutaka
George and Alice Kuwahara
Pvt. Roy Kuwahara
Yoshitomo and Akino Kyono
Hon. Bill Leonhart
Kyoko H. Linehan
Helen Loguirato
Loved Ones
Janie Low
PFS Harry F. Madokoro
Junichi and Tetsuye Maeda
Kinsuke Maeda Family
1st Lt. Saburo Maehara
Sentaro and Midori Maeyama
Caeli Mahon
Jenna Mahon
Kumakichi and Matsuye Maida
Torayoshi and Kane Maida
Wilson Makabe
Henry S. Makeshima
Harry E. Makoto
Mr. & Mrs. Keitaro Mameda
George Mamiya
Mac Mamiya
Mr. Masami Mamiya
Royal Louis Manaka and The Service Company
Chise and Lillian Manji
Many Japanese American Friends
Manzanar
Jacque M. Martin
Mr. & Mrs. Sanichi Maruko
Mr. & Mrs. William Marumoto
Tomi Marutani
Honorable William M. Marutani
Mrs. Mary Maruyama
Dr. Yosh Maruyama
Yoshio Masada
James Masaichi
Fumio Masaki
Harry K. and Kinu Masaki
George Masako
Frank Masami
James Masamori
Ben, Ike and Hank Masaoka
Mike and Etsu Masaoka
Tad Masaoka
Ariya Masuda
Kazuo Masuda
Rusiko Masuda
Tokiye Sakai Masuda
Toshio Masuda
Viola K. Masuda
Fred and Faye Masumoto
Fumiyo Masumoto
Pvt. George Masumoto
James Masumoto
Yaeko K. Masumoto
George Masunaga
Kamematsu and Taki Masunaga
Mr. & Mrs. Magoki Masunaga
Shiro Masunaga
J. Masunaga Family
Mrs. Tane Masuo
Masy Masuoka
Shig Masuoka
Takashi Masuoka
Matthew M. Masuoka, DMD
Hisao Masuyama
Rev. & Mrs. Kionin Matano
Hiroshi Matoba
Kumaji Matoba Family
John and Koyuki Matsubara
Frank Matsuda
Hiroshi Matsuda
Ken Matsuda
Mitsugu Matsuda
Toshio Matsuda
John Matsudaira
Daniel R. Matsukage

Alice Abe Matsumoto
Frank Y. Matsumoto
George Matsumoto
Hisao Matsumoto
Masakazu and Shizuye Matsumoto
Masao Matsumoto
Mr. & Mrs. Otogoro Matsumoto
Rinichi and Masae Matsumoto
Sakaye Matsumoto
Sei Matsumoto
Sugitaro and Toyo Matsumoto
Susumu S. Matsumoto
Ted Matsumoto
Tom Matsumoto
Tsuka Matsumoto
Kelly Matsumura
Phil Matsumura
Sadahiko and Sumiyo Matsumura
Jim Matsumura
Min Matsunaga
Hon. Spark M. Matsunaga
Tomokichi and Kazuko Matsunaga
Yoshiko Matsunaga
Towako Matsuno
Shoichi Matsuo
Jack Matsuoka
Harry K. Matsushima
Tadashi James Matsuura
Mrs. Barbara Matsuyama
Mr. & Mrs. Tomozo Matsuyama
Charles R. and George M. Mayeda
Dyke Mayeda
Edward Y. Mayeda
Ekutaro and Tsutsu Mayeda
Jim and Akimi Mayeda
Mr. & Mrs. Minoru Mayeda
Takashi Mayeda
Tamiki Mayeda
John R. McCormick
Albert Y. Menda
Mitsuyo Menda
Allen Meyer
Gertrude Meyers
Dorothy Mihara
Masao Miho
Tadao Mikasa
Ken Miki
Robert Miki
Tadafumi and Anna Mikuriya
Col. Virgil R. Miller
Walter and Sue Minaai Family
Ichiro Minabe
George Y. Minakata
Henry Minami
Judith Minami
Mr. & Mrs. Nobuichi Minami
Tatsuichi Minayo
Kikue Mine
Hon. Norman Mineta
Fred Minoru
William Miroto
MIS Veterans
David Mita
Roy G. Mita
Kazuo Mito
Matomi Mitsunaga
Tom J. Mitsuyoshi
Sachiko H. Miura
Toshio Miura
G.E. Miwa
Haruji Miya
Charles Y. Miyada
William H. Miyagi
Ben Miyahara
Hiro Miyahara
T. Miyahara and family internees
Patricia A. Miyahira
Joe Miyake
Manabu J. Miyake
Mr. & Mrs. T. Miyake
Yukie Miyake
Genichi and Hatsuyo Miyamoto
Mr. Mike M. Miyamoto
Noboru N. Miyamoto
Shizuko Miyamoto
Takashi K. Miyamura
Hershey H. Miyamura
Tom L. Miyanaga
Elyse H. Miyao
Martin S. and Yukiko Miyao
Torataro and Okuno Miyao
Mr. & Mrs. Shikataro Miyaoka
Robert Miyasaki
Mr. & Mrs. Shintaro Miyasaki
T. Miyasaki
Peter T. Miyashiro
Gerald Miyata
Tsuyoshi Miyoga
Charles and Hamako Miyoshi
Teiko Mizota
Jimmy M. Mizote
Mr. & Mrs. Harry K. Mizoue
Kakuhei and Misayo Mizoue
Larry and Isao Mizuno
Merio Mizutani
Rev. & Mrs. Seikan Mizutani
T/Sgt. Yukitaka Mizutari

In Honor Of

Minoru and June Mochizuki
Tara Mochizuki
Yoshino and Mary Mochizuki
Momii Veterans
Jimmie Momoi
Mr. Charles S. Mori
Sgt. Elmer Mori
Roy T. Mori
Yoneo Mori
Haluto Moriguchi
Miyoko Moriguchi
Chieko Morihata
Kiichiro Moriki
Arthur and Virginia Morimitsu
Frank Morimitsu
Jack K. Morimitsu
Virginia Morimitsu
Kiyono Morimoto
Noboru Morimoto
Sam and Edith Morimoto
Soichi and Tei Morimune
Masato Morinaga
Akira and Hiroko Morio
George Morisato
Fred A. Morishige
Joseph Morishige
Mr. Shig Morishige
Shun Morishige
Emi Kusumi Morishima
Ataka and George Morishita
Ernest K. Morishita
Itoye Morishita
Ray J. Morishita, Sr.
Gunji Moriuchi
Art Moriya
Ken Moriyama
Sadao Morodomi
Shigenori Motoike
Katsumi Motooka
Maoo M. Motooka
MSgt. Junichi R. Mugihira
Bryan T. Mukai
Cromwell D. Mukai
Frank T. Mukai
Mr. & Mrs. George Mukai
Hachiro Mukai
Roy A. Mukai
Bette N. Mukasa
Helen K. Mukoyama
Mrs. M. Mukoyama
Miye Mukoyama
Mrs. Mukoyama
Sam Mune
Sadao Munemori
Munemori Family
Jack S. Munemura
Akira Murakami
Chizuko Murakami
George and Cora Murakami
George and Judy Murakami
Mark Y. Murakami
Mary C. Murakami
Dr. Raymond S. Murakami
Richard M. Murakami
Sego and Haruko Murakami
Takashi Murakami
Toshio Murakami
Harry Murakashi
George Muramatsu
George G. Muramoto
Mr. & Mrs. Minejiro Muramoto
Mr. & Mrs. Roy T. Murano
Shigeyoshi Murao
Carol Muraoka
Charles M. Murase
Mantsuchi and Moto Murase
Teruyo Murashima
Teruo I. Murata
Sonoko S. Murayama
George S. Muto
Kazuo Muto
Mr. & Mrs. R. Mutobe
Ikuto Iky Nabeta
Kikue Kathryn Nabeta
Betty Nagai
Kooru Nagai
Teikan Nagamine
Mr. & Mrs. G.S. Nagata
Kaz Nagata
Kiyo Nagata
Kiyono Nagata
Cmdr. Scott S. Nagatani
Masatoshi Nagatomi
Akira Naguwa
Mr. & Mrs. S. Naito
Tak Naito
Mr. Toru Naito
Henry Nakada
Pershing Nakada
Mary Nakadate
Masaru Nakagaki
Bunny Nakagawa
Harvey and Tom Nakagawa
Jack Y. Nakagawa
Michiko Nakagawa
Mutsuo Nakagawa
Sharon Nakagawa

Tetsuzo Nakagawa
Tom T. Nakagawa
Yatsuji Nakagawa
Mr. & Mrs. Yusaimon Nakagawa
Yusuke and Misuyo Nakagawa
Nakagawa Family
Masaichi W. Nakagiri
May H. Nakahara
Suwako Nakajima
Hidetaka Nakaki
Robert Nakamoto
Stanley Y. Nakamoto
Nakamoto Family
Ellen Nakamura
Mr. & Mrs. George Nakamura
Mr. & Mrs. Jennosuke and Sam Nakamura
Kiyomi and Ellen Nakamura
Kiyomi Kay Nakamura
Mr. & Mrs. Naojiro Nakamura
Mr. Ned T. Nakamura
Patti Nakamura
Ralph K. Nakamura
Ray M. Nakamura
Toshio H. Nakamura
Uji Nakamura
Yoshinari Nakamura
James J. Nakanishi
Joe M. Nakanishi
Kameichi and Col. (Ret) Toshio Nakanishi
Mary Nakanishi
Tsugio Nakanishi
Kiyotaro and Kikuno Nakano
PFC Masayoshi Nakano
Sono Nakano
Yosuke and Teru Nakano
Emil and Mieko Nakao
George K. Nakao
Tom Nakao
Tom M. Nakasaki
Sam and Jeanette Nakashige
Mr. & Mrs. Gentaro Nakashige Family
Mr. & Mrs. Henry K. Nakashima
Mr. & Mrs. Kohei Nakashima
Lester T. Nakashima
Masayuki Nakashima
Mits and Mikiye Nakashima
Walter Y. Nakashima
William and Yone Nakashima
Mr. & Mrs. Matsukichi Nakasone
George M. Nakata
Gerry Nakata
Nao Nakata
Nobuo Nakata
Takeno Nakata
Tokizo and Misa Nakatogawa
Wallace T. Nakatsu
Mr. & Mrs. Atsuma Nakatsuka
Mr. & Mrs. J.A. Nakatsuka
Sembe and Some Nakawatase
Mr. & Mrs. David Nakayama
Dr. Denny Nakayama
Dr. & Mrs. Don Nakayama
Kiichi Nakayama
Masako Nakayama
Min Nakayama
Mrs. Mineko Nakayama
Nebo Nakayama
William S. Nakayama
Sam H. Nakazono
Sam Narahara
John Narimatsu
Chiyokichi and Sen Natsuhara
George M. Negoro
Paul Negoro
Masao and Miyeko Nehira
Sadaichi and Kikuyo Neishi
Mr. & Mrs. Nakagoro Ni
Mr. & Mrs. Nigo
Tsumoru Nii
Yuzuko Nii
Henry M. Niizawa
Zitaro and Take Niizawa
Tamizo and Miyono Nimura
Ben Ninomiya
Mr. Casey Ninomiya
Takao Ninomiya
Dick Nishi
Hito and Ivy Nishi
Masakazu Nishi
Nick and Helen Nishi
Seijiro Nishi
Sumio and Grace Nishi
Masaru Nishibayashi Ph.D.
Faye Nishida
Kenneth K. Nishida
Malcolm M. Nishida
Jill T. Nishikawa
Sekiyo Nishikawa
Hiro Nishikubo
Mr. & Mrs. Kirohachi Nishimori
Elmer Y. Nishimoto
Hugo Nishimoto
Joe Nishimoto
Miyuki Nishimoto
Tom T. Nishimoto
Frank and Haru Nishimura
Masaru and Haruo Nishimura

Tom Nishimura
Wilfred K. Nishimura
Mr. & Mrs. Nishimura
George M. Nishinaka
Kinori Nishino
Yemi Nishino
Torazo Nishio
Mr. & Mrs. Nishioka
Masako Nishiyama
Tsuru Nishizaki
Alice Nitta
Jiro and Yaye Nitta
Kiyoshi Nitta
Mae Nitta
S. John Nitta
Moriye and Flora Nobori
K. Nobusada
Bunsaku and Sawa Noda
Joe and Art Noda
Ruth and Bob Noda
Takeo Nogaki
Frances Nogawa
David M. Noguchi
Toshio Noma
Fred S. Nomiya
Richard Nomura
Tokuo and Michiye Nomura
Fumi and Kameo Nose
Ben Noto
Mr. & Mrs. Wallace Nunotani
Stanley T. Oba
Noboru Obana
Col. Benjamin Obata
Bonnie Obata
Ted Obata
Obayashi Family
Virginia Ochi
Mr. & Mrs. Kensaku Ochi and family
Heihachi and Yaye Oda
Kazuo Oda
Dr. Margaret Y. Oda
Toshiye A. Oda
Yoshinobu Oda
Ima Ogami
Hiroki Ogata
Yoshiye and Shizuye Ogata
Edward Ogawa
George Ogawa
Reginald T. Ogawa
Valiant "Butch" and Kelly Ogawa
Dorothy M. Ogino
Richard Ogura
Mr. Taka Oguri
T/Sgt. Abraham G. Ohama
Ben Ohama
Kuni Ohama
Ohama Family
Jerry J. and Misao Ohara
Masayuki Ohara
J.K. Ohashi
Arnold Ohki
Shigeto and Satsuyo Ohmura
Mr. Kazuo and Isao Ohsawa
Sadako Oishi
Evelyne G. Oka
Sadao and Shizuko Oka
Mr. & Mrs. Satoru Okabe
Peter and Muts Okada
Seichi and Kiyome Okada
Shigeo Okada
Bill T. Okamoto
Itsuto Okamoto
James G. Okamoto
Kiyoshi Okamoto
Matsuo and Ida Okamoto
Parents of Jeffrey A. Okamoto
Peg and Kim Okamoto
Tom T. Okamoto
Tosh Okamoto
Mr. & Mrs. Toshikazu Okamoto
Tsuya and Manzo Okamoto
Togo Okamura
Uso Okamura
Takeshi Okawa
Frank K. Okazaki
Ginta and Tazu Okazaki
Johnny M. Okazaki
K. George Okazaki
Mary Y. Okazaki
Minoru Okazaki
Mike Okazi
Hideichi and Kimi Okida
Tameichi and Kirie Okimoto
Tetsuro Okimoto
Laura Okimoto, US Army Nurse Corps
Okinawans
John S. Okizaki
Ben T. and Susan S. Okubo
Mr. & Mrs. George Okubo
James Okubo
Mume I. Okubo
Sue Okubo
Mr. & Mrs. Tamotsu Okubo
James K. Okubo, MOH
Matsuo Okumoto
Esuo and Mitsuye Okumura
Seisuke and Tome Okumura

Benny T. Okura
George Okura
Mrs. Hisayo Okura
Susumu Okura
Seinosuke Okuye
Masao Omachi Family
Jitsuzo and Kane Omata
James M. Omoto
Mas and Claire Omura
Shomatsu and Shizuko Omura
1st Lt. Curtis J. Onchi
Jinichi and Tsuna Onizuka
Kohei and Tsuya Ono
Tom Ono
Yoneshiro and Tome Ono
Kaun Onodera
PFC Lloyd M. Onoye
Ichiro Onuma
Carl and Marie Ooka
Seikichi and Momose Osaka
Frank H. Osaki
Tad Osaki
Hiroshi L. Osako
John Oshida
Seikichi Oshiro
Hisayo H. Oshita
Kai Oshita
Fred K. Ota
Hajime Ota
Hisano Ota
Kinuyo Ota
Koichi and Tomi Ota
Rev. Tosuke and Hideko Ota
Kanematsu and Kumae Otagaki
Masaru Otaguro
Rev. Andrew Otani
Matsujiro and Kane Otani
George T. Otsubo
Mrs. Sei Otsuji
Charles I. Otsuka
Dentaro and Tsuma Otsuka
Fumi Otsuki
Our beloved Issei parents
Our Issei Parents
Frances Owan
Emiko Owashi
Owashi Family
Riki and Tomekichi Oya
Akira and Harumi Oye
Garry Genya Oye
Mr. & Mrs. I. Oye
Mr. & Mrs. Tsunetaro Oye
Mike Ozaki
Robert Y. Ozaki
Frank and Matsuji Ozawa
Mr. & Mrs. Frank N. Ozawa
Jack K. and Bill H. Ozawa
Parents and family
Mary Pattishall
Sai Mandai Pramenico
Sai Mandai Pramenico
Dr. E.M. Rallings
Ray Randall
Peggy S. Rattenbury
Henry F. Reavey
Harold Reibesell
David Richnerger
Mr. & Mrs. J. Ryugo
Mr. & Mrs. F. Sagami
Masa Sagara
Masa Sagara
Thomas T. Sagimori
S/Sgt. Atsuo Sahara
Risuke and Akiko Sahara
Shigako Sahara
Mr. Y. Sahaue
Dr. Deborah Saiki
Yasaburo and Shige Saiki
Buffy, Bambi and Fanny Saito
T/Sgt. Chuji Saito
George Saito
George and Calvin Saito
Harold T. Saito
Keiji Saito
Kenneth K. Saito
Koemon Saito
Mrs. Lillian Saito
Shuji Saito
Tadao, Shinji, Masazo and Akira Saito
Saito Family
Yasu Saito, 8K-3-A (Amache, CO)
Masao Sakagami
George T. Sakaguchi
Taylor T. Sakaguchi
Hachiro and Mitsu Sakai
Hiroshi Sakai
John Sakai
Mrs. Miyo Sakai
Naoko Sakai
Sadao Sakai
William Sakai
Yohei Sakai
Sakai Family
Heiji and Mitsuji Sakakibara
Lt. Col. Richard M. Sakakida
Mrs. Tama Sakakura
Harry Sakamoto

Kiyoshi and Kazue Sakamoto
Masa Sakamoto
Samuel M. Sakamoto, 100th Inf. Bn.
Fumie Sakano
Fred Sakasegawa
Mr. & Mrs. Frank Sakata
Joe Sakata
Koretsuge and Shizue Sakata
Robert Jr., Vicki and Lani Sakata
Pvt. Sam Sakata
Mr. & Mrs. Tatsugo Sakata
Sgt. Teruo Sakata
Takami and Sadako Sakatani
Yoshio Sakaue
William Sakayama
Harry Sakohira
Tod Sakohira
Tadashi Sakuma
Hideaki Sakuraba
Tomio Sakurai
C.W. Sallas
Hanzo and Sumi Samejima
Mr. & Mrs. Chosaburo Sameshima
Herman and Beatrice Sanders
Raymond and Marion Sanford
George Sankey
Shig Sano
Harold H. Sasahara
Sasai Family
Akira Sasaki
Asako Sasaki
Everett Sasaki
Fujiko F. Sasaki
Fuju Sasaki
Fukumatsu, Yoi, Lloyd and Harvey Sasaki
Hideo Sasaki
Itsuo Sasaki
Jinjiro and Shimoyo Sasaki
Kaichiro Sasaki
Mary S. and John K. Sasaki
Raymond Sasaki
Sam I. Sasaki
Susumu Sasaki
Tadashi Sasaki
Tamaki and Asaz Sasaki
Thomas T. Sasaki
Rev. & Mrs. Yonosuke Sasaki
Yoshio, Lloyd and Harvey Sasaki
Michiyo and Akira Sasano
Ben Sato
Carl K. Sato
Hanako O. Sato
Karen A. Sato
Kisa Sato
Mr. & Mrs. Masamori Sato
Robert S. Sato
Steve S. Sato
Susie Sato
Mr. Susumu Sato
Tadao Sato
Dr. & Mrs. Tomejiro Sato
Mrs. Tomoe Sato
Torazo and Yoneko Satow
Motoye Sawada
Yukio and Motoye Sawada
Sawada Family
Celia S. Schectman
Ms. Marjorie F. Schweiger
Kazuji and Misuye Segawa
Carol, Sathya, Sai and Sahanti Seigel
Toll Seike
Joe Seikichi
Ruby K. Seino
Ms. May Seitz
Lloyd Seki
Kenichiro Sekiguchi
Koichi K. Sekimura
Takasaburo Sekino
Shika Sekitani
Hanna and Thomas Semba
Senseis at Ann Arbor and Fort Snelling
Seto Brothers
Grace Setsuda
Hana U. Shepherd
Harry Shibata
M/Sgt. Koichi Shibuya
Tak Shibuya
Janet Yoshiko Shields
Sakiko Shiga
Tetsuo Shigaya
Edha K. Shigekawa
Kiyoshi Shigekawa
Michael Shigekawa
Shina Shigekawa
Tsunetaro and Shina Shigekawa
James T. Shigemasa
Noboru Morimoto Shigeru Kiba
Howard K. Shigeta
Ichiji Shikano
Buck H. Shima
Mr. Min Shimada
Masayo and G. Gentoku Shimamoto
Gladys Shimasaki
Kurazo, Hatsu and Tom Shimasaki
Tom T. Shimasaki
Harry and Yoshi Shimazaki
Roy S. Shimazu

Mr. & Mrs. Arthur T. Shimidzu
Dave and Craig Shimizu
Jimmy T. Shimizu
Mary Shimizu
Sada Shimizu
Rev. & Mrs. Sojiro Shimizu
Shikiye Shimojima
George and Shimayo Shimokochi
Tsugiye F. Shimokubo
Itaro and Sawano Shimomura
Hugh Shimotsu
James N. Shimoura
Seiji and Yukiye Shimura
Lincoln M. Shinidzu
Mr. & Mrs. Geo. Shinmoto
Henry and Haruno Shinmoto
Kameichi and Haruno Shinmoto
Tony Shinmoto
Carl Shinoda
Shigenori and Mutsumi Shinoda
James Shinohara
Michi Shinomura
Ernest S. Shinozaki
Fred Shinso
Kiyoshi M. Shintaku
K. Jean Shintani
Mr. Saichi Shintani
Yasuo Shinzaki
Stanley T. Shioi
Will Shiomi
Shiro and Catherine Shiraga
Noboru Shirai
John K. Shiraishi
Mr. & Mrs. Sentaro Shiraki
Dr. Takao Shishino
Joseph T. Shoji
Mr. & Mrs. Rinai Shoji
Toshiaki Shoji
John Shundo
Tokutaro Slocum
Dr. Robert Smith
Smith Family
Butler Barron Smith, Jr.
Sadako Soeda
Francis Y. Sogi
Noboru and Mitsuyo Sogi
Machiko Sogo
Grace M. Stern
Lyn C. Stern
Herbert L. Stern Jr.
Marguerite Stock
Stockton Aichi-Ken Immigrants
Calvin K. Suemori
Mr. & Mrs. Kiujiro Sugai
Mr. Michael Sugai
Ray Sugai
Susumu Sugai
Tomojiro and Tome Sugai
William A. Sugano
Takeshi Sugawara
Saichiro R. Sugidono
Chiomo Sugihara
Thomas T. Sugimori
Susie and Henry Sugimoto
Masako Sugino
Otono Sugioka
Tokuo Sugioka
Isa Sugiura
Senkichi and Sadako Sugiura
Dr. Tetsuo and Mary Yoshiko Sugiyama
Aiko Suguro
Sgt. Takeo Suma
Yoshio Sumi
Grandpa and Grandma Sumida
Harry, Bull, Max and Chang Sumida
Harry, Edward, Makoto and Richard Sumida
Mitsuru Sumida
Robert Sumida
Setsuya Sumida
Takeo Sumida
Sumio Sumihiro
Shig Sumioka
Dan K. Sunada
Sgt. George W. Suyama
Masato Suyama
Shoichi Suyama
Mr. & Mrs. Tom Suyama
Suyama 50th Wedding Anniversary
William S. Suyeyasu
Chiyosaku and Aki Suzuki
Frank Suzuki
John T. Suzuki
Lester Suzuki
Flyer Tabata
Joe M. Tabata
Misao T. Tachibana
Richard and Hideko Tachibana
1st Lt. Yoshi Tachino
Ormal E. Tack
Kazuo Tada
John T. Tadano
Terri Tagami
Yoshio Taguma
Yoko and Tetsu Taira
Tsuneo Tajima
Dr. George S. Takahashi
Harry H. Takahashi

Sgt. Iwao A. Takahashi
Kiyomi and Fumi Takahashi
Shig Takahashi
Mr. & Mrs. T. Takahashi
Dr. Toyoko Mae Takahashi
Yoshibei and Shizuyo Takahashi
Dr. Harry H. Takaki
James and Frank Takaki
Yutaka D. Takaki
Mr. & Mrs. Norikazu Takamine
George Takanashi
George Takaoka
Charlie Takata
Fred T. Takata
Mr. & Mrs. Harry Takata
Tomie Takata
Tosh Takata
Yoshihiro Takata
Shizue Takatani
William Takatsuki
Takayama Brothers
Toshio and Katsuya Takechi
George Takeda
Henry Takeda
William J. Takei
Kaneji Takekawa
Kay Takemori
Ben T. Takemoto
Celia Takemoto
Hiroshi Takemoto
Kay Takemoto
Ray Takemoto
Shiro and Margaret Takemoto
Takeo F. Takemoto
Gail Takeoka
Robert Takeshita
Thomas and Lillian Takeshita
Mr. & Mrs. Thomas K. Takeshita
Betty S. Inouye Taketa
Henry Taketa
James Taketa
Miyuki Taketa
Tarozo and Yoshino Taketa
Tom M. Taketa
Chiyo C. Taketoshi
Hideo Takeuchi
Itsuki Takeuchi
Kochiyo Takeuchi
Mr. & Mrs. Koichi Takeuchi
Steve H. Takeuchi
Tadashi Takeuchi
Paul A. Takiguchi
Mr. & Mrs. William K. Takimoto
Minoru Takiuchi
Gentaro and Natsuyo Tamaki
Thelma Tambara
Hiroshi H. Tamura
Masaru Tamura
Sadao and Haruko Tamura
Tadashi Tamura
Toku Tamura
Toshio Tamura
Yoshio Tamura
Anthony and Kyogo T. Tanabe
H. Del Tanabe
Henry Tanabe
Hiroshi H. Tanabe
Isamu S. Tanabe
James Y. Tanabe
Kyogo T. Tanabe
Yoshihiko Tanabe
Yoshijiro and Asano Tanabe
Gihei and Tora Tanada
Toshiye Tanada
Lt. Kei Tanahashi
Bert M. Tanaka
Carolyn Tanaka
Chester Tanaka
Frank and Maki Tanaka
George Tanaka
Harley Tanaka
Harry Tanaka
Mrs. Haru Tanaka
Isama G. Tanaka
John M. Tanaka
Ken Tanaka
Capt. Paul A. Tanaka
Shigeo Tanaka
Mr. & Mrs. T. Tanaka
T. Jim Tanaka
Yoshiko and Hisako Tanaka
Mr. & Mrs. Shigeyuki Tanaka
Tanaka Family
Frank Tanamachi
PFC Saburo Tanamachi
Shimataro Tange
Ernest M. Tani
Dr. George Tani
Henry N. Tani
James F. Tani
Saitaro and Chikaye Tani
Koichi and Taniyo Taniguchi
Mr. & Mrs. Taniguchi
Chisato Tanimura
Charles Tanioka
Tom and Mary Tanita
Mitsuo Tanji, F Co., 442nd RCT

Toshio Tano
Mitch Tanouye
Frank K. Tashima
Mack Tashima
Masaru Tashima
M/Sgt. Ken and Teruko Tashiro
Shigezo and Kayoko Tashiro
Thomas Tateishi
Jim Tatsuda
Kunio Tatsui
Tut Tatsuno
Tosh Tawara
Masao Tayama
Nobuko U. Taylor
Teachers at MILS
Masaru Tengan
PFC Yoshio Tengwan
Roy Terada
Yoshio and Sumiko Terada
Frank Y. Teranishi
Mrs. Masae T. Teranishi
Dr. Paul Terasaki
Chiyoko Teshima
The experiences and treatment while in
    USAF stationed near Tachikawa, 1965-1967
Molly Thomas
C.H. Thornburg
Those who gave the "ultimate"
Those who gave their lives, fortune and honor
Those Who Served in WWII
Those who toiled and suffered
Carolyn Tirada
Tadao Tochioka
Ken and Jean Toda
Ms. Mary Toda
Dr. Terry M. Toda
Toda Family
Hachiro John Togashi
Mr. & Mrs. Shinsaburo Togashi
Mr. & Mrs. Shigetaro Togo
Fred S. Toguchi
Akira Tohei
George Tohinaka
Yaeno and Yahay Tojo
Jon S. Toki
Moriye and Mariko Tokubo
Thomas S. Tokuhisa
Mr. & Mrs. Asataro Tokunaga
Mr. & Mrs. Atsushi Tokunaga
Lincoln Tokunaga
Shinkichi and Mary Tokunaga
Shiro and Jim Y. Tokuno
Michelle M. Tomasa
James S. Tomasu
Yoshimi Tomatani
Ruth H. Tominaga
Mrs. Tominaga
Frank Tomino
Dick K. Tomita
Hirochi Tomita
Melvin K.S. Tomita
Richard T. Tomita
Todd S. Tomiyama
Toyokuma and Kane Tomooka
Warren G. Tonaki
Jack and Mary Tono
Harley M. Tonooka
Tom T. Tora
Albert N. Torii
John Toriumi
Okamoto Tosh
Dora Toyama
Bob Toyoda
Umekichi and Itsuyo Toyohara
Shichizo Toyota
Mr. Albert Trousdale
Joe J. Tsuboi
Masao Tsuboi
Will Tsuchida
Hal Tsuchiya
Kurao Tsuchiya
Ray and Kiku Tsuchiya
Frank Tsuchiya, Sr.
Ben T. Tsudama
June O. Tsuji
Yento Tsuji
Ken and Mary Tsujioka
Fusakichi and Kyo Tsukahara
Alfred and Mary Tsukamoto
Keitaro Tsukamoto
Kuzo and Ito Tsukamoto
Mary Tsukamoto
Henry Tsukimura
George Tsunayoshi
Mr. & Mrs. Tsunehara
Warren Tsuneishi
Aiko Tsurui
James M. Tsutsui
Jimmy Tsutsui
Kumakichi and Sawaye Tsutsui
Umematsu Tsutsumi
Mr. & Mrs. Soyomatsu Tsutsumida
Tadao Uchi
Frank Uchida
Kimimoto P. Uchida
Uchida Family
Mr. & Mrs. Gonzo Uchiyama

Kazuo Ueda
Vic T. Ueki
James Morio Ueno
Kiku Ueyama
M. Ujifusa Family
Sam and Frances Umade
Aiko A. Umeda
Jujiro and Tokiyo Umeda
Mr. & Mrs. Juzo Umemura
Umomota Family
Shigeo Uota
Ernest H. Ura
Yoshioko Uragai
George M. Uramoto
James Urano
Hango and Mashi Uratsu
USAF Base in Tachikawa
Mr. & Mrs. Jirokichi and Masuye Ushiyama
Blossom C. Usuki
Richard Uto
Alice Uyeda
Florence Uyeda
Tomochika Uyeda
Alfred S. Uyehara
Edward T. Uyemura
Harry Uyemura
Uyemura Family
Dr. & Mrs. Ben Uyeno
Ichiyo Uyeno
Mr. & Mrs. Joe Uyetaki
George Uzawa
Honorable J. Valk
Veterans of Service Company
VFW L.A. Post 9938 Reunion
Frank Wada
Mr. & Mrs. Genjiro Wada
Ryukichi and Sueko Wada
Tamakichi and Akiyo Wada
Wada Family
Bob Wagatsuma
Henry Wakabayashi
Lynn Wakabayashi
Mrs. Fumiko Wakamatsu
Joseph Wakamatsu
Edward M. Wake
Mrs. Reiko Wake
George and Mae Waki
Taeno and Hanhichi Wakiji
Noboru Wakumoto
Cosma Walter
Washington High Students
Washington State Nisei
Andrew R. Watada
Toku Watamura
Boris Tsugio Watanabe
Juzo and Hana Watanabe
Mary Watanabe
Robert M. Watanabe
Samual and Matsue Watanabe
Takuzo and Mitsuko Watanabe
Taul Watanabe
Masakichi and Haru Watanuki
Tsukasa Wataya
Michi Weglyn
Connie A. Weimer
Fusae N. Wiegand
Takimori William
Eugene N. Wilson
Alice Wiser
Jenny Wishnack
Mr. & Mrs. Walter Woodward
WWII Veterans
Ken Yagi
Nancy M. Yagi
Takeo Yagi
Tadao J. Yagura
Jack T. Yagura
George Yaki
Yakuno Family
Tom Yamachika
Frank and Mary Yamada
Fred Yamada
Masayo and Masaaki Yamada
Parents of Gordon and Kiyo Yamada
Ryojiro and Seki Yamada
Sachio Yamada
Shigeko Yamada
Shigeto and Hatsuyo Yamada
Yas Yamada
Mr. Thomas Yamagata
Mr. & Mrs. Yamagata
Joseph Yamagiwa
George Yamaguchi
Masu and Tomoichiro Yamaguchi
Niso and Tami Yamaguchi
Peggy Yamaguchi
Tadashi Yamaguchi
Roy S. Yamahiro
Rev. & Mrs. Yamaka
Helen S. Yamakoshi
Beverly Yamamoto
Charley K and Mary Yamamoto
Fred Yamamoto
Hiro Yamamoto
Hiroji and Yoshino Yamamoto
Kongo Yamamoto
Mits Yamamoto

Shoichi Yamamoto
Tokuo Yamamoto
Mr. & Mrs. Toraichi Yamamoto
Yukimi Yamamoto
Mr. & Mrs. Sahichi Yamamoto
PFC Thomas I. Yamanaga
Mrs. Eshi Yamane
Kasuke and Misao Yamane
Mark O. Yamane
Dr. Eiji Yamane
Mr. & Mrs. T. Yamanishi
Yahichi and Taniyo Yamanishi
Toyoatsu and Kikuno Yamanouchi
Frank and Toshiko Yamasaki
Hiromi Yamasaki
Ruby T. Yamasaki
Sam and Sumiko Yamasaki
Sarah H. Yamasaki
Youko Yamasaki
Yukio Yamasaki
Mr. & Mrs. Midori Yamashiroya
Irene Yamashita
Kiyoo Yamashita and Family
Anna F. Yamauchi
Mr. & Mrs. Shigeaki Yamauchi
Thomas T. Yamauchi
Alice Yamazaki
Rev. John M. Yamazaki
Thomas Yamazaki
Mrs. Shig Yamono
Yanaga Family Members
Shigeo Yanai
Shigeo and Florence Yanaru
Ronald K. Yanehiro
Steve M. Yano
Pvt. Joe R. Yasuda
Haruhiko Yasuhara
Mr. & Mrs. Henry Yasuhira
Masuo and Shidzuyo Yasui
Minoru Yasui
Tatsumi and Hideo Yasui
Hero and Ivy Yasukochi
Koma Yasukochi
Takejiro and Chieko Yasumoto
Edward Yasumura
Yasumura Family
Tadashi Yasunaga
Hide Yasutake
Richard Yasutomi
James and Peggy Yatabe
Mary Yatabe
Tut Yates
Itsuto Yokomi
Rev. & Mrs. Luke T. Yokota
Paul H. Yokota
Mr. & Mrs. Tsukane Yokota
Aya Yokoyama
Tom and Mitsi Yokoyama
Yokoyama Family
Glenn M. Yomogida
Yooko Yoneda
Miyuki Yonemoto
1st Lt. Hiroshi Yonemura
Toshi J. Yorioka
George Y. Yoshida
Mrs. Kikuno Yoshida
PFC Minoru M. Yoshida
Rudy Yoshida
Yasohichi and Marie Ann Yoshida
Yukio Yoshida
James M. Yoshimaru
Dempei and Shigeno Yoshimi
Fumiko N. Yoshimoto
George Yoshimoto
Mr. & Mrs. K. Yoshimoto
Katsuo and Hana Yoshimoto
Koji K. Yoshimoto
Mary Y. Yoshimoto
Ray Yoshimoto
Arthur T. Yoshimura
Fudeko Yoshimura
Kazuo and Fude Yoshimura
Alice A. Yoshinari
David A. Yoshinari
Yoshinari Family
John Y. Yoshino
Mr. & Mrs. Kichisaburo Yoshino
Y.J. Yoshino
Yasuo Yoshino
Patricia K. Yoshino-Jordan
George and Giichi Yoshioka
Joseph and Dorothy Yoshioka
Ken Yoshioka
Marion Yoshioka
Mr. & Mrs. Toragu Yoshioka
Yukino Yoshishige
Chaplin Israel A.S. Yost
Chiyeko Yukawa
Douglas Yuki
Yuki Yukinori

Board of Directors

What the members of the Board
had in common was a determination
to create a Memorial worthy
of the Japanese American experience.

Left to right first row: Hideto Kono, Tom Masamori, Cherry Tsutsumida, Elizabeth Yamada, Jean Kariya, Rita Takahashi, Mike Shimizu.
Second row: George Aratani, Emma Boers (staff), Don Tokunaga, Peter Okada, Tomio Moriguchi.
Third row: Florence Miyahara, Mae Takahashi, James Suzuki, Harry Abe, Kelly Kuwayama
Fourth row: Karen Tani, Bill Hosokawa, Jim Mukoyama, Cressey Nakagawa, Paul Terasaki, Gerald Yamada
Fifth row: Bob Sakata, Ray Murakami, Mel Chiogioji, Harry Fukuhara, Shiro Shiraga, Phil Ishio
Sixth row: Rodney Shinkawa, Bruce Kaji, Mas Funai, Dennis Otsuji, Grant Ujifusa

USDA Honors Asian American Farm Families

On April 27, 2001, commemorating National Asian Pacific American Heritage Month, the United States Department of Agriculture honored five prominent Asian Pacific American farming families for their contribution to agriculture.

Agriculture Secretary Ann M. Veneman stated, "The achievements highlighted by these families have helped develop vital markets throughout the world for US commodities."

The Tanimura families, of Salinas, California, is a parthership of the Tanimura brothers in the T&A Produce Company, the largest independent grower/shipper of lettuce in the United States.

The George Higashi family of Salinas, California, owns/operates Easton Enterprises and are partners in NewStar Fresh Foods, a company employing over 400 people that ships 14 million cartons of produce annually.

The Clarence Nishizu family of Orange County, California, is helping to construct the Orange County Agricultural & Nikkei Heritage Museum at the California State University at Fullerton campus.

In addition, two NJAMF Board members Robert Sakata of Sakata Farms in Brighton Colorado and Mae Takahashi of Clovis and their families also received awards. Sakata Farms is an innovative domestic and exporter of corn, broccoli and onions. Dr. Takahashi who was the President of Valley Medical Pharmacy was a former member of the USDA Citizens Advisory Council on Civil Rights from 1990 to 1992. Her family have been farming since the 1930's in the Fresno area.

Family Record

Family Name: _____

Father: _____ Mother: _____

Dates of Arrival in the United States: _____

Birthplace of Parents : _____

Children: _____

Prewar Residence: _____

City: _____ State: _____

Occupation: _____

Date of Evacuation: _____ Family Number: _____

Assembly Center: _____ Assembly Center Address: _____

WRA Camp: _____ Camp Address: _____

Date of Release: _____

Camp Job Assignment(s): _____

_____

_____

Relocated to: _____

_____

_____

Service Record Including Place(s) of Service:

_____

Medals Earned: _____

Postwar Addresses: _____

_____

Education and Accomplishments of Children: _____

_____

_____

_____

Morbidity Record:

Father (date): _____ *Mother (date):* _____

Children (names and dates): _____

Other Notes: _____

_____

_____

_____

_____

_____

_____

_____